Marihuana
Reconsidered

2nd EDITION REPRINT

Marihuana Reconsidered

Lester Grinspoon, M.D.

QUICK AMERICAN ARCHIVES
Division of Quick Trading Company
Oakland, CA

ISBN 0-932551-13-0

Fourth Printing, June 1999

Printing History

First edition printed by Harvard University Press in 1971
Second edition printed by Harvard University Press in 1977
        ISBN 0-674-54833-7 (cloth)
        ISBN 0-674-54834-5 (paper)
Library of Congress Catalog Card Number 77-76767

This edition published by Quick American Archives, a division of Quick Trading Company.

Distributed by: Quick Trading Company
                   P.O. Box 429477
                   San Francisco, CA 94142-9477
                   (510) 533-0605

                   Publishers Group West

Publisher's Cataloging in Publication

Grinspoon, Lester, 1928 –
        Marihuana reconsidered / Lester Grinspoon. - - 2nd ed.
        p. cm.
        Includes bibliographical references and index.
        ISBN 0-932551-13-0

        1. Marijuana. 2. Drug abuse. I. Title

HV5822.M3G75 1994   362.2'95
                                                     QBI94-90

Printed in the United States of America

Children are the greatest high of all

In memory of Danny

On Further Reconsideration
Introduction to the 1994 Reprint Edition
Lester Grinspoon, M.D.

I first became interested in cannabis when its use increased explosively in the 1960s. At that time I had no doubt that it was a very harmful drug that was unfortunately being used by more and more foolish young people who would not listen to or could not believe or understand the warnings about its dangers. When I began to study marihuana in 1967, my aim was to define scientifically the nature and degree of those dangers. But as I reviewed the scientific, medical, and lay literature, my views began to change. I came to understand that I, like so many other people in this country, had been misinformed and misled. There was little empirical evidence to support my beliefs about the dangers of marihuana. By the time I had completed the research that formed the basis for this book, originally published in 1971, I was convinced that cannabis was far less harmful than I had believed. The book's title, *Marihuana Reconsidered*, reflected that change in view.

After three years of research on cannabis, I concluded not only that it was much less harmful than alcohol and tobacco, but also that no harm it might cause was nearly as serious as the damage attributable to the annual arrest of 400,000 mostly young people on marihuana charges. I naively believed that once people understood that marihuana was much less harmful than drugs that are already legal, the laws against it would be repealed. I confidently predicted that cannabis would be legalized for adult use within the decade. I had not yet learned that there is something peculiar about illicit drugs: if they don't always make the drug user behave irrationally, they certainly cause many nonusers to behave that way. Instead of making marihuana legally available to adults, we have continued to criminalize many millions of Americans. Hundreds of thousands of mostly young people are arrested on marihuana charges each year, and the political climate has now deteriorated so severely that it has become difficult to discuss marihuana openly and freely. It could almost be said that there is a climate of psychopharmacological McCarthyism.

In the years following publication of *Marihuana Reconsidered*, it became increasingly clear that there were no valid scientific reasons for the ban on marihuana. The Anslinger-era notions on which the 1937 Marihuana Tax Act was based — that marihuana caused violent crime, "sexual excess" (whatever that is), and addiction, and that it served as a "stepping-stone" to "harder drugs," had been thoroughly discredited. Since these arguments were no longer plausible, groups opposed to liberalization of the marihuana laws now began to talk about "new research" supposedly proving that marihuana caused other kinds of harm. It was in this atmosphere that the federal government provided greatly expanded support, largely through the National Institute on Drug Abuse, for studies designed to uncover new health hazards. Thus we heard in the early '70s that marihuana destroyed brain cells, caused psychoses, lowered testosterone levels and sperm counts, led to breast development in adolescent males, damaged memory and intellectual functions, compromised the immune system, and caused chromosome breakage, genetic damage, and birth defects. The publication of these findings followed a typical pattern. Each one would be reported in front-page stories with alarmist commentary. Then, over the next few months or years, investigators would report that the finding could not be replicated. When this contradictory evidence was reported at all, the story would usually appear as a short item in the back pages. The public was often left with the impression that the existence of the latest health hazard had been scientifically demonstrated.

By 1977 enough genuine new knowledge had accumulated to justify a second edition of *Marihuana Reconsidered* with a new chapter in which James B. Bakalar and I reviewed research and social developments over the intervening six years. Undeterred by the failure of my prediction in 1971 that marihuana would be legalized within the decade, we concluded the second edition with the following words: "Whatever the cultural conditions that have made it possible, there is no doubt that the discussion about marihuana has become more sensible. We are gradually becoming conscious of the irrationality of classifying this drug as one with a high abuse potential and no medical value. If the trend continues, it is likely that within a decade, marihuana will be sold in the United States as a legal intoxicant."

We had reason to be optimistic at that time, three years before Ronald Reagan was elected President. In 1971 the National Commission on Marihuana and Drug Abuse, appointed by President Nixon, had recommended eliminating penalties for possession of marihuana for personal use and casual non-profit transfers of small amounts. In 1973 Oregon had become the first state to decriminalize marihuana, making possession of less than an ounce a civil offense penalized by a small fine. In 1975 Alaska had eliminated all penalties for private possession and cultivation of less than four ounces. President Carter had endorsed decriminalization, as had the American Medical Association, the American Psychiatric Association, the American Bar Association, and the National Council of Churches. By 1977 most states had reduced simple possession to a misdemeanor, and by 1980 eleven states had actually decriminalized possession.

Unfortunately, this trend did not continue. The marihuana reform movement peaked in the late 1970s. In 1978 Dr. Peter Bourne, the White House drug advisor who had helped President Carter move toward reform, resigned and was replaced by Lee Dogoloff, a hardliner. In that same year the proportion of the population favoring marihuana legalization began to fall from its 1977 high of 28%; today it has dropped to 15%. Under President Reagan the government instituted a program of "zero tolerance." By 1983 it was spraying the dangerous insecticide Paraquat on domestic marihuana crops and using military methods to uproot cannabis plants and arrest their growers in northern California.

In 1987 a Supreme Court nominee had to withdraw under pressure because he had smoked marihuana as a law professor. In 1989, under President Bush, the federal government began Operation Green Merchant; it confiscated lists of people who had ordered indoor plant growing equipment and raided their homes. The Bush administration also worked hard to persuade Alaska to recriminalize marihuana possession, and succeeded in 1990. That same year Congress passed a bill calling for federal transportation funds to be withheld from states refusing a six-month suspension of the automobile licenses of people convicted of marihuana possession.

It is important to remember that these increasingly harsh government measures (and the growing hysteria of anti-marihuana citizens' groups) did not reflect any new knowledge about the dangers of this drug. The quarter of a century since the publication of the first edition of *Marihuana Reconsidered* has produced remarkably little laboratory, sociological, or epidemiological evidence of serious health or social problems caused by marihuana. The present attitude of the government and anti-marihuana crusaders bears the same relationship to reality that the film "Reefer Madness" bore in 1936. But the dissonance is even more striking now, because we know so much more. Since 1971 millions of dollars have been spent to study the dangers of cannabis, and this vast research enterprise has completely failed to provide a scientific basis for prohibition. Although evidence against the toxicity continues to accumulate, the government persists in escalating its war on cannabis users. To justify this policy (usually with the Drug Enforcement Administration (DEA) as its voice) it distorts, stretches, and truncates research findings to an extent worthy of Procrustes.

The government's commitment to gross exaggeration of the harmfulness of cannabis has made it necessary to deny the drug's medical usefulness in the face of overwhelming evidence. In 1991 the DEA was inundated with requests for marihuana from people with AIDS. In response, James O. Mason, head of the Public Health Service, announced that the compassionate IND program, which had helped a handful of patients to use marihuana legally as a medicine, would be suspended. He explained that this program undercut the administration's opposition to the use of illegal drugs: "If it is perceived that the Public Health Service is going around giving marihuana to folks, there would be a perception that this stuff can't be so bad," Mason said. "It gives a bad signal. I don't mind doing that if there is no other way of helping these people. . . . But there is not a shred of evidence that smoking marihuana assists a person with AIDS."

In 1971 I pointed out that since marihuana had been used by so many people all over the world for so many thousands of years with so little evidence of significant toxic effects, the discovery of some previously unknown serious health hazard was unlikely. I suggested that the emphasis in cannabis research should be shifted to its medical uses and its potential as a tool to advance our understanding of brain function. Although few resources have been committed to either of these fields, there have been compelling developments in both.

In 1990 researchers discovered receptors in the brain stimulated by THC. This exciting discovery implied that the body produces its own version of cannabinoids for one or more useful purposes. The first of these cannabinoid-like neurotransmitters was identified in 1992 and named anandamide (ananda is the Sanskrit word for bliss). Cannabinoid receptor sites occur not only in the lower brain but also in the cerebral cortex, which governs higher thinking, and in the hippocampus, which is a locus of memory. These discoveries raise some interesting questions. Could the distribution of anandamide receptor sites in the higher brain explain why so many cannabis users claim that the drug enhances some mental activities, including creativity and fluidity of associations? Do these receptor sites play a role in marihuana's capacity to alter the subjective experience of time? What about the subtle enhancement of perception and the capacity to experience the physical world with some of the freshness and excitement of childhood? Perhaps further research on these receptors, which may not be limited to the brain alone, will also promote a better understanding of the remarkable medical versatility of cannabis.

Despite conditions that deter medical researchers, medical applications of cannabis have seen considerable progress since 1971 under the most unusual and difficult of circumstances. New drugs are generally escorted over the complicated federal regulatory obstacle course by pharmaceutical companies, which devote vast resources to the task of taking a chemical with therapeutic potential and transforming it into a marketable property. For many reasons, including the fact that patent protection is impossible, no drug company is ever likely to undertake this effort on behalf of cannabis. Furthermore, the United States government has been steadfast in its opposition to recognizing the medical utility of cannabis. Yet ever larger numbers of people are using marihuana medically.

Several developments have greatly increased interest in cannabis as a medicine. In the early 1970s many people noticed that cannabis could relieve the intense nausea and vomiting induced by cancer chemotherapeutic substances, which were then new. Marihuana often proved to be more effective than legal anti-nauseants. At about the same time it was discovered that marihuana reliably lowered the pressure on the optic nerve in people suffering from open-angle glaucoma; many patients learned, mostly from one another, that cannabis was more effective than conventional medications in retarding the progressive loss of vision caused by this disorder. In the mid-1980s people with AIDS discovered that cannabis relieved the nausea caused by their illness or by the medicines taken to counteract it. In addition, cannabis often improved their appetite and enabled them to stop losing or even to gain weight. Like most medical users of cannabis, AIDS patients have found that smoked marihuana is more effective than the synthetic THC (Marinol) that was made legally available as a prescription drug in 1985.

The effort to make cannabis itself available as a prescription drug was initiated in 1972 by the National Organization for the Reform of Marihuana Laws and worked its way through the legal system with excruciating slowness. In 1986 the administrator of the DEA finally announced that he would hold the public hearings ordered by the courts seven years before. Those hearings, which began in 1986 and lasted two years, involved many witnesses, including both patients and doctors, and thousands of pages of documentation. The DEA's own Administrative Law Judge, Francis J. Young, reviewed the evidence and rendered his decision in 1988. Young said that approval by a "significant minority" of physicians was enough to meet the standard of "currently accepted medical use in treatment in the United States" established by the Controlled Substances Act for a Schedule II (prescription) drug. He added that "marihuana, in its natural form, is one of the safest therapeutically active substances known to man. . . . One must reasonably conclude that there is accepted safety for use of marihuana under medical supervision. To conclude otherwise, on the record, would be unreasonable, arbitrary, and capricious." Young went on to recommend "that the Administrator [of the DEA] conclude that the marihuana plant considered as a whole has a currently accepted medical use in treatment in the United States, that there is no lack of accepted safety for use of it under medical supervision, and that it may be lawfully transferred from Schedule I to Schedule II."

The DEA disregarded the opinion of its own Administrative Law Judge and refused to reschedule marihuana. As the agency's lawyer remarked, "The judge seems to hang his hat on what he calls a respectable minority of physicians. What percent are you talking about? One half of one percent? One quarter of one percent?" DEA Administrator John Long went further, calling claims for the medical utility of marihuana a "dangerous and cruel hoax." In the last twenty years, as the medical potential of cannabis has become increasingly clear, I have witnessed the growing frustration of patients who cannot obtain it legally. The United States government must accept responsibility for the unnecessary suffering produced by a policy that can only be described as ignorant and cruel, and for forcing its citizens to engage in criminal activity. Despite government obstructionism, many patients have learned to use marihuana therapeutically and many more are discovering its benefits. Unfortunately, they have to endure the anxiety imposed by the threat of arrest and their feelings about breaking the law, and they are compelled to pay exorbitant street prices for a medicine that should be quite inexpensive[1].

Re-reading *Marihuana Reconsidered* now, I find that some chapters, such as those on chemistry, pharmacology, and medical uses, are out of date. Some of the ideas expressed in the book now seem a little quaint to me as well. The tone is more conservative than it would be if I were to undertake the same task today. Although I still believe that marihuana is not harmless, I am convinced that it is one of the least dangerous, if not the least dangerous, of all psychoactive drugs, legal or illegal, recreational or medicinal.

Another impression I have in re-reading the book is a certain neglect of uses of marihuana that are neither strictly medical nor strictly recreational. I wrote in 1971 that "My intention is to present a reasonably accurate and comprehensive account of the drug and its properties and to put into perspective its dangers and utilities." At that time, largely because of my ignorance, "utilities" referred only to medicine. Experience over the last twenty years has compelled me to take much more seriously the claims of those who believe that cannabis has useful properties that cannot be described as medical.

---

[1] For a detailed account of the growing place of cannabis in the treatment of a variety of disorders, see Lester Grinspoon and James B. Bakalar, *Marihuana, the Forbidden Medicine* (New Haven: Yale University Press, 1993).

For example, I no longer doubt that marihuana can be an intellectual stimulant. It can help the user to penetrate conceptual boundaries, promote fluidity of associations, and enhance insight and creativity. Some people find it so useful in gaining new perspectives or seeing problems from a different vantage point that they smoke it in preparation for intellectual work. I suspect that these people have learned to make use of the alteration in consciousness produced by cannabis. Other ways in which cannabis is useful probably have less to do with learning. It can enhance the appreciation of food, music, sexual activity, natural beauty, and other sensual experiences. Under the right conditions and in the right settings, it can promote emotional intimacy. For almost everyone it has the capacity to highlight the comical in life and catalyze a deep and salutary laughter.

Perhaps in part because so many Americans have discovered for themselves that marihuana is both relatively benign and remarkably useful, moral consensus about the evil of cannabis is uncertain and shallow. The authorities pretend that eliminating cannabis traffic is like eliminating slavery or piracy, or like eradicating smallpox or malaria. The official view is that everything possible has to be done to prevent everyone from ever using marihuana. But there is also an informal lore of marihuana use that is far more tolerant. Many of the millions of cannabis users in this country not only disobey the drug laws but feel a principled lack of respect for them. They do not conceal their bitter resentment of laws that render them criminals. They believe that many people have been deceived by their government, and they have come to doubt that the "authorities" understand much about either the deleterious or the useful properties of the drug. This undercurrent of ambivalence and resistance in public attitudes towards marihuana laws leaves room for the possibility of change, especially since the costs of prohibition are all so high and rising. At the present time more than 300,000 people a year are arrested on marihuana charges, contributing to the clogging of courts and the overcrowding of prisons.

Besides the measurable billions wasted on prohibition, there are costs more difficult to quantify. One of them is lost credibility of government. Young people who discover that the authorities have been lying about cannabis become cynical about their pronouncements on other drugs and disdainful of their commitment to justice. Another frightful cost of prohibition is the erosion of civil liberties.

The use of informers and entrapment, mandatory urine testing, unwarranted searches and seizures, and violations of the Posse Comitatus Act (which outlaws the use of military forces for civilian law enforcement) are becoming more common. It is increasingly clear that our society cannot be both drug-free and free.

It is also clear that the realities of human need are incompatible with the demand for a legally enforceable distinction between medicine and all other uses of cannabis. Marihuana use simply does not conform to the conceptual boundaries established by twentieth-century institutions. It enhances many pleasures and it has many potential medical uses, but even these two categories are not the only relevant ones. The kind of therapy often used to ease everyday discomforts does not fit any such scheme. In many cases what lay people do in prescribing marihuana for themselves is not very different from what physicians do when they provide prescriptions for psychoactive or other drugs. The only workable way of realizing the full potential of this remarkable substance, including its full medical potential, is to free it from the present dual set of regulations — those that control prescription drugs in general and the special criminal laws that control psychoactive substances. These mutually reinforcing laws establish a set of social categories that strangle its uniquely multifaceted potential. The only way out is to cut the knot by giving marihuana the same status as alcohol — legalizing it for adults for all uses and removing it entirely from the medical and criminal control systems.

Given my record as a prophet, it may be foolhardy for me to make any further predictions about the fate of marihuana. Yet I still believe that eventually the people of the United States and the world will recognize the individual and social benefits of this drug and the enormous cost of the present prohibition. One day, I hope, we will look back and wonder why our societies were so perverse as to treat cannabis as they did for the greater part of the twentieth century.

Preface to the Second Edition, 1977

This edition contains a new chapter in which James B. Bakalar and I have attempted to summarize the major developments in cannabis research since *Marihuana Reconsidered* was first published. We have touched on the changing social and legal aspects of the growing use of marihuana in this country, but our major involvement is with current clinical and laboratory findings relative to the potential health hazards of cannabis. These investigations have resulted in the passing of most old concerns and the appearance of some new ones. We have tried to relate these more recent findings to what was known in 1971 and with them put marihuana in perspective as a medical and social issue. Finally, we have reviewed the possibilities arising from an aspect of marihuana research that is attracting increased interest and funding: the therapeutic potential of cannabis. Works that reflect these developments have been added to the Selected Bibliography.

Lester Grinspoon, M.D.
Boston, Massachusetts
April 1977

Preface to the First Edition, 1971

Most of this book is addressed to the nonspecialist reader, although Chapter 3, "Chemistry and Pharmacology," demands some background in chemistry or medicine. It was included as part of an overall effort to provide a reasonably comprehensive view of the current state of knowledge of cannabis and its derivatives. The reader who does not have the appropriate background might skip this chapter; its omission will not significantly diminish his comprehension of the remainder of the book.

I had originally planned, also primarily for the sake of completeness, an opening chapter on the early history of cannabis. However, I soon found that because the literature contained so many contradictions, discrepancies, uncertainties, difficulties in obtaining primary sources, and statements which appeared more mythological than factual, it would be impossible to do more than contribute another largely apocryphal account. For that reason the chapter was abandoned, and those aspects of the early history which are relevant to particular topics appear in the corresponding chapters.

During the course of writing this book I incurred indebtedness to a number of people. It was Murray Chastain of Harvard University Press who encouraged me to undertake this project, and for this I am now grateful. William von Eggers Doering, Richard E. Schultes, Donald Berman, Carl Sagan, David Vigoda, and Jack R. Ewalt read parts of the manuscript and offered many invaluable criticisms and suggestions. R. David Hill and Craig Wood helped with the research, Kathleen Karant did much of the typing, and the entire manuscript benefited from the editorial skills of Kitty Dexter.

Susan Payne, librarian at the Massachusetts Mental Health Center, spared no effort in seeking out particular books or papers, some of them rather obscure. I am particularly indebted to Peter Hedblom, who in addition to helping with much of the research, suggested some of the formulations which appear in several of the chapters. I am also most grateful to Linda Twing and my wife, Betsy, for their devotion to this project and the many ways each contributed to it. Finally, for his unique contribution to Chapter 4, I am most indebted to Mr. X.

L. G.

Acknowledgements

The author wishes to acknowledge his appreciation and gratitude to the following authors, publishers, and publications for permission to quote from the works listed below:

Quotations from *Marijuana* by Erich Goode are reprinted by permission of the publisher, Atherton Press, Inc., copyright © 1969, Atherton Press, Inc., New York, all rights reserved; quotations from *Marijuana: America's New Drug Problem* by R. P. Walton are reprinted by permission of the publisher, J. B. Lippincott Company, copyright © 1938, J. B. Lippincott Company, Philadelphia, Penn.; quotations from "Pot: A Rational Approach" by Dr. Joel Fort originally appeared in *Playboy* magazine, copyright © 1969, HMH Publishing Company, Inc.; quotations from "Marihuana and Temporal Disintegration," F. T. Melges, *et al.*, *Science*, 168 (May 29, 1970), 1118–1120, are reprinted by permission of the publisher, *Science*, copyright © 1970 by the American Association for the Advancement of Science; quotations from "First Manifesto to End the Bringdown" by Allen Ginsberg are published with the author's permission, copyright © 1966, Allen Ginsberg; quotations from "Marihuana Psychosis: A Case Study" by G. D. Klee, *Psychiatric Quarterly*, 43 (1969), 719–733, are reprinted by permission of the publisher; quotations from *Marijuana, The Facts, The Truth* by W. Oursler are reprinted by permission of the publisher, Paul S. Eriksson, Inc., copyright © 1968, Paul S. Eriksson, Inc., New York; quotations from "A Comparison of Marijuana Users and Non-Users," N. E. Zinberg and A. T. Weil, *Nature*, 226 (April 11, 1970), 119–123, are reprinted by permission of the publisher; quotations from *Drugs: Medical, Psychological and*

Social Facts by P. Laurie are reprinted by permission of Penguin Books Ltd., copyright © 1967, P. Laurie; quotations from "Marihuana and Aggressive Crime" by W. Bromberg are reprinted by permission of *The American Journal of Psychiatry*, 102 (1946), 825–827, copyright © 1946, the American Psychiatric Association; quotations from "Marihuana Intoxication: A Clinical Study of Cannabis Sativa Intoxication" by Walter Bromberg are reprinted by permission of *The American Journal of Psychiatry*, 91 (1934), 303–330; quotations from "Experiments with Hashish" by V. Robinson are reprinted by permission of the *Ciba Symposia*, formerly published by Ciba Pharmaceutical Company, copyright 1946; quotations from "Who Says Marijuana Use Leads to Heroin Addiction?" by J. Mandel are reprinted by permission of the *Journal of Secondary Education*, 43 (1968), 211–217; quotations from "The Hashish Club," D. Solomon, ed., *The Marihuana Papers*, are reprinted by permission of R. J. Gladstone, trans., and the publisher, Bobbs-Merrill, New York, copyright © 1966, R. J. Gladstone; quotations from *The Drug Beat* by A. Geller and M. Boas are reprinted by permission of the publisher, Cowles Book Company, Inc., New York, copyright © 1969, A. Geller; quotations from "Notes and Comments," *The New Yorker*, August 30, 1969, pp. 17–19, are reprinted by permission of the publisher; quotations from "Marihuana and Sex" by Erich Goode are reprinted by permission of the publishers, *The Evergreen Review*, 66 (May 1969), and Basic Books, Inc., New York, copyright © 1970, Basic Books; quotations from *The Odyssey*, trans. Robert Fitzgerald, are reprinted by permission of Doubleday and Company, Inc., copyright © 1961 by Robert Fitzgerald; quotations from "Marijuana" by Lester Grinspoon, *McGraw-Hill Yearbook of Science and Technology 1971*, are reprinted by permission of the publisher, McGraw-Hill Book Company; quotations from *The Marihuana Problem in the City of New York* by the Mayor's Committee on Marihuana are reprinted by permission of the publisher, the Ronald Press Company, copyright © 1944 the Ronald Press Company, New York; quotations from "Notes on the Use of Hashish" by Sheldon Cholst appeared in D. Solomon, ed., *The Marihuana Papers*, published by Bobbs-Merrill Co., New York, copyright © 1965 by Sheldon Cholst; quotations from "Multiple Drug Use Among Marijuana Smokers" by Erich Goode, in *Social Problems,* vol. 17, no. 1 (summer 1969), pp. 48–64, are reprinted by permission of the Society for the Study of Social Problems; quotations from *Outsiders: Studies in the Sociology of Deviance* by H. S. Becker are reprinted by permission of the publisher, the Free Press of Glencoe (division of the Macmillan Company), and the University of Chicago Press and the Society of Applied Anthropology; quotations from *Marijuana* by Edward R. Bloomquist are reprinted by permission of the publisher, Glencoe Press, Beverly Hills, California (division of the Macmillan Company), copyright © 1968 by Edward R. Bloomquist; quotations from "Interview with Allen Ginsberg," *Writers at Work: The Paris Review Interviews,* 3rd ser., are reprinted by permission of The Viking Press, Inc., and Martin Secker and Warburg, Ltd., copyright © 1967, The Paris Review, Inc.; quotations from "The Change: Kyoto-Tokyo Express," in *Planet News* by Allen Ginsberg are reprinted by permission of the publisher, City Lights Books, copyright © 1968, Allen Ginsberg; quotations from *Miserable Miracle* by Henri Michaux are reprinted by permission of the publisher, City Lights Books, copyright © 1963, Louise Varese; quotations from "Drug Dependence— A Socio-Pharmacological Assessment" by W. D. M. Paton, in *Advancement of Science* (December, 1968), pp. 200–212, are reprinted by permission of the British Association for the Advancement of Science; quotations from *Light Through Darkness* by Henri Michaux are reprinted by permission of the publishers, the Orion Press, Inc., Librairie Gallimard, and Bodley Head, copyright © Librairie Gallimard, 1961, copyright © the Orion Press, Inc., 1963.

Marihuana
Reconsidered

Contents

Introduction 1

1 The History of Marihuana in the United States 10

2 From Plant to Intoxicant 30

3 Chemistry and Pharmacology 42

4 The Acute Intoxication: Literary and Other Reports 55

5 The Acute Intoxication: Its Properties 117

6 Motivation of the User 173

7 Turning On 185

8 The Place of Cannabis in Medicine 218

9 Addiction, Dependence, and the "Stepping-Stone"
Hypothesis 231

10 Psychoses, Adverse Reactions, and Personality
Deterioration 253

11 Crime and Sexual Excess 291

12 The Campaign against Marihuana 323

13 The Question of Legalization 344

14 Marihuana: Six Years of Reconsideration
(with James B. Bakalar) 372

Abbreviations 403

Selected Bibliography 407

Notes 417

Index 463

Introduction

Marihuana is the North American name of a weedlike plant whose unusual products have enjoyed a long, frequently strange, and, especially in the West, ambivalent association with mankind. Definitively labeled *Cannabis sativa* by Linnaeus in 1753, the plant is in most parts of the world better known by its popular name, Indian hemp. Requiring little more than a climate with hot summers, cannabis can be, and is, grown both legally and illegally all over the world, wild or cultivated, for utilitarian or intoxicant use, from Calcutta to Beacon Hill.

At least as interesting as its fascinating psychoactive properties and as ancient as its medicinal applications is the controversy its use as a euphoriant has invariably generated. The first recorded use of marihuana is to be found in the *Herbal*, an ancient equivalent of the *U.S. Pharmacopoeia*, written about 400 to 500 B.C. And even then there were those who felt that the road to Hades was lined with hemp plants, and others who felt that the path to Utopia was shaded by the freely growing *Cannabis sativa*.

Few drugs in the United States have produced as much affective heat as cannabis, particularly during the last decade. The controversy essentially revolves around the question of how dangerous or safe the drug is. The established belief views marihuana as an addicting drug that leads to personality deterioration and psychoses and to criminal behavior and sexual excess. For many, its use seems to forebode such catastrophe to the individual and the country that only laws that are Draconian in intent and execution will contain the threat. This view is epitomized in several of the Southern states — Georgia, for example, where the first offense for the transfer or sale of marihuana from an older person to one below the age of 21 carries the penalty of life imprisonment, a second offense carries the penalty of death, and there is naturally, no provision for a third offense.

The polar view asserts that it is no more harmful than aspirin, and therefore should be equally available. While there are relatively few who will go this far, a view expressed increasingly often is that the single greatest risk encountered by the user of marihuana in any state in this country is that of being apprehended as a common criminal, incarcerated, and subjected to untold damage to his social life and career. Many would maintain further that this risk varies not so much with the quantity, form, or potency of the cannabis, but rather with the user's background and family, and such things as the length of the hair on his face and head and other evidence of deviance from social norms, perhaps even his political views and activities.

It was inevitable with the explosive growth of the use of marihuana over the last decade, particularly among young people and, more recently, older middle-class people, that the governor's son, the socially important person's daughter, the senator's grandson, and prominent academic people would be busted. And if these dramatic events gave some visibility to the fact that smoking pot was now becoming a middle-class phenomenon, they more strikingly suggested the extent to which its use was hidden from view. The very burgeoning of the use of marihuana in this country makes it abundantly clear that, whatever else they are, the laws dealing with the distribution and use of cannabis are quite ineffective. And, although it is not so apparent, it is equally true that the application of the law has been inequitable, often barbaric, and counterproductive.

With the increasing public concern over the drug problem, considerable interest has arisen in reexamining the punitive measures attached to its use. In several challenges of the law in court and deliberations about changing the law in legislative hearings, the nuclear question has always been, "What is the nature and the degree of the danger of using marihuana?" In advocate situations, expert witnesses have always been found who claim that there are great dangers and others who assert just as authoritatively that the drug is completely without danger. The partisans of these respective positions can find in the marihuana literature considerable material, if not data, to support their positions. The listener ends up totally bewildered and often finds himself compelled to conclude that not enough is known about the drug to warrant any change in approach to its distribution, possession, and use. High government medical officials testifying before legislative bodies generally take this position. They go on to reassure us that now that this information gap has been discovered, the government, particularly through the National Institutes of Health, is itself undertaking a broad program of research to provide the much-needed data upon which, sometime in the future, changes might be made. In the meantime, they say, we should continue to frighten, perhaps unnecessarily, many people, throw some in jail, and witness the greatest disregard of a law since the Volstead Act. It is certainly true that more and better research on marihuana is needed, but it does not necessarily follow that we do not know enough about the drug to define a more rational policy with regard to its social use than the one that exists today.

There is in an absolute sense a fairly large body of literature on cannabis. In 1951 the *Bulletin on Narcotics* of the United Nations published a comprehensive list of titles that included a total of 1,104 references. At the request of the Commission on Narcotic Drugs, a more complete bibliography was prepared in 1965. It included 1,860 titles. O. J. Kalant corrected this bibliography for errors and duplications and brought it up to date so that it now includes nearly 2,000 titles, only 377 of which appeared before the year 1900. The United Nations bibliography is comprehensive and includes the periodical literature of the nineteenth and twentieth centuries, pamphlets, books, theses, ancient documents from various parts of the world, literary works, and a substantial number of League of Nations and United Nations documents. Kalant estimates that, of these works, those of a sound medical or scientific character probably do not account for more than half of the total bibliography. I believe that this is probably a generous estimate. The language distribution of the titles of the Kalant revision of the U.N. bibliographies is as follows: English, 1,073; French, 309; German, 232; Portuguese, 116; Spanish, 85; Italian, 38; others, 111; total, 1,964. Less than 40 papers per decade were written before 1840. From that time until 1879, an average of about 40 titles per decade appeared. From 1800 to 1929, the number of publications averaged about 120 per decade. From 1930 to 1959 there appeared about 300 titles per decade.[1] The number of titles in the 1960's probably exceeds 500.

When one considers that this most fascinating and controversial drug has been used for thousands of years and by millions of people throughout the world, 2,000 publications does not appear to be a very large literature. Moreover, only a fraction of these are reasonably sound medical or scientific articles. Another intoxicant, which also has an ancient history, has been written about much more widely; the number of selected scientific papers in the Classified Abstract Archive of the Alcohol Literature was given as 11,847 in 1966. This is not to speak of the nonscientific papers. The list of papers on amphetamines, which were introduced as recently as the late 1920's, presently consists of more than 2,000 titles.

One is compelled to ask why there is so little literature on a drug whose properties are as interesting as its use is widespread. Until relatively recently, hemp was not very much used as an intoxicant in the more scientifically oriented Western countries. Had its use been earlier established, no doubt there would be a larger collection of scientific papers devoted to it. The heyday of Western medical exploration of cannabis as a possible therapeutic tool from about 1840 to 1900 did not establish it as the hoped-for panacea, but one might have expected that such an attempt, with the promising leads that were generated, would not have been so soon almost totally abandoned. One would certainly have expected that after the early 1940's, when the tetrahydrocannabinols had been identified as pure substances having cannabislike action, the search for marihuana's therapeutic utility would have been pressed with considerable vigor, as is the case with so many classes of drugs that exhibit psychoactive properties. Such an expectation is especially reasonable in the case of cannabis, which has through the ages served as an indigenous medicine in vast areas of the world and for which many undocumented anecdotal claims for therapeutic utility in various ailments have been made. Research prior to the early 1940's was hampered by the necessity of using the raw plant or various crude, ill-defined chemical extracts that were notoriously unstable and of inconsistent potency, but this problem was largely overcome with the development of the ability to prepare pure tetrahydrocannabinol. That the burst of research activity which might have been anticipated at this time did not develop may, in large part, be due to the drug's bad reputation and the restrictions and harassment imposed on researchers after the passage in 1937 of the Marihuana Tax Act.

Just because there has been a relative vacuum of research on every aspect of this drug since the early 1940's, the nature of the information now available is, on the whole, considerably less precise than it might be had studies of it been unfettered by its bad name and paralegal problems. Thus, with the exception of a few recent studies, cannabis has escaped the more critical scrutiny and finer resolution power of modern laboratory techniques, research designs, and methodologies. The isolation and identification of tetrahydrocannabinol by R. Adams in the early 1940's certainly opened the door to more precise investigation.[2] This development should have made it unnecessary to have to qualify all of the studies reviewed in this volume with the statement that no two of them involved the same amount of the same substance; further, no two studies used comparable or representative samples of individuals, nor did they observe or measure comparable behavior with comparable instruments.

Tetrahydrocannabinol has been used in some recent studies, but there is no question that in most of the various laboratory studies the substances used and their potencies varied considerably. In some studies, for example, an alcoholic fluid concentrate may have been used, whereas in others finely chopped flowering tops and leaves of Indian hemp plants from different areas of the world were smoked. Furthermore, these whole preparations contain more than just stereoisomers of tetrahydrocannabinol, and it is possible that other cannabinol derivatives do have pharmacological activity. It is not known exactly what the active constituents of marihuana smoke are, except that they probably are not the same, at least in quantity, as those of ingested cannabis.

In addition to this problem of comparable potency and substances, there is the problem of set and setting. Experienced laboratory investigators as well as users of marihuana know that the effects of this drug are influenced by the physiological characteristics and condition of the individual, by his psychological makeup and state, by his reasons for using the drug, by his fantasies about the effect of the experience, and by the physical and social factors that define the setting in which the drug is used or administered. A precise laboratory experiment on the effects of marihuana should take these variables into consideration.

The situation is even more complicated than this. It is a principle of psychopharmacology that the effect of any single substance may vary with the route of administration. The routes of administration used in these studies were frequently different; the drug can be absorbed through the digestive tract or through inhalation, and both routes were used. Another principle of psychopharmacology is that the effect of a drug bears a relationship to the dose. There is the dose required to produce the defined effect in 50 percent of the subjects (the effective dose or ED50), the dose required to produce toxicity, depending on how one defines toxicity, in 50 percent of the subjects (the toxic dose or TD50), and finally the dose which leads to the death of 50 percent of the subjects (the lethal dose or LD50). Again, in almost all of the extant studies, the dosage is not precisely defined, and if it is taken into account at all, it is usually in terms of "high" and "low" dosage levels, which means that the different effects are difficult to relate to those of other investigations. Most of what has been said so far with respect to human laboratory studies applies equally to studies involving animals.

Further difficulties are imposed by the fact that these studies cannot be performed on a group of human subjects who, like a litter of laboratory mice, are nearly identical to each other. If it is true that "the psychological effects of marihuana are as varied as the range of human personality and as complex as the factors which influence the user each time he smokes," then it is extremely difficult to control human laboratory studies on marihuana even under the best of circumstances.[3] The fact of the matter is that much of the human laboratory research completed to date has used subjects as diverse as inmates of mental hospitals and prisons and bright, healthy, young students. Another tenet of modern psychopharmacology is that one designs into the study a control, that is, half of the subjects are randomly selected, unbeknownst to them or to the laboratory personnel who are administering the drug and measuring the effects, to receive a placebo, while the other half receives the drug being studied. This is an effective way of ferreting out what is truly an effect of the drug from what may be an effect of extraneous variables such as the subject's expectations. As the reader may have surmised by now, few cannabis studies are properly controlled.

Any attempt at a critical assessment of the properties of cannabis must allow for these weaknesses in laboratory studies. Cannabis is not peculiar in this respect, however. It has suffered more than others, largely because it has not benefited from as much recent attention as it should have, but there are relatively few really good studies of any psychoactive drug. Where human laboratory drug studies are concerned, because of such problems as subject selection, proper controls, and ethical considerations, no study is perfect. Nonetheless, within the limits imposed by these difficulties, there is much need for psychopharmacological studies of cannabis that take advantage of the more rigorous modern research designs, methodologies, and statistical techniques.

Better laboratory studies of cannabis can and will be made. But what are we to do in the meantime? Are we to assume that there is no baby in all of that bathwater? Are we simply to dismiss any attempt to review the present approach to the problem of the explosively growing social use of marihuana simply because we do not have very much modern data? Will the geometrically growing number of cannabis devotees stop using it until we have such data? Or can we, through a careful and critical assessment of the extant studies, arrive at, at the very least, a global, albeit qualified, understanding of the psychopharmacological properties of this drug? I believe that we can discern this much from the studies which already exist. More subtle understanding of the psychopharmacological properties will have to await the maturity of the new generation of cannabis investigations, just now undergoing birth and not without considerable pain. And again we have to question how much an increment of sophistication about the psychopharmacological properties will bear on the problem of how society should address itself to its increasing popularity. Clearly this new knowledge will be of great importance, but I think more for what it will teach us about the human organism as a biochemical, physiological, and psychological system than for any revelation of dangers to men and their societies which are not already apparent. I think research is just as likely to lead to new clinical utilities as it is to establish cannabis as an etiologic agent in organic or functional illnesses.

While knowledge about any drug which can be obtained from the laboratory, both human and animal, is essential to an understanding of both its usefulness and harmfulness, in the case of a widely used, self-administered intoxicant there are other domains for the collection of information. And with respect to the question of the dangers of acute intoxication with and long-term use of cannabis, studies exploiting the fact that millions of people are and for a long time have been using hemp products may provide data that are actually far more relevant to the question of how its use as an intoxicant should be dealt with than are data generated in the laboratory. Needless to say, there are vast problems with these naturalistic studies. They are, in general, uncontrolled studies of self-selected populations of individuals who have used a number of different hemp products in different doses and ways over varying conditions and periods of time. But much the same can be said of cigarette smokers and users of alcohol, and we have been able, through studies of populations of smokers and drinkers, to delineate the dangers of these self-administered drugs and in a rough fashion to relate these risks to dose.

Studying the medical consequences to users of drugs in this fashion is quite similar to studying the natural history of a disease. While the modern laboratory is essential to the ever-growing body of knowledge of the etiology, treatment, and prevention of all diseases, descriptions of most diseases and what was likely to happen to an afflicted person were well established long before the development of modern laboratory techniques. Of the body of knowledge known as modern medicine, the clinical segment particularly was largely derived from observations and studies which could hardly be considered controlled, rigorous, or even scientific. And just as even before the development of modern laboratory, epidemiologic, and statistical techniques it was possible to have considerable clinical knowledge of most diseases, so it is possible to know much about cannabis from the imperfect descriptions and studies, the natural history, as it were, of its acute and chronic use.

We are at present a long way from knowing all we eventually must to be completely successful in the prevention and treatment of disease, but long before the advent of modern medicine we knew that phlebotomization as a treatment method was completely ineffective; yet we continue to make use of a kind of bloodletting when it comes to the treatment of the use of marihuana. The important question with respect to the existing information about cannabis is whether or not it presently provides evidence convincing enough of its dangers to the individual and society to justify the continuance of the present punitive approach on the part of law enforcement agencies.

My purpose in this study is not — as some will certainly think — to attempt to establish that cannabis is a harmless drug. It is not possible to do that for any drug, let alone one with psychoactive properties. Nor is it possible at this time, I am convinced, to write a completely objective statement concerning marihuana. My intention is to present a reasonably accurate and comprehensive account of the drug and its properties and to put into perspective its dangers and utilities. It is important to do this now, because use of the drug is growing explosively, and if we are to reexamine our present approach to the problem, we must try to divest ourselves as much as possible of the mythology, distortion, and hyperemotionalism surrounding the drug. The studies presently available are less than perfect, but until better ones are completed we quite obviously cannot declare a moratorium on either the use of cannabis or the punitive reaction to this use. What we can do is to use critically the available data to approximate a body of knowledge about this drug and to update it as new and better-designed scientific studies are completed. Such a body of knowledge may help to light the way to a more reasoned approach to the use of cannabis. It is still better to light one candle than to curse the darkness.

1 The History of Marihuana in the United States

During the course of its history, the United States has both zealously embraced and vigorously outlawed the cannabis plant and its various products. Cultivation of the plant for its fibrous content was practically simultaneous with the founding of the early American colonies. Until the Civil War, hemp fiber continued to be a cash crop, the source of the rope that rigged many of the world's sailing ships and the rough fabric that covered westward-bound American pioneer wagons. Following the decline of the hemp rope and canvas industry in the second half of the nineteenth century, ingenious American entrepreneurs discovered other uses for Indian hemp. Paper industries began to use the fiber in the manufacture of fine-grade papers, including those used in Bibles and paper currency. In addition, birdseed manufacturers rated the cannabis seed, rich in sugar and albumin, second in quality only to the sunflower seed as an ingredient in their mixtures. It appeared as a reliable therapeutic in the *U.S. Pharmacopoeia* and *National Formulary,* and until 1937 tincture of cannabis could be prescribed by physicians as a remedy for a variety of ailments.

For centuries of American history, the use of the plant as an intoxicant was exceedingly rare. Indeed, it is generally assumed that knowledge of the plant's intoxicating properties was nonexistent; certainly Kentucky pioneers cultivated tons of hemp without a single recorded use of the plant as an intoxicant. As R. Blum has pointed out, there is no evidence that, simply because a plant is native or even cultivated as hemp is for fiber, there will be knowledge of its psychoactive properties.[1] However, as a result of the increase of marihuana smoking in the southern states during the

1920's, the United States Federal Bureau of Narcotics, under the direction of Commissioner H. J. Anslinger, conducted a campaign against cannabis that resulted in the Marihuana Tax Act of 1937 and the dramatic end of America's unsupervised romance with Indian hemp and its products. Although the Tax Act was styled as a revenue-producing measure, it prohibited use of cannabis as an intoxicant and effectively circumscribed the "legitimate" industrial uses of the plant.

America's early relations with hemp were a compulsory inheritance from the mother country. England had long relied on the hemp plant for a number of important items: windmill and ship sails, fine napkins, sheets and altar cloths, meal bags and horse blankets, and flags were all produced from the 5- to 15-foot-long white bast fiber located in the pericycle of the hemp stalk. Caulking made from old hemp rope was another important product. Hemp was so useful that Henry VIII required its cultivation by English farmers. The home supply of hemp apparently dwindled, however, as the expansion of the English fleet during Elizabeth's reign increased the demand for fiber. Domestic flax, whose strands were short, was unsuitable for making rope or sails, and England's trade conflict with the Dutch, whose ships were to have supplied her with hemp grown in the Baltic and Dutch East Indies, made the shortage acute. The first American crop of Indian hemp, planted in 1611 near Jamestown, Virginia, thus represented an attempt to ameliorate an economic crisis.

The climate of the American colonies was considered ideal for growing hemp and flax, and the English looked forward to an abundant yield. King James I ordered the settlers to produce "iron, cordage, hemp, flax and silkgrass . . ." and firmly corrected Sir Walter Raleigh when the latter suggested that energy might be better put to the cultivation of tobacco, which was just being introduced into Europe. The Virginia Company made the cultivation of hemp a part of its contract agreement.[2]

The hemp grown in America proved to be excellent for bagging, webbing, twine, and marine rope. In addition, according to one source, by 1630 half of the winter clothing of Americans and nearly all of their summer clothing was made from hemp fiber.[3]

During and after the Revolution, American settlers continued to grow hemp, chiefly in the area of what became Kentucky. Hemp farming became a respectable, often familial occupation. In fact, one of America's founding fathers, George Washington, was actively engaged in hemp farming, and devotees of the intoxicant properties of cannabis have read much into some scanty entries he made in his diary in 1765. G. Andrews and S. Vinkenoog, in citing these entries, preface them as follows:

> The . . . entries from George Washington's Diary show that he personally planted and harvested hemp. As it is known that the potency of the female plants decreases after they have been fertilized by the males, the fact that he regrets having separated the male from the female plants too late (after fertilization) clearly indicates that he was cultivating the plant for medicinal purposes as well as for its fibre.

> 1765   May 12–13   Sowed Hemp at Muddy hole by Swamp.
>   August 7   began to separate [sic] the Male from the Female hemp . . . rather too late.[4]

The belief that unfertilized female plants are more productive of resin than fertilized ones is apparently in error. E. M. Houghton and H. C. Hamilton in careful studies found products from each to be equally active.[5]

The crop grew easily, and required only sufficient hand labor to sow and harvest it. Black slave labor brought the crop to yield. Despite the relative ease of actually growing and harvesting hemp, however, commercial farmers were plagued by a number of difficulties which included wildly fluctuating prices and competition with higher-quality Russian hemp.[6]

The Civil War discouraged the industry beyond all hope of resuscitation. Union embargoes of southern ports caused a crisis in the southern cotton production. Because hemp products had come to be used heavily in the cotton baling process, the decrease of the cotton production indirectly curtailed hemp production. Also, the industry's labor supply disappeared with the freeing of the slave. Finally, with the radical decline of sail-ship building and the introduction of Philippine Island hemp, the industry entered a slump from which it never recovered.

In the 1940's it was estimated that 60 percent of the world's hemp came from Russia, with the United States contributing less than 1 percent. Because of the Japanese occupation of the Philippines during World War II, which had cut off the American supply of sisal rope, the United States government briefly encouraged domestic hemp cultivation during the 1940's. After the war, however, with foreign imports supplemented by the development of synthetic fibers, the market for domestic hemp dwindled again to nothing.

Other uses for hemp fiber were found. The United States Department of Agriculture published in 1916 the results of a study investigating the possibility of using hemp "hurds," the inner woody portion of a hemp stalk, in the manufacture of various fine-grade papers. Thus the plant which later came to be termed "Devil's Weed" began to be used in the production of Bibles. And its seeds found a number of uses, some of which were described by V. Robinson in 1925 as follows:

> The plant is also cultivated for its seeds, which contain a large quantity of oil, and is therefore used in pharmacy for emulsions, and in the domestic arts because of its drying properties. But the seeds are chiefly used as a favourite food for birds. In fact, some birds consume them to excess, which should lead us to suspect that these seeds, though they cannot intoxicate us, have a narcotic effect on the feathered creatures, making them dream of a happy birdland where there are no gilded cages and where the men are gunless and the women hatless. The seeds also contain sugar and considerable albumin, making them very nutritious; rabbits eat them readily. They are consumed also by some human beings, but are not as good as the sunflower seeds . . .[7]

Prior to 1937, the legitimate use of cannabis as a medicine was familiar in the United States. Although the plant had been used for centuries as a folk medicine, Europe and America became acquainted with the therapeutic possibilities of the plant only after 1839. Between 1839 and 1900 more than one hundred articles appeared in scientific journals describing the medicinal properties of the plant. The instability of the medicinal preparation, "Cannabis indica," contributed to the uncertainty of the potency of many of the preparations used. This uncertainty was reflected in a widespread concern that it was impossible to grow plants rich in the drug in the United States. The problem was investigated by Houghton and Hamilton, who grew the plants in Mexico, Kentucky, and Michigan and harvested them for medical purposes. They tested solid and fluid cannabis extracts in dogs and from their results concluded that the American-grown products were just as potent as the foreign imports. However, they noted that the plants had to be grown in certain parts of the United States and Mexico and that they had to be grown and harvested, and the products prepared, in the proper way. They noted that plants grown for fiber content should be planted in warm wet areas with rich loamy soil, while those cultivated for the production of the drug should be planted in hot, dry areas with soil that is somewhat sandy.[8]

After the introduction of injectable opiates in the latter half of the nineteenth century and of specific synthetic analgesics and hypnotics in the first decades of the twentieth century, the use of cannabis as a medicine decreased. However, as late as 1937 the Committee on Legislative Activities, in protesting the impending 1937 Marihuana Tax Act, reported to the American Medical Association: "There is positively no evidence to indicate the abuse of cannabis as a medicinal agent or to show that its medicinal use is leading to the development of cannabis addiction . . . [and] it would seem worthwhile to maintain its status as a medicinal agent for such purposes as it now has." [9] While the Tax Act did not proscribe the medical use of cannabis, it imposed a registration tax and record keeping which made its use so cumbersome that other drugs were invariably prescribed in its place, and "cannabis indica" was soon no longer to be found in the *U.S. Pharmacopoeia* and *National Formulary*.

A good deal of mystery and uncertainty surrounds the story of the "reefer's" debut in the United States. It is generally assumed that in the early decades of this century the custom of smoking the weed in cigarette form traveled with groups of itinerant Mexican workers across the Texas border into the southwestern and southern states. In 1910 the reefer began attracting some slight attention in New Orleans. By 1926, according to R. P. Walton, who studied the problem "on location," the city was wet with the habit. Supplies of marihuana came occasionally from Texas and more often by boat from Havana, Tampico, and Vera Cruz. Using New Orleans as a distributing center for the intoxicant, enterprising sailors became traffickers. The dried plant leaves were shipped from New Orleans up the Mississippi to various river ports and thence cross-country to large cities. It is said that by 1930 there was not one major American city which did not boast

among its ranks a few marihuana smokers. The national newspapers carried horror-filled stories of the "Marihuana Menace."
In 1936 a state narcotics officer attributed 60 percent of the crimes
committed that year in New Orleans to use of the intoxicant.[10]

In its early American years, however, the reefer did not cause a
great deal of consternation, perhaps because it was used almost
exclusively by minority groups. Marihuana smoking was familiar
among Mexican-Americans and it became a favorite of Negroes,
particularly jazz musicians, in urban centers. Milton Mezzrow, one
of the few whites to master the black jazz idiom, and a smoker of
marihuana, provided the following description of the effects of
the drug:

> The first thing I noticed was that I began to hear my saxophone
> as though it was inside my head, but I couldn't hear much of the
> band in back of me, although I knew that they were there. . . .
> Then I began to feel the vibrations of the reed much more
> pronounced against my lip, and my head buzzed like a loud-
> speaker. I found I was slurring much better and putting just
> the right feeling into my phrases — I was really coming on. All
> the notes came easing out of my horn like they's already been
> made up, greased and stuffed into the bell, so all I had to do was
> blow a little and send them on their way, one right after the
> other, never missing, never behind time, all without an ounce
> of effort.[11]

A subculture with its own system of slang grew up around this
early use of the drug by musicians; the user was called a "viper,"
and one of the names for a joint was a "mezz." It is interesting to
note that in 1933 Mezzrow was approached by a successful radio
booking-agent who wanted the musician to form a company to sell
on a national scale Mezzrow's special type of marihuana cigarette.
Perhaps anticipating the impending prohibition of the drug,
Mezzrow declined, thus foreclosing what might have been an interesting and possibly quite significant chapter in the history of
marihuana in the United States.[12]

Marihuana started getting into trouble in the South in the
1920's. In Louisiana, the *New Orleans Item* pointed a critical
finger at the "moota," and hostilely claimed that the habit seemed
to be most widespread among groups of foreign extraction. Reporters for the *Item* became involved in undercover work among

the peddlers of the intoxicant. According to Walton, these reporters

> not only heard of but saw a large number of boys of school age buy and smoke "mootas". . . . Inquiries were made of 60 children all under 15 years of age, some of whom were girls. All knew what "mootas" were, where they could be bought and what effects could be expected. Most of these children were of poorer families and of foreign parentage.[13]

Perhaps some of the fury aroused by marihuana can be attributed to fear of that which is alien and un-American, which would make the drug seem a particularly dangerous and degenerate intoxicant. An especially blatant example of this sort of prejudice was published in the *New Orleans Medical and Surgical Journal* in 1931:

> The debasing and baneful influence of hashish and opium is not restricted to individuals but has manifested itself in nations and races as well. The dominant race and most enlightened countries are alcoholic, whilst the races and nations addicted to hemp and opium, some of which once attained to heights of culture and civilization have deteriorated both mentally and physically.[14]

In 1930, the year in which the Federal Bureau of Narcotics was founded, only sixteen states had laws prohibiting the use of marihuana. In contrast, by 1937, nearly every state had adopted legislation outlawing marihuana. Sociologists have speculated that pressure from the liquor lobby figured among the more subtle factors in this sudden legal onslaught. Following repeal of the 1919 Volstead Act in 1933, liquor manufacturers looked forward to a golden era of prosperity which the sudden emergence of a cheap popular intoxicant such as marihuana would endanger.[15]

More important, lack of scientific understanding concerning the effects of the drug enabled the alarmist propaganda of the Federal Bureau of Narcotics to go substantially unchallenged. In the 1930's, articles on the physiological and psychological effects of marihuana, most of them inaccurate, were rife. Each of them contributed to the atmosphere of dimly perceived danger that led the way to congressional action. One of the more amusing of these reports ran in the *Boston Herald*:

The weed itself looks and smells not unlike cat-nip. Have you ever seen the family cat under the influence of cat-nip? Well, that is something what the effects of the cigarettes are supposed to have on people.[16]

Scientists and officials with their lack of information did little to diminish the burgeoning fear that marihuana was a "killer drug," that it led not only to crime, but to insanity and moral deterioration as well. In fact, alarmist statements such as the following from Walton were the order of the day in the mid-thirties:

During the next few years New Orleans experienced a crime wave which unquestionably was greatly aggravated by the influence of this drug habit. . . . Youngsters known to be "muggle-heads" fortified themselves with the narcotic and proceeded to shoot down police, bank clerks and casual by-standers . . . Mr. Eugene Stanley, at that time District Attorney, declared that many of the crimes in New Orleans and the South were thus committed by criminals who relied on the drug to give them a false courage and freedom from restraint. . . .[17]

The Federal Bureau of Narcotics, spearheading an educational campaign to alert the American public to the dangers of marihuana, portrayed the drug as releasing great hostility and aggression and inciting normal people to commit all manner of crimes and violence. The Federal Bureau of Investigation joined in the campaign and issued alarmist warnings concerning the marihuana user:

He really becomes a fiend with savage or "cave man" tendencies. His sex desires are aroused and some of the most horrible crimes result. He hears light and sees sound. To get away from it, he suddenly becomes violent and may kill.

Contributers to the campaign against marihuana were plentiful. Mr. F. T. Merrill, a member of the Opium Research Committee of the Foreign Policy Association, wrote with assurance:

While numerous crimes were traced to its abuse, its peculiarly virulent effect, leading sometimes to insanity, makes its use dangerous to the individual and to society in general . . . intense over-excitement of the nerves and emotions leads to uncontrollable irritability and violent rages, which in most advanced forms cause assault and murder.

In 1938 the Foreign Policy Association published accounts of 10 cases, "culled at random from the files of the U.S. Bureau of Narcotics," of murder and assault caused directly by marihuana. These same cases, published in a number of other journals and popular magazines, gave the reader the impression that the marihuana user was a violent criminal given to rape, homicide, and mayhem. W. Bromberg reports as follows on one of the cases published by the Foreign Policy Association:

> Among the ten patients, the second, J. O., was described as having confessed how he murdered a friend and put his body in a trunk while under the influence of marihuana.
>
> J. O. was examined in this clinic; although he was a psychopathic liar and possibly homosexual, there was no indication in the examination or history of the use of any drug. The investigation by the probation department failed to indicate the use of the drug marihuana.[18]

Apparently much of the evidence of a crime-marihuana relationship came from voluntary statements by prisoners, who may well have been hoping for lighter sentences by thus attributing their crimes to the influence of a drug. In these cases of self-confessed evidence, there was, as Bromberg notes, no "opportunity for objective tests or other corroborative check, as in the case of other drugs, e.g. heroin or morphine." [19]

In 1934 Bromberg published the results of his study of 2,216 convicted felons indicted by the Court of General Sessions, New York County. All the individuals were examined psychiatrically. Bromberg reported:

> Of the 361 individuals diagnosed as psychopathic personality in the routine psychiatric examination 32 (9 percent) were drug addicts and of these only seven had smoked marihuana for any period of time. None of the assault cases could be said to have been committed under the drug's influence. No crimes were committed in this group during or immediately after intoxication. Of the sexual crimes (rape, sodomy, impairing morals of a minor, etc.) there were likewise none due to marihuana intoxication.[20]

In contrast to this sober academic study, which never achieved wide circulation, the Federal Bureau of Narcotics was at about the same time portraying the drug as "the Killer Drug 'Marihuana' — a powerful narcotic in which lurks *Murder! Insanity! Death!*" (see Fig. 6, Chap. 12).

Many of the nation's newspapers were aiding the efforts of the Federal Bureau of Narcotics. H. S. Becker reports that of seventeen articles on marihuana published within 1937–1939, "ten either explicitly acknowledged the help of the Bureau in furnishing facts and figures or gave implicit evidence of having received help by using facts and figures that had appeared earlier." Becker adds, "One clear indication of Bureau influence in the preparation of journalistic articles can be found in the recurrence of certain atrocity stories first reported by the Bureau." [21]

The following case study found in the files of the U.S. Bureau of Narcotics and reported by Anslinger in *The Traffic in Narcotics* provides a sense of the sensationalism and inadequate documentation of cases used by the Federal Bureau of Narcotics:

Del Rio, Texas. 1940. One Eleutero G. while allegedly under the influence of marihuana, shot to death two women and then committed suicide by literally slicing himself to bits about the abdomen, heart, and throat, in a manner which indicated that he was bereft of all reasoning. Law enforcement officers believed that G. was under the influence of marihuana at the time of the double murder and suicide and that he had previously used marihuana. It was the opinion of the doctor who saw G. just before he died that no one could so mutilate himself unless he was unable to feel "shock" and the only thing he knew that would produce such a condition, to such a degree, is marihuana. G. had wandered around in the fields for hours after the killing and after his self-mutilation.[22]

A few moderate voices emerged, but were for the most part lost in the welter. Walton acknowledged that no American agency had made a thorough study of the situation and cited the famous Indian Hemp Drugs Commission Study of 1894 as a possible model for such a study. The American Army added a judicious element to the debate. The physiological and psychological effects of marihuana smoking, as practiced by U.S. soldiers stationed in the Canal Zone, was reviewed. Published in 1933, the study concluded that the drug was relatively harmless and did not cause maladjustment in the user.[23]

Perhaps the least hostile article to appear in popular journals was published in the January 1937 issue of the *World Digest*. The article described a Negro "tea" or marihuana party:

> With their uncanny power for wheedling melody out of even the worst pianos, it wasn't long before the crowd was humming, softly clapping hands or dancing in sensuous rhythms that have never been seen in night-clubs. There is little noise; windows are shut, keeping the smell of smoking weeds away from what might be curious nostrils.
>
> Nor is there any of the yelling, dashing about, playing of crude jokes or physical violence that often accompany alcoholic parties; under the effects of marihuana one has a dread of all these things. Sensuous pleasure is the beginning and the end.[24]

The 1937 Tax Act was the culmination of a series of efforts on the part of the Federal Bureau of Narcotics to generate antimarihuana legislation. According to Becker, "The Federal Bureau of Narcotics cooperated actively with the National Conference of Commissioners on Uniform State Laws in developing uniform laws on narcotics, stressing among other matters the need to control marihuana use. In 1932 the Conference approved a draft law." In 1936 the Bureau was agitating with increased zeal, declaring that in the absence of federal legislation which would enable the Bureau itself to carry on an open "war" with the drug, narcotics agents were restricted to impressing upon the various states the urgent need for "vigorous enforcement of local cannabis laws," preparing "articles" on marihuana at the request of organizations dealing with the general subject of narcotics, and attempting to solicit "intelligent and sympathetic public interest." [25]

The legislative judgment that marihuana is a "harmful" substance was made in 1937 when the Federal Marihuana Tax Act was passed. A reading of the hearings that preceded the passage of the legislation demonstrates quite clearly how little empirical data was found to support that legislative judgment. Indeed, the enactment reflected far more the mass hysteria surrounding the subject than any concrete evidence of the drug's harmfulness. Congressional legislative action against marihuana began on April 14, 1937, when Representative Doughton of Tennessee introduced H.R. 6906 to the House of Representatives. Following introduction to the House, the bill was sent to the House Ways and Means

Committee, and hearings began on April 27. Witnesses in favor of the bill appeared first.

C. Hester, Assistant General Counsel for the Treasury Department, the initial witness, stated that the bill employed

> the Federal taxing power not only to raise revenue from the marihuana traffic, but also to discourage the current and widespread undesirable use of marihuana by smokers and drug addicts and thus drive the traffic into channels where the plant will be put to valuable industrial, medical, and scientific uses.

Hester explained that by differential taxation of registered and unregistered marihuana transactions, the federal government could restrict use without impinging on the rights of drug regulation reserved to the states according to the Tenth Amendment to the Constitution. The Tax Act provided that: (1) all individuals using the plant for defined industrial or medical purposes must register and pay a tax of $1.00 per ounce; (2) individuals using marihuana for purposes undefined by the Act must pay a tax on unregistered transactions of $100. per ounce; and (3) any individual failing to comply with the above regulations was subject to penalties for tax evasion, or (under section 12 of the Act) a fine of not more than $2,000. and/or a prison sentence of not more than five years.[26]

While theoretically the bill was only a means of raising revenue, the real motivation for its enactment was thinly veiled. By making the individual who wished to smoke marihuana pay $100. tax per ounce, the government would effectively force the user to purchase it in an underground market, thereby exposing himself to the risk of tax evasion — an oblique, even in a sense underhanded, attempt at control of the social use of the drug.

The congressional hearings were characterized by brevity and lack of information. Little expert medical, sociological, or other scientific evidence was produced or listened to. Mr. Anslinger in his introductory statement presented a superficial and hyperbolic history of cannabis.

> This drug is as old as civilization itself. Homer wrote about it, as a drug which made men forget their homes, and that turned them into swine. In Persia, a thousand years before Christ, there was a religious and military order founded which was

called the Assassins, and they derived their name from the drug called hashish which is now known in this country as marihuana. They were noted for their acts of cruelty and the word "assassin" very aptly describes the drug.[27]

While there is no consensus on the matter, some scholars believe that Homer's nepenthe may have been cannabis or a combination thereof. The only two cases recorded by Homer of men forgetting their homes or being turned into swine are found in *The Odyssey,* and it was not nepenthe, but the lotus that made men forget their homes — "Those who ate this honeyed plant, the Lotus, never cared to report, nor to return: they longed to stay forever, browsing on that native bloom, forgetful of their homeland." Similarly there is no indication in the only case of men being transformed into swine that nepenthe was involved. The reference occurs after Circe had lured some of Odysseus' men into her palace:

> On thrones she seated them, and lounging chairs,
> while she prepared a meal of cheese and barley
> and amber honey mixed with Pramnian wine,
> adding her own vile pinch, to make them lose
> desire or thought of our dear father land.
> Scarce had they drunk when she flew after them
> with her long stick and shut them in a pigsty —
> bodies, voices, heads and bristles, all
> swinish now, though minds were still unchanged.[28]

Anslinger's reference to the relationship between the Assassins and hashish is equally distorted (see Chap. 11). As J. Mandel in his study of the original sources of the myths of the Assassins puts it:

> Religion leads to assassinations, not hashish. The supposed hashish-induced "visions of paradise" are as responsible for the assassinations as the religiously fortifying drinking of wine and eating of wafers are responsible for the bloody crusades.[29]

During the questioning that followed his initial statement, Anslinger disposed of the results of Bromberg's 1934 study:

> He argued one way and then he argued another way. His conclusions were based on a study made of those men who had been sentenced to prison. But that is not a fair conclusion because

at the present time we have so many in prison in the several states sent up as the result of using marihuana.

I think in some States today that study would show a fairer conclusion than he arrived at, although in one part of his article he did say he believed that this excited to crime a man who would be less likely to commit a crime.[30]

Anslinger's concern about the conclusions not being "fair" reflects a difference in opinion as to proper methodology. Bromberg's sample consisted of all prisoners including those imprisoned for drug use; apparently Anslinger would select only those who had committed serious crimes and then attempt to establish the use of marihuana. Had Anslinger read the paper carefully, he would have found that Bromberg also specifically examined criminals convicted of the crimes marihuana was supposed to incite and reported "none due to marihuana intoxication." As for Anslinger's comment about exciting "to crime a man who would be less likely to commit a crime," Bromberg's statement was that cannabis was a:

"breeder of crime" only when used by psychopathic types in whom the drug allows the emergence of aggressive, sexual or anti-social tendencies.[31]

Dr. J. C. Munch, a Temple University pharmacologist, testified as to the physiological effects of marihuana on humans and animals. He considered marihuana harmful, because "any drug that produces the degeneration of the brain is harmful." With a little help from Representative McCormack, Munch enlarged on the dangers of marihuana:

Mr. McCormack: In some cases does it not bring about extreme inertia?
Dr. Munch: Yes; it does.
Mr. McCormack: And in other cases it causes violent irritability?
Dr. Munch: Yes; it does.
Mr. McCormack: And those results lead to a disintegration of personality, do they not?
Dr. Munch: Yes; it does.[32]

Having satisfied itself that it understood the nature and dangers of the drug, the committee attended to the complaints of the various industrial concerns which depended upon cannabis for some part of their product. Representatives from oilseed and birdseed concerns were heard, and complaints from fiber industrialists were entertained. Pending considerations to outlaw all use of any part of the cannabis plant were deemed unwise, and provisions were then made to accommodate industrial concerns. Agreements were worked out to the effect that hemp seed used in birdseed would be sterilized with heat before being placed on the market, and provisions were made to exempt oilseed producers from supervision and taxes.

The single seriously dissident voice heard during the whole proceedings was that of Dr. W. C. Woodward, Legislative Counsel for the American Medical Association. While he acknowledged limited medical use for cannabis at that time, he attempted to persuade the congressmen to initiate less restrictive legislation because of the possibility "that future investigators may show that there are substantial medical uses for cannabis." Woodward then went on to attack the evidence proffered by the Treasury Department on the "marihuana problem."

> The newspapers have called attention to it so prominently that there must be some grounds for their statements. It has surprised me, however, that the facts on which these statements have been based have not been brought before this committee by competent primary evidence. We are referred to newspaper publications concerning the prevalence of marihuana addiction. We are told that the use of marihuana causes crime.
>
> But as yet no one has been produced from the Bureau of Prisons to show the number of prisoners who have been found addicted to the marihuana habit. An informal inquiry shows that the Bureau of Prisons has no evidence on that point.
>
> You have been told that school children are great users of marihuana cigarettes. No one has been summoned from the Children's Bureau to show the nature and extent of the habit, among children.
>
> Inquiry of the Children's Bureau shows that they have had no occasion to investigate it and know nothing particularly of it.
>
> Inquiry of the Office of Education — and they certainly should know something of the prevalence of the habit among the school children of the county, if there is a prevalence of the habit — indicates that they have had no occasion to investigate and know nothing of it.[33]

With the completion of his initial statement, the committee began questioning Woodward concerning his educational background, his relationship to the American Medical Association, and his views on medical legislation of the previous fifteen years. His questioning by Mr. Dingell is fairly representative of the committee's treatment of him:

Mr. Dingell: We know that it is a habit that is spreading, particularly among youngsters. We learn that from the pages of the newspapers. You say that Michigan has a law regulating it. We have a State Law, but we do not seem to be able to get anywhere with it, because, as I have said, the habit is growing. The number of victims is increasing each year.

Dr. Woodward: There is no evidence of that.

Mr. Dingell: I have not been impressed by your testimony here as reflecting the sentiment of the high-class members of the medical profession in my State. I am confident that the medical profession in the State of Michigan, and in Wayne County particularly, or in my district, will subscribe wholeheartedly to any law that will suppress this thing, despite the fact that there is a $1. tax imposed.

Dr. Woodward: If there was any law that would absolutely suppress the thing, perhaps that is true, but when the law simply contains provisions that impose a useless expense, and does not accomplish the result —

Mr. Dingell (interposing): That is simply your personal opinion. That is kindred to the opinion you entertained with reference to the Harrison Narcotics Act.

Dr. Woodward: If we had been asked to cooperate in drafting it —

Mr. Dingell (interposing): You are not cooperating in drafting this at all.

Dr. Woodward: As a matter of fact, it does not serve to suppress the use of opium and cocaine.

Mr. Dingell: The medical profession should be doing its utmost to aid in the suppression of this curse that is eating the very vitals of the Nation.

Dr. Woodward: They are.

Mr. Dingell: Are you not simply piqued because you were not consulted in the drafting of the bill? [34]

Woodward at no time during the hearings expressed opposition to the overall objectives of the proposed legislation. He did object to the form of the proposed bill; he estimated it would cost American physicians $1,000,000. per year to comply with it. However, he did not endear himself to the members of the committee by objecting to the quality of the evidence and to the manner in which it had been brought forth. In the end, Woodward's testimony was cut off with the admonition:

> You are not cooperative in this. If you want to advise us on legislation you ought to come here with some constructive proposals rather than criticisms, rather than trying to throw obstacles in the way of something that the Federal Government is trying to do.[35]

None of Woodward's testimony was harkened to. The House hearings were concluded without any substantial changes in the proposed bill, and the Senate hearings were conducted in a similar fashion. On August 2, 1937, the bill was signed into law by the President, and it took effect on October 1, 1937. In its wake many state laws, just as punitive and hastily conceived, were legislated.

Very few in public office responded rationally to the "marihuana problem." An exception was New York's Mayor Fiorello La Guardia. In 1938 he gathered from the New York Academy of Medicine a team of scientists to study the medical, sociological, and psychological aspects of marihuana use in the city of New York. Serving on the committee were two internists, three psychiatrists, two pharmacologists, one public health expert, and the Commissioners of Correction, of Health, and of Hospitals, and the Director of the Division of Psychiatry of the Department of Hospitals, ex officio. Work was begun in 1940, and detailed findings were published in 1944 under the title *The Marihuana Problem in the City of New York*. Although the report represented the only reliable American study undertaken on marihuana, it remained largely disregarded by the general public. It dispelled many of the myths that had spurred passage of the Tax Act. Among the more important findings reported were: that no proof existed that major crimes are associated with the practice of smoking marihuana; that marihuana smoking does not lead to aggressive or antisocial behavior; that marihuana does not alter the basic personality structure of the smoker or cause sexual overstimulation; and that no evidence of acquired tolerance for the drug exists.[36]

Shortly before the publication of the La Guardia Report and independent of it, Col. J. M. Phalen, editor of the *Military Surgeon,* in an editorial of 1943 entitled "The Marihuana Bugaboo," dismissed the exaggerated dangers, stating: "The smoking of the leaves, flowers, and seeds of *Cannabis sativa* is not more harmful than the smoking of tobacco, or mullein or sumac leaves." Phalen added: "The legislation in relation to marihuana was ill-advised . . . it branded as a menace and a crime a matter of trivial importance." [37]

The La Guardia Report was bitterly attacked by outraged critics. Even before it appeared, rumors circulated that it was going to be suppressed, and upon publication the Federal Bureau of Narcotics began an onslaught. Anslinger commented upon the report:

> There has also been a climate of public opinion which has favored the spread of narcotic addiction. Contributing to this was a very unfortunate report released some years ago by the so-called La Guardia committee on marihuana. The Bureau immediately detected the superficiality and hollowness of its findings and denounced it.[38]

In September 1942, the *American Journal of Psychiatry* published a paper by Doctors S. Allentuck and K. M. Bowman entitled "The Psychiatric Aspects of Marihuana Intoxication" in which, among other things, they asserted that habituation to cannabis is not as strong as to tobacco or alcohol. This report grew out of the studies they carried out under the auspices of the La Guardia committee. The *Journal of the American Medical Association* subsequently published (in December 1942) a reasoned, informative editorial on their work which was described as "a careful study." In reviewing the major findings of the study, the editorial proceeded to mention some possible therapeutic uses that might be made of the drug's properties. Those mentioned were the treatment of depression, the treatment of loss of appetite, and the possible treatment of addicts to opiate derivatives. However, following the *Journal's* publication of letters from Anslinger (January 1943) and R. J. Bouquet, Expert on the Narcotics Commission of the League of Nations (April 1944), both of which denounced the La Guardia Report, the American Medical Association made an extraordinary about-face and joined the Federal Bureau of Narcotics in the denunciation of the La Guardia Report. This switch was heralded by an editorial which appeared in the *Journal of the American Medical Association* in April 1945:

> For many years medical scientists have considered cannabis a dangerous drug. Nevertheless, a book called "Marihuana Problems" by the New York City Mayor's Committee on Marihuana submits an analysis by seventeen doctors of tests on 77 prisoners and, on this narrow and thoroughly unscientific foundation, draws sweeping and inadequate conclusions which minimize the harmfulness of marihuana. Already the book has done harm. . . . The book states unqualifiedly to the public that the use of this narcotic does not lead to physical, mental or moral degeneration and that permanent deleterious effects from its continued use were not observed on 77 prisoners. This statement has already done great damage to the cause of law enforcement. Public officials will do well to disregard this unscientific, uncritical study, and continue to regard marihuana as a menace wherever it is purveyed.

With this editorial the *Journal of the American Medical Association,* in the words of A. S. deRopp, "abandoned its customary restraint and voiced its editorial wrath in scolding tones. So fierce was the editorial that one might suppose that the learned members of the mayor's committee . . . had formed some unhallowed league with the 'tea-pad' proprietors to undermine the city's health by deliberately misrepresenting the facts about marihuana." [39]

In contrast to the *Journal of the American Medical Association* editorial is a report of the La Guardia study that appeared one month later (May 1945) in *Science*:

> This report includes a thorough study of the ancient hashish vice as it currently exists in New York City. Primarily intended as a local project, the findings have considerable value of a general nature . . . the New York report represents a substantial contribution to existing clinical and pharmacological knowledge of the subject. Earlier impressions with sporadic measurements are now supported by concerted observations

using the methods of the modern clinical laboratory. . . . Conclusions, previously recognized but now better supported with these studies, are to the effect that marihuana smoking, at least as ordinarily practiced in this country, does not lead directly to mental or physical deterioration, does not develop addiction or tolerance as is characteristic of opiates, and is not a direct causal factor in sexual or criminal misconduct.[40]

Over the past twenty-five years the American Medical Association has been steadfast in maintaining a position on marihuana closely allied to that of the Federal Bureau of Narcotics. A great deal of misinformation and fear-generating mythology has come to surround this drug, and, judging by the published statements of the Council on Mental Health of the American Medical Association, the medical community has been both a victim and an agent of this unfortunate process.[41] And as we shall see in Chapter 12, this position is reflected in the editorial policy of the *Journal of the American Medical Association* which apparently "disregards" as "unscientific" and "uncritical" any study that does not demonstrate marihuana to be "a menace wherever it is purveyed."

2 From Plant to Intoxicant

In 1753 Linnaeus gave the name *Cannabis sativa* to Indian hemp. Thus one of the oldest psychoactive plants known to man formally entered modern botanical literature. Centuries earlier (eighth century B.C.) the Assyrians had called the plant *Quonoubou Qunnapu,* whence the following roster of ancient epithets: the Hebrew *Qanneb,* the Arabic *Qannob,* the Persian *Quonnab,* the Celtic *Quannab,* and the Greek *Kannabas.* Some scholars assert that, excluding alcohol, hemp was indeed the original intoxicant.[1] However, R. Wasson, an authority on "hallucinogens," has suggested that a cult of "hallucinogenic" mushroom worshippers may have existed thousands of years before the hemp intoxicant was introduced.[2]

Early man must certainly have been acquainted with many of the plants now known to have psychoactive properties. These plants are currently classified as members of one of two groups: those — variously called "hallucinogens," psychotomimetics, and "psychedelics" — which can produce subjective perceptions of that which does not exist; and, second, those yielding psychotropic drugs which normally calm or stimulate the central nervous system. Only one plant narcotic, opium, is known to cause addiction and to be physically dangerous to the user. Marihuana, one form of *Cannabis sativa,* is a mild mind-active drug, and lacks the powerful consciousness-altering properties of either mescaline-bearing peyote or the psilocybin-bearing mushrooms.

The number of plants capable of producing mind-active substances remains undetermined. The total number of these species, however, forms a relatively small portion of the members of the kingdom. Of the 400,000 to 800,000 plant species, perhaps 60 species of flowering and nonflowering plants are known to have been used as "hallucinogens." [3] Of these 60, only 20 have been used to any significant extent, and most of these are found in the New World. Botanists are quick to point out that most of the plants (*Cannabis sativa* is one of the exceptions) in this small group owe their psychoactive properties to the activity of alkaloids, which at least 5,000 higher plants also possess.

Although the chemistry of the active constituents of many "hallucinogenic" plants is at this time incompletely known, a classification has been made according to whether the plant's potency is due to nitrogenous or nonnitrogenous principles. Cannabis belongs to the latter group, as does the common spice nutmeg (*Myristica fragrans*) which has been employed as an inebriant to many in prison whose access to more powerful and less easily obtained drugs is otherwise cut off.

The lore of the more exotic "hallucinogens" is extensive. Psychotropic mushrooms called "Flesh of the Gods" played a part in the sacraments of the ancient Aztecs.[4] Nine tribes of Mexican Indians still use a variety of psychotomimetic mushrooms, many of which contain the substance psilocybin.[5] Many North American Indians presently practice a religion in which the ingestion of the peyote button plays an important part.[6] Morning glory seeds rich in lysergic acid derivatives closely related to lysergic acid diethylamide were used in Mexico by the ancient Aztecs for divinatory and "hallucinogenic" purposes; today in England, after a rash of misuse which resulted in several serious illnesses, a proposal to prohibit the sale of the seeds is under consideration.[7] Perhaps the most fascinating of all is the mystery of the plant *soma*. Carried into the north of India some 3,500 years ago by the Aryan invaders, the plant has been celebrated as a divine intoxicant in more than a thousand hymns of the *Rig Veda,* one of the oldest of the Hindu scriptures. While some botanists believed that the drug was purely mythical, others have thought that it was derived from the hemp plant. However, the hypothesis that *soma* was cannabis disguised under yet another name has been largely rejected. The botanical identity of *soma* remains unknown; the fly agaric is the most recent suggestion.[8]

The common hemp is one of the least exotic of the plants which produce mind-active drugs. Botanically speaking, *Cannabis sativa* is a herbaceous dioecious plant belonging, with the hop plant (*Humulus lupulus*), to the Cannabaceae. The genus *Cannabis* consists of a single species, *Cannabis sativa* (L.), including perhaps many "varieties" or races. The hemp plant, then, either male or female, is a weedy annual closely akin to the hop and not distantly related to the stinging nettle and the fig tree. It is the source of hemp fiber, a seed oil, and an intoxicant.

Cannabis is probably the most widely diversified of all the psychoactive-drug-producing plants. A native of central temperate Asia, perhaps the Irytsh region, it is now common in nearly all parts of the world, capable of escaping from cultivation and growing naturally in any fertile or waste area.[9] Hemp appears scattered along roadsides and in fields, thriving in a variety of climatic conditions. In the United States, the presence of such wild marihuana plants has resulted in a most disturbing development. In 20 counties of 10 central states, the Justice Department has begun a pilot program designed to eradicate the plants through the use of the dangerous weed-killer *2, 4-D.* They are enlisting the help of local weed specialists and county extension agents in implementing this insidious program, one which potentially can cause far more harm to people and their environment than the existence of wild hemp plants. When burned, *2, 4-D* may give off extremely toxic chemicals called dioxins, which are capable of causing birth defects. Marihuana could be extremely hazardous if treated thus and then smoked.[10]

The names borne by various forms of hemp intoxicants read like a gazetteer. In India the hemp drug is called *bhang, ganja,* and *charas (churrus);* in Algeria and Morocco, *kif;* in South Africa, *dagga;* in Brazil, *machona* or *liamba;* in Turkey, *kabak;* in Tunisia, *takrouri;* in Central Africa, *djoma;* in Syria and Lebanon, *Hashish el Keif.* Americans have generated a variety of colloquialisms to signify marihuana, among them muggles, reefers, joints, weed, Texas tea, tea, gage, loco-weed, sticks, grass, boo, jive, rope, gates, goof-butts, mooters, and Mary Jane. The most common epithets among current American colloquialisms are pot, grass, tea, and weed.

The plant may reach a height of 16 to 20 feet, or reach maturity at 1 foot, depending on varying conditions. It has been shown that the larger plants which produce superior fiber quality are normally less productive of resin. In the temperate regions of Europe, Indian hemp commonly reaches a height of a little more than 6 feet, a phenomenon which the amateur botanist, François

Rabelais, took into account in naming a fictionalized version of the plant after his giant hero: "This plant is also called Pantagruelion out of resemblance. For when Pantagruel was born into the world, he was as big as this plant I am telling you of." [11]

The stem is upright and hollow — the source of the strong hemp fiber used for production of rough cloth, twine, and rope. The mature stalk may measure as much as 2 inches in diameter. The plant's short fragile branches are rather rough. Its lanceolate, serrated, unequal leaves fan out radially from the stalk. The dark green leaves measure 3–10 inches at maturity and somewhat resemble those of a poinsettia. The segments of the leaves generally number five or seven, although there may occasionally be nine or eleven. This combination of numbers delighted Rabelais: "The leaves are arranged in rows around the stock, at equal distances apart, with five or seven in a row; for Nature so cherishes the Pantagruelion that she has endowed its leaves with those two odd numbers, which are so divine and mysterious." [12]

The male and female plants differ markedly in appearance. The smaller and more slender male plant, which is thought to possess little value as an intoxicant, has a shorter period of vegetation. After flowering and fertilizing the female, it withers and dries fairly rapidly. The female plant, though taller, appears more compact and robust. At the height of its development it is a full bushy plant. The greater frailty of the male was formerly a source of confusion, for the male plant was often believed to be the female. Both male and female plants bear flowers. The small auxiliary male flowers are born in panicles and often have five yellow-green or purple sepals. The auxiliary female flowers are born in profusion. Of the plant's rather rank smell, particularly strong in the female at the time of flowering, Rabelais remarked, "Its odor is strong, and none too pleasant to delicate nostrils." [13]

The fruit is the hemp seed, and in ancient times a preparation from the seed was used medically as an emollient. Herodotus reports that the Scythians and Thracians intoxicated themselves with fumes given off by roasting the seeds on white-hot stones:

The Scythians, then, take the seed of this hemp, and creeping under the felt covering of the tent they throw the seed on the stones glowing with heat from the fire, and there it smoulders and makes such a steam as no vapour-bath in Greece could surpass, and the steam makes the Scythians howl for joy. This serves them for a bath, for they never wash their bodies in water.[14]

Borne at the top of the plant, the seeds are tan, hard, and covered with a thin coat. They yield an economically useful oil, and seed-oil-cake can be made from them. Formerly used for lighting purposes and in soap making, the oil currently plays a part in the manufacture of varnish and linoleum and, substituting for linseed oil, is used as an ingredient in the manufacture of artist's paints. The hemp-seed oil-cake is used as bait for fish, and also as a fertilizer.[15] Hemp-seeds have been mentioned as added touches in making "tarts and fritters" [16] as well as in making the Oriental *majun*. The crushed seed is used as nourishment in eastern Europe, especially in times of famine.[17] The seed is also an important food for birds, in which form it acts as a general tonic and helps maintain healthy plumage.

The chemical compounds responsible for the intoxicating effect of cannabis are commonly found in a sticky, golden resin which, during periods of the growing season's greatest heat, is exuded from the female flowers and is found also in the adjacent leaves and stalks. Although it is generally held that the plant's active agents are found solely in the resin produced by the female flower parts, there is insufficient evidence to support this hypothesis. It is possible that other parts of the female and male plants may contain active substances.[18] Detailed phytochemical studies of plants originating in many different regions will be needed before this statement can categorically be made.

The plant grows in areas of sufficiently varied altitudes and periods of sun and rain as to create ecotypes or races differing in morphology and physiological action. Seeds from identical stock, when sown in France, produce plants six feet in height, but in Virginia give rise to plants nine to fourteen feet in height; when sown in North Africa, they produce plants which barely attain five feet in height.[19] Hemp plants also exhibit a bewildering capacity for changing sex. Botanical literature includes the report of an experiment in which 90 percent of hemp plants reversed their sexual expression following removal from the field and being planted in a greenhouse during the winter months.[20] Moreover, hemp is reported capable of becoming monoecious (with the sexes on one plant) in extremely unfavorable conditions.[21]

Growing conditions also affect the degree of the plant's intoxicating power. Plants grown in the northern hemisphere produce less resin, and it also seems clear that psychoactive potency decreases directly as the plant is grown in more northern regions. Experienced users of marihuana maintain that differing growth conditions lead to differences in the quality of the high produced as well as in potency; according to these statements, some types are more likely to produce merely physical symptoms, whereas others emphasize distortions of perception or "hallucinations."

Perhaps because of such varying characteristics, some botanists in the past were convinced that the genus *Cannabis* included several species, and they differentiated *C. sativa* from *C. indica* on the grounds that the former was the source of fibers, the latter of the intoxicant. This distinction fails to convince contemporary botanists. Currently there have been attempts to instate the following varieties: *C. erratica, C. Foetens, C. lupulus, C. macrosperma, C. gigantea, C. excelsa, C. compressa, C. sinensis*. Botanists now generally agree that there is but one species, *Cannabis sativa*, and many unstable "varieties" or races which are, in effect, ecotypes. According to R. J. Bouquet, a variety once distinguished with the epithet *sinensis* when introduced in France in 1827 rapidly manifested the characteristics of the typical form. In summary, hemp seems, in part, at least, to differ from or approach the characteristic type in response to the conditions under which it is grown.[22]

Cultivation of the plant is singularly easy. A citation in a pharmaceutical handbook, *Les Remèdes galéniques*, describes the process of preparing hemp for medicinal purposes as requiring essentially only tilling and manuring.[23] Since the plant has many tap roots, light, sandy soil is ideal for planting. Choice of soil generally depends upon the purpose for which the plant is grown. Moist loamy soils are best to develop fiber production; dry thin soils are most suitable for hemp grown to produce the intoxicant. Although various soluble nitrogen fertilizers are ideal, either horse or cow manure is excellent. The seeds should be sown about 20 cm apart, in order to facilitate hoeing and thinning. It has been remarked that plants sown a good distance apart tend to produce a superior resin crop, although the quality of the fiber suffers.

Germination of the male and female plants occurs simultaneously. Some signs of life should show six days after planting; in two weeks, the seedling should bear strong healthy leaves. Growth decreases as both plants approach maturity, and the plants' energy is spent in the processes of reproduction. Wind carries pollen to the female plants; insects, interestingly enough, apparently have nothing to do with fertilization.[24] Following pollination, the dry male plants with negligible or no resin production are generally cleared from the field. In India, the male plants may be destroyed as soon as they show their sex, because of the belief that a fertilized female plant produces an inferior intoxicant.[25] In certain areas of India where production of cannabis is economically important, a relatively highly paid consultant is the "ganja doctor," whose job it is to weed out the male from the female plants at an early age. Generally speaking, the female plants are harvested about a month after fertilization, when it occurs. Time of harvesting varies. In Europe the plants are harvested in September; in North Africa, in July.

Resin production increases until the female plant has reached maturity. A multitude of pluricellular glandulose hairs then grow over the top of the female plants. These shiny hairs are so abundant that the plant appears to be covered with dew. The hairs produce the light, amber-colored oleoresin containing the intoxicant, and this is stored between the cuticle and the middle part of the cell. When the temperature skyrockets, or secretion is especially heavy, the cuticle splits, and the liquid resin oozes out onto the adjacent leaves, where it later dries to a golden yellow mass. Most resin is produced between the time when the flowers first appear and the seeds reach maturity. Resin production ceases when the seeds are fully ripe.

It is generally assumed that resin production is a defensive reaction of the plant against high temperatures and lack of moisture in the air.[26] According to this theory, the female plants require a protective coat as they are flowering and preparing the ovaries for the shelter and formation of the seeds. The hardened resin acts as a kind of varnish under which the sap carries to the fertilized ovules the elements necessary for their development. A plant grown in areas of fairly high altitude and high temperature tends to produce a greater amount of resin than a plant grown in northern Europe. In those regions where heat and lack of moisture is not marked, hemp tends to secrete less of the protective resin and becomes instead a tall thick plant with many leaves and strong fiber. It follows, then, that plants cultivated for the production of fiber would thrive in moist, warm, temperate climates and that plants cultivated for intoxicant resin are best grown in hot dry regions such as Tunisia, Lebanon, and parts of Iran. In the Americas, Mexico is particularly appropriate for the resin-producing hemp plant.

The resin and resin-bearing parts of hemp are prepared for use in a variety of ways. Three grades of the drug are prepared in India and serve as a kind of standard against which preparations produced in other parts of the world are compared for potency; they are *bhang, ganja,* and *charas.* The least potent and cheapest preparation, *bhang,* is derived from hemp grown in the plains areas. Because *bhang* can be prepared in a variety of ways, it is exceedingly difficult to determine if a preferred or more common method of producing this poor man's "friend" actually does exist. The intoxicant may consist simply of hemp leaves picked from dooryard plants, dried, and then crushed into a coarse powder. Frequently, however, the leaves are mixed with male and/or female inflorescences and with seeds and small stems. The resulting drug is of inferior quality and may be smoked or made into a decoction. Occasionally *bhang* is chewed by beggars or fakirs who consider it the giver of long life and a means of communion with the divine spirit.[27] To the wealthier Hindu, *bhang* is a crude substitute for *ganja,* somewhat akin to the difference between beer and fine scotch. In the words of W. B. O'Shaughnessy, writing of the medical uses of *bhang* in India in 1839: "*Bhang* is cheaper than *gunjah* and though less powerful, is sold at such a low price, that for one pice enough can be purchased to intoxicate an experienced person."[28] *Bhang's* special importance to us is that it is, under the name of marihuana, the most commonly used hemp product in the United States.

Ganja, the second strongest hemp intoxicant, is prepared from the flowering tops of cultivated female plants. The dried pistillate tops with their exuded resin are generally smoked, sometimes mixed with tobacco leaves. Occasionally the preparation is eaten or made into a drink. *Ganja,* variously estimated as being two or three times as strong as *bhang,* is consequently more desirable and costlier.

India produces three kinds of *ganja:* flat *ganja,* round *ganja,* and *Cur-ganja,* or *Rora.* The preparation of flat *ganja* is simple. As soon as the plant begins to flower, the large leaves and branches are removed. This allows the leaves and brackets of the inflo-rescences to agglutinate into a sticky mass as the resin oozes out. Field workers then crop the stalks of the plants approximately six inches above the ground.[29] After being exposed to hot sunlight for several hours, the flowering tops of the plants are arranged in a circle on the ground. The flower clusters are then trampled and kneaded until they are flattened and the resin expressed. Fresh bundles are laid atop the pressed ones, and the process is repeated until the circle reaches a foot in height. Harvesters sub-sequently remove the flowering twigs and sort them according to length and breadth of stem. Flat *ganja* is sold in local market places in dusky green bunches, resinous to the touch and pleasantly sweet-smelling.

Round *ganja* is shaped into little pellets by rolling and pressing the flowering twigs between the hands until they are tapered. The pellets usually are sold packed twenty-four to a bundle. *Rora* is the name given to *ganja* prepared from hemp flowers that have been accidentally broken off from the flat or round *ganja,* or inten-tionally plucked from the plants. *Rora* is sold as a coarse yellowish-green powder. Of these different types of *ganja,* it is thought that only the flat *ganja* is well known in Europe.

Pure resin of the pistillate flowers is called in India *charras* or *charas*. Examined under the microscope, *charas* appears as masses of pluricellular hairs stuck together in yellowish clumps, mixed with scraps of inflorescences and leaves. *Charas* is the most potent hemp intoxicant. While the female hemp tops contain 8 to 12 percent resin, unadulterated *charas* contains approximately 40 per-cent.

The resin of the hemp plant has been used as an intoxicant for millennia. Originally cultivated in Chinese Turkestan, *charas* production soon spread to the Hindustan, where it was observed with interest, particularly in the nineteenth century, by British colonialists. In a letter addressed to the President of the Medical Society at Edinburgh, dated August 17, 1849, a Mr. Jameson (then Director of the Botanic Gardens at Saharunpore, India) devoted himself to describing the care given to the production of hemp by the Indians:

> In October, in crossing the Himalayas from Almora to Mussuri, I have passed through dozens of villages 6,000 to 8,000 feet above

the level of the sea, and seen hundreds of men, women and children, all employed in making churrus.[30]

At the time of Mr. Jameson's description, *charas* was not generally known in Britain except as an occasional, unimpressive, walnut-sized exhibit in botanical museums.

Unlike *bhang, charas* can be obtained only from plants growing at high altitudes. The superior-grade resin is gathered by various exotic methods from uncut plants; the slightly weaker grade is taken from the tops of harvested plants. From the moment that the small unripened flowers begin to exude the resinous drops until the time when the fully mature flowers yield the main crop, harvesters are busy with a variety of methods of collecting *charas* from the growing plants. Dressed in leather garments, or sometimes naked, laborers run through the hemp fields, brushing against the resin-covered plants. The sticky resin clings to the clothes, or, less hygienically, to the sweating bodies, and is later scraped off with a blunted curved knife made especially for this purpose. Occasionally the plant is simply pressed between the palms of the hands, after which the exuded greenish-yellow secretion is removed. In some areas, harvesters pass a leather thong over the resinous parts of the plant and later run the thong over the edge of a receptacle.[31]

Resin is collected from cut plants by a variety of methods: by pressing the plant between fine mattings to which the resin adheres; by threshing the dried plants, so that the resin drops onto pieces of cloth placed on the ground; or simply by vigorously rubbing the tops of the plants between coarse cloths.

The crude impure secretion thus gathered then undergoes a variety of treatments before it is sold and consumed. The resin is sifted to eliminate dirt and other impurities and is then kneaded with a little water into a sticky lump. The material is stored for a few days in an airy dry place; dampness causes the resin to deteriorate. The first-grade resin, obtained from uncut plants, may be purified by hand in copper pans and shaped into tiny tapering sticks. This variety of *charas* is relatively rare and very highly valued. The second-grade resin gathered from cut plants is sliced up into sheets 3–6 cm thick when it has dried.

Producers of *charas* in Chinese Turkestan may use one of two means to prepare their second-grade *charas* for market. The powdery resin is collected in bags which are steamed above a pan of boiling water. The resin, after being cooled and compressed, slowly agglutinates and is moulded into a block. Similar methods of preparation are used in Asia Minor, Syria, and Lebanon.

A second method of preparation is in use in Chinese Turkestan. After being harvested in October, the resin powder is sifted and stored in large ten- to fourteen-pound rawhide bags during the four or five months of winter. When the warm season arrives, the resin is exposed to the sun and allowed to melt. The adhesive mass is then kneaded with wooden rods until an oily substance covers its surface. Each bag yields one or two pounds of this oil, which is then freshly packaged and ready for sale.

Charas reaches the market in a variety of forms. The most expensive kind usually arrives as small sticks or cakes of a medium brownish color. Second-grade *charas* is often sold as brownish-green lumps or flattened in bags of rawhide (*turbahs*).

Charas is called *hashish* in Egypt, Asia Minor, and Syria and *chira* in northern Africa. Roughly speaking, *hashish* and *chira* correspond to the second grade of Indian *charas*. *Hashish* is sold as flattened cakes or as a thin sheet shaped like the sole of a shoe. Occasionally, both the *turbahs* and the soles bear stamps of origin and inscriptions proudly describing details of manufacture. Soles stamped with quaintly designed lions and airplanes have been discovered by customs officers.

Although *charas* is most frequently smoked, often in water pipes, both confections and macerations are prepared from it. When it is smoked, the small sticks of resin are broken up and inserted into cigarettes. Drunk as an infusion, the resin is mixed with alcohol and perfumed syrups or jams which have been thinned with such exotic potions as rosewater, jasmine-water, or orange-blossom water.

Various sweetmeats made from the resin are common in the Near East and Orient. A small cake, variously called *Magoon* (India), *Majun* (Turkey), and *Madjun* (North Africa) is prepared from a mixture of honey, *charas,* and spices. The paste is then rolled into small pellets. A second type of confection, called *Manzul,* is prepared from a mixture of *charas,* sesame seed oil, cocoa butter, powdered chocolate, and various spices. In the north of Africa, stuffed dates and Turkish delight may also contain various forms of the hemp resin. *Charas* sweets may contain any of the following ingredients, and more: almonds, walnuts, pistachios, cinnamon, cloves, vanilla, musk, nutmeg, and belladonna berries. The ingenuity of the *charas* confectioners is indeed impressive. With their innumerable spices and condiments, they create a wide variety of intoxicating delectables.

Most Westerners, and certainly most Americans who use cannabis, take it in the form of cigarettes, despite Alice B. Toklas's recipes for Arab-style marihuana cookies. The "joint" is roughly comparable to Indian *bhang* in content, mode of preparation, and potency. As such it is, at most, about one-fifth to one-eighth the potency of Indian *charas*. Despite the occasional triumph of a marihuana cake or a marihuana spaghetti sauce, the hand-rolled cigarette predominates in the United States.

3 Chemistry and Pharmacology

By the middle of the nineteenth century, the euphorigenic agent
of *Cannabis sativa* was determined to be an alkali-insoluble, nitro-
gen-free principle.[1] Between 1840 and 1895 most chemical investigations of cannabis and its extracts were attempts to find tests that
would identify a hemp extract. The "Beam Test" became a favorite. Hemp extract produces a purple color when treated with 5-
percent methanolic potassium hydroxide, and the test was assumed to indicate the active principle of the extract. Later, however, R. Adams and his coworkers were to show that the test does
not indicate a substance with marihuana activity.

Around 1895, T. B. Wood, W. T. N. Spivey, and T. H. Easterfield isolated cannabinol from cannabis extracts.[2] Cannabinol
was considered to be the active principle until about 1932. Wood
and the others also tried to determine the structure of the cannabinol molecule. However, the Cambridge chemists were unable
to complete their investigative program because of a series of
tragic accidents. Wood, after taking some cannabinol at the time
he was preparing zinc ethyl, lost consciousness; the zinc ethyl
ignited, and but for a difficult rescue he would surely have per-
ished. Easterfield lost his life in a violent laboratory explosion
while attempting to hydrogenate cannabinol, and Spivey suffered
a similar fate while studying nitro-cannabinolactone.[3] Cannabinol
was not isolated again until R. S. Cahn succeeded in 1932.[4] Cahn
determined the structure of the molecule in all but the orientation
of the substituent groups. He also cast doubt on the euphorigenic
activity of cannabinol.

Not long after Cahn's work, University of Illinois chemists led
by R. Adams isolated cannabinol by a method different from
Cahn's; as a result of their procedure they isolated a new con-

stituent, cannabidiol. They, in collaboration with pharmacologists at Cornell Medical College, reported both substances to be inactive. Their study of cannabidiol structure, however, led to determination of cannabinol structure (1-hydroxy-6,6,9-trimethyl-3-pentyldibenzopyran; *c*, Fig. 1), which in turn led them to the

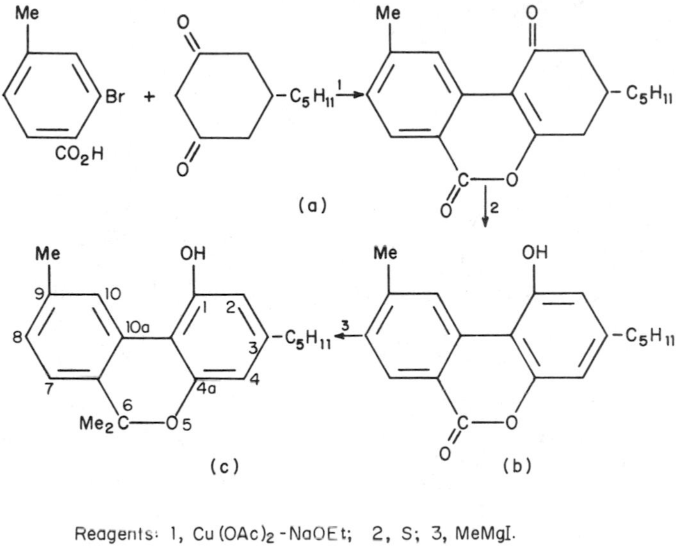

(a)

(c)   (b)

Reagents: 1, Cu(OAc)$_2$-NaOEt; 2, S; 3, MeMgI.

Fig. 1. Adams's synthesis of cannabinol.

euphorigenic tetrahydrocannabinols. Heating cannabidiol with an acid catalyst converted it into a mixture of stereoisomers and double-bond isomers of tetrahydrocannabinol. They suspected such a mixture to be present in natural cannabis. Adams and the others found the acetates of tetrahydrocannabinol active also, though much less so than the unacetylated compounds. Catalytic reduction of the tetrahydrocannabinols yielded hexahydrocannabinol, which was also less active than the original compound.[5] Adams's synthesis of cannabinol was from dihydroolivetol (5-pentylcyclohexane-1,3-dione; *a*, Fig. 1), which was prepared by catalytic reduction of olivetol. Condensation of that diketone with 2-bromo-4-methylbenzoic acid in the presence of sodium ethoxide and cupric acetate, and dehydrogenation of the product with sulfur, gave the pyrone (*b*, Fig. 1), which gave cannabinol (*c*, Fig. 1) when combined with methylmagnesium iodide.[6]

Todd and his coworkers arrived at the structure of cannabinol at about the same time as Adams's group. Todd's synthesis of cannabinol included tetrahydrocannabinol as an intermediate. His method (Fig. 2) was to condense olivetol with 4-methyl-2-oxo-cyclohexanecarboxylate, combine methylmagnesium iodide with the resultant dibenzopyrone, to give tetrahydrocannabinol (*a*, Fig. 2), which was dehydrogenated by palladium or selenium to cannabinol (*b*, Fig. 2).[7]

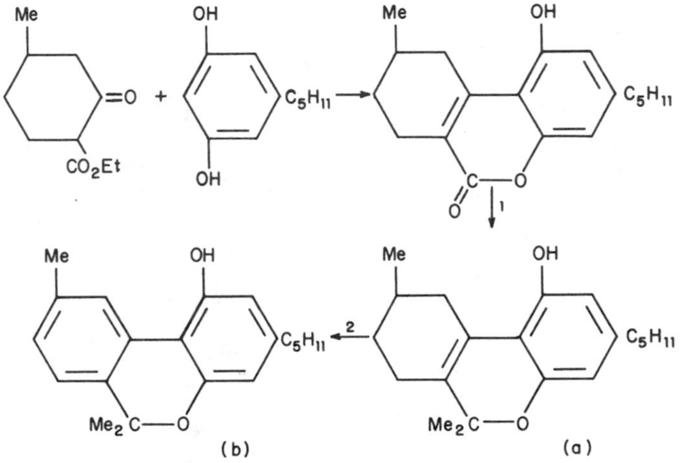

Reagents: 1, MeMgI; 2, Pd or Se.

Fig. 2. Todd's synthesis of cannabinol.

Adams's group went on to synthesize compounds with activity similar to that of natural tetrahydrocannabinol. One isomer, for example, with the double bond conjugated to the benzene ring proved to have marihuana activity of about one-tenth the natural form.[8] Adams's group in 1940 also tried to synthesize the isomer with an 8,9 double bond. Although Adams's group failed, E. C. Taylor and E. J. Strojny (1960) successfully adapted Adams's method to the preparation of tetrahydrocannabinol model compounds.[9] They found that isoprene reacts readily with coumarins substituted with an electronegative group in the 3-position (CO Et, CN) to give the adduct (*a*, Fig. 3; R = CO Et or CN). Hydrolysis yields dicarboxylic acid (*b*, Fig. 3) which on lactonization produces a separable mixture of *cis*- and *trans*- lactones. Treatment of each lactone with methylmagnesium iodide, followed by cyclisation with toluene-p-sulphonic acid in xylene, results in the *cis-* and *trans-* 6a, 7, 10, 10a-tetrahydro-6,6,9-trimethyldibenzopyrans (*c*, Fig. 3). These two isomers lack the 1-hydroxy- and the 3-pentyl-groups of the corresponding tetrahydrocannabinols.

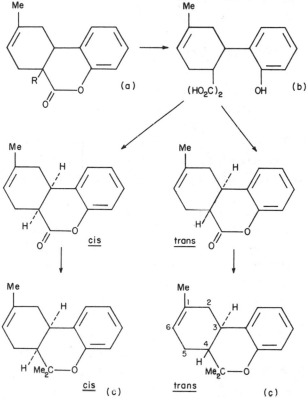

Fig. 3. Taylor and Strojny's synthesis of model tetrahydrocannabinols.

A large number of the tetrahydrocannabinol homologues have been prepared, especially compounds such as in Figure 4 (R = alkyl).[10] Such compounds usually have been tested by one or both of the two tests used in the pharmacological study of marihuana. These are the "dog ataxia" test and the Gayer "corneal anaesthesia" test. In the series R = n-alkyl (see Fig. 4), the 1-hexyl compound is the most potent in animal tests. Its activity is surpassed by R = 1-methylheptyl and by the 1′,2′-dimethylheptyl compound. The compound represented in Figure 4 by R = hexyl is known as "parahexyl," "pyrahexyl," or "synhexyl" and is one of the few members of the series tested for euphorigenic activity in man.

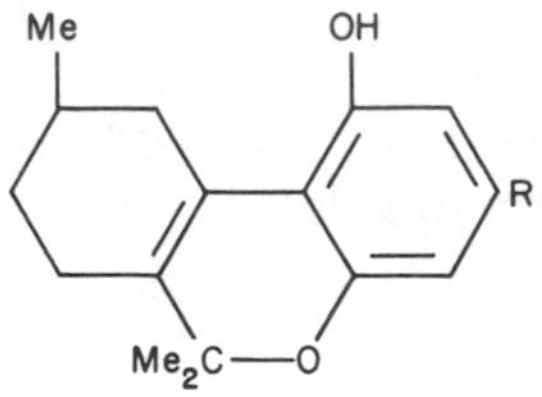

Fig. 4. Model tetrahydrocannabinol compound.

Its effective dose was found to be 5–15 mg per man. D. F. Downing, however, reported the activity threshold at 200 mg per man, but this claim is not adequately substantiated.[11]

Almost all earlier workers, including those of the 1940's, obtained their materials from purified resin and hemp extracts called "red oil" of hemp. Adams's description of red oil is as follows:

> After extraction with an organic solvent, filtration of the solution thus obtained, removal of the solvent and vacuum distillation of the residue, a highly viscous, physiologically active oil results, red in color and boiling over a wide range. Fractionation of the oil leads to the concentration of the active components in the portion boiling from 180–190° (1mm) which is commonly known as "purified red oil." This . . . has been shown definitely to be a welter of closely related substances which are very difficult to separate from each other and which occur in varying proportions depending on the source of the hemp.[12]

Investigations during the last decade have established the biogenetic precursors of cannabidiol and have identified and synthesized two tetrahydrocannabinol isomers in natural cannabis. Y. Gaoni and R. Mechoulam (1965), with methods such as nuclear magnetic resonance and infrared spectroscopy, reported that the Δ^1-3,4-*trans* isomer of tetrahydrocannabinol is the major active constituent of natural cannabis.[13] They were able to synthesize that isomer in 1966 (Fig. 5) and also identified a new active constituent, cannabichromene.[14] Earlier they had isolated cannabigerol, yet another new constituent.[15]

The other naturally occurring isomer of tetrahydrocannabinol is Δ^6-3,4-*trans*.[16] It is similar to the Δ^1 form in marihuana activity. Taylor et al. produced it and two additional isomers, *dl*-Δ^1-3,4-*cis*

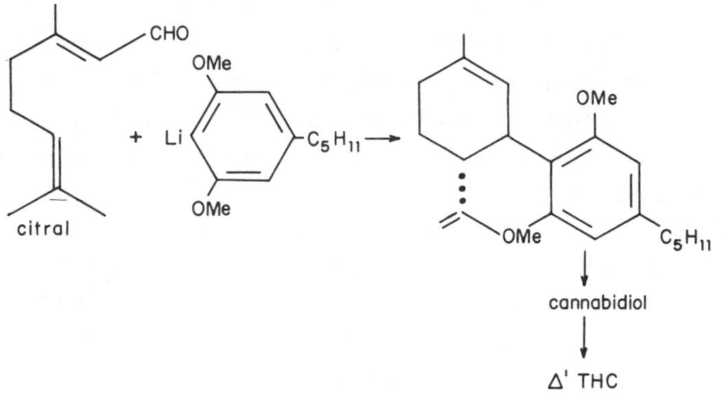

Fig. 5. First total synthesis of dl-Δ^1THC.

and dl-Δ^6-cis-tetrahydrocannabinol in 1966.[17] Their one-step synthesis gives the *trans* isomer in 20-percent yield under very mild conditions. They have also used nuclear magnetic resonance to distinguish between Δ^1 and Δ^6 *trans* isomers by a difference in the locations of the olefinic double bond. Both Taylor and Hively note that because of easy thermal isomerization, euphorigenic activity due to smoking marihuana may actually come from the Δ^6 isomer rather than from the Δ^1 isomer. It might be possible to link this thermal isomerization to the difference in effect between ingested and smoked marihuana, although the major differences reported have been in time of incidence and duration of effects rather than in the quality of the effects themselves. However, Mechoulam asserts that the most recent work indicates that the isomerization of Δ^1 to Δ^6 THC which has been thought to occur with both storage and smoking is of minor importance. While it is true that Δ^1 THC decreases as marihuana ages, in absolute figures Δ^6 THC does not increase. Because the rate of deterioration (oxidation) of Δ^1 THC is higher than that of Δ^6 THC, the observed change does not necessarily reflect a conversion of Δ^1 THC to Δ^6 THC.[18] As for the higher activity following smoking as compared with ingestion, Mechoulam suggests that this is due to the fact that inactive THC acids are converted with smoking to active Δ^1 THC.[19]

Most early investigations were made upon extracts of the Indian variety of *Cannabis sativa*. Recent German workers, such as F. Korte and H. Sieper, and others, have extracted materials from non-Indian varieties.[20] They have also used chromatographic and counter-current distribution methods to isolate crystalline cannabidiol and probably tetrahydrocannabinol from the extract. With these techniques they have acquired two crystalline isomers from synthetic tetrahydrocannabinol resin and have also isolated cannabidiolcarboxylic acid.

L. Grlic et al. have reported on variation in chemical composition and potency of cannabis of different age and provenance.[21] Variation results mainly because some of the constituents are unstable and change form. Cannabidiolic acid is regarded as a genuine natural precursor of cannabidiol; it was isolated in 1958 by O. E. Schultz and G. Haffner,[22] and independently by Z. Krejčí, M. Horak, and F. Santavý.[23] With age cannabidiolic acid converts by decarboxylation to inactive cannabidiol which in turn yields by intramolecular condensation the active tetrahydrocannabinols. Further aging converts tetrahydrocannabinol into inactive cannabinol by spontaneous dehydrogenation. These changes are faster in tropical areas than in temperate areas, so that various samples of a given age can produce varying effects. Ecological and geographical factors also are important in euphorigenic effects, because the resin of *Cannabis sativa* (where most of the active constituents are presumed concentrated) is produced in greater quantities by plants growing in hot dry climates.

Numerous studies of the physiological effects of cannabis and its constituents in both animals and man may be found in the literature; however, the results are highly varied and even confusing. Experiments with whole cannabis or with its resins may vary with the source of the plant and probably with the concomitant varying of constituents. Experiments with isolated tetrahydrocannabinol probably have varying results because the "tetrahydrocannabinol" was in fact a mixture of isomeric compounds. Experiments with individual, clearly identified chemical principles are rare.

S. Gershon (1970) provides us with an up-to-date review of cannabis pharmacology and bioassay.[24] Early studies give only general information on the behavioral effects of marihuana extracts; more detailed analyses have appeared only during the last ten years. Many of the animal studies, however, are elaborations of two observations by S. Loewe: (1) amytal alone, in doses below the threshold of hypnotic effectiveness, will produce ataxia in dogs. Marihuana exerts no synergistic hypnotic influence, but a mixture with amytal increases ataxia. (2) A combination of marihuana and benzedrine produces a synergism of marihuana effects twice that of marihuana alone.[25] Tetrahydrocannabinols prolong both the barbiturate sleeping time and amphetamine excitation.[26] This latter finding is taken as evidence that microsomal enzyme function is inhibited by cannabinol constituents of marihuana.[27]

E. Joël found that no marihuana effect is seen in decerebate cats; only swaying occurs in decorticated cats; whereas swaying, decrease in motility, cataleptic perseverance, and general inhibition occur in normal cats.[28] The conclusion is therefore that marihuana acts preponderantly upon the hemispheres. B. C. Bose et al. made electroencephalographic (EEG) studies in rabbits which indicated initial depression of the parietal area of the cortex with a simultaneous stimulation of the frontal regions, followed by depression of both. Recovery was characterized by increased excitability of neurons.[29] In 1964, three members of the Department of Pharmacology of the M.G.M. Medical College at Indore, India, ran a series of experiments in which they found that rabbits treated with a dose of cannabis equivalent to that usually required to produce the characteristic "high" in humans showed in their EEG's an increased frequency of cycles in the frontal and parietal regions, which was interpreted as indicating stimulation. This initial stimulation was followed by a depression and a gradual return to normal EEG readings after about five hours.[30]

In gross behavior, Gershon states, "Most authors have shown that extracts of marihuana induce stimulation and excitement in animals, followed by general depression. Other behavioral effects include catalepsy, excitation, aggressiveness, and also sedative and hypnotic effects."[31] Rats given cannabis resin every day for five months showed depression followed by normal or hyperexcitability, followed again by depression. After five months, treated rats showed a lower level of reproductive activity than the controls. The newborn of treated rats developed normally.[32]

E. S. Boyd et al. studied two synthetic tetrahydrocannabinols — the dimethylheptyl and the methyloctyl derivatives — in cats. Above doses of 20 mcg/kg, the dimethylheptyl compound produced a typical depression of performance. The methyloctyl compound produced a similar response but was not as potent.[33]

In maze-learning experiments by E. A. Carlini and C. Kramer (1965), rats receiving cannabis extract before the trials were better performers. After the sixth trial, their performance was significantly better than the control group. This effect was not observed in the rats injected *after* the trials; their running time was longer than the control running time, but the number of errors was the same. Studies by these authors on tolerance in rats are inconclusive, and no effect has been found on the RNA in the rat brain.[34]

The question as to the effect of marihuana on brain waves in humans as measured by the EEG is still not established. According to L. S. Thompson and R. C. Proctor, who used pyrahexyl in the treatment of depressed and addicted subjects, cannabis produces an increase in the frequency of the alpha wave in electroencephalographic recordings, "thus indicating increased relaxation." [35] They are in conflict with E. G. Williams et al. who found that in six of eight experiments (in four subjects), the alpha frequency did not change significantly when the subjects were given single doses of 30 mg and 120 mg of pyrahexyl. They also found that in four of the eight the alpha percentage dropped significantly, and in none of the remaining four was there a significant increase. When in five subjects the medication was continued, on the twelfth day "three . . . subjects . . . [showed] significant diminution in alpha frequency. The alpha percentage was increased in one and decreased significantly in two subjects, while in the remaining two the changes were within the limits of experimental error. . . . In one of the two cases in which there was a diminution in alpha percentage the alpha was replaced with delta activity, while in the other there was no replacement. Considerable delta activity also appeared in one record in which there was no significant over-all change in alpha percentage." [36] When Williams et al. tested the effects of smoking from one to four marihuana cigarettes on the EEG in twenty-two experiments on eighteen subjects, they found no significant uniform change in alpha frequency. "The effects on the alpha percentage, however, were more significant and uniform, an average decrease of 19 percent being observed in eight cases while in only one case was it increased." [37] In addition, the electroencephalographic changes occurring during continued daily smoking of marihuana cigarettes were observed in six subjects. Regarding the effects of "continued daily smoking . . . [it was] noted that in only one instance was the alpha frequency altered significantly. The changes in alpha percentage were not uniform, three showing significant increases and two decreases." [38] R. Adams in his 1942 Harvey Lecture stated that marihuana "produces definite increase in the frequency of the alpha wave in electroencephalographic recordings, thus indicating increased relaxation." [39]

The question of the effect of marihuana on the eyes, especially the pupil size, is one that has interested investigators and users alike, since it has long been thought that the use of marihuana tended to cause dilation. According to A. T. Weil et al., "About 9 out of 10 marijuana users we have interviewed (we have now interviewed many hundreds) have told us they are certain marijuana dilates the pupils of their eyes when they are high. An even higher percentage of law-enforcement agents have told us the same thing." [40] But there are other factors besides the particular drug(s) in one's system that affect pupil size — chiefly the degree of illumination; and marihuana is usually smoked in a dark room. Also, the distance at which one's eyes are focused is a factor; pupils constrict for near vision. Weil et al. claim that their study is the first to measure the effects of marihuana on pupil size while holding all other variables constant; they found that there was no change in pupil size before and after smoking marihuana in either users or nonusers.[41] The only report other than that of Weil et al. that I have found that also appears to be correct regarding pupillary dilation is by H. Isbell et al.: "Pupillary size remained unchanged throughout, a result at variance with much of the literature in which change in size (evaluated by simple clinical observation) has frequently been described." [42] Isbell determined pupillary size by photography under constant lighting conditions.[43]

Weil et al. did find that "significant reddening of conjunctivae due to dilatation of blood vessels occurred in one out of nine subjects receiving placebo, three of nine receiving the low dose of marihuana, and eight of nine receiving the high dose. It occurred in all eight of the chronic users receiving the high dose and was rated as more prominent in them. The effect was more pronounced 15 minutes after the smoking period than 90 minutes after it." [44] S. Allentuck and K. M. Bowman noted the same reddening of conjunctivae, and also report photophobia, lacrimation, tremulousness of the eyelids, and nystagmus upon lateral gaze, but ophthalmoscopic examination revealed nothing unusual in the nerve head, vessels, or retina.[45] It is interesting that they mention lacrimation, since Weil et al. suspect there is a decrease in the flow of tears (and saliva, also reported by Allentuck and Bowman).[46]

Cannabis does have an effect on the heart and circulatory system: the effect on the blood pressure is uncertain but apparently slight; a number of investigators have reported an increase in blood pressure, others a decrease, and still others no change in blood pressure.[47] Investigators are more consistent in reporting an increase in pulse rate.[48] Weil et al. found that in marihuana-naive subjects, marihuana in low dose or high dose was followed by increased heart rate 15 minutes after smoking, but they were unable to demonstrate that the effect was dose-dependent. The high dose caused a statistically greater elevation in the heart rates of chronic users than in those of the naive subjects 15 minutes after smoking. They concluded that cannabis increases heart rate moderately.[49] Isbell et al. observed a consistent elevation in pulse rate, both resting and standing, in all subjects.[50]

Cannabis has long been considered to affect blood sugar level, but again the reports are contradictory, with some authors reporting hypoglycemia and others hyperglycemia.[51] Weil et al. in a controlled study found that marihuana at dose levels approximating or slightly higher than those used by typical "chronic" users had no effect on the level of blood sugar.[52]

The studies of Isbell et al. are very important because they are the first demonstration of marihuanalike activity of tetrahydrocannabinols of known chemical structure in man.[53] Δ^1-*trans*-tetrahydrocannabinol was given to patients orally and by smoking. By either route of administration this isomer caused no significant changes in systolic and diastolic blood pressures, respiratory rate, pupillary size, or threshold for elicitation of the knee jerk. Pulse rates were consistently elevated and subjects developed injection of the conjunctivae after larger doses. Furthermore, response to the tetrahydrocannabinol is statistically reproducible if the same patients are used under the same conditions. Δ^1-tetrahydrocannabinol was three times as potent when smoked as when taken orally; some thermal conversion of Δ^1-tetrahydrocannabinol to Δ^6-tetrahydrocannabinol may have occurred in smoking, but such a change is unproven. The conclusions of this study may be summarized as follows: (1) Δ^1-tetrahydrocannabinol causes subjective effects similar to or identical with those of marihuana; (2) the effects include alterations in mood, sensory perceptual distortion, and, in high doses, depersonalization, delusions, and "hallucinations"; (3) the drug in high doses is a psychotomimetic agent; (4) these tetrahydrocannabinols can be assayed quantitatively in man using either the subjective responses or increase in pulse rate; (5) synthetic cannabidiol dimethyl ether and cannabichromene are much less active than Δ^1-tetrahydrocannabinol or have no activity at all in man; (6) the activity of crude extracts of cannabis resin correlates best with their tetrahydrocannabinol contents.[54]

What is so striking about the pharmacology of cannabis is that it has such limited and mild effects on human nonpsychic function. This is consistent with the equally striking observation that there has never in its long history been reported an adequately

Name	Formula	Pharmacological Properties
cannabidiolic acid		sedative and antibacterial pulse elevating activity
cannabidiol		no psychotomimetic activity
Δ^1 - trans- tetrahydro- cannabinol		euphorigenic activity pulse elevating activity

Name	Formula	Pharmacological Properties

Δ^6- trans-tetrahydro-cannabinol — euphorigenic activity / probable pulse elevating activity

cannabinol — no psychotomimetic activity

cannabigerol — no psychotomimetic activity

cannabichromene — mild or no euphorigenic activity

Table 1. Two systems of numbering appear in the literature. Under the system shown in Figure 1, the two tetrahydrocannabinols are Δ^9 and Δ^8, corresponding to the more frequently encountered Δ^1 and Δ^6, respectively, which are shown in Table 1.

documented case of lethal overdosage. Nor is there any evidence of cellular damage to any organ. This is not to say that future studies will not reveal other effects of cannabis on the body; but, inasmuch as the above represent the major findings reported to date, it seems unlikely that any major deleterious effects will be discovered.

In summary, the name, chemical structure, and (if known) physiological activity of the major constituents of cannabis known to date are listed in Table 1.

4 The Acute Intoxication: Literary and Other Reports

Perhaps the most meaningful way of conveying an appreciation of the nature of the acute cannabis intoxication is through the accounts of some of those who have recorded their own experiences. Among the most articulate of these descriptions are those of some of the nineteenth-century literary figures who experimented with the drug. Their accounts are important not only because they were so successful in putting into words some of the more subtle aspects of the experience, but because they have enormously influenced the general impression of the nature of the acute cannabis intoxication. The effusive descriptions of such writers as Gautier, Taylor, Baudelaire, and Ludlow are, however, often excessive and distorted and frequently have little to do with the moderate use of cannabis (e.g., the smoking of marihuana), for they were written about and under the influence of large amounts of ingested hashish, sometimes admixed with other drugs. Nonetheless, these writings, so influential in creating the Western impression of cannabis, deserve considerable study, just because they do illuminate some of the quantitative and qualitative differences between the intoxication produced by large amounts of ingested hashish and that of moderate doses of smoked marihuana.

It is helpful to regard the French reports of hashish intoxication as offshoots of a literary revolution. Viewed in such a light, many excesses and exaggerations concerning the effects of hashish become less puzzling; in many cases it was not the hashish alone, but the excitement engendered by a new approach to literature, combined with the intoxication of the writers' already exceptional powers of imagination and narration, that caused the fantastic and unbelievable claims for the magical, supra-mundane effects of the drug. A fact that helps to establish this hypothesis of the direct relationship of the French Romantic literary revolt to the use of hashish is the absence of any subsequent writings about hashish that even approximate the extreme nature of the reports from Gautier, Baudelaire, and others. Cannabis did not become popular immediately in the West, despite its availability (it could be purchased without a prescription at any pharmacy, in various preparations) and the lack of any legal prohibitions. But as the literary interest in hashish vanished with the waning of the French Romantic movement, the medical and scientific interest that began with W. B. O'Shaughnessy's report of 1839 gathered headway and provided a more sober perspective, restoring balance to these literary accounts of the effects of cannabis.[1]

Another factor which must be taken into consideration, especially when reading Baudelaire and Fitz Hugh Ludlow, is that most of the literary accounts were written by men who had read De Quincey's description of his extremely uncommon reactions to opium, published in 1822 as the *Confessions of an English Opium-Eater*. De Quincey's 17-year-long use of opium, as he recounts it, seems to give the lie to the conception of opium as an analgesic and soporific. De Quincey took his opium in the form of laudanum, a mixture of opium and alcohol, and some have suggested that it was not the opium but the alcohol which produced the fantastic "dreams" that De Quincey claims are the real reason for his confessions. It is more likely that it was not laudanum alone but the combination of laudanum and De Quincey's fascinating mind that was responsible for the results. The basic point is one that is well kept in mind when reading nearly all of the "literary" reports of the use and effects of hashish; with minds that are unpredictable in their general imaginative and creative functionings, it is not surprising that the effects of hashish are just as often unpredictable.

Further, as will be seen, nearly all the "literary" cases must be evaluated in terms of a combination of other factors which would tend to result in atypical effects.

Pierre Jules Théophile Gautier was born at Tarbes, near the Pyrenees, on August 31, 1811. His father, who worked in the civil service, was transferred to Paris in 1814. When he was 11, Gautier was sent away to board at the College Louis-le-Grand, but he was so miserable with homesickness that his parents soon transferred him to the College Charlemagne, where he was a day student. There he met the first of a long series of literary and artistic friends, Gerard de Nerval, who was instrumental in Gautier's early decision to become a painter. Around 1830, however, Gautier changed his mind, deciding to devote himself to poetry and literature. The opening of Hugo's play *Hernani*, with the general furor it created, was probably the turning point in his shift from painting to writing. Gautier led the supporters of Hugo, with the battle cry, "Death to the old fogies [*perruques*]!" in his soon-to-be-famous rose-red waistcoat. July 1830 saw the publication of his first volume of poetry; he soon became a leader in the group which aimed to restore some life to French literature under the aegis of Hugo. Gautier began writing romances and criticism, and he attained a good deal of fame and notoriety at the age of 24 (1835) with the appearance of his novel *Mademoiselle de Maupin*, described as "the most daring novel . . . that even a full-fledged Romanticist could write." [2] In it Gautier described in detail the adventures of a transvestite experimenter. In the preface, Gautier declared that he would rather "give a large premium [prize] to anyone inventing a new pleasure; for enjoyment appears to me to be the end of life, and the only useful thing in the world," than create "a Prix Monthyon as the reward of virtue." In this preface he also sounded the motto of the French literary Romantic Revolt, "Art for Art's sake." [3] In fact, Gautier was an artist before he was anything else. He had no interest in politics, religion, current events outside the literary world, or morality; he had trained himself to see, not merely to glance or look at. Beauty, fine and of pleasing proportion, vivid detail, aesthetic excellence of expression were his goddesses. This fact, together with Baudelaire's observations that hashish does not warp or destroy the user's basic personality, but on the contrary, mirrors, enlarges, reveals, and draws forth what is already latent in his mind — that, in other words, hashish visions or "hallucinations" are dictated by the user's basic personality — helps to explain the great differences between the hashish experiences of Baudelaire and Gautier — and, for that matter, among all users of hashish. This is not to minimize the importance of other considerations in causing different responses, but it goes a long way toward indicating why Baudelaire, for example, who was constantly involved in philosophical and moral and metaphysical speculation, typically experienced overpowering abstractions dealing with problems of God and the devil, whereas the artist Gautier entered a world of fantastic shapes, colors, and visual detail when under the influence of hashish. Gautier, unlike Baudelaire, had no desire to analyze what he "saw"; for the most part he merely reported it, in a prose that at times strives to outdo his "hallucinations" in its rhetorical flourish and ornate style.

Gautier seems to have found the man deserving of his handsome prize — the psychiatrist Dr. Jacques Joseph Moreau (de Tours). Moreau (de Tours), who experimented clinically with hashish, introduced Gautier to the drug in the form of the preparation known as *dawamesk*, which he imported from Algeria. *Dawamesk* was a sort of a mash or jam made of cannabis, sugar, vanilla, almonds, musk, pistachio, cinnamon, orange extract, cloves, cardamom, nutmeg, and very often a small amount of a cantharides for aphrodisiac effect (an addition which greatly raised the potential for serious damage to the user, since the lethal dose of cantharides is relatively low, and varies greatly from person to person).

Following his first use of cannabis, Gautier, along with Fernand Boissard and F. B. de Boisdenier, was instrumental in founding "Le Club des Haschischins," the members of which, in addition to themselves, included Hugo, de Nerval, Balzac (who, according to Baudelaire, never used hashish), Dumas *père*, and, of course, Baudelaire, along with a number of lesser known artists and writers. In 1845 Moreau (de Tours) published a monograph on his experiments in the administration of hashish and his own experience with the drug: *Du Hachich et de l'aliénation mentale*.[4] Gautier appended a report of one of his own hashish episodes, which later appeared separately in *Revue des deux mondes* in February 1846 and earlier in *La Presse medicale*.[5] In reading it one should keep in mind what has already been said about Gautier's style, and also Gautier's psychological "set," which was apparently one of nervous expectation raised to a high degree, and the general "setting," which, granted the environment of the Hotel Pimodan, where the "club" met, was at the very least macabre.

One striking quality of Gautier's writing is apparent from the first sentence; from his tone, his choice of words, the atmosphere he attempts to create, there does not seem to be a great difference between his descriptions of his perceptions while straight and those under the influence of the drug: "One December evening, in answer to a mysterious summons drawn up in enigmatic terms understood only by the knowing and unintelligible to others, I arrived in a remote section, a sort of oasis of solitude in the midst of Paris, which the river, surrounding it with both its arms, seems to defend against the encroachments of civilization: an old mansion on the Isle Saint-Louis, Pimodan House built by Lauzun, was where the bizarre club of which I was a recent member held its monthly sessions, which I was attending for the first time." [6] Gautier continues in the same vein, delaying the account of his arrival at the hotel to give a full account of the stormy, foreboding atmosphere of the night. Finally he reaches the hotel, rings, and is admitted "with the usual precautions"; this despite the fact that there existed no overly harsh punitive legislation — Gautier appears to be striving for effect.

He approached the Doctor (Moreau), who hands him a "piece of greenish paste or jam, about the size of one's thumb," informing Gautier at the same time, " 'This will be subtracted from your share in Paradise.' " After each member (but one, for reasons eventually made clear) has taken this hashish preparation, the group sits down to dinner ("Le Club des Hachichins," p. 124). Gautier launches into an etymological explanation of the derivation of "assassin," and then remarks that "surely, those who saw me leave my home at the hour when ordinary mortals take their nourishment had no notion that I was on my way to the Isle Saint-Louis, . . . to consume a strange dish, which, several centuries ago, served an imposter sheikh as an inducement to drive his zealots to assassination. Nothing in my perfectly ordinary appearance could have drawn suspicion to such an excess of orientalism; I rather seemed some nephew on his way to dine at his aunt's, than a believer about to taste the joys of Mohammed's heaven in company with twelve exceedingly French Arabs" (p. 125).

He takes a good deal of trouble to describe not only the food served, but also the utensils and general arrangement of the table. The guests are "long-haired, bearded, moustached or singularly shorn." As the dinner comes to an end, Gautier notes that some of the guests are beginning to feel the effects of the hashish; as for himself, he first notes that his taste has undergone "a complete transposition . . . water . . . seemed to savor like the most delicate wine, the meat turned to raspberries in my mouth, and conversely. I could not have told a cutlet from a peach" (p. 125). He then notes that the faces of his fellow-diners are changing shape and color, as they pass through the various stages and states of the hashish intoxication; some are sinking into a stupor, some become agitated, some are soon fighting with all their strength to raise a glass, some are roaring with irrepressible mirth. Gautier himself becomes aware that his reason and his perceptive powers are ebbing and flowing like waves; this, in fact, is a typical sensation throughout hashish intoxications, reported by many users. At this point he simply states: "Hallucination, that strange guest, had set up his dwelling place in me" (p. 126). Immediately the group was called to the drawing room to listen to the "celestial choirs," for the musicians had been waiting for some time. Gautier sought out a low seat by the chimney and surrendered to the effects of the drug. After a few minutes, he felt that his companions had vanished, leaving only their shadows behind, which were soon absorbed into the atmosphere. At this point, he claims that he was no longer conscious; what he means is that he was not aware of any of the other occupants of the room or even of the room itself, but his mind was far from inactive. Suddenly "a red flash passed beneath my eyelids, innumerable candles burst into light, and I felt bathed in a warm clear glow." Although this is somewhat delayed in coming after the clear onset of the first hashish symptoms, it is at least analogous to the "thrill" reported by Ludlow, Taylor, and others. Gautier knew that he was in the same place, but he felt that the surroundings had as little relationship to his perception of them as a sketch has to a finished painting: "Everything was larger, richer, more gorgeous. Reality served as a point of departure for the splendors of the hallucination" (p. 126; see discussion of "hallucinations" in Chap. 5). Although he could see no one, he "divined the presence of a multitude." Suddenly an "enigmatic character" appeared before him. He was like a bird in most aspects of his appearance with a curved hook for a nose, three brown rings around his green eyes, and, in his cravat, a visiting card with the identification, "Daucas-Carota, of the Golden Pot." His legs were "made of a bifurcated mandrake root," and they continually danced and twitched. The "uninvited guest" suddenly burst into weeping, and then proclaimed in a mournful tone, " 'It is today that we must die laughing.' " Gautier looked at the ceiling and perceived a multitude of "bodiless heads like cherubims', with such comical expressions" that he was forced to join in their hilarity. Gradually the drawing room filled "with extraordinary figures such as one finds only in the etchings of Callot and the aquatints of Goya: . . . hodgepodges of spangles and rags of human and bestial figures," but there was nothing at all menacing about them; they were all entirely benign. Gautier became the center of a circle of these shapes, who approached him to whisper banter in his ear which he found immensely humorous at the time, but later could not recall (p. 127). "With each new apparition, a Homeric, Olympian, immense, dumbfounding laugh" burst about him. The tempo of the hilarity increased until he felt assaulted by the "phantoms," while beyond he was dimly aware of "hybrid creatures, formless mixtures of men, beasts, and utensils; monks with wheels for feet and cauldrons for bellies." It was, as Gautier remarks, a veritable Walpurgis Night (p. 128). He sought refuge in a corner, from which he could watch the figures begin to dance more rhythmically. Daucas-Carota was "performing inconceivable pirouettes and leaps, . . . [and] repeating in farcically piteous tones, 'Today is when we must die laughing.' "

Gautier makes a slightly disguised reference to the writing of Rabelais on cannabis: "What bizarrely contorted faces [he saw leaping about before him]! . . . What abdomens, huge with Pantagruelion mockeries!" (p. 129). Of course, it is possible that the reference is mere coincidence, and that Gautier was unaware of the real subject-matter of chapters 49 52 of Book III of *The Great Gargantua,* in *The Histories of Gargantua and Pantagruel* (1516).[7] It is more likely, however, that he was aware of Rabelais's subject matter when Rabelais refers to "the plant Pantagruelion." Throughout what Gautier describes as an "unterrifying nightmare," Gautier perceived flashes of images, caricatures, not all of which were "monstrous or burlesque: gracefulness too showed itself." The figure of gracefulness was a "small head with peachlike cheeks," and it "uttered a high-pitched, vibrant, silvery, prolonged burst of laughter embroidered with trills and organ-bursts." By now the general laughter had reached a peak, and "turned into grunts . . . : Daucas-Carota's words were about to come true." The guests began to writhe and twist on the floor: "It was time to throw a drop of cold water on this seething vapor, lest the boiler burst" (p. 129). Accordingly, the guest who had refrained from partaking of the drug sat down to play the piano, to soothe those in the full delirium. The music seemed like a "celestial melody, . . . [and] soon dissipated the ridiculous visions. . . . The grimacing ghosts withdrew, . . . and again I seemed to be alone." His description of the music suggests an element of synesthesia: "The notes quivered with such power that they entered my breast like luminous arrows; . . . sounds sprang forth, blue and red, in electric sparks."

Gautier notes that after the "convulsive gaiety of the beginning, an indefinable feeling of well-being, a boundless calm, took over." This state he identifies with the "blessed state . . . which the Orientals call *al-kief*." Gautier could no longer feel his body; he seemed to move "by sheer willpower in an unresisting medium" (p. 130). The ecstasy was untinted by anything of a material nature: "No terrestrial desire marred its purity. Love itself . . . could not have increased it." It is interesting, with regard to the continuing dispute as to the aphrodisiac powers of cannabis, to read Gautier's account: "With a peaceful though fascinated eye, I watched a garland of ideally beautiful women, who diademed a frieze with their divine nudity; I saw the gleam of their satin shoulders, the sparkle of their silvery breasts, . . . the undulation of opulent hips, without feeling the least temptation."

Gautier also experienced a not rare sensation while under the influence of acute cannabis intoxication: "After several minutes of contemplation I would melt into the object looked at, and I myself would become that object" (p. 131). This depersonalization and "entry" into the contemplated object is more typical of the more powerful "hallucinogens," LSD especially, and is an indication that the amount of the drug Gautier had taken was considerable. But soon the *al-kief* turned into a nightmare: Daucas-Carota appeared, and "fixed his blazing eyes upon me," contorting and writhing his limbs. Gautier felt a cold breath, and heard a voice inform him: " 'That wretched Daucas-Carota, who sold his legs for drink, has purloined your head and replaced it, not with an ass's head as Puck did to Bottom, but with an elephant's head!' " Gautier went straight to the mirror, and, to his horror, saw that the voice appeared to be telling the truth (p. 131). He began to chase Daucas-Carota in blind fury, finally grabbing him and knocking him against the edge of a table until his own head was restored. But the same voice returned: " 'Beware, you are surrounded by enemies; the invisible forces are seeking to attract you and hold you. You are a prisoner here: try to leave, and you will see.' " Immediately it "became clear" to Gautier that he was indeed trapped, and "that the members of the club were nothing other than cabalists and magicians who wanted to drag me down to my perdition" (p. 132).

With a great deal of effort, Gautier managed to rise and head for the door leading from the drawing room. It took him, according to his estimate at the time, at least ten years to reach the door, "for some unknown force compelled me to take one step backward out of every three." Daucas-Carota followed, mocking him. Once in the next room, he was struck by an unaccountable change in size; the room had "lengthened out . . . indefinitely." At this point he felt that his legs were turning into marble; every step demanded a supreme effort. The half-lit stairs had taken on "Cyclopean, gigantic proportions," and seemed to stretch from heaven to hell (p. 132). Looking up, he indistinctly saw innumerable landings; when he looked down, he saw "abysses of steps, whorls of spirals, dazzling circumconvolutions." As he started down the stairs, he felt that each step he passed immediately returned to be below him again; he estimated it took him a thousand years to reach the vestibule. There he encountered another horror: a "chimera holding a candle in its paws . . . was barring my way with clearly hostile intent, . . . and Daucas-Carota was urging it on." But Gautier, in a sudden access of courage, pushed past into the courtyard. Again, everything was altered: "The courtyard had taken on the proportions of the Champs-de-Mars, and . . . had become bordered with giant buildings set out against the horizon in a tracery of steeples, domes, towers, gables, and pyramids" (p. 133). At this point the chimera attacked him and dragged him back into the drawing room, from which he had just escaped with so much effort. Gautier became dizzy, then "insane, delirious." Daucas-Carota, cavorting about, informed Gautier that he had returned the latter's head, but only after taking out the brains with a spoon. At this point, after reaching up and feeling that the top of his head was indeed missing, he "passed out." When he came to, a funeral for time was in progress, for time had died: " 'Eternity was worn out; there had to be an end,' " as one participant put it (p. 134). At this point the piano player, the only present nonindulger in hashish, felt it appropriate to enliven the situation with a few cheerful melodies, which seemed to annoy Daucas-Carota exceedingly; indeed, he was so vexed that he gradually dissolved, and Gautier realized that the spell cast by hashish had worn off. Back in his room an hour later, he felt as lucid as ever, and stated that he could have reviewed "a pantomime or comic play, or . . . [written] three-lettered rhyming verses" (p. 135; compare his reaction with that which Baudelaire describes as typical after the intoxication). It is interesting that the deep sleep which generally terminates a hashish intoxication apparently did not come to Gautier; although there is no way to determine for how long he "passed out," it was eleven o'clock when he left the hotel. But it is unclear whether that was A.M. or P.M.; if the former, his experience was not unique.

The next major literary report that has survived is something of an anomaly. It was written, not by a member of "Le Club des Haschischins," but by an American, as a part of an account of his travels through Europe and the East. Bayard Taylor's *The Land of the Saracens; or, Pictures of Palestine, Asia Minor, Sicily, and Spain* appeared in 1855, about five years before Baudelaire's *Les Paradis artificiels* (although this is not altogether fair to Baudelaire, since, as we shall see, part of his well-known work is largely an elaboration of a much shorter article he had written in 1851, "Du Vin et du haschisch").[8] Although Taylor was not as given to literary imaginative exaggeration as Gautier and the other French Romantics, neither was he known for his understatement. Still, it is doubtful that the reader must be as wary in reading him as in approaching the works of the French group.

It was in Damascus that Taylor tried hashish in a significant amount for the first time, as he relates in the chapter entitled "The Visions of Hashish." The reason he gives for his experiment is his insatiable and wide-ranging curiosity, in which he seems to take particular pride. He had once before tried cannabis in Egypt, but the rather mild results had only further aroused his curiosity and made him determined "to throw myself, for once, wholly under its influence." The effects he had experienced at that time were not so very different from those experienced by many today who smoke marihuana: a sense of lightness (physically) and "a wonderfully keen perception of the ludicrous, in the most simple and familiar objects." But at no time, he claims, was he unable to note all the changes that were taking place in him, including "the fine sensations which spread throughout the whole tissue of my nervous fibre, each thrill helping to divest my frame of its earthly and material nature." [9] This state lasted only a half-hour, after which he gradually sank into a deep and refreshing sleep. If this is so, Taylor seems to have experienced the opposite from the usual effect. It seems at least possible that the effects lasted for some time longer than half an hour, since one's judgment of time under the influence of cannabis is notoriously inaccurate. The cannabis user usually reports that time "slows down," that which seems to take place over many hours often is discovered to have taken up only a few minutes of actual clock time.

Taylor records that the custom in Syria is to take a small amount of hashish just before the evening meal, so that the food will slow absorption and make the effects more gentle. This was the procedure he wished to follow, but, according to him, "my friends, fearing that its operation might be more speedy upon fresh subjects, and thus betray them into some absurdity in the presence of the other[s]," talked him into taking it after dinner, at which time the group would retire to an upper chamber.

The dose for all present (the exact number is not mentioned) was one teaspoonful of a mixture procured by a servant of their host. This was approximately equal, Taylor estimated, to the amount he had taken in Egypt, thus assuring no danger of an overdose. Even though he realized that the strength of the present sample must be far stronger than the first he had tried, since it was distinctly "bitter and repulsive" instead of merely sweet, the fact that no effects were felt by any of the group after an hour prompted Taylor to suggest that they each take another half teaspoonful, followed with hot tea ("Visions of Hasheesh," p. 44). Shortly afterward, as Taylor was sitting slightly apart from his friends and talking with them, he felt "the same fine nervous thrill" that he had previously experienced. But this time it was far more intense and accompanied by a burning sensation in the stomach. In addition, instead of coming on gradually, it "came with the intensity of a pang, and shot throbbing along the nerves to the extremities of my body." Taylor also experienced a massive sense of relief, as if all confinement of the senses within the body were dissolved. "The walls of my frame were burst outward and tumbled into ruin; . . . I felt that I existed throughout a vast extent of space." Taylor stresses the difficulty of adequately describing the sensation or the rapidity with which this sensation overcame him. The chief factor, as well as he could recall, of this state was that "all sensations . . . suggested more or less coherent images. They presented themselves to me in a double form: one physical, and . . . to a certain extent tangible; the other spiritual, and revealing itself in a succession of splendid metaphors." For example, he relates that the physical feeling of expansion was accompanied by the "image" of a meteor exploding continuously, without dying out, and with its center of explosion the very center of his burning stomach (p. 45). The sensation is one he describes in terms of light radiating from his body, and this is a metaphor — light as epitomizing the hashish intoxication, especially in the early stages — that appears throughout the literary reports.

At this point Taylor felt that he had satisfied his curiosity; he was entirely possessed by hashish, and he implies that he would have been satisfied to return to his normal conscious state immediately. But instead the "thrills . . . became more rapid and fierce, accompanied with sensations . . . [of] unutterable rapture." As he was attempting to explain his feelings to his companions, who had not yet been affected by the drug, he suddenly, without the slightest warning, found that he was at the base of the pyramid at Cheops (p. 45). He wished to climb it; immediately he found himself on the top, thousands of feet high. He was struck by a sense of the ludicrous that was overwhelming, beyond words to express. All he could do was writhe in his chair "in an agony of laughter," which lasted until the "vision" melted away, to be soon followed by "another and more wonderful vision."

Taylor writes that the more he recalls the next "scene," the more he fears he will never be able to describe it adequately. He was moving over a desert of gold in a "barque" of mother-of-pearl, studded with jewels. Again he mentions the quality of light around him; it made the air seem radiant. All his senses were gratified to the highest degree. He inhaled the most pleasing perfumes; he heard music like that which Beethoven "may have heard in dreams, but never wrote"; in front of him, for what seemed a thousand leagues, stretched rainbows of colors like gems. But stronger than the euphoria induced by the satisfaction of the senses raised to a degree he had never before experienced was the triumph he felt: "My journey was that of a conqueror — not of a conqueror who subdues . . . , either by Love or by Will, for I forgot that Man existed — but one victorious over the grandest as well as the subtlest forces of Nature . . . Light, Color, Odor, Sound, and Motion were my slaves" (p. 46).

Taylor experienced, at this point anyway, the usual time-distortion of the hashish intoxication; although it seemed to him that this "vision" persisted for thousands of years, during which he rode over the desert through rainbows, he guesses that in fact it was only about five minutes. Eventually this "vision" also dissipated, and, still "bathed in light and perfume, I found myself in a land of green and flowery lawns, divided by hills of gently undulating outline." But for Taylor the most striking feature of what he calls "these illusions" was that even though and precisely when he was most under their influence, he also simultaneously knew that he was sitting in a room, among friends, that he had taken hashish, and that the drug was the cause of the "strange, gorgeous, and ludicrous fancies which possessed me." At the exact moment that he looked at the Nile, so he claims, he also saw the room in which he sat, and his companions watching him. Both "sensations" were equal in terms of reality and, he insists, "metaphysicians" to the contrary notwithstanding, both were simultaneous: "I was conscious of two distinct conditions of being in the same moment," yet there was no conflict felt between them. At the same time as he was fully able to enjoy his "visions, . . . undisturbed by the faintest doubt of their reality; . . . in some other chamber of my brain, Reason sat coolly watching them, and heaping the liveliest ridicule" on them.

But soon after this experience of double-awareness, the drug effects became stronger and much less pleasant. Taylor believes this is because the full strength of the hashish (which he later asserts was enough to produce severe intoxication in six men) was not felt until the retarding effects of the meal taken before the drug had worn off. At any rate, his new visions were not only "grotesque," but he suffered from a pervasive and painful tension. His next "vision" was that he had been transformed into a mass of jelly, which someone was trying to pour into a twisted mould: "I threw my chair aside, and writhed and tortured myself for some time to force my loose substance into the mould." He admits that his contortions must have seemed highly humorous to an observer; for him, however, they were hellish, and his misery was compounded by "the sober half," which went into fits of laughter over his condition. This laughter was enough to shift his "vision," and the tears that fell from his eyes on account of his laughter each became a large loaf of bread, which piled up around a baker, threatening to smother him.

At this point Taylor felt his perceptions growing dimmer and more confused. "I felt that I was in the grasp of some giant force; and . . . grew earnestly alarmed, for the terrible stress under which my frame labored increased every moment." The heat from his stomach became almost unbearable, radiating throughout his system; his mouth and throat felt as dry and hard as brass, and his tongue felt like a "rusty iron." Drinking large amounts of water gave him no relief (p. 48). He screamed for someone to help him drive out the demon that had taken possession of him, but could no longer perceive the room or his friends, although he heard one remark: " 'It must be real; he could not counterfeit such an expression as that. But it don't look much like pleasure.' "

It was midnight by this time, and Taylor had gone well out of the "Paradise of Hasheesh, and was plunged . . . into its fiercest Hell." He felt that the blood was rushing through his body at a disastrously high rate: "It was projected into my eyes until I could no longer see; it beat thickly in my ears, and so throbbed in my heart, that I feared the ribs would give way." He tried to take his pulse, but felt two different hearts, one beating at a rate of 1,000 beats per minute, and the other with only a slow, dull rhythm. His throat felt as if it were filled with blood, and he could feel blood pouring from his ears. In desperation he fled from the house in a mad, goalless flight, and found himself on the roof (p. 49). For a moment he contemplated suicide by jumping, but "there was an invisible hand at my breast which pushed me away from the brink." He returned to the room with no lessening of his suffering; on the contrary, he felt himself sinking deeper and deeper into what he feared was insanity. Taylor writes that he was not conscious of any real physical pain, but of a "sensation of distress which was far more severe than pain itself." He felt "the remnant of will" with which he struggled against the effects of the drug growing weaker, and this made every effort to preserve his sanity a fearful one. Death seemed to him, or so he writes afterward, a preferable fate than the route he seemed to be descending (p. 50).

Finally he sunk into a stupor, probably, he guesses, about three o'clock in the morning, five hours after the hashish had taken effect. For thirty hours he lay in a "state of gray, blank oblivion, broken only by a single wandering gleam of consciousness," when he heard a friend's voice. Afterward he was told that in the midst of his near-coma he arose, tried to dress, drank two cups of coffee, and lapsed again into this state, but he had no memory of this when he finally awoke. He describes himself awaking "with a system utterly prostrate and unstrung, and a brain clouded with the lingering images of my visions." His food and drink were tasteless, and he had to force himself to understand when spoken to, as "a veil now and then fell over my mind." But the servants who were in charge of caring for him apparently understood his condition, for they gave him "a glass of very acid sherbet," which provided him with "instant relief" (p. 51). (This is perhaps the most obvious parallel with Fitz Hugh Ludlow's account of his experiences with hashish, for Ludlow at one point remarks that he has learned that hashish users in the East use sherbet to recover from severe hangovers, and he accordingly finds much relief in lemonade, which he attributes to its acidity. The many similarities of experience and expression between the two accounts suggest very strongly that Ludlow had read Taylor; in fact he admits this early in his account. But it is at least possible that Taylor's account did more than merely stir Ludlow's imagination and curiosity; it may be that many of Ludlow's reported experiences were borrowed from Taylor, just as he, and perhaps Baudelaire alike, may have, through identification, borrowed a good deal from De Quincey, representing a literary experience as if it were a personal one.)

Although the sherbet brought immediate relief to Taylor, he was still under the "spell" for two or three days, and "subject to involuntary fits of absence," which he tried to battle "with a constant effort to reunite my divided perceptions."

Yet, despite his suffering, he writes that he does not regret having made the experiment, for it "revealed to me deeps of rapture and of suffering which my natural faculties never could have sounded. It had taught me the majesty of human reason and of human will . . . and the awful peril of tampering with that which assails their integrity." Taylor ends his account with an expression of hope that his story will forestall others from experimenting with hashish, but if he merely succeeds in arousing more curiosity, and leads others to try the drug, he begs them to take a dose sufficient for one man, and not for six (p. 52).

Charles Baudelaire was born on April 9, 1821, at Paris, into a complex and confusing family situation. His father, François Baudelaire, was a wealthy man of 62; his mother was 28. She taught Charles English from the beginning, and it is generally agreed that she instilled in him notions of sin, a personal devil, and the inevitability of retribution for evil-doing, forces which can be seen operating strongly in his later writing and life. When he was older Baudelaire remembered his father with only the warmest feelings, but it is difficult to imagine how the youth could have looked on the old man as anything but a grandfather; perhaps some of the usual Oedipal antagonisms were deflected to his much older half-brother, Claude. But his father died when Baudelaire was only six, and for a very short time he became the sole focus of his mother's affection and attention. Less than two years after the death of François Baudelaire, she married again, this time to a man who must have impressed the youngster as a definite competitor. Major Aupick was still in his thirties, handsome, with a fine military record and prospects, later fulfilled, for a first-rate military career. The mother's remarriage could hardly have had a worse effect on Charles. He felt that he had been displaced, first, while his father was alive, as a co-sharer of his mother's love, and now, with her remarriage, as her main and only love-object. His stepfather, despite what seem to have been good intentions, was not a type who could reach the moody, increasingly introspective, and always highly sensitive boy of seven and a half. Himself a self-made military specimen, he could conceive of no other way of raising his wife's son than by discipline and strict training. Although it is probably true that Aupick had a genuine fondness for his stepson, he could hardly see him as anything but a rebellious recruit who needed to be "broken" in his obstinacy and stubbornness and constantly reminded of his "duties" and "obligations."

Although the report that Baudelaire never forgave his mother for remarrying may be untrue, Baudelaire did say, "When you have a son like me, you don't marry again." [10] To the extent that Oedipal wishes remained unresolved, it may well be the case that Baudelaire was unaware, until much later in his life, of his true feelings generated by these wishes. For example, when he was eighteen, he wrote to his mother: "Persuade him if you can that I'm not a scoundrel, but a good boy"; and again, when his step-father was promoted to general, Baudelaire wrote him a letter of congratulation and high praise.[11] But gradually he came to see Aupick in another light; first as the embodiment of all the middle-class hypocrisy that he despised, and then, more personally, as the person chiefly responsible for his misery. This shift appears quite definitely after 1842, by which time Baudelaire had begun using opium, alcohol, and perhaps hashish.[12]

The exact date when Baudelaire was introduced to the use of drugs is undetermined, although there are helpful indications. In 1839 his mother and stepfather suggested that he apply for a position at the Foreign Office, but Baudelaire flatly refused, having made up his mind that his life work was to be literature. After he received his *baccalauréat* in 1839, his parents acquiesced, his step-father more graciously than his mother, and Baudelaire immediately entered the Bohemian life of the Latin Quarter. He began drinking heavily, but this was not unusual for the circle he moved in.[13] If he did try opium or hashish at this time, it was probably only an isolated experiment; there is no evidence either way. There have been rumors that a contemporary and former school-mate of Baudelaire's, Louis Menard, introduced Baudelaire to opium (probably in the form of laudanum, which also contained alcohol) and/or hashish as early as 1839; these remain only rumors.[14]

But Baudelaire's first venture into the literary-Bohemian world was short-lived; his mother, and to some extent his stepfather, were becoming increasingly alarmed at the friends he was making and decided to send him on a long sea-voyage to India in the hope that he might return to what they considered a safer and saner existence. Baudelaire was strongly opposed to the journey, but, since he was under twenty-one, he had no choice. There is dispute as to whether Baudelaire did actually reach India; there is some reason to believe that if he did he tried hashish at least once. But even if he did not, the long sea-voyage opened and deepened in him the love of reverie. "He came back from the East with a romantic yearning for rich, warm countries, for exotic splendour, and beauty impossible to achieve in this world." [15] If he had not already used drugs, he was set to experiment with them now.

Soon after returning early in 1842, Baudelaire took living quarters at the Hotel Lauzum, shortly after renamed the Hotel Pimodan, and joined the new "Le Club des Haschischins," to which he was introduced by the painter F. Boissard, who, with Gautier, had been one of the founders. This association is often cited, perhaps erroneously, as conclusive evidence that Baudelaire was a user of hashish. Similarly, his writings, particularly *Les Paradis artificiels,* are often cited as authoritative and revealing commentary on the subject of hashish. It is, therefore, important to consider this work in some detail.

In *Les Paradis artificiels* (1860), after making the distinction between "pure" or "true" hallucinations versus those "hallucinations" induced by hashish or other drugs, and noting that hashish does not alter or add to the basic personality of the user, but only draws forth what is already latent, he summarizes the ideal conditions under which hashish should be taken.[16] It is interesting to note that his message is very much reminiscent of Leary's and other recent writers' references to the importance of "set" and "setting" in taking any drug, although these writers refer mainly to LSD and related drugs. The individual should be in a state of "perfect leisure," without any interfering "duties to accomplish that require punctuality, exactitude; no domestic cares, no love pangs" should be occupying his mind. His warning as to what may happen if these precautions are not taken sounds very much like a description of a bad LSD trip and is an indication that Baudelaire was taking high doses. He suggests "a favorable environment, such as in the midst of a picturesque landscape or in a room artistically decorated," and also that music be available.[17]

Baudelaire described four distinct stages of the acute intoxication of hashish: (1) This is the stage of the breaking up of the individual's customary thought patterns. Baudelaire mentions the novice's typical response of impatience and the complaint that he is experiencing slow or no effects, which Baudelaire attributes mainly to anxiety in the face of the new, the unknown.[18] In the earlier article he had written: "It is funny to watch the first effects appear and grow even while these protestations of disbelief are being made." [19] The first major observable effect is "a certain hilarity, irresistible, ludicrous, which takes possession of you." This arises, according to Baudelaire, from a sudden and strange sense of the incongruous that pervades all: "The simplest words, the most trivial ideas, take on new and strange shapes; you are even astonished to have found them so simple." These minor attacks of hilarity mixed with a sense of incongruity are interspersed with "intervals of stupor during which you vainly try to collect yourself." He emphasizes the rapidity and fleeting quality of mental associations at this stage, exemplified by "interminable puns, comical absurdities, . . . associations impossible to foresee," and writes that "the Demon" has the hashish user in "His" possession.

Another subjective phenomenon common to this first stage is what Baudelaire calls a "silent, lazy, soft benevolence." But he warns that there is a possibility of sudden seizures of terror, usually arising spontaneously without any apparent "cause" and interrupting this deepest (early stage) pleasure. Baudelaire asserts that this exaggerated fear is most apt to arise if the individual feels any necessity to hide his true condition — if, for example, he is obliged to attend a formal dinner while under the influence of hashish. In this same connection, he mentions the tremendous efforts required when he had to mask his condition from others. (Ludlow, as we will see, states it becomes gradually easier for the hashish eater to feign complete sobriety.)

(2) The transition to the second stage is marked by a "momentary lull." [20] But quite soon definite physical symptoms of coldness, which particularly characterized Baudelaire's second stage, begin to be felt. Typically, he experienced a pronounced coldness in his extremities, usually accompanied by "a great weakness in the limbs," trembling hands, and a mental state of "awkward stupor and stupefaction. [One's] eyes dilate, . . . [the] face becomes pallid, . . . [the] lips thin, as if they were sucked into the mouth by the act of inhaling which characterizes the ambitious man a prey to great projects, oppressed by vast thoughts, or saving his breath to get a better start. The throat is contracted, so to speak; the palate is tormented by a thirst it would be infinitely sweet to slake if the delights of idleness were not more agreeable and were not opposed to the slightest disturbance of the body. You heave deep, raucous sighs, as if your old body could not endure the desires and activity of your new soul. From time to time you shudder, and this forces you to make an involuntary movement, like those nervous jumps which, at the end of a day's work or during a stormy night, precede one's sleep." [21]

Baudelaire relates an anecdotal case study of a man who had

" 'taken a moderate dose of *extrait gras*,' " and then was obliged to attend the theater. His first impression was that the actors seemed exceedingly small, but still he was able to perceive " 'distinctly, not only the most minute details of their costumes, such as the pattern of the material, the seams, buttons, etc., but also the edge of the wig, the blue, white, red, and all the rest of the make-up.' " This appears to be an example of a heightening of sensory discrimination, which often accompanies the earlier period of the acute hashish intoxication. The actors appeared to Baudelaire's acquaintance as if " 'bathed in a cold, clear, magic brilliance, like that given by a glass neatly adjusted to an old painting.' " [22]

(3) The third stage is characterized by a very strong subjective sense of expanded consciousness: "A new sensitiveness, a superior acuteness, manifests itself in all the senses. Sight, smell, hearing, touch participate equally . . . The eyes have a vision of Eternity. The ear hears almost inaudible sounds in the middle of a vast tumult." It is at this point that the "hallucinations" begin. Baudelaire is very careful to distinguish these from "true" hallucinations: "A very subtle distinction characterizes the pure hallucination, such as doctors have often had occasion to study, from the hallucination or rather from that misapprehension of the senses during the mental state caused by Haschisch . . . The drunken eyes of the man who has taken Haschisch will see strange shapes; but, before being strange or monstrous, these shapes were simple and natural . . . The second [hashish "hallucination"] has its roots in the environment, while the former ["pure" hallucination] has no such roots in the present." [23]

Simultaneously or immediately after the onset of the "hallucinations" come what Baudelaire calls "equivocations," which are, for the most part, various instances of synesthesia: "Sounds take on colours and colours contain music." He asserts that there is nothing essentially "supernatural" in these interminglings of the usual sensory pathways, and that any sane, poetical mind can easily imagine such experiences vividly enough to be at the point of actually experiencing them.[24] This is in line with his statements that hashish does not generate in the user visions or "hallucinations" that cannot be traced directly to some stimulating factor in the environment, and that hashish only exaggerates, has only a quantitative, not a qualitative, effect.

Baudelaire mentions a specific subtype of hashish-induced synesthesia: "Musical notes become numbers, . . . and . . . melody, audible harmony . . . transforms itself into a vast arithmetical operation in which numbers beget numbers." [25] (Fitz Hugh Ludlow experienced the same phenomenon in a slightly altered form; he must have felt it important, because he titled his book: *The Hashish Eater: Being Passages from the Life of a Pythagorean*. This title is explained when Ludlow recounts one of his hashish experiences, during which he was able to comprehend in a new mode the concept of a pervasive, universal harmony based on numbers, and his "insight" was induced by music: "While that music was pouring through the great heavens above me, I became conscious of a numerical order which ran through it, and in marking this order, I beheld it transferred to every movement of the universe . . . An exquisite harmony of proportion reigned through space, and I seemed to realize that the music which I heard was but this numerical harmony making itself objective through the development of a grand harmony of tones.")[26] But this is clearly more than a mere synesthesia. In fact, Baudelaire uses the term "equivocation" to cover a variety of diverse phenomena; for example, he includes the loss of sense of self (depersonalization), and the transformation of sense of self into the sense that the self is projected onto an external object: "Objectivity . . . develops so abnormally that the contemplation of objects outside yourself makes you forget your own existence, and causes you to lose yourself in them." [27] Accordingly, if one intoxicated by hashish stares at a tree long and deeply enough, he is likely to feel that he has become the tree. Baudelaire uses a helpful metaphor: the hashish-intoxicated individual is like one *living* "some fantastic novel" instead of reading it.

Baudelaire gives an analysis of typical hashish symptoms and reactions that cut across his four-part division: (1) Temporary lulls occur, during which the individual feels he is back to "normal," but which are merely "deceptive calms and intermissions." (2) He suggests that these are linked to the frequently experienced "voracious hunger," and "voracious thirst." Although he describes the hunger and thirst as "tyrannical, . . . [involving] an immense amount of labour" to appease them — for any physical effort becomes extremely difficult — he does not try to explain this phenomenon, except to note that "man believes himself to be so far above material things, or rather he is so overwhelmed by his intoxication, that he has to summon a great deal of courage to grasp a bottle or fork." (3) But, he claims, in many instances, food or drink only cause a "new paroxysm, . . . [a] vertiginous crisis." (4) This is followed by a "series of enchanting visions" which are sometimes "lightly coloured by fear."

Baudelaire writes that the third stage is typically characterized by an experience of "what the Orientals call the *Kief*. It is no longer something whirling and tumultuous; it is a calm and motionless beatitude, a glorious resignation," [28] a state of what would today be referred to as "expanded" or "cosmic" consciousness, in discussions of LSD especially. This indicates, as will be discussed later, that Baudelaire was in the habit of using a preparation much more powerful than marihuana, or even most kinds of so-called "hashish" presently available in the United States.

Near the end of the third stage, "for quite a while you have not been master of yourself, but you are completely unconcerned. Sorrow and the sense of time have disappeared," and even if they should happen to recur, they "would be transfigured . . . and they would then be, as compared to their habitual form, what poetical melancholy is to positive sorrow." [29]

(4) Baudelaire describes the ultimate stage of the hashish experience as one that is not always reached, but the one that is by far the most overpowering. His description is close to some reports of the effects of LSD, especially, for example, Alan Watts' *Joyous Cosmology* — although, as Watts points out, this stage is difficult for some individuals to achieve, even with high doses of LSD.[30] This state has been described in many ways: *satori;* the ultimate religious experience; the feeling of total identification with the All; self-transcendence; conversion (in the sense that William James used it); a sense of complete loss of the self by a merging into the "external, out-there" all-encompassing whole; "The Beatific Vision"; "Being-Awareness-Bliss"; "Sat Chit Ananda," etc.[31] Baudelaire writes as follows about this condition: "My imaginary man — the spirit of my own choice — has thus arrived at that peculiar state of joy and serenity in which he is *constrained* to admire himself. All contradiction disappears, all philosophical problems become clear, or at least seem to . . . The plenitude of his actual existence inspires in him an immeasurable pride. A voice speaks inside him . . . and says to him: 'You now have the right to consider yourself superior to all men; no one knows or could un-

derstand all that you think and all that you feel; they would even be incapable of appreciating the good-will with which they inspired you. You are a King, unrecognized . . . who lives alone in his belief; but why care? Do you not possess a sovereign contempt that strengthens the soul?' " He admits that "from time to time a biting memory enters and corrupts that joy," but asserts that the effects of hashish are stronger than and overcome any memory of wrong-doing: "The man who takes Haschisch will courageously face these reproachful ghosts of memory . . . , and he will find in these hideous reminiscences new reasons for pride and pleasure." [32]

Continuing his "analysis of this victorious monomania," Baudelaire presents the hashish habitué as one who "supposes himself to be the centre of the Universe . . . , [who] becomes the living and exaggerated embodiment of the proverb that says that passion creates passion." Ultimately he comes to believe that "all these things [he mentions museums, cities, ships, libraries, musical instruments, even women] have been created *for me, for me, for me* . . . No one should be astonished at the final, the supreme thought born in the dreamer's mind: *I have become God!* . . . But soon this storm of pride changes to a calm, silent, restful beatitude; the universality of man is announced colorfully, and lighted as it were by a sulphurous dawn." [33]

Baudelaire attempts a personality analysis of the type most prone to the habitual use of hashish. He lists such characteristics as "a temperament half nervous and half splenetic . . . ; a cultivated mind, given to the study of form and color; a tender heart, made weary by unhappiness, but still youthful; . . . with past faults, and, . . . if no positive remorse, at least a regret for time ill-spent and profaned." Further predisposing factors are "a taste for metaphysics," some knowledge of various philosophies of human existence and meaning, a love of "abstract, stoic, or mystical virtue," and, finally, a "delicate sensibility." This type of individual is first entranced by the ability of hashish to enhance appreciation of color and form, but, according to Baudelaire, the drug insidiously undermines powers of mental discrimination and judgment until the "first object seen becomes the perfect symbol." [34]

Baudelaire begins the final chapter of the "Poem to Hashish" ("Moral") with a damnation of the hangover-like aftereffects of the "terrible day after," with its symptoms of exhaustion, "a desire to weep," and the complete impossibility of accomplishing any sustained work. This occurs because "man is forbidden, on the pain of intellectual death and decay, to upset the primordial conditions of his existence and to disturb the equilibrium of his faculties with the environment for which they were intended." Regarding "the immoral character of Haschisch," he writes that it is nothing but a slow, bloodless suicide, worse than a quick and bloody suicide, because it, "like all solitary pleasures, makes the individual useless to men and makes society superfluous for the individual, driving him to a singular kind of self-admiration and . . . pushing him toward the luminous gulf." [35]

He raises a question that he has been often asked: "What if a man could, at the expense of his dignity, of his honesty, and of his free-will, still derive certain spiritual benefits from Haschisch, make a sort of thinking machine, a fruitful instrument, out of it?" His answer is strongly negative: "To begin with, as I have explained at length, Haschisch never reveals to the individual more than what he is himself." In fact, he has only *asserted* this many times; he has given no real explanation, and many of his anecdotal case studies seem to imply an opposite position. However, for the sake of argument, he is willing to suppose for the moment that hashish might bestow, or at least reveal and increase, "genius"; but the other side is inescapable: hashish "reduce[s] willpower, and thus grant[s] on one side what it withdraws from the other, that is to say, imagination without the ability to profit by it." Moreover, there is the "fatal, terrible danger, . . . inherent in all such habits. They soon become necessities. One who has recourse to poison *in order* to think, will soon be unable to think *without* taking poison." [36] Note that Baudelaire is not referring to addiction in the sense of a need for higher doses over time in order to achieve the desired effect, on account of increasing tolerance, nor does he mean withdrawal symptoms experienced on abrupt discontinuation of drug use. To the extent that he is writing about hashish he is describing what is now called "psychic dependence."

As mentioned above, Baudelaire's detailed accounts of his hashish experiences are very often cited as authoritative sources for those who wish to illustrate the powerful effects of this drug and, indeed, its capacity to destroy a great and talented man. However, for those who wish to establish the validity of such claims, the crucial questions are whether or not Baudelaire did in fact use hashish and to what extent his literary descriptions are actually of *his* use of *this* drug.

A collection of poems by three young French writers, published in 1842, includes one poem with a direct reference to Baudelaire's habit of taking drugs, although the type of drug is unspecified.[37] But, on the other hand, there is the report of Varlet, in *Au Paradis du haschisch*, that Baudelaire had very little or no experience with hashish, and that he completely discontinued any use of the drug before 1845.[38] But he apparently did not abandon either opium or alcohol until much later when he knew, or suspected, that he was dying from syphilis; A. Marx wrote (*Indiscrétions parisiennes*, 1866) that he more than once saw Baudelaire swallow enough opium to kill five men.[39] In two letters, one to his mother (December 4, 1847) and the other to Ancelle (January 1, 1850), Baudelaire mentions that he habitually took large doses of opium.[40] Starkie suggests that he gave up opium in the late 1850's, returning to it sometime after 1858, when he was in almost continual pain.[41] There are frequent references to his use of opium in letters written during 1858. Starkie is also of the opinion that he finally abandoned the opium habit just before 1865, since a letter to his mother, written from Belgium that year when he was extremely ill, speaks of his use of opium as a thing of the past and expresses extreme horror at opium's effects.[42] But this evidence is inconclusive: in a letter dated February 17, 1866, he wrote to his mother, "As for opium, you well know that I have had the habit for many years, to the extent of taking 150 drops without any danger." [43] However, the point is largely irrelevant as to whether he means that he is or is not still taking the drug, since by the time he wrote the letter he was nearly dead.

In 1851 Baudelaire published an article in *Le Messager de l'Assemblée*, "Du Vin et du haschisch." This was later expanded and published as the first section of *Les Paradis artificiels*, "The Poem of Hashish." [44] In the early article Baudelaire compared the two drugs (alcohol and hashish) and came out strongly in favor of alcohol. He wrote that the two had only one property in common: "the excessive poetic development of a man . . . [but] liquor . . . aids digestion, strengthens muscles, and enriches the blood. Even taken in large quantities, it only causes brief disorders; . . . [whereas hashish] interrupts the digestive functions, weakens the limbs, and can cause an intoxication of 24 hours. Wine exalts the will; haschisch annihilates it . . . Wine makes one good and sociable; haschisch isolates one . . . Wine is useful, it produces fruitful results. Haschisch is useless and dangerous." [45]

It is clear that Baudelaire was addicted to alcohol by 1851; his bias is easy to understand.[46] But there is a good deal of evidence that he was on much less familiar ground when he wrote of hashish. It is at least possible, even probable, that most of the effects he ascribes to hashish were in fact effects produced by opium. If Varlet is correct, Baudelaire had not taken hashish for six years when he wrote the article, which appeared nine years before *Les Paradis artificiels,* but he had continued to use alcohol and opium throughout this period for nearly fifteen years.[47] Furthermore, Baudelaire makes a curious statement in the 1851 article: "Haschisch is made from a decoction of Indian Hemp, butter, and a small amount of opium." [48] Either this mixture is the drug which Baudelaire did take and referred to as hashish, in which case we can never be certain whether he is writing about the effects of hashish or some mixture containing opium also; or else he was, in 1851, largely ignorant concerning hashish. But then where did he get the accurate and extensive information concerning not only the effects, but the processing, history of use, "mythology," and so forth, of hashish? An answer is suggested in the *Notes et éclaircissements* appended to Crépet's 1928 edition of Baudelaire's complete works: he got his information from his wide reading. A surprising number of French writers before Baudelaire had written about their own experiences and knowledge of hashish. Crépet writes:

> In August, 1848, while Baudelaire was writing for *L'Esprit public,* M. Souquère published in four articles a review of the book by Dr. Moreau de Tours, *Of Haschisch and Mental Alienation* . . . It is quite certain that Baudelaire knew well . . . the articles of M. Souquère, or, at any rate, the work of Dr. Moreau de Tours . . . Not only Moreau de Tours, and after him Souquère, but many others, several better known than these, had written on haschisch; for example, in addition to Hammer and Silvestre de Sacy, cited by Baudelaire, Aubert Roche, Liataud, Forvault, . . . Gastinel, Jacquet, Lallemand, Theophile Gautier, and many others . . . Perhaps you mentioned

. . . the work of Brierre de Boismont — *Hallucinations* . . .
When one reads it carefully, it becomes clear that this book, the
first edition of which appeared in 1845, was one of those most
studied by Baudelaire and from which he frequently drew. Are
supplementary proofs necessary? In "Curiosités Esthétiques,"
allusion is made to the famous prediction of Cazotte. This prediction is found in Brierre de Boismont . . . The above is certainly enough to prove Baudelaire's familiarity with de Boismont's work . . . The reader curious about predecessors of
Baudelaire in this area could look to advantage among the
sources provided by M. le Dr. Henri Moreau in his *Study on
Haschisch* (J. Rousset, 1904) and, among the authors mentioned
there will find explorers, savants, doctors, pharmacists, rubbing
elbows with writers.[49]

Thus it seems clear that Baudelaire did not lack for material that
he could present as his own experience or thought. This fact is
essential to a consideration of *Les Paradis artificiels*.

Les Paradis artificiels was planned as a two-part work, the main
title to be *L'Idéal artificiel*, and the subsections *Haschisch* and
Opium, although all were later changed. Baudelaire wrote the
first part very quickly and easily, mainly because it was an elaboration of the second part of his 1851 article. The first section was
published in October 1858 as "Le Poème du haschisch," in *La
Revue contemporaire*. But the second section caused Baudelaire
much more difficulty and was not completed until March of 1859;
neither he nor his publisher were pleased with the final form. His
troubles in writing this section may have been simply a result of
his attempt to relate the experiences with opium of De Quincey
(from the *Confessions*) instead of his own. He found it distinctly
uncongenial to select passages from a mass of sometimes dull and
tedious writing, translate some parts and paraphrase others, at
times inserting his own invention.[50] But another, more subtle
reason is suggested in a letter to his mother, dated December 11,
1858: "My 'Opium' is causing me a great deal of trouble, and I
feel I've produced something rather nasty!" [51]

Perhaps Baudelaire's work inhibition on this project had a complicated basis: if it is true that the first section, supposedly about
his own hashish experiences, was actually, for the most part, a
disguised report of his opium experiences or of his experiences

with mixtures of various drugs, or of his reading about the effects of both opium and hashish on others, and since in writing the "Opium" section he was not attempting a straight translation, but rather a rendition or adaptation into which he admitted that he had introduced many of his own ideas, he may simply have felt that he had nothing further to say on the subject of opium; hence his paralysis.[52] To repeat essentially what he had already written in the "Haschisch" section, he may have feared, would be to expose himself as a fraud, or at least one whose authority and veracity were of little value. Suppose that "Haschisch" described nothing but his opium experiences (not those of another, and with no exaggeration); might he not have felt acute embarrassment and considerable guilt at the prospect of a task of rendering into French a more complete, direct, and authentic report? And might he not have decided on the pseudotranslation method as a dodge — to cover his tracks by obscuring, as much as possible, exactly where the drug experiences of De Quincey left off and his own began?

Whether or not Baudelaire did in fact write about hashish in the places he claimed to do so, he has been largely accepted at his word by the vast majority of readers. Because of the combination of his powerful intellect, at least until his final years, his eloquence, his magnetic personality, his eventual fame as a poet, and his contemporary notoriety — he enjoyed spreading rumors about himself, especially that he was a pederast[53] — as an artistic personality whose popular reputation placed him among the select group of ultimate decadents, he may be considered the most important figure, literary or otherwise, in establishing a sense of what the hashish experience consists of, in its most extreme forms, and of what the inevitable result is for one who uses it to excess. But what if, in ostensibly relating the effects of hashish, he was really reporting about the effects of an entirely different drug, or of a combination of different drugs? If Baudelaire was not writing about his own experiences with hashish, a whole mythology begins to crumble. It is a known fact that he had used laudanum since around 1841–1842. By the time he admitted this in a letter to his mother of December 16, 1847, in which he also blames his lack of any worldly success on the abuse of drugs, in particular of laudanum, he was probably addicted to both of the ingredients of laudanum; certainly he was addicted to alcohol.[54] It is questionable whether he ever gave himself a real chance to have a pure hashish experience, or, if he did, whether it could have provided him with enough material to write the work he did write.

In direct support of this, G. T. Clapton and T. Varlet have concluded, working independently although simultaneously, after a careful study of De Quincey's full texts (the *Confessions* of 1822 and the later sequel, *Suspira de profundis* of 1845, to which Baudelaire had access), and an examination of Baudelaire's omissions and re-renderings, that he had far less personal, first-hand knowledge of or experience with hashish than he claimed or implied, and that many of his alleged descriptions of hashish use were descriptions of opium use, some his own, but many lifted from his reading of De Quincey.[55] From his reading in the contemporary or recent books on the subject of hashish he obtained enough material and information to make his report seem genuine. These two researchers have established beyond any reasonable doubt that Baudelaire was using opium, and not hashish, during and before the time he wrote *Les Paradis artificiels,* only the first part of which alleges to treat his hashish use of *some fourteen years earlier.* Again, Baudelaire's 1851 remark that hashish is composed of opium must be given some consideration.

Thus, we discover that we have from Baudelaire what is at best a mixed report, and to unravel the genuine descriptions of his own use of hashish from his use of other drugs — especially mixtures — or of his reading about hashish and opium, is, as far as I can see, impossible. It should be remembered that, even after due allowance has been given to his love of hyperbole and dramatic exaggeration, he did habitually take extremely high doses of opium, alcohol, and other mixtures, some with hashish in them. But nowhere in his writing is there any evidence that he was concerned with or even aware of some of the essential differences between opium and hashish (for example, that opium is addictive in the usual medical sense, whereas prolonged use of hashish is believed to result in what is called psychic dependence, but not true addiction). I believe that this is another indication that he was never a heavy user of hashish, if he used it at all.

Although Baudelaire's psychosis and death have been popularly attributed to overindulgence in hashish (or, more rarely, opium or even alcohol), this is clearly a myth. True, "his story is the story of a very slow, very painful decomposition," which began quite early, but even if he had used as much hashish as he claimed, it is extremely doubtful that the effects could have been cumulatively lethal.[56] Nor is it likely that his death, at least not as it did occur, can be attributed to the fact that what he called hashish might frequently, if not usually, have been mixed with high doses of opium or laudanum. What killed him was tertiary syphilis. Sometime between the autumn of 1839, when he left home, and early June of 1842, when he left on his sea journey, Baudelaire contracted syphilis. In a letter dated May 6, 1861, he wrote to his mother: "You know that when I was very young, I contracted a venereal disease, which I thought later was completely cured. It broke out again in Dijon after 1848, and it was once more checked. Now it has returned in a new form." [57] Evident was the usual progressive nature of the disease toward death including the typical symptoms of paralysis, seizures with or without temporary loss of consciousness, psychotic episodes, all complicated in his case by alcoholism. Further, the stigma attached to both his venereal disease and alcoholism, their complexity, and the difficulty of a permanent "cure" for either, combined with his persistent sense of inadequacy and failure, indicate that he may have been almost eager to displace the blame for his misery onto one specific agent, even one that he knew little about, and had used for only a short period of time, if at all — hashish.

Perhaps the best brief summation of Baudelaire's weltanschauung is his own statement, from the first section of *Les Paradis artificiels,* Chapter 1, "The Taste of the Infinite": "Man will never believe that he has entirely given himself over to evil." [58] Baudelaire felt the truth of this to his very core, and his life may be seen as a prolonged acting out of this belief. I think that it is safe to assert that the only valid or defensible relationship between Baudelaire's death and his alleged use of hashish is that his personality structure, critically influenced by some early, moulding circumstances and experiences (e.g., the age of his father, his father's death when Baudelaire was only six, his relationship to his mother, and her remarriage) generated conflict and guilt which drove him to self-destruction. This operated perhaps most plainly in his use of various drugs; hashish may have been one of these, but it is certainly not the one that caused Baudelaire the most difficulty.

I can find no better concluding comments on the mystery that is Baudelaire than those of Sartre:

But we should look in vain for a single circumstance for which he was not fully and consciously responsible. Every event was a reflection of that indecomposable totality which he was from the first to the last day of his life. He refused experience. Nothing came from outside to change him and he learned nothing. General Aupick's death scarcely altered his relations with his mother. For the rest, his story is the story of a very slow, very painful, decomposition. Such he was at the age of twenty; such we shall find him on the eve of his death. He is simply gloomier, more nervous, less alive, while of his talent and his admirable intelligence nothing remains except memories. And such no doubt was his singularity, that "difference" which he sought until death and which was only visible to others. He was an experiment in a retort, something like the *homunculus* in the Second Part of *Faust*; and the quasi-abstract circumstances of the experiment enabled him to bear witness with unequalled eclat to this truth — the free choice which a man makes of himself is completely identified with what is called his destiny.[59]

Fitz Hugh Ludlow is the first American writer after Bayard Taylor to discuss hashish at any length. He usually is not regarded as the equal of Baudelaire on the subject of hashish use, and I believe that he, like Baudelaire, should be trusted less than he is. There are a number of indications that Ludlow may have exaggerated, plagiarized, and invented many of his alleged "hashish experiences."

Ludlow was born September 11, 1836, in Poughkeepsie, New York, the son of an abolitionist minister. His early education was thorough, and he indulged in a wide range of reading outside the prescribed school curriculum. In particular, his reading of the *Arabian Nights* and Bayard Taylor's *Land of the Saracens* stirred his imagination and eventually led or at least influenced him to try hashish. Ludlow graduated from Union College in 1856, and after teaching at the high school level for one year in Watertown, New York, he studied law and was admitted to the bar in 1859. But he did not practice law, preferring to earn his living by writing music, art, and drama criticism. In 1863 he traveled to Oregon and then California, but before leaving on his journey west, and just after graduating from college, he wrote anonymously the tale of his interior journeys: *The Hasheesh Eater: Being Passages from the Life of a Pythagorean* (published in late 1857). The book was a success; one Mrs. M. E. W. Sherwood recalled that "he held the town [New York City] in his slender right hand at one time." [60]

The brief preface deals with the relationship of what Ludlow has written to the *Confessions* of De Quincey. He admits a deep admiration for the English opium eater, although the "recital . . . of . . . [his own] career . . . may fall far short of the Opium Eater's, and . . . was not coincident and but seldom parallel with his, . . . still [it] ran through lands as glorious, as unfrequented, as weird." He foresees that many will compare his account with De Quincey's and charge him with unintentional imitation or even outright plagiarism. He tries to forestall such criticism: "In the first place, this book . . . is a resume of experiences which, so far from being fiction, have not been given even adequate representation. . . . The fact of my speaking truths, so far as they can be *spoken*, out of my actual memory, must shield me . . . from the imputation of being a copyist of incidents." Second, he maintains that to copy another's style, careful study and rewriting are essential, but he has published his first draft. Third, Ludlow claims that he refrained from looking at De Quincey's work while writing his own. But he does admit "actual resemblances both in incident and method." He justified this by asserting that they both did in fact experience many of the same phenomena, and also he chose the same, because most natural, narrative: "I divide my narrative into use and abandonment of hasheesh, and speculations upon the phenomena after abandonment, . . . [and] in this arrangement I follow Nature, who begins, goes on, and finishes, and reflects the past in her progress, so that I should seem no copyist on that score." But even if he has been influenced by De Quincey, "I feel that the influence must necessarily have been beneficial to my own efforts. . . . If in any way, therefore, except servilely, I seem to have followed De Quincey, I am proud of it." [61] This statement is extraordinary; not only does it in effect cancel out most of his previous argument, but it ignores the alleged essential differences between the experiences of De Quincey and those of Ludlow. De Quincey used opium, which is strongly addictive in the medical sense, while Ludlow claims to have used strong concoctions of hashish, at what were probably high doses (although this point is difficult to ascertain, because the compounds that Ludlow used were quite variable and unstable). While cannabis can lead to what is known as "psychic dependence," it is not addictive. Accordingly, when we come to Ludlow's account of his battle to free himself from his "addiction," we are reading nonsense. "There is no such thing as genuine addiction to *hashish* or any other preparation of cannabis. Those terrible and agonizing withdrawal symptoms which chain the opium addict to his poison do not affect the *hashish* eater. He can take the drug or leave it alone. It is, by all unbiased accounts, even less habit-forming than tobacco. So Ludlow's literary lamentations over his terrible 'slavery' must be taken with a large grain of salt, as must a good many of his other remarks." [62]

Ludlow's introduction begins with the admission that he was "set" for hashish use by reading the *Arabian Nights*. He has written his book "as a key to some of the . . . manifestations of the Oriental mind, as a narrative interesting to the . . . student of the human soul and body, and the mysterious network of interacting influences which connect them, . . . [and for] the investigation of general readers" (*The Hasheesh Eater*, pp. xii–xiii).

It is clear from the opening pages of *The Hasheesh Eater* that Ludlow was no drug-naive individual when he began taking hashish. It was at "the shop of my friend Anderson the apothecary," where he was in the habit of studying "the details of surgical or medical experiment," and where he also "with a disregard to my own safety which would have done credit to Quintus Curtius . . . made upon myself the trial of the effects of every strange drug and chemical which the laboratory could produce . . . , until I had run through the whole gamut of queer agents within my reach." He mentions chloroform and ether and refers to "other opiates and stimulants." Ludlow is insistent that "it was research and not indulgence" that was his aim in these experiments, so that "I never became the victim of any habit in the prosecution of my headlong investigations." When he thought he had tried all the drugs available, he "sat down like a pharmaceutical Alexander, with no more drug-worlds to conquer" (pp. 15–17).

But then his "friendly apothecary" obtained some "Tilden's Extract" of cannabis which he described to Ludlow as "a preparation of the East Indian hemp, a powerful agent in cases of lockjaw." Ludlow was about to taste some of the "olive-brown extract, of the consistency of pitch, and . . . [with] a decided aromatic odor," when the apothecary stopped him, shouting that the drug was "deadly poison." Ludlow spent the rest of the morning consulting various medical texts and arrived at three conclusions: (1) His friend was "both right and wrong" — "a sufficiently large dose of the drug, if it could be retained in the stomach, would produce death, like any other narcotic"; habitual use of the drug "had always proved highly injurious to mind and body, . . . [but] moderate doses of it were never immediately deadly, and many millions of people daily employed it as an indulgence similar to opium." (2) He concluded that this was the substance referred to by Bayard Taylor, whose account of a hashish experience "months before had moved me powerfully to curiosity and admiration." (3) He decided: "I would add it to the list of my former experiments." Accordingly, he stole and immediately swallowed 10 grains, expecting to feel the results within three to four hours, but he experienced nothing, so thought that the dose had been too low. He waited several days, then repeated the experiment, increasing the dosage to 15 grains. Again nothing happened. He took a dose of 30 grains, late in the afternoon. Ludlow "had now almost come to the conclusion that I was absolutely unsusceptible of the hasheesh influence." He went about his usual social affairs, visiting a friend's home. By ten in the evening, three hours after ingestion of the hashish, he was convinced that this "experiment" would be as fruitless as the previous; nothing had happened (pp. 17–20).

Suddenly, without any warning, he felt a "thrill, . . . a shock, through my entire frame, leaping to my fingers' ends, piercing my brain, startling me till I almost sprang from my chair." He had no doubt: "I was in the power of the hasheesh influence." His first reaction was nearly uncontrollable terror, "a sense of getting something which I had not bargained for." He felt no physical pain, but rather an "unutterable strangeness" which isolated him from all that had seemed most familiar only three hours before. The usual "endeared faces . . . were not with me in my loneliness." He barely managed to answer questions and to laugh at a joke. But when he tried to speak his voice seemed to be "perhaps one which I had far away and in another time and place." He felt out of touch with his immediate environment; then, for a moment, he would slowly and indistinctly recall a remark, as if it were "some trait of a dream . . . [that] will return after many days."

A "fitful wind" had been blowing all night. It seemed to increase "into the steady hum of a vast wheel" that resounded through all space. Then slowly it diminished to a "reverberating peal of a grand cathedral organ, . . . [which] filled . . . [Ludlow] with a grief that was more than human." It is clear that the "hallucination" of the "vast wheel" was based on an environmental stimulus. The origin of the organ "hallucination" is more ambiguous; Ludlow does not say whether, for example, anyone was playing an instrument, or if perhaps a church bell had just chimed. He searched the faces of those present for some sign that they too heard the music, because he had a "full conviction that all I heard and felt was real," but apparently no one else had; there were no signs of appreciation on any faces. He began to wonder whether he was acting strangely and soon this wonder turned into a mild paranoid reaction, as he anticipated hearing the accusing word "hasheesh" at any time. His fears were groundless; the conversation went on as it had before. But still he felt that his replies were "as mechanical as an automaton," and again he "became convinced that it was some one else who spoke, and in another world" (pp. 20–22).

The hashish affected his time perception. He also experienced a peculiar personality split or "double consciousness"; as a part of him was whirled along by the effects of the hashish, another "sat looking down from a height upon its double, observing, reasoning, and serenely weighing. . . . This calmer being suffered with the other by sympathy, but did not lose its self-possession," and soon warned him to go home, lest he do something frightening. He rose to leave, but, in advancing toward the table, perceived it moving away from him with each step. Finally, after what seemed an interminable time, he got to the street, where "the view stretched endlessly away." Although the journey home at first seemed to be infinite and distances frighteningly extended, Ludlow soon ceased to be aware of anything external, and dwelt in a "marvellous inner world." He "existed by turns in different places and various states of being: . . . Venice, . . . [the] Alps, . . . some unexplored tropical forest . . . My soul changed to a vegetable essence." At times he briefly returned to a more or less normal state, especially when passing some familiar house, but then he would relapse into a dreamlike state. At the corner of his own street, a new phenomenon greeted him: "Out of a blank wall at my side a muffled figure stepped into the path before me. His

hair . . . [was] white as snow; . . . he carried also a heavy burden." As Ludlow stepped aside, lamplight fell on the stranger's
face: "Horror unspeakable! I shall never, till the day I die, forget that face. Every lineament was stamped with the records of a
life black with damning crime; it glared . . . with a ferocious
wickedness and a stony despair." Ludlow, in an agony of fear,
tried to escape, but the apparition grabbed him "with a bony
hand," and slowly shifted the burden over from his own to Ludlow's shoulders, saying: "You shall bear my burden with me."
Ludlow finally pushed him aside and ran away; he finally arrived
home, to find that a "family connection had arrived." It demanded
an intense effort for him to hide his condition, especially since he
was not sure whether the relative might not also be a "phantom."
After the greetings and salutations, he felt "terrific" sensations, not
of pain, but of "the tremendous mystery of all around me and
within me." He was directly aware of "all the operations of
vitality which, in our ordinary state, go on unconsciously," and he
could "trace the circulation of the blood along each inch of its
progress . . . every sense was preternaturally awakened." The
beating of his heart seemed so loud that it must be audible to
anyone nearby; he began to conceive of his heart as a "great foun-
tain," whose "jet played upward with loud vibrations," until "the
stream became one continuously pouring flood, whose roar resounded through all my frame." He feared immediate and violent
death. But then he realized that his bounding and accelerated
heartbeat might be merely imagination. He took his pulse and
discovered that his condition was not so extreme as he had feared;
his pulse was not extraordinarily rapid, and gradually slowed to
about 90. This comforted him, but only briefly, for he began to
imagine "apoplexy, congestion, hemorrhage, a multiplicity of
nameless deaths." As a last recourse, he decided to seek out a
doctor. Going down the stairs he had the experience of being
forced to descend endlessly, into a fathomless abyss. He almost
gave up, but then it occurred to him that if the distance was infinite, he was immortal, so he persevered. After a "league-long,
year-long journey," he was on the street again (pp. 26–28).

When he reached the doctor's house, he was unable to recall
whom to ask for. He finally solved the problem by free association;
he recalled the doctor's daughter's name, and deduced that the
doctor's must be the same. When he told the doctor that he had

taken hashish and thought that he was dying, the doctor calmly inquired as to the amount, took Ludlow's pulse, and, finding it only "triflingly accelerated," told him to go home to bed, ridiculing Ludlow's fears of apoplexy.

Returning home, he was greatly relieved to see light in a window, for he had begun to fear that all life had vanished from earth. (Later he treats the hashish-induced fear of darkness and the extremely painful and negative experiences it can produce.) He left the light on for a more peaceful sleep and, after what again seemed a journey of years, reached his bed (pp. 29–34). But his journey was not over yet, for the moment he closed his eyes,

> a vision of celestial glory burst upon me. I stood on the silver strand of a translucent, boundless lake, across whose bosom I seemed to have been just transported. A short way up the beach, a temple, . . . like the Parthenon . . . lifted its spotless and gleaming columns; . . . [yet the temple] as much excelling it as the godlike ideal of architecture must transcend that ideal realized by man. . . . [It was] unblemished in its purity of whiteness, faultless in the unbroken symmetry of every line and angle, . . . draped in odorous clouds, whose tints outshone the rainbow. It was the work of an unearthly builder, and my soul stood before it in a trance of ecstasy. . . . The temple-doors opened noiselessly before me, but it was no scene of sublimity which thus broke in upon my eyes [Note the rapid shift from an extreme of enjoyment to another of fear, wonder, or despair, which is typical of most of his experiences]. I stood in a large apartment, which resembled the Senate-chamber at Washington. . . . Its roof was vaulted, and at the side opposite the entrance the floor rose into a dais surmounted by a large armchair. The . . . house was occupied by similar chairs disposed in arcs; the heavy paneling of the walls was adorned with grotesque frescoes of every imaginable bird, beast, and monster, which . . . were forever changing, like the figures of a kaleidoscope. . . . My attention was quickly distracted . . . by the sight of a most witchly congress, which filled all the chairs. . . . On the dais sat an old crone, . . . I beheld that she was the product of an art held in preeminent favor among persons of her age and sex. She was *knit* of purple yarn! In faultless order the stitches ran along her face; in every pucker of her reentrant

mouth, in every wrinkle of her brow, she was a yarny counterfeit of the grandam of actual life, . . . the occupants of the
seats below were all but reproductions of their president, and
both she and they were constantly swaying from side to side,
forward and back, to the music of some invisible instruments,
whose tone and style were . . . Ethiopian. Not a word was
spoken, . . . but with untiring industry they were all knitting,
knitting, knitting ceaselessly, as if their lives depended on it. I
looked to see the objects of their manufacture. They were
knitting old women like themselves! . . . ever and anon some
completed crone sprang up from the needles which had just
achieved her, and, instantly vivified, took up the instruments of
reproduction, and fell to work as assiduously as if she had been
a member of the congress since the world began. "Here," I
cried, "here, at last, do I realize the meaning of endless progression!" and, though the dome echoed with my peals of laughter,
I saw no motion of astonishment in the stitches of a single face,
but, as for dear life, the manufacture of old women went on un-
obstructed [by my presence] . . . [I felt] an irresistible desire
to aid in the work, . . . [and] the next moment I had been a
partner in their yarny destinies but for a hand which pulled me
backward through the door, and shut the congress forever
from my view.

For a season I abode in an utter void of sight and sound, but I
waited patiently in the assurance that some new changes of
magnificence were preparing for me . . . [Suddenly I saw]
three intense luminous points; . . . through each of them shot
twin attenuated rays of magic light and music . . . I . . . felt
that I was noiselessly drifting toward those radiant and vocal
points . . . before long I could distinguish plainly three colossal arches rising from the bosom of a waveless water . . . On
each side of me ran a wall of gnarled and rugged rock, from
whose jutting points, as high as the eye could reach, depended
stalactites of every imagined form and tinge of beauty, while
below me, . . . lay a level lake, whose exquisite transparency
wanted but the smile of the sun to make it glow like a floor
of adamant. On this lake I lay in a little boat divinely carved
from pearl . . . ; I floated as I list . . . upon a horizonless sea
. . . I looked out, and met no boundaries of space. Often . . .

have I beheld the heavens and the earth stretching out in parallel lines forever, but this was the first time I had ever stood un-"ringed by the azure world." [pp. 34–41]

He describes a number of "regions and circumstances" through which he passed, still in the shallop, each different from the others, except for one common characteristic: "Everywhere . . . [there was] godlike peace, the sum of all conceivable desires satisfied." When he awoke it was morning, "and not a hasheesh hallucination." His first response was one of relief at finding "things again wearing a natural air," even though "the last experience of which I had been conscious had seemed to satisfy every human want, physical or spiritual, I smiled on the four plain . . . walls, . . . and hailed their familiar unostentatiousness with a pleasure which had no wish to transfer itself. . . . It was like returning home from an eternity spent in loneliness among the palaces of strangers" (pp. 41–43).

Ludlow was wary, suspecting some hangover effects, but soon discovered, to his delight, that there was not "one trace of bodily weariness nor mental depression. Every function had returned to its normal state, with . . . one exception . . . : memory could not efface the traces of my having passed through a great mystery." He claims that despite having spent many hours in extreme torture, he never experienced anything like a hangover, and never felt any diminishment in strength or "buoyancy" the next day, but his testimony, especially toward the end of the book, seems to indicate that his claim is largely wishful thinking (p. 43).

About a week later Ludlow tried the drug again and went for a walk with his friend Dan. He notes that it is possible for a person with some imagination and sympathy to lead a hashish-intoxicated companion "through visions of incomparable delight," often by merely making a few suggestions. His companion was able to do so, and so they "passed on through Asia." A plank walk became the Wall of China; a young couple approaching in a carriage were "an eminent mandarin of the interior, . . . of the order of the Blue Button, and by name Fuh-chieng, who, with his sister, at this season every year takes the tour of the provinces" (pp. 51–55).

The issue of the subjective reality — the extent to which the hashish-intoxicated individual believes that his "hallucinations" are "real" or are entirely drug-induced, and the extent to which

"reality" affects the tone, quality, and subject matter of the "hallucinations" induced by hashish — is treated by Ludlow in various
places throughout the book. But on this subject he is inconsistent.
Concerning his "China" trip, he wrote: "Truly, this was imagination; but to me, with eyes and ears wide open . . . , an imagination as real as the soberest fact" (p. 57). Later he writes of an experience during which he "traveled" through Italy: "But in a
very short time, . . . much shorter than I supposed, every suspicion of the imaginary utterly vanished from my mind, and I
no more doubted our being in some fair Italian city than I
doubted my own existence" (p. 96). Again, he writes that "at the
acme of the delirium there is no consciousness remaining in the
mind of its being an unnatural state. The very idea of the drug
is utterly forgotten, and present reality shuts out all inquiry into
grounds for belief" (p. 107). This loss of objectivity seemed dependent on dose, for at low levels (5 to 15 grains), which Ludlow
took at one point when he was trying to "taper off," he experienced no loss of "insight" or awareness as to what was the cause
of any mild "hallucinations" or even more gentle "visions." Ludlow claims that with practice, he was able to learn a "self-retent,"
that is, a silence, to hide his condition. This may have been
merely a derivative of another phenomenon which Ludlow and
others describe; the steady use of hashish over some time does not
lead to the development of tolerance, but apparently enables
the user to get the same results with a lower dose. At this lower
dose the user can, because of the part of him that stands aside,
control any observable manifestations of his condition much
more easily.

A peculiarity of the hashish experience that Ludlow discusses is
that its effects are wavelike. "At intervals, . . . there occurred sea-
sons of a quieter nature than the ravishment of delirium, when
my mind, with a calm power of insight, penetrated into some of its
own kingdoms" (p. 165). In these comparatively lucid intervals
Ludlow not only maintained objectivity, but was able to work out
complicated etymological connections, most of which seemed
valid to him and others after he had returned to normal consciousness. He also enjoyed himself with some humorous and complicated punning.

When he had used up his original supply of Tilden's Extract,
he "procured a small jar of a preparation of the same drug by

another chemist, which, I was told, was much weaker than the former" (p. 65). But he discovered that it was impossible to judge relative strengths of hashish preparations. Judging that about 50 grains of the new preparation would be equal to his previous maximum dose of 30 grains of Tilden's Extract, Ludlow swallowed that amount at eight o'clock in the evening, then went to bed around midnight. He noticed no effects, and therefore supposed that the new preparation was even weaker than he had been told. However, the new preparation was nowhere near as weak as he had supposed; he awoke suddenly in the middle of the night "in a realm of the most perfect clarity of view, yet terrible with an infinitude of demoniac shadows" (p. 67). The ensuing episode was hellish; he was turned into a corpse lying on a bier and tortured by demons with white-hot pitchforks.

Ludlow admits that "It may be thought strange that, after that experience of infinite agony, . . . I should ever take hasheesh again." But the morning after he felt "as vigorous and buoyant as I ever was in my life . . . [although] mentally, I had the conception of being older by many years." He did, however, make a private resolve to cease all "experiment with the drug of sorcery" (p. 85). But slowly he forgot the pain, and gradually he began again to "thirst . . . for insight, adventure, strange surprises, and mystical discoveries" (p. 86). Eventually he took hashish again.

Ludlow's remarks on his visions during his next "trip" (mainly through the Ukraine) are a mixture of private mysticism and a highly moralistic religious attitude: "Hasheesh is indeed an accursed drug, and the soul at last pays a most bitter price for its ecstasies; moreover, the use of it is not the proper means of gaining any insight. . . . In the jubilance of hasheesh, we have only arrived by an improper pathway at the secret of that infinity of beauty which shall be beheld in heaven and earth when the veil of the corporeal drops away, and we know as we are known. . . . [p. 91] I had caught a glimpse through the chinks of my earthly prison of the immeasurable sky which should one day overarch me; . . . [p. 92] my scope of sight was infinite. I was invested with a grand mission to humanity, and slowly it dawned upon me that I was the Christ, come in the power and radiance of his millennial descent, and bearing to the world the restoration of perfect peace. I spoke, and it was done: with a single sentence I regenerated the Creation" (p. 96).

When he awoke the next day, Ludlow experienced what marks the beginning of his break from hashish: after "a succession of vague and delicious dreams, I had not yet returned to the perfectly natural state. I now began to experience a law of hasheesh which developed its effects more and more through all the future months of its use. . . . the effect of every successive indulgence grows more perduring until the hitherto isolated experiences become tangent to each other; then the links of the delirium intersect, and at last so blend that the chain has become a continuous band. . . . The final months of this spell-bound existence, be it terminated by mental annihilation or by a return into the quiet and mingled facts of humanity, are passed in one unbroken yet checkered dream" (p. 98). Yet he was able to "forgive" hashish all the misery it had brought him on account of "the glimpses of supernatural beauty and sublimity" that it had afforded him. And "I still suppose that I was only making experiments, and that, too, in the most wonderful field of mind which could be opened for investigation."

Ludlow's further hashish experiences included one in which he felt a definite impulse — almost a compulsion — to commit suicide. A voice, in a "hot and hissing whisper," urged him repeatedly: "Kill thyself! kill thyself!" (p. 125). He had his knife out and was ready to obey, when, "I felt the blow of some invisible hand strike my arm, . . . [from] an awful angel of midnight blackness . . . [who] floated, with poised wings, on the sky" (p. 126).

Shortly after this escape from suicide, Ludlow "first experienced those sufferings which are generated by a dose of hasheesh taken to prolong the effects of the preceding one" (p. 132). This experience, although repeated twice, marks the second major event in Ludlow's break from hashish. Strangely, during the agonies brought on by this dual dose, he discerned the "very principles of being." It was the omnipresence of *symbols* that characterized this episode: "They flashed forth the apocalypse of utterly unimagined truths. All strange things . . . were explained — all vexed questions solved" (p. 138). One representation "still retains its full significancy to my mind, and is communicable also to others": the sight of a "serene old prophet, whose face was radiant with divine majesty" standing on a mountain peak (p. 139). As Ludlow knelt before him, he heard a voice: " 'Behold man's soul in primeval grandeur, as it was while yet he talked with God.' " Ludlow hurried away, and soon came upon a dwarf, "hideous . . . , deformed in body, but still much more terrible in the soul." The same voice spoke to him again: " 'Behold thine own soul!' " Ludlow cried out for a reason, and the voice answered: " 'Thou hast perverted thy gifts, thou hast squandered thine opportunities, thou hast spurned thy warnings, and, blind to great things, thou playest with bawbles. Therefore, behold thyself thus!' " (p. 140). Ludlow broke down: "All my violations of the principles which I saw revealed fell down upon my head from the heights of the Past." He screamed for the "discords which I had caused in the grand harmony of universal law." It made no difference whether the remembered "violation" was "a deliberate falsehood or a fictitious addition, for the sake of symmetry, to an otherwise true recital. . . . It was not consequences to happiness that troubled me, but something of far mightier scope, for I looked upon some little pulse of evil which, at its time, had seemed to die away in the thought, and lo, in all the years since then, it had been ceaselessly waving onward in consecutive circles . . . there was no such thing as a little wrong in all the universe" (p. 141).

Many of the bad experiences Ludlow reports have a distinct religious tenor. He seems in many ways a walking reservoir of religious guilt (he was the "fallen" son of a highly respectable clergyman, etc.) and it seems likely that the hashish intoxication did much to mobilize this guilt. Many experiences which would be religiously "neutral" for most people struck Ludlow as of the utmost personal religious-spiritual significance.

Ludlow expresses frustration at not being able to communicate fully his hashish episodes. "I was lifted entirely out of the world of hitherto conceivable being, and invested with the power of beholding forms and modes of existence which, on earth, are impossible to be expressed, for the reason that no material emblems exist which even faintly forshadow them" (pp. 146–147). Under the influence of hashish, "a virtual change of worlds has taken place, through the preternatural scope and activity of all his . . . [the hashish-user's] faculties. Truth has not become expanded, but his vision has grown telescopic; that which others see only as the dim nebula, or do not see at all, he looks into with a penetrating scrutiny." When the intoxicated hashish eater tries to convey his subjective state to another, he fails; he finds that even "the symbols which convey the apocalypse to his own mind are meaningless, because, in our ordinary life, the thoughts which they convey have no existence; their two planes are utterly different" (p. 148).

One of the most difficult experiences to convey to those not familiar with hashish, according to Ludlow, is the "interchange of senses"; that is, synesthesia (p. 149). He also notes that under the influence of hashish, objects which appear to ordinary, utilitarian, pragmatic, goal-oriented thought and perception as irrelevant take on sudden and surprisingly fresh meanings. Since he had walked, talked, and reclined to dream under the influence of hashish, Ludlow decided he would listen to music and watch drama, to "note the varying phenomena, if any occurred" (p. 153). To do so, he sailed down the Hudson to New York City with some college friends and repeated a double-dose (by his standards) "experiment," again with hellish results. This time, however, the element of paranoia in his reaction was much more distinct. Upon recovering, he felt certain, for the first time, that he could "never again, in the hasheesh state, be secure in the certainty of unclouded visions. The cup had been so often mingled, that its savor of bitterness would never wholly pass away." Yet he still rationalized, ascribing his torture to "some unfavorable state of the body," and supposing that by keeping a more careful watch over his general health he would be free to experiment at will with hashish without suffering (p. 161). Accordingly, he waited only until the next evening before he took approximately 25 grains and then went to the theater, where he experienced "a most singular phenomenon." He could distinguish the exact notes played by each of two different violinists, both playing the same part, and both in the middle of the full orchestra "as distinctly as if the violinists had been playing at the distance of a hundred feet apart, and with no other instruments discoursing near them" (p. 162).

Another reaction to hashish which Ludlow describes as typical, especially at doses lower than those needed to cause "delirium," is the feeling of universal benevolence — what Ludlow calls a "catholic sympathy, a spiritual cosmopolitanism."

The next stage in Ludlow's use of hashish, also the next in his abandonment of the drug, was marked by "a new element . . . [which] began to develop itself toward a terrible symmetry. . . . This was the appearance of Deity upon the stage of my visionary

life, now sublimely . . . wrathful, or avenging. . . . [p. 188]
At length the reasons of my punishment were shown me . . . as
audibly as man talks with man, I was told, 'Thou hast lifted
thyself above humanity to peer into the speechless secrets before
thy time; and thou shalt be smitten — smitten — smitten' " (p.
189). His religious background and guilty nature continued to
contribute an increasingly gruesome tone to his hashish-use: "It
was the wrath of God which had whelmed that city . . . [ancient
Memphis]; my heart, therefore, lay under that wrath. Yet I would
appeal submissively to the Supreme, that he might perchance
have mercy on me. I looked heavenward, but what a vision there
unveiled itself! In the most intimate recess of a sable, cloudy
cavern flamed vengefully two burning, soul-penetrating eyes.
Their gaze dissolved me" (p. 193).

But Ludlow continued to take hashish, and even increased the
frequency, until "life became with me one prolonged state of
hasheesh exaltation." He endured "hours of wretchedness from
superhuman threatenings such as I would not, if I could, tran-
scribe. . . . Repeatedly, as I have said, was I menaced by voices.
Yet the threatening sometimes took other forms, and none of
them were more terrific than the exhibition to me, as frequently
occurred, of all nature abominating me" (p. 196). In one of his
worst episodes he imagined that he had become the tongue of a
huge bell, and was annihilated when "my head smote against its
side. It was not the pain of the blow, though that was inconceivable, but the colossal roar that filled the universe, and rent my
brain also, which blotted out in one instant all sense, thought,
and being. . . . When I awoke out of the hasheesh state I was
as overwhelmed to find myself still in existence as a dead man of
the last century could be were he now suddenly restored to
earth. . . . and to this day I have so little lost the memory of
that one demoniac toll, that, while writing these lines, I have
put my hand to my forehead. . . . It is this persistency of impressions which explains the fact of the hasheesh state, after a
certain time, growing more and more every day a thing of agony.
It is not because the body becomes worn out by repeated nervous
shocks; . . . [rather] the universal law of constantly accelerating
diabolization of visions held good . . . in my case."

Ludlow was becoming more and more obviously dependent:
"It now became my practice, the moment that I began to feel

the hasheesh change come over me, to run for sympathy to some congenial friend" (p. 203). While he was in the company of such a person, Ludlow experienced what reads like the most horrible of all his hashish experiences. He pleaded with a "voice," promising that he would never take hashish again, if only his sufferings might be alleviated. The voice reminded him that he had made the same promise many times before, and always broken it, but still informed him that " 'Once more shalt thou go free — remember — *once!*' " (pp. 208–209). Ludlow heeded this warning — for a few days. Then he began to take hashish again, but in a way he thought would enable him eventually to abandon it entirely: "This end I sought to accomplish by diminishing the doses of the drug." The highest dose he had taken (although, as noted, comparative doses of the extract he used are relatively meaningless) was 60 grains; he "now reduced my daily ration to ten or fifteen grains. The immediate result of even this modified resumption of the habit was a reinstatement into the glories of the former life. I came out of my clouds; . . . and the lethal torpor of my mind was replaced by an airy activity" (pp. 214–215). Ludlow continued with his new regimen for "a number of weeks, . . . sometimes diminishing the doses, then returning to the boundary, but never beyond it. As the diminutions went on by a tolerably regular but slow ratio, I flattered myself that I was advancing toward a final and perfect emancipation. But the progress was not that painless one with which I had flattered myself." In fact, Ludlow relates that "one of the most bitter experiences of hasheesh occurred to me about this time" (p. 219), during which he imagined that he was the crucified Christ. During this period he also made the mistake of taking a short trip to Niagara Falls without his hashish — his "staff of life" — although "at the Falls, . . . and once grown enthusiastic, I fared much better than I had expected" (p. 221). He discovered that "a use of tobacco, to an extent which at other times would be immoderate, was a preventive of the horrors of abandonment. . . . I smoked incessantly when out of the immediate presence of the waters" (p. 222). He also found some psychological comfort in gazing at "the stony figure [of Profile Rock] . . . with its look of calm endurance. . . . In many a vision afterward did he appear to me as a silent consoler" (p. 224). But Ludlow soon fled "to a place where hasheesh was within reach . . . for relief as into an ark." He discovered "that gradual was almost as difficult as instant abandonment." It was the most he could do to keep the upper level of his daily ration at 15 grains, although "there was no suffering from absolute intellectual lassitude, . . . [but] there still, ever and anon, arose a longing more or less intense for the former music and ecstatic fantasia. . . . Yet I struggled strenuously against the fascination to a more generous ration, and hoped against hope for some indefinite time at which the dangerous spell might be entirely unbound."

Upon his return from Niagara Ludlow, having taken his usual "ordinary dose without yet feeling its effect . . . strolled into a bookseller's to get the latest number of Putnam's [magazine]." He happened by chance upon an anonymous article, "The Hasheesh Eater" (pp. 226–227), which told the story of one who had become "addicted" to hashish, experienced many hellish episodes similar to Ludlow's, and finally, after a hard struggle, through which he was helped by a doctor friend, managed to abandon the use of hashish completely. The article was published in *Putnam's Magazine* in September 1856, just before Ludlow began his teaching duties at Watertown Academy.[63] Previously, he had sufficient leisure for the trip to Niagara, and, according to his own report, his reduced dose regimen enabled him to function tolerably well. This would be irrelevant, except that the supposedly "anonymous" article reads so much like Ludlow's own account (his book has the same title), and contains so many curious, coincidental resemblances to Ludlow's experience and reading, that it is at least possible that Ludlow himself wrote the article (his book was also published anonymously). Perhaps he did so to give credence to his own exaggerated report and to bolster sales of his soon-to-be-published work, or perhaps as a first experiment and attempt at expiation (the book certainly seems to serve, among other functions, that of the confessional type of self-therapy). It is not only the similarity in style, vocabulary, structure, syntax, and general tone that suggests the possibility that Ludlow perpetrated such a hoax; many details of the article can be traced to experiences he recounts in his book or to books that were important in arousing his curiosity about hashish. For example, the article begins with the statement: "It was at Damascus that I took my first dose of hasheesh," and Damascus is where Bayard Taylor conducted the experiment, the report of which Ludlow claims aroused his curiosity and led to his own first "experiment" with hashish.[64] Taylor's article also refers to Damascus in the opening words. But there are other, more significant similarities: the highly moralistic tone of the "anonymous" article and Ludlow's book; the mention in the article of the phenomenon of separation of body and soul — one of Ludlow's favorite topics; the "anonymous" author's mention of his "legal profession" — Ludlow was admitted to the bar, although he never practiced law; the great psychological comfort that the "anonymous" author received from his sympathetic doctor friend — Ludlow extols the virtues of the medical profession in general and one doctor in particular, who gave him the same sort of aid described in the article; the similarity in pattern of use for Ludlow and the "anonymous" author, beginning with one "experiment" and ending with "daily" use; the mention in the article and Ludlow's book that use of hashish is "insanity"; the exaggerated and overblown account, in each report, of the tremendous difficulty in abandoning hashish. There is even a passage from the article that reads as if it were lifted unchanged from Ludlow's book. It is a recital of how all the animal — and inorganic — world turned hostile and of being rejected by his best friends. Perhaps most outstanding is the similarity between the reports of the ultimately horrible experience; both are focused on a "vision" of Christ and a voice from "heaven" that threatens, warns, and — eventually — leads, in both cases, to an (alleged) total abandonment of hashish.

At any rate, Ludlow claims that he wrote to the author of the article (after having found his name through the editorial office of *Putnam's*) and received not only genuine sympathy, but real aid with regard to various methods for alleviating the pains of hashish deprivation.

Although Ludlow goes into great detail concerning his sufferings when he stopped taking hashish, and even if every word is part of an unexaggerated and truthful account, he nowhere gives a description of true withdrawal symptoms. Just as his continued attraction to hashish had been a matter of psychic dependence, so his cessation resulted in no more than psychic discomfort. Nonetheless, Ludlow certainly makes the most of his chance to portray the "hell" he somehow survived.

Again, as with Baudelaire, there is the question of the cause of Ludlow's early death. Many have attributed it to his use of hashish, but that seems in error; all the evidence is that he died of tuberculosis. Indeed, if there is any causal connection at all between his use of hashish and his death it might be through the large amount of tobacco he reports that he resorted to in his efforts to find a "harmless" substitute for hashish. Ludlow was on his way to a sanatorium in Switzerland when, just one day after his thirty-fourth birthday, he died in Geneva. He had made reference to what he called "pulmonary spasms" in an article he wrote in late 1863 about his travels from San Francisco to the Columbia River.[65] Less than seven years later he was dead from the disease which caused these symptoms.

To read Allen Ginsberg's accounts of his experiences with cannabis, after having read the reports of the French Romantics, Taylor, and Ludlow, gives a sense of relief and is comparable to listening to the mild, objective report of a wine taster after having endured the ravings, impossibly extreme promises, exaggerated fears, and general overreactions of a drunk. This may be because the basic premise behind Ginsberg's use of and attitude toward cannabis is not that it is a drug offering an easy escape from the harsh realities of awareness, but rather that it is an agent, a *natural* agent (as an herb), that offers one the chance to experience a true expansion of consciousness, an increase in awareness, a general improvement and heightening of perception of all kinds. Ginsberg gladly acknowledges that the marihuana-high state is not "normal," but this carries no negative or evil connotations to one who believes, with Ginsberg, that "normal" ordinary consciousness and/or awareness is a state in which one is at least half blind, deaf, and alive.

One of the most interesting efforts by Ginsberg is the article that originally appeared in the *Atlantic Monthly*.[66] The special value of this paper is that the first half was written while the author was smoking marihuana, in the hope that he would be able to demonstrate the shift "*from* habitual shallow, purely verbal guidelines and repetitive secondhand ideological interpretations of experience to *more direct, slower, absorbing, occasionally microscopically minute, engagement with sensing phenomena during the high* moments or hours after one has smoked" (Ginsberg's italics). He feels that there is "much to be revealed about marijuana especially in this time and nation for the *general* public, for the actual experience of the smoked herb has been completely clouded by a fog of dirty language by the diminishing crowd of fakers who have not had the experience and yet insist on being centers of propaganda about the experience." [67]

Concerning his own experiences with marihuana, he begins by asserting that "although most scientific authors who present their reputable evidence for the harmlessness of marijuana make no claim for its surprising *usefulness*, I do make that claim: Marijuana is a useful catalyst for specific optical and aural aesthetic perceptions. I apprehended the structure of certain pieces of jazz and classical music in a new manner under the influence of marijuana, and these apprehensions have remained valid in years of normal consciousness." [68] This last point is especially interesting, for Ginsberg has recently given up the use of drugs in favor of " 'the primacy' of his own body and emotions." [69] However, one suspects this abandonment (which was, according to *Playboy*, the result of conversations with Martin Buber and "various holy men" in India) is not in any way a lifelong commitment, especially when one reads Ginsberg's accounts of his marihuana and other drug-induced "visions."

In the article written for the *Atlantic Monthly*, Ginsberg mentioned that marihuana enabled him to perceive Cézanne's paintings for the first time: "I perceived ('dug') for the first time Cézanne's 'petite sensation' of space achieved on a two-dimensional canvas." [70] In an earlier *Paris Review* interview (1965) he elaborated on this experience:

> I smoked a lot of marijuana and went to the basement of the Museum of Modern Art in New York and looked at his water colors and that's where I began really turning on to space in Cézanne and the way he built it up. . . . I suddenly got a strange shuddering impression looking at his canvases, partly the effect when someone pulls a Venetian blind, reverses the Venetian — there's a sudden shift, a flashing that you see in Cézanne canvases. Partly it's when the canvas opens up into three dimensions and looks like wooden objects, like solid-space objects, in three dimensions rather than flat. Partly it's the enormous spaces that open up in Cézanne's landscapes. And it's partly that mysterious quality around his figures. . . . They look like great huge 3-D wooden dolls, sometimes. Very *uncanny*

thing, like a very mysterious thing — in other words, there's a strange sensation that one gets, looking at his canvases, which I began to associate with the extraordinary sensation — cosmic sensation, in fact — that I had experienced catalyzed by Blake's "Sun-flower" and "Sick Rose" and a few other poems. . . . he produced a solid two-dimensional surface which when you looked *into* it, maybe from a slight distance with your eyes either unfocused or your eyelids lowered slightly, you could see a great three-dimensional opening, mysterious, stereoscopic, like going into a stereopticon. . . . Particularly there's one of rocks, I guess "Rocks at Garonne," and you look at them for a while, and after a while they seem like they're rocks, just the rock parts, you don't know where they are, whether they're on the ground or in the air or on top of a cliff, but then they seem to be floating in space like clouds, and then they seem to be also a bit like they're amorphous, like kneecaps or cock-heads or faces without eyes. And it has a very mysterious impression. Well, that may have been the result of the pot. But it's a definite thing that I got from that.[71]

It is clear from the rest of what Ginsberg says in the interview that his first appreciation of Cézanne after having smoked marihuana was the beginning of a fairly long learning process that continued after all effects of the marihuana had worn off: "I could imagine someone not prepared, in a peculiar chemical-psychological state, peculiar mental state, psychic state, someone not prepared who had no experience of eternal ecstasy, passing in front of a Cézanne canvas, distracted and without noticing it, his eyes traveling in, to, through the canvas into the space and suddenly stopping with his hair standing on end, dead in his tracks, *see*ing a whole universe." [72] Ginsberg himself undertook a prolonged study of Cézanne, "studiously investigating Cézanne's intentions and method, and looking at all the canvases of his that I could find, . . . and all the reproductions I could find, and I was writing at the time a paper on him. . . . And the whole thing opened up, two ways: first, I read a book on Cézanne's composition by Earl Loran, who showed photographs, analyses and photographs of the original motifs, side by side with the actual canvases — and years later I actually went to Aix, with all the postcards, and stood in the spots, and tried to find the places where he painted Mont-Sainte-

Victoire from, and got in his studio and saw some of the motifs he used." [73]

In the same interview Ginsberg discusses at length his "Blake experience" of 1948, when he underwent an intense mystical episode (during which he believed that he actually heard Blake intoning his own poems) without the aid of any drugs, contrary to the report given in *Playboy*. The interviewer asks if his use of drugs was an attempt to extend this experience, and Ginsberg replies: "Well, since I took a vow that this was the area of, that this was my existence that I was placed into, drugs were obviously a technique for experimenting with consciousness, to get different areas and different levels and different similarities and different reverberations of the same vision. Marijuana has some of it in it, that awe, the cosmic awe that you get sometimes on pot. . . . It's a normal state also, I mean it's a holy state of some sort. . . . So — summing up then — drugs were useful for exploring perception, sense perception, and exploring different possibilities and modes of consciousness, and exploring the different versions of *petites sensations,* and useful then for composing, sometimes, while under the influence." [74]

He also talks about his "giving up" drugs:

Well, the Asian experience kind of got me out of the corner. I painted myself in with drugs. That corner being an inhuman corner in the sense that I figured I was expanding my consciousness and I had to go through with it but at the same time I was confronting this serpent monster, so I was getting in a real terrible situation. It would finally get so if I'd take the drugs I'd start vomiting. But I felt that I was duly bound and obliged for the sake of consciousness expansion, and this insight, and breaking down my identity, and seeking more direct contact with primate sensation, nature, to continue. So when I went to India, all the way through India, I was babbling about that to all the holy men I could find. I wanted to find out if they had any suggestions. And they all did, and they were all good ones. First one I saw was Martin Buber, who was interested. . . . I was thinking like loss of identity and confrontation with nonhuman universe as the main problem, and in a sense whether or not man had to evolve and change, and perhaps become nonhuman too. Melt into the universe, let us say — to put it awkwardly and inaccurately. Buber said that he was interested in man-to-man relationships, human-to-human — that he thought it was a human universe that we were destined to inhabit. . . . And he said, "Mark my word, young man, in two years you will realize that I was right." He was right — in two years I marked his words. Two years is sixty-three — I saw him in sixty-one. . . .

Then there was Swami Shivananda, in Rishikish in India. He said, "Your own heart is your guru." . . . [I] suddenly realized it was the heart that I was seeking. In other words it wasn't consciousness, it wasn't *petites sensations,* sensation defined as expansion of mental consciousness to include more data — . . . the area that I was seeking was heart rather than mind. In other words, in mind, through mind, . . . one can construct all sorts of universes, . . . and with lysergic acid you can enter into alternative universes and with the speed of light; . . . Anyway, a whole series of Indian holy men pointed back to the body — getting *in* the body rather than getting out of the human form. . . . So now the next step was that the gurus one after another said, Live in the body: this is the form that you're born for. That's too long a narration to go into. . . . But it all winds up in the train in Japan, then a year later, the poem "The Change," where all of a sudden I renounce drugs, I don't renounce drugs but I suddenly didn't want to be *dominated* by that nonhuman any more, or even be dominated by the moral obligation to enlarge my consciousness any more. Or do anything any more except *be* my heart.[75]

It is clear from the *Atlantic* article that Ginsberg's "renouncement" was temporary. Perhaps the important point is that he thought that he had to abandon drugs, including even marihuana, when he felt they were taking him away from a direct involvement with life, and leading him into preoccupation with the inorganic. Yet even in the article (written in two parts, one a month after the first, 1965) he states that marihuana enabled him to see "anew many of nature's panoramas & landscapes that I'd stared at blindly without even noticing before; thru the use of marijuana, awe & detail were made conscious. These perceptions are permanent — any deep aesthetic experience leaves a trace, & an idea of what to look for that can be checked back later. I developed a taste for Crivelli's symmetry; and saw Rembrandt's *Polish Rider* as a sublime Youth on a Deathly horse for the first time — saw myself in the rider's face, one might say — while walking around the Frick Museum high on pot. These are not 'hallucinations'; these are deepened perceptions that one might have catalyzed not by pot but by some *other* natural event (as natural as pot) that changes the mind, such as an intense Love, a death in the family, a sudden clear dusk after rain, or the sight of the neon-spectral reality of Times Square one sometimes has after leaving a strange movie. So it's all *natural*." [76]

Although "Ginsberg likes to call his own well-known experiments with marijuana and the hallucinogens 'pious investigations' [and] . . . often compares himself, in this respect, to the French symbolist poets, and, like them, he has kept a faithful record of his investigations in poems and journals written over the years and under a variety of influences," [77] his writings on the subject of marihuana are understated, mainly lucid, entirely believable reports which *show* instead of merely *telling* about the cannabis experience. Of course it should be remembered that Ginsberg, while writing the first part of his article, was under the influence of a dose of marihuana *much* smaller than that customarily consumed as hashish by members of "Le Club des Haschischins," or by Taylor or Ludlow. But his statement that he has spent about as much time "high as I have spent in movie theatres — sometimes three hours a week, sometimes twelve or twenty or more, . . . with about the same degree of alteration of my normal awareness," [78] read after the effusive hyperbole and self-dramatization of Gautier, Ludlow, and even Baudelaire, is a good indication of the wide difference between the effects of marihuana used in comparatively low doses and the effects of the much more potent preparations used in extremely high doses by Ginsberg's literary predecessors. He states that one of the aims of his article, which he dedicates to those who have never smoked marihuana, is to give an example of "the phenomenon of transmuting to written language a model of the marijuana experience, which can be understood and related to in some mode by those who have not yet met the experience but who are willing to slow their thought and judgment and decipher the syntax clause by clause." [79]

It is interesting that although the effects of the marihuana on

Ginsberg's style are sometimes obvious, his ability to think and express himself does not appear to be significantly impaired. In fact, he marshals an impressive and detailed and appropriate selection of footnote references to articles and studies on the effects of cannabis, some of them not very well known or generally ignored.

He attributes the anxiety and paranoidlike reactions that many users of marihuana have reported, as well as his own similar responses, to "the effects on consciousness . . . of the law and the threatening activities of the U.S. . . . Bureau of Narcotics," and not at all to cannabis. He states that he smokes marihuana less frequently when in America than "in countries where it is legal. I noticed a profound difference of effect. The anxiety was directly traceable to fear of being apprehended and treated as a deviant criminal & put thru the hassle of social disapproval, ignominious Kafkian tremblings in vast court buildings coming to be judged, the helplessness of being overwhelmed by force or threat of deadly force and put in brick & iron cell." [80]

The second part of the essay begins with Ginsberg's decision to let the first part stand as written, "for the reader who has not smoked marijuana, [let it remain] a manifestation of marijuana-high thought structure in a mode which intersects our mutual consciousness, namely language." [81]

Ginsberg admits that there are some people who do not like the marihuana sensation, "and report back to the language world that it's a drag and make propaganda against this particular area of nonverbal awareness. But the vast majority all over the world, who have smoked the several breaths necessary to feel the effect, adjust to the strangely familiar sensation of Time slow-down, and explore this new space thru natural curiosity, report that it's a useful area of mind-consciousness to be familiar with, a creative show of the silly side of an awful big army of senseless but habitual thought-formations risen out of the elements of a language world: a metaphysical herb less habituating than tobacco, whose smoke is no more disruptive than Insight — in short, for those who have made the only objective test, a vast majority of satisfied smokers." [82]

The following biography is approximately accurate. Mr. X is a professor at one of the top-ranking American universities, head of an organization producing important new research results, and is widely acknowledged as one of the leaders in his specialty. In his early forties, X has lectured at virtually every major American university, and his scientific and popular books have been best-sellers of their kind. His productivity has steadily increased over the last decade. He has won many awards and prizes given by government, university, and private groups, is happily married, has a wife and children, and asks that his anonymity be respected. I am grateful to another scientist for putting me in touch with Mr. X. In view of the reports which precede his, it is of interest to note that Mr. X has read none of the other authors whose accounts of their experience with cannabis make up this chapter.

"It all began about ten years ago. I had reached a considerably more relaxed period in my life — a time when I had come to feel that there was more to living than science, a time of awakening of my social consciousness and amiability, a time when I was open to new experiences. I had become friendly with a group of people who occasionally smoked cannabis, irregularly, but with evident pleasure. Initially I was unwilling to partake, but the apparent euphoria that cannabis produced and the fact that there was no physiological addiction to the plant eventually persuaded me to try. My initial experiences were entirely disappointing; there was no effect at all, and I began to entertain a variety of hypotheses about cannabis being a placebo which worked by expectation and hyperventilation rather than by chemistry. After about five or six unsuccessful attempts, however, it happened. I was lying on my back in a friend's living room idly examining the pattern of shadows on the ceiling cast by a potted plant (not cannabis!). I suddenly realized that I was examining an intricately detailed miniature Volkswagen, distinctly outlined by the shadows. I was very skeptical at this perception, and tried to find inconsistencies between Volkswagens and what I viewed on the ceiling. But it was all there, down to hubcaps, license plate, chrome, and even the small handle used for opening the trunk. When I closed my eyes, I was stunned to find that there was a movie going on on the inside of my eyelids. Flash . . . a simple country scene with red farmhouse, blue sky, white clouds, yellow path meandering over green hills to the horizon. Flash . . . same scene, orange house, brown sky, red clouds, yellow path, violet fields . . . Flash . . . Flash . . . Flash. The flashes came about once a heartbeat. Each flash brought the same simple scene into view, but each time with a different set of colors . . . exquisitely deep hues, and astonishingly harmonious in their juxtaposition. Since then I have smoked occasionally and enjoyed it thoroughly. It amplifies torpid sensibilities and produces what to me are even more interesting effects, as I will explain shortly.

"I can remember another early visual experience with cannabis, in which I viewed a candle flame and discovered in the heart of the flame, standing with magnificent indifference, the black-hatted and -cloaked Spanish gentleman who appears on the label of the Sandeman sherry bottle. Looking at fires when high, by the way, especially through one of those prism kaleidoscopes which image their surroundings, is an extraordinarily moving and beautiful experience.

"I want to explain that at no time did I think these things 'really' were out there. I knew there was no Volkswagen on the ceiling and there was no Sandeman salamander man in the flame. I don't feel any contradiction in these experiences. There's a part of me making, creating the perceptions which in everyday life would be bizarre; there's another part of me which is a kind of observer. About half of the pleasure comes from the observer-part appreciating the work of the creator-part. I smile, or sometimes even laugh out loud at the pictures on the insides of my eyelids. In this sense, I suppose cannabis is psychotomimetic, but I find none of the panic or terror that accompanies some psychoses. Possibly this is because I know it's my own trip, and that I can come down rapidly any time I want to.

"While my early perceptions were all visual, and curiously lacking in images of human beings, both of these items have changed over the intervening years. I find that today a single joint is enough to get me high. I test whether I'm high by closing my eyes and looking for the flashes. They come long before there are any alterations in my visual or other perceptions. I would guess this is a signal-to-noise problem, the visual noise level being very low with my eyes closed. Another interesting information-theoretical aspect is the prevalence — at least in my flashed images — of cartoons: just the outlines of figures, caricatures, not photographs. I think this is simply a matter of information compression; it would be impossible to grasp the total content of an image with the information content of an ordinary photograph, say 108 bits, in the fraction of a second which a flash occupies. And the flash experience is designed, if I may use that word, for instant appreciation. The artist and viewer are one. This is not to say that the images are not marvelously detailed and complex. I recently had an image in which two people were talking, and the words they were saying would form and disappear in yellow above their heads, at about a sentence per heartbeat. In this way it was possible to follow the conversation. At the same time an occasional word would appear in red letters among the yellows above their heads, perfectly in context with the conversation; but if one remembered these red words, they would enunciate a quite different set of statements, penetratingly critical of the conversation. The entire image set which I've outlined here, with I would say at least 100 yellow words and something like 10 red words, occurred in something under a minute.

"The cannabis experience has greatly improved my appreciation for art, a subject which I had never much appreciated before. The understanding of the intent of the artist which I can achieve when high sometimes carries over to when I'm down. This is one of many human frontiers which cannabis has helped me traverse. There also have been some art-related insights — I don't know whether they are true or false, but they were fun to formulate. For example, I have spent some time high looking at the work of the Belgian surrealist Yves Tanguey. Some years later, I emerged from a long swim in the Caribbean and sank exhausted onto a beach formed from the erosion of a nearby coral reef. In idly examining the arcuate pastel-colored coral fragments which made up the beach, I saw before me a vast Tanguey painting. Perhaps Tanguey visited such a beach in his childhood.

"A very similar improvement in my appreciation of music has occurred with cannabis. For the first time I have been able to hear the separate parts of a three-part harmony and the richness of the counterpoint. I have since discovered that professional musicians can quite easily keep many separate parts going simultaneously in their heads, but this was the first time for me. Again, the learning experience when high has at least to some extent carried over when I'm down. The enjoyment of food is amplified; tastes and aromas emerge that for some reason we ordinarily seem to be too busy to notice. I am able to give my full attention to the sensation. A potato will have a texture, body, and taste like that of other potatoes, but much more so. Cannabis also enhances the enjoyment of sex — on the one hand it gives an exquisite sensitivity, but on the other hand it postpones orgasm: in part by distracting me with the profusion of images passing before my eyes. The actual duration of orgasm seems to lengthen greatly, but this may be the usual experience of time expansion which comes with cannabis smoking.

"I do not consider myself a religious person in the usual sense, but there is a religious aspect to some highs. The heightened sensitivity in all areas gives me a feeling of communion with my surroundings, both animate and inanimate. Sometimes a kind of existential perception of the absurd comes over me and I see with awful certainty the hypocrisies and posturing of myself and my fellow men. And at other times, there is a different sense of the absurd, a playful and whimsical awareness. Both of these senses of the absurd can be communicated, and some of the most rewarding highs I've had have been in sharing talk and perceptions and humor. Cannabis brings us an awareness that we spend a lifetime being trained to overlook and forget and put out of our minds. A sense of what the world is really like can be maddening; cannabis has brought me some feeling for what it is like to be crazy, and how we use that word 'crazy' to avoid thinking about things that are too painful for us. In the Soviet Union political dissidents are routinely placed in insane asylums. The same kind of thing, a little more subtly perhaps, occurs here: 'Did you hear what Lenny Bruce said yesterday? He must be crazy.' When high on cannabis I discovered that there's *somebody inside* in those people we call mad.

"When I'm high I can penetrate into the past, recall childhood memories, friends, relatives, playthings, streets, smells, sounds, and tastes from a vanished era. I can reconstruct the actual occurrences in childhood events only half understood at the time. Many but not all my cannabis trips have somewhere in them a symbolism significant to me which I won't attempt to describe here, a kind of mandala embossed on the high. Free associating to this mandala, both visually and as plays on words, has produced a very rich array of insights.

"There is a myth about such highs: the user has an illusion of great insight, but it does not survive scrutiny in the morning. I am convinced that this is an error, and that the devastating insights achieved when high are real insights; the main problem is putting these insights in a form acceptable to the quite different self that we are when we're down the next day. Some of the hardest work I've ever done has been to put such insights down on tape or in writing. The problem is that ten even more interesting ideas or images have to be lost in the effort of recording one. It is easy to understand why someone might think it's a waste of effort going to all that trouble to set the thought down, a kind of intrusion of the Protestant Ethic. But since I live almost all my life down I've made the effort — successfully, I think. Incidentally, I find that reasonably good insights can be remembered the next day, but only if some effort has been made to set them down another way. If I write the insight down or tell it to someone, then I can remember it with no assistance the following morning; but if I merely say to myself that I must make an effort to remember, I never do.

"I find that most of the insights I achieve when high are into social issues, an area of creative scholarship very different from the one I am generally known for. I can remember one occasion, taking a shower with my wife while high, in which I had an idea on the origins and invalidities of racism in terms of gaussian distribution curves. It was a point obvious in a way, but rarely talked about. I drew the curves in soap on the shower wall, and went to write the idea down. One idea led to another, and at the end of about an hour of extremely hard work I found I had written eleven short essays on a wide range of social, political, philosophical, and human biological topics. Because of problems of space, I can't go into the details of these essays, but from all external signs, such as public reactions and expert commentary, they seem to contain valid insights. I have used them in university commencement addresses, public lectures, and in my books.

"But let me try to at least give the flavor of such an insight and its accompaniments. One night, high on cannabis, I was delving into my childhood, a little self-analysis, and making what seemed to me to be very good progress. I then paused and thought how extraordinary it was that Sigmund Freud, with no assistance from drugs, had been able to achieve his own remarkable self-analysis. But then it hit me like a thunderclap that this was wrong, that Freud had spent the decade before his self-analysis as an experimenter with and a proselytizer for cocaine; and it seemed to me very apparent that the genuine psychological insights that Freud brought to the world were at least in part derived from his drug experience. I have no idea whether this is in fact true, or whether the historians of Freud would agree with this interpretation, or even if such an idea has been published in the past, but it is an interesting hypothesis and one which passes first scrutiny in the world of the downs.

"I can remember the night that I suddenly realized what it was like to be crazy, or nights when my feelings and perceptions were of a religious nature. I had a very accurate sense that these feelings and perceptions, written down casually, would not stand the usual critical scrutiny that is my stock in trade as a scientist. If I find in the morning a message from myself the night before informing me that there is a world around us which we barely sense, or that we can become one with the universe, or even that certain politicians are desperately frightened men, I may tend to disbelieve; but when I'm high I know about this disbelief. And so I have a tape in which I exhort myself to take such remarks seriously. I say 'Listen closely, you sonofabitch of the morning! This stuff is real!' I try to show that my mind is working clearly; I recall the name of a high school acquaintance I have not thought of in thirty years; I describe the color, typography, and format of a book in another room. And these memories do pass critical scrutiny in the morning. I am convinced that there are genuine and valid levels of perception available with cannabis (and probably with other drugs) which are, through the defects of our society and our educational system, unavailable to us without such drugs. Such a remark applies not only to self-awareness and to intellectual pursuits, but also to perceptions of real people, a vastly enhanced sensitivity to facial expressions, intonations, and choice of words which sometimes yields a rapport so close it's as if two people are reading each other's minds.

"Cannabis enables nonmusicians to know a little about what it is like to be a musician, and nonartists to grasp the joys of art. But I am neither an artist nor a musician. What about my own scientific work? While I find a curious disinclination to think of my professional concerns when high — the attractive intellectual adventures always seem to be in every other area — I have made a conscious effort to think of a few particularly difficult current problems in my field when high. It works, at least to a degree. I find I can bring to bear, for example, a range of relevant experimental facts which appear to be mutually inconsistent. So far, so good. At least the recall works. Then in trying to conceive of a way of reconciling the disparate facts, I was able to come up with a very bizarre possibility, one that I'm sure I would never have thought of down. I've written a paper which mentions this idea in passing. I think it's very unlikely to be true, but it has consequences which are experimentally testable, which is the hallmark of an acceptable theory.

"I have mentioned that in the cannabis experience there is a part of your mind that remains a dispassionate observer, who is able to take you down in a hurry if need be. I have on a few occasions been forced to drive in heavy traffic when high. I've negotiated it with no difficulty at all, although I did have some thoughts about the marvelous cherry-red color of traffic lights. I find that after the drive I'm not high at all. There are no flashes on the insides of my eyelids. If you're high and your child is calling, you can respond about as capably as you usually do. I don't advocate driving when high on cannabis, but I can tell you from personal experience that it certainly can be done. My high is always reflective, peaceable, intellectually exciting, and sociable, unlike most alcohol highs, and there is never a hangover. Through the years I find that slightly smaller amounts of cannabis suffice to produce the same degree of high, and in one movie theater recently I found I could get high just by inhaling the cannabis smoke which permeated the theater.

"There is a very nice self-titering aspect to cannabis. Each puff is a very small dose; the time lag between inhaling a puff and sensing its effect is small; and there is no desire for more after the high is there. I think the ratio, R, of the time to sense the dose taken to the time required to take an excessive dose is an important quantity. R is very large for LSD (which I've never taken) and reasonably short for cannabis. Small values of R should be one measure of the safety of psychedelic drugs. When cannabis is legalized, I hope to see this ratio as one of the parameters printed on the pack. I hope that time isn't too distant; the illegality of cannabis is outrageous, an impediment to full utilization of a drug which helps produce the serenity and insight, sensitivity and fellowship so desperately needed in this increasingly mad and dangerous world."

5 The Acute Intoxication: Its Properties

The major difficulty in any discussion of the "properties" of acute cannabis intoxication is that the effects of this herb are extremely variable and unpredictable — from one occasion to the next for each individual, and, more strikingly, from one person to another. However, while it is true that no single account includes all the effects which this drug is capable of producing, it is possible to give an admittedly overly inclusive or overly comprehensive list of all the effects which have been experienced and/or observed during the acute intoxication. It should be kept in mind that the set, the setting, and the individual's general physical and psychological condition, as well as his basic personality structure prior to use of cannabis, are all crucial factors.[1]

The diversity of reactions to cannabis has led to some curious descriptions of the characteristics of the acute intoxication; for example: "Its physiological effects have been likened to those of the atropine group of drugs, and its psychic effects to those of alcohol."[2] A main complaint of experts on and students of cannabis has long been the supposed "scarcity" of accurate and objective experimental investigations and reports. "The recorded medical literature is most confusing. The reports are contradictory, and the description of the drug varies from one which is habit-forming and which with constant use is as harmful to the system as morphine, to one which is almost completely innocuous with a stimulation not far remote from that of alcohol."[3] Much of the criticism of cannabis studies grows out of the assertion that no two of the studies involve the same amount of the same substance administered to or used by comparable or representative samples of individuals who are observed or measured for comparable behavior with comparable instruments. I think there are two basic flaws in this general type of criticism: first, the degree to which two or more studies are not susceptible to comparison need not be taken as an indictment of the specific findings of any one study, provided the aims, procedure(s), drug(s) used, doses administered, findings, conclusions, and the nature and background of the experimental subjects are all carefully noted; second, although wide variations in individual responses to cannabis are common, even a cursory glance through the literature will reveal that there are particular responses or effects which recur almost constantly. In fact, one authority writes of the "relatively uniform symptomatology" of the acute "intoxication of transitory nature . . . of the drug in the smoked form (when inhaled)." [4] Perhaps more troublesome is the hidden or thinly disguised bias for or against the use of cannabis which distorts so many reports. For example, one author (of a book on marihuana) does not reveal his strong anti-marihuana bias until a question-and-answer appendix.[5] But not all biases are primarily connected with attitudes concerning the use of cannabis: one experiment "was set up to study the effects of this compound [pyrahexyl] . . . on . . . [musical] performance as measured by the Seashore tests of musical talents in order to determine objectively whether or not marihuana affects musical ability." [6] This "Seashore" study was apparently inspired by an article in *Life* magazine relating how "the swing musician ascends to new peaks of virtuosity" when high on marihuana, plus R. P. Walton's attack on this popular belief: "There is very little probability that an individual's performance is in any degree improved over that of his best capabilities. As judged by objectively critical means, the standards of performance are no doubt lowered." [7] He attributes the view expressed in *Life* magazine to a general lowering of inhibitions, which may allow hidden or suppressed talents to emerge, or which may evoke a more intense emotional performance, and he also notes that the feeling of improved performance is probably entirely subjective and would not stand up under any objective scrutiny. But, as C. Winick has pointed out regarding the "Seashore" study's failure to demonstrate enhanced musical ability, "A test in which non-musicians are given objective questions on matters like the consonance of pitch between two sounds can hardly be compared to the musical creativity and expertise required of the jazz musician playing in a group situation which is based on mutual reinforcement and in which improvisation may be extremely important." [8] Furthermore, it has been "discovered . . . that this drug ["synhexyl," which is another term for "pyrahexyl," also spelled "parahexyl"] . . . fails to produce the exact effects of marihuana. The pharmacological properties of synhexyl, although in many ways similar to those of the cannabis drug, exhibit several important qualitative differences in the human system," [9] apparently including — with synhexyl — the development of tolerance to the drug's effects, which does not occur with marihuana.

In evaluating the various reports on the effects of marihuana, the problem of relative potency, stability, dosage-level, and means of administration of marihuana or synthetic analogues rates second to the problem of bias or prejudice. First, marihuana of the grade usually smoked in the United States is nowhere near as powerful as the hashish used by Baudelaire, Taylor, Gautier, Ludlow, and others, and the reports of these highly imaginative individuals could well be criticized on the grounds that they exaggerate even the hashish experience. "While both are essentially the same, there are differences of degree which at times seem to make almost qualitative differences in the resulting picture." [10] "*Marijuana* is a cheap and very crude preparation of hemp consisting of the flowering tops of the female plant in various stages of development. In relation to refined preparations such as *charas* [hashish] . . . it stands as *vin ordinaire* does to fine champagne." [11] The usual estimates are that Mexican-grown marihuana, the type used most frequently in the United States, is from one-fifth to one-eighth as potent as hashish;[12] furthermore, much of the "marihuana" smoked in the U.S. is even weaker, since it is not uncommon for "dealers" to adulterate the marihuana with oregano or other herbs.[13] In addition, much of the reputed "Mexican grass" is grown in the south central part of the United States or even in such unlikely places as Vermont.

Second, the dose is crucial because many (although not all) of the effects of cannabis are directly dose-related. For example, whereas some of the physical or physiological effects of marihuana may be dose-independent, most of the psychological and mental phenomena associated with cannabis use are distinctly enhanced by an increased amount or increased potency of the drug.[14] Although the usual reaction to relatively small or low-potency doses is a subjectively positive experience, with "larger doses of the drug

. . . feelings of anxiety, and in some cases, of physical distress, such as nausea, overcame the pleasurable sensations. The subject's confidence was eroded until feelings of insecurity became pronounced enough to evoke generally negativistic attitudes." Also, the duration of many effects of cannabis usually increases with an increase in dose.[15]

Third, Isbell et al. have shown that l-Δ^1-3,4-$trans$-tetrahydrocannabinol (usually abbreviated to Δ^1-THC, or simply THC), which "has marihuana-like activity" in man, is 3 times as powerful when smoked as when taken orally if subjective peak positive response is the criterion, and 2.6 times as powerful when peak pulserate change is the criterion (so long as all other variables are held as constant as possible).[16] Three possible explanations have been suggested for this phenomenon: "(1) more effective and rapid absorption from the lungs, (2) less rapid detoxification of the drug because of bypassing the liver, (3) conversion of the substance [Δ^1-THC] . . . to a more active substance [possibly Δ^6-THC, which has been reported [17] as one of the conversion-products of Δ^1-THC when the latter is heated — as it is in smoking] . . . by heat." [18] Moreover, the great variation of response to cannabis, which one study suggests is due to occasional faulty or slow absorption (although this would seem to apply only to the oral route of administration),[19] indicates that it is important that the subject be his own control.

The basic personality structure is of prime importance; many persons are simply unable to enjoy the cannabis experience, and others are unable to feel any effects whatsoever. One of the most adequate explanations for this lack of response is given by H. S. Becker: the enjoyment of marihuana is a learning process in which the neophyte must first learn the correct technique of smoking the drug, then learn to distinguish the effects of the drug, and finally learn to define them (or redefine them) as pleasurable.[20] However, there is another theory, based mainly on the observation that individuals do not seem to get high the first time, or the first few times, that they smoke marihuana, even if they smoke it correctly. This hypothesis "suggests that getting high on marihuana occurs only after some sort of pharmacological sensitization takes place." [21] There are problems with both of these theories and at present little data to support either one; the question remains unanswered.

Fourth, many early investigators concluded that the active constituents of marihuana were unstable — perhaps this is the reason why the sale of cannabis throughout India is limited by the government to preparations no older than one year.[22] According to Geller and Boas, the La Guardia Report confused the issue by claiming that samples derived from hemp plants stacked outdoors for several years were as potent as samples from hemp grown on the same ground and immediately processed and smoked; further, distilled psychoactive oils from hemp could be preserved without any loss of potency for several years, whether or not the oils were vacuum sealed and stored at low temperatures or left open at room temperatures. But N. R. Farnsworth, writing with the advantage of having studied the results of more recent work, stated that "variation in the chemical composition and biological activity of *Cannabis sativa* results primarily from the fact that some of the constituents are unstable and change form. It has been explained that, on aging, cannabidiolic acid (inactive) is gradually converted to cannabidiol (inactive), then to tetrahydrocannabinols (active) and finally to cannabinol (inactive). These biological conversions proceed at a more rapid rate in tropical areas than in more temperate zones. As a result, samples of varying age give rise to different biological effects in humans" (see Chap. 3, above).[23]

In addition to the four difficulties enumerated above, there is also apt to be a wide range of response to cannabis depending on whether or not the subjects have used marihuana previously, and how often. The possible explanations for this phenomenon were mentioned above, in the discussion of the two opposed hypotheses of "pharmacological sensitization" and "the learning process." It is almost invariably the case, as noted, that the first or first few experiences with cannabis are subjectively nil, even when others, especially experienced users, are able to detect that the neophyte is showing all the signs which are ordinarily criteria for calling someone "high." [24] But, strangely, users sometimes declare that the first time they did get high (as opposed to the first time[s] they used cannabis) was the best. There are many easily observable differences in the reactions of the beginner, after he has become high, and the long-time (two years or more) user: "The neophyte usually is ecstatically euphoric, laughs loudly and has an increased appetite and thirst. A subject, who has taken it for, say 2 years, is much more repressed in his laughter and general boisterousness." [25] This general tendency is reported by one author to continue throughout the period during which the individual uses marihuana, often eventually terminating in cessation of use altogether[26] (this may be an analogue of the "maturing out" process that heroin and other "hard" drug addicts sometimes go through, in which they inexplicably cease using a drug which supposedly has an unbreakable, or nearly unbreakable, hold over them). Usually beginners require a higher dose in order to experience the same or similar effects as the long-time user. Further, as will be discussed in more detail in a later chapter, there is a discernible difference in reactions to cannabis depending on whether it is smoked (or, more rarely, ingested) alone (which is also relatively rare) or in a group — especially a congenial group.[27]

According to P. Laurie, the physiological and psychomotor effects "are slight and unimportant, compared to the spectrum of mental effects." [28] When marihuana is smoked, the onset of effects is almost instantaneous, due to rapid absorption into the blood from the lungs. The first observable effects are ordinarily a result of the (usually) euphoric mood swing, which is often manifested by a sudden volubility,[29] but almost as often by a dreaming, lolling state, or, less frequently, by general agitation and hyperactivity.[30] Anxiety, which may approach panic, usually associated with fears of death,[31] and sometimes an indefinite "oppressive foreboding and feeling of apprehension" [32] are not uncommon, but usually give way within a few minutes to an increasing sense of calmness,[33] which usually shifts into a mild to strong sense of euphoria.[34] The general nature of this mood shift is usually related to what the individual was thinking about, or to his mood, just prior to smoking,[35] although even in subjects who experience mainly unpleasant sensations, an element of euphoria is nearly always present to some degree.[36] Its particular expression is also largely dependent upon whether or not the person is alone (which, as noted, is rare), in which case he may "trip off" and be quiet and drowsy or he may sit and watch the passing parade of technicolor illusions which may occur, or in a group (which is much more common), in which case he may be talkative and hilarious, with "bursts of singing and dancing, . . . amusing antics . . . [and] much contagiousness of laughing and joking." The same report notes that "the occurrence of a euphoric state, in one or another form, was noted in most of the subjects. But except for those who were allowed to pass the time undisturbed, the pleasurable effects were interrupted from time to time by disagreeable sensations." [37] This may be related to the "wavelike aspect of the experience . . . [which] is almost invariably reported for cannabis." [38] The "wavelike aspect" is mentioned specifically by several observers;[39] although J. H. Jaffe mentions that "there are often marked alterations of mood," he writes that the most predominant affect is "a feeling of extreme well-being, exaltation, excitement, and inner joyousness (described as being 'high') often followed by a moody reverie, but occasionally the depressed mood may be the initial and predominant reaction." [40] Walton summarizes the findings of F. Fraenkel and E. Joël, and states that "All this is accomplished not as a continuous development but rather as a continuous change between the dreaming and waking state, a lasting, finally exhausting alternation between completely different regions of consciousness; this sinking or this emerging can take place in the middle of a sentence." [41] Walton himself calls attention to the "alternating character of the effects. . . . The delirium approaches after the manner of a tropical storm. Each succeeding disturbance becomes more intense and prolonged and the intervening periods become shorter and shorter." [42] It is interesting how his negative bias is revealed in his vocabulary; he gives no justification for using words with such emotional connotations as "delirium," "storm," "disturbance," "intense." Nor is there any reason for supposing that the wavelike character of the cannabis experience, when it does occur, is in any way unpleasant, or diminishes the degree of euphoria felt.

One of the frequently mentioned effects of the acute intoxication is a subjective feeling of "unreality": Walton states that "a peculiar sense of unreality is one of the first sensations experienced. . . . A type of sensory anesthesia" is what he believes "contribute[s] to this sense of unreality." [43] Whereas others write of a "dreamy state of altered consciousness," "fantasy type mentation," or assert that marihuana "creates . . . a false reality," or causes "tormenting doubts of the reality of things," [44] Walton connects this special sensation with another, more frequently mentioned effect: various sensations of lightness and/or heaviness in the limbs, or head, and sometimes throughout the body.[45] Paresthesia — an abnormal sensation of prickling, itching, etc., — reported by W. Bromberg and Walton (as "crawling sensations"), is probably the mildest form of this sensation.[46] Bromberg has given one of the earliest, perhaps overinclusive, but still satisfactorily objective accounts of the acute intoxication. He was able to maintain a high degree of objectivity (and memory function) even though his curiosity had prompted him to smoke "two . . . [marihuana] cigarettes . . . within 40 minutes. . . . Immediately after the second a feeling of lightness in [the] vertex of the head was felt." This was followed by the feeling that his head was "expanding," along with a "mild excitement," and next a sensation of heaviness in his head, which soon alternated with feelings of lightness. He also mentions "a sensation as though the top of the head were lifted," accompanied by "a definite feeling of lengthening in the legs . . . [and] a feeling of the arms rising up in the air." Bromberg considers all these sensations significant, especially since they may mark early elements in the etiology of a panic or anxiety reaction: "Simple sensations of itching, and paresthesias are often present and form the basis, along with disordered visual perceptions, of . . . terrifying hallucinations." Similarly, "Feelings of elevation of the extremities, of lengthening and increase in the diameter of the limbs, of enlarging of the head . . . [give rise to] a feeling that the integrity of the body is being assailed — an inner perception of the breaking up . . . of the personality. . . . the personality may react to the threat against the unity of the body by an anxiety or panic reaction." [47]

Other investigators have reported similar sensations: "The extremities become tremulous, and there are involuntary twitching, . . . a sensation of 'floating in air,' 'falling on waves,' lightness or dizziness in the head, . . . and heaviness in the limbs." [48] One subject reported: "Man, when I'm up on weed I'm really livin'. I float up and up and up until I'm miles above the earth. Then, Baby, I begin to come apart. My fingers leave my hands, my hands leave my wrists, my arms and legs leave my body and I just floooooooat all over the universe." [49] Jaffe notes that "the head often feels swollen and the extremities seem heavy." R. D. Johnson has described "dizziness to some degree, tremors, . . . and an unpleasant floating sensation," but only as a result of "overindulgence." (He does not explain why the floating sensation is "unpleasant.") V. Robinson relates a subject's account (while Robinson's "experiments" were not conducted under laboratory conditions, and his reports tend toward anecdote, his "subjects" were "normal" friends — not prisoners, mental patients, paid or even volunteer experimentees in the usual sense): "The first symptom which told me the drug was beginning to take effect was a feeling of extreme lightness. I seemed to be hollowing out inside, in some magical manner, until I became a mere shell, ready to float away into space. This was soon succeeded . . . by a diametrically opposite sensation of extreme solidity and leaden weight." Another comparable report from a physician relates: "I begin to rise horizontally from my couch. No walls impede my progress, and I float into the outside air . . . an unhindered wanderer through unending space." This particular sensation does not always occur at the beginning of the acute intoxication. Robinson describes how, about three hours after the ingestion of cannabis extract, one of his friends complained of a "heavy feeling . . . creeping over him," which soon turned into its opposite: " 'Ah, I'm beginning to get light again. It's much nicer to be light.' " [50] L. S. Goodman and A. Gilman claim that "the head often feels swollen and the extremities seem heavy" to the intoxicated individual only when higher doses of marihuana are used.[51] The La Guardia Report, which is to date the most thorough and detailed "collection of factual findings in the whole body of scientific literature on marihuana — a literature that goes back thousands of years" [52] (with the possible exception of the relatively unavailable British Army Hemp Drugs Commission Report of 1894, which runs to over 3,000 pages and 7 volumes) reports that "a feeling described as lightness, heaviness, or pressure in the head, often with dizziness, was one of the earliest [symptoms], and occurred in practically all subjects, irrespective of dose." [53] The La Guardia Report notes another aspect of this drifting or floating sensation; the subject feels less need or compulsion to accomplish any particular task, even one that has seemed worth doing before taking marihuana.[54]

Michaux writes about one of his experiences while under the influence of hashish: "I was looking through a magazine at some photographs of those amazing divers of the New Hebrides who, held back (more or less) by long lianas, leap head-first from a rustic tower fifty feet or so high, landing on the ground sloweddown . . . I was conscious of the distances, I estimated them as though I were up there on top of the tower, myself the man, or with the man who was about to jump, even having the sensation of dizziness, and even after turning the page, still feeling myself on top of the tower, still at that terrifying height. At the time I did not know that the sensation of floating in the air, of being weightless, was one of the characteristics of hashish. The flying carpet is not just a legend, but an old reality in Persia and Arabia where for centuries Indian Hemp made people float on air and travel through the skies." [55]

Another related early sign of the acute intoxication which usually, but not always, occurs is some degree of hypermotility, or at least some distinct change in motor impulses and behavior. Walton writes that "in most cases there is hypermotility and the subject is impelled to move rapidly or dance about." He also mentions that Professors W. Straub, F. Kant, and E. Krapf of the Psychiatric Clinic at Munich, in a series of self-experiments with a fairly low dose-range of marihuana, found that "the inclination to motor activity was much increased. 'It felt as if all the joints of the body were freshly lubricated.' The subjects mimicked common movements such as riding or dancing." [56] Bromberg states that the tendency of motility is toward mania, and that "walking becomes effortless." [57] The point that may need to be stressed at this juncture is the interconnection of many of the responses to marihuana: hypermotility is related to the just-discussed alterations of feeling in the extremities, sensations of floating, twitching, and so on. N. B. Eddy et al. mention "hypermotility . . . *without impairment of coordination*" (italics added).[58] S. Allentuck and K. M. Bowman see the "increased psychomotor activity" as one of the many manifestations of general euphoria, and describe the typical cannabis-intoxicated individual as "hyperactive"; Jaffe claims that even "with the smaller doses, behavior is impulsive . . . ; violent or aggressive behavior, however, is infrequent." [59] R. Adams has reported that the use of a cannabis synthetic ("tetrahydrocannabinol") in the treatment of drug addicts undergoing withdrawal resulted in a feeling of enhanced strength and in increased psychomotor activity; there are a number of other reports which mention the same type of effect.[60]

But there is another, perhaps confusing, side. Many investigators and commentators report a finding close to that of the La Guardia Report, that the simplest physical tasks may appear to require such Herculean effort that situations demanding no physical effort are preferred. Another account states that "high school and college youth alike report that this desire to stay put, this passivity, is a main reason why they do not consider themselves a menace on the highways." [61] A series of tests done with rats and mice, using a "hashish extract," found one of the main effects to be "reduced spontaneous locomotor activity." [62] A way of reconciling these apparently contradictory findings is suggested by the La Guardia Report: even though marihuana's general property of decreasing inhibitions may lead to a desire to be more active, or to general, nonfocal restlessness, the typical incoordination and clumsiness (despite the statement of Eddy et al., above) of which the user is in most cases aware, prevent him from attempting many activities.[63] (As a number of articles report, "These behavior symptoms are in direct contrast to those produced by alcohol, which usually induce [*sic*] overt expression of the released inhibitions, as opposed to the turning inward of the marijuana smoker." [64])

Perhaps the most noticeable effect, both subjectively and from the investigator's point of view, is in the general area of appetite, hunger, thirst, and other metabolic effects. Almost every account of the effects of cannabis mentions increased appetite or hunger, and very often bulimia or excessive eating.[65] There had been two competing explanations for this phenomenon; recent investigation has strongly suggested that one is untenable. For a long time, it was not known whether the hunger and seemingly compulsive eating were the result of a lowering of the blood sugar level (hypoglycemia) or simply the result of an actual increment in ability to enjoy eating, probably due to a general lowering of inhibitions, or possibly due to some central physiological change other than blood sugar level. But when A. T. Weil et al. conducted their experiments in 1967, they decided to determine, among relatively few physiological parameters, the blood sugar level in subjects who had smoked marihuana. Possibly one of the reasons for this decision was their annoyance at the American Medical Association who, "on the basis of no evidence whatever" (according to Weil et al.), reported in 1967 that hypoglycemia was one of the effects of cannabis use.[66] Weil et al. found that "there was no significant change in blood sugar levels after smoking." They comment: "A first step [in looking for an explanation for the hunger-type effect] . . . would be careful interviewing of users to determine whether they really become hungry after smoking marihuana or whether they simply find eating more pleasurable." [67]

Along with hunger, thirst is almost always reported as one of the most apparent effects of cannabis.[68] The thirst is usually accompanied by a dry mouth and/or throat, and one writer notes inflammation of the mucous membranes of the mouth.[69] According to the La Guardia Report, one of the side effects of the craving for food — especially sweets — and liquid was that it prevented the subjects from getting too high.[70] It is interesting that a number of researchers and reporters have observed that alcohol is rarely used with or after marihuana, unless the individual feels that he is "too high" and wants to "come down," in which case light wine or beer is generally preferred over any stronger liquor.[71] As Walton has pointed out, although most individuals experience hunger and thirst, some become nauseous to the point of vomiting, which he takes as an indication that "most of these effects are simply secondary to the central-nervous-system effects or even directly mediated by central-nervous-system changes." [72] The La Guardia Report stated that "the sensation of hunger and an increase in appetite, may be considered results of central nervous excitation, producing peripheral effects through the autonomic nervous system"; it also included "nausea and vomiting" under this explanation.[73] Reports generally agree that there may occasionally occur nausea and vomiting.[74] Some investigators report that subjects complained of a bitter or metallic taste.[75]

The La Guardia Report mentions that the subjects preferred smoking to oral ingestion of the "concentrate" because — for one reason — they were able to control or "titrate" the amount of cannabis absorbed, and stop at the right point, before any unpleasant effects were felt.[76] Not only is the effect of smoked marihuana felt almost immediately, but, when it is taken orally, the onset of effects may be delayed up to three or four hours, although one hour is more usual.[77] According to Walton, cannabis taken orally is more "abrupt" in the onset of its effects than cannabis smoked.[78] He does not mean that the oral route increases the potency, or, if he does, he is mistaken, as Isbell et al. have shown.[79] What he probably means is explained as well as anywhere in a rather informal and humorous book:

Usually you creep slowly into a stoned condition, inch by inch sliding upward, but if you've eaten it, it may come on you suddenly, and strike you full force in the middle of a word. If the latter happens, it may sound like this: "So while I was shopping in the market I saw this fantastically beautiful chick, and I wanted to meet her. I was just about to use the 'drop the mustard on her foot' ploy, when she . . . uh . . . what? What were we talking about?" And if the people you're talking to are stoned, they won't remember either.

Getting stoned suddenly and with full force most often is typical of having eaten rather than having smoked the grass. The reason is probably that an hour after you've eaten the grass, you've partially forgotten about it, and are therefore unconscious of the early barely perceptible signposts of being stoned.[80]

Euphoria is not the only typical mood-shift brought on by cannabis, although it is the most consistent. Some writers stress the disinhibiting activity of marihuana: "The old cry used to be that the drug was aphrodisiac, but that claim has been discredited. The correct terminology now is that it is an inhibition-releasing drug." R. J. Bouquet refers to "a state of exhilaration, well-being and bliss." W. H. McGlothlin states that "the experienced user is able to achieve consistently a state of self-confidence, satisfaction, and relaxation." A. R. Lindesmith cites "exhilaration, loss of inhibitions" as the first two noticeable effects of marihuana. According to S. Cohen, "What most users seek is a feeling of relaxation with a dissolution of the tensions and frustrations of the day." The chief danger he cites is the possibility of "strong feelings of grandiosity . . . [or] an overestimate of one's own capabilities." [81]

Along with this the marihuana-high individual may find that he is incapable of or unwilling to exert himself in order to carry through what strike him — while high — as worthwhile projects. This incapacity and/or unwillingness to act occurs during the period of time for which the drug effects last. The lassitude induced by marihuana is usually expected, so the inability or disinclination to do more than talk about various magnificent projects is not usually at all upsetting to the user, but rather a part of what he comes to call "being high."

C. Winick, in his study of the use of marihuana by jazz musicians, noted that a significant number of respondents stated that they used marihuana *after* playing, because "many musicians are fairly 'keyed up' after playing emotionally demanding music like jazz for five or six hours, up to the early morning hours, and drugs help them to 'unwind.' " [82] One of the eleven tests used by the

La Guardia researchers to determine the existence and extent of change in emotional reaction and basic personality structure was the Downey will-and-temperament test, which was used (in this investigation) solely to determine what, if any, changes cannabis caused in self-evaluation. The findings are summarized as follows: "Under the influence of marihuana changes in personality as shown by alterations in test performance are slight. They are not statistically significant." [83] The observed personality changes were described as (typically) a lowering of incentive or drive, a lessening of aggressive trends, and a basically more favorable attitude on the part of the subject toward himself (together with a slight loss of objectivity in judging situations). These changes were attributed to an enhanced sense of relaxation and loosening of inhibitions, together with an increase in self-confidence. But perhaps the most important finding of this research team was that, unless taken in very high doses, cannabis did not alter the basic world view, general attitudes, or personality structure of the individual, with very few exceptions, and in those cases the alteration was slight. Introspective subjects tended to become more introspective, more demonstrative participants tended to show more emotion and an increase in responsiveness to others, and so on — in short, marihuana tended to magnify or accentuate the basic personality, with very little warping or distortion.[84]

One fairly common characteristic of the acute intoxication is a particular kind of laughter, which Bromberg describes as uncontrollable, explosive, and without any apparent reason: "If there is a reason it quickly fades, the point of the joke is lost immediately." [85] Other writers have noted that "uncontrollable laughter and hilarity at minimal stimuli are common," especially when the user is with others.[86] E. R. Bloomquist suggests that the source of this laughter is to be found in the fact that "the flow of thoughts . . . is so overwhelming that, try as they may, they cannot communicate their ideas. This usually strikes the user as hilariously funny, and he begins to titter the high-pitched, giggly laughter so common to cannabis users." [87] H. Michaux offers a less specific suggestion as to the cause for the laughter: "Just as a serious and quite commonplace figure of speech, just as an ordinary sentence can, more readily than any other, send the subject under the effect of hashish off into gales of laughter which go on endlessly, renewing themselves mysteriously, finding within themselves a new source and a new investment of comicality, so a banal idea . . . [can] exceed in fabulousness . . . the most entrancing visions." [88] Michaux also writes: "For a great many people Indian Hemp manifests itself in these outbursts of laughter, although, especially at first, they have not yet noticed anything funny. Then, having been *massaged* by laughter, *by laughter-waves,* by a vibratory tickling that is so characteristic, little by little they begin to find things funny, particularly when there is nothing funny about them. The absurdity lies precisely in the contrast between what is non-comical and the person's own overwhelming sense of absurdity, and in the object's perfect seriousness which their own state of hilarity is about to get the best of. A certain kind of seriousness becomes fairly irresistible. It will not, however, be laughter of the back-slapping sort but, true to its origin, it will be a laugh that is delicate, though intense, born of tenuous vibrations, a laugh that is 'in the know,' that grasps the infinite subtleties of an infinitely absurd world." [89]

Nearly all of Robinson's acquaintance-subjects displayed the same particular type of laughter; the following is a description of Robinson's observations of one subject: "It had begun: the flood of laughter was loose, the deluge of mirth poured forth, the cascade of cachinnation rushed on till it swelled into a torrent of humor while the waves of snickering and tittering mingled with the freshets of hilarity and jollity till the whole flowed into a marvelous Niagara of merriment. What a pity the audience was so small! . . . How the belly of Aristophanes would have thundered a loud *papapappax,* how Scarron would have grinned, . . . how Rabelais would have raised the rafters with his loud ho-ho-hos! Mr. C. was a Leyden-jar of laughter, charged to the limit." [90] Robinson's article is interesting because he also presents the subject's own report (written after the acute intoxication): "When my laughter began it seemed for an instant to be mechanical, as if produced by some external power which forced air in and out of my lungs; it seemed for an instant to proceed from the body rather than from the mind; to be, in its inception, merely physical laughter without a corresponding psychic state of amusement. But this was only momentary. After the first few moments I enjoyed laughing immensely. I felt an inclination to joke as well as to laugh, and I remember saying: 'I am going to have some reason for this laughing, so I will tell a story; if I have to laugh anyway, I'm going to supply good reasons for doing so, as it would be idiotic to laugh about nothing.' I thereupon proceeded to relate an anecdote. Although I knew that my condition was the result of the drug, I was nevertheless filled with a genuine sense of profound hilarity, an eager desire to impart similar merriment to others, and a feeling of immense geniality and mirth, accompanied by sentiments of the most expansive good-will." [91]

This feeling of general benevolence and "expansive good-will" is also described by a respondent to another investigator: "Smoking pot, she says, makes her more understanding of others, more compassionate and willing to accept others, more cosmic and universal in her attitudes. 'You have your hangup, your thing. So have I. We each have our problem, our thing, whatever it is. But when you're high you begin to understand, to know.' " [92] The highly favorable attitude toward others is sometimes more egocentric: "I felt myself the centre of a world-pervading love," although the same writer relates how he was "eager to share my bliss with all the other guests who had seemed to me [before smoking cannabis] . . . a somewhat ragged, poverty-stricken crew." [93]

One of the more interesting accounts of a related effect of cannabis is given by Dr. S. Cholst, who smoked some hashish, and then wrote the following:

Hashish I think . . . makes you

> Younger by far
> Than ever you are.

So it makes you a child again — in mind or emotions or soul or unboring restless behavior. You move easily in thoughts . . . — one to another like a child. . . . Now after the wearing off of the effect, . . . [he believes] the hashish affects the pyramidal tract in some way producing the minor changes listed before and is similar to hypnotic age regression. Thus I was adult and child at the same moment. . . . under hashish . . . [one] need no longer be concerned about the environmental dangers which he previously concerned himself with and compromised with, for in the real world the concern with danger, insecurity, fear of evil, have made him dress a certain way, listen to rules, frustrate himself, keep himself from being free — "able to do what he wants when he wants to do it!" Were he able to do so as an adult at will (and only the good and decent truly want this freedom) he would continuously feel "high" and would know of no difference in states. That society causes pressures against absolute freedom goes without saying, and so the artist — that individual most desirous of freedom — . . . longs the most for the hashish release so that he can pursue and feel his joy in self as a child — for the child is the most free — not having yet been brainwashed into conformity — and the artist (and also the great artists, geniuses) retains always part of himself as this curious, naive, child-like self, the self that probes, that does not take rules easily, that does not believe unless he has checked it out himself. . . . How joyous is this state — like love — for in love with another one is completely free to be oneself in its noblest meanings. . . . this poisoner of frustrating reality, this antidote for restlessness that is frustrated, this instant joy and relaxation, this chemical age-regression that allows us to be young and old at the same moment of time.[94]

One common effect of the acute marihuana intoxication is that individuals often experience a peculiar sensation of "double-consciousness." Walton mentions that people often speak of being aware that they "undergo the hashish delirium, of being thoroughly conscious of the conditions of their intoxication yet being unable or unwilling to return to a state of normalcy." [95] The reader will recall that Ludlow trained himself to appear to the casual observer to behave fairly normally even though heavily intoxicated with cannabis. As W. Oursler puts it, the person high on marihuana "admits . . . that a stop light may look like a lovely red Christmas ball hanging in the sky, but on another level, . . . [he] still knows that it is a traffic light and he will react to it as such." [96] At least one writer equates this phenomenon with "depersonalization," [97] but specific case reports indicate that the situation is more complex: "I took it [marihuana, smoked], and it was pretty much the same thing and then all of a sudden I was walking from one room to another and I fell down on the floor — no, I didn't fall down, I let myself down — and I began turning, back and forth, and back and forth, and I imagined that I was someplace in a jungle. . . . My friends really got worried. And they

said, 'What's the matter?' You know . . . And I liked the sensation, you know . . . it was interesting . . . very interesting. You
had the feeling you were watching yourself. I remember that distinctly. . . . I was myself watching myself. . . . I imagined myself as three different things." [98] Another respondent perceived the
phenomenon in slightly different terms: "Q. Is it true that if you
don't have this double perception, if you aren't sort of standing to
one side and observing yourself having this experience, you aren't
getting all you should out of the drug? A. I think what you're asking me is how do you know you're high. My way is asking myself
if I am high, and at the point at which I begin to wonder, then I
know I'm high. The wonder is the first sign of it — you're feeling
a little different, a little dislocated. And you're wondering, 'Is this
me or is it the drug?' That's the first sign. . . . Marijuana can be
an introspective experience. Some people have the first experience
of communicating with themselves." [99]

Still, there are many writers who insist on labeling this experience "the feeling of being a dual personality," or that "there may
be delusions of a dual personality." [100] One of Robinson's friends
reported that "Throughout the experiment I experienced a peculiar double consciousness. I was perfectly aware that my laughter, etc., was the result of having taken the drug, yet I was powerless to stop it, nor did I care to do so, for I enjoyed it as thoroughly
as if it had arisen from natural causes." [101] In fact, a number of
subjects have noted that the attempt to analyze or convey to another their condition resulted in a "bringdown": "Although I
was in an altogether abnormal state, my thoughts it would seem
were not in any way unreasonable; and the sole annoyance I experienced was the trifling one that when I strove to analyze my
impressions and find them in my mind, they seemed to yield like
melted wax under pressure." [102] Or, as one of Robinson's subject-
friends described it: "Against the effects of the drug, much as I enjoyed and yielded to it, there was opposed a preconceived intention. I had determined to tell my friend Victor Robinson, who was
taking notes . . . , just how I felt. . . . The result was that I
repeatedly summoned all the rational energy that remained to me,
and fought desperately to express the thoughts that came to me,
whether ridiculous or analytical. . . . I believe that this acted as
a great resistant to the effect of the drug. The energy of the drug

was dissipated, I think, in overcoming my will to observe and analyze my sensations, and it was probably for this reason that I did not pass very far on this occasion into the second stage in which laughter gives place to grandiose visions and charming hallucinations." [103] Isbell et al. describe much the same "double-consciousness" in terms of "insight": "Most patients retained insight and ascribed these psychotomimetic effects to the drug." [104]

In the area of speech some of the most strikingly obvious effects occur. As Walton relates the summary of Fraenkel and Joël, "The intoxicated subject usually reports in a form which varies considerably from the normal. The associations become difficult because of the frequent sharp separation of each recollection from that which preceded. Conceptions cannot be expressed well in words." [105] As already noted, the basic euphoria "is first manifested . . . in volubility. . . . His [the marihuana-high individual's] . . . stream of talk may be circumstantial; his mood may be elevated, but he does not harbor frank abnormal mental content such as delusions, hallucinations, phobias, or autistic thinking." [106] Bromberg notes, with regard to speech, that it is usually rapid and flighty, giving the individual the impression that he is being witty and brilliant: "Ideas flow quickly. Conclusions to questions seem to appear, ready-formed and surprising in their clarity." He attributes this to a subjective conviction that the flow of thoughts has speeded up tremendously; the consequent disconnection in speech is a result of this conviction combined with "weakness in storing memories, so that thoughts are forgotten even as they are expressed." [107]

Again the interconnectedness of many of the effects of cannabis is apparent: speech impairment or disruption, in fact, can be viewed as a secondary effect of the more important and basic effects on memory, general mentation, distortion of time perception, and, perhaps, "chemical age-regression." Weil et al. examined speech behavior in their subjects by taping five-minute samples before and during the period of intoxication. They tested long-time users and marihuana-naive individuals, all of whom were left alone with a tape recorder and asked to describe an interesting or dramatic situation in their lives. They found that "in our user population . . . the nature of a verbal sample changed in several important ways" after smoking. For instance, before smoking, the

users, along with the novices, tended to talk about some incident
from their past experience. But after smoking, the users "abandoned narrative format and tended to talk about the present" —
usually about what they believed to be happening in the immediate physical and psychological environment. "They also
tended to become more intimate and to think in free associative
patterns. . . . The imagery they used became less concrete and
more dreamlike." [108] Jaffe states that "random ideas are quickly
translated into speech," [109] which might be a result of the general
disinhibiting capacity of cannabis. Bloomquist, along with many
others, notes the importance of a (preferably congenial) group as
an inducement to verbal expression.[110] Again, another statement
stresses the effect of the preintoxication state: "The ideas that pass
through the psyche seem at first to be uncontrollable, fantastic,
and so rapid that for the novice smoker it is usually akin to a
revelation. After a while he will try to communicate these ideas,
but since his mind works far more rapidly [I question whether this
may not be entirely a subjective evaluation, directly related to the
usual effect of marihuana on the sense of the passage of time,
which will be discussed shortly] . . . than his ability to verbalize,
he may end up spouting fragments of sentences and incoherent
verbiage. [Again, there is a connection with memory function,
which also is discussed below.] Whatever was on the mind of the
individual before lighting up a joint is usually connected with the
broken sequence of ideas going through his head. Concentration
is impossible, though, and the mind tends to jump from one train
of thought to another. It is very common for the smoker to stop in
the middle of a sentence and ask his fellow smokers what he was
talking about." [111] Similarly, the "flow" is not always easy and free:
"I hear my sister come home from the opera. I wish to call her.
My sister's name is Margaret; I try to say it, but I cannot. The
effort is too much. . . . It occurs to me that I may achieve better
results if I compromise on Marge, as this contains one syllable
instead of three. Again I am defeated. I am too weary to exert myself to any extent, but I am determined. I make up my mind to
collect all my strength, and call out: Marge. The result is a fizzle.
No sound issues from my lips. . . . I give it up . . . utterly exhausted and devoid of all energy," although his "brain teems." [112]
Clearly the difficulty in speech is not here connected with any too-
rapid flow of thought, but with the passivity and indolence that

many individuals experience, especially when alone, as was this respondent.

Michaux has some interesting observations on a speech-related activity. In "Experience G: Reading while under the influence of hashish," he writes: "After an average dose of hashish [he does not specify what he considers "average," nor is it clear if he is referring to a *charas*-type preparation when he uses the word "hashish"] . . . one is unfit for reading. This is well known. Even a literary text can be followed only with difficulty . . . followed at the same pace line after line. Nevertheless I have found hashish to be an admirable detector. Some of the greatest authors of literature and of mystical theology have not resisted its 'penetration' for a minute. You can hear the authors in person, they are no longer imposing. . . . You meet them as certain cool-headed men, meeting them during their lifetime. . . . Words no longer play any part. The man who is behind them comes out in front. . . . A highly revered saint is suddenly shown me. What a disappointment! No doubt she has devoted herself, worked, made progress. She still had a long way to go. Garrulous dame that she was, she proved to be nothing but a lightweight. I shall never be taken in by her again. Others, rare wonders, have something to say to you, are really behind their words, which are true, without emphasis. . . . The text, at whatever point you pick it up, becomes a voice, the very voice that suits it, and the man speaks behind this voice. The one who wrote it is there, . . . immediately engaged in thinking, in expressing himself, finding his way among his ideas. . . . An end of abstractness, of vagueness. The man behind his name comes with his weight, his lack of weight. . . . hashish . . . sees quicker than we do, pointing to what we have not yet understood. At the outset, and each time, there is an effort to be made. Which is the reason why it [hashish, cannabis] . . . has not been used to this end. It is doing violence to the hashish-smoker to call upon him to make an effort just when by letting himself go he can experience so many wonders. He has to force himself to make the contact, to maintain it, to pierce through. But once the contact has been made in depth, what an experience! . . . Hashish opens the inner spaces of sentences, and the concealed preoccupations come out, it pierces them at once. It is curious that this hashish, when I used it to test a few authors, never proved vain, or eccentric. Set at the quarry, it never faltered. It was diligent as a falcon. The author thus unmasked never altogether recovered his mantle or his former retreat." [113]

The La Guardia Report noted that one of the effects of marihuana was to free the subject from his customary, self-imposed restraints and in general enable him to speak more freely: "Metaphysical problems which in the undrugged state he would be unwilling to discuss, sexual ideas he would ordinarily hesitate to mention, jokes without point, are all part of the oral stream released by the marihuana." [114]

The effect of cannabis on perception in general and time, space, visual, auditory, and tactile perception in particular is striking. In fact, if there is one property that nearly every researcher and writer recognizes for marihuana, that one is probably the effect on time perception. Further, almost without exception, all agree that the effect is fundamentally the same, no matter how it is described. Walton's summary of Fraenkel and Joël is tinged with the usual negative connotations: "The dream-like phases have an influence on the often grotesque over-evaluation of periods of time, which likewise is a characteristic hashish phenomenon." [115] But Walton himself is more objective, and also perceives some of the interconnections between memory function and time sense that recent investigations[116] have established and carried further. Walton writes: "The exaggeration of the sense of time is one of the most conspicuous effects. It is probably related to the rapid succession of ideas and impressions which cross the field of consciousness. Similarly, the paralysis of the function of memory destroys a sense of continuity which may also be closely related to the sense of time." According to Bromberg, "Activities speed up tremendously and time is slow in passing." In relating his own experience with marihuana, he wrote that he "had a sensation a few minutes after smoking that all this had been going on for hours. There was also a feeling as if the present were a dream, . . . [there was a] change in time passage subjectively. 'Passage of time on my watch does not seem strange but my inner sense of time has long lapses in it.' " [117] Three different authorities, including the American Medical Association, in one of its position statements on marihuana, simply state that marihuana causes "distortion of time perception." [118] Others give slightly more detailed descriptions, although often too vague to be of any real value: "Time intervals subjectively appear elastic," [119] "[There is] frequent . . . temporal distortion," [120] "Minutes seem to be hours, and seconds seem to be minutes," [121] "Time is often slowed," [122] "Awareness, touch, and perception are considerably altered, particularly as they relate to time," and, by the same writer, "Time and space [space is included with time in many of these brief statements] . . . seem distorted and unimportant," [123] "Concepts of time . . . are altered," [124] "[There is] a changed sense of time," [125] or "Perhaps some distortion of perception and time sense, depending on the dose," [126] or "Disturbances of time and space perception." [127] Isbell et al. reported that at medium doses, i.e., 100 mcg/kg smoked or 240 mcg/kg ingested orally (using Δ^1-THC), "alterations in time sense were frequently reported." [128] Winick, writing about drug use among jazz musicians, found that from a sample of 409 persons interviewed, only "a few (2 percent) observed that the musician's altered perception of time and space could permit him to perceive new space-time relationships which might enable him to play either better or worse on different occasions. They pointed out that by expanding the musician's conception of space and time, marijuana seemed to retard the beat of the music. The musician thus felt that he had leisure to express his musical ideas, which might be either an advantage or a disadvantage in individual cases." [129]

Weil et al. found that "before smoking, all nine naive subjects estimated . . . [a] five minute [period used as a test for time judgment] . . . to be 5 ± 2 minutes. After placebo, no subject changed his guess. After the low dose three subjects raised their estimates to 10 ± 2 minutes, and after the high dose, four raised their estimates." Further, "Several subjects mentioned that 'things seemed to take longer.' Below are examples of comments by naive subjects after high doses.

Subject 1: '. . . Things seemed to go slower.'
Subject 2: 'I think I realize why they took our watches. There was a sense of the past disappearing as happens when you're driving too long without sleeping. . . .'
Subject 9: 'Time seemed very drawn out. I would keep forgetting what I was doing. . . .' " [130]

One of the most fascinating reports on the effect of marihuana on time perception is Michaux's: first he presents a long poem,

"Conveyer Belt in Motion," written while he was under the influence of cannabis, and then he gives a part-by-part analysis of the poem. The opening lines read as follows:

> I go forward, fast
> Shovels fly
> then cries
> I free myself
> a moment later, Naples.

He comments: "At the time that hemp augments the intensity of evocation, it augments its speed of apparition and of disappearance. Throughout these pages I could have repeated *the next instant*. Indeed each instant, or small squad of micro-instants, exceptionally independent, appears sharp, without flow, without connection either with the preceding one or the following one. In a completely raw state. The nonsense line therefore is its line, is its style, which is the absence of stylization, of preparation. None of them leans on its neighbors. Series which stop by falling, by pure and simple annulment. Especially hiatuses, except in the phase of peace, of beatitude." [131] In another shorter book, chiefly concerned with the effects of mescaline, but with a chapter devoted to hashish, Michaux observes that: "The tendency to elongate objects and men, characteristic of mescaline, . . . was not very apparent with Hashish, but not entirely absent. It was, however, very much stranger, and, as befits Ha [sic], which is secretive, it was there as if hidden, known only to one's own obscure interior. One has the feeling of prolongation, certainly, but of what? Of time rather than space, and of non-interruption rather than time, of distance above all, of a distance that never reaches its limit." [132]

Perhaps the most original and thorough investigation into the effects of cannabis on time perception is that reported by F. T. Melges et al. They have attempted to determine the effects of marihuana in inducing "temporal disintegration," which they define as "difficulty in retaining, coordinating, and serially indexing those memories, perceptions, and expectations that are relevant to the goal . . . [an individual] is pursuing." They have found that: "(a) high oral doses of THC induce temporal disintegration in normal subjects; (b) the phenomenon stems partly from impaired immediate memory; and (c) temporal disintegration is associated with disorganized speech and thinking." [133] Perhaps the best quality of their work is the clear appreciation they indicate of the interconnection among the various effects of cannabis or THC, reflecting the conception of the person as an interacting conglomeration of mutually dependent processes, an organic gestalt, and not as an automaton or machine which can be taken apart or viewed in a way that stresses the independence of "parts" or "functions." The basic test employed, the Goal Directed Serial Alternation test (GDSA), was used as follows: the subject was given a number at random between 46 and 54 (after having received an oral dose of 20, 40, or 60 mg of Δ^1-THC, or a placebo), then instructed to subtract 7 serially from a starting number (arbitrarily picked in the range of 106 to 114) and after each subtraction to add either 1, 2, or 3, and to continue this alternate addition and subtraction until the initially assigned number was reached. This test "required that the subject simultaneously hold in mind and coordinate information as well as mental operations relevant to pursuing a goal." They also employed two simpler tests to measure short- and long-term memory, the Regular Serial Subtraction of Sevens (RSSS), in which the subject began at a specified number somewhere around 100 ($+$ or -1 to 4), and subtracted seven until past zero. The other test was the Digits Spans Forward and Backward (DSFB), in which the experimenter read a series of digits at random "at a steady rate of 1/sec. He then recorded as the subject's digit span, forward or backward, the largest number of digits that the subject could reproduce without error on two successive trials." [134] The findings were that: (1) "increased doses of THC progressively impaired GDSA performance," especially increasing the number of errors in "the serial or 'working' functions of immediate memory" as doses were increased, and also increasing the number of errors in reaching the goal. "Of particular relevance . . . is the mistake of disregarding the goal." (2) Performance on the RSSS was "not significantly impaired by THC . . . [indicating that] sustained attention and long-term memory operations . . . appear not to be affected by THC." (3) Performance on the DSFB was impaired by THC, indicating short-term memory impairment, although the difference in dose apparently had no appreciable effect.[135] The report concludes with a hypothetical linkage between the effects of marihuana on time perception and on memory: "This temporal incoordination of recent memories with intentions may account, in part, for the disorganization of speech patterns that occurs under marihuana intoxication. As one subject remarked, 'I can't follow what I'm saying . . . can't stay on the same subject . . . I can't remember what I just said or what I want to say . . . because there are just so many thoughts that are broken in time, one chunk there and one chunk here.' These difficulties are similar to the breakdown of goal-directed serial operations during performance of the GDSA. In this regard, the construction of meaningful speech requires that words and phrases be hierarchically ordered in a goal-directed fashion. If there is a deficiency in immediate memory, the components of speech become poorly interconnected over time, and the person is apt to lose his train of thought. Hence, 'loose associations' emerge, since ideas are determined primarily by very recent or current stimuli rather than by a more extended temporal context of what has already been said and what is intended." [136]

The same group has reported in another paper that "impairments in immediate memory from marihuana intoxication do not follow a smooth time-function, but rather are episodic, brief in duration, and not always under volitional control. These episodes often interrupted the speech patterns of our subjects and seemed to be associated with the intrusion of extraneous perceptions and thoughts." They quote two subjects: "I just felt very confident and able to remember the numbers . . . then when it came time to give them back, I'd see and hear, mostly see, I think, all kinds of numbers . . . [note the element of synesthesia here]. And I wouldn't know which ones were the right ones." Another subject: "I can understand what I'm thinking, but I can't understand what I'm saying. . . . Because there are so many thoughts in between what I'm saying." They conclude that immediate memory dysfunction "may result from the intrusion of irrelevant material into the user's awareness," and call attention to "an additional factor in THC-induced cognitive impairment . . . [which] entails intermittent lapses in attention." [137]

Years ago Bromberg had mentioned "loss of memory for what he [Bromberg] . . . had in mind to say" and that he was confused and "found it difficult to think of needed words." He states that he was " 'trying hard to understand what goes on in my mind when I have these little "absences" of memory but cannot express myself.' " He also mentioned as characteristic of the cannabis intoxication a "weakness in storing memories, so that the thoughts are forgotten even as they are expressed." [138] Fraenkel and Joël found that "long-buried recollections appear, whole scenes and situations project into the present." [139] Walton, in fact, suggested that "the paralysis of the function of memory destroys a sense of continuity which may also be closely related to the . . . exaggeration of . . . the sense of time." [140] Jaffe states that individuals under the influence of marihuana are able to recall what has long been forgotten, at the same time as they forget the well known. Bloomquist mentions that memory is impaired but does not differentiate between short- and long-term memory. Rosevear, however, has noted that some events from the remote and obscure past may come clearly to mind, while at the same time experiences and mental transactions only a few seconds old are often forgotten. It is on the basis of this property that the recommendation for its use in the treatment of absentmindedness is to be found in the ancient Herbal of the Chinese Emperor, Nung. In 1938 Yawger reminded readers that "John Stuart Mill, philosopher, wrote of its [cannabis's] power to revive forgotten memories, and in my inquiries, smokers have frequently informed me that while under its influence, they are able to recall things long forgotten." [141]

The La Guardia study measured the effects of ingested and smoked marihuana on memory, using tests for rote memory (digit series recall), rote memory plus "mental control" (digits reversed), object memory (in which the subjects were shown ten small objects on a flat surface for three seconds and then asked to list as many as they could), and visual memory (in which "Army designs" were shown for ten seconds to the subjects, who were then asked to reproduce them as accurately as possible). In this last test, the element of practice interfered to some extent, since there is only one form for the test. The results for oral ingestion of marihuana were slightly different from those obtained after smoking: although there was no significant change in simple digit repetition after either oral ingestion or smoking, and, after smoking, no change in reversed repetition, after ingestion "the repetition of digits reversed was affected adversely. . . . The impairment was comparatively small, but it seems to have been related to the amount of drug taken." [142] In the object memory test, smoking marihuana did not affect performance adversely, but when marihuana was taken orally, "there was a loss of about 9 per cent in the subject's ability to recall objects which had been exposed to his vision for three seconds when he took the test under the influence of 2 cc. of marihuana, while after the ingestion of 5 cc. the impairment was less, being only about 5 per cent." The report attributes this "seemingly contradictory result" to the effects of practice.[143] It is interesting that after smoking the subjects showed a slight but definite increase in object memory.[144] With regard to visual memory, both smoking and oral ingestion of marihuana had an adverse effect on test performance: "After the ingestion of 2 cc. of marihuana there was a 6 per cent drop . . . , while under 5 cc. there was a 24 per cent drop . . . [and after smoking] there was . . . an impairment of about 8 per cent." [145] Probably the only genuinely significant figure is the 24-percent decrement in visual memory after ingestion of 5 cc, and it should be noted that this amount of this extract contained a good deal more marihuana than the ordinary user would take by smoking. Another interesting aspect of this series of tests was that whereas after oral ingestion "the same difference was observed in intensity of the effect upon user and non-user," after smoking, "the difference in intensity of effect . . . on the user and on the non-user was not the same. . . . The user was usually more affected by smoking marihuana than was the non-user, probably because the non-user did not smoke as much or as intensely as the user and was not as much under the influence of the drug." [146]

The effects of marihuana on perception of space are often described along with its effects on time perception, although not as frequently. Walton states that "distortion of the space sense is commonly noted and this again . . . [like time perception] is evidently a matter of cortical narcosis." [147] However, unlike time perception, which seems always (or almost always) to be affected in the same general way (i.e., the cannabis-intoxicated individual feels that time has "slowed," that, for example, many hours have passed in the space of a few minutes), space perception may be distorted in a number of ways, and there is no particular pattern. "Distance and time intervals subjectively appear elastic";[148] "Space may be broadened and near objects may appear far distant." [149] Most observers simply mention "disturbances" [150] or "altered . . . concepts" [151] or "distortion" [152] in spatial perception. Michaux, in analyzing the line "A pipe line with a wild beast's jaws springs at me (known!)," from his poem written while under the influence of cannabis, remarks: "An extreme lengthening of objects really seen or seen in inner vision is common. . . . The pipe line comes from this lengthening." [153] In writing of one of his experiences while under the influence of cannabis, he describes a ride in a taxi, during which the slowness and general ineptitude of the driver became so intense (to him) that he deliberately abstained from observing all spatial or distance relationships. But "at home again, I next found myself observing a certain situation, the main element of which was defined by the word 'distance,' which I wrote down. Having written it, it magically stripped itself of its meaning, of its importance, to the point of becoming insignificant, then stripped itself of the adjoining meaning which I had seen in it in writing the actual reflection on the situation, which moreover I could no longer find, then of the meaning that it habitually has for me. It stood there, unrecognizable. All it had left to do was to become meaningless. It did. It now no longer had any meaning. . . . But in leaving the word, the meaning of it lodged in me, giving me suddenly, totally, actorly, the character of a distant man. And even distant from myself, so that I had difficulty also in approaching myself. The spiriting away of the meaning had made the meaning spread on my person!" [154]

The effects of cannabis on visual perception are perhaps the most variable of all "perception effects," both between two persons and for the same person at different times and under different circumstances. Bromberg writes that after approximately 30 minutes (from the time of smoking marihuana), the user "may begin to see visual hallucinations which may start as misinterpretations and illusions. Characteristically there are at first flashes of light or amorphous forms of vivid color which evolve and develop into geometric figures, shapes, human faces, and pictures of great complexity. The depth of the color and its unusually arresting tone strike the subject." [155] When he smoked marihuana himself, "suddenly he saw images of legs and arms in a dissecting room which were terrifying . . . [he remarked that] 'every object seems to stand out with crystal like clearness. . . . The imagery I have is so luminously clear, it stands out in the background like sharply cut figures in a frieze.' " [156] He further states that "the symptomatology of cannabis smoking illustrates in the visual sphere a primitive level of perceptive integration." After noting that L. Kanner and P. Schilder, in a study of the behavior in normal subjects of optic images, found various changes occurring in the image representing a primitive level of perception, he argues that in "the cases of hashish intoxication, visual phenomena indicate that disintegration to primitive levels occurs under the cortical influence of the drug. The symptoms of Case 8 who saw flying masses of color; . . . the amorphous character of the optic perceptions (Case 7); the distortion of optic images (Case 4), all show the primitive form which the perception assumes under intoxication." [157] According to Walton, Fraenkel and Joël found that "colors become brighter and more luminous. . . . It is remarkable that variations take place in all animate things; they assume expressions of mask-like fixity and lifelessness. Physiognomies turn to gypsum, wax, and ivory. True hallucinations are rarely experienced." [158] The last sentence is one which needs emphasis; nearly all of the so-called "hallucinations" are misinterpretations or "variable seeings" of objects in the immediate environment, especially at dose levels usually taken by those who smoke marihuana. Walton also reported a German study that found, among other effects, "Impressions of light . . . seemed extraordinarily exaggerated. The light from a table lamp blinded the eyes. . . . Illusionary misconceptions developed. 'I see now that you have become much more square. Now you have a very sharp-pointed chin.' " [159]

Micropsia and macropsia (or megalopsia) have been frequently reported.[160] Bloomquist asserts that "not infrequently the user experiences phantasmagoria — the sensation that figures are rushing toward him at tremendous speed, increasing in size as they approach. Conversely, they may depart from him, decreasing in size. As one user described this, 'It's like a zoom lens on a TV camera.' " [161] Isbell et al. state that at "threshold doses [of Δ^1-THC] . . . (25 mcg/kg by smoking or 75 mcg/kg orally) . . . alterations in sensory perception were not prominent and hallucinations, delusions, and illusions never occurred." But beginning around 100 or 240 mcg/kg (by smoking and oral ingestion, respectively) they note "reports of perceptual distortion such as 'colors are brighter,' . . . [and] the majority of the patients had . . . illusions, delusions, and hallucinations." [162] However, the authors do not consider the question of whether or not it is accurate to call these subjective alterations true hallucinations, that is, hallucinations that arise spontaneously, independent of any environmental stimuli. The whole question of whether or not marihuana can in fact be said to induce true hallucinations is un-settled. Walton's summary of the findings of Fraenkel and Joël states that: "All these oppressive forces cannot be dispelled by simply saying 'This is not reality, it is only the effects of a drug.' The character of the delusions, for example, cannot be evolved at will; one recognizes that they are hashish phenomena, yet they remain unaltered. These delusions are mostly illusionary trans-formations of the outer world, which at first had become very strange and singular." Allentuck and Bowman state flatly that the marihuana-intoxicated individual "does not harbor frank ab-normal mental content such as delusions, hallucinations, phobias, or autistic thinking." Jaffe asserts that "when larger doses are used [he does not specify relative levels] . . . extremely vivid hallucinations may be experienced; these are often pleasant, but their coloring, sexual or otherwise, is more related to the user's personality than to specific drug effects." Eddy et al. claim that high dosage and repeated administration will result in "hallucina-tions, illusions, and delusions that predispose to antisocial be-havior," which seems to be an unwarranted assertion. Another authority claims that "visual hallucinations, seeing faces as gro-tesque, . . . are also common." S. F. Yolles writes that "in acute intoxication, especially when ingested, it [marihuana] . . . may also produce visual hallucinations." Bloomquist writes that "with increased doses [again, the levels are not specified] . . . hallu-cinations may appear. If they are pleasant the user will usually trip on them and remain high. If they are unpleasant he may experience deathly fear." According to Keeler, Bouquet states that "illusions, visual and auditory hallucinations . . . occur," but no particular dose level is described. Robinson's accounts of his friends' experiences under the influence of cannabis are full of references to what seem to be genuine — that is, not causally re-lated to the environment — hallucinations.[163] Oursler quotes A. Ginsberg on the matter: "These are not 'hallucinations.' These are deepened perceptions that one might have catalyzed by some other natural event." In an interview with a remarkably intelli-gent individual who happens to have used marihuana, Oursler reports the following dialogue: "Q. Are the hallucinations stronger on *hashish*? A. I don't know anyone who really hallu-cinates on either *hashish* or marijuana. The experts seem to spend their time quoting each other about that. Q. Can *you* say anything? A. It's hard to generalize. You're talking about something that affects psychological centers. I just don't happen to know anyone who hallucinates, and I don't either. Personally, I think the people who hallucinate on *hashish* or marijuana are the ones who would hallucinate on a glass of water if someone told them they would. There's an awful lot of that — you know, like what you're told you're supposed to experience, you experience. Anyway, how do you define hallucination? It's hard to define. Is it the actual visible total visual phenomenon or is it a subtle distortion of what's visibly valid?" Another interviewee responded: "Q. What effects or hallucinations did you have? A. Well, I don't believe in hallucinations. I sort of — well, it turned back toward watching my sister die which then was the big thing in my life, the only thing really. I concentrated on this. It brought it all back to me. I watched it, and saw it all go by. . . . But it really wasn't a hallucination or anything. It was just because I was stoned." Oursler states his own view: "The evidence of those who use it, with some regularity, . . . is that . . . when they achieve a 'high' they often have somewhat psychedelic experiences and what might be called in layman's language mild or semihallucinations." He went on to state: "Only one of the subjects our researchers interviewed reported hallucinations. Yet analysis of their statements to interviewers gives the very clear impression that they at times *did* hallucinate. One might ask, did they hallucinate and simply would not admit it? Or, did they merely imagine certain things to have happened because they had read that this was the way in which they were expected to react to marijuana? In this climate, even their indecision may be a valid clue when such studies can be made." [164] It seems reasonable to conclude that those phenomena commonly reported as "hallucinations" in connection with the acute marihuana intoxication are probably not true hallucinations except possibly in cases where very large amounts of the drug have been consumed. Such a degree of intoxication is rarely achieved through the smoking of marihuana in the United States today.

The effects of marihuana on auditory perception have not been as thoroughly reported as other perceptual effects. Walton, citing the German study of F. Kant and E. Krapf at Munich, writes that "Impressions of . . . sound seem extraordinarily exaggerated. . . .

ordinary noises, such as the ticking of a clock, resounded loudly. An inconclusive but suggestive experiment indicated that the actual threshold of sound stimuli was lowered; steps in an adjoining room, which were imperceptible to other people, were heard and counted correctly." [165] Walton himself observes that "sounds appear to be tremendously magnified. . . . There is little doubt, at least, regarding an apparent increase in auditory faculties. Some orchestra leaders declare that they are much more sensitive to sound and rhythm when under the influence of the drug. They insist that there is a special capacity for voluntarily hearing one instrument to the exclusion of others." In this connection he mentions the experience of Fitz Hugh Ludlow, who described the same phenomenon in *The Hasheesh Eater* (see Chapter 4, above). Reference has already been made to some of Walton's comments on "musical performance" while under the influence of cannabis (see beginning of this chapter). He further states that: "The very common idea of improved performance is based on several features which can give considerable apparent support to such an impression. There is an increased sensitivity to sound and a keener appreciation of rhythm and timing. These phenomena, as judged by objective criteria, probably do not exist except during certain early phases of the drug's effects. The release of inhibitions may uncover latent talents which previously had been subject to personality restraints. The wild, emotional character of performance can be intensified and for certain audiences this may represent improvement although it would not be so acknowledged by an individual of cultivated musical appreciation." [166] It is interesting that Ludlow and another hashish-taker both independently reported an improvement in performance as judged objectively. Ludlow gave hashish to a friend and carefully watched his reactions.

> He now possessed a power of melodious creation unknown in his highest natural states. Setting his lips so as to send forth sounds in imitation of a bugle, he played in my hearing a strain of his own impromptu composition so beautiful that it would have done credit to any player upon wind instruments that ever attained celebrity.[167]

However, it should be noted that it is not clear that Ludlow was not also under the influence of hashish. An anonymous user of the drug described a similar incident which occurred while under the influence of hashish.

> Under ordinary circumstances I am a poor player; yet I have a good ear and improvise with tolerable facility. My friend, therefore, expected to hear what he had often heard before from me — a trivial air, perhaps, and some vulgar variations upon it; and he was accordingly astonished when I began a wild melody like some of the quaint creations of Saint-Saens, and played it (so my friend says) with brilliancy.[168]

Eddy et al. report a "lowering of the sensory threshold . . . for . . . acoustical stimuli," and McGlothlin reports "increased sensitivity to sound." But, according to the La Guardia Report, "Auditory acuity is not affected by marihuana." A related finding of the La Guardia Report was that a few subjects experienced "ringing or pressure in the ears." H. France "experienced, besides, an unspeakable pleasure in listening to the wild, barbaric music," although at the same time "I kept telling myself, . . . [that] the orchestra that ravishes my soul . . . [was nothing but] a jumble of discordant noises." Michaux noted: "I also seem to be hearing in an unusual way. A sound so faint that I would not ordinarily have heard it at all, is perceptible through three closed doors. I can even follow all its shiftings though very slight, follow them as I would a flying swarm of bees. I am experiencing stereoaudition." [169]

The reported effects of cannabis on tactile perception and body-sense in particular show perhaps the greatest range of findings, at least under the general heading of "perception." Walton, reporting the findings of Fraenkel and Joël, reports: "In the haptic sphere there often develops a disintegration of the feeling of the body's coherence. There are also dynamic sensations such as that of being hurled through space [which should be distinguished from the more frequently reported sensations of floating, weightlessness, etc.] . . . as by a powerful centrifugal force." [170] He also reports the findings of the Munich investigators in this area: "Sensations of heat coursed in waves from the feet to the head or seemed to locate in specific organs . . . along with a slight feeling of numbness." [171] Walton reports that "some of the sensory perceptions are depressed. Rumpf described experiments in which skin sensitivity was considerably diminished. Two-point sensitivity on the volar surface of the forearm decreased from 3.8 cm. to 5.8 cm." [172] As mentioned previously, Bromberg believed that the changes in the individual's perception of his own body have important psychological repurcussions: "There is a feeling that the integrity of the body is being assailed. . . . Narcissism in a sense depends on the perception of an intact organism and the personality interprets its dissolution as a threatened loss of unity." He traces an "interesting relationship between the feelings evoked by the change in the subjective sensation due to the drug and the subjective feelings entertained by schizophrenics. . . . From a psychoanalytic point of view the problem seems to revolve around the narcissism of the individual and its changing value for the ego. . . . The dissolution of the integrity of the motor hierarchy parallels the change in the structure of the sensory world. . . . The disintegration of the sensory sphere, of the motor sphere, and consequently of the total perceptive personality, reacts on the ego. The various mental states — anxiety, depersonalization, panic, manic or schizophrenic episodes, depending on the underlying personality pattern — appear as total reactions of the personality to the intoxication." [173]

In a brief note on the effects of cannabis and alcohol during labor, the American Medical Association in 1930 noted that after the administration of cannabis the "sensation of pain is distinctly lessened or entirely absent and the sense of touch is less acute than normally." However, Allentuck and Bowman report that there is "increased sensitivity to touch, pressure, and pain stimuli." Jaffe states that with "larger doses . . . the body image may seem distorted"; McGlothlin notes that there are frequent reports of "perceiving various parts of the body as distorted, and depersonalization." Isbell et al. simply mention that at the middle dose-levels (of the three administered), there are frequently "changes in body image such as body feels light, etc." One of Robinson's friends felt that "the surfaces of my body seemed to communicate to my consciousness a metalliferous feeling; and I imagined that if struck I would give forth a metallic ring." According to Keeler, the "user feels that he is unusually aware of the function of his limbs." G. M. Carstairs mentions that one of the typical effects of cannabis "taken alone and in moderate strength" is "sensory hyperesthesia." [174]

The question of the effects of marihuana on mental performance is an intriguing one; the reports seem to hold to some variety of two polar positions: (1) that cannabis has a detrimental
effect on all mental functioning, which is, in most instances, directly related to the dose; (2) that cannabis has no, little, or even
a positive effect on intellectual and/or mental performance and
functioning. One element which is apt to cause confusion on this
general point is the question of how long the individual has been
using cannabis regularly; when Weil et al. tested a group of nonusers and a group of regular users, they found that the regular
users actually improved their scores on two out of three tests
(improvement on the Digit Symbol Substitution Test — "a simple test of cognitive function often used on I.Q. tests"; improvement on the Pursuit Rotor Test — to measure coordination
and attention), and showed no change on the third (the Continuous Performance Test, one which "measures a subject's capacity for sustained attention"), whereas the marihuana-naive subjects showed impairment on both of the two tests for which the
regular users showed improvement, and no change on the same
test for which the regular users' scores were not affected. Accordingly, it is possible, say the authors of the report, for a habitual
user to ignore any adverse effects on mental functioning, focus
on a specific task, and actually improve his performance. (They
also note that although the scores for the habitual users were
improved, "they started out from good baseline scores," obtained
when they were not under the influence of cannabis.) They do
not try to explain this apparently paradoxical phenomenon, but
they assert that the habitual user can apparently learn to adapt
to or compensate for up to 100 percent against any nonspecific
adverse effects of marihuana. However, the *improvement* would
seem to indicate that the users actually did more than merely
compensate or adapt for any nonspecific adverse effects on cognitive functioning, although the question could only be finally
settled if the researchers had been able to test the users before
they began to use marihuana regularly, since the apparent improvement may have reflected nothing but a return to (higher)
scores which they could have achieved before becoming regular
users.[175]

Allentuck and Bowman assert that "attention, concentration
and comprehension are only slightly disturbed, as is evidenced

by the fact that the results in his [the marihuana intoxicated individual's] . . . educational achievement tests are only slightly lowered." [176] One of Robinson's friends found that, despite "a thousand other fancies [in his] . . . excited brain," he was able to correctly quote a "stanza from a favorite poem." [177] Of course, this is not an indication that marihuana does not adversely affect mental performance, for the factor of compensation or adaptation must be considered. On the other hand, it is interesting that many "intelligence tests" strike a marihuana-high individual as simply irrelevant, just as tests to measure "intelligence" devised by someone high would strike an individual who was not intoxicated as irrelevant. As one writer, an artist, expresses it, "Pot puts your head in a different place." The same writer goes on to note:

> Like most people, I formed certain habits of perception and modes of thought at an early age. These methods served me well until I was about thirty when doubts began to crowd me; I realized that my empirical stance was not strong enough to withstand the thrust of new ideas. . . . Most marijuana smokers agree that the senses are heightened by grass. This is a visually oriented culture. We've developed high visual acuity at the expense of the other senses. When I smoke grass, I find that the other senses are heightened in receptivity, while the visual sense is often diminished. . . . When I'm straight I often see things not as they are objectively, but as I believe them to be. . . . The banana . . . is viewed through the memory of every artificial commercially-produced banana I've ever seen. . . . But when I'm high, it looks to me like a pulpy plant, fibrous and almost alive. . . . Often, marijuana insights are accompanied by an emotion which reinforces the conviction that a fragment of Truth has been discovered. We call this kind of learning "revelation," and it seems to me as valid as logic or reasoning. Certainly five senses are limited in their range and their sensitivity. Man has many other sensory receptors which we are only dimly aware of, and these have been sadly neglected by our empirical age. By shifting our focus of consciousness from the visual to the audial, or from the outer senses to the inner ones, we may experience revelation of a profound and trenchant nature. I find that marijuana helps me in this process.

I do not subscribe to the point of view that insights come

from outside the individual. Rather, we know much more than we *think* we know, and grass is one way of tapping that rich field of knowledge, insight, and revelation. . . . by adulthood our pattern of thinking, of bringing out . . . thoughts, have become pretty rigid. Old patterns of thought are repeated. . . . But the unconscious has other answers locked away; marijuana may be seen as a key to that attic. . . . If we can think of the brain as a computer, then perhaps grass, by temporarily altering the chemistry of the brain, stimulates new connections, linking up memories and information in unusual ways. By this kind of synthesis, fresh concepts are formed. . . .

Whereas my thinking is normally structured along traditional lines of linear thought, reasoning, building from particulars to generalities, and vice versa, and drawing associations, corollaries, various conclusions based on other ideas, when I think behind grass, I frequently think in flashes of insight. . . . So thought is not so architectural and not so linear, but more "mosaic." The pot smoker sometimes makes conceptual *leaps* that are difficult for others to follow. Sometimes if the listener is also high he can keep up. . . . My mind *plods* when I'm straight; it leaps and flies ahead when I smoke. . . . When I write I generally turn on, do a first draft, and then re-write when I'm straight. I find that my style is fresher and more original than it was before . . . I've found that what I write high is freer and more honest. . . . The point is that, freed from conventional processes, the mind can produce more vivid, more original images and thoughts. . . . When I'm stoned, my mind leaves the linear plane and moves into new dimensions. Montage and synthesis are the media of perception and expression. The images are symbolic and mosaic, rather than logical and linear.[178]

That is one side. The "authorities" are in nearly unanimous agreement on the other. The American Medical Association states that among the results of smoking cannabis are "impaired judgment and memory, irritability and confusion." Cohen states that "an overestimate of one's own capabilities is not infrequent. Often mental productions are not as highly assessed when they are later examined in the sober state." Yolles agrees: "It may . . . lead to heightened suggestibility and a faulty perception, really an exaggerated notion of thinking more clearly, profoundly and creatively." [179] Other typical remarks: "The . . . individual . . . becomes less aware of his inadequacy, and . . . feels more capable of meeting the demands made upon him. . . . [The] effect gives him a false sense of well-being; he feels more ambitious and more successful. He therefore has a distorted view of his ability and performance, which when checked objectively is found to be far from satisfactory." Jaffe is less judgmental: "Ideas come in disrupted sequences. . . . ideas seem disconnected, uncontrollable, and freely flowing." Bloomquist states that "Self-confidence, often unwarranted, is one of the usual reactions. . . . his judgment and memory are impaired." Bromberg: "The subject has the impression that his conversation is witty, brilliant; ideas flow quickly. Conclusions to questions seem to appear, ready-formed and surprising in their clarity. The feeling of clarity is, of course, spurious: it is merely a subjective feeling. . . . The rapid flow of ideas gives the impression of brilliance of thought and observation. The flighty ideas are not deep enough to form an engram that can be recollected — hence the confusion. . . . Along with the retention defect is a slowing of concentration and comprehension; what is heard or otherwise perceived can only be attended to for a few seconds: the focus of attention shifts momentarily. . . . often there is a subjective feeling . . . that each idea or perception stands out. . . . Mennier believes that the special lucidity and brilliance of thought apparent to the subject is due to emotional stimulation (elation) and not to any increase in comprehension." [180] Laurie cites Murphy: the chief mental effect is "dulling of attention." However, he states that "the drug increases imagination but reduces concentration. Intelligence-test scores are slightly lower or unchanged, and if attention is held, say in a game of poker, an expert player can more than hold his own against other good players." [181] The La Guardia Report found that "with both pills and cigarettes many of the men had difficulty in concentrating and maintaining a fixed goal" and also that "marihuana taken either in pill or in cigarette form has a transitory adverse effect on mental functioning. . . . The extent of intellectual impairment, the time of its onset, and its duration are all related to the amount of drug taken. . . . The degree of intellectual impairment resulting from the presence of marihuana in the system varies with the function tested. The more complex functions are more severely affected than the simpler ones. . . . In general, non-users experience greater intellectual impairment for longer periods of time than the users do. . . . The falling off in ability which occurs when an individual has taken marihuana is due to a loss in both speed and accuracy. . . . Indulgence in marihuana does not appear to result in mental deterioration." Keeler writes that "the power to focus concentration is lost or relinquished. Associations are rapid and disorganized." Johnson emphasizes that "mental functioning is affected by marihuana in relation to the amount of drug taken both in degree and duration. Complex functions are more seriously disrupted than simple ones." He relates an anecdote concerning a graduate student who was at a seminar discussion "stoned" on marihuana. "His conduct and comments were deemed normal by all observers and no one was the wiser until he disclosed his state at the seminar the following day. He had been 'lost' in most of the discussion but was able with difficulty to relate the content to the previous day's discussion and thus make some comments. The fellow participants found it hard to reconcile his subjective disorientation with his relatively normal objective behavior. Decreased intellectual ability is due to diminished speed as well as accuracy." [182]

But, still, there are authorities who take a less critical stand: "Heightened suggestibility, perception of thinking more clearly and deeper awareness of the meaning of things are characteristic." [183] Weil et al. note that the 1933 Panama study found unchanged performance on psychological and neurological tests, although the amounts of the drug were not specified.[184] Even apart from the findings of Weil et al., there is evidence that marihuana is of real value to the artist, although, even at the time when he is creating under the influence of marihuana, he would be likely to score lower on standard "intelligence" tests. William Burroughs has written that "unquestionably this drug is very useful to the artist, activating trains of association that would otherwise be inaccessible, and I owe many of the scenes in 'Naked Lunch' directly to the use of cannabis. . . . Cannabis serves as a guide to psychic areas which can then be re-entered without it." [185] The views of Allen Ginsberg are given in Chapter 4; they are mainly an extension and elaboration of Burroughs' comments. But despite the claims of the writers, artists, and other creative individuals, the medical and psychological experts and would-be experts continue to maintain that any apparent gain in creativity is illusory, with a few exceptions. Eddy et al. attribute the "[feeling of] intensified appreciation of works of art" to the "lowering of the sensory threshold." The American Medical Association states flatly that "while some persons assert that marijuana improves artistic and other creative endeavor, there is no evidence that this is so." Bloomquist categorically denies that marihuana "opens the mind and enhances creativity." Concerning music he writes: "The myth exists that jazz musicians play much better when on cannabis. It is true that they are less inhibited and probably tire less easily, but there it stops." He cites the "Seashore" study of C. K. Aldrich as confirmation of this claim, but ignores entirely the study of Winick, who traces in some detail the undeniable connections between jazz and cannabis use. However, although Winick does establish a definite connection between the use of marihuana and the phenomenon of jazz, he asserts that "there appears to be no significant relationship between . . . the marijuana user and the degree of professional success attributed to him by his peers." [186]

One of the most disputed "properties" of marihuana concerns its alleged aphrodisiac effects. This subject is discussed in Chapter 11; in passing, however, it should be mentioned that the effects of marihuana on sex are probably as important for the *user* as any other effects, even if it be true that cannabis has no specific aphrodisiac properties, as most medical and scientific investigators — but not most users — assert.

One of the areas of effects of the acute intoxication that has received little systematic or well-defined study until quite recently is concerned with the intoxicated individual's ability to perform specific tasks or tests, some of them connected with normal societal functioning, but many of them artificial, or reflecting the norms of a particular socioeconomic segment of the population. In my opinion, most "intelligence" and psychological tests fall into the second group, but unfortunately, these have been used in the majority of instances. Walton reports that Fraenkel's study of hashish-intoxicated individuals' responses to the Rorschach (inkblot) test showed, generally, that the persons tested "attribute an abnormally significant importance to details. The detail tends to break its boundaries, it tends to emancipation. Accordingly, it ceases to be a detail. Interpretations of detail are collectively reduced and, in turn, changed in character. It no longer simply stimulates affectivity, it becomes epic in character." [187] It seems to be often the case that, under the influence of cannabis, usual tasks, tests, and activities appear to have less relevance. As Ginsberg has already been quoted, "The marijuana consciousness . . . shifts . . . to *more direct, slower, absorbing, occasionally microscopically minute, engagement with sensing phenomena during the high* moments or hours." [188]

According to the La Guardia Report, marihuana-high individuals given the Rorschach test responded with a "slight increase in the actual number of interpretations made," and also "the amount of talking and extraneous comment increased. The subject played around with answers and often repeated them. He seemed anxious to get his every thought clearly across. . . . More than this, he was much freer in the type of interpretation he allowed himself . . . [he often] offered . . . lengthy tirades . . . on topics which in his undrugged state he would undoubtedly feel were beyond him. . . . In some instances the 'cockiness' induced by his drugged condition produced an entirely new attitude in the subject. Instead of the customary deferential, almost ingratiating approach there was now a confident 'know-it-all' manner." In comparing the responses of the users and nonusers, the report concluded that "the effects . . . on user and non-user were essentially the same . . . except that on the whole the alterations which did occur were more marked for the non-user than for the user. Thus, for example, while the average number of responses given by the user increased only 11 per cent, those of the non-user rose 26 per cent. Again, the user when drugged gave only 6 per cent fewer whole answers as against a decrease of 15 per cent in the whole responses of the non-user. . . . The user showed a 29 per cent increase in small detail interpretations, the non-user 31 per cent. There was only a 2 per cent drop in good form interpretation by the user as against a 12 per cent drop for the non-user. Only in the loss of popular interpretations did the user exceed the non-user, his falling-off being as great as 31 per cent as compared with 24 per cent for the non-user." Although the report admits that the number of individuals tested was too small to draw any but tentative conclusions, "the trend seemed to indicate that the ingestion or smoking of marihuana has a greater adverse or disorganizing effect on the neophyte." [189] Again, it could be objected that the use of words with the connotations carried by "disorganizing" is indicative of a fairly subtle bias against seeing the primary effects of marihuana as consciousness-expanding and facilitating a mental condition in which the irrelevance of the inkblot tests was apparent to the subjects, except when they became engrossed in detail. In reading the La Guardia Report, and to a greater degree in reading most other reports of various tests and tasks given to marihuana-high individuals, I was reminded of Bob Dylan's words (as applicable to the testers) when he sings of Mr. Jones' knowing that *something* is happening, but having no sense of what it is.[190]

Rosevear notes that marihuana is often used in social situations. For example, it may be smoked while playing card games, such as bridge or poker. Other games, such as Monopoly or Scrabble, may be more difficult for the inexperienced user, but if the smoker becomes only mildly intoxicated while playing these games his skill and judgment are not significantly impaired, although he may think "too much" about his play. Rosevear also notes that with more frequent use, the ability of the user to "compensate" (as Weil et al. have put it) is increased to the point where he is able to do anything, or nearly anything, that he could do when not high, although many habitual users prefer to be "straight" when performing certain activities.[191]

Bloomquist, however, has written that "surprisingly the user can walk on the street without appearing to the casual observer to be in any but a normal state. He talks with his usual ability, although sometimes hesitantly and with a slight slur. On the surface he seems quite coherent. But underneath he is probably tripping on the beauty of the sky, the noises of traffic or the smell of some nearby flowering bush or tree. If he is placed under stress or required to coordinate he may fail miserably in performance." [192] One wishes that Bloomquist had given some indication as to the source(s) for this statement, since at least two recent experiments show that it is, if not downright false, at least greatly exaggerated. One experimental project concerns the effects of marihuana as compared to alcohol on driving performance as tested by a driving simulator, which has been studied and found to be a valid tester of driving ability.[193] The experimental team found, using a fairly rigorous and systematic procedure of control and double-blind technique, that "subjects experiencing a 'social marihuana high' accumulated significantly more speedometer errors than when under control conditions, whereas there were no significant differences in accelerator, brake, signal, steering, and total errors. The same subjects intoxicated from alcohol accumulated significantly more accelerator, brake, signal, speedometer, and total errors than under normal conditions, whereas there was no significant difference in steering errors." [194] The driving test was 23 minutes long, and included a total of 405 checks, broken down as follows: accelerator — 164; brake — 106; turn signals — 59; steering — 53; speedometer — 23. Because the simulator was so constructed that the driver could not control the rate of the filmed stimuli, the speedometer checks "are not an indication of speeding errors, but of the amount of the time spent monitoring the speedometer." [195] But, as the researchers note, "comments by marihuana users . . . report alteration of time and space perceptions, leading to a different sense of speed which generally results in driving more slowly." [196] Although the selection of subjects was from a group of regular marihuana users (who also were "familiar with the effects of alcohol — there were no teetotalers or chronic alcoholics"), and accordingly the results of the study might seem vulnerable on the grounds that the "nature of selection probably resulted in subjects who preferred marihuana to alcohol and, therefore, had a set to perform better with marihuana," the study effectively eliminated the possibility of any such subject bias. "The main safeguard against bias was that subjects were not told how well they did on any of their driving tests, nor were they acquainted with the specific methods used to determine errors. Thus, it would have been very difficult intentionally and effectively to manipulate error scores." [197] Perhaps the most striking finding of the study was that "simulated driving scores for subjects experiencing a normal social marihuana 'high' and the same subjects under control conditions are not significantly different. However, there are significantly more errors ($P < .01$) for [alcohol] intoxicated than for control subjects (difference of 15.4 percent). . . . the mean error scores of the three treatments [were] . . . control, = 84.46 errors; marihuana, 84.49 errors; and alcohol, 97.44 errors." [198] Another interesting observation was that "Impairment in simulated driving performance does not seem to be a function of increased marihuana dosage or inexperience with the drug." [199] This was suggested by "retesting four subjects after they had smoked approximately three times the amount of marihuana used in the main experiment. None of the subjects showed a significant change in performance. Four additional subjects who had never smoked marihuana before were pretested to obtain control scores, then given marihuana to smoke until they were subjectively 'high' with an associated increase in pulse rate. . . . All subjects showed either no change or negligible improvement in their scores." [200]

Another recent investigation of the effects of marihuana on auditory and visual thresholds states that "The most provocative comment was the frequent report of the ability to 'turn-off' the 'high' at time of stimulus presentation, thus enabling S to perform as in a normal or nondrugged state." In this study many of the subjects

reported the "turn-off" phenomenon to be a *normal* concomitant of the marihuana experience. This apparent ability to turn-off the marihuana "high" during periods requiring short attention spans raises the issue whether such tests (which constitute the majority of those used in studies reported to date) are valid indicants of the marihuana experience or simply measures of an interesting concomitant of the drug's effect, namely, the ability to respond normally at will? Whether this phenomenon is possible only for tasks of short-term duration or would be manifest in sustained performance tests is partially answered in the Weil et al. study (1968) where marihuana users *improved* from baseline levels on digit symbol substitution and pursuit rotor tests, both being more sustained performance tasks than any used in the present study. Furthermore, no performance decrements were observed for a 5-minute continuous performance test following marihuana smoking for either naive or experienced Ss. Moreover, Crancer et al. (1969) have reported no impaired performance for marihuana-intoxicated Ss in a simulated driving condition. All tests, however, were basically meas-

ures of eye-hand coordination, whereas the present study measured pure sensory response data. Since simulated driving is a
relatively complex motor-coordination task and since Crancer's
Ss were administered large doses of marihuana (viz., 1700 mg.
of 1.312% delta⁹-THC concentration) [Δ^1-THC is sometimes
referred to as Δ^9-THC; Δ^9 follows standard chemical abstracts
nomenclature, whereas Δ^1 follows terpene nomenclature which
was used by Mechoulam and Gaoni and which is preferred. See
Chap. 3] the relationship of task type and complexity to level of
intoxication warrants further study.[201]

It seems as accurate as any statement I have read to assert that
whereas cannabis will not provide motivation or incentive, will
not induce one to act, if a habitual or relatively frequent user has
a specific self- or other-assigned task or test or project to carry
out, he will be able to do so as effectively while experiencing a
social marihuana high as he would if he were entirely drug-free,
and, in some cases, he may perform more efficiently or accurately
or effectively. Although he may feel unmotivated, this can usually
be dispelled by outside encouragement or praise for any work
already done and outside enthusiasm for any anticipated project.
However, in spite of the findings of the simulated driving experiment, it is not at all clear that the effects on a nonuser will
not largely prevent him from accomplishing any such task, test,
or project. Also, with increasingly larger doses, the likelihood of
impairment of performance in general is increasingly likely. Since
one of the properties of marihuana is to intensify one's predrug
state of mind,[202] the degree to which one is "set" to perform a
particular activity is crucial.

With regard to the alleged ability of cannabis users to "turn
off" the high, it is interesting that the La Guardia Report stated:
"Just as strong extraneous sensations will bring the sleeper [the
report compares the "high" induced by marihuana to "the twi-
light state between sleeping and waking in which the individual
floats pleasantly and does not allow outside stimuli to impinge"]
face to face with reality, so the insistence of the examiner that the
subject perform certain tasks served to destroy his general feeling
of well-being. Aside from the test situation, any unpleasant circumstances can serve as a 'bring down.' This 'bring down' apparently only results in destroying the subject's pleasure." [203]

Synesthesia is not as frequently reported in the literature on effects and/or properties of marihuana as one might suppose. Bromberg mentions the phenomenon: "A subject suddenly realizes in the midst of a sentence that an unknown quantity of time has passed while he has been speaking. In such a period the author likened the experience to time spent in a vacuum and had at the same time a visual image of himself standing at the edge of an empty chasm. This type of combination of categories of existence, a kind of 'synesthesia,' is not uncommon in hashish intoxication." The link that Bromberg claims to exist between the altered sense of the passage of time and "synesthesia" seems at best rather tenuous, but his definition ("combination of categories of existence"), if recognized by more experimenters and observers, would probably mean that there would be far more reports of synesthesia as a property of the acute intoxication. Walton includes the phenomenon under the general heading "space sense distortion," which seems even more surprising than Bromberg's classification. "Distortion of the space sense is commonly noted and this again is evidently a matter of cortical narcosis. The illusions frequently experienced are probably more intense manifestations of the same effects. Interpretative functions are specially narcotized and the subject 'sees sounds and hears colors.' . . . The drug here is acting in a manner similar to fever toxins which produce delirium." McGlothlin writes that "merging of senses (synesthesia)" is common in cannabis intoxication. One of Robinson's friends reports an experience that probably would be classified as an instance of synesthesia by Bromberg, although it may be that his metaphorical language is getting in the way of an accurate report of his actual experience: "I hear music. . . . The anthem is far away, but in its very faintness there is a lure. In the soft surge and swell of the minor notes there breathes a harmony that ravishes the sense of sound. A resonant organ, with a stop of sapphire and a diapason of opal, diffuses endless octaves from star to star." [204]

One of the most basic questions with regard to the properties of the acute intoxication, and one about which there is considerable dispute, concerns the question of whether it is correct to call the effects of cannabis depressive or stimulating. Aside from the generally recognized soporific effect, typically observed after a period of time no more than three to six hours from the onset of the intoxication, should marihuana be classified as a general stimulant or a general depressant? Walton asserts that "the predominant effect of the drug is depressant and . . . the effect is on the higher centers of the central nervous system." [205] Others agree with Walton, but many assert that the depressant effect occurs only if the smoker is alone. [206] But the majority of writers side with Bloomquist, who writes that "marijuana is a true hallucinogen [which is not, strictly speaking, correct at all] which possesses elements of both stimulation and depression." He attributes the lack of any "specific pattern of behavior" to this. [207] Rosevear asserts that the intoxication comprises both excitation and depression. The American Medical Association stated in 1930 that: "its chief effects are on the central nervous system. There is a mixture of depression and stimulation similar to that occasionally seen under morphine." Robinson quotes Alfred Stillé, comparing alcohol and cannabis: "As the latter [alcohol] . . . excites or depresses, . . . so does the former [cannabis] . . . give rise to even a still greater variety of phenomena." Robinson himself writes that "it primarily stimulates the brain." Lindesmith also compares the "stimulating" effects to those of alcohol, although he notes that "they differ qualitatively from those of alcohol." In the 1868 *Pharmacopoeia* of India, E. J. Waring wrote that the properties of cannabis were "primarily stimulant," but also, secondarily, "anodyne, sedative, and antispasmodic." [208] Various medical reports, especially those written prior to 1937, stress the analgesic effects of cannabis; after 1937 this effect is mentioned, but not emphasized. [209]

The duration of the effects of marihuana, as usually smoked in this country, is from one to three or four hours, in most cases. [210] However, Allentuck and Bowman state that the physical effects of the drug last "for about twelve hours," although they note that the user ordinarily falls asleep after about six hours. [211] If cannabis is ingested, the effects are slower in onset (usually about one hour, but sometimes as long as three or four), and last longer. [212]

Perhaps the last effect to be experienced, which is almost invariable, is somnolence, followed by a sleep that is usually deep and as close to natural sleep as that induced by any drug. [213]

One of the major differences between the cannabis and the alcohol intoxication is the relative absence of any noticeable aftereffects when cannabis is used. Walton notes that Fraenkel and Joël found that: "The recollection of the intoxication is particularly clear." Walton himself writes that "following the episode it often happens that there are no disturbing after-effects and some have declared that they felt keener and more refreshed. With larger doses, some residual effects may persist. . . . There are frequent instances of a mild headache following moderate doses and most every observer is agreed that the recollections are particularly vivid." [214] Although Allentuck and Bowman state that "the aftermath of marihuana intoxication resembles an alcoholic 'hangover,' " they note that "in contrast to alcoholics, marihuana users do not continue their indulgence beyond the point of euphoria, and soon learn to avoid becoming ill by remaining at a pleasurable distance from their maximum capacity for the drug." [215] Most other reports agree that there are no hangover-like effects the following day, and some even report (with Walton) that the subject feels better, and generally feels keener and refreshed.[216] Oursler quotes two users: "I got used to it at Harvard. Now, just like then, it certainly is cheaper than the legitimate theatre, and you are more certain of getting your money's worth. I don't get hangovers, which is a plus"; "Q. You don't have hangovers? A. Not really, but at first, you have this marijuana haze after you go to sleep. You sleep very well." [217] Most authorities are clear in stating that the acutely intoxicated individual has a clear recollection of all that he did or said while under the influence of marihuana, although Gaskill mentions "temporary . . . amnesia" as one of the effects.[218] However, the La Guardia Report states that "both the subject and the examiner felt that the drug produced a 'hang-over' which in most cases continued into the following day. The subject complained of being headachy, sleepy, and unable to work at his usual level, and the examiner also noted that the subject did not work as well or as quickly when called upon to do something on a day following marihuana ingestion." [219] It should be noted that this statement concerns ingested, not smoked marihuana. Smoking enables the experienced user to regulate his intake more exactly so as to avoid any hangover; furthermore, there may be some as yet unknown factor involved in the absorption of orally ingested marihuana that is more apt to cause a hangoverlike effect.

It may be helpful at this point to summarize some of the most commonly observed properties of the acute intoxication. Most writers agree that the effects from smoking marihuana are usually noticed within ten to thirty minutes and last for two to four hours, while the effects from ingestion may take from thirty minutes to an hour to become noticeable, and may last anywhere from five to twelve hours. The initial reaction may be one of anxiety and agitation, especially if the user is inexperienced or if the setting in which the drug is taken is not supportive. Fear of death or vague sense of distress sometimes occur, but the presence of supportive friends often helps to alleviate these anxieties in the new user. Experienced users may also feel anxious, but not infrequently they describe it in paradoxically positive terms such as, for example, "happy anxiety." It is still anxiety, but somehow it has a desirable quality to it. Soon the user feels more calm and relaxed and begins to experience a sense of euphoria or high. Often this feeling of elation and well-being comes in waves alternating with periods of almost dreamlike repose. Somatic sensations too are high; generally the user is slightly dizzy and light-headed; his body feels weightless, often with a floating sensation; walking is effortless. On some occasions, however, the head and limbs feel heavy, and there is an unpleasant sensation of pressure in the head. Although some users find the euphoria merely a calm and blissful state, hilarity and uncontrollable laughter are not uncommon. Frequently the stimulus to a contagion of mirth is minimal and is quickly forgotten. Users find that their thoughts dart quickly in and out of awareness and associations become freer.

There are, of course, users who engage in serious conversation and study while high. In fact W. C. Burroughs claims to have written much of *The Naked Lunch* while high. Often there is the impression of great clarity and importance of thought, but attempts to convey this either verbally or through writing generally fail.

Along with the sense of acceleration of thought, there is a heightened sensitivity to external stimuli. And while there is a sense of attention flitting from one topic to another, there is at the same time higher focusing and concentration on details that would ordinarily be overlooked. Macropsia is occasionally reported; more common is micropsia. Colors may seem brighter, and new qualities and hues may be seen. Works of art which previously had little or no meaning now say something of value to the viewer. It is claimed that there is a similar enhancement in the appreciation of music. Many jazz musicians claim to perform better under the influence of marihuana, but this has not been objectively confirmed.

Perhaps related to the sense of acceleration of thought is a distorted sense of time. Most commonly time seems to stretch out so that ten minutes seems like an hour, and there is ample time for thought between the notes of a piece of music. Occasionally a user will have a sense of two different simultaneous meters of time. This is closely related to what has been described as "double consciousness." The user experiences the high and is at the same time an objective observer of his own intoxication. It is perhaps this quality of being able to remain at least in part objective about the intoxication that allows many experienced users to train themselves to act perfectly sober in public despite the fact that they may be quite high. Paranoid thoughts are not uncommon to some users while getting high (see Chap. 10); curiously, these users, while seeing the thoughts are paranoid, may at the same time laugh or scoff or even in a sense enjoy the paranoid ideation. For others the paranoid thoughts may be quite frightening.

The physical signs and symptoms of cannabis intoxication are few and usually not marked, and this is one of the reasons why it is difficult to make this diagnosis. There is, it seems certain now, no dilatation of the pupils but there may be slight tremors and ataxia (see Chap. 3). Perhaps the most noticeable sign is injection of the conjunctivae. The user often experiences dryness of the mouth and throat with consequent thirst. Occasionally nausea, vomiting, and diarrhea occur, but these are more frequently associated with the ingestion than with the smoking of cannabis. An invariable physiological effect is a significant increase in pulse rate and a very common and striking symptom is hunger. There is something special about the sense of hunger, however, in that it involves an exquisite appreciation of food so that the user may approach an ordinary dish with much the same anticipation and appreciation as a gourmet relishes a very special culinary treat.

Before leaving the topic of the acute intoxication, it may be of value to compare cannabis with other drugs which are generally classified as "hallucinogens." Among these other drugs are LSD (d-lysergic acid diethylamide), peyote, mescaline, and psilocybin, the "hallucinogens" about which most is known. There are, however, newer synthetic ones which have recently been developed and about which less is known; many are powerful "hallucinogenics." They include STP (2,5-dimethoxy-4-methylamphetamine), sometimes called DOM. A substance developed by the Dow Chemical Company, it first hit the streets in the summer of 1967 and developed a reputation for "bad trips." This substance is illicitly distributed in tablet form generally of 9-mg strength, but apparently 3 mg is the amount suggested for a "trip." DMT (N,N-dimethyltryptamine) and the closely related substance DET (N, N-diethyltryptamine) are also manufactured in clandestine laboratories. Both are mixed with tobacco and then smoked; the average street dose is 200 to 300 mg per cigarette. Another is DPT (dipropyltryptamine). Aside from the fact that it is apparently a clandestinely manufactured "hallucinogen," little is known about it at this time. PCP (phencyclidine hydrochloride) is a prescription veterinary drug manufactured by Parke-Davis and Co. under the trade name of Sernyl. It is an injectible anesthetic for primates and is currently being manufactured in underground laboratories as a "hallucinogen"; the street dosage is 15 mg. It is also known as "the peace pill" and sometimes sold as synthetic marihuana. MDA (3,4-methylenedioxyamphetamine) is another substance developed by Dow Chemical Co. and now produced in clandestine laboratories. Street dosage is about 150 milligrams per capsule. Some varieties of morning glory seeds contain lysergic acid amidelike alkaloids, derivatives which apparently have about one-tenth the potency of LSD. A tea or brew may be prepared from the seeds or they may simply be chewed. There are other "hallucinogens," some of which are just beginning to be experimented with, such as Hawaiian Woodrose and nutmeg, and now there are reports of dried seahorses and small starfish being ingested to produce a new type of "trip." [220]

Cannabis sativa is often classified as a mild "hallucinogen" even though hallucinations of any type are by no means an invariable consequence of the intoxication and are only one of the many effects the drug may produce. In fact there is a serious question whether these phenomena, which are usually referred to as such, should be considered to be true hallucinations.

Baudelaire was perhaps the first person to make the distinction between true or "pure" hallucinations and the "hallucinations" induced by hashish. Clinically speaking, a hallucination is a perception of an object, person, place, and so on, that has no analogue, no causative equivalent, in the "external," "real" world that we all must assume we share and must believe is revealed to us through our perceptions. In other words, a true hallucination is spontaneous in the sense that there is no discoverable relationship between anything in the immediate environment and what is "seen" by the individual. A person with a perceptual disorder may experience a true visual or auditory hallucination but, in nearly all the literary reports of "hallucinations" (excepting perhaps some of Ludlow's), there is a stimulus of some sort, which a person not under the influence of any drug could perceive, which forms the basis, the starting point, the primer, for the "hallucination." Moreover, hashish-type "hallucinations," as reported by Baudelaire, Gautier, and others, almost invariably have a progressive nature; they do not occur without premonition, but rather have a gradual onset, and there is almost always at least an element of volition, of *willing* the "hallucination" to develop further, of allowing the imagination to "go where it will," which is not seen in the true, clinical instances of hallucinations. "Sounds may seem to say strange things, but there always was a sound in the first place. Strange shapes may be seen, but before becoming strange the shapes were . . . [perceived as] natural. *Hashish,* in short, may distort but it does not create that which is not there." [221]

S. Cohen notes that almost any drug, "if ingested in sufficient quantities by a person sensitive to its effects, can produce a delirium." He described a delirium as a "confusional state marked by disorientation, delusional thinking and hallucinations." He means "pure" or true hallucinations, and he therefore objects to the use of the term "hallucinogen" as it is commonly applied to drugs that have effects quite different from mere stimulation, sedation, or even delirium, and which involve "other, more interesting dimensions of awareness." He suggests the term "pseudohallucinogens" for these drugs, but recognizes it is awkward and too long. He might have added that it also has some disadvantageous connotations; that is, that the state induced by these drugs is somehow less real, is to be taken less seriously, is more artificial, is more a subjectively induced state than that occurring in true hallucinations. He thinks that "illusinogen" is a more accurate term, but doubts that it will be adopted. He carries the point made by Baudelaire a step further, claiming that the phenomena generated by what he would prefer to have called something like "illusinogen" are perceived but evaluated by the perceiver as "fictitious," unreal, not really "out there." An illusion, as he uses the term, is merely "an error in seeing based upon some sensory cue — for example, a crack on the wall which is identified as a snake." He states that most LSD-induced "visual phenomena" are of this sort — an "elaboration of something 'out there' into a misperception." [222]

Cohen also mentions the term "psychotomimetic" which, as he notes, is found most frequently in scientific and medical reports, although there seems to be a tendency away from this usage. The term was first applied because researchers thought that the group of drugs so distinguished actually "mimicked" psychoses when the first close studies were begun, but subsequent work has shown several important differences between clinical cases of endogenous psychoses and those states induced by drugs. "Mysticomimetic" is another term sometimes suggested; as are "phantasticant," "psychoticant," "psychotogen," and "schizogen." [223] Cohen suggests that the unlikely term "psychotomystic" may be the most appropriate term insofar as it covers "the gamut of possible response forms." He notes that Osmond's choice of "psychedelic" (from the Greek, meaning "mind-manifesting") was an attempt to avoid any of the connotations of mental illness that most of the other choices carry.[224] However, "hallucinogen" is the term most commonly employed nowadays, and it seems likely to continue to be the term of choice. In this volume, whenever "hallucination" or "hallucinogen" is surrounded by quotation marks, the indication is that the mental state or substance is hallucinatory or hallucinogenic only in the special sense already described.

Many of the phenomena associated with LSD and LSD-type substances can be produced by cannabis. With LSD the wavelike aspect of the experience is often reported, as is the distorted perception of various parts of the body, spatial and temporal distortion, and depersonalization. Other phenomena commonly associated with both types of drugs are increased sensitivity to sound, synesthesia, heightened suggestibility, and a sense of thinking more clearly and having deeper awareness of the meaning of things. Anxiety and paranoid reactions are also sometimes seen as a consequence of either drug.

While it is clear that cannabis has much in common with the other "hallucinogens," it is equally clear that there are important differences between it and such drugs as LSD, peyote, mescaline, psilocybin, DMT, and so forth. For one thing the effects of these latter drugs are longer lasting. Perhaps of equal importance is the fact that cannabis is especially amenable to control, so that desired effects can usually be titrated when smoked. Michaux, in exploring his own reactions to a number of "hallucinogens," writes, "Compared to other hallucinogenic drugs, hashish is feeble, without great range, but easy to handle, convenient, repeatable, without immediate danger." [225] This ability to titrate the amount of marihuana and the motivation of the user to control the high is borne out by the La Guardia Report. When the subjects were given the extract orally, the effect could not be accurately controlled, and although euphoria was the most commonly reported experience, the subjects also demonstrated anxiety, irritability, and antagonism. On the other hand, when the experienced subjects smoked marihuana, they carefully limited the intake to produce the desired high. Though they were offered more cigarettes, they refused more than was necessary to maintain a "euphoric state with its feeling of well-being, contentment, sociability, mental and physical relaxation, which usually ended in a feeling of drowsiness." [226] Thus the agonizingly nightmarish reactions which even the experienced LSD user may endure are quite rare to the experienced marihuana smoker, not simply because he is using a far less potent drug, but also because he has much closer and *continuing* control over the extent and type of reaction he wishes to induce.

Before leaving the comparison of cannabis with other "hallucinogens," some other differences should be noted, some of which make it possible for experienced drug takers to distinguish with ease between the effects of the two types of drugs. Cannabis has a tendency to produce sedation, whereas LSD and the LSD-type drugs may induce long periods of wakefulness and even restlessness. Unlike LSD, marihuana does not dilate the pupils nor materially heighten blood pressure, reflexes, and body temperature. On the other hand, it is more likely to increase the pulse rate (see Chap. 3). Marihuana only infrequently and in doses larger than those ordinarily used in this country produces even the type of "hallucinations" described above, and it is highly questionable whether it can produce true hallucinations. A very important difference is the fact that tolerance rapidly develops with the LSD-type drugs, but not at all with cannabis. Finally, there is the most important fact that marihuana lacks the potent consciousness-altering qualities of LSD, peyote, mescaline, psilocybin, and so on. These differences, particularly the last, cast considerable doubt on marihuana's credentials for inclusion in this group.

6 Motivation of the User

Cannabis has a long history of ceremonial use in religion in some primitive tribes of Africa and South America, as well as in India, where legal restrictions do not necessitate concealment and where cannabis is still used to a considerable degree as an indigenous medicine. In fact, one contemporary Indian author has pleaded that cannabis continue to be available to the Ayurvedic practitioners, for whom it is an important part of the traditional armamentarium, at least until the use of modern drugs is introduced to the villages.[1] Moreover, cannabis, usually in the form of *bhang* or *ganja*, is frequently taken by laborers at the end of the day to alleviate fatigue. I. C. and R. N. Chopra note that this results in a 50-percent increase in cannabis consumption in certain parts of India during the harvest season. They write that "a common practice amongst laborers engaged in building or excavation work is to have a few pulls at a ganja pipe or to drink a glass of bhang toward the evening. This produces a sense of well-being, relieves fatigue, stimulates the appetite, and induces a feeling of mild stimulation which enables the worker to bear more cheerfully the strain of the daily routine of life."[2] Writing in 1913, C. J. G. Bourhill stated that *dagga* smoking was not only permitted, but actually encouraged, among African mine workers because "after a smoke the natives work hard and show very little fatigue." The usual mine practice was to allow three smokes a day.[3] R. P. Walton noted that the same practice is or was "traditional in the Southwest and in Mexico . . . laborers will usually work better if allowed a moderate amount of the drug. They perform their duties with fair effectiveness and say they do not 'feel work.' "[4] Thus, for many people around the world the importance of cannabis as an intoxicant, per se, is apparently secondary to its use as a ceremonial adjunct, a folk medicine, and a refreshing tonic.

In North America there is no recognized religious practice that makes ceremonial use of cannabis. The primary psychoactive drug widely used as an integral part of religious expression in the United States today is alcohol. Wine is used to symbolize the blood of Christ in the Roman Catholic and the Eastern Orthodox masses and in some Protestant communion services (e.g., Episcopal). The only other psychoactive drug that plays a vital part in an established religion in the United States today is peyote (mescaline).[5]

The attraction to marihuana as a folk medicine and tonic by the downtrodden in the United States is suggested in survey studies conducted from the mid-twenties through the forties. In New Orleans in 1926 a group of reporters became interested in the widespread use of marihuana among Negro dock workers and undertook to get first-hand information. They were frequently told "that marihuana made them [the workers] feel better and work better providing they didn't smoke too much at one time." [6] That people whose lives are oppressed and dreary may be more motivated toward the use of cannabis is further supported by the fact that until fairly recently in this country most of the marihuana was consumed by ghetto Negroes, Puerto Ricans, and people of Mexican origin. The preponderance of use among Negroes is supported by four studies (all conducted in the mid-forties) that demonstrated that 87 percent or more of users in the Army were Negro.[7]

One study of 310 marihuana users in the United States Army attempted to determine why the soldiers used marihuana. Two hundred eleven were frequent users, 75 were occasional users, and 24 merely tried marihuana once or twice. Many of the frequent users indicated that they smoked it because it was "like whiskey," and some said that they smoked only when they could not get liquor. Others stated that they used it because it gave them "a good feeling." Other comments from this group were: "I feel bad all the time — weeds make me feel better." "I feel good and don't care." From the group where use was considered occasional, typical comments were: "I used it sometimes for the kick of it, occasionally to feel high and good." "Makes you feel good once in a while." "Off and on when I can't get whiskey." Most of the comments from the smaller group of soldiers whose use was limited to one trial indicated that smoking marihuana had made them sick; they were not inclined to try it again. The frequent and occasional users often mentioned the medicinal uses ascribed to marihuana, usually the relief of some kind of pain — often headaches. Many used it for their "nervous system." One soldier said, "Because I been nervous all my life; anything for my nerves. Reefers make me feel fine. My headaches stop, and I can remember good. I know what I'm doing then." Another asserted: "It makes me sleep and eases my pain." [8]

Many responses from this group suggest that some sort of psychic pain is relieved by marihuana: "I feel high and good." "I feel like I own everything." "It makes me feel like I'm a man; it springs me up. Without it I'm beat." "It normally gets your worries off your mind." "I feel like I don't give a damn if the world was turning." "Makes you feel alive." "I feel drunkified and happy." Of this frequent type of response, H. L. Freedman and M. J. Rockmore say, "[They] reflect some of the personality inadequacies for which compensation is obtained in the fantasy enjoyed under the influence of marihuana. Repeatedly there is an expression of an inability to cope with everyday problems of living. The use of marihuana apparently either supplies the means of escape or provides the expedient which closes the breach between this overwhelming reality and the individual's wish." [9] This suggests that some persons may use the drug in an attempt to deal with personal inadequacies and frustrations and also to cope with anxiety and depression, with or without somatic symptoms.

What motivates people to use cannabis in the United States today is, as one would expect, an extraordinarily complicated question. Like many other forms of human behavior, it is multidetermined: many different motives act and interact in concert to produce it. And as with other behaviors, cannabis use is influenced not only by drives and conflicts within the individual (many of which are unconscious), but also by the individual's experience of what is "outside" him — his relationships with people who matter to him and, in a broader sense, his relations in a shared social and political world.

In a recent study of 54 white, middle-class college graduates, all of whom were between the ages of 18 and 30 and were either psychiatric in- or out-patients, curiosity and the desire to "go along" with friends were cited as the major motivation for the initial marihuana experience. Forty of them continued to use marihuana, and of these, 65 percent said that they sought primarily to relax, to feel good, to forget their worries, to get relief from tension and inhibitions, and to experience a state in which they could "blow off steam." Eighty-five percent of them reported that they experienced a greater sense of well-being than they could with alcohol. Those who used marihuana as an intoxicant believed that it was superior to alcohol for many reasons: it was less expensive; the high, although different, was better than that induced by alcohol; it was quicker to act than alcohol; the effects wore off more rapidly; it did not cause a hangover. Several subjects said that they used marihuana to heighten perception, and two stated that their principal motivation was to experience the enhanced fluidity of mental associations produced by marihuana. Others said their principal interest in the drug was as a means of helping them to gain insight into their own psychological problems. A few were seeking a mystical experience, and some were primarily interested in the "hallucinogenic" or psychotomimetic effects. It is interesting to note why 14 of the 54 did not continue to use marihuana or confined their use to a few puffs and then only if the drug was offered to them. Three of these subjects had unpleasant experiences, either anxiety or depression. Four users who had enjoyed the marihuana intoxication stopped using the drug because they had become adherents of the teachings of Meher Baba, an Eastern religious leader who opposes the use of all drugs. Four discontinued, not because of any unpleasant experience, but simply because they did not find marihuana particularly enjoyable. Two, who found the effects quite pleasant, decided that the pleasure was not sufficient to balance their reservations about the use of drugs. But only one stopped because of the legal risks involved.[10]

Much of the increased use of marihuana has occurred on and near the campus, and it has aroused the most intense feelings. Generally speaking, this concern does not distinguish between marihuana and the "hallucinogenic," psychedelic, or psychotomimetic drugs like LSD (d-lysergic acid diethylamide), psilocybin (the active substance in the Mexican "sacred" mushroom), mescaline (the active ingredient in peyote), DMT (N,N-dimethyltryptamine), DET (N,N-diethyltryptamine), and STP (2,5-dimethoxy-4-methyl-amphetamine). The different drugs are lumped together as are the individuals who use them, even though different people use different drugs for diverse reasons and under a wide range of sets and settings and to varying degrees. Although it is true that student drug use is rapidly increasing, the widely believed estimates that half of the seven million college students in the United States have used or are using these drugs are grossly exaggerated — at least for the present. However, I believe that drug use may very well reach the every-other-student rate, perhaps sooner than we expect. In a most recent (1970) survey conducted by the Becker Research Corporation, 48 percent of college students at five colleges in Boston admitted to having smoked marihuana during the past year, and fully 60 percent of these students stated that they used it occasionally or frequently. When they were asked to express an opinion about the extent of marihuana smoking, their estimates were even higher than the admissions; their impression is that more than half of their number have experimented with marihuana.[11] The widespread impression that enormous numbers of American college youths are using marihuana and "hallucinogens" derives from the fact that there are high rates of drug use in those colleges which are most visible; the Boston colleges are among these. K. Keniston points out that the correlation between the "intellectual climate" of a college and the rate of drug use on its campus is very close. The highest rates are found at small, progressive liberal arts colleges with a high faculty-student ratio, high student intellectual capacity as measured by College Boards, close student-faculty relationships, and considerable value on academic independence, intellectual interest, and personal freedom for students.[12] At a number of such colleges, it is probably true that half or more of the students have tried marihuana or one of the "hallucinogens," but the great majority of the nation's 2,200 colleges have a lower intellectual climate, are often noted for their practical orientation, a relative absence of serious student intellectual pursuit, and an emphasis on fraternity life and sports. It is estimated that between 10 and 25 percent of the students on such campuses use these drugs.[13]

Within any school there is likely to be a concentration of drug users in the traditionally humanistic fields such as history, music, art, literature, and psychology. Conversely, fewer drug users are found in the more practical applied departments like business and engineering. A survey conducted at one liberal arts college indicated there is evidence that students who use drugs also get higher grades than those who do not. As Keniston points out, "The demographic evidence suggests a strong relationship between intellectuality and drug use within the college population." He believes that some schools, those with more "intellectual climate," attract those students whose character make-up is such that they are potential drug users and then expose them to a milieu which enhances the probability that they will use drugs.[14]

A student who enters a drug-using campus climate usually soon experiences pressure, sometimes subtle, sometimes overt, to try these drugs, particularly marihuana. One obvious source of pressure is the fact that so many of his friends use pot; not to use it is deviant within the context of the group that matters to the student. He wants to be part of the youth "scene," a subculture in which marihuana use may be one of a number of expected patterns of behavior (e.g., adopting certain preferences in music and clothes). While this use, viewed from a larger social perspective, may seem alienating, it is in fact in the service of the gratification of a particularly urgent adolescent need, that of belonging. How many parents of these same young people took their first drinks of liquor, whose taste and effects they may have found unpleasant, out of similar kinds of pressures? Furthermore, despite all the dreadful things he may have heard about marihuana, the student discovers that, for example, a much-liked, sophisticated roommate, or an admired, brilliant English major who writes good poetry, or a friend who has made the tennis team all use pot without any deleterious effects that he has been able to observe.

Of those students who decide to try marihuana, probably relatively few confine their experience to one or even several trials. For one thing, the initiate is told by the pot cognoscente that he will very probably experience little, if anything, on his first trial, and that he may have to smoke a number of times before experiencing a high. After initial experimentation with marihuana, students may become occasional users or frequent users or "potheads." The occasional or casual user is one who smokes irregularly and generally only as a result of someone else's having provided him with the opportunity. The frequent or "social" user is one who smokes two or three times a week or only on weekends, but not necessarily every weekend, and who, while he plans to continue to use marihuana, has by no means oriented his life around it. If he were to decide to give it up, he would not consider it a great deprivation. On the other hand the "pot-head" has made marihuana an important part of his life. He is more likely to be interested in experimenting with LSD, DMT, mescaline, STP, and so forth; sometimes he is even willing to experiment with an altogether new drug that he knows little or nothing about. It is within this group that a fair amount of psychopathology exists, frequently in the same forms for which drug use is most dangerous, such as severe depression, marked anxiety, some form of cognitive disturbance, or depersonalization. In a small number of students, disturbances such as these undoubtedly play a part in motivation to use the drug, on the one hand, and enhance the risk of its use, on the other.

The "social" user is likely to be intellectual, introspective, hardworking, and a better-than-average student. He often comes from an upper-middle-class background and commonly is much more concerned than his parents with any one of a number of urgent social and political issues. As Keniston points out, "They are not in any systematic way 'alienated' from American society, but they have not really made their minds up whether it is worth joining, either." [15] More important than grades is the search for truth and meaningful experience. Cannabis provides a new domain of experience for them; it heightens (or so they assert) their capacity to feel, to appreciate, to perceive, and to share. It often provides an increased sense of self-awareness, which is very important to these students. They seem remarkably sensitive to the war in Southeast Asia, the draft, the facts of the arms race, overpopulation, poverty, racial injustice, and pollution — issues that promote a gnawing anxiety within them. Cannabis may periodically provide relief from this burden. It may also provide some measure of intermittent relief from the enormous pressures which many of today's students experience, particularly at the better schools, as they try to cope with the problems of having to master much more information and material than their predecessors of just a few decades. Of course, this anxiety may be more in the nature of a displacement from some unconscious conflict, but regardless of its ultimate origin, pot may provide the student with a much-needed respite from his disquieting feelings. Similarly, depression, most frequently of the reactive type, is associated with the beginning or increased use of marihuana. A major loss frequently precedes a period of intensified use of cannabis. This loss may be of self-esteem following examinations or a break-up with a girlfriend, or it may be the loss of old and cherished life-orienting values which the student felt compelled to abandon in his often lonely search for truth and meaning. During such periods, which are generally self-limited, the promise of euphoric escape will increase his interest in the use of marihuana. It is important, however, not to think of everyone who uses marihuana as having some kind of problem. In fact, a very strong case could be made on some campuses today, that if a young man goes through four years of college without having tried marihuana, his abstinence is suggestive of a rigidity in his character structure and a fear of his impulses that can hardly be considered desirable.

If a student is more troubled, he is more likely to use marihuana frequently and to experiment with other drugs, as well, particularly the "hallucinogens." Those students for whom drug use becomes the central focal point of life and whose friends and activities are largely determined by their relationship to the use of drugs are known as "pot-heads" or "heads." Keniston describes the "head" as follows:

> heads are genuinely alienated from American society. Their defining characteristic is their generalized rejection of prevalent American values, which they criticize largely on cultural and humanistic grounds. American society is trashy, cheap and commercial; it "dehumanizes" its members; its values of success, materialism, monetary accomplishments and achievement undercut more important spiritual values. Such students rarely stay involved for long in the political and social causes that agitate many of their activist classmates. For alienated students, the basic societal problem is not so much political as aesthetic. Rejecting middle-class values, heads repudiate as well those conventional values and rules that deem experimentation with drugs illicit. For heads, the goal is to find a way out of the "air-conditioned nightmare" of American society. What matters is the interior world, and, in the exploration of that world, drugs play a major role.[16]

The "pot-heads" constitute a subculture that is infatuated with the mystique of the pot experience. They create a sense of mutuality among themselves as they become alienated from many of their fellow students, the faculty, and the administration.

For most, this movement into the drug-using "hippie" subculture is limited to a few months, or, at the most, a year or so. Probably the greatest risk these young people expose themselves to during this period of time is that of being labeled and apprehended as a felon, and it is this which most jeopardizes their otherwise probable, gradual reentry into the more conventional world of accomplishment and commitment. Before the war in Southeast Asia escalated, with the resultant increased draft calls of the late 1960's, "dropping out" usually meant leaving school, most often for a term or a year, and very often, but not always, exploring the "hippie" subculture. Under the pressure of the draft, students who otherwise would have "dropped out" remained in school, often to "drop out" in spirit if not in body. In the process they brought a flavor of the "hippie" subculture and attitude toward drugs to the campus.

The importance of boredom must also be considered in any discussion of motivation for marihuana use. Especially in the late adolescent, boredom may reflect a maladaptive control of unacceptable sexual and aggressive impulses. Some seek relief in drugs from the tension and boredom that result from unsuccessful sublimation of these impulses. There may also be heightened interest in danger, travel, unusual modes of expression through words, music, and clothes, and the need to experience contact with the mainstream of society primarily through friction and opposition.

In an attempt to determine their motivation for using marihuana, D. L. Farnsworth interviewed numerous college students during the summer of 1967. The reasons the students gave included curiosity, the acquiring of a sense of group identification, pressure from friends, and the search for a symbol of their defiance toward adult authority. In connection with the last-cited reason, it was important for most that their parents knew that they were using the drug, and several stated that their parents' belief that the drug was harmful was only one example of parental hypocrisy.[17]

Although much is made of the use of marihuana as an act of defiance against older generations, it is much more than simple defiance. It is an identification with, a modeling after, a generation that has legitimized the taking of drugs. The miracle of modern medicine seemed to provide a solution to every problem in the form of a prescription, and in fact 70 percent of prescriptions are for psychoactive substances. The quarrel is not that the younger people take drugs, but what drugs they choose.

To carry this one step further, to some extent, at least, young people are acting out some of the repressed unconscious wishes of their parents. It is a well-known psychoanalytic fact that parents may — not explicitly of course — communicate their own unconscious wishes to their progeny and achieve some measure of gratification through their offsprings' acting out of these wishes, while at the same time the parents consciously condemn such behavior. Accordingly, it is not surprising that one of the concerns uppermost in many parents' minds is that marihuana leads to antisocial behavior and sexual promiscuity.

There are some persons for whom the drug experience, particularly the use of more potent "hallucinogens" like LSD, represents a kind of "proving oneself." It is not unlike the game of "chicken," but instead of testing oneself against the fear of a high-speed head-on collision with another automobile, the "contest" is an internal one which tests one's ability to come as close as possible to a psychotic "crash" or even go over the line and then to return unscathed. It is doubtful that even fairly large amounts of smoked marihuana can be used in this way, but it is certainly possible with the more potent "hallucinogens." Such drug use is a kind of Russian roulette, and just as games like "chicken" are played by young men who, at least at this time of their lives, have a lot of uncertainty about their manliness, so one wonders if the use of "hallucinogens" suggests the user's uneasiness with respect to his mental health. Unfortunately, as I have already indicated, it may be just these people for whom such drugs are both a manifestation and precipitant of serious psychopathology.

Today's students in general have less interest and commitment to past traditions than students before them, and they are at the same time profoundly uncertain about their future. Their sense of being adrift, isolated, and powerless, which this lack of connection with a relatively stable past and future generates, is experienced as a vague anxiety by some. Activity, particularly that which at least unconsciously has some palliative meaning with respect to the source of the anxiety, is the most immediate way of dealing with it. For many who experience this sense, political and social activism is the most healthy and successful adaptation.

Others find their solution in focusing on the present, on the here and now. If the past is irrelevant and the future is ominous, one's meaningfulness must be found within the immediate context of one's own present experience. But in fact it is not just found; it is created largely from within. Such experiences as encounter groups, transcendental meditation, sensitivity training, psychotherapy, and, to some extent, sexual exploration, are all means toward this end. What better catalyst than cannabis and/or the "hallucinogens"?

In a similar vein, as the external world becomes more crowded, and consequently both esthetically less interesting and more restricting, there may be increased interest in exploring facets of the internal world. As experiencing the physical world comes more and more to mean bumper-to-bumper travel through neon corridors and foul air to beaches slicked with oil and cesspools that were once rivers and lakes, the attraction to a fantasy of internal travel to new experiences becomes more compelling.

Just as with other behavior, individual wishes and needs are often counterbalanced by various kinds of social controls. Where the use of cannabis is concerned, these controls are rapidly changing. Valued or esteemed behavior is rewarded, and bad or negatively valued behavior is punished in one way or another. How good or how bad an activity is judged is to a large extent communicated by people who are highly regarded. Whereas just a decade or two ago it would have been impossible to find any such person who would not have condemned cannabis, the situation is not the same today. Many teachers whom students most admire openly acknowledge using marihuana, and in fact students and faculty sometimes smoke together. In the past, in order for a person to begin to use marihuana, he ordinarily had to participate in a group which he considered criminal or deviant. But it is now fairly readily available to him, most often through fellow students. In fact, not long ago marihuana users were secret deviants. Today, because many of the people the novice knows and respects use the drug, the concept of deviance exerts little pressure against its use. Initiates no longer fear that nonusers who discover that they are users will in some way punish or exclude them.

What, then, does act to discourage or inhibit people from the continued use of drugs? Already there is evidence that less LSD is being used today than a few years ago. Students relate this decrease to their learning about reports of the possible chromosomal damage and other deleterious effects which began to be published several years ago. (A recent study of the alleged chromosome-damaging effects, however, suggests that these early findings may have been in error.)[18] Whatever else drug use among young people may represent, it is not, except in rare cases, a conscious wish for self-destruction, and most will respond to credible evidence of significant danger to a particular drug. Despite the continued mass media advertising and the obstructionism of the tobacco lobby, education about the very real dangers of cigarette smoking gained momentum in the late 1960's, and it is estimated that two to three million Americans have given up smoking. What has apparently not been effective with respect to drug use, any more than it was with respect to alcohol during prohibition, is the threat of severe punishment. It may make the determined drug user more clandestine in his activities and may make him pay more for the drugs he wishes to use. It may make the quality and the exact quantity of the drugs he uses less certain. The threat of incarceration may make him more anxious and distrustful, but for the most part it has not and will not deter him from drug use.

7 Turning On

One of the basic and still unsettled questions about the cannabis experience concerns exactly what occurs when a person "turns on" for the first time. This question arises mainly because it is almost invariably true that the first time, or the first few times, a person smokes marihuana, he experiences no psychic change.[1] As far as he is concerned, he might as well be smoking seaweed. A. Weil et al. refer to the puzzling phenomenon that many if not all people do not become high on their first exposure to marihuana even if they smoke it correctly; this phenomenon, they point out, can be discussed from either a physiological or psychosocial point of view.[2] The sociological approach is perhaps best detailed in H. S. Becker's *Outsiders: Studies in the Sociology of Deviance.* He states that psychological attempts to explain why a person becomes a user of marihuana rely on "the premise that the presence of any particular kind of behavior in an individual can best be explained as the result of some trait which predisposes or motivates him to engage in that behavior. In the case of marihuana use, this trait is usually identified as psychological, as a need for fantasy and escape from psychological problems the individual cannot face." [3] He cites a number of articles which assume or state such a premise as examples of this approach.[4] But Becker believes that these types of psychological approaches are neither sufficient nor necessary to account for the phenomenon of *learning* to use marihuana for *pleasure.* Two points should be emphasized here. First, Becker considers that the entire sequence of events (which he claims was consistent in all his 50 interviewed users) marking the transition for any particular person from initial "vague impulses and desires" or simple curiosity to steady or habitual use of marihuana comprises a definite *learning process,* in which there are three distinct stages.

Second, he concentrates on the "lower" of the two "castes" which Bloomquist claims have evolved with "the entrance of the intellectual into the cannabis drug community," the "caste" including all users who simply "trip," that is, experience "the bizarre effect of the drug for the effect alone." He ignores the "upper caste," members of which "take the drug to 'maintain' and to explore themselves and the infinite. To 'maintain' . . . is to defer the enjoyment of the pleasurable effects of the drug and to utilize the experience to better understand one's inner self and rid oneself of his 'hangups.' " [5] Becker is solely concerned with the process by which a person arrives at the point where he "answers 'Yes' to the question: 'Is it [marihuana smoking] . . . fun?' " [6] He rejects all psychological theories because (1) they are "based on the existence of some predisposing psychological trait . . . [but] have difficulty in accounting for that group of users . . . who do not exhibit the trait or traits which are considered to cause the behavior," [7] and (2) they cannot account "for the great variability over time of a given individual's behavior with reference to the drug. The same person will at one time be unable to use the drug for pleasure, at a later stage be able and willing to do so. . . . These changes, difficult to explain from a theory based on the user's needs for 'escape' are readily understandable as consequences of changes in his conception of the drug." [8] Becker enumerates three discrete, consecutive phases through which the initially "curious, . . . ignorant, . . . and . . . [often] afraid" individual passes as he becomes "willing and able to use the drug for pleasure." [9] The first step is learning the technique, and, according to Becker, this learning is a direct function of the individual's participation in a group using marihuana, members of which are able to instruct him in the correct techniques for inhaling, and so on, in order to introduce into his bloodstream a "sufficient dosage for the effects of the drug to appear." [10]

Next, the new user must learn to perceive the effects. Getting "high consists of two elements: the presence of symptoms caused by marihuana use and the recognition of these symptoms and their connection by the user with his use of the drug." This second learning process takes place because "typically . . . the novice has faith (developed from his observations of users who do get high) that the drug actually will produce some new experience and continues to experiment with it until it does. . . . One symptom of being high is an intense hunger." [11] Becker relates part of a case history in which the neophyte became high only after he became aware of his intense hunger and gorging of food, and he became aware of this only when it was pointed out to him by members of the group with which he was smoking.[12] "The novice, . . . eager to have this feeling, picks up from other users some concrete referents of the term 'high' and applies these notions to his own experience. The new concepts make it possible for him to locate these symptoms among his own sensations and to point out to himself a 'something different' in his experience that he connects with drug use. It is only when he can do this that he is high. . . . for use to continue, it is necessary not only to use the drug so as to produce effects but also to learn to perceive these effects." [13] Becker cites two kinds of evidence at this juncture: (1) those who are or "become heavy users of alcohol, barbiturates, or opiates cease to experiment with marihuana, because they are not able to differentiate the effects of the cannabis from those of the other drugs"; (2) if — and this is relatively rare — a novice begins to use marihuana almost constantly so that "he is always high, he is apt to feel the drug has no effect on him," since he has no psychic base-line for comparing with his perpetual high state in order to perceive the essential qualities of being high. "In such a situation, use is likely to be given up completely, but temporarily, in order that the user may once again be able to perceive the difference." [14]

Finally, the potential user must learn to enjoy the effects that he has previously learned to perceive. "Marihuana-produced sensations are not automatically or necessarily pleasurable. The taste for such experience is a socially acquired one, not different in kind from acquired tastes for oysters. . . . The user feels dizzy, thirsty, his scalp tingles; he misjudges time and distance. Are these things pleasurable? He isn't sure. If he is to continue marihuana use, he must decide that they are. . . . The novice's naïve interpretation of what is happening to him may further confuse and frighten him, particularly if he decides, as many do, that he is going insane. . . . Given these typically frightening and unpleasant first experiences, the beginner will not continue use unless he learns to redefine the sensations as pleasurable. . . . This redefinition occurs, typically, in interaction with more experienced users who, in a number of ways, teach the novice to find pleasure in this experience which is at first so frightening. They may reassure him as to the temporary

character of the unpleasant sensations and minimize their seriousness, at the same time calling attention to the more enjoyable
aspects." [15] Becker presents an experienced user's account of how
he helps novices:

> Well, they get pretty high sometimes. The average person isn't
> ready for that, and it is a little frightening to them sometimes.
> I mean, they've been high on lush [alcohol], and they get higher
> that way than they've ever been before, and they don't know
> what's happening to them. Because they think they're going to
> keep going up, up, up, till they lose their minds or begin doing
> weird things or something. You have to like reassure them, ex-
> plain to them that they're not really flipping or anything, that
> they're gonna be all right. You have to just talk them out of be-
> ing afraid. Keep talking to them, reassuring, telling them it's all
> right. And come on with your own story, you know: "The
> same thing happened to me. You'll get to like that after a while."
> Keep coming on like that; pretty soon you talk them out of be-
> ing scared. And besides they see you doing it and nothing hor-
> rible is happening to you, so that gives them more confidence.[16]

Becker also notes that the experienced user teaches the novice
to regulate the amount of smoke he holds in his lungs after inhalation and, more importantly, "to regard those ambiguous experiences formerly defined as unpleasant as enjoyable. . . . Enjoyment is introduced by the favorable definition of the experience
that one acquires from others." [17] Becker emphasizes that enjoyment of the experience is crucial not only at the outset of a marihuana "career," but also "represents an important condition for
future use. It is quite common for experienced users suddenly to
have an unpleasant or frightening experience, which they cannot
define as pleasurable. . . . The user has sensations which go beyond any conception he has of what being high is [because of a
larger than usual amount smoked or a more potent variety of mari-
huana]. . . . He may blame it on an overdose and simply be more
careful in the future. But he may make this the occasion for a re-
thinking of his attitude toward the drug and decide that it no
longer can give him pleasure. When this occurs and is not followed
by a redefinition of the drug as capable of producing pleasure, use
will cease. The likelihood of such a redefinition occurring depends
on the degree of the individual's participation with other users.

Where this participation is intensive, the individual is quickly talked out of his feeling against marihuana use. . . . The direction his further use of the drug takes depends on his being able to continue to answer 'Yes' " to the question "Is it fun?" It also depends on his response to awareness that society disapproves of his smoking marihuana, according to Becker.[18] However, the climate of general opinion, especially among what Bloomquist calls the "upper caste," has changed considerably since 1963, when Becker published his book, and the analysis just considered was fully presented in an article published ten years earlier, in 1953. Negative attitudes toward marihuana use appear to be declining at an increasing rate, simultaneously with a diminishing concern over questions of the social ethics or morality of continued marihuana use in the general population of the country.

Becker attaches major importance to the power of the group as influencing the smoker at each of the three learning stages. E. Goode has recently asserted that marihuana is unique among drugs (with the possible exception of LSD and other related substances) in that it is "sociogenic." He presents seven criteria for determining whether a drug is sociogenic; marihuana meets them all: (1) the drug is typically used in a group; (2) the other persons with whom one shares the drug experience are "usually intimates, intimates of intimates, or potential intimates, rather than strangers"; (3) the relations that the user has with others in the group are generally "long-term continuing social relations"; (4) the group shares many of the same values; (5) "a value convergence will occur as a result of progressive group involvement"; (6) in turn, the drug-oriented activity of the group continually reaffirms its solidarity; (7) "participants view the activity as a legitimate basis for identity — they define themselves, as well as others, partly on the basis of whether they have participated in the activity or not." [19]

Goode interviewed about 200 marihuana users, whose names he obtained in two ways: (1) from drawing up a list of about 25 persons who he knew used marihuana, and, after interviewing them, asking for the names of a few other users; (2) by employing another technique, "also resulting in about one hundred interviews, . . . [which] involved access to several places of employment at which high proportions of marijuana smokers worked. These organizations were two large New York universities, a medium-sized market research firm, and a very large publishing firm." [20] Many of his findings and observations could be used as direct support for Becker's analysis: "Being 'turned on' for the first time . . . is a group experience. Only three percent of my respondents were alone when they had their first marijuana experience." [21] (It is not clear whether "experience" means first use of marihuana or first achievement of the "high" state.) "It is clear . . . that the neophyte marijuana smoker, at the point of his first exposure to the drug, is subject to group definitions of the desirability of the experience, as well as the nature of its reality. Marijuana use, even at its very inception, *is simultaneously participation in a specific social group*. This generalization holds equally as strongly for the *continued* use of marijuana. . . . Marijuana cannot be understood apart from the web of social relations in which it is implicated. Moreover, the *nature* of the group-character of marijuana use also significantly determines its impact. Marijuana is not merely smoked in groups, but it is also smoked in *intimate* groups. The others with whom one is smoking are overwhelmingly *significant* others. One rarely smokes with strangers." [22] Goode mentions various ritualistic aspects of the typical marihuana experience, including its symbolic elements, the strong feelings of brotherhood and/or sharing of something of value (as the joint is passed around), and he also suggests that the illegality and therefore clandestine nature of the "ritual" adds an element of mystery and excitement. He further notes that a distinct "mythology" is connected with the history of marihuana use and with particular minor ceremonies which have gradually come to be considered essential for "turning on." [23]

However, in spite of the support that Goode renders Becker's sociological approach, an alternative hypothesis concerning the process by which one becomes a regular or habitual or frequent user has been proposed. Becker's is one extreme of the sociopsychological approach; Weil et al. suggest that a purely physiological explanation may be as valid and perhaps account for some otherwise inexplicable phenomena. One of the major findings of a recent study conducted and reported by Weil et al. was that nonusers react significantly differently from regular users, "not only subjectively but also physiologically." [24] They suggest that the observed set of differences in response can only be *fully* explained by assuming that a "pharmacological sensitization" occurs fairly early in an individual's use of marihuana, although they do admit that it is apparently true that users teach nonuser friends how to notice the effects of marihuana, especially the more subtle effects. They suggest that the phenomenon of "reverse tolerance" (a hybrid term which refers to the lesser amount of marihuana required to get a user, as opposed to a marihuana-naive individual, high) may be a manifestation of or signal for this "pharmacological sensitization." [25] Also, there is at least a suggestion that "people who have used LSD . . . are much more attuned to getting turned on. Marijuana usually sends them much much higher than it does others." [26] If this is so, then it might follow that LSD accomplishes the same "sensitization" in a single trip, and perhaps even has the effect of "super-sensitization."

The confirmed "pot-head" often claims that he is able to sense, immediately on entering a room, and before speaking with any person present or hearing any conversation, whether or not anyone is high. The "pot-head" claims that he can sense whether or not others are high by the so-called "vibrations" they emit, and he means this altogether seriously and literally. It remains to be experimentally determined whether or not this phenomenon actually does exist, and if so, the exact nature of the "vibrations." A related, but explainable phenomenon is the "contact high." This is described by two authors as follows: "When someone is in a room with one or more people who are smoking, and that person can't or won't smoke, he'll often get very high merely by the superfluity of the smoke in the air. Many people turn on for the first time this way without knowing it. . . . people [also] use the term . . . to mean that someone . . . [who] is with others who are high will start to act high too, although there is no smoke around." [27] The first type of contact high is self-explanatory; the second is probably related to the degree of susceptibility or mood which a person characteristically or occasionally displays. The degree to which one is capable of being influenced by the behavior of others — that is, one's sensitivity to suggestion — is a crucial factor here, as is one's attitude toward the use of marihuana. It is possible for a person to be with others who are high, not know they are high, and yet feel and act as they do; but this behavior is usually not referred to as a "contact high." Further, if the individual who is not partaking of the marihuana disapproves of the practice, it is not only very unlikely that he will experience any sort of high, but also possible that he will act as a "bring down" for the others, even if he does not verbalize his feelings and attitudes about the use of the drug. Such a person is usually referred to by users as a "bummer" — the same term which is applied generally to a wide variety of unpleasant (usually psychological) reactions to marihuana or LSD.

Goode found that the more one used marihuana, the higher his chances of having taken "LSD-type drugs" at least once.[28] Whether or not this indicates that the LSD experience is ever sought out as a means of enhancing the marihuana experience is an open question, but it remains at least a possibility. Weil et al. suggest the possibility of testing "in a systematic manner the hypothetical explanations of the phenomenon" of their "suggested difference between user and non-user," that is, "pharmacological sensitization." One approach they suggest is to continue to administer high doses of marihuana to the naive subjects according to the experimental protocol described in their report. If originally marihuana-naive subjects began to report significantly increased responses to the drug after several exposures in the absence of "psychedelic" settings, suggestions, or manipulations of mood, then the likelihood that marihuana induces a true physiological sensitization or that experience reduces psychological inhibitions, permitting real drug effects to appear, would be increased. If subjects failed to become high, it could be concluded that learning to respond to marihuana requires some sort of teaching or suggestion.[29] That is, if the naive subjects failed to get high, the indication would be that Becker's theory, or one resembling it, is the correct one. Weil et al. appear to hedge somewhat when they mention a lowering of inhibitions as a possible explanation for getting high, since this hypothesis would not meet the requirements of either a purely physiological or a strict sociological explanation.

At any rate, it does seem clear that after a relatively small number of trials, a change in attitude toward marihuana takes place almost inevitably for persons mildly opposed, ambivalent, or uncertain concerning marihuana use in general, and their personal use in particular, and the *usual* shift of attitude is toward a more positive view of the drug and those who use it, whether or not this shift leads to further marihuana use by the individual.

The sociophysical setting in which marihuana is typically used in this country has undergone a remarkable change from the time of the La Guardia investigations (begun in 1938; findings published in 1944). The Mayor's Committee was investigating the marihuana "problem" in New York City, and most of the known users of cannabis lived in or near Harlem, with a few residing near Broadway from Forty-second to Fifty-ninth streets. At that time, cannabis was mostly smoked in "tea pads." These were usually single rooms or apartments, comfortably furnished to suit the preference of the fairly steady clientele, usually dimly lighted, with blue being the predominate color, and music — radio, phonograph, or jukebox — available. The "owner" was ordinarily the supplier, although independent pushers also sold marihuana on the streets. While the number of tea pads and independent pushers was about the same (500), most of the smoking was done in the tea pads, and apparently the owners did not object when individuals smoked marihuana obtained elsewhere.[30] In fact, many owners worked in liaison with the pushers, who would sell cigarettes to the owners and recommend their pad as a good place to smoke. Incense was a usual feature of these rooms, employed mainly to mask the distinctive aroma of cannabis. The La Guardia Report comments:

> The marihuana smoker derives greater satisfaction if he is smoking in the presence of others. His attitude in the "tea-pad" is that of a relaxed individual, free from the anxieties and cares of the realities of life. The "tea-pad" takes on the atmosphere of a very congenial social club. The smoker readily engages in conversation with strangers, discussing freely his pleasant reactions to the drug and philosophizing on subjects pertaining to life in a manner which, at times, appears to be out of keeping with his intellectual level. A constant observation was the extreme willingness to share and puff on each other's cigarettes. A boisterous, rowdy atmosphere did not prevail and on the rare occasions when there appeared signs indicative of a belligerent attitude on the part of a smoker, he was ejected or forced to become more tolerant and quiescent. One of the most interesting setups of a "tea-pad," which was clearly not along orthodox lines from the business point of view, was a series of pup tents arranged on a roof-top in Harlem. Those present proceeded to smoke their cigarettes in the tents. When the desired effect of the drug had been obtained they all emerged into the open and engaged in a discussion of their admiration of the stars and beauties of nature.[31]

The La Guardia Report also notes that smoking marihuana was "very common in the theatres of Harlem. . . . in some instances, perhaps few in number, employees actually sold cigarettes on the premises." [32] It also reports that marihuana was smoked in the lavatories and sometimes the main floor of Harlem dance halls.[33] Of the group studied by the La Guardia Report (as opposed to the larger and more general subculture inside the city of New York which investigators also observed to be using marihuana), slightly over half were Negro or Puerto Rican.[34] The fractions for users outside can be readily and probably quite accurately ascertained by noting the location of the tea pads (almost always in Harlem) and the frequent references to Harlem dance halls and movie theaters. Although the report claims that the group of 72 subjects "constituted an excellent sample of the class in New York City from which the marihuana user comes," it is doubtful that the proportion of white to nonwhite users in the city was as high.[35]

It is probably the case (as the La Guardia and other reports maintain) that the use of marihuana as an intoxicant traveled from New Orleans to other American cities with the migration north of various jazz musicians, most of whom were Negroes.[36] Also, it is undeniable that "the use of cannabis seems to mitigate the force of some of the problems facing certain Negroes, . . . [and accordingly] use of the drug by this group continued at a relatively high level. . . . Cannabis use was not . . . limited to this group by any means, but it did seem to offer this particular segment of society more than any other a much appreciated escape from the pressures of life." [37] (And a much-deserved escape from the "pressures of life," which were and are unlike any experienced by white Americans. Allen Ginsberg has suggested that the "suppression of its [marihuana's] . . . use . . . has been one of the major unconscious, or unmentionable, methods of suppression of Negro rights.")[38]

The situation has changed today, but the change is not as simplistic as one rather naive and facile account would have it: "With the coming of the civil rights movement and racial integration in the Fifties and the hippie movement in the Sixties, social forces mingled black with white, and users with nonusers. Cannabis use increased. Further, the spread of contemporary versions of the hedonist philosophy has encouraged many to experiment with a drug alleged to bring only pleasure and to have no ill effects." [39] In fact, the supposed "racial integration" of the 1950's turned out to be at the best mere token integration, as has recently been clearly shown as the government appears to be backing down on enforcement of many of the decisions of the Supreme Court which were intended to bring about integration. On the other hand, it is true that many young civil rights activists may have been influenced to try marihuana for the first time through their association with some of the black people for whom they were crusading. With regard to the fifties, it should also be noted that for the beatniks, who were in some ways precursors of the hippies, the Negro was the hero, whereas for the hippies, who openly scorn all kinds of hero-worship (while maintaining an intense dedication to a select number of rapidly shifting heroes, many unknown or hardly known to the "straight world"), the Negro is simply irrelevant. There are not many black hippies: " 'How can a Negro drop out?' asks a New York hippie. 'He's there, at bedrock, all the time.' The difference is reflected not only in the contrast between Norman Mailer's 1957 beat manifesto, *The White Negro,* and the 'white Indian' affiliation of the hippies, but also in the apolitical nature of hippie philosophy as well. Mailer's model was a white activist who shared the Negro's sense of rage at injustice; the Indian whom many hippies emulate is a primitive man whose ego is submerged in a Jungian tribal consciousness." [40]

Another factor contributing to the spread of cannabis use beyond specific minority groups is the great increase in international travel among United States citizens, and not only among civilians; World War II, and, to a greater extent, the Korean War and present Vietnam–Cambodia–Laos "War" have introduced many young (and a few not-so-young) individuals to an entirely different attitude toward the use of cannabis from that which prevails in the United States.[41] The general equalizing or socio-leveling effect of the military experience (for the typical G.I.) has had some effect in breaking down many of the customary barriers that exist between various minority groups and the huge American middle class; one consequence has been that the *concept* of marihuana use has spread more widely and rapidly from various minority groups traditionally supposed to show a higher incidence of marihuana use than it would have if civilian norms prevailed. In both 1925 and 1931 the Army conducted investigations concerning soldiers' use of cannabis in the Panama Canal Zone, largely on account of pressure from antimarihuana advocates.[42] The two reports reached practically identical conclusions: marihuana was found to be not habit-forming, and it was reported as the cause of no deleterious influence on those soldiers using it.[43] But the Army findings created much concern in nonmilitary newspapers and magazines, which "attacked them viciously for they saw one of their most lurid topics of reportage snatched away from them." [44] The Army in turn responded with an article entitled "The Marihuana Bugaboo" which stated in part that "the smoking of the leaves, flowers and seeds of *Cannabis sativa* is no more harmful than the smoking of tobacco or mullen or sumac leaves. . . . It is hoped that no witch hunt will be instituted in the military service over a problem that does not exist." [45] The military chose to decide there was no problem, but openly admitted that many soldiers stationed abroad were turning on. During World War II and the Korean War the widespread but not truly large-scale use of marihuana among the troops was regarded as a trivial issue; indeed it was minor compared to the problem of opium addiction, especially for soldiers stationed in the Far East.[46] But the period following World War II saw a decided change. The civilian and especially ex-G.I. use of marihuana was no longer limited to various underprivileged or unprivileged groups, with a small sprinkling of users among "the bohemian fringe of writers, intellectuals, artists, and musicians. . . . Many of the young men who had fought in the war returned with more than just their battle experiences; a good number of them had sampled marijuana. . . . A decade had passed since the 'Marijuana Menace' scare of the thirties and, although the propaganda of the anti-marijuana groups still hung heavily in the air, the war veterans studying on the GI Bill spread its usage to campuses across America. The drug entered a whole new stratum of society. College students now encountered marijuana users of their own social class." [47] And, perhaps as important, the students met marihuana users of their own skin color. With the gradual escalation of the United States' involvement in Vietnam, the situation changed rapidly. In 1967 more and more newspapers reported widespread use of marihuana among the American troops fighting in Vietnam.[48] Perhaps the most publicity was achieved by John Steinbeck IV, who stated, in numerous articles with a popular audience, that approximately 75 percent of the soldiers stationed in Vietnam were smoking marihuana.[49] The Army again preferred to make light of the situation, "despite the fact that in 1967 more United States servicemen in Vietnam were arrested for smoking marijuana than for any other major single offense." [50] As Steinbeck notes: "Until recently, practically no civil or military controls were used in Vietnam to inhibit the smoking of marijuana, and it's doubtful the current furor will be very thorough or long-lasting. This is not so much a matter of kindly indulgence, though. It's simply that with all its other problems, the military has neither time nor inclination to try to jail such a huge part of its fighting force by stomping on marijuana. To enforce a prohibition against smoking the plant would be like trying to prohibit the inhalation of smog in Los Angeles. The military does not take as provincial a view of marijuana as American civil law-enforcement agencies do." [51] Other newsmen "found that many a pointman or rifleman on patrol in enemy territory turns on not because he's looking for a different kind of kick, but simply to overcome a basic human and particularly martial emotion: fear." [52] These reporters also noted that the boredom of much of the behind-the-lines inaction coupled with the constant threat of attack from unsuspected persons or groups contributed to the high level of cannabis use: "Lighting up a joint doesn't make time go faster but it does make a task of drudgery easier to bear, according to many GI's." [53] Still, one recent study of marihuana use in Vietnam states that only about 35 percent of the troops turn on,[54] and two writers state that "military officials estimate that one out of every two hundred GI's in Vietnam has smoked pot at least once . . . [that is, about 0.5 percent have *ever even tried* marihuana]. GI opinion [agreeing with Steinbeck] . . . puts this figure much higher. Of ninety-five inmates questioned in the Long Binh stockade in 1967, seventy-nine admitted having smoked pot. Ten percent indicated they had their first smoke in the military; forty-five percent had smoked before [entering the Armed Forces] . . . and the remaining forty-five percent began the practice in Vietnam." [55]

However, when a soldier in Vietnam is apprehended for using marihuana, he is very rarely if ever given a general court-martial, the outcome of which is almost inevitably five years at heavy labor plus dishonorable discharge. Almost always he is tried before a special court; the usual penalty is six months in the stockade and loss of pay. "Such lenience is . . . to be explained by the military's unstated awareness that smoking marihuana does, in some cases, give a lift to lonely, frightened, or disheartened soldiers who are fighting an unpopular war thousands of miles from home." [56]

"One twenty-one year old Pfc . . . claims that 'You just couldn't fight if you didn't have any pot. You wouldn't be of any use because you'd be too scared. The NCO's and the officers know that and they don't hassle us about it.' " [57] On the other hand, the Army does try to limit exportation of marihuana: "The American authorities are, however, very serious about pot sent through the mail from Vietnam. Some GI's stationed in rear-line posts such as Saigon have made this practically a full-time occupation, salting away a sizeable nest egg by the time their tour of duty is up. . . . the generations now fighting the war in Vietnam may well be influential. It will take many years before their impact will be felt. No doubt, young soldiers, having smoked pot and liked it, are thinking of ways to combat the old bugaboos." [58] Yippie Jerry Rubin asks: "What's going to happen when all those Amerikan [sic] GI's come home? 'What do you mean, we're old enough to fight and die but not old enough to smoke?' " [59]

But to return to the shift that has taken place since the La Guardia Report (for if one lesson is clear from the recent past, it is that there is an increasing sense of futility and irrelevance felt toward and sometimes even implied in *predictions* of sociopsychological changes in this country): the impact of the current American idealization of youth, even though at times it takes the form of covert jealousy or overt repression by members of older generations, has helped establish a totally new "marihuana environment" in this country. The increased use of marihuana on campuses may have been initially a result of the returning World War II G.I.'s, but the specific patterns and rituals that have developed in marihuana use, as well as the ever-growing number of college users, do not rely to any appreciable extent on methods or attitudes that returning soldiers use or hold.

Perhaps the most obvious determinant in marihuana use is that it is illegal, and the penalties, even for the possession of a small amount, are harsh: "As a smoker becomes more acquainted with the drug, he will find that many occasions lend themselves to a marihuana intoxication. He is always plagued by the law, however, and must filter his desires through the 'being caught' possibility before he can think of lighting up." [60] However, even this pattern of general apprehension is changing, as noted in the previous chapter. Mass gatherings of young people (such as occurred at Woodstock) often eventuate in mass "open-air" smoking in full view of police; in such instances the insurance against arrest is not provided by a locked door or pulled shade, but by the sheer number of users and the difficulty of making mass arrests. The legal sanctions against the use of marihuana no longer reflect society's outright condemnation; the concepts of defiance and deviance are becoming increasingly irrelevant to marihuana use. Still, since mass "turn ons" are relatively rare, and marihuana is much more frequently smoked in fairly small groups, certain precautions are usually taken, "all connected with the rite itself. It is a good idea to make certain the door is locked, for instance. . . . so severe are the marihuana laws that the smokers play another game with the police, . . . the game of 'stash.' " [61] This practice probably dates to earlier (i.e., post 1937) days when the comparatively few numbers of users felt a greater fear of being "busted." [62] Marihuana is "stashed" by concealment in "such places as the toilet tank, under loose floor boards or tiles, behind the plate of a light switch, or in a variety of holes as artfully crafted as a set of Chinese boxes. Before stashing . . . some . . . even take the precaution of wrapping the drug in a substance such as lard, which neutralizes the smell of pot. . . . Others prefer to hide their contraband outside the home — in the hollow of a tree, on the rooftop, on a stairway landing, in the backyard, or in a locker at a bus or air terminal." [63] But there is frequently a minor inconvenience in such stashing: "Always in transit, the stash can frequently become lost, it has been hidden so well. The smoker, after hiding his marihuana under the refrigerator for a few months, frequently thinks that *of course* the police will look there, and so he changes places. Yet after a while the smoker realizes the whole procedure is hopeless, and begins to leave the bundle not quite so hidden, yet not quite so in plain sight. . . . The absurdity of stashing and restashing is a long-standing joke among pot smokers. . . . LEMAR [an organization whose title is an acronym for "Legalize Marihuana"] . . . has gone so far as to have regular competition called 'The Best Stash Contest' . . . Some smokers hide their stash in a museum, or unsuspecting public place." [64]

The most usual contemporary mode of marihuana use is by smoking cigarettes, as it was at the time of the La Guardia Report, although there is a steadily increasing interest in and use of a variety of pipes, many specially designed, and also food — including liquid — preparations. The method described for rolling cigarettes in the La Guardia Report is practically unchanged today: "Two gum-edged cigarette papers . . . [are] stuck together with saliva from the tongue and then rolled with the ends twisted together. The old [circa La Guardia Report] . . . practice was to wet the whole cigarette with saliva for the purpose of making the joint burn slowly. This is not done today simply for hygienic reasons and possibly because the present generation of smokers is more affluent than its forerunner." [65] However, a booklet directed to an audience of neophyte smokers, published in 1969, suggests licking the paper just before smoking to retard the burning speed somewhat.[66] The marihuana cigarette is (and was) considerably slimmer than the average tobacco cigarette — about half the diameter[67] — because marihuana is generally scarce, a smaller cigarette can be consumed to its maximum worth, and little is needed for a satisfying smoke. Whereas with regular cigarettes much of the smoke goes to waste, most of the marihuana that is burned can be inhaled and absorbed.[68] Two papers are used for three particular reasons: to prevent loose twigs from puncturing the paper (especially in the case of lower-quality marihuana, i.e., marihuana containing pieces of stem and therefore a lower resin level), to slow the burning and prevent some of the smoke from escaping, and to simplify the actual rolling process — the double thickness makes rolling easier.[69] Sometimes, after the joint has been rolled and any bulges or uneven sections have been squeezed out, another (third) paper is wrapped around the outside of the twin papers.[70] The cigarette is then examined to see which end will probably draw better — since homemade cigarettes are not as even or standardized as machine-made ones — and then the correct procedure for lighting is followed.[71] Lighting a joint is not so easy as lighting a commercial cigarette; the usual method is to hold "the flame and cigarette end where they can be observed closely, which is usually at eye level a short distance from the face. The thin cigarette is then turned and twisted so that the flame starts the end of the joint evenly." [72]

The actual smoking process (i.e., frequency and depth of inhalation, length of time the smoke is held in the lungs, etc.) is not the same as for tobacco. In fact, one of the interesting findings of Weil et al. was that when marihuana-naive individuals were being

trained in the "correct" method for inhaling marihuana by prac-
ticing with *tobacco* cigarettes, five became too ill to continue the
experiment — they developed "acute nicotine reactions," although
they had all claimed to be "heavy" smokers.[73] "The object of
marihuana smoking is to get the smoke into the lungs in the most
efficient way, taste and flavor be damned. The throat is opened
and the smoke drawn directly into it." [74] Mezz Mezzrow has
written about his first experience: "I didn't feel a thing and I told
him so. 'Do you know one thing?' he said. 'You ain't even smokin'
it right. You got to hold that muggle so that it barely touches
your lips, see, then draw in air around it. Say *tfff, tfff,* only
breathe in when you say it. Then don't blow it out right away,
you got to give the stuff a chance.' " [75]

The cigarette, when it is nearly consumed, is usually referred
to as a "roach." These are highly valued by the "true pothead,
. . . [who] believes [probably correctly] . . . that the potency
gathers in a roach so that it is the last third of a marihuana cigarette that packs the biggest punch." [76] Accordingly, several
methods have been devised to enable the smoker(s) to use as much
as possible of each cigarette: the "cocktail" method, in which the
roach is inserted into a regular filter-tip cigarette from which all
but the last inch or so of tobacco has been emptied; the "West
Coast Crutch" method, in which a paper matchbook cover is torn
free of matches and wrapped around the roach like a cigarette
holder; a method in which the roach is inserted into a special
narrow slit that many marihuana pipes have built into the bowl;
or a method in which a paper clip or pin or tweezers are used to
protect the smoker's fingers; the "can" method, in which beer
cans, plastic (water-based) glue bottles, milk bottles, cocoanut
shells, and even the lower portion of a ballpoint pen are used.
The roach is stuck into an end of the container, and a hole
punched (if needed) in the opposite end, the device thereby acting
as a holder and something of a cooler. This last method allows the
usual circle smoking to be maintained. The thumb is held over
the mouth-end as the container is passed to each smoker; this pre-
vents any smoke from escaping.[77]

As mentioned, many users prefer pipes to "reefers," "joints,"
"sticks," "twists" (a few of the names given marihuana cigarettes).
There are at least two to three hundred different varieties of pipe,
the most popular being those which have some smoke-cooling

method designed into them — either a long stem or forcing the smoke to pass through water. Pipes are smoked differently than cigarettes: for one thing, a greater volume of smoke is obtained from each inhalation, because of the relative absence of any filtering effect from the marihuana through which the smoke passes when a joint is smoked. The pipe, like the cigarette, is usually smoked in company; after inhalation it is passed immediately from one smoker to the next, in order to minimize smoke-loss. The actual method is closer to puffing than with reefers, which are more deeply inhaled.

Perhaps the best-known user of marihuana who was not a smoker was Alice B. Toklas, the lifelong companion of Gertrude Stein. Toklas included a recipe for marihuana fudge in her cookbook. "She said that anyone could whip it up on a rainy day and recommended it as an 'entertaining refreshment for a ladies' bridge club or a chapter meeting of the Daughters of the American Republic [sic].' " [78] When marihuana is used in foods, it is usually crushed to a very fine-grain consistency, but this operation tends to reduce the resin level and hence the potency (the resin remains on the sifter).[79] Accordingly, a larger amount of marihuana is generally used to gain the usual "high" effect. Some of the more popular recipes that include marihuana are tea, cake, fudge, and spaghetti sauce.[80] The hippies in particular have also adopted many Indian and some Middle Eastern recipes. Although these edible concoctions have nowhere near the popularity of smoked marihuana in the United States, "American students who have travelled in North Africa have become the innovators on the United States drug scene by bringing marihuana out of the joint or pipe and into the kitchen. The effects of marihuana eaten as 'brownies' or otherwise are much longer in coming, usually about an hour after ingestion," whereas when marihuana is smoked, the effects are felt almost at once.[81]

The massive increment in number of people using cannabis in America is linked with many contemporary youth-culture phenomena: the underground newspaper system, the "new music" initiated by the Beatles, the hippie-derived colorful costumes, and so on. Perhaps the strangest phenomenon is the unique sense of potential power and actual powerlessness that the great mass of young people feel today. Contemporary music is another interesting phenomenon, and the exchange, the intense communication, between the various acid-, hard-, Nashville-, and so forth, -rock sound-makers and their audiences has acted as a special type of mutual reinforcement in the solidification of attitudes — toward the use of marihuana, among other things. "Because pot heightens the senses [or gives the illusion of a greater receptivity] . . . including hearing — smokers . . . have helped to make popular the psychedelic rock of dozens of new groups," who feed back to their audience an extremely positive attitude toward the use of marihuana.[82] "There can be no question but that these sudden new developments in musical tastes and other art forms have been influenced . . . by an increasing use of marijuana over the past five years by persons in all walks of life." [83] No longer is the young user a deviant in the eyes of his friends; in fact, it is the nonuser who is more apt to be considered somewhat "out" by his age peers. Furthermore, the young "doctors, lawyers, executives, and housewives of today have emerged from the group of youngsters who smoked their first marijuana cigarettes during the fifties and early sixties. . . . Although the language may be somewhat different, their gatherings do not deviate much from the standard cocktail party. Respectable types in the larger cities — lawyers, college instructors, advertising copywriters, journalists, fashion designers, artists, TV producers and writers — gather at a friend's house to smoke and socialize, to 'turn on' and 'drop out' temporarily from their nine-to-five world. Some individuals from a still older generation, the middle-aged doctor, business man, corporation executive — those who did not encounter marijuana during their college years — are now crossing over to the other side of the generation gap." [84] But it is still true that the older smokers are leading "a more stable life than the smokers in the ghettoes, the students, or the hippies, . . . [and one consequence of their relative stability is that] they have a more difficult time obtaining marijuana and therefore do not smoke as often . . . [yet still] the over-thirty . . . who smoke marijuana cut a wide swathe in society. . . . [However,] they're usually settled in their habits and life style and do not smoke as frequently as their younger counterparts. . . . Other individuals with fairly well regulated lives who reside in the suburbs and are employed in various respectable businesses and professions, frequently obtain their supplies from people they have smoked with in their youth and with whom they have kept in contact for this purpose. . . . Because the over-thirty

smoker has more to lose and has developed more respect for society . . . [that is, for his own generation's definition of "society"]
he is usually the most cautious type of smoker. Yet there is almost no risk at all for this group of smokers, if they choose their
sources carefully — for who would suspect marijuana smoking in
the suburbs?" [85] But it is still a fact that only in the last few years
has there been any real spread of marihuana use from the less
achievement-oriented youth culture and hippie and ghetto sub-
cultures to the more career-minded middle class a generation or
two older.[86] Judy Collins has described the division between
youth and the older generation(s) as one between the "marijuana
generation" and the "alcohol generation." [87] A Jesuit priest and
psychologist, Father Carlo Weber, from Loyola University, says
that "the older generation lives in an achievement culture, zeroed
in on alcohol as symbolized by the cocktail party where people go
to become anonymous and dip into a great cloud of escape. The
new generation doesn't want to run away. It wants to look at the
ultimates." [88] According to E. Z. Friedenberg: "Alcohol primarily
relieves anxiety and promotes optimism. It makes the society and
what one has to do with society okay. Pot, on the other hand,
turns you inside yourself. Imagine a twenty-fifth college reunion
with pot, not flasks." [89]

There are no doubt myriad ways of classifying marihuana users.
Even in the United States Bloomquist refers to an upper and a
lower "caste": "Each is characterized by the way the user enjoys
his drug. The lower-caste user is totally unconcerned about the
intellectual advantages of philosophizing and self-exploration
which intrigue his educated counterpart. The lower-caste user
simply 'trips,' that is, he experiences the bizarre effect of the
drug for the effect alone. . . . Until recently, when the high
school, college, and postgraduate crowd entered the drug arena,
most cannabis users were lower-caste users, both as to their origins
and as to their mode of use of the drug.

"The upper caste, still growing in size and now the major
contemporary group, is composed of intellectuals — students, pro-
fessionals, artists, musicians, actors, and professors, who take the
drug to 'maintain' and to explore themselves and the infinite. To
'maintain' in this parlance is to defer the enjoyment of the pleasurable effects of the drug and to utilize the experience to better
understand one's inner self and rid oneself of his 'hang-ups.' This

is not to imply that the upper-caste user does not 'trip.' He does. Not infrequently this is his principal goal at a given cannabis session. But whereas the upper-caste user will both trip and maintain, the lower-caste user seldom sees any benefit in maintaining per se. This user considers cannabis primarily as fun or as a recreational or escapist thing to enjoy without the complications of intellectual overtones." [90] This sounds plausible enough, until one stops to consider some of its implications and some reports from objective observers of persons "intoxicated" with cannabis. First, Bloomquist's schema assumes a definite evaluative-judgmental stance closely connected to the Puritan ethic (or perhaps a direct hangover from it) in its assignment of "higher" caste to the more intellectual, probably more introspective, and certainly more self-concerned user. This author — whether he would agree or not — seems to be saying that the relatively superior beings are those who mainly forsake pleasurable aspects of the cannabis experience for the sake of what the group that Bloomquist calls "lower-caste" might well label an "ego-trip." Also, it is difficult to believe that the individuals who claim or imply that they are members of this "upper-caste" are not often indulging in a form of rationalization induced by a strong sense of guilt. Instead of openly admitting that the cannabis experience is simply fun, and an experience that can be appreciated regardless of intellectual or intelligence level, these individuals must apparently justify their use of cannabis on grounds of "self-exploration." Perhaps they are simply less honest than Bloomquist's "lower-caste" users. Second, many reports stress that subjects under the influence of marihuana are apt to engage in philosophical and metaphysical conversation that would normally be foreign to them, because above their (apparent) level of intellect.[91] Perhaps another way of putting this would be to ask whether it is in fact possible to have the *full* cannabis experience without recognizing and giving in to the strong element of simple enjoyment, pleasure, nondirected, free-flowing thought, which allows the drug to lead, perhaps to a genuine and viable personal insight, but equally likely to a "mere" sense of returning to the world of the child, where almost everything was fresh, interesting, and plain *fun*.[92] Those who insist that they must "maintain" are apparently convinced they must ignore the present immediacy of the objects, persons, and events that cannabis enhances and instead delve into their past in a sort of amateur self-analysis. Sometimes they also try to determine how they "should" behave in the future. In doing so, they often miss the essential property of the cannabis experience, which is, I believe, an intensification of the present, an increased awareness of the here-and-now, however trivial it may seem to someone not high. "To see the world in a grain of sand" seems closer to what the "lower-caste" user does, and this activity, in my opinion, is certainly not to be denigrated, even on "intellectual" grounds.

But the more usual way of classifying users of marihuana is related primarily to the frequency of use for the individual, and also to his motivation for marihuana use. First, there is the occasional or casual user, who smokes irregularly and sporadically, *if* he enjoyed his first experience of turning on. (If he did not, the chances are that, unless he relearns, in Becker's terminology, to view the experience as pleasurable, he will not smoke again.) This user is not apt to keep his own supply of marihuana, but he will not usually turn down a joint offered to him at a social gathering where marihuana is being used, nor will he express disapproval of those who use marihuana more frequently than he does, although he may have definitely negative views concerning the "pot-head" (the third major type). He is actually on the fringe of the marihuana subculture, but he may become more involved, even to the point where he passes over from being an occasional or casual user to a member of the second major group, the "social" or frequent users.

This transition is usually marked by the casual users' purchase usually of a fairly large amount (i.e., a pound, or sometimes a "kilo" or 2.2 pounds). Often this transition is partially the result of a feeling of embarrassment on the part of the occasional user, who doesn't like to be continually asking his friends for small amounts, or even for a joint. The major preventive factor in this transition is probably the fear that specific nonusers of the drug will discover that he has smoked marihuana (a fear that the occasional user does not have to deal with, since the pattern of his marihuana use is such that it quite effectively insures that he will not come into contact with nonusers while he is high) and express various degrees of disapproval: "If a . . . [marihuana] user's family, friends, or employer discover that he uses marihuana, they may impute to him the auxiliary status traits ordinarily assumed to be associated with drug use. Believing him to be irresponsible and powerless to control his own behavior, perhaps even insane, they may punish him with various kinds of informal but highly effective sanctions, such as ostracism or withdrawal of affection. . . . a set of traditional views has grown up, defining the practice as a violation of basic moral imperatives, as an act leading to loss of self-control, paralysis of the will, and eventual slavery to the drug. Such views are commonplace." [93] However, the climate of general opinion regarding the occasional user is undergoing such rapid changes — almost always shifts to a more liberal view — that much of what Becker has written in this regard is less applicable or even entirely irrelevant today. The other "social controls" that he mentions, which were probably not as important or effective in 1953, may today be on a par with the one just described, although it is probably true that these controls also have lost a good deal of authority. They are, according to Becker, "control through limiting of supply and access to the drug" and "control through definition of the act as immoral." [94] The overcoming of the fear of all three of these controls is, Becker claims, essential if a person is to move from occasional smoking to frequent use. He mentions two alternatives often adopted in overcoming the fear of social disapproval; the frequent smoker may take "the attitude that marihuana use can be carried on under the noses of nonusers" without detection, or, alternatively, the frequent user may embrace a new living pattern "which reduces contacts with nonusers almost to the zero point." [95] The other controls are comparatively easy to avoid or overcome; the activity of procuring marihuana will be treated at some length below and, in overcoming the fear that others will define the act as immoral, the regular user has many options. Becker suggests a few. Perhaps the most common is abstaining altogether for a specified time (usually about a week), to prove to oneself that one has in fact not "become the slave of a vicious habit." [96] For the psychoanalytically or psychologically more sophisticated individual, the common rationalization that mere awareness of *possible* harmful moral implications is enough — the "notion that to be aware of the problem is to solve it" [97] — although transparent enough to most nonusers, often suffices for the regular user. Another option is to adopt an attitude of pity, superiority, and exclusion toward those who condemn use of marihuana.

The frequency with which the "social" user turns on varies considerably from individual to individual, and, for each such user, over periods of time. He may use it every day (or night), every other day, two or three times a week (probably the most usual frequency), or only on weekends, but there is almost invariably a regular pattern, even though it may be interrupted from time to time, for a variety of reasons. These include the above-mentioned "testing" by abstinence for a short period, non-availability through loss of contact with one's "connection," or even a change in general living habits (such as, for example, taking on a night or second job). Also, since the "social" user almost universally (and by definition) still prefers to smoke in the company of other "social" or regular users, his use will be regulated to some degree by the frequency with which others that he knows well and smokes with "turn on." Even though the regular user is "usually a secure person who does not feel that he has to prove anything by turning on," especially if he has begun to smoke after adolescence, and even though "more often than not, he is considered successful in conventional terms," he still must lead something of a double life.[98] Sometimes this is true only to the extent of, say, hiding his habit of regular use from his employer. The "social" user is also much more likely to grow some of his own cannabis than is the occasional user, although the amount is ordinarily so small that the act is more of a symbolic gesture of defiance or of a status-seeking activity than it is his sole source of supply. However, some "social" users, especially those who live in secluded regions of the south or west, may be able to grow enough to satisfy all their needs. But this practice, on a fairly large scale, is much more widespread among the third main type of user, commonly known as the "pot-head." [99] Whereas the occasional and "social" users are mainly distinguished by a difference of degree — like the difference between the person who has a drink or two at a cocktail party and the one who more or less regularly has a cocktail before dinner and on social occasions — the "pot-head's" whole existence, or nearly all of it, focuses on the procuring, use, and sometimes sale of marihuana. But the primary activity of the "pot-head" is getting and staying high, usually for days at a time, sometimes all the time, to some degree. "To the pothead any contact with reality is a bring-down and for this reason he is happiest when he is high." [100] The attitude of the "pot-head" is one of almost complete alienation from the values and mores of even the most liberal members of the "straight" world, and, if anything or any person forces him to make a choice between ceasing to use cannabis or continuing his drug career, he will probably opt for the latter. However, some commentators are of the opinion that the typical "pot-head" does not continue this career for long: "He is usually a person in his late teens or early twenties who is trying to come to grips with himself and society. His hang-ups are those usually associated with the young. . . . Once he has settled these conflicts, he usually does not remain a pothead much longer. He will gradually diminish his smoking as he finds new interests and his place in society. After a year or two at the most, he will have cut down to the level of the social smoker. He will have discovered that the pleasures of marijuana are greatest when enjoyed in moderation, making each turn-on a fresh departure from the everyday." [101] Although it is very unlikely that he will become a complete abstainer, he will regulate his smoking to the level of a less crucial concern and begin to explore other areas of experience, in many ways a reversal of his "pot-head" life-style.

Since the "pot-head" does smoke daily, he is more apt to smoke alone at least a few times than either the occasional or "social" user, unless he establishes a living situation where he is in daily contact with other "heads." The latter choice seems to be the one of preference, and many — but by no means all — of the communes that have sprung up over the last few years throughout the United States are made up almost exclusively of "pot-heads," with a few "social" smokers, and hardly ever an occasional or nonsmoker. One interesting aspect of the "pot-head's" mode of existence is the degree of paranoia he exhibits, or the apparently paranoidlike attitude he holds. It often strikes an observer that the "pot-heads" deliberately cultivate this stance toward the world, mainly as a means of justifying their continued mode of existence. For unless the "head" firmly believes that various police agents and drug-abuse law enforcement personnel are out to get him, personally, and put him away for as long as possible, he will have difficulty in maintaining his attitude of ultimate disdain for and rebellion against the values which he believes the law and drug-abuse enforcement groups represent, which he usually refers to as those of the "Establishment."

Whereas the "pot-head" lives in a distinct subculture, with its own values, lifestyle, and particular rituals, his language has influenced popular jargon, not only of the "social" and occasional user, but also of society in general. The specific subculture of the "pot-head" is a major source for many of society's — particularly youthful society's — latest fads, especially in speech. "The language of youth culture is found in the current idioms of adult language," and this language is derived to a considerable degree, especially in its normative and evaluative functions, from that of the marihuana user. "How many of us are 'doing our thing'? How many of us casually describe ourselves or others in terms of this or that 'bag'?" [102]

One of the problems in discussing the language of a subculture is that by the time the terms most meaningful to its users have reached some sort of public use and/or acceptance as a part of the national idiom, these terms have long since been discarded by the members of the subculture. By the time that Mr. Jones figures out that he's "square," the group(s) first using the term have found another way to describe him. Even the word for marihuana seems to change at approximately three- to five-year intervals. Although any user will know what is referred to if one mentions "pot," "weed," "smoke," or perhaps "gauge" (although the word dates to the 1930's), most users in this country currently refer to cannabis as "grass," and "dope" seems to be gaining in popularity. A general descriptive term that gained perhaps the widest currency among both users and society in general over the past few years is "head," perhaps because it can be applied to almost any person who takes almost any drug, and even to many who do not. For example, not only can one be described as a "pot-head" or an "acid-head" (LSD user), but one can be a "book-head," or a "fabric-head," or a "movie- (or flic-) head." However, the rapid spread of the term has effectively undermined its use among those who "know what's happening," and the replacement, "freak," as in "grass-freak," "music-freak," "camera-freak," and so on, is also used less nowadays by the cognoscenti than by the "straight" world. It is interesting how very often words such as "freak," which are first used with strong negative or derogatory connotations, are gradually applied to persons and activities without carrying the same (or any) such negative connotations. The verb to "freak out" originally meant to lose one's self-control, to be obviously agitated and disturbed, but the term has acquired much less negative and/or derogatory connotations, and it is used in the general sense of changing something or somebody radically, if even for a short period of time, i.e., "freaking" a car is painting it in day-glo colors, and "freaking" a person is now widely used to describe only a mild "put-on." But there is one term, probably the ultimate expression of disdain for most regular and heavy users of marihuana, which seems unlikely to become more or less neutral in connotation, and that is "plastic." If there is any other word that approaches this one in the immutability of its negative-derogatory connotations, it is "up-tight." Both are frequently used by young smokers, especially the relatively apolitical hippies, in their wholesale condemnation of the "Establishment," which is a shorthand word for nearly every conceivable power structure or authority symbol or group.

But it should be remembered that an important impetus to the use of a special and rapidly shifting vocabulary is, for the young marihuana user, the same as it was (and still is) for the black man in America: to exclude the "outsider"; to establish a sense of group solidarity; to protect the members of the group from (in the case of marihuana) legal apprehension or discovery by those whom the users do not wish to know "what's happening"; and, although it may seem a minor point, to allow members of the group to exercise creativity in one of man's most important social activities — speech.

Although Becker is describing jazz musicians, much of the following is relevant to those who use marihuana to the extent that it becomes the focal point of their lives:

> The process of self-segregation is evident in certain symbolic expressions, particularly in the use of . . . slang, which readily identifies the man who can use it properly as someone who is not square and as quickly reveals as an outsider the person who uses it incorrectly or not at all. Some words have grown up to refer to unique professional problems and attitudes of musicians [for marihuana smokers this could be changed to "unique problems in obtaining a supply of the drug and attitudes of smokers"]. . . . Such words enable musicians to discuss problems and activities for which ordinary language provides no adequate terminology. There are, however, many words

which are merely substitutes for the more common expressions without adding any new meaning. . . . The function of such behavior is pointed out by a young musician who was quitting the business: "I'm glad I'm getting out of the business, though. I'm getting sick of being around musicians. There's so much ritual and ceremony junk. They have to talk a special language, dress different, and wear a different kind of glasses. And it just doesn't mean a damn thing except 'we're different.' " [103]

One valid generalization can be made concerning the "new language" of the young marihuana users, and that is that they do, for the most part, earnestly believe that their ever-shifting vocabulary is an honest mode of expression, infinitely more open and direct than what they see as the polite verbal manipulations and double-talk of their parents' generation.

Perhaps the major change that has taken place among cannabis users in the United States since the days of the La Guardia Report lies in the general activity of acquiring the drug. Geller and Boas divide "people who purchase pot in this country into five main groups. Their buying patterns, as with any other product, dictate the ways marijuana is sold." The five groups are: "(1) the urban minority groups (including the ghetto groups — the Negroes, Puerto Ricans, and other Spanish-speaking people); (2) the rural minority groups (consisting mainly of poor farm workers, many of them Negroes and Mexican Americans); (3) the white middle-class students (*who are a relatively new market but seem to be outnumbering all the other groups*); (4) the hippies (who make use of not only marijuana but also the more potent hallucinogens — peyote, mescaline, LSD, as well as speed); and (5) the group over thirty (artists, intellectuals, writers, and beatniks who went 'straight,' people who learned to smoke in college or in the service)" (italics added).[104] The third group is of special interest, not only because it is reportedly the largest, but because it has effected a whole new approach to the distribution and sale of marihuana, one that is as far from the stereotyped view of the sleazy streetcorner pusher whose real aim is to get his customers "hooked" on heroin as is the view that every bartender wants to turn all of his customers into alcoholics. Although it is true that the five groups enumerated above do have one common characteristic — they are all, technically, criminals guilty of the same crime: the possession, sale, or even the giving away of cannabis — and although it is true that they all do get their marihuana from the same regions — either Mexico, Central America, or the Caribbean — the resemblance soon ends. For the third group has demonstrated an initiative and degree of imagination in foiling the U.S. Bureau of Narcotics and Dangerous Drugs that far outstrips the efforts of any of the other groups. It could be argued — and this is where I think the five-group classification breaks down — that the fifth and the third groups are, for all practical purposes, indistinguishable, since the fifth group is an offshoot of the third in that it is largely comprised of members of the third group who have grown a few years older. But the important point is that the young, middle-class, college age (and usually college-attending) users have altered, if not broken, the usual and traditional methods of distribution and sale of marihuana. As mentioned, by far the largest amount of marihuana used in the U.S. has traditionally come from Mexico, and to a lesser extent, the Caribbean and Central America. This aspect of distribution remains unchanged. In fact, the Deputy Commissioner of Customs of the Treasury Department stated as recently as 1962 that "ninety-nine percent of our marijuana comes from Mexico," which was in accord with a statement to the same effect released by the Bureau of Narcotics at the same time.[105] This is true despite the illegality of marihuana in Mexico, where the law against smoking it is rarely enforced. However, the Bureau of Narcotics and Dangerous Drugs has taken upon itself the task of supplying Mexican police with arms, equipment,[106] and, recently, a special spray that has no apparent effect on the crop, but when it is smoked (or ingested), it causes severe nausea and vomiting. The attitude of the Mexican population toward their antimarihuana laws is apparently even more contemptuous than that of the regular marihuana user in this country; however, Mexico signed the United Nations Single Convention Narcotic and Drug Act of 1961, so the law-enforcement authorities evidently feel obliged to present at least token opposition toward the mass production of marihuana (while almost universally ignoring the small patch that perhaps every other farmer grows for his own needs), realizing that if they were as successful as the Bureau of Narcotics and Dangerous Drugs wished, they would eliminate a significant percentage of Mexico's annual income.[107] The enforcement of the antimarihuana laws is especially lax in the small towns throughout Mexico, where "the small-town officials, whose first allegiance is to the farmers, seldom give much assistance to the federal Mexican police officials." [108]

Prior to 1964 (when the Single Convention Act came into force after the necessary ratification by the fortieth participating country)[109] there was little or no effort on the part of the Mexican officials to eliminate a source of income from their wealthy northern neighbor. "For many years the Mexican government has pretty much ignored its commitments on drug control. It pays lip service to the laws; occasionally it wipes out a few opium fields in the mountains of northwestern Mexico where opium grows and cannabis grows, and where the owners reap sizable profits and local officials in many cases seem unable or unwilling to do anything very drastic about it." [110] B. Fitzgerald, a staff assistant to the United States Commissioner of Narcotics, believes that the widespread and serious economic poverty in Mexico is the basic problem. He quotes a Mexican as saying: "The ambition of every poor Mexican is to sell enough pot so that he can get rich enough to get drunk on alcohol." [111] However, very few Mexican farmers manage to get rich by raising cannabis, despite the relatively high prices that the product will bring once it arrives in major cities and college towns throughout the United States. On the average, the Mexican farmer can expect to receive about $7.50 per *pound,* which means that he would have to grow and harvest a full ton to take in $15,000, and from this amount he must pay off the middleman (very few purchasers buy directly from the farmer), local officials, local police, and, occasionally, the Mexican federal agents.[112] By the time the marihuana reaches the streets or the campus, the price has risen to anywhere from $100 to $300 per pound, depending on a number of factors: distance from the border, local supply and demand, quality of the product, and so forth. But this is not the final step in sale-distribution, in most cases. The pounds (or kilograms equaling 2.2 pounds) will be broken down into ounces, which sell for anywhere from $20 to $35. Sometimes the ounces (which are often "short") are further broken down into "nickel bags" — usually a fifth of an ounce, for which the standard price is indicated by the name — $5.00. A nickel bag is good for approximately 15 to 20 cigarettes, depending on how thickly they are rolled. On rare occasions nowadays (although the practice was much more frequent in the days of the La Guardia Report), the nickel bags themselves will be broken down and sold as separate cigarettes, usually for less than a dollar each.[113]

Traditionally, or at least at the time of the La Guardia Report, the marihuana user has been regarded as the final "link in a chain of supply usually made up of individuals and groups operating outside the bounds of conventional society." [114] The La Guardia Report stated that the average user bought marihuana in the form of separate joints, either from a street pusher or at a tea-pad,[115] and, although the marihuana changed hands many times (with consistent escalation of price) before it reached the eventual user, no one syndicate controlled the underground market in marihuana.[116]

The difficulties in the way of any organized monopoly of the market are due to the nonaddictive nature of the drug and also its weedlike character; it will grow almost anywhere, with a minimum of cultivation (although, as noted in Chap. 2, the potency tends to fall off unless the climate is sufficiently dry and the plant receives a good amount of sunlight). Most of the cannabis used in this country is grown by independent, usually fairly small, Mexican farmers, and they would probably tend to resist any efforts to organize or standardize production. Although there are wholesalers who are connected with the Mafia, there are many more who are not; there are also middlemen, purchasing from the wholesalers and acting as wholesalers themselves. Then there are the street pushers, the true retailers, who buy marihuana by the pound or the kilo and sell mainly $5.00 and $10.00 bags. Also, there is a growing number of individual entrepreneurs — especially on college campuses and among the hippie or pseudo-hippie groups, many of whom make trips to Mexico themselves instead of buying from a middleman or wholesaler. Finally, there are many more-or-less casual users who by chance or with little planning come across a fairly large amount of marihuana, keep some for themselves, and sell the bulk in small quantities, mainly to friends, at cost or slightly above. Accordingly, methods of distribution and sale of marihuana in the United States vary considerably, depending on who the seller is and to whom he is selling. It is a highly competitive but relatively open field; anyone who wants to go into business for himself need make only a small investment.

Still, for the risks and effort involved, the economic reward is slight. In the days of the La Guardia Report, the large number of wholesalers, middlemen, street pushers, and tea-pad sellers would seem to have given "the Italian Mafia, the Spanish-speaking Mafia and the loosely-formed mobster crime syndicate" more opportunities for entering the distribution-sale complex than is the case today.[117] Not only has the "tea-pad" almost entirely vanished, but the largest group of users (according to Geller and Boas's classification of users by methods of purchase) does "not exactly relish the idea of having to go into town and hang around some seedy neighborhood waiting for their connection. Knowing someone on campus makes the procedure a lot easier. Rather than spend an hour or a day waiting around to obtain a supply, it is far more convenient to obtain marihuana from someone close by — invariably a student himself." [118] The campus users are generally more imaginative, have been exposed to more options in ways of living, and are far more mobile than their counterparts in the ghetto; their source is not restricted to the local pusher. Many a well-established campus dealer began his deviant career after returning from Mexico on a vacation with a large or fairly substantial amount of marihuana hidden in his car or suitcase — marihuana which he had not gone to Mexico for the explicit purpose of buying, but which he realized would be a profitable and highly marketable item back on the campus. Since this beginner, semiamateur often is his own complete organization (i.e., he makes his own contact with the farmer in Mexico, smuggles his purchase across the border alone, and sells it himself), he effectively cuts out the profit which was traditionally taken by the middlemen. Furthermore, it is not even necessary for the campus dealer to travel, since he often has friends permanently or temporarily residing in Mexico who will ship him his supply — and the precautions taken in concealing and wrapping are thorough and always changing. A paragraph from an article in *Esquire* magazine, written by a student pusher, provides a sense of the motivation and attitude of the campus dealer:

I pushed in my senior year at the University of Michigan, starting I remember after I quit this incredibly boring job showing early-morning educational movies. We were sick of buying lousy grass at exorbitant prices around Ann Arbor, so over Thanksgiving we all chipped in and bought a pound in New York through one of our business associates who lived there and knew a fairly reliable contact. It cost four of us about thirty-five dollars apiece and after weighing it . . . we each wound up with four honest ounces. Then the idea hit — we could sell a couple, make back our investment, and still have buckets to smoke ourselves. So, we cut the stuff up — this is a technique we eventually got down to a real science — and packaged the ounces in baggies. Now we had to find a market. . . . So I phoned up a chick I knew who smoked quite a bit and asked her to look around. About a half hour later she called back with an order for three ounces. We were in business. Our pound went within two days and people were lined up begging for more. What could we do? You have to understand that this is a pretty common way for pushers to get started. They're not these crummy, slinky, little junkies you read about turning school kids on to pot and dirty pictures. It's the puritan ethic, people, the capitalist way — make a buck. Sure, simple supply and demand — like loan companies and . . . Gimbel's basement. Nobody's a nonprofit organization . . . : just business as usual in the true American tradition.[119]

8 The Place of Cannabis in Medicine

Cannabis has long been used as an indigenous medicine in the south of Africa, South America, Turkey, Egypt, and many areas of Asia including India, the Malays, Burma, and Siam. The heyday of the medical application of cannabis occurred in the Western world in the period from 1840 to 1900. During this time more than 100 articles were published recommending it for various ailments and discomforts. Physicians of a century ago knew far more about it and were much more interested in exploring its therapeutic potential than are physicians today. While its use was already declining somewhat in the earlier part of this century, primarily because of the introduction of synthetic hypnotics and analgesics, the attendant difficulties imposed on its use by the Tax Act of 1937 completed its medical demise, and it was removed from the *U.S. Pharmacopoeia* and *National Formulary* in 1941. Nonetheless, a spate of papers published prior to that time have established for it a compelling potential as a medically useful substance. Some of the indications are only suggestive; some are more definitive; but this potential has yet to be realized, largely because of ignorance on the part of the medical advisory establishment, the bad reputation of cannabis, and the legal difficulties involved in doing the kinds of basic and clinical research that would long since have been stimulated in any other group of substances with such promising possibilities. Despite the extreme difficulties of doing medical research with these drugs, some studies have been completed, and these have, to some extent, confirmed the century-old promise of the medical utility of cannabis products. With the relaxation of the restrictions on research and the chemical manipulation of the various cannabinol derivatives, this potential will doubtless eventually be realized.

His interest excited by accounts of medical applications of cannabis products in the Orient, W. B. O'Shaughnessy, then a thirty-year-old assistant surgeon and professor of chemistry in the Medical College of Calcutta, undertook some simple observational experiments with hemp on dogs and kids. Having satisfied himself that the drug was a safe one, he began to experiment with it in patients suffering from rabies, rheumatism, epilepsy, and tetanus. He found tincture of hemp to be an effective analgesic and to have anticonvulsant and muscle-relaxant properties, which he reported in 1839. O'Shaughnessy, particularly impressed with the anticonvulsant properties of the previously untried *materia medica*, expressed his "belief that in Hemp the profession has gained an anti-convulsive remedy of the greatest value." [1] Stimulated by O'Shaughnessy's report, a number of Western physicians proceeded to explore the clinical possibilities of cannabis, and within the next two decades, a number of papers on the usefulness of cannabis were to be found in the medical literature.

In 1860, Dr. R. R. M'Meens reported on the findings of the Committee on Cannabis Indica before the Ohio State Medical Society. After acknowledging their indebtedness to Dr. O'Shaughnessy, he reviewed the symptoms and conditions for which hemp was found useful. These included tetanus, neuralgia, the arrest of uterine hemorrhage, as an analgesic during labor, in dysmenorrhoea, convulsions, the pain of rheumatism, asthma, postpartum psychoses, gonorrhea, and chronic bronchitis. Indian hemp was assigned "a place among the so called hypnotic medicines next to opium; its effects are less intense, and the secretions are not so much suppressed by it. Digestion is not disturbed; the appetite rather increased; . . . The whole effect of hemp being less violent, and producing a more natural sleep, without interfering with the actions of the internal organs, it is certainly often preferable to opium, although it is not equal to that drug in strength and reliability." [2] M'Meens, as did O'Shaughnessy, emphasized the remarkable capacity of cannabis to stimulate appetite. In fact, this is such a universally reported property of the drug that it is a wonder that psychiatrists in their frequent frustration with the results of the present-day symptomatic treatment of anorexia nervosa, an emotional disturbance involving pathological and sometimes life-endangering loss of appetite, have not seized upon cannabis as potentially quite useful in this distressing syndrome.

M'Meens was also impressed with its use as a sedative, and in support of his view that this utility of the drug has been long recognized, he notes that "some high Biblical commentators maintain that the gall and vinegar, or myrrhed wine, offered to our Saviour immediately before his crucifixion, was in all probability a preparation of hemp, and even speak of its earlier use." [3]

Even as early as 1891 Dr. J. B. Mattison lamented the fact that cannabis indica was falling into disuse as an analgesic-soporific, and he attributed this to the arrival of new drugs. He compared it to the disuse that befell the use of digitalis for a period, and he urged upon physicians "the use of a drug that has a special value in some morbid conditions, and the intrinsic merit and safety of which entitles it to a place it once held in therapeutics." [4] Much the same could be said about it today. He reviews its usefulness as a general analgesic and emphasizes its worth as a soporific; he comments particularly on its use in dysmenorrhoea, chronic rheumatism, asthma, and gastric ulcer. He asserts that "it has proved an efficient substitute for the poppy." One of the morphine addiction cases he described was "a naval surgeon, nine years a ten grains daily subcutaneous morphia taker . . . [who] recovered with less than a dozen doses." [5] Actually this use had already been reported. E. Birch in 1889, approaching modern research techniques, treated one chloral-hydrate addict and one opium addict with cannabis indica. In both, the drug of addiction was replaced by unidentified pills containing cannabis, which was subsequently slowly withdrawn. Birch noted in each case a prompt response with the return of appetite and sound sleep.[6] Its usefulness in the treatment of delirium tremens Mattison described as "the best." He asserts that "its most important use is in that opprobrium of the healing art — migraine." In reviewing his own experience and that of others, Mattison concludes that this drug is not only important in the arresting of the pain from a migraine attack but is as well most useful in preventing attacks.[7] This view was amplified years later by William Osler, who said of migraine, "Cannabis indica is probably the most satisfactory remedy," and a prolonged course of treatment was recommended.[8] So convincing are the data and arguments Mattison and others present for the application of this drug to the treatment of migraine that it seems a pity that today's migraine sufferers who do not get satisfactory relief from modern treatments cannot have the opportunity for a therapeutic trial of cannabis. Dr. Mattison concludes his report on a wistful note:

> Dr. Suckling wrote me: "The young men rarely prescribe it." To them I specially commend it. With a wish for speedy effect, it is so easy to use that modern mischief-maker, hypodermic morphia, that they [young physicians] are prone to forget remote results of incautious opiate giving.
>
> Would that the wisdom which has come to their professional fathers through, it may be, a hapless experience, might serve them to steer clear of narcotic shoals on which many a patient has gone awreck.
>
> Indian hemp is not here lauded as a specific. It will, at times, fail. So do other drugs. But the many cases in which it acts well, entitle it to a large and lasting confidence.
>
> My experience warrants this statement: cannabis indica is, often, a safe and successful anodyne and hypnotic.[9]

Dr. J. R. Reynolds, in 1890, summarized thirty years of experience with cannabis indica. Of the patient with senile insomnia — that is, an elderly person who is fidgety at night, goes to bed, gets up again, fusses over his clothes, believes that he has some appointment to keep and must dress himself toward that end — a condition which we, at the present time, are not always very successful in managing — Reynolds states: "In this class of case I have found nothing comparable in utility to a moderate dose of Indian hemp."[10] Furthermore he assures us that it is successful for months, indeed years, without any increase in the dose. In his experience it was most valuable in the treatment of various neuralgias including tic douloureux. He, too, attests to its usefulness in the treatment of migraine: "Very many victims of this malady have for years kept their sufferings in abeyance by taking hemp at the moment of threatening, or onset of the attack."[11] He found it useful in certain epileptoid states, depression, and sometimes useful in asthma and dysmenorrhoea. He also enumerates a number of illnesses and syndromes for which he has used the drug with little or no success. Finally, he cautions the reader about the frequency with which preparations are found to be inactive and the importance of gradually arriving at the appropriate dose for the individual patient in order to avoid toxic effects.[12]

H. A. Hare, in 1887, made the same point with respect to potency in the use of cannabis indica for the treatment of pain: "Owing to the variations found to exist as to its activity, it has not received the confidence which I think it now deserves." [13] He, too, asserts that hemp is a most valuable agent in subduing the pain and preventing other attacks of migraine. He stresses that this is true in even the most intractable of cases. He also recommends its use in terminal cases for its effect of "quieting restlessness and anxiety, and by turning the mind of the patient to other channels. . . . Under these circumstances, the patient, whose most painful symptom has been mental trepidation, may become more happy or even hilarious." [14] He believes it to be as effective as opium in the relief of pain, and he describes this property of hemp as follows:

> During the time that this remarkable drug is relieving pain a very curious psychical condition sometimes manifests itself; namely, that the diminution of the pain seems to be due to its fading away in the distance, so that the pain becomes less and less, just as the pain in a delicate ear would grow less and less as a beaten drum was carried farther and farther out of the range of hearing.[15]

Hare also notes its usefulness as a topical anesthetic, particularly with respect to the mucous membrane of the tongue.[16] Dentists of a century ago were apparently quite familiar with this property of the drug.

One might have expected these promising clinical leads to have been followed up with a great deal of research activity, especially after 1942, when it was possible to study congeners of tetrahydrocannabinol. That the analgesic properties were not pursued is largely due to the increased use of opiates in the United States in the latter half of the nineteenth century. The hypodermic syringe, which was introduced from England in 1856, accelerated this use, for the water-soluble opiates could now be conveniently administered through this route with fast relief of pain; hemp products are insoluble and cannot be administered parenterally. The speed, reliability, and convenience of opiate administered in this way led to its widespread use during the Civil War. In fact it was used and misused so widely that opiate addiction became known as the "soldier's disease." With the development of synthetic analgesics such as aspirin, and synthetic hypnotics such as chloral hydrate and barbiturates, physicians lost interest in cannabis indica for its analgesic and hypnotic properties, for it was far less stable and primarily for that reason less reliable than the synthetics. Still one would have supposed that once some of the disadvantages of the newer drugs were realized — for example, the fact that there are about 500–1,000 deaths per year in this country from aspirin and countless deaths from addiction to barbiturates — physicians pressing the search for better analgesics and hypnotics would have turned to the study of cannabinol substances, especially at a time when new analogues could be elaborated, quite possibly both more stable and specific.

A rare exception to this neglect is to be found in a short paper written by J. P. Davis and H. II. Ramsey in 1949. They did a study of the anticonvulsant activity of two tetrahydrocannabinol congeners in five institutionalized epileptic children, all of whom had severe symptomatic grand mal epilepsy which was inadequately controlled by the usual treatment of phenobarbitol and Dilantin or Mesantoin. Three responded at least as well as to previous therapy. The fourth became almost completely and the fifth entirely free of seizures.[17]

Another exception is the work of some Czechoslovakian investigators who followed up earlier hints that cannabis might have antibacterial properties. J. Kabelík, Z. Krejčí, and F. Santavý have furnished evidence that cannabis extracts containing cannabidiolic acid produce impressive antibacterial effects upon a number of gram positive microorganisms including *Staphylococcus aureas* strains which are resistant to penicillin and other antibiotics. This finding, if borne out clinically, may prove especially important nowadays when such a high percentage of staphylococcus diseases are resistant to penicillin. The authors report one case of a pathologist who sustained an injury to his thumb in the dissecting room; the infection became so severe that it threatened amputation, as the infecting microorganisms were absolutely resistant to available antibiotics. Upon treatment with the cannabis extract the infection was overcome.[18]

Another medical use for cannabis is suggested by an observation made by Dr. H. H. Kane in 1881.[19] One of his patients was a 38-year-old English woman who deliberately took up the use of hashish in an effort to replace alcohol, to which she had become a slave. She smoked it daily in a pipe, liked it, and often claimed that if she wished she could stop it without any difficulty. While

Kane's description of her physical condition is hardly suggestive of robust health, it must be borne in mind that she had been an alcoholic for some years prior to this change. It is at least interesting to speculate whether had she made this conversion earlier she might not have fared better, at least physically. This highly speculative possible usefulness of cannabis makes the assumptions that there are some people who are bound and determined to be chronic users of some intoxicating substance, that cannabis may be substituted for alcohol as the intoxicant, and that cannabis has less devastating effects on the health of an individual than alcohol. As has already been mentioned, Birch, in 1889, used hemp successfully in treating addictions to opium and chloral hydrate, and Mattison, in 1891, found it an "efficient substitute for the poppy."

Doctors S. Allentuck and K. M. Bowman in 1942 found cannabis-derivative substitution superior to both gradual and sudden withdrawal from opiates. In a study of 49 cases they found that with substitution of a marihuana derivative, "the withdrawal symptoms were ameliorated or eliminated sooner, the patient was in a better frame of mind, his spirits were elevated, his physical condition was more rapidly rehabilitated, and he expressed a wish to resume his occupation sooner." [20] L. J. Thompson and R. C. Proctor reported quite favorable results from the use of pyrahexyl, a synthetic cannabis preparation, in the treatment of patients withdrawing from alcohol, barbiturates, and various narcotic agents. They agreed with Allentuck and Bowman that the use of cannabis did not give rise to biological or physiological dependence and that the discontinuance of the drug did not result in withdrawal symptoms.[21] Again, in view of these most suggestive early studies, it is striking how few clinical and basic research studies in this area have been made. Because there is a fairly good suggestion that cannabis has utility in the treatment of various addictions, one would expect that there would be more studies in this area and some large comprehensive clinical trials. Perhaps in addition to general difficulties in obtaining the drug and the paralegal problems involved in its study, such investigations are impeded by the fact that cannabis is still thought of as an addicting agent, and investigators are loathe to substitute one such agent for another.

It was also during the mid-nineteenth century that cannabis was first seriously proposed in Western medical literature as an agent useful in the treatment of various psychiatric illnesses. In 1845,

J. J. Moreau (de Tours) wrote of its use in the treatment of melancholia (particularly with *idée fixe*), hypomania, and chronic mental illness in general.[22] There followed a number of papers which supported and disputed its utility in the treatment of various mental illnesses. In 1947, G. T. Stockings administered synhexyl (the British name for the same synthetic cannabis preparation which in the United States is called pyrahexyl) to 50 depressive patients of whom 36 showed a definite improvement. Obsessive ruminations (Moreau's *idée fixe*) were significantly lessened in 6 out of the 7 patients of the obsessive type. However, this study, like most of the others of this drug, was not controlled.[23] D. A. Pond, in 1948, attempted to duplicate Stockings' results with another uncontrolled study. He was unable to find evidence that the drug was valuable in the treatment of depression.[24] In 1950, C. S. Parker and F. W. Wriggly conducted a double-blind study involving 57 patients suffering from melancholia or neurotic depression. They were unable to demonstrate a significant difference between synhexyl and placebo — this despite the fact that in their pilot studies, patients with melancholia and neurotic depressions consistently improved. However, because of the sedative effect of the drug, these investigators were compelled to give smaller doses (10 to 20 mg) than they would have wished, and it is possible that the amount of drug given did not produce a sufficient euphorigenic effect to counterbalance the depression.[25] That the failure of these authors to confirm the drug's utility in the treatment of depression may have been due to insufficient dosage is suggested by the fact that their dosage was less than that of Stockings' (15 to 90 mg), and in fact D. F. Downing claims that the euphorigenic activity threshold for synhexyl in man is 200 mg.[26] If it is possible to develop synthetic cannabis preparations whose euphorigenic to sedative ratio is higher than that of synhexyl, it may yet prove to be a useful substance in the symptomatic treatment of depression.

Cannabis has been written about, albeit infrequently, as an adjunct to psychotherapy.[27] The limited data available at this time are not altogether convincing. Moreover, my own experience in treating patients who are high on pot, while limited, is not impressive. The patient often has the conviction that there is heightened communication, understanding, and insight, a sense which I as a therapist have usually not been able to experience. The drug does, however, appear to promote associational fluidity and, in view of this property, deserves more study as an adjunct to psychotherapy.

T. H. Mikuriya, after reviewing the medical literature, summarized the possible therapeutic applications of cannabinol products as follows:

1. analgesic-hypnotic
2. appetite stimulant
3. antiepileptic — antispasmodic
4. prevention and interruption of the neuralgias, including migraine and tic douloureux
5. antidepressant — tranquillizer
6. psychotherapeutic aid
7. antiasthmatic
8. oxytoxic (a medicine that accelerates childbirth)
9. antitussive
10. topical anesthetic
11. an agent which facilitates withdrawal in addictions to opiates and alcohol
12. childbirth analgesic
13. antibiotic[28]

The mystery of the nature of the present relationship between cannabis and organized medicine in the United States is not simply that physicians have ignored this drug for 30 years and allowed themselves to become ignorant of its uses and its potential, but that they also condemn it as medically worthless and even dangerous. It has not always been that way. In 1937, members of the Committee on Legislative Activities of the American Medical Association, physicians who might at that time have used cannabis indica in their practices, wrote in protesting the impending 1937 Marihuana Tax Act: "There is positively no evidence to indicate the abuse of cannabis as a medicinal agent or to show that its medicinal use is leading to the development of cannabis addiction. Cannabis at the present time is slightly used for medicinal purposes, but it would seem worthwhile to maintain its status as a medicinal agent for such purposes as it now has. There is a possibility that a restudy of the drug by modern means may show other advantages to be derived from its medicinal use." Almost prophetically, it goes on to state, "Your committee also recognizes that in the border states the extensive use of the marihuana weed by a certain type of people would be hard to control." [29] Thirty years later, a *Journal of the American Medical Association* position paper, written by men who have apparently had little if any experience with the use of cannabis drugs and apparently as little familiarity with the medical literature, asserts: "Cannabis (marihuana) *has no known use in medical practice in most countries* of the world, including the United States." [30] In a position paper a year later there is a specious argument about potency: "The orders of potency [of cannabis resin] on a weight (milligram) basis are greater than those for many other powerful psychoactive agents, such as barbiturates. They are markedly greater than those for alcohol." [31] Here there is a clear implication that cannabis is an extremely toxic substance as compared to barbiturates and alcohol, and this in a journal that has been less than aggressive with respect to the toxicity of cigarette smoking, and often seems more sensitive to the needs of its drug company advertisers than the toxic effects of their products. Mikuriya compared the toxicity of cannabis to barbiturates and alcohol.[32] His comparison is modified and summarized as follows:

	Effective Dose	Lethal Dose	Safety Factor (Lethal Dose/ Effective Dose)
Secobarbital	100–300 mg	1,000–5,000 mg	3–50
Alcohol	0.05–0.1%	0.4–0.5%	4–10
Tetrahydro- cannabinol	50 mcg/kg	2,160,000 mcg/kg*	40,000 *

* Because no human fatalities have been documented, the figures given are for the human effective dose and the lethal dose for mice.

Thus, it can be seen that secobarbital (Seconal), whose effective dose as a hypnotic is usually 100 mg but may be as much as 300 mg, has a lethal dose of 1,000 to 5,000 mg. Thus a dose which is only three to fifty times the effective dose may prove fatal. With alcohol, the blood level required for intoxication is between 0.05% and 0.1%. Since the fatal dose is 0.4% to 0.5%, the safety factor is 4 to 10. The effective intoxicating dose of tetrahydrocannabinol is estimated to be between 25 and 50 micrograms per kilogram weight. Because there is no data on human fatalities, the lethal dose had to be extrapolated from data on mice, and from this the safety factor can be estimated to be something on the order of

40,000. Thus, to the extent that the most extreme, acute toxic effect of death may be considered a measure of a drug's toxicity, cannabis, contrary to the American Medical Association's position, is an extremely safe drug compared with secobarbitol and alcohol.

In fact it is invariably reported that no instances of death resulting from the use of cannabis have ever been recorded. I have encountered only four exceptions to this claim. G. F. W. Ewens, the superintendent of the Punjab Lunatic Asylum, Lahore, India, reported seeing two instances in 1898. In both cases the victims were prisoners who had previously been "addicted" to *charas,* but had been compelled on confinement to relinquish its use. Each is said to have suddenly obtained possession of a large amount and taken a greater dose than he had been in the habit of taking even before confinement. The effect was the rapid development of coma, emesis, and stertorous breathing, and coldness of the body surface. The only postmortem finding he reported was a curious congestion of all the organs of the body. Skepticism about these two poorly documented cases of Ewens's is enhanced by the fact that the reference to death following a larger than usual dose clearly suggests that the actual drug leading to death may have been opium.[33] The third case was a death from taking Indian hemp, reported by S. Deakin in the *Indian Medical Gazette* in 1880. In this case a man who had been using *bhang* struck himself on the head and apparently died of a subdural hematoma resulting from the blow. The role of cannabis, if any, was quite indirect.[34] The fourth case, a recent one (1969), is to be found in the Belgian literature. Here a 23-year-old man was found dead, and it was established that he had been using cannabis; how much and over what period of time is not known. The evidence is presumptive, but not conclusive.[35] Still, it is difficult to believe that there is any drug which does not, at the very least in the circumstances of gross ill-health on the part of the user and the taking of very large amounts, lead to death in some cases. Yet one of the curious things about the cannabis literature is that these four poorly substantiated cases are the only ones as far as I know in which death has been reported, despite the fact that the drug has been used by countless people for a very long time. I think it is safe to conclude that death from cannabis must be extremely rare and will only occur under conditions of extraordinary dose and unusual circumstances.

Some research on tetrahydrocannabinol has been done during

the last decade. The Department of Defense in its never-ending search for new weapons, became interested in cannabis in the early 1960's. They let contracts with Arthur D. Little, Inc., whose chemists have synthesized a number of new classes of compounds that are molecularly like tetrahydrocannabinol, but differ in some respects from the naturally occurring forms. Rather than new weapons, some compounds with exciting therapeutic potentials were discovered. When I asked to review this data, I was told that it would not be possible, inasmuch as the Department of Defense continued to classify this material. However, in one paper recently presented by this group success in synthesizing two water-soluble Δ^1-tetrahydrocannabinols is reported.[36] Although the Department of Defense has apparently given up on cannabis, the drug companies are becoming interested. What can be learned now about these new compounds suggests that they may be useful in three areas.

1. *Analgesics.* Apparently some of the new compounds have generated encouraging data in animal procedures designed to evaluate pain-relieving drugs. They appear to have properties in common with mood elevators as well as analgesics, and this combination could make them unique and potentially useful drugs.

2. *Blood pressure reduction.* Some of the new agents lower the blood pressure, apparently through mechanisms which are entirely different from drugs presently used to treat hypertension.

3. *Psychopharmacotherapeutic agents.* Again there is apparently some preliminary data which indicates that some of the new compounds have antidepressant and antianxiety properties and that these properties are quite different in their mode of action from those in drugs presently used.[37]

Thus, while whole cannabis preparations are unstable, vary greatly in strength, are insoluble in water, and have an onset of action which is slower than that of other drugs, they have the advantage over other analgesics, hypnotics, and sedatives in that they do not lead to the development of either physical dependence or tolerance, they have extraordinarily low toxicity, and lead to no disturbance of vegetative functions. Furthermore, from what we know about other classes of drugs, it is altogether possible that when new congeners of the various cannabinol derivatives are developed — if indeed some have not already been — many or all of these problems will be overcome. Equally likely is the possibility that medical utilities already known will be enhanced and new ones discovered.

9 Addiction, Dependence, and the Stepping-Stone Hypothesis

To clarify the issue of whether or not marihuana is an "addictive" drug, and the related question whether or not it is a drug that causes what is generally referred to as "psychic dependence" or "habituation" (which do not, in fact, mean the same thing, but which are not generally distinguished) it may be helpful to determine just what the criteria for (opium or opium-related) addiction are: (1) the individual, once addicted, has undergone some sort of long-lasting change such that even if he abstains for years he can be readdicted by relatively few doses;[1] (2) if the addicted individual is deprived of his drug, he experiences severe and highly unpleasant physical and psychological withdrawal symptoms, characterized (usually) by yawning, rhinorrhea, lacrimation, excessive perspiration, and a fitful restless sleep (6 to 12 hours after the last dose), increasing restlessness, back and leg pains, twitching of various muscle groups, hot and cold flashes, and chills (after 24 hours). Other signs of disordered function of the autonomic nervous system appear, including elevation of both temperature and blood pressure, increase in both rate and depth of respiration, and dilation of previously constricted pupils. By 48 hours the withdrawal syndrome reaches its peak with nausea, retching, vomiting, diarrhea, anorexia, and rapid weight loss. After 72 hours the abstinence syndrome begins to subside slowly, and after about 5 to 10 days most of the signs and symptoms have disappeared, but there may continue to be some weakness, insomnia, restlessness, and muscle pains in legs and back for several weeks. Four to 6 months elapse before some physiological variables approach a stable level, and, even 6 months after withdrawal, hyperresponsitivity of the autonomic nervous system has been reported;[2] and (3) usually there is a strong craving for the drug, which may be partly or entirely psychological and induced by fear of withdrawal, although the exact nature of this craving, which is perhaps the model for compulsion, is not known.[3] Often associated with true addiction, and usually referred to as an "essential attribute," is the development of tolerance, which refers to the phenomenon that on repeated administration of the same dose of the drug there is a declining effect of the drug or, conversely, a necessity to increase the dose on repeated administrations in order to obtain the initial degree of effect. Tolerance almost always occurs with prolonged, addictive use of opiates, but it is not correct to consider it an absolute criterion for addiction, since it may also develop when generally recognized nonaddictive drugs (LSD, for example) are used. Addiction includes physical dependence, but (unless the term is expanded beyond the usual definition, which is roughly equivalent to the inevitability of onset of withdrawal symptoms) it is not limited by this phenomenon. The three criteria, along with tolerance in almost all cases, do not separately indicate addiction; they are criteria only in the sense that all of them must be present or potential in true addiction.

It is interesting that the Expert Committee on Drugs Liable to Produce Addiction of the World Health Organization has revised its views on addiction and rewritten their definition in terms of "drug dependence." In 1950 this committee defined "drug addiction" as follows: "a state of periodic or chronic intoxication, detrimental to the individual and to society, produced by the repeated consumption of a drug (natural or synthetic). Its characteristics include:

1. An overpowering desire or need (compulsion) to continue taking the drug and to obtain it by any means.
2. A tendency to increase the dose.
3. A psychic (psychological) and sometimes a physical dependence on the effects of the drug." [4]

However, in 1964 this same committee gave its endorsement to the following statement: "Drug dependence is a state of psychic or physical dependence, or both, on a drug, arising in a person following administration of that drug on a periodic or continuous basis. The characteristics of such a state will vary with the agent involved, and these characteristics must always be made clear by designating the particular type of drug dependence in each specific case; for example, drug dependence of morphine type, of barbiturate type, of amphetamine type; etc." [5] The term "addiction," along with the term "drug habituation," was not mentioned. An unfortunate effect of this revision is that it has helped to reinforce the general transfer of the connotations of "addiction" to "drug dependence" ("of the psychic type" in the case of cannabis).

There is no longer any doubt that marihuana is not a drug of addiction. As early as 1904, G. F. W. Ewens, Superintendent of the Punjab Lunatic Asylum in Lahore, and an author who had little use for the drug, wrote: "In the first place it is universally believed that this habit has a great advantage over that of opium or alcohol or even tobacco taking in that it may be at any time relinquished without difficulty, and though I do not know whether this is absolutely true, I can certainly testify that no ill-effects follow its sudden forcible stoppage against the will of the patient." [6] The 1925 Panama Canal Zone Governor's Committee, "after an investigation extending from April to December 1925, . . . reached the following conclusions: There is no evidence that marihuana as grown here is a 'habit-forming' drug in the sense in which the term applies to alcohol, opium, cocaine, etc." [7] Not only are there no withdrawal symptoms, but there is no necessity to increase dosage over time. [8] In fact there is a suggestion that more experienced users are able to get the desired effect with less of the drug than inexperienced users. [9]

In 1934 W. Bromberg stated that "there is a definite difference . . . between marihuana addicts and morphine or heroin addicts . . . morphine and heroin affect deeper layers of the personality. The morphinist feels the need of his drug more strongly because it is involved with basic instinct structures. . . . Addiction among marihuana users is unlike addiction among the users of morphine or heroin. In the latter two drugs the tolerance developed in the body is a potent factor in addiction — the victim must have increasing doses of the drug to feel normal. With marihuana the user wants to recapture over and over again the ecstatic, elated state into which the drug lifts him. There is no physical disturbance on withdrawal of the drug: no real tolerance is developed. The addiction to cannabis is a sensual addiction: it is in the services of the hedonistic elements of the personality." [10]

Although Bromberg's final sentence may strike the reader as somewhat moralistic, his particular terminology should not obscure the possibility that a psychic dependency can develop in some people. While most authorities agree that cannabis does not lead to either physical dependence or tolerance, there are many who assert that there is nevertheless drug dependence because of its capacity to generate psychic dependency. However it is not at all clear that this type of dependency is essentially any different from that which a man may develop with respect to his trousers, his automobile, or his wife. The crucial question, one that neither Bromberg nor any of the antimarihuana crusaders raise, is whether or not this dependency causes individual or social harm. Psychological dependency, despite the negative connotations the term has for many people, is not in and of itself dangerous. Even one of the most vociferous opponents of the legalization of marihuana in England, W. D. M. Paton, admits that "life is in fact built up of such dependencies . . . [he is referring to his habit of eating Kellogg's cornflakes each morning]. Any habit represents one: some dependences are trivial, some benign and pleasurable, some not so benign: some, such as dependences on friends and family and work, are part of what makes you what you are." [11] The possibility of harm to the individual or society is not a function of dependency per se, but rather of the harmfulness of that which is depended upon. In the case of marihuana, the dangers are not well established. Furthermore it is not clear just how habituating cannabis is. While one Egyptian survey suggests considerable psychological dependence, inasmuch as 65 percent of hashish users wished to rid themselves of the habit, it is, on the other hand, asserted by S. Allentuck and K. M. Bowman that habituation to cannabis is not as strong as to tobacco and alcohol. [12] This is borne out by the study of 34 soldier users by J. F. Siler et al. in which they found that only 15 percent missed marihuana when deprived of it, and 71 percent stated that they preferred tobacco. [13] The disparity between this study and the Egyptian one may have to do with the difference between marihuana (*bhang*) and hashish, as well as differences in culture and set and setting. L. S. Goodman and A. Gilman assert that an overwhelming preoccupation with the continued use of marihuana is extremely rare; as most users in this country express it, "I can take it or leave it alone." [14] Whether this is also true of the more potent synthetics or of the more concentrated cannabis preparations used more commonly in other parts of the world is still unsettled.

Nonetheless, for some, the desire to use cannabis can apparently be most compelling, and it is certainly possible that a psychic dependency may develop in those people whose psychological makeup is such that one of the euphoriants becomes an essential catalyst to the experience of pleasure or, perhaps more accurately in others, a respite from psychic pain. Those who become psychologically dependent on marihuana to this degree are undoubtedly people with character disorders, anxiety, depression, feelings of inadequacy, or intolerable life situations; that is, people who are particularly susceptible to dependency on *any* of a number of euphoriant drugs.

But can it be said that even people who use marihuana in this fashion are abusing it? If the term drug abuse has been difficult to define with respect to other intoxicants, it is particularly difficult with regard to cannabis, because it is not altogether clear what, if any, is the danger of protracted use to the individual, society, or both. Furthermore, since the definition of drug abuse is largely socially determined, it will vary from culture to culture, and even within a culture. In the United States chronic alcoholic inebriation is considered abuse, but occasional inebriation and "social drinking" are not. The dangers of protracted and even the social use of alcohol have been established; those of the casual and even protracted use of marihuana in this country have not been clearly established.[15] In fact, the clearest risk to the user of marihuana in this country is the one imposed by the present laws, that of conviction of a felony or misdemeanor with its attendant permanent social and career damage.

It is generally conceded that marihuana is not addicting, but there are still those who believe that smoking it will lead to the use of narcotics.[16] In fact, this is offered as a major argument in justification of the existing laws. The present position of the Bureau of Narcotics and Dangerous Drugs with reference to the necessity of maintaining the stringent and overly harsh legal sanctions against the use, possession, or sale of marihuana has changed considerably from the position expressed in 1937 by the then Commissioner of the Federal Bureau of Narcotics, H. Anslinger. At that time, in testimony before the House of Representatives Ways and Means Committee, Anslinger based his strong opposition to marihuana entirely upon its supposed crime-inducing effects. When he was questioned by Representative John Dingell of Michigan as to whether "the marihuana addict graduates into a heroin, an opium, or a cocaine user," Anslinger gave the following reply: "No, sir; I have not heard of a case of that kind. I think it is an entirely different class. The marihuana addict does not go in that direction." [17] In the same year Anslinger also testified before a Senate subcommittee which was considering the bill requested by the Federal Bureau of Narcotics, stating that "there is an entirely new class of people using marihuana. The opium user is about 35 to 40 years old. These users [of marihuana] are 20 years old and know nothing of heroin or morphine." [18] In the same year, 1937, Anslinger and C. R. Cooper wrote an article in which they emphasized the capacity of marihuana to lead to violence and deviant behavior; they made no mention of a linkage between marihuana and opiate use.[19]

However, the "official" position of the Federal Bureau of Narcotics had shifted 180 degrees by 1950, when Deputy Commissioner G. W. Cunningham, testifying in place of Anslinger before Congress's Committee on Appropriations, stated that most young heroin addicts gave "a history of having started by smoking marijuana." [20]

J. Mandel has found that during the years 1920 to 1948, "more than 70 percent of the major articles . . . dealing with marijuana made no mention of the danger [that use of marihuana would lead to use of opiates, and this] . . . was also found to be true in professional literature, there being no mention of a marijuana-opiate connection in eighteen papers; on law enforcement and criminology, in eight lay articles and books; and in eighteen other publications." [21] As early as 1931, Dr. A. E. Fossier, in an article written for the *New Orleans Medical and Surgical Journal*, asserted that marihuana users "become engulfed in the abyss of drug addiction," by which he meant addiction to opiates, although the focus of the article was for repeal of prohibition, on the grounds that prohibition of alcohol leads directly to "the possible substitution of alcohol for a greater evil [sic] . . . [i.e., marihuana and then heroin or other opiates]." [22] Other articles and books published before 1949 that mentioned the "stepping-stone" hypothesis were either publications of various prohibition or temperance groups or "unofficial statements by unnamed federal agents, or the 'New Orleans school' of experts such as Dr. Fossier."[23] The absurdity of most of the positions on the "stepping-stone" hypothesis can be seen by examining some of the ways authors cited each other as their sole supporting evidence for the theory. One F. R. Gomila, who was a colleague and co-worker with Fossier, wrote a book about marihuana, which he condensed into an article in 1938. R. P. Walton reprinted Gomila's article (on the "stepping-stone" hypothesis) in his book, *Marihuana, America's New Drug Problem*.[24] In 1943 P. O. Wolff used Walton's reprint as the sole supporting evidence in an article advocating the "stepping-stone" hypothesis.[25] Another article that advanced the "stepping-stone" hypothesis appeared in 1937, listing Fossier's article as one of the five bibliographic references given.[26] In all, there were only 15 works printed during the period 1931 to 1948 that advanced this hypothesis.[27] This figure includes a 1938 booklet published by the now-defunct White Cross organization, entitled *On the Trail of Marihuana*. This is an interesting example of the kind of "argument" that was typically advanced in favor of the "stepping-stone" notion: naive and innocent individuals are depicted as falling prey to vicious pushers who "bait" them with marihuana, and then when the "thrills" provided by that herb are no longer strong enough (an argument which assumes what has to all intents been established as *not* occurring with marihuana use, i.e., the development of tolerance to the effects of the drug), get them hooked on heroin. But the White Cross went back a step further in this causative train, just as another antimarihuana crusader, the "hyperactive reformer and alarmist of the period, Earle Albert Rowell," had done.[28] Rowell asserted in 1939 that he had spent the previous 14 years in a personal campaign against not only marihuana, but also tobacco, because he was convinced that there was a direct *causal* connection between the use of, first, tobacco; second, marihuana; and, finally, heroin.[29] This was essentially the same argument advanced by the White Cross publication: "The organization claimed that the chain of evil, 'the descent into hell,' started with smoking ordinary cigarettes and subsequently it saw a direct link between the government-licensed tobacco companies and the peddler flogging [*sic*] his drugs. In their view, the stepping stones on the route to addiction led inevitably from tobacco to marijuana and thence to the opiates and the needle. It was never clarified just how this progression came about; it was accepted as fact and as such it was readily absorbed by the mass media and the public at large. Pot, they declared, might be the lesser of the drug evils, but it was the likely place for the occasional smoker on his way to permanent addiction to the opiates." [30]

Besides Anslinger and Cooper, only a few writers attempted any refutation of this theory: "Opiate effects and users were differentiated from those of marihuana in three articles in professional journals for psychiatrists, in a professional journal for police (*Police and Peace Officers Journal,* June 1934), several issues of the WCTU's *Union Signal* after 1935 [prior to that time, between late 1934 and early 1935, three articles appeared in the same publication asserting that there was a direct link between the use of marihuana and addiction to heroin], and in the vehemently anti-marijuana book *Marihuana — The New Dangerous Drug* by F. T. Merrill (1938). . . . The retired chief of the Public Health Service convincingly attacked some basic arguments used by advocates of stepping stone'ism in a 1946 article for probation officers (*Federal Probation*)." [31] During this same period, the La Guardia Report stated: "We have been unable to confirm the opinion expressed by some investigators that marihuana smoking is the first step in the use of such drugs as cocaine, morphine, and heroin. The instances are extremely rare where the habit of marihuana smoking is associated with addiction to these other narcotics." [32]

In 1949, however, there was an abrupt shift in the pattern of decreasing public interest in drug abuse. "This time the 'problem' was teenage heroin use. Marijuana was considered a relatively mild danger, and almost exclusively because of long-run indirect effects — namely, as a 'starter' drug." [33] Mandel cites a 1949 *Collier's Magazine* article on drugs, written by Broadway gossip columnist Earl Wilson, as the first clear and widely read indication of a broad shift in attitude toward the use of marihuana — a shift which included and was in fact based on adoption of the "stepping-stone" theory. However, Wilson's "evidence" that users of marihuana "stepped up" to the use of harder drugs was nothing more than personal comments made to him by Los Angeles narcotics agents.[34] Despite a level or declining rate of opiate use and an increase of marihuana use during the period 1930–1950, the Federal Bureau of Narcotics, within one year after the publication of Wilson's article, was testifying that the main danger of marihuana use was no longer the pre-1937 charges of immediate near-compulsion to commit murder, rape, theft (coupled with the onset of insanity), but rather that marihuana use provided "schooling" for future heroin and other opiate addicts.

Within three years from the publication of Wilson's article, at least nine mass media articles on drugs asserted that the *only* danger of marihuana was that it tended to "start" heroin users; another five articles mentioned, but slighted, any dangers of marihuana other than its alleged effect of causing users to "graduate" to stronger drugs, usually heroin specifically.[35] The authors of these articles offered no supporting data; apparently they realized that the mass media audience had been sufficiently propagandized to accept the "stepping-stone" theory as self-evident, and, had they presented what little data was available — for example, the rise in cannabis use was simultaneous with a leveling-off or even a declining rate of opiate addiction over the preceding twenty years — they would have done very little to support their claims.[36]

But what was the cause of this apparent about-face in the attitudes of both the mass media and the Federal Bureau of Narcotics? As Mandel suggests, and as a 1943 *Life* magazine article predicted, the 1949 shift was a delayed reaction to the drug-traffic (and opiate-traffic specifically) slow-down caused by World War II — a slow-down that amounted to a nearly complete stoppage.[37] In 1943 *Life* reported that:

Today agents of the Treasury's Bureau of Narcotics are kept busy with . . . petty cases. . . . From the current crop of offenders it would almost seem that the U.S. has little or no narcotics problem. And indeed, so long as the war lasts, this is true. Traditional sources of narcotics supply — Yugoslavia's Vardar Valley, Occupied China and Java, are cut off entirely and wartime strictness in customs inspection and the general difficulty in moving from one place to another over the oceans have made large-scale drug smuggling virtually impossible. The only sources left open . . . are Iran, Turkey, and Afganistan. . . . Yet officials of the Bureau of Narcotics and officials of the

League of Nations now in Washington are deeply concerned about the future. They foresee the very real danger of a post-war epidemic of drug addiction.

They have cogent reasons for so thinking. One is that addiction usually has increased alarmingly after major wars in the past. . . . A second reason is that when the war ends, enormous quantities of narcotics may be available to illicit merchants. . . . At the same time, in the general chaos of the postwar months, it will be difficult to police all the narcotics manufacturers and growers whose war markets will suddenly have disappeared.[38]

As Mandel notes, the actual use of narcotics on a much wider scale than during the war years began no later than 1947, although it was not "reflected by the national panic" until 1949.[39] G. Connery of the American Medical Association's Washington, D.C., office made the same prediction as that given by *Life* (although much later): "In 1947, when there was some talk of closing the Lexington [narcotic] hospital as surplus, Mr. Anslinger advised against it. He told the Public Health Service that an increase in addiction, in his opinion, would occur in a very few years." [40] Still, the question why marihuana was implicated in this increase in opiate use is puzzling, especially when one realizes that although the rise in opiate use was considerable compared with the war-year levels, it was only a little above the level in 1940 (if one considers arrests as an indication of use), and 1940 was supposedly a year in which "the national [opiate] situation was well in hand." [41] The number of opiate arrests by the Federal Bureau of Narcotics rose from 3,009 in 1940 to 3,779 in 1949, whereas the number of federal marihuana arrests rose from 950 to 1,643 over the same 9 years — a 26-percent increase in opiate arrests vs. a 73-percent increase in marihuana arrests.[42] If these figures indicate anything significant with regard to usage, they would seem to show that despite a large increase in the use of marihuana, there was a relatively slight increase in the use of opiates: a finding that directly contradicts the implications of the "stepping-stone" hypothesis.

In 1955 Anslinger appeared before a Senate subcommittee investigating the traffic in illicit drugs. Senator Price Daniel questioned Anslinger whether "the real danger there [in the use of marihuana] is that the use of marihuana leads many people eventually to the use of heroin, and the drugs that do cause complete addiction; is that true?" Anslinger hedgingly replied: "That is the great problem and our great concern about the use of marihuana, that eventually, if used over a long period, it does lead to heroin addiction." [43] At the same time, Anslinger played down considerably the crime-inducing effects of marihuana — those alleged effects that had been the mainstay of his 1937 arguments. Senator Welker questioned him: "Is it or is it not a fact that the marihuana user has been responsible for many of our most sadistic, terrible crimes in this nation, such as sex slayings, and matters of that kind?" Anslinger replied: "There have been instances of that, Senator. We have had some rather tragic occurrences by users of marihuana. It does not follow that all crimes can be traced to marihuana. There have been many brutal crimes traced to marihuana, but I would not say that it is a controlling factor in the commission of crimes." [44] Clearly Anslinger remembered enough of his exaggerated statements during the thirties, but just as clearly he wished to indicate that, in the eyes of the Federal Bureau of Narcotics, the real danger of marihuana was no longer its propensity to induce crime, but rather its propensity to lead to the use of heroin and other hard drugs. This is the same line that the Federal Bureau of Narcotics has stuck to ever since: in 1967 the former Commissioner, H. L. Giordano, echoed an earlier statement of his predecessor Anslinger, who has stated that "they start on marihuana, then graduate to heroin." [45] Giordano asserted that "the individual who starts using marihuana usually is looking for some kicks, and after a while marihuana kicks are not enough and they go on to heroin." [46] The present Director of the Federal Bureau of Narcotics and Dangerous Drugs, J. E. Ingersoll, is talking the same line: "And it is a matter of record that the explosion in marijuana use has been accompanied by a sharp upturn in heroin use. . . . Now, looking at the problem from the other end, we know that the overwhelming majority of those who use heroin or LSD in the U.S. and England have had prior experience with either marijuana or hashish. Thus, it seems reasonable to assume that if many individuals did not get involved with marijuana, they would never get around to using the more potent and dangerous drugs." [47] This statement is instructive as an example of what is perhaps the basic fallacy of all arguments for the "stepping-stone" hypothesis, which I like to call the *fallacy of the reversed apparent equation*. For example, when Emerson wrote, "To be great is to be misunderstood," he did not mean to imply that every person who is misunderstood is therefore great, although many people who are often misunderstood and like to confuse obscurity with depth of thought would have it so.[48] In the same way, when Ingersoll urges us to look "at the problem from the other end," he is falling into the same trap. Moreover, he assumes that consecutiveness implies causality, and he introduces another point of confusion by seeming to equate the "stepping up" from cannabis to either LSD *or* heroin, when, in fact, as at least one recent study has clearly shown, regular users of marihuana, if they use any other drug, are much more apt to use LSD or another similar drug than they are to use heroin.[49]

If one attempts to analyze the argument of the Federal Bureau of Narcotics by examining relative statistics, one is immediately met with a simple but frustrating fact: there is a dearth of reliable statistical data relating to use of marihuana or heroin, except perhaps in the state of California. But also, even the California statistics are only for the number of individuals arrested, and whether or not this type of figure is a valid indication of comparative incidence of use is in no way known. It would seem that the heroin addict is perhaps more likely to be arrested, but it is also quite obvious that, with the present widespread use of marihuana throughout the country, the law enforcement officials simply cannot crack down "on the street-level trafficker in drugs — the 'pushers.' There are just too many of them. For every one you pick up, there are 20 waiting to take his place" — as Director Ingersoll himself admits.[50] But still, the statistics from most cities and states are useless. "For New York City, Chicago, and Detroit, the available published official statistics are useless for testing the 'stepping stone' proposition for there was no attempt made to differentiate between marijuana and opiate violations."[51] The California statistics, however, *do* make this distinction; and a perusal of these data from 1960 indicates that they form a case *against* the "stepping-stone" theory. "From 1960 to the present, opiate arrests have declined while marihuana arrests have increased over 400 per cent."[52] But even these statistics are weighted: because "about 90 per cent of all California opiate law violators from 1960–66 have had past opiate records," much closer checks — parole and probation — have been kept on these individuals than on those arrested for marihuana violations. However, California has also kept statistics for drug law violators who have *not* had a past record of involvement with opiates, and from an examination of *these* data, Mandel has reached the following conclusions:

> Dangerous drugs (amphetamines, barbiturates, etc.) are more often "starters" towards opiates than is marijuana.
>
> . . . Opiate use *without* a past history of marijuana is seven times likelier than opiate use *with* a past record of pot smoking.
>
> . . . On the average, over 60 times as many Californians are arrested for marijuana without having a history of "hard drugs" than appear to "graduate" from marijuana to heroin.[53]

As Mandel notes, each of these could be used to refute the "stepping-stone" view.

There are other sources of data which are less comprehensive but indicative of identical conclusions with regard to the validity of the "stepping-stone" hypothesis. In a study of 100 heroin users in the Chicago area in 1952, it was found that "only eleven . . . admitted having . . . [any history of] using marihuana. . . . Most of them began directly with heroin." [54] A study conducted in New York in early 1951 found that "marijuana had virtually disappeared from the [Harlem adolescent drug] scene; it is now considered 'kid stuff'!" [55] The New York City Youth Board, in a study of 15 heroin users from one street gang, found *no* prior history of marihuana use, although there was one of alcohol use.[56] Two major studies of adolescent heroin users in New York City in the early 1950's concluded that marihuana use was not a causal element in the etiology of heroin use.[57]

Other, usually unpublished, studies of prior drug use among *incarcerated* opiate addicts have indicated that the figures for prior use of marihuana range from 40 percent to 90 percent. However, none of these studies indicate the length of time the average opiate addict had smoked marihuana before using heroin for the first time, nor do any even mention how frequently he used marihuana, nor do they suggest any factors indicative of a causal connection between use of the two drugs.[58] There is one report from a surprising source that is an exception to this apparently high rate of association (40–90 percent) between the use of the two drugs; in 1950 the Federal Bureau of Narcotics ran a random study of 602 cases pulled from their files of opiate convictions and found that only "seven per cent of them started on marihuana." [59] Again, the indication is that the assumption that previous marihuana use is a causative factor is entirely spurious.

The Task Force on Narcotics and Drug Abuse of the President's Commission on Law Enforcement and Administration of Justice asserted in 1967 that approximately 50 percent of heroin users have had some prior experience with marihuana. However, this same group noted that most of the heroin users studied had also had previous experience with alcohol and tobacco. [60] It might have been noted that most of them had had experience with milk, Coca-Cola, or sex. Such retrospective studies of this problem give no clue as to the existence of any conceivable typical "escalation"; there is simply no valid evidence of anything inherent in cannabis or cannabis use which would make the marihuana user likely to become a heroin or other opiate user. Marihuana is, as far as has yet been determined, a precursor of only further marihuana use. One conclusion of a follow-up study on an in-depth investigation of 63 subjects by N. E. Zinberg and A. T. Weil was that there was remarkably little use of drugs other than marihuana by the participants, despite heavy marihuana use by many of them. The authors stated that their results provided "absolutely no evidence" that cannabis users "progress" to hard drugs. [61]

Recently, however, a British pharmacologist, W. D. M. Paton, has attempted to establish "the association between cannabis and heroin" in a different manner. He writes that

> the idea that cannabis might "escalate" to heroin has been canvassed really seriously in this country; and one can find some quite wise authorities who have said that they can see no evidence for it. I have reached a different conclusion. But first one must be clear what one is saying: not that every person who takes cannabis is bound to go on to heroin; nor that I can identify *a priori* a process, started by cannabis, which must, physiologically or chemically, go on to heroin. It is simply a question of public health statistics: is there evidence or is there not, that taking cannabis gives an enhanced risk of addiction to opiates, and, if so, by how much? If there *is* such an enhance-

ment, then the social cost of cannabis includes . . . that of the harder drugs to which it may lead.

The approach I would like to make is to set up, in contrast, a different hypothesis; that is that cannabis and heroin have nothing to do with each other, and then to test this hypothesis. . . .

A second approach would be to look at the growth, on the one hand of cannabis-taking, on the other hand of heroin addiction. . . .

Finally one can approach it statistically. Again let us suppose that cannabis and heroin-taking have nothing to do with each other. In that case the incidence of cannabis-taking among known heroin-addicts should be the same as that of the general population.[62]

Paton is here proposing three separate arguments for the "stepping-stone" hypothesis; each one deserves careful examination. In the case of his first argument, he maintains that the hypothesis "that cannabis and heroin have nothing to do with each other" would be supported if "one could for instance show that the age at which people come to take cannabis is in fact later than the age at which they take heroin." [63] He cites the findings of a Dr. Glatt to show that the opposite is true. However, the first weakness in his first argument is revealed when he asserts that Glatt "has shown . . . that in a group of heroin addicts, their history showed that on the average they began to take cannabis *or amphetamines* at around 16 or 17, [and] they began to take heroin at around 18 or 19" (italics added).[64] Clearly, if these young users began to take *either* amphetamine or cannabis previous to taking heroin, there is no reason to single out cannabis and exclude amphetamine as the first "step" to hard-drug addiction; yet, as far as I know, neither Paton nor anyone else has made the "stepping-stone" claim for amphetamines. Furthermore, this argument is merely a variation of the "consecutiveness equals causality" or "chronological-use-pattern indicates causality" fallacy. If there is any relationship between the reported earlier age for initial cannabis use and reported later age for heroin use, it might possibly be explained by the fact that once the users have established what the law defines as a criminal activity, entailing contact(s) with the underworld — in some, but probably not many cases — it is relatively easy for them to be persuaded or to persuade themselves that experimentation with heroin would be no more dangerous than with cannabis. If this were so, any relationship between the two drugs would be a direct result of the repressive and punitive legislation that (in this country, although not in England at the present time) equates marihuana use with heroin use. But one need not even go so far as to assume that it was contact with sellers of heroin that influenced the marihuana users to first try the harder drug; doubtless they all drank milk, ate food, read comic books, wore clothes, and rode bicycles before they used either cannabis or heroin, yet, so far as I know, no one has maintained that any of these activities lead to cannabis or heroin use. And furthermore, even if Paton's argument (number one) were entirely acceptable, all that it would indicate is that the suggestion that marihuana leads on to heroin is not nonsense.

With regard to Paton's second argument, he claims that "over the years from 1959 to 1967, after a relatively stable period up to 1958, there was, both in cannabis offenses and heroin addicts, a 20-fold growth." [65] The first major methodological error that is obvious is his comparison of "offenses" with "addicts" — he does not indicate exactly what kinds of cannabis offenses were committed, nor does he give his source for the number of addicts, although he apparently means those known to the Home Office. Furthermore, a closer look at the data which he cites (in the form of a graph) as evidence reveals some discrepancies Paton does not mention. For example, in 1956 the number of cannabis offenses was about 100, and the number of heroin addicts was about 50. In 1957, the number of cannabis offenses dropped to below the number of heroin addicts, which increased to approximately 55. By 1959 the number of cannabis offenses had risen to about 200, whereas the number of heroin addicts was the same as for 1957. Between the years 1959 and 1962, the number of cannabis offenses rose to about 600, whereas the number of heroin addicts rose only to about 175. From 1962 to 1965, the number of cannabis offenses remained constant (always around 600), whereas the number of heroin addicts rose from about 175 to just below the 600 level.[66] But there are factors other than marihuana use which help to account for this apparent "explosion" in the number of British heroin addicts. The British system "has an interpretive joker in it which in practice legalizes lifelong addiction for addicts [to heroin] without appearing to do so in a statutory sense. The Dangerous Drugs Act of 1920 is presently interpreted so that narcotics may be legally administered to addicts by physicians 'where it has been . . . demonstrated that the patient, while capable of leading a useful and relatively normal life when a certain minimum dose is repeatedly administered, becomes incapable of this when the drug is entirely discontinued.' In effect, this interpretation enables physicians legally to supply addicts with enough narcotics to gratify their euphoric needs, since the authorities demand no proof that the addicts in question are leading normal and useful lives or that the drug is essential and is given in the minimum doses necessary for this purpose." [67] The author, writing in 1960, notes that the number of addicts known to the officials was "too small to be credible, and the high *per capita* consumption of legal narcotics suggests the existence of much masked addiction." [68] This in turn suggests the possibility that the apparent rise from 1962 to 1965 may have been simply the result of more of the "masked" addicts reporting their condition, in order to insure their supply. Another possible explanation, which also has nothing to do with the apparent rise in cannabis use, may be provided

by the flight of addicts from Canada's new penal drug code of 1958. The first arrived at the end of 1959, and by the end of 1962 about 70 had come, some with criminal, trafficking backgrounds. . . . We must also take into account the general change in teenage attitudes at the end of the fifties, with the shift of interest away from the crude external power relationships of gangs to rather more private worlds of experience expressed in clothes and music. . . . With a sudden rush of new young addicts, the Brain Committee was reconvened in 1964; . . . What it ignored, however, was one important aspect of the new wave: the favorable, indeed grasping attitude to publicity of many young drug users. . . .

In the Welfare State it is difficult to reach the heights of self-immolation of the classical, American drug user. Drugs are available free from almost all the doctors who supply addicts; from the others they cost about a shilling a grain, so a week's supply might cost £3. (This passage was written before the implementation of the Brain Report in 1968; it is now more difficult to get heroin, but the principles are the same.) In law an addict under the care of a doctor is sick; if the doctor will issue the necessary certificate he can draw National Assistance and, if his card is stamped, National Insurance benefits. . . . It has been remarked that the most striking characteristic of the new adolescent addicts is their desire for publicity. The inquirer, thinking that it is going to be difficult to meet drug users, is immediately overwhelmed by them showing off their spiritual sores like medieval beggars; willing to discuss their most intimate affairs at exhaustive, and soon tedius, length. It is clearly no use being drug dependent in London unless one is seen to be so.[69]

These phenomena would seem to account fully for the rise in identified (that is, known to the Home Office) addicts, without any need to put the blame on increased cannabis use.

Paton's third argument is the most easily refuted. He asserts that "the incidence in the general population [of marihuana use] is something of the order, according to rather rough estimates, of 1 in 2,000, that is, an incidence of about 0.05 per cent." [70] He compares this with his claim that 80 to 100 percent of heroin addicts have used cannabis. Paton asserts that he has proved by Bayes's theorem that 7 to 15 percent of cannabis users go on to heroin. However, there are a number of weaknesses in this argument: (1) Bayes's theorem is itself the subject of considerable controversy, and it is not at all clear that the theorem, used mainly by astronomers, "for whom comparable difficulties exist in making *direct* experiments on their objects of study," is at all applicable to this kind of calculation with human subjects;[71] (2) "a study made of 25 per cent of the known addicts, who were seen . . . during a single year, indicates that 66 per cent had smoked cannabis, but that an equal proportion had taken barbiturate[s] . . . [and] 75 per cent had used amphetamine tablets, and 88 per cent had used methedrine by injection";[72] and (3) the crucial factor in Paton's "proof" is his estimate of the total number of cannabis smokers. "This figure [Paton's] is preposterously small and seems to have been based on misreading a 'very approximate' estimate made by a member of the Wootton committee on the basis of conviction figures which are now out of date . . . it is easily arguable on the basis of figures for convictions and reconvictions that the actual number of cannabis smokers in Britain is about 500,000. It may well be that Paton has arbitrarily loaded the odds in his favor by a factor of 20. I can perfectly well argue that the chances of becoming a heroin addict are approximately one in 500, rather than one in 10." [73]

Another claim that Paton makes offers a good example of the wariness with which one should approach statements that have no substantiation other than "obviously." "It is obvious that the natural field for recruitment of heroin addiction is the population of those youngsters who have tried one drug for pleasure and might like to extend the experience," that is, those who have tried marihuana and might like to try heroin. However, there is strong evidence that, if it is correct to speak of any sort of drug "progression" from cannabis, one can only refer to an increased likelihood that an individual who has used marihuana may "progress" to LSD and related "hallucinogens," and not to heroin. J. T. Carcy asserts that "The rationales for using hallucinogenic drugs preclude any interest in heroin. Its use is considered antithetical to the value of opening up one's perceptions. Hence dealers in marihuana and LSD do not usually stock heroin as a service to their customers." [74] E. Goode, in his study of approximately 200 users of marihuana, found that "in spite of the commonly-stated belief that marijuana use will 'lead to' the use of and eventual addiction to, heroin, this powerful and potentially dangerous narcotic was used by only a small minority of the sample. Twenty-seven respondents, or 13 percent of the sample, had used heroin at least once. Further, extremely limited use was more common than repeated usage, whether 'chippying' or actual addiction. Over half of the heroin users took it fewer than a dozen times — and of these, eleven tried it three or fewer times — and five, or about 2½ percent of the sample, claimed to have been addicted — although none was, or claimed to be, at the time of the interview." [75] Goode also claims to have found that marihuana use often "leads to" experimentation with hard drugs "in a working class urban area not because of the search for an even bigger and better 'kick,' but because the associations one makes as one's use level moves upward are increasingly also likely to experiment with the narcotics. Obviously the process is anything but inevitable — indeed, a minority of even heavy marijuana smokers ever makes this move. . . . In contexts other than the slum, marijuana use does not imply experimentation with narcotics; on the college campus, for instance, heroin use involves a very tiny segment of even the drug-using contingent, and its use is distinctly frowned upon." [76] However, the same author asserts that frequent use of marihuana

> in middle-class users increases one's chances of using any of the LSD-type drugs. . . . There is a linear relationship between marijuana use and use of the hallucinogenic drugs. Involvement with marijuana leads to social relations which strengthen one's commitment to psychedelic values, to opportunities for use, for favorable definitions of hallucinogenic drug taking.

> Heavy marijuana use on the college campus almost implies at least one-time use of one of the heavier psychedelics. . . . A certain degree of prestige is generated by having tried a wide range and a large number of drugs. . . . But to get "hung-up" on a drug — to need to take the drug — is seen as losing "cool." The narcotics addict is viewed with pity and scorn specifically because of his loss of cool. He is the prime example of the individual who has ceased to exercise choice. The drug adventurer, on the other hand, sees himself as precisely exercising choice; he views the "straight" person, the individual who refuses to take any drugs, as unduly restricted.[77]

In *Drugs on the College Campus,* H. H. Nowlis asserts that "although many heroin addicts have used cannabis, they have more frequently used alcohol before using either heroin or cannabis, and the large majority of cannabis users do not progress to heroin." She also points out, after noting that WHO in 1965 dropped the term "addiction," and substituted "dependence," that an important fact about "drug dependence is the finding that individuals differ greatly both in their tendency to repeat a particular drug experience and in their tendency to become dependent on any one drug." [78] She quotes Jaffe in this connection with regard to alcohol: "It seems obvious that the effects of the drug *per se* [alcohol] do not compel a normal individual to use the drug repeatedly, and we readily accept the idea that social and psychological factors play major roles in the abuse of alcohol. It is sometimes erroneously assumed that opiates and related narcotics are different, that they regularly produce such pleasurable effects (euphoria) that it is difficult to avoid repeated use." [79] P. H. Hoch asks, "Why is it, for example, that out of every 100 individuals who experiment with narcotics ('joy-pop' in the argot of the addict) only a relatively small percentage become addicted?" [80] H. Brill asserts: "Careful inquiry indicates that not all who try heroin become addicted." [81] Nowlis writes: "It appears that no known drug has effects which in and of themselves compel a normal individual to use them repeatedly. In other words, as with alcohol, we have to discover and identify for each drug the social and psychological factors which deter or facilitate repetitive use and the development of dependence." [82] Even more clearly, while some individuals who have used marihuana subsequently use more dangerous and addicting drugs, there is nothing to indicate that the use of marihuana is one of the causal factors behind this heavier use of more dangerous substances. We must look instead at the reasons — the psychological and social needs of the individual — in order to determine just why some of these individuals seem compelled to "graduate" to heroin use.

Although there is no definite or indicative evidence of any causal "stair-step" phenomenon by which the use of marihuana necessarily leads to the use of harder drugs, and specifically to the use of heroin, there is evidence that an initial interest in drugs — which may amount to no more than a healthy (from a psychiatric point of view) curiosity, but which must because of prohibitive laws be expressed first in an illegal act — may lead to an expansion of the one-time user's drug interests and, eventually, to a commitment to a way of life that revolves around or is focused on drugs. But what is surprising is the slight relationship between the use of cannabis and opiates (again, heroin in particular), inasmuch as a major effect of the 1937 antimarihuana legislation was to drive prices for cannabis high enough to make it profitable for dealers in other "high-risk" drugs to handle marihuana also.[83] Many dealers in cannabis quickly realized that they were in the same legal class, in terms of punishments, as opiate dealers, and that they would take on no further legal risks, although they might increase their profits considerably, if they handled heroin as well as marihuana. It would seem to have been predictable that this increased potential for expansion on the part of the seller (with regard to types of drugs) would have led to a significant positive relationship between the use of marihuana and heroin, but this has not proved to be the case.

A position paper of the Committee on Alcoholism and Drug Dependence, Council on Mental Health, American Medical Association, states that four major categories of "drugs can lead to dependence through abuse"; the last of these is "the hallucinogens, such as LSD and marihuana." [84] The paper further states that the effects of marihuana are "similar in kind to those produced by LSD and other potent hallucinogens." [85] In the next sentence, however, the American Medical Association asserts that the "chief danger" of marihuana is that it leads to "stronger substances, including heroin." They underline this logical contradiction only four paragraphs further on: "A sizable minority [of marihuana smokers] . . . will turn to heroin, but more of the discontented will try other drugs, particularly LSD, because they don't want to risk physical dependence." [86] Although this statement makes the preceding argument for a causal connection between marihuana and heroin use plainly untenable, the description is probably as close to the true situation as the American Medical Association comes at any point in its advocacy of the "stepping-stone" theory. As Mandel notes, "The advocacy of stepping stone'ism has rarely been based on any demonstrable evidence of this tie. Rather, that idea has a life of its own apart from, and often quite contrary to, the published data. Could such a long-standing and agreed-on notion be wrong? [He must intend irony, since the notion has only been "officially" accepted since around 1950.] Well, it would not be the first time in the history of American ideas towards marijuana. Past notions of pot's immediate deadly effects [and past notions of pot's immediate crime-inducing effects as well] . . . and past rejections of the 'stepping stone' proposition, have been 'instantly' dropped from their place as the core of the anti-marijuana arguments. But if one dismisses the notion that all current popular conceptions on drugs are right, then should the 'stepping stone' proposition be the keystone of anti-marijuana legislation? Could our leading narcotics [and medical] officials be leading us astray?" [87]

The answer is yes.

10 Psychoses, Adverse Reactions, and Personality Deterioration

The literature on the relationship of cannabis to the development of psychosis is both vast and exceedingly confused, and as one reads through its more noteworthy contributions, a definite dichotomy, one based largely on locale and observer, becomes evident. Authors from India, Egypt, Turkey, Africa, and other Eastern lands are largely in agreement that their psychiatric institutions are populated by a large number of cases of insanity which can be directly attributed to hashish. In the late 1800's and early 1900's particularly, but even as late as 1967, papers and official statements appeared which adamantly condemn the drug as harmful both to the mental health of the individual and to the integrity of the social fabric of their countries. It is striking that numerous discussions of the psychotogenic effects of cannabis in Western literature (notably those written recently in the United States) are in quite an opposite vein; they either exonerate marihuana from these charges or else cite only a handful of cases to support the contention that its use leads to the development of psychoses. Clearly, there are some discoverable factors or circumstances which account for the existence of such a wide dichotomy in world medical opinion. A critical look at this literature may reveal some reasonable conclusions that can be drawn with regard to cannabis and psychosis.

Examining first the Eastern literature, one is immediately impressed with the magnitude of the role that cannabis apparently plays in admissions to psychiatric facilities. Authors from the East would have us believe that anywhere from one-fourth to nine-tenths of the admissions to their institutions result from the use of this drug. There are seemingly endless numbers of reports written by staff members and superintendents of Egyptian and Indian insane asylums that are frequently cited as evidence of the psychotogenic effects of cannabis. An article by J. H. Tull-Walsh serves the useful purpose of summarizing 21 of these reports written from the 1860's through the 1870's; many of them cite huge percentages of the patient population of their institutions as cases of "cannabis insanity." [1] For example, J. Wise, the Superintendent of the Dacca Asylum, writing in 1873, stated that "between thirty and fifty percent of the admissions in the Indian asylums was due exclusively to the effects of hemp drugs." [2] A. Eden, the Secretary to the Government in Bengal, estimated that "four-fifths of all the cases where the cause is known" are due to *ganja*.[3] The "Annual Report Dacca Lunatic Asylum for 1863" estimates that "165, or 50 per cent. of the total number treated, have been distinctly traced to that cause [*ganja*]"; in writing the "Annual Report" for this same institution in 1869, H. C. Cutcliffe states, "Of 312 patients, no less than 123 are alleged to have become insane from *gánja* smoking and drinking." [4] Similarly, G. F. W. Ewens, in 1904, reported that 161 of the 543 cases of mania in male admissions to the Punjab asylum during the period 1900 to 1903 were attributable to excessive indulgence in hemp drugs.[5] R. F. Hutchinson, writing in 1865, reports that 90.6 percent of all cases in asylums in Bengal were due to indulgence in *ganja, bhang,* opium, or spirit, and that if these "causes were checked or removed the asylums would speedily be depopulated." [6] However, one discovers in reading these and similar reports that the authors based their findings of "hemp insanity" largely on inadequate or circumstantial evidence riddled with discrepancies.

To begin with, a number of authors mention that a diagnosis of "hemp insanity" is often taken directly from police reports which are required to state a reason for psychiatric hospitalization.[7] Cannabis is the easiest and least complicated reason for the police to use. Apparently it is common knowledge, even to the asylum superintendents, that this is the usual practice; yet no effort is made to correct this matter on the records subsequent to the patient's admission. In addition, as A. J. Payne notes, repeated readmissions are included in these figures, even when they are not cases of recurrent insanity but only repeated intoxication; in other words, the diagnosis of "hemp insanity" once made, persists.[8] Another group of readmissions wrongly included in these figures are those patients "removed by relatives and brought back from difficulty or expense in managing them at home." [9] In addition, many of the reports citing these high figures were generated by institutions admittedly so overcrowded and understaffed that accurate record-keeping was impossible. J. Wise, Superintendent of the Dacca Asylum, writes: "An attempt has been made this year to distinguish between those cases of insanity clearly due to *gánja* smoking and those in which the use of *gánja* has only been occasional, and, therefore, insufficient to excite insanity. The attempt has not been successful. For want of any other reason, it has been necessary to enter under the heading *gánja* several who were merely reported to have indulged in its use." [10]

These are just a few of the ways in which the figures for so-called "cannabis insanity" have swelled to a point totally out of keeping with the facts. There are other less obvious but equally important contributing factors which will be discussed in greater detail, but even at this point one can unequivocally state that Eastern reports are exaggerated and inaccurate. Tull-Walsh himself estimates that "want of accuracy in ascertaining a cause renders about 50 per cent. of the cases of insanity, said to be due to *gánja,* etc., doubtful." [11] Sandwiched among these reports one can find another note of reason by A. MacKenzie who, in writing a government resolution in 1871, stated that

> the number of cases attributed to *gánja* is 169 out of 230 admissions in which a cause was known, but it may be that it has become a habit to attribute insanity to *gánja*. The Lieutenant-Governor would be glad to have it specially noted in the reports if there are generally good grounds for setting down this drug as the cause in so many cases.[12]

An Egyptian report which is frequently quoted as incriminating cannabis as a cause of insanity was written by J. Warnoch, Medical Director of the Egyptian Hospital for the Insane in Cairo at the turn of the century, and the first to institute some record-keeping procedures in what was then the only, and accordingly very crowded, psychiatric facility in Egypt. Some difficulties common to most Eastern reports are especially evident in this one. In investigating the hypothesis that hashish is instrumental in causing a large proportion of the insanity in Egypt, Warnoch developed five categories of "hashish insanity." Aside from those cases of temporary intoxication (type 1) or pleasant, dreamlike states, which do not require hospitalization, he reported observing numerous instances of the following hashish-induced conditions:

2. *Delirium from hasheesh,* which is accompanied by hallucinations of sight, hearing, taste, and smell, often of an unpleasant kind. Delusions of persecution often occur. The idea that the subject is possessed by a devil or spirit is common. Great exaltation and the belief that the individual is a sultan or prophet may occur. Suicidal intentions are rare. . . . Hasheesh delirium is a less grave state both physically and mentally [than delirium tremens]. Some cases are stuporous in type.

3. *Mania from hasheesh.* — This varies in degree of acuteness from a mild short attack of excitement to a prolonged attack of furious mania ending in exhaustion or even death. Most cases are exalted, and have delusions of grandeur or of religious importance; persecutory delusions occur frequently, and provoke violence towards others, but not suicide. Restlessness, incoherent talking, destructiveness, indecency, and loss of moral feelings and affections, are all ordinary symptoms. A certain impudent dare-devil demeanour is a characteristic symptom. Hallucinations are not so marked as in alcoholic mania, but those of hearing and taste are not uncommon; delusions of being poisoned are often based on the latter variety. A few cases are more melancholic than maniacal in demeanour, and exhibit extreme depression and terror with hallucinations of hearing (threatening voices, etc.).

4. *Chronic mania from hasheesh,* including a form of mania or persecution. Many of these cases are not distinguishable from ordinary chronic mania.

5. *Chronic dementia from hasheesh* describes the final stage of the preceding forms.[13]

Warnoch is by no means the only author who developed a symptomatology for "hashish insanity." Ewens did so in great detail, as did J. E. Dhunjibhoy, who wrote: "In India, hemp drugs, whether taken in excess or moderation, over a prolonged period, produce a special form of mental disorder, which is characterized by a definite train of symptoms which is fairly uniform in character." He enumerated as typical of a "hemp insanity" case: "intense excitement, grandiose ideas, tendency to willful violence and destruction, the peculiar eye condition, . . . total amnesia of all events, . . . with a history of a drug habit." [14]

What is obvious about the syndromes established by Warnoch and the typical symptoms listed by Dhunjibhoy (excluding the eye condition and drug habit) is that they cannot be ascribed exclusively to the effects of hashish. They describe both schizophrenia and, to a lesser extent, manic-depressive psychoses (particularly manic phase), and it is not unlikely that many if not most of the vast number of schizophrenics and manic patients admitted to psychiatric facilities in the East, especially in the past, have been sheltered under the diagnostic umbrella of "hemp insanity." In fact this possibility has been noted by another Eastern author, F. Kerim, who has studied the problem of hashish in Turkey; his observations of patient populations similar to those studied by Warnoch led him to take a broader perspective, one probably more consistent with the reality. He writes, "The symptoms [of "hashish insanity"] are not unlike those in cases of schizophrenia, with bizarre hallucinations and delusions, impulsive and compulsive phenomena, paranoid formations, fear reactions, etc. Differentiation between them and transitory schizophrenic episodes is difficult." [15]

Since Warnoch acknowledges that there is no pathognomonic symptom of "hasheesh mania," how then did he differentiate cases of "hasheesh insanity" from schizophrenia and other forms of mental disease? The following is his account:

> The discovery of hasheesh in the patient's clothing, or concealed in his ears or mouth, occasionally betrays the nature of the case. On admission every male patient is questioned with regard to hasheesh, and a report made on the amount he takes and his attitude towards the charge; excited protests and denials of the habit are known by experience to indicate a hardened hasheesh smoker. As the mental state of the patient improves, he is again questioned about hasheesh, and before discharge he is invited to give full details of his habit. By comparing the repeated statements and by noting his knowledge or ignorance of the various details of hasheesh smoking, such as the price of the gozeh, the different qualities of the drug, etc., it is not difficult in most cases to form an opinion as to whether the case is one of hash-

eesh. The evidence of relatives is occasionally of use, but it is less reliable than the repeated cross-examination of the patient; numbers of the Cairo cases are known to be frequenters of hasheesh cafés from being seen there by hospital employés.[16]

From the above it is clear that at least in Warnoch's report the diagnosis of "hemp insanity" was based not on the existence of certain clear-cut signs and symptoms, but solely on more or less substantiated reports that the patient had been a hashish user at the time of his hospitalization. Thus, of two patients exhibiting the same symptoms of mental disturbance, one, whose wife acknowledged him to be a user, could have been included in Warnoch's figures as a case of "hemp insanity," while the other, whose relatives were not as willing to speak, would have been placed in some other diagnostic category — most probably schizophrenia. Figures compiled in such a fashion, if they are of any use at all, provide more of a sense of the number of psychotics who use hashish rather than the number of hashish users who become psychotic.

A more modern study than Warnoch's, and, like his, one which is frequently referred to by those who assert that hemp produces psychosis, is that of A. Benabud.[17] His study, like Dhunjibhoy's, is largely dependent on the contention that there is a specific syndrome entity, the "cannabis psychosis." [18] He asserts that a significant proportion of the patient population at the Berrechid Hospital in Morocco suffers from this type of psychosis. He notes that in 1955 the number of genuine "cannabis psychotics" was 239 out of 1,017 hospitalized male Moslem patients, 72 percent of whom admitted to some experience with *kif*. In 1956, the figure fell to 68 percent; the number of "cannabis psychoses" was 328 out of 1,252 male Moslem admissions. However, the clinical data which Benabud presents are unclear. First, it is not possible to define those particular clusters of symptoms and signs which distinguish a "cannabis psychosis" from other acute toxic states, and, particularly in Morocco, from states associated with malnutrition and endemic infection. Secondly, Benabud asserts that the number of *kif* smokers "suffering from recurrent mental derangement" is not more than 5 per 1,000. Now this is on the low side of the estimates of active prevalence rates for total psychoses from different parts of the world. Therefore, we would have to assume either (1) that there is a much lower prevalence of psychoses other than "cannabis psychoses" among *kif* smokers in Morocco, or (2) that there is no such thing as a "cannabis psychosis," and that the drug is contributing little or nothing to the prevalence rate for psychoses. Two highly respected Indian authors, I. C. and R. N. Chopra, completed a study of 466 cannabis smokers in which they found 9 cases of insanity; in a second study of 772 cannabis drinkers they found 4 such cases. The data from these two samples yielded active prevalence rates of 1.93 percent and 0.52 percent, respectively.[19] These rates do not differ significantly from the active prevalence rates for total psychoses found in surveys in both Europe and North America, rates which range from 0.6 percent to 2.1 percent of adult populations.[20] This further supports the contention that the use of cannabis does not contribute significantly to the prevalence of psychoses.

It is possible that the widespread use of a drug which, with excessive dosage, may cause toxic psychoses, could, providing those toxic psychoses are short-lived, lead to an increased incidence of psychoses without significantly elevating the prevalence rates for psychoses. In considering hospital-admission figures from the East, we are in fact dealing to a large extent with individuals who consume large quantities and potent forms of cannabis. As Ewens writes, "I have repeatedly met with instances in which after recovery a man has attributed his insanity to a single large dose of *bhang* or *charas* generally stated to have been administered by a *faqir*. . . . The history always given is that they have been induced to partake of a large amount, that they fell into a state of *nasha* (intoxication) and remember nothing more until finding themselves in custody or in the asylum." [21] Even Warnoch states: "Probably only excessive users, or persons peculiarly susceptible to its toxic effects, become so insane as to need asylum treatment. Whether the moderate use of hasheesh has ill effects I have no means of judging." [22] Tull-Walsh writes that there are "a number of cases in which the abuse of Indian hemp drugs, either alone or combined with datura or alcohol, has produced a violent and prolonged intoxication followed by a maniacal, melancholic, or demented condition. In these cases recovery takes place in a very short time; indeed, in many of them the individuals are sane, or almost sane, when they reach the asylum." [23] I believe that the episodes for which Tull-Walsh's cases were hospitalized may be considered short-lived toxic psychoses and that they do not differ substantially from some of the episodes of Gautier, Ludlow, and Taylor which were described in Chapter 4. Large amounts of cannabis — particularly, if not almost exclusively, ingested hashish — can lead to such a degree of intoxication that the extreme perceptual distortion, anxiety to the point of panic, and temporary loss of capacity to test reality produce a clinical picture which is often indistinguishable from other toxic psychoses. These, however, are self-limiting episodes and quite different from functional psychoses such as schizophrenia or what is meant by those who believe in the "cannabis psychosis."

W. Grossman touches on this subject in reporting on "emotional disorders" of six Westerners who used native hashish while visiting in India. "One shouldn't confuse American marijuana with what is commonly available in India: They are different! Indian hashish or 'marijuana' has a high that can last up to 3 days, the high consisting of severe anxiety and confusion," [24] according to one such user. As was illustrated in Chapter 4 by the reactions of, for example, Bayard Taylor as compared to Mr. X, this American discovered there is quite a difference between the ordinary use of marihuana (*bhang*) and large doses of *ganja* or *charas*. It is possible, writes Grossman, that "the observed frequencies of serious adverse reactions to cannabis products in different areas may merely represent different segments of a dose-response curve to THC." [25] All but a very few of the Eastern reports refer exclusively to *ganja* or *charas* in citing mental-hospital admission statistics; it seems clear that to the extent that cannabis plays a significant role in hospital admissions it is a drug which, when used excessively in its most potent forms, may lead to the development of a short-lived toxic psychosis.

To an undiscoverable extent one is also dealing with *ganja* which has been adulterated with other substances such as opium or datura, and these substances may modify or enhance the effects of the intoxication. Tull-Walsh says that this is a common practice, but it is impossible, at this time, to determine how great an influence it might be in the number of cases of toxic psychosis. [26]

Another point, made by Warnoch and by A. Boroffka, is the existence in any population of some individuals who are "particularly susceptible to its [hashish's] toxic effects." [27] Such persons are already suffering from some form of mental instability, and in this view the drug serves as an exciting agent; the excited or irrational behavior may be considered more a manifestation of that predisposition than a direct effect of the drug. As Tull-Walsh puts it:

> It is not very improbable that, owing to the fact that these persons are of a neuropathic diathesis, and in them a tendency to insanity exists, and has always been latent, hemp drugs in excess, or even in quantities which would not damage a man of robust nervous constitution, have acted as an *exciting cause*, making manifest a mental weakness which might not have shown itself in the absence of such indulgence.[28]

A last but equally important factor that undoubtedly contributes to the numbers of those reported to be suffering adverse effects from cannabis use is the environment. In underdeveloped countries such as Egypt or India there is a lack of sufficient food for good nutrition for large portions of the populace; juxtaposed with this fact is the observation that "the violent intoxicating effects [of *ganja* or *charas*] are less marked, or not seen at all, in persons having a regular and wholesome supply of food." [29] This is supported by observations of the Ramawats "who are the greatest smokers in Eastern Bengal, [and] seldom, if ever become mad. They, as well as other natives who exceed in smoking *gánja*, invariably live very well, and they maintain that as long as plenty of food is taken its effects are innocuous. . . . During the last six years none of these luxurious mendicants have been admitted into the asylum, although they are very numerous in the city of Dacca." [30]

In addition to being deprived of sufficient food and thus being more susceptible to the adverse effects of any drug, the poorer people in these countries also exist in extremely overcrowded living conditions which, from a public health standpoint, are deplorable at best. A sense of general despair and hopelessness prevails which nourishes mental illness, and individuals living in such environments may be seen as among those particularly susceptible to both the use and the adverse effects of cannabis.

In summary, the Eastern cannabis literature must be read with caution. The large numbers of cases diagnosed as "cannabis psychosis" are often a result of the "fact that no distinction is made between drug induced symptoms and independent schizophrenia," and they are greatly increased through both the purposeful and the inadvertent inclusion of cases for which no proper diagnosis has been made.[31] Furthermore, there are vast cultural and economic differences between East and West, and essential differences in the forms in which the drug is used. With all this in mind one can then acknowledge that some unknown (probably small) percentage of the cases cited by these authors as "cannabis insanity" are, in fact, related to use of the drug, in that large doses may lead to the development of a toxic psychosis of short duration, and, in already emotionally unstable and susceptible people, it may excite psychotic-like symptoms.

What of the reports linking cannabis to psychosis in the North American literature? The number of reports contending that such a relationship exists has diminished considerably since the 1920's and 1930's; as H. S. Becker points out, such reports after the 1940's are relatively rare despite the very large increase in the use of the drug.[32] In their study of 310 soldiers who had used marihuana for an average duration of 7.1 years, H. L. Freedman and M. J. Rockmore found no history of psychoses.[33] Of the 60 marihuana users studied by S. Charen and L. Perelman, 77 percent began to use marihuana before the age of 18; the average length of time for smoking marihuana was approximately 6 years, during which some smoked from one to two marihuana cigarettes a day, others as many as ten, but most from four to six daily. None of the patients had a history of psychosis.[34] In the more than 150 marihuana-using patients observed by H. S. Gaskill, there was only 1 who was questionably psychotic.[35] The 34 cannabis-using soldiers who volunteered to be studied by J. F. Siler et al. had used the drug for from 2 months to 4 years, the average period being 1 year and 2 months. They smoked between one and twenty cigarettes daily; the average was five. None was found to exhibit psychotic symptoms.[36] In the La Guardia study there was a high incidence (9 out of 77) of history of psychoses; but this is to be expected inasmuch as these patients were located through hospitals and institutions.[37] In fact, S. Allentuck and K. M. Bowman, during the course of their study of these subjects, became convinced that "marihuana will not produce a psychosis de novo in a well-integrated, stable person." [38]

In the North American literature the most frequently cited study in support of the psychotogenic effect of cannabis is probably the one published by W. Bromberg in 1939.[39] But, as H. B. M. Murphy has pointed out, of the 31 patients whose psychoses were reported in this paper to be related to the use of cannabis, 7 were functional psychoses precipitated by the drug, 7 patients were presented as acute toxic psychoses but were readmitted to a mental hospital within two years with the diagnosis of schizophrenia, and another patient, with a similar picture, was readmitted with a manic-depressive psychosis.[40] Further scrutiny of the case material in Bromberg's paper leads me to the impression that an additional number of these patients may have had unrecognized early acute schizophrenic reactions of the type that reconstitute quite rapidly (the so-called "five day schizophrenia"). In the same paper Bromberg reports on 67 prisoners who were users of marihuana; there were among them neurotics and personality disorders, but none were found to be psychotic.

More recently there have appeared a number of case reports which are meant to illustrate, sometimes quite alarmingly, the psychotogenic effects of marihuana. For example, D. Perna recently published a very brief paper in which she presented a case which she asserted demonstrated "that marihuana may have a psychotogenic effect even in an individual with a healthy premorbid personality." [41] However, the information she presented about this patient leads one to question seriously how healthy he was; he had suffered from nocturnal enuresis until he was 18 years of age, and at age 16 suffered from depression serious enough to require six months of psychotherapy, and he was depressed again at the time he used marihuana. Her statement that this schizophrenic reaction developed in a healthy premorbid personality stretches the concept of premorbid health.

The opening sentences in a much more detailed report titled "Marihuana Psychosis: A Case Study" suggest that the author, G. D. Klee, is determined to avoid such a mistake. He states: "I have seen numerous patients, however, who have had a wide variety of psychiatric difficulties associated with marihuana use. Most of these patients, however, have had pre-existing psychiatric disturbances and have also taken other drugs, so that it is difficult to establish a definite cause-effect relationship between marihuana use and the ensuing psychiatric disturbance." [42] After this preface he asserts: "The case to be presented is unique in that the relationship between marihuana use and the psychiatric disturbance is unmistakable." [43] The author records in considerable detail the accounts of a 26-year-old man and his girlfriend in which they relate the horrors of his psychotic experience, which occurred after they had smoked two marihuana cigarettes between them (they had on four or five previous occasions used cannabis without any adverse effects). In summary, the episode was punctuated by "unbelievably horrible" visions of death and hell, during which he became so irrational and violent that his girlfriend called in neighbors who helped her to tie him up. However, the impression that the author is discussing a stable young man with no preexisting psychiatric difficulties who is suddenly crazed by marihuana is completely dispelled by consideration of the facts disclosed in the past and family-history sections of the report. The young man came from a home "filled with tension" where violent behavior between father and sons often erupted; in fact, just two days prior to taking marihuana there had been a "violent episode at home." His girlfriend related how insecure, unpredictable, and impulsive he had been, and she equated the marihuana episode to his behavior when drinking. "Although usually jolly at such times [when intoxicated with alcohol], he can become very irritable and nasty. It has been only when he was drinking that they have had fights. He apparently is quite angry about her refusal to agree to marriage and expresses this anger when drunk. At times, and especially during the marihuana reaction, she has felt that, 'There is something about me that . . . [he] hates very much.' What it might be, she cannot say. She also reported that during the psychotic episode and while tied up in the blanket, . . . [he] was talking about his friend Danny, and moving in such a way as to suggest that they were having enjoyable homosexual relations. This she has not told him, because she believes he feels quite insecure about his masculinity. He also imagined himself having sexual relations with her, and said, 'It's wrong, it's wrong.' " [44] She reported that, on the only occasion that they had sexual intercourse, "he expressed feelings of guilt and inadequacy about his sexual performance." [45] In discussing his past history, the young man denied "any history of previous psychiatric symptomatology of any nature. . . . He does report, however, that on a few occasions he has had unusual and alarming reactions to alcohol. Although not a habitual or usually a heavy drinker, he has used liquor many times. On a few occasions, usually when high (on about a half pint of whiskey), he has been explosive and assaultive. On very slight provocation he has fought and beaten one, two, three, or four other men — friends or enemies — sometimes much larger than himself. On these occasions he has been quite vicious, continuing to beat and kick his victim after knocking him down. His memory after the event tends to be rather hazy. These occurrences are described more with an air of alarm than of braggadocio. Only on rare occasions, in adult years, has he ever been violent when not under the influence of alcohol. He came in search of psychiatric help after the realization that there was something dangerously explosive inside of him that was brought out by alcohol and marihuana." [46] The author directly acknowledges at the close of the paper this man's "latent psychopathology" and further reports the patient admits: "On occasion, drugs, or as he puts it fearfully, 'almost anything else' which interferes with ego functions, might bring out the latent psychopathology. . . . In other words, the marihuana augmented his psychopathology and vice versa." [47]

Thus, the author presents a young man who has a poor self-image, intense guilt feelings, an impulse disorder with a propensity for violence, and who by his own acknowledgment is so shaky that "almost anything" could have precipitated a temporary psychotic state. This paper ("Marihuana Psychosis: A Case Study"), the title of which commends it to those who wish to emphasize the alleged dangers and horrors of cannabis, might just as easily have been written about the dangers of alcohol for such a susceptible person; but a paper about so common an occurrence would undoubtedly not have been accepted for publication.

Another common flaw in reports linking marihuana and psychosis is the apparent willingness on the part of those whose bias is antimarihuana to gloss over the fact that the persons involved are often multiple-drug users. P. Dally has written of four cases of mental disorder which in his opinion incriminate marihuana as a causative factor.[48] An examination of these case summaries leads to considerable doubt regarding this opinion, and in turn reveals some of the discrepancies and weaknesses which are often observed in reports addressed to the psychic dangers of cannabis. Two of these case reports are as follows:

An art student of 19 experimented with lysergic acid diethyl-amide (L.S.D.) over a period of several months without obvious ill effect. At a party he took 100 mg. [*sic*] L.S.D. by mouth and smoked two "reefers." He felt "depersonalized, about to disintegrate, and go mad." He became extremely anxious. He was treated with trifluoperazine 2 mg. three times a day and chlordiazepoxide 10 mg. three times a day for a fortnight, and symptoms subsided. A week later he again smoked a "reefer." Anxiety immediately returned and he experienced fleeting visual hallucinations.[49]

The initial symptoms were much more likely to have been caused by the LSD than the cannabis. It is probable, however (as will be discussed later), that the symptoms he presented "a week later," the flashbacks of his experiences with LSD, were precipitated by the use of marihuana. The author remarks, "After full recovery he was resolved not to smoke marijuana again." [50] It is regrettable that his resolve did not include LSD; if the aim of this paper was anything but making a case against marihuana, the author would have noted this.

This [next] case concerned a man who "under the influence of marijuana" tried to drill a hole through his skull. He was "under the influence of a group of people who believe that, after a suitable period of preparation with L.S.D. and marijuana, trepanning of the skull, by releasing cerebral pressure, will enable an individual to conquer time." [51]

The author summarizes: "Although he showed no overt psychotic signs, other than what amounted to a delusional belief in this idea, his history suggested schizophrenia simplex." [52] Why is this case cited as one illustrating the undesirable effects of marihuana? If one is considering causes for the irrational act of trepanning the skull, then indictments should first be made against this individual's "history of suggested schizophrenia simplex," next his involvement with a group of people suffering a shared delusion, and then quite possibly the use of LSD. The only reasonable statement to be made here about marihuana is that it could have been one of several possible contributing factors. Thus, to title this piece "The Undesirable Effects of Marihuana" and then attribute to this drug the probable effects of LSD and preexisting psychic disturbance is misleading and contributes to the long list of misconceptions about marihuana.

Another recent addition to the American literature on the subject of marihuana and psychoses further obfuscates the matter. The causal relationship between the smoking of marihuana and what J. A. Talbott and J. W. Teague describe as "toxic psychoses" is quite shaky and based on only three detailed cases described as representative. In one case they attempt to establish marihuana as the precipitant of a reaction with the statement: "He had smoked a pipeful of 'strange tasting tobacco' two days previously and had felt light-headed and 'funny.' " [53] Furthermore, many if not most psychiatrists would have diagnosed these cases as acute panic states, not toxic psychoses. By their own acknowledgment, up to 65 percent of soldiers in Vietnam have used cannabis at least once during their tour of duty; they further assert that approximately 50 percent of the cannabis preparations seized in Vietnam are laced with opiates. Yet these authors insist that the reactions they have described are due to cannabis. One would expect in any war zone that there would be a number of short-lived acute psychotic states; the key question, to which these authors do not address themselves, is whether there is a higher incidence of these states among soldiers using marihuana than among those abstaining. While these authors acknowledge that the incidence of combat reactions in Vietnam is low in comparison with other wars, a possibility which apparently never occurred to them is that widespread use of cannabis may indeed to some extent be protecting that population from psychoses.[54]

The psychiatric incidence rate for U.S. Army troops in Vietnam was reported to be 12 per 1,000 strength per year during the calendar years 1965 and 1966. This rate is much lower than that recorded for both the Korean War (73 per 1,000 strength per year July 1950 to December 1952) and World War II (between 28 and 101 per 1,000 strength per year September 1944 through May 1945). During World War II, 23 percent of all cases evacuated for medical reasons were psychiatric cases; the percentage for the comparable group in Vietnam has been approximately 6 percent.[55] Many factors have undoubtedly played a part in this decreased incidence, including changes in rotation policy, improvements in training, early treatment at forward areas, etc. (One would imagine that a difference tending toward an increased psychiatric incidence rate among the soldiers in Vietnam, as compared with World War II and the Korean War, is the fact that many soldiers experience conflict over the Vietnam War's morality and legality and the part they are compelled to play in a foreign policy which often seems genocidal.) It is certainly possible that these differences between the Vietnam War and the two preceding ones account for the dramatic decrease in psychiatric illness, but it is also at least conceivable that another major difference, the much more widespread and frequent use of cannabis, may also be playing an important role. One soldier in Vietnam, writing to his mother in May 1970, puts it this way:

> Is it any wonder people take advantage of the pot over here? It really helps. It's helped me more to get my mind right than the stuff I'm supposed to be taking. The only medication I do use from the Witch Doctor is the sleeping pills. I have a hard time going to sleep at night.
>
> Like I said before, I don't want you or anyone else to be worried over me. I can assure you that my mind is really above this mess and I'll make it through. I found out you can't ask yourself "Why?" or you'll go crazy trying to find an answer. Sure, you can argue all night at some party in the comfort of the World but not here where it happens. There is no answer to Why? on the ground after a firefight. Just bodies. So don't look at your dead friend and ask Why. I think that's what was messing me up.[56]

It is a curious fact that while a great deal of attention has been devoted to the hypothesis that cannabis has a causal relationship to psychosis, very little has been written about the possibility that it might protect some people from psychosis. An outstanding feature of many of the surveys cited above is that while few or none of the users were found to be psychotic, many of them did suffer from neuroses or personality disorders. I think that it is safe to say that any population of marihuana users will embrace more mental disturbances of varying types and degrees than a comparable one of nonusers. Thus, one would expect that the prevalence of psychoses among cannabis users would be greater than that of the general population. This does not appear to be so and suggests the possibility, which also occurred to H. B. M. Murphy, that the use of this drug may indeed be protecting some individuals from psychoses.[57] Here one might suppose that the drug serves to provide relief from, or at any rate dull, the impact of unbearable anxiety or an overwhelming reality.

Fortunately, recent literature also contains a number of studies and reports which do not appear to harbor either a pro- or an anti-marihuana bias and appear to be scientifically sound. One such study, published in 1968, is that of L. J. Hekimian and S. Gershon. They conducted a survey of 112 randomly selected, hospitalized drug abusers. Two senior psychiatrists took careful and thorough patient histories within 24 hours of admission. They included demographic and social data, psychiatric anamnesis, and paid particular attention to the history of illnesses that occurred before these patients were hospitalized. In each case a drug was presumed to have played a part in the development of the illness for which they were hospitalized. Eight of the patients had been admitted to the hospital because of psychiatric difficulties that appeared after they had used marihuana. What of their history? Six of the eight had previously taken LSD; seven had had previous psychiatric treatment or hospitalization. Six manifested primary and secondary symptoms of schizophrenia prior to smoking marihuana; one was a schizoid and one was a depressive personality prior to smoking marihuana. The authors write, "The schizophrenics were paranoid or undifferentiated on admission, but several days later, when there no longer were drug effects, their illnesses were well documented." [58] If it were not for these careful history-taking procedures and the candor of the authors, these eight cases could easily have been presented as clear and uncomplicated examples of marihuana-induced psychosis.

W. Keup recently completed a survey of those psychiatric patients admitted to the Brooklyn State Hospital who had a history of drug abuse. Of the 126 who were thoroughly studied, 14 "were found to have suffered, at some time from cannabis induced psychotic behavior of a more serious nature." [59] Careful psychiatric interviewing and testing revealed that "only 6 of the 14 patients had cannabis-related symptoms at the time of admission, in the remaining 8 patients the symptoms occurred in the past. . . . Only in 2 patients cannabis abuse seemed the direct cause of admission, in 4 other patients it contributed to the events leading to hospitalization." Thus "only in 0.9 per thousand of all [psychiatric] admissions was cannabis found to be the direct cause of hospitalization." [60] Of the two cases where cannabis was labeled as the direct cause, one was diagnosed as a toxic psychosis, and the other as a panic reaction.

Such figures are indeed in striking contrast to those cited by Eastern authors which often run as high as 750 per 1,000. If there is any factual basis for the contention that marihuana, as it is used in the United States, causes psychosis, then one would expect the tremendous increase in its use would directly occasion a *substantial* increase in the number of cases diagnosed and admitted to hospitals and written about in scientific journals and the press. That this hasn't happened is substantiated by some observations of D. E. Smith. Unlike a clinician who occasionally sees one or two drug cases, he is Medical Director of the Haight-Ashbury Medical Clinic and Consultant on Drug Abuse at the San Francisco General Hospital; in this capacity he has had extensive experience with large numbers of marihuana users, and he has conducted research into the drug practices of a marihuana-using subculture. He writes: "At San Francisco General Hospital 5000 acute drug intoxications were treated in 1967. Despite the high incidence of marijuana use in San Francisco, no 'marijuana psychoses' were seen. In fifteen months of operation the Haight-Ashbury Clinic has seen approximately 30,000 patient-visits for a variety of medical and psychiatric problems. Our research indicated that at least 95% of the patients had used marijuana one or more times, and yet no case of primary marijuana psychosis was seen. There is no question that such an acute effect is theoretically possible, but its occurrence is very rare." [61]

Isbell et al., in a controlled study of over 30 subjects (all former opium addicts), found that the dose level of Δ^1-THC which would lead to a positive mood change, "with patients frequently reporting that they felt happy, gay, silly, and relaxed," was 25 mcg/kg smoking or 75 mcg/kg orally.[62] When they reached dose levels of 200 mcg/kg smoking or 360 mcg/kg orally, "the majority of the patients had 'psychotomimetic effects,' including marked changes in body image, illusions, delusions, and hallucinations." [63] (The authors do not raise the point whether it is accurate to call these subjective alterations "true" hallucinations — see Chap. 5.) They state that while most of the subjects did maintain "insight and ascribed these . . . effects to the drug," two subjects lost insight, did not realize that the effects they were experiencing were drug-induced, and "even after they had recovered, had difficulty in accepting the fact that their psychotic experiences were due to a drug and more particularly that they were due to a drug isolated from marihuana." [64] There are two problems with this report insofar as it has been used to support the claim that marihuana induces psychoses. First, the smoked dose of marihuana required to produce the "psychotic experiences" in two subjects was *eight times* the dose required for the usual high. There are a number of drugs which are not ordinarily thought of as psychotogenic, but which, if given at a dose level eight times the ordinary dose, will almost inevitably precipitate a toxic psychosis. Second, it is unjustifiable to draw the conclusion that marihuana will lead to psychoses in normal people when the subject population in this study was composed of former opium addicts who also revealed, according to the authors, "evidence of character disorder." [65]

That adverse reactions to marihuana are not seen more frequently is a point which H. S. Becker deals with at length. There has developed in this country a marihuana-using subculture whose members share a knowledge of techniques, a definition of effects, an awareness of the drug's typical course, and the ability to deal with anxiety attacks and other adverse reactions:

> When someone experiences disturbing effects, other users typically assure him that the change in his subjective experience is neither rare nor dangerous. . . . They redefine the experience he is having as desirable rather than frightening . . . What they tell him carries conviction, because he can see that it is not some idiosyncratic belief but is instead culturally shared. . . . In all these ways, experienced users prevent the episode from having lasting effects and reassure the novice that whatever he feels will come to a timely and harmless end.[66]

Furthermore, the supportive ministrations of this subculture could not possibly have any effectiveness if the drug did produce, quite apart from the user's interpretation, any permanent damage to the mind. Though in some instances transitory adverse reactions do occur, the reassurance of companions and the passage of a day or so will convince the user that the effects he has experienced are not permanent.

It is difficult to understand how, in the face of all the evidence to the contrary, prominent medical men, newspaper reporters, lawmakers, law enforcers, judges, and others are still publicly stating that the use of marihuana commonly leads to the development of psychoses (see Chap. 12). One problem may be that they latch onto a few of the early Eastern reports telling of asylums overflowing with raving "cannabis psychotics" and without any further knowledge or investigation transpose this horrifying picture to the growing use of marihuana in this country. One such author, an attorney writing in 1966, summarizes his case against marihuana by stating:

> A marijuana addict is more easily cured in the early stages than is a morphine, heroin, or cocaine addict. However, as a general rule, more of this drug is used by the addict, and there is a great danger that his brain will sooner or later suffer a complete breakdown and that he will have to spend the rest of his life in an insane asylum. Its use often eventuates in mania and dementia. In the complete distortion and demoralization of the brain, due to the rapidity of its inroads, marijuana is even more harmful than morphine.[67]

Such a statement presents, at the very least, a distorted, semi-hysterical view of the consequences of marihuana use, but undoubtedly, and regrettably, many of the readers of *The Medico-Legal Journal,* in which it was published, did not recognize it as such, and have and will continue to base their medical and legal judgments on such blatantly false and misleading grounds.

While there is little evidence for the existence of a "cannabis psychosis," it seems clear that the drug may precipitate in susceptible people one of several types of mental dysfunction. The most serious and disturbing of these is the toxic psychosis already mentioned. This is an acute state that resembles the delirium of a high fever and is caused by the presence in the brain of toxic substances which interfere with a variety of cerebral functions. Generally speaking, as the toxins disappear, so do the symptoms of toxic psychosis. This type of reaction may be caused by any number of substances taken either as intended or inadvertent overdoses. The syndrome often includes clouding of consciousness, restlessness, confusion, bewilderment, disorientation, dreamlike thinking, apprehension, fear, illusions, and hallucinations. The latter part of the earlier described experience of Bayard Taylor is that of a toxic psychosis induced by a very large dose of hashish; it is also possible that Fitz Hugh Ludlow experienced this syndrome. In any event, cannabis can induce a toxic psychosis, but it generally requires a rather large ingested dose. Such a reaction is apparently much less likely to occur when cannabis is smoked, perhaps because not enough of the active substances can be absorbed sufficiently rapidly, or possibly because in the process of smoking those cannabinol derivatives which are most likely to precipitate this syndrome are modified in some way, as yet unknown.

There are people who may suffer what are usually short-lived, acute anxiety states sometimes with and sometimes without accompanying paranoid thoughts. The anxiety may reach such proportion as properly to be called panic. Such panic reactions, while they are not very common, probably constitute the most frequent adverse reaction to the moderate use of smoked marihuana. During this reaction the sufferer may believe that the various distortions of his perception of his body mean that he is dying or that he is undergoing some great physical catastrophe, and similarly he may interpret the psychological distortions induced by the drug as an indication that he is losing his sanity. Panic states may, albeit rarely, be so severe as to incapacitate, usually for a relatively short period of time. Set and setting undoubtedly contribute to this type of reaction; that is, a person who expects some sort of severe mental dislocation is more likely to experience one; similarly, if he smokes marihuana in an unpleasant or frightening social setting he is more likely to react pathologically. Conversely, in a setting where use of marihuana as a recreational intoxicant is casual and well accepted and the smoker is experienced and comfortable, this type of adverse reaction is less probable. According to A. T. Weil, in communities where marihuana is well accepted as a recreational intoxicant, these reactions are extremely rare; they constitute about 1 percent of all responses to the use of marihuana in such settings. However, where use of the drug represents a greater degree of social deviance, as many as 25 percent of people using it for the first time may experience panic.[68] These reactions are self-limited, and simple reassurance is the best method of treatment. Perhaps the main danger of this type of reaction to the user (aside from the fact that it is quite uncomfortable) is that he will be diagnosed as having a toxic psychosis, an unfortunately common mistake.

Users with this kind of reaction, while they may be quite distressed, are not psychotic inasmuch as the sine qua non of sanity, the ability to test reality, remains intact, and the panicked user is invariably able to relate his discomfort to his use of the drug. There is no disorientation, nor are there "true" hallucinations.

Sometimes this panic reaction is accompanied by paranoid ideation. The user may, for example, believe that the others in the room, especially if they are not well known to him, have some hostile intentions toward him, or that someone is going to inform on him, often to the police, for smoking marihuana. Generally speaking, these paranoid-type ideas are not strongly held, and simple reassurance dispels them. Set and setting are again very important. Allen Ginsberg asserts that the anxiety and paranoid ideation are not so much a pharmacological effect as one determined largely by the fact that in the United States there is a real basis for them; here one can be apprehended for using marihuana and treated as a deviant criminal.[69] Curiously enough, as one peruses the psychiatric literature from different parts of the world, the emphasis on the anxiety-paranoia symptoms does not appear to be prominent in areas where penalties for the use of hemp are either nonexistent or not overly severe.

With respect to paranoia and the importance of set and setting, the following experience, reported by D. L. Farnsworth, is instructive. A student concerned about the widespread use of marihuana on his campus remonstrated to the dean against the lack of official action taken against those who were using the drug. The student said, "You have a list, you know, and why don't you get after the students who are smoking marijuana?" The dean denied that he had such a list, whereupon the student said, "You have one now," and gave the dean such a list.[70] The dean, concerned that he might be remiss in his duties if he did nothing, appointed a committee of faculty members and administrators to investigate the problem on campus, and shortly thereafter a student known to be selling drugs was apprehended. Because he feared that discussion of the case would violate the apprehended student's privacy, the dean refused to discuss the case and remained silent. However, his silence apparently increased the anxiety among those using marihuana; rumors about more lists and crackdowns ran throughout the campus. Among the rumors was one that the health services regularly turned over to the administration the names of students using drugs. Despite the fact that no such betrayal was demonstrated and the punitive action on the part of the college authorities had been taken against only the one student supplier of drugs, fear and suspicion continued to spread. The patients at the health service who were already troubled and using drugs became increasingly guarded when talking with their psychotherapists, and within two weeks six patients became so paranoid that they required hospitalization. The usual rate for hospitalization at this particular college does not exceed two or three students per year.

Rarely, but especially among new users of marihuana, there occurs an acute depressive reaction which resembles the reactive or neurotic type. It is generally rather mild and transient but may sometimes require psychiatric intervention. This type of reaction is most likely to occur in a user who has some degree of underlying depression; it is as though the drug allows the depression to be felt and experienced as such. Again it must be supposed that set and setting play an important part, inasmuch as the same individual who on one occasion has this type of reaction will not have it on another occasion.

According to Weil, there are some rare reactions that occur in people who have previously taken "hallucinogenic" drugs. One is the recurrence of "hallucinogenic" symptomatology, the so-called "flashbacks." This type of reaction has been reported independent of marihuana use, and it usually consists of the recurrence of a "hallucination" first experienced during an earlier LSD or mescaline trip. However, and this too is quite clear, in some individuals a "flashback" may occur during a marihuana high. For some this is an enjoyable experience; for others it is distressing. Some see the "flashback" phenomenon as a specific instance of a more general change in the nature of the marihuana high, which may be experienced after the use of "hallucinogens." Generally this type of reaction fades with the passage of time. There is one report that is suggestive of the possibility of something like this reaction occurring in the absence of a prior history of use of "hallucinogens." [71]

Quite rarely there are some people who, subsequent to their use of "hallucinogens," suffer psychotic reactions which may not become apparent until several months after the taking of a "hallucinogen." The reactions may appear unrelated to any previous suggestion of mental illness, and in some cases they seem to have been precipitated by an acute marihuana intoxication. It is, of course, unknown whether they would have occurred without the use of marihuana.[72] Quite apart from any previous use of "hallucinogens," while it has not been conclusively established that marihuana may precipitate a psychosis, it stands to reason that a person maintaining a delicate balance of ego functioning — so that, for instance, the ego is threatened by a severe loss, or a surgical assault, or even an alcoholic debauch — may also be overwhelmed or precipitated into a schizophrenic reaction by a drug which alters, however mildly, his state of consciousness. The concatenation of factors — a person whose ego is already overburdened in its attempts to manage a great deal of anxiety and to prevent distortion of perception and body image, plus the taking of a drug which, especially in some individuals, seems to promote just these effects — may indeed be the last straw in precipitating a schizophrenic break. Of 41 acute schizophrenic patients studied by the author at the Massachusetts Mental Health Center, it was possible to elicit a history of marihuana use in 6. In 4 of the 6 it seemed quite improbable that the drug could have had any relation to the development of the acute psychosis, because the psychosis was so remote in time from the drug experience. Careful history taking and attention to details of the drug experience(s) and changing mental status in the remaining 2 patients failed to either implicate or exonerate marihuana as a precipitant in their psychoses.

Another peculiarity of the marihuana literature is that it is replete with claims that the long-term use of the drug leads to degeneracy. However, the few survey studies that exist, and are reasonably sound methodologically, generated data which fail to support this claim. One of the earliest was the report of the Indian Hemp Commission published in Simla in 1894 in the form of seven volumes comprising over 3,000 pages. As N. Taylor notes, there was suspicion that the real motive for the inquiry on the part of the British was to establish that Scotch whiskey, from which a large tax revenue could be derived, was less dangerous than hemp products.[73] Hemp products, with the exception of *charas*, were only about one-twentieth as expensive as whiskey and more difficult to tax. Nonetheless, the inquiry was carried out with typical British impartiality and meticulous examination of 800 doctors, fakirs, yogis, coolies, superintendents of insane asylums, tax collectors, *bhang* peasants, clergy, hemp dealers, *ganja* palace operators, and so forth. They concluded as follows:

1. There is no evidence of any weight regarding mental and moral injuries from the moderate use of these drugs.
2. Large numbers of practitioners of long experience have seen no evidence of any connection between the moderate use of hemp drugs and disease.
3. Moderation does not lead to excess in hemp any more than it does in alcohol. Regular, moderate use of ganja or bhang produces the same effects as moderate and regular doses of whiskey. Excess is confined to the idle and the dissipated.[74]

In the La Guardia study, 17 of the 77 subjects were chronic cannabis users. One can calculate from the data given (in Table 42 of that study) that the duration of usage ranged in these men from 2½ to 16 years, with a mean of 8 years, and the number of cigarettes smoked per day varied from 2 to 18, with a mean of 7.2.[75] Despite the fact that this dosage would be considered to be rather on the high side of marihuana use in the United States, the investigators were able to establish that the marihuana users were not inferior in intelligence to the general population and that they had suffered no mental or physical deterioration as a result of their use of the drug. Nor could Freedman and Rockmore, whose 310 users had a history of an average of 7.1 years of cannabis use, find any evidence of mental or physical decline that could be attributed to drug use.[76] Furthermore, Bromberg's 67 criminal offenders who were users of marihuana revealed no peculiarities of psychopathology which would distinguish them from a non-marihuana-using group of criminal offenders.[77] Although in the study of Siler et al. the subjects were young (an average age of 23) and their experience in using the drug averaged only two years, it was also not possible to demonstrate any evidence of mental or physical deterioration.[78]

Still, it is difficult to ignore the numerous reports from the East, particularly Egypt and parts of the Orient, which characterize the long-term cannabis user as a passive, nonproductive, even slothful degenerate. One possible explanation is that the excessive use of the stronger cannabis preparations may indeed lead to some physical and mental deterioration, as may the chronic excessive use of alcohol and other substances. Another is that among whole populations that are already hungry, sick, and hopeless, there are many who have given up, are passive and nonproductive, and use relatively large quantities of an available and inexpensive drug to soften and distort the impact of an otherwise unbearable reality. A similar problem exists with regard to the "pot-heads" in the United States. Here again it is uncertain which comes first, the drug on the one hand or, on the other, the unbearable conflict, the depression or the personality disorder. D. L. Farnsworth cites six cases to illustrate the relationship of marihuana use to the development of emotional disturbance in college students, but in all of them serious conflict or depression existed well before the student began to use the drug.[79] In fact, it appears that the use of marihuana was one of the means these students tried for dealing with conflict, anxiety, and depression. Some of them took advantage of an opportunity to get psychotherapy, made good use of it, and had less need to use marihuana. However, it can be assumed that for many psychotherapy is not sought or is not available. Here the use of the drug is not causative, but symptomatic, and the conscious intent on the part of the user is not self-destructive, but restitutive.

It seems clear that among populations of illicit drug users there will be found more psychopathology than among nonusers. But the critical questions are whether the drug use comes first, and, if it does, whether it is causally related to the development of the psychopathology, either as a precipitating factor or a synergistic one, or whether the drug use is completely independent of the psychopathology or at the most an expression of it. Recently M. Cohen and D. F. Klein studied 70 patients who occasionally or frequently used "marijuana, amphetamines, barbiturates, LSD, other psychotogens, and opiates." [80] The 70 were among 224 consecutive in-patient voluntary admissions, under 25 years of age, to the Hillside Hospital between December 1966 and November 1967. All the 224 patients were hospitalized for nondrug reasons.

The patients were assigned to three groups:

1. An extreme drug-use group whose members indicated almost habitual use of two or more drugs on a daily basis for at least a one-month period; many had used drugs for several years. There were 39 patients in this group.

2. A moderate mixed-drug-use group composed of patients who made moderate use of two or more drugs or moderate to excessive use of only one drug, *except* marihuana. The 16 patients in this group used the drugs on an irregular basis, for instance, weekends or parties only.

3. A moderate marihuana-only group made up of those patients who had used *only* marihuana on either a regular or an irregular basis. The 15 patients in this group did not include those who had used the drug only once or twice.

In addition there was a nondrug control group selected from the non-drug-using patient sample and matched with the preceding groups for age and sex.[81]

Of the demographic variables taken into account there were no significant differences between drug and control groups except for total WAIS IQ scores. Extreme drug-use patients had significantly higher scores (113.08) than either the moderate marihuana group (102.15) or the control group (103.26). The mean WAIS score for the moderate mixed-drug group (110.86) was close to that for the extreme group. Thus the authors found that the patient groups most involved with drugs were also the most intelligent. They also found that there were significantly more character disorders (85 percent) and fewer schizophrenic patients (5 percent) among the extreme drug-use patients than among any of the other three groups. The percentages of character disorders among the two moderate drug-use groups and the control patients were similar to those of the entire hospital population under 25 years of age (50–55 percent). Forty-five percent of the character disorders among the extreme drug-use group and 33 percent of those in the two moderate drug-use groups were found to be the "Emotionally Unstable" type as compared with 6 percent of the character disorders among the controls. Within the latter group, 44 percent of the character disorders were Passive-Aggressive/Dependent as compared with 30 percent among the extreme group and 18 percent among the combined moderate groups. "Combining all drug groups, there were significantly more Emotionally Unstable character disorders (21/51, 41%) among drug patients than among the controls (1/16, 6%, $z = 3.76$, $p < .01$); and significantly more Passive-Aggressive/Dependent character disorders among the controls (7/16, 44%) than among the drug patients

(13/51, 26%, z = 2.13, p < .05)." [82] The authors also demonstrated that there were significantly more psychotics among moderate drug users and controls than among the extreme drug users.

Two points should be emphasized regarding this study. First, neither the moderate mixed-drug-use group nor the moderate marihuana-only drug-use group had a higher prevalance of character disorders than did the control group or the entire hospital population under 25 years of age. (In fact an examination of the data in Table 3 of the study reveals that the percentage of character disorders among the moderate marihuana group was smaller than any other group and almost identical to that of the control group, 47 percent as compared with 46 percent; similarly, if one looks at the percentages for the prevalence of schizophrenia among the groups, with the exception of the extreme drug group of 5 percent, the moderate marihuana group with 20 percent is lower than the other drug group and half that of the control group.)[83] Second, with respect to the extreme drug-use group, among which there is a higher prevalence of character disorders, there is no way of determining whether the extreme use of drugs in some way contributed to the existence of those disorders or whether, as seems more likely, people with this much and kind of psychopathology are more likely to use drugs and use them excessively.

That there are personality characteristics associated with the use of marihuana is becoming increasingly clear. R. Hogan et al., in a study of 148 male undergraduates at two universities, delineated some of these characteristics. The investigators defined three levels of marihuana use: (1) Users — students who reported that they had smoked or were still smoking marihuana; (2) Nonusers — students who reported that they had not smoked marihuana; and (3) Adamant nonusers — students who said that they had not and never would smoke marihuana. Through a biographical questionnaire and the California Psychological Inventory (a scale designed to measure "aspects of interpersonal behavior which arise in every day social living and are found in all cultures and societies"), they arrived at the following conclusions:

> Users tended to major in the humanities and social sciences, and could be generally described as socially poised, open to experience, and concerned with the feelings of others. On the other hand they also tended to be impulsive, pleasure seeking,

and somewhat rebellious. In contrast, adamant non-users showed no clearly defined academic preferences, and were responsible and rule-abiding. However, they also tended to be rigid, conventional, and narrow in their interests. Finally, users and adamant non-users could not be distinguished in terms of a well-validated index of social maturity, and both groups appeared as less than morally mature on two scales designed to predict moral behavior.[84]

The authors are careful to emphasize that these personality characteristics are merely associated with the use of marihuana and do not imply any causal relationship. However, there is no reason to suppose that the use of marihuana has any more to do with the personality traits associated with the user than its nonuse with those of the adamant nonuser. Unfortunately, the investigators do not distinguish between heavy and moderate users of marihuana.

A study that did compare heavy users with moderate users is the recent one of S. M. Mirin et al. They tested 12 "heavy users" (i.e., persons "using marihuana . . . 30 to 40 times per month") and 12 "casual smokers" (i.e., persons "using marihuana between 1 and 4 times per month") along a number of parameters; they obtained apparently paradoxical results from "two measures of hostility. . . . The Buss-Durkee Scale . . . [which is] a self-report of one's willingness to indulge in aggressive behavior," showed no significant difference between the two types with regard to general level of hostility, but the "Psychiatric Outpatient Mood Scale . . . [which is] an indicator of current mood," and which was administered at the end of the testing, indicated that "the group of heavy users scored significantly higher in hostility compared to the 'casuals' (p < .05; two-tailed t-test)." [85] The researchers offer several hypotheses to account for this apparent discrepancy: "the 'establishment' setting, the interviewers themselves, or the interview material. Casual users closely approximated the life style of their interviewers. In contrast, it is possible that discussion of multiple drug use coupled with questions about work, social and sexual adjustment [all of which were done prior to the Psychiatric Outpatient Mood Scale test] made our heavy users defensive, and then hostile." [86] Another finding of this same study, which confirmed other reports, was that "heavy marihuana use is frequently associated with use of more potent mind-altering agents." [87] The authors, however, were careful to avoid concluding that "this data . . . implicate[s] marihuana as a cause of amphetamine or hallucinogen use." Instead, they tried to discover, "given this syndrome of multiple drug use and the preference of our Ss for marihuana . . . what it was in the marihuana experience that prompted its repetitive and frequent use." [88] They found that both the heavy and the casual users "cited the drug's pleasurable effects (i.e., euphoria, relaxation)" when questioned as to their reasons for continued drug use; "only the heavy users, however, mentioned the search for insight and/or the wish for a sense of harmony or union as part of their motivation for continuing." [89]

The report concludes with the following statement: "Psychological dependence [which is not defined and which is attributed solely on the basis of the subjects' own reports] and the search for insight or a meaningful affective experience appear to be correlated with heavy marihuana use. Multiple drug use is also associated with poor work adjustment. Goal directed activity and the ability to master new problems is diminished. By traditional psychiatric standards, social adjustment in heavy users is poor as are their relationships with women. There is also evidence of a less than satisfactory sexual adjustment in this group." [90]

When these findings are compared with an equally recent study by Zinberg and Weil, a somewhat different picture of the "chronic" marihuana user emerges: "Although we assigned them to the three groups — N, NN and C — the actual drug use of some of the NN [persons not naive to marihuana] approached that of the Cs [chronic marihuana users]. All but two in each of the three groups [the totals for each group were N — marihuana naive — 25; NN — 28; C — 9] were students in eight different institutions of higher learning in the Boston area. Of the rest, all but one (an N, diagnosed as a chronic schizophrenic . . .) were employed." [91] One interesting finding was that as marihuana use became more and more regular (or "chronic"), "the use of alcohol, especially distilled spirits, declined proportionately or even more steeply. . . . In the C group, with one exception, no subjects drank alcohol except as part of the marijuana smoking ritual when they sipped cold beer or wine to relieve dryness of the mouth. In fact, three of the nine C subjects virtually never drank alcohol, and one other reported a definite distaste for drink even before he started using marijuana." [92] The authors present the results of their attempt to put each individual subject "on a rough gradient of personality traits ranging from extreme compulsiveness to extreme hysteria. The entire gradient is considered to fall within the limits of 'normal' character structures." [93] They predicted that persons tending toward hysteria would be more susceptible to the influence of marihuana, and the results of their interview-ratings bore out this prediction in an interesting fashion: "The N group showed a general tendency towards compulsiveness; the NN group tended towards more hysterical traits, and regular users (at least once a week) within the NN group clearly fell towards that end of the scale [i.e., hysteria]. Most subjects in both groups fell within the limits of the scale (that is, within the spectrum of normal personalities). By contrast, five of the nine C subjects fell off the scale and one more was only questionably within it. We shall call these personality distortions aberrations, although four of the six seemed well stabilized in their chosen environments." [94] They further noted that the C group was "easily differentiable from the other two" on a number of counts: they viewed their use of marihuana as the central and most significant aspect of their life-patterns; they showed a "constancy of attachment to female partners" that was "not only out of line with the rest of . . . [the] sample but significant compared with their age group in the general population or with a selected group matched for family background and educational achievement"; they displayed "extreme anxiousness and vague paranoia . . . during the interviews and persisting into the experiments." [95] However, they also note that "in appearance the C group split about fifty-fifty with five recognizably hippy (long-haired and costumed) and four 'clean-cut.' " Although two or three from each of the other two groups wore "unusual clothes, . . . none was as distinctive as the hippy members of the C group." [96]

One of the more striking results of the report was purely unintentional: when the article was printed in *Nature,* an error of omission was made. Instead of the authors' statement: "There were no signs of overt intellectual deterioration in the C interviewees," the published article read as follows: "There were signs of overt intellectual deterioration in the C interviewees." [97] The *Washington Post* for 14 April 1970 ran a short article "summarizing" the report of Zinberg and Weil, with this lead headline: "Daily Pot-Smokers Erode in Intellect, Researchers Claim." [98] Since then Zinberg has publicly stated that the omission of the crucial negative occurred somewhere in the publication process and was not omitted from the final draft submitted to *Nature*.

A final conclusion of the research was that the attitudes of the C group were "quite negative toward society, which they saw as blindly conformist." [99] In attempting to arrive at a valid explanation for these observed differences between the C and the other two groups, the research team considered three hypotheses, but felt that none was "satisfactory by itself: (a) the C group members . . . were generally more neurotic than the average person before they began using marihuana," and "it was their need to express some personality distortion . . . that pushed them into being chronic users of an illegal drug. (b) The Cs were 'weaker' [*sic*], more suggestible persons who had succumbed to heavy marijuana use, and the drug itself caused the distortions now observed. (c) Choice of marijuana as a means of self-expression marks one as a deviant in the eyes of society and leads to fear of the police and other agents of the prevailing social order. Impact of these experiences on the C group produced the personality changes recorded in the interviews." [100] The members of the C group preferred to think that the last of the three proposed hypotheses was the correct one, and even "saw it as a factor in their early decisions to marry. They were uniformly bitter about society's attitude toward marijuana use and said this feeling affected their lives. Many reported that being defined as a deviant and law-breaker for something they could not accept as criminal had driven them into increasingly negative attitudes toward the larger society. Three subjects were especially articulate in tracing the shift of their values that led them to seek out individuals and groups who shared their positions and who used marijuana as frequently." [101] The contentions of these members of the C group are bolstered by the observation that "although 60 percent of the NN subjects were regular users, all began use after 1966 while all the Cs began use before 1965. The social atmosphere at the time that the NNs began to use marijuana accepted the use more thoroughly, contemporaries were less likely to differentiate people as special (rebels or heroes) simply because of the drug use." [102]

One completely unexpected finding surprised the investigators, since it contradicted a number of earlier studies (see note 87, above): "A negative finding that deserves some attention . . . was the low frequency of use of drugs other than cannabis in the NN and C groups. . . . if a single experiment with a drug ('one taste') is disregarded, then only 20 per cent have used any drug other than cannabis. [It is not clear if alcohol is included as a drug here.] And in those two cases (LSD and mescaline twice, and LSD three times) the use of these drugs was seen as a careful intellectual or philosophical exercise and was repeated ostensibly only for that purpose." [103]

In closing, the authors return to a discussion of alcohol and cannabis: "In the case of the moderate use of alcohol associated with late adolescence and the early twenties, marijuana smoking seems to be a functional equivalent, not simply a further drug habit. . . . Possibly, a history of initial and persistent dislike of alcoholic effect will turn out to be correlated with subsequent chronic marijuana use." [104]

In a survey of drug use on two eastern campuses, E. S. Robbins et al. administered a self-rating questionnaire in the classroom to 287 students, all but 1 of whom completed it. The investigators recognized the limitations of this sample, because it did not include absentees and drop-outs. From their data they characterized a typical marihuana user as "a liberal arts student, who reported somewhat looser religious ties than his non-drug-using classmates. Many marihuana users classified themselves as agnostics or atheists, or reported preferring an Eastern religion such as Zen to the one their parents professed. Half the marihuana smokers expressed dissatisfaction with their school, in contrast to 20 percent of the nonusers." [105]

The data from their self-assessment personality scale revealed that the drug user (meaning those who used illicit substances such as marihuana, LSD, and heroin or medicines such as amphetamines or barbiturates) "described themselves as usually anxious, bored, cynical, disgusted, impulsive, moody, rebellious, and restless significantly more often than did nonusers. They also saw themselves as never ambitious, secure, or slow. The nonusers were much more positive in their self-reports, selecting ambitious, contented, decisive, and secure as traits that usually depicted them. They felt that they were never helpless, hopeless, lonely, useless, or worthless significantly more often than the drug users." [106] The authors note that the marihuana smokers tended to describe themselves as more moody and unhappy than the nonsmokers and considered that the differences might be due to a greater tendency to "respond along conventional, socially acceptable lines on the part of the nonusers of marihuana. The marihuana smokers might have been responding in terms of quite different norms than their classmates, with their ideal image more likely that of a searching, self-preoccupied, and restless individual. Within the context of this study, it is not possible to determine whether the marihuana smokers were more tense than the others when they began to smoke, or whether smoking made them more moody and depressed." [107] A. Braiman, in discussing this paper, noted that K. Keniston had previously remarked that "alienated students are quick to admit their confusions, angers, anxieties, and problems. Given a list of neurotic symptoms, they check them all, describing themselves as socially undesirable, confused, depressed, angry, neurotic, hostile and impulsive." [108] For this reason Keniston is cautious in interpreting the self-descriptions as realistic barometers of psychopathology:

> The inference that these students are grossly disturbed can only be made with reservations. For one, they reject the value assumptions upon which most questionnaire measures of "maturity," "ego-strength," and "good mental health" are based. Furthermore, they make a great deal of effort to undermine any so-called "defenses" that may protect them from unpleasant feelings. For most of these students, openness to their own problems and failings is a cardinal virtue, and they make a further point of loudly proclaiming their own inadequacies.[109]

There are some striking parallels between personality traits of cigarette smokers and marihuana users. C. McArthur et al. have studied for almost twenty years "252 Harvard alumni [from the classes of 1938 and 1942] who were selected during their sophomore years for lack of visible abnormality" in an attempt to delineate a psychology of smoking.[110] Of this work they write:

> In summary, then, we may hypothesize that starting to smoke is largely brought about by one's social environment but that reactions to smoking, once it has started, seem to depend in good part on the personal needs that the newly-established habit is able to gratify. Some people seize on the habit compulsively. These people may often be emotionally constricted types for whom there is great gain in a simple "flight into

behavior" or they may be restless, active men, for whom smoking is just one more impulsive activity. It would also seem that anxious people can seize on smoking as a tension reducer if they have already, for other reasons, been oriented toward it. In short, the habit, once well available, increases in strength if it serves well the person's emotional economy.[111]

If one looks at the "psychiatric labels" which describe their "heavier smokers" who cannot stop smoking, they are close to those one would imagine might popularly be applied to a group of heavy marihuana users: "Weak Basic Personality, Asocial, Lack of Purpose and Values, Introspective, Ideational, and Inhibited." [112] In another paper they state, "Within the smoking group, one can make a case for the poorer integration of the heavy smoker's personality. The heavy smokers are often given to what the psychiatrists call 'acting out.' " [113]

In a more recent study (involving Harvard freshmen from the classes of 1958 and 1961) it was found, with respect to the examining physicians' ratings on "Personality Integration," that "the percentage of smokers marches upwards as the ratings become less favorable." [114] Similarly, in relation to the examining physicians' prediction of "College Adjustment," percentages are again related to predictions of poorer adjustment: "Both these findings from the physicians' ratings would seem to parallel the study findings that smoking went with psychiatric ratings suggesting poorer mental health." [115] What is so strikingly different in this paper is that, unlike those which deal with the association of personality traits and the use of marihuana, there is no hint or implication that cigarette smoking may be in any way responsible for the psychopathology described.

Of the various personality changes that allegedly occur with the chronic use of cannabis, those which together constitute what has been called the "amotivational syndrome" have been written about by several authors.[116] Those who suffer from this "syndrome" are described as being passive, nonproductive, achievement-eschewing, sloven, apathetic, and ineffective. It has even been suggested that those who use marihuana regularly may be "actually performing chemical self-leukotomies," that is, destroying areas of the frontal lobes of the brain which when accomplished surgically leaves "the individual more comfortable but less able to carry out complex long-term plans, endure frustration, concentrate for extended periods, follow routines, or successfully master new material (learning) with the same ease as before." [117] The description of the "amotivational syndrome" is based on some clinical observations in which no attempt has been made to distinguish between preexisting personality traits and this particular alleged sequela of chronic cannabis use.

W. H. McGlothlin and L. J. West, in a paper titled "The Marihuana Problem: An Overview," assert that "clinical observations indicate that regular marihuana use may contribute to the development of more passive, inward-turning, amotivational personality characteristics. For numerous middle-class students, the subtly progressive change from conforming, achievement-oriented behavior to a state of relaxed and careless drifting has followed their use of significant amounts of marihuana." [118] Yet in another paper, "Flight from Violence: Hippies and the Green Rebellion," in the same issue of the *American Journal of Psychiatry,* West and Allen, attempting to establish a close relationship between hippies and the use of marihuana, describe the following four "stages of hippiedom":

> The hippie way of life apparently evolves with the individual's passage through a series of stages that may be listed as follows: *Step 1:* Dissatisfaction and frequently a sense of impotence in dealing with the world, usually symbolized by one's middle-class parents. While our subjects ranged in age from 17 to 52, the vast majority of the hippies were intelligent, college-educated 20-year-olds of white middle-class background, from which they were trying to escape — less with a feeling of anger than with disillusionment and the sad conviction that their parents were unable to offer relevant models of competence. These were mostly thoughtful, sensitive youngsters with liberal, idealistic values — values perhaps articulated but not necessarily practiced by their parents.
> *Step 2:* A search for meaning in the light of a good educational background and from an initial posture of financial — not interpersonal — security. The search was directed toward the Haight-Ashbury by the mass media, hot and cool, establishment and underground. They supplied guidebooks and manufactured stereotypes for the youth to live out.

Step 3: Association with other searchers, some of whom seemed to have discovered a Way.

Step 4: Turn on (with drugs). Tune in (on the hip scene). Drop out (from the competitive life of society).[119]

It is not difficult to imagine that an adolescent with an inchoate adult identification who has truly passed through the first three stages of this Odyssean schema would appear different in his orientation to life and his behavior whether or not he had ever used marihuana. Inward-turning young people who have embraced such a profound rejection of the life style of their goal-oriented, achievement-seeking, well-dressed, and materially secure parents may very well adopt, in most cases transiently, an identification and style of living that is shared by a large group of their peers, a style in which they present themselves as passive, nonproductive, and sloven. There is, then, the question whether the "amotivational syndrome," assuming for the moment that it is a clinical reality, is necessarily a product of the chronic use of cannabis; and beyond that, there is the question whether or not this syndrome is truly a manifestation of personality deterioration or even change.

Personality has been defined in a multitude of ways. A psychodynamic approach sees personality as evolving over time and within the limits of genetic potentials through a prolonged series of stages of social experiencing into a system of more or less enduring and consistent attitudes, beliefs, desires, capacities for affective expression, and patterns of adaptation, which make each individual unique. The distinctive whole formed by these relatively permanent patterns and tendencies of a given person is spoken of as his personality. Once it is fully formed it is rather resistant to change; even a profound experience like psychoanalysis, one which is calculated to effect personality change, very often leads to limited differences, and they are often so subtle that they elude attempts at objectification and quantification. There can be no doubt that certain personality types are more attracted to the use of marihuana, but it is questionable whether its use, certainly its moderate use, leads to personality change. I think however, that of all the deleterious effects which cannabis use is alleged to cause, personality change, especially with regard to heavy use, is the most difficult to refute. Data from well-designed, prospective, longitudinal studies which bear directly on this point are simply not available at this time.

As has been noted, there are clinicians who have reported what they discern as personality change, and they relate this to the use of cannabis. I would agree that when a young person gives up a more or less conventional mode of living for one which is or is closer to that of the hippie, one may observe in him changes in behavior and attitude, changes which, taken together, may constitute what has been called the "amotivational syndrome." I am not so certain, however, that these differences constitute personality change; it may be more accurate to consider them manifestations of a purposeful and extensive change in life-style, one involving ideology, values, attitudes, dress, social norms, and many aspects of behavior. This type of change may be likened to that which a girl who decides to join a convent may undergo; she certainly appears different with respect to her values, dress, goals, behavior, and so forth, but beneath her habit the same pre-convent personality resides. Similarly, it seems more than likely that behind the hirsuteness and the hip patinas are personalities which have not undergone significant and basic change.

The use of marihuana is almost always one manifestation of this kind of change in life-style; whether it may also contribute in some way to the change is unknown. However, it appears that the determinants of this type of change are more likely to be found in predisposing personality problems and in disaffection with the social system than in the moderate social use of the drug marihuana.

11 Crime and Sexual Excess

When one surveys the history of cannabis use in the United States with regard to the alleged direct causal connection between marihuana use and the commission of serious crime, one is struck by the widespread influence a nine-hundred-year-old myth has had on this belief. The myth of the eleventh-century Persian "Assassins" has for years served as an ultimate source for those who have sought to establish a connection between marihuana and crime. Marco Polo is usually credited with having introduced the story of the Assassins to the Western world. The Commissioner of the Federal Bureau of Narcotics, H. J. Anslinger, made the following statement on the subject in 1937:

> In the year 1090, there was founded in Persia the religious and military order of the Assassins, whose history is one of cruelty, barbarity, and murder, and for good reason. The members were confirmed users of hashish, or marijuana, and it is from the Arabic "hashshashin" that we have the English word "assassin." [1]

Anslinger succinctly outlines the myth in the form which has had the strongest impact on nearly all who are aware of any part of it, or even of any connection between the words "hashish" and "assassin." In order to appreciate just how misinformed the view reiterated by Anslinger is, an examination of some aspects of the historical basis for the myth is helpful.

The story goes back at least to the middle of the seventh century, when the Moslem saint Husein (also spelled Hussein), the second son of Ali, who was a first cousin of Mohammed, unsuccessfully claimed to be the caliph, that is, the head of the Islam theocratic organization and a direct agent of God. After Ali's death, Islam split into a number of sects; at least four individuals declared themselves the caliph and managed to attract a following. "Of these Aliites . . . a chief sect, and parent of many heretical branches, were the Ismailites. . . . About A.D. 1090 a branch of the Ismaili stock was established by Hassan [full name usually rendered in English as "al-Hasan ibn-al-Sabbah," abbreviated to "Hasan"], son of Sabah, in the mountainous districts of Northern Persia; and, before their suppression by the Mongols, 170 years later, the power of the quasi-spiritual dynasty which Hassan founded had spread over the Eastern Kohistan, at least as far as Kain. Their headquarters were at Alamut ('Eagle's Nest'), about 32 miles north-east of Kazwin," [2] a strategic point 10,200 feet above sea level, along the shortest but difficult route between the Caspian Sea and the Persian highlands.[3] "The Assassin movement," as it has come to be known, was called the "new propaganda" by its members. Hasan's motives were evidently personal ambition and desire for vengeance. As a young man in al-Ravy, al-Hasan received instruction in the Batinite system, and after spending a year and a half in Egypt, he returned to his native land as a Fatimid missionary.[4] The possession of Alamut was the first historical fact in the life of the new order. The agnosticism of Hasan's secret organization aimed to free people from the rigidity of doctrine, enlighten them as to the superfluity of prophets, and encourage them to believe nothing and dare all. Below the grand master stood the grand priors, each in charge of a particular district, and below them came the ordinary propagandists. The "fida'is" (or "Fidawi"), who stood ready to execute whatever orders the grand master issued, were the lowest degree of the order.[5]

The assassination in 1092 of the illustrious vizir of the Saljuq sultanate, Nizam-al-Mulk, by a fida'i disguised as a Sufi, was the first of a series of mysterious murders which plunged the Muslim world into terror. . . . attempts by caliphs and sultans [to capture Alamut] proved . . . futile until finally the Mongolian Hugalu, who destroyed the caliphate, seized the fortress in 1256 together with its subsidiary castles in Persia. Since the Assassin books and records were then destroyed, our information about this strange and spectacular order is derived mainly from hostile sources.

As early as the last years of the eleventh century the Assassins

had succeeded in setting firm foot in Syria and winning as con-
vert the Saljuq prince of Alappo, Ridwan ibn-Tutush (died in
1113). By 1140 they had captured the hill fortress of Masyad and
many others in northern Syria. . . . Even Shayzar (modern Say-
jar) . . . was temporarily occupied by the Assassins. . . . One
of their most famous masters in Syria was Rachid-al-Din Sinan
(died 1192), who . . . [was known to the Crusaders] as "the old
man of the mountain." It was Rashid's henchmen who struck
awe and terror into the hearts of the Crusaders. After the capture of Masyad in 1260 by the Mongols, the Mamluck Sultan
Baybars in 1272 dealt the Syrian Assassins the final blow. Since
then the Assassins have been sparsely scattered through northern
Syria, Persia, 'Uman, Zanzibar and especially India, where they
number about a hundred and fifty thousand and go by the name
of Thojas or Mowlas. They all acknowledge as titular head the
Aga Khan of Bombay, who claims descent through the last
grand master of Alamut from Isma'il, the seventh imam, receives over a tenth of the revenues of his followers, even in
Syria, and spends most of his time as a sportsman between Paris
and London.[6]

In considering Polo's account of the myth that has become associated in the Western world with Hasan and his followers, it
should be remembered that Polo visited the remains of the palace
and garden at Alamut during 1271–1272, approximately 158 years
after Hasan's death and 15 years after the Mongolian Hulagu had
seized the entire region, destroying all books and written records
and dispersing the followers. Polo therefore could not have personally witnessed any of the events that he recounts (as he admits
himself):

Concerning the Old Man of the Mountain

MULEHET is a country in which the Old Man of the Mountain dwelt in former days; and the name means *"Place of the
Aram."* I will tell you his whole history as related by Messer
Marco Polo, *who heard it from several natives of that region.*
[italics added.]

The Old Man was called in their language ALOADIN. He
had caused a certain valley between two mountains to be en-
closed, and had turned it into a garden, the largest and most

beautiful that ever was seen, filled with every variety of fruit. In it were . . . palaces the most elegant that can be imagined, all covered with gilding and exquisite painting. And there were runnels too, flowing freely with wine and milk and honey and water; and numbers of ladies and of the most beautiful damsels in the world, who could play on all manner of instruments, and sung most sweetly, and danced in a manner that it was charming to behold. For the Old Man desired to make his people believe that this was actually Paradise. . . . And sure enough the Saracens of those parts believed that it *was* Paradise!

Now no man was allowed to enter the Garden save those whom he intended to be his ASHISHIN. . . . He kept at his court a number of the youths of the country, from 12 to 20 years of age, such as had a taste for soldiering, and to these he used to tell tales about Paradise. . . . Then he would introduce them into his garden, some four, or six, or ten at a time, having first made them drink a certain potion which cast them into a deep sleep, and then causing them to be lifted and carried in. So when they awoke, they found themselves in the Garden. . . .

When therefore they awoke, . . . they deemed that it was Paradise in very truth. And the ladies and damsels dallied with them to their hearts' content, so that they had what young men would have; and with their own good will they never would have quitted this place.

Now this Prince whom we call the Old One . . . made those simple hill-folks about him believe firmly that he was a great Prophet. And when he wanted one of his *Ashishin* to send on any mission, he would cause that potion whereof I spoke to be given to one of the youths in the garden, and then had him carried into his Palace. So when the young man awoke, he found himself in the Castle, and no longer in that Paradise; whereat he was not over well pleased. He was then conducted to the Old Man's presence, . . . The Prince would then ask whence he came, and he would reply that he came from Paradise! and that it was exactly as Mahommet had described it in the Law. This of course gave the others who stood by, and who had not been admitted, the greatest desire to enter therein.

So when the Old Man would have any Prince slain, he would say to such a youth [as wished to enter Paradise]: "Go thou and slay So and So; and when thou returnest my Angels shall bear thee into Paradise. And shouldst thou die, natheless even so will I send my Angels to carry thee back into Paradise." So he caused them to believe; and thus there was no order of his that they would not affront any peril to execute, for the great desire they had to get . . . into that Paradise. . . . And in this manner the Old One got his people to murder any one whom he desired to get rid of.[7]

This is traditionally considered to be the origin of the myth that was repeated by Anslinger as actual history. However, when one compares Anslinger's with Polo's account, it is clear that there are a number of wide discrepancies. In the first place, in Polo's account, the entrance into Paradise was the reward, and not the cause, of the political crimes. Second, Polo tells us that the "Fidawi" acted on the promise of entering what others described as "Paradise" — they were not acting under the influence of the "potion," since they had never taken it: "It is not those who have tasted of the hashish-tinted paradise who will willingly kill but those who have not been there, (just as it is not the sated satyr who kills for sex but the horny 'have-not')." [8] Third, as Mandel has noted, Polo does not mention hashish or cannabis at all. "In fact, close reading of Marco Polo suggests the presence of two drugs: probably an opiate used for drugging young men to sleep for purposes of entering and exiting them without their knowledge, and free-flowing conduits of wine." [9] The Modern Library edition of Polo, revised from Marsden's translation (1818) and edited by Manuel Komroff, is probably the most accurate, compact, and well-written of all the translations. It should be noted that Polo himself never actually wrote the book attributed to him: he dictated it to a fellow prisoner in Genoa named Rusticien, after the Venetian fleet in which Polo was sailing was captured on September 7, 1298, without a single ship escaping. Polo, according to Komroff, had told his story many times during the three years between his return to Venice and his capture by the Genoese, but "to his listeners it all seemed incredible . . . there is, indeed, no record to prove that a single one of his contemporaries really believed much of the story he told." [10] But in prison he had sufficient leisure and a willing amanuensis. Because even the first copy was not direct from Polo's hand, and with each copying further variations in words and meaning crept into the text, and since the entire work was transcribed in only a few months, it is vain to look for complete accuracy or agreement among the approximately 100 different "first edition" manuscripts now preserved in various museums, no two of which are exactly alike. The Komroff edition states that the Old Man "at certain times . . . caused *opium* [italics added] to be administered to ten or a dozen of the youths" before they were carried into the garden; there is no mention in this edition of either cannabis or hashish.[11] In 1854 T. Wright revised the Marsden edition, and in 1926 J. Masefield revised the Marsden-Wright edition. None of these mention cannabis or hashish; *all* mention opium specifically.[12] Mandel accordingly notes that it would be more accurate to call the young fanatics "alcoholins" or "opiins" or even "frustratins" than "assassins."[13] According to A. A. Lubecensis, writing in 1659, a group known as the "Heissessin" used a special "potion," about a century before the time described in Polo's account, which "carried them away in ecstasy or frenzy, intoxicating them and producing a kind of fantastic, magic dream, filled with joy and delightfulness of a foolish sort."[14] Primarily on the basis of this statement, Walton suggests that the "magnificent gardens, if they existed at all, were chiefly products of the hashish delirium."[15] He may be correct, but there is no reason to suppose that these gardens were not the products of opium delirium.

Yet the term "assassin" is listed by every dictionary as etymologically derived from "hashish," and sometimes "Hasan." "Philologists dispute whether the word *assassin* derives from *Hasan* or from *hashish;* some maintain that *hashish* itself derives from *Hasan.* . . . One thing is certain, however; *Hasan, hashish,* and *assassin* were all tied together in the days when the Fidawi were strewing corpses across the Moslem crescent."[16] However, this derivation — in either form — is not at all certain. E. Fitzgerald, translator of O. Khayyam's *Rubaiyat,* is of the opinion that "Assassin" is derived from "Hasan," and not from "hashish" (or the alternative spelling "hashshaschin," used to refer to the Fidawi and mentioned by Anslinger).[17] However, one of the leading historians for the period during which Hasan's men were supposedly "strewing corpses across the Moslem crescent," B. Lewis, cites a "Jewish writer in Constantinople in the mid-twelfth century . . . (who) says that the Hashishiyah were so called because they dismissed the things of this world as so much grass (hashish)."[18] One surprising piece of evidence for this theory comes from the Dutch Biblical scholar C. Creighton, who argues that cannabis, although never mentioned directly, is implicitly referred to in a number of passages of the Old Testament. This hypothesis was suggested to him by the guess that the "grass" which Nebuchadnezzar ate was in fact hashish, or at least some form of cannabis, and because the Arabian word for "grass" was the same as the word for "cannabis": "hashish." [19] Creighton suggests that Saul's madness, Jonathan's and Samson's strength, and especially the first chapter of Ezekiel, which does sound like a description of an intense cannabis intoxication — an almost psychedelic experience — are all to be explained by the use of cannabis.[20]

The earliest proponent of the theory that "assassin" derives from the name of the drug used by Hasan's henchmen appears to be that of Sylvester De Sacy, writing in 1809: "Those who abandon themselves to its use are still called today *Haschischin* and *Haschaschin* and these two different expressions make it clear why the Ismaeliens have been named by the historians of the Crusades, now *Assissini*, now *Assassini*." [21] Although De Sacy may have been the first to derive "assassin" in this manner, Alexander Dumas probably had a much greater effect in popularizing and perpetuating the etymology, in his widely read *Count of Monte Cristo*, published in 1845.[22]

Lewis makes the point that "the stories told by Marco Polo and other Eastern and Western sources of the 'gardens of paradise' into which the drugged devotees were introduced to receive a foretaste of the eternal bliss that awaited them after the successful completion of their missions are not confirmed by any known Isma'ilite source." [23]

It appears that Polo was either presenting a pure fabrication of his imagination (not a very likely hypothesis), or else that he was passing on as historical fact a tale which had already been recognized by many inhabitants of the East as a myth, and an ancient myth, which had not always been connected only with Hasan or even with the areas over which his descendants ruled. One scholar had noted: "Romantic as this story [of Hasan and his band] is, it seems to be precisely the same that was current over all the East. It is given by Odoric [who wrote a generation after Polo] at length, more briefly by a Chinese author, and again from an Arabic source by Hammer in the *Mines de l'Orient*." [24] All these accounts are

similar in the important respects, but it is interesting that one particular similarity that runs through them appears to have had a
longer life:

> As an instance of the implicit obedience rendered by the *Fidâwi*
> or devoted disciples of the Shaikh [of Syria], Fra Pipino and
> Marino Sanuto relate that when Henry Count of Champagne
> (titular King of Jerusalem) was on a visit to the Old Man of
> Syria, one day as they walked together they saw some lads in
> white sitting on the top of a high tower. The Shaikh, turning
> to the Count, asked if he had any subjects as obedient as his
> own? and without giving time for reply made a sign to two of
> the boys, who immediately leapt from the tower, and were killed
> on the spot. The same story is told in the *Cento Novelle Antiche,*
> as happening when the Emperor Frederic was on a visit (imagi-
> nary) to the Veglio. And it is introduced likewise as an incident
> in the Romance of Bauduin de Sebourc. . . .

> [Footnote reads:] This story has been transferred to Peter the
> Great, who is alleged to have exhibited the docility of his sub-
> jects in the same way to the King of Denmark, by ordering a
> Cossack to jump from the Round Tower at Copenhagen, on the
> summit of which they were standing.[25]

As Lewis points out, the only sources for any knowledge concerning the Assassins were their enemies, who included practically
all other Persians and Syrians, and perhaps especially the Crusaders. Mandel refers to the Assassins as the "red-baited victims of
their time, analogous to the Tito'ists of 1950 — labelled barbaric
murderers by their Western adversaries and a hated and maligned
radical sect by their fellow, if more orthodox, members of the
larger religious order." [26] For it is only as a sect of distinctly religious *and* politically oriented fanatics that the Assassins can be understood. Even if it is proved that the Assassins did use hashish (and
it does not seem that this will be the case), and insofar as it may
have been as a means of preparation for violent or warlike acts, the
further question as to the degree of barbarity and atrocity, as compared to the other opposing groups in the same general region,
leads in to some interesting conclusions. As has been noted, it can
truthfully be said that the Assassins had a "bad press." Although
it is doubtful that Hasan or his followers will ever qualify for

sainthood, their tactics were "not without precedent. Three hundred years before Hassan ben Sabbah an Isma'ilite sect had 'practiced the strangling of opponents with cords as a religious duty. . . .' Further, 'the adjoining provinces of Dailam and Azerbaijan had long been centers of extremist heresy, and offered a ready recruiting ground from which al-Hassan formed his corps of fida'is. . . .' " [27] Thus, the Assassins "seem almost typical for their time and place, and need not have resorted to hashish or any other drug. There might even have been reasonable cause for their vicious tactic"; they might have rightly believed that the only alternative which would enable them to have any chance of survival was to frighten the Crusaders to the point where the latter would believe *any* tale concerning Hasan's followers.[28]

I believe, however, that the story of the Assassins, seen in conjunction with the other stories which obviously resemble it, and viewed from a slightly more comprehensive stance than is usually taken, must be regarded as mythological in the strictest sense of the word, that is, as a "traditional story of ostensibly historical events that serves to unfold part of the world view of a people or explain a practice, belief, or natural phenomenon," [29] in which deities, or a single deity, are important figures, and (usually, but not always) there is both a feudal type of hierarchy of duties and obligations between members of different "castes" or social levels, together with a very strong cultural or patriotic identification as a result of the unifying force of the commonly shared myth.

But after the mythological nature of the story of the Assassins is acknowledged, the crucial matter concerns the ways in which Polo's account was gradually warped until popular knowledge — as far as it has ever existed — agreed largely with the view expressed by Anslinger. It is indeed true that eleventh-century folklore should not be a foundation for an important twentieth-century prohibition, but it is just as surely true that in fact this is the case. When the antimarihuana forces in this country were making their first case against the legal sale of cannabis, they relied heavily on the myth of the Assassins and the subliminal, pervasive, and highly subtle (and often unconscious) link between the use of marihuana and violent crime that the myth both epitomized and fostered. In addition to Anslinger's statement, there were others, many even more misguided. In 1931, a Dr. A. E. Fossier of New Orleans wrote concerning "this diabolical, fanatical, cruel and murderous tribe [referring to the followers and descendants of Hasan]. . . . under the influence of hashish those fanatics would madly rush at their enemies, and ruthlessly massacre every one within their grasp." [30] Here it is clear that the doctor has altogether given up so far as the facts or even the myth are concerned; he is determined to prove that cannabis induces crime, so he will, quite naturally, rely on the "evidence" furnished by the Assassins, even if it is entirely apocryphal, and, in short, a complete fabrication. He does not even appear to grant the Assassins the intelligence that their enemies did; the picture conveyed is that of the classic "dope fiend," gone completely berserk, with no control over his violent impulses to destruction and crime. It seems nearly incredible that such statements were made, not in the popular press, but in a medical journal. But this was not the earliest such account to appear in a medical journal. In 1927 Dr. R. Kingman, writing for the *Medical Journal and Record,* quoted Polo to the effect that hashish was used as the reward, and not the cause, of murders, but then, apparently forgetting the basis for his account, he went on to assert that the Assassins took cannabis "as a preliminary to each errand of murder to which they were assigned." [31] And still earlier in 1912, Dr. V. Robinson had presented his version of Polo's account (again in a medical journal):

> When a Devoted One was selected to commit murder, he was first stupefied with hasheesh, and while in this state was brought into the magnificent gardens of the sheikh. All the sensual and stimulating pleasures of the erotic Orient surrounded the excited youth, and exalted by the delicious opiate he had taken, the hot-blooded fanatic felt that the gates of heaven were already ajar, and heard them swing open on their golden hinges. When the effect of the drug disappeared and the Devoted One was reduced to his normal condition, he was informed that through the generosity of his superior he had been permitted to foretaste the delights of paradise. The Devoted One believed this readily enough — disciples are always credulous — and therefore was eager to die or to kill at a word from his master. From these hasheesh-eaters, the Arabian name of which is hash-shashin, was derived the term "assassin." [32]

This, the earliest account of the Assassins, is the closest to Polo's story, although it errs in asserting that the devotees who were willing to die or kill at a word from the Old Man had already experienced the drug (whether opiate or cannabis). But after Robinson, practically no writer, with a very few recent exceptions, appears even to have looked at Polo's account.

The popular press uncovered the Hasan-hashish-crime connection in the 1930's, and magazines like the *American Mercury*,[33] the *Christian Century*,[34] *Hygeia* (a publication of the American Medical Association, but mainly a nontechnical publication directed to the general reading public),[35] and *Forum and Century*[36] echoed some version of two alternatives presented in *Popular Science Magazine* in 1936:

> "Assassin" has two explanations, but either demonstrates the menace of Indian hemp. According to one version, members of a band of Persian terrorists committed their worst atrocities while under the influence of hashish. In the other version, Saracens who opposed the Crusaders were said to employ the services of hashish addicts to secure secret murders of the leaders of the Crusades. In both versions, the murderers were known as "haschischin." [37]

The official reasons given by the Federal Bureau of Narcotics for its opposition to the use of marihuana shifted entirely during 1949–1950 from the claim that use of marihuana led to crime and violence to the claim that marihuana use led to heroin use. But in 1954 a former Chief Medical Officer at the Narcotics Farm in Lexington, Kentucky, wrote a book in collaboration with a professor of English and humanities, in which it was stated that

> marihuana is a form of hashhish [*sic*], a most dangerous drug in its unadulterated form. We get the word *assassin* from the Italian *assassino,* which in turn is derived from the Arabic *hashshashin,* meaning one who uses hashish; this etymology reflects rather accurately the cultural pedigree of the drug, which has been known for centuries to release impulses toward violence. It is still used in the Middle East to prepare warriors for combat or massacre.[38]

Even as recently as 1961, Oakland Police Chief T. Brown, who is considered an expert on narcotics and drugs, wrote that the " 'assassin' weed . . . [was] used by the Mohammedan secret order which . . . practiced secret murder committed under the influence of hashish." [39] Evidently there is still a strong undercurrent of the "discarded" crime-cannabis linkage among supposedly knowledgeable persons and persons in positions of power with respect to enforcement of the antimarihuana legislation. And wherever this alleged relationship is proffered, the myth of the Assassins is almost invariably cited as if it were an ultimate and indisputable source of supporting evidence.

But beyond the myth, what data exist that bear on the question of whether or not the use of cannabis is criminogenic, and particularly whether it leads to crimes of violence? In 1938 the Foreign Policy Association published accounts of ten cases, "culled at random from the files of the U.S. Bureau of Narcotics," involving instances of murder and assault allegedly caused directly by marihuana.[40] These same cases, published in a number of journals and other popular magazines, gave the reader the distinct impression that the user of marihuana was a violent criminal who was given to rape, homicide, and mayhem. However, in a study of 31 cases of persons brought to Bellevue Hospital who had also smoked marihuana at some point, W. Bromberg has this to say about the Foreign Policy Association findings:

> It is difficult to evaluate these statements, because of their uncritical nature. . . . Among the ten patients [of the allegedly random sample drawn by the Foreign Policy Association], the second, J.O., was described as having confessed how he murdered a friend and put his body in a trunk while under the influence of marihuana.
>
> J.O. was examined in this clinic; although he was a psychopathic liar and possibly homosexual, there was no indication in the examination or history of the use of any drug. The investigation by the probation department failed to indicate use of the drug marihuana. The deceased, however, was addicted to heroin.[41]

Bromberg's study covered all cases of convictions in the Courts of General and Special Sessions for the five and a half years from 1932 to 1937; during the same period of time he and his team conducted "routine interviews with some 17,000 offenders, several hundred [of whom] have been found who had direct experience with marihuana." He also analyzed the statistics of the two courts for the same period: there were 16,854 offenders convicted in the

Court of General Sessions, which handles felonies, and 200 of these were found to be drug users; there were about 75,000 offenders in the Court of Special Sessions, which handles misdemeanors, of whom about 6,000 were drug users. The main difference, so far as drug use is concerned, between the two types of convicted individuals is reflected in the fact that the Court of General Sessions covers cases of possession with intent to sell, whereas the Court of Special Sessions handles cases of mere possession. Of the group of 200 users of drugs who were convicted in the Court of General Sessions, 67 were marihuana users. Of these 67, 46 had been convicted of possession with intent to sell, and 21 had been convicted on other charges: 8 for burglary, 5 for grand larceny, 3 for robbery, 2 for assault, and 1 each for petty larceny, forgery, and first-degree murder. Accordingly, 16 of the 21 can be accounted for under burglary, grand larceny, and robbery. The most interesting finding was: "In only nine cases of the sixty-seven was the criminal record found to commence with a drug charge, indicating that there was not in those cases a close relationship between drugs and the beginning of a career of crime." [42] For an examination of the data from the Court of Special Sessions (misdemeanors), a random sample of the records of 1,500 offenders (25 percent of the total of about 6,000) was considered. Of the 1,500, 135 had been charged with possession of marihuana. Extrapolating from these figures, Bromberg calculated that about 540 offenders — only 9 percent of all *drug* offenders appearing before this court — were marihuana users. Of the 135, 93 had no previous charge or record, 8 had been charged previously only with regard to drugs, 5 had previous records that included drug as well as other charges, and 29 had records that did not include drug charges. In summarizing the significance of these data, Bromberg wrote that "as measured by the succession of arrests and convictions in the Court of General Sessions [felonies] . . . , it can be said that drugs generally do not initiate criminal careers. Similarly, in the Court of Special Sessions [misdemeanors], only 8 per cent of the offenders had previous charges of using drugs and 3.7 per cent had previous charges of drugs and other petty crimes. In the vast majority of cases . . . then, the earlier use of marihuana apparently did not predispose to crime, even that of using other drugs. . . . The expectancy of major crimes following the use of cannabis in New York County is small, according to these experiences." [43]

Some five years earlier, the Army had published the results of two studies of soldiers stationed in the Panama Canal Zone, the first conducted in 1925 and the second in 1931. The results of both studies were published in the same article in 1933. With regard to the findings of the 1925 study, the authors stated: "There is no evidence that mariahuana [sic] as grown here . . . has any appreciably deleterious influence on the individuals using it. . . . [It is recommended that] no steps be taken by the Canal Zone authorities to prevent the sale or use of mariahuana, and that no special legislation be asked for." [44] With regard to the 1931 findings, the conclusions reached were practically the same: "Delinquencies due to mariajuana smoking which result in trial by military court are negligible in number when compared with delinquencies resulting from the use of alcoholic drinks." The report continued with the assertion that there was no tendency to combativeness or destructiveness, that marihuana presented no threat to military discipline, and that "no recommendations . . . to prevent the sale or use of mariajuana . . . are deemed advisable." [45]

In 1946, Bromberg, who was then serving in the U.S. Navy, wrote an article in conjunction with Lieutenant Commander T. C. Rodgers, "Marihuana and Aggressive Crime." The article is perhaps one of the best summaries to that date of the "most controversial point" as to "the influence of marihuana on the antisocial impulses of its users, and its influence on crime causation." [46] The authors note that there appears to be a major disagreement:

> The older and recent literature differ on this issue, depending on the area of observation, toxicity of the drug (hashish, ganja, or marihuana) and the specific social psychology of the users. For example, Dr. J. Bouquet, an eminent Tunisian author finds that cannabis has most serious consequences, resulting in a propensity for theft and crime. Stanley found a high percentage of marihuana addicts [sic] among criminals in New Orleans. A recent article by Marcovitz and Myers describing delinquents in the U.S. Army was utilized by the editorial writer of the Journal of the American Medical Association to contradict the conclusions of the New York City Mayor's Committee on Marihuana. Bowman, a member of this committee, replied to these criticisms and defended the findings

of the committee. Observers in India indicate a frequent relation between the use of hemp and crime. On the other hand,
the senior author [Bromberg], in a study of major crime in
New York City over a period of six years (1932 to 1937 inclusive) found marihuana users to constitute but .004% of all
offenders convicted of felonies. Of the total of 16,000 felons
examined, 67 were marihuana users; among these only 16
cases of serious assault occurred. Similarly, the report of the
New York City Mayor's Committee on Marihuana stated that
there was no specific relation between marihuana and crime.

In an attempt to shed light on this problem, the frequency
of marihuana usage among naval and marine prisoners at the
U.S. Naval Prison, Portsmouth, New Hampshire was studied.[47]

The authors note that the preliminary psychiatric screening
given to all new members of the Armed Forces effectively excluded the more obvious instances of "proven drug addicts,
psychopathic personalities, felons, or obviously mentally sick
individuals. . . . Therefore, the total number of marihuana
users convicted of offenses while in the naval service can be
expected to be less than within the general population."[48]

The total number of convicted offenders between January 1,
1943, and July 1, 1945, at Portsmouth was 8,280; forty, or .0048
percent, were found to be marihuana users. The breakdown of
naval offenses in this group of 40 was: AWOL or AOL = 32;
assault or striking an officer = 3; theft = 3; narcotics charge = 2.
For the same group, the following table (Table II in the study)[49]
indicates the previous civilian offenses:

Assault	3
Theft	3
Violation of Mann Act	1
Gambling and Narcotics	1
Drunkenness	1
Draft Dodging	1
Traffic Violations	3
None	28

Of the same group of 40 users, "23 were users to excess, 10 were
moderate users, and 7 were light users. *Only 2 gave a history of
being more aggressive while under the influence of marihuana*"

(italics added). The authors also note that "there is a suspicion that these claims may have been mere rationalizations. One . . . — a repeated offender — was a moderate user and only his present offense had occurred under the influence of the drug." [50] In order to contrast the users with non-marihuana-using prisoners, 40 nonuser prisoners were drawn at random and their naval and civilian offenses were subjected to the same breakdown as for the users. A comparison of the data from these two groups showed that "the non-user group . . . committed more aggressive crime . . . than the users. Conversely, the negative [characteristically nonaggressive] offenses predominate in the user group — 32 (AWOL or AOL offenses) to 25 in the non-users." The investigators also found a "preponderance of psychiatric disorders in the user group over the non-users." [51]

Three specific conclusions were reached: "1. There is no positive relationship between aggressive crime and marihuana usage in the Naval service; . . . 2. . . . there is no significant causal relationship between aggressive crime in civilian life [of the naval offenders studied] and the use of marihuana. . . . 3. Marihuana usage is but an aspect of some type of mental disorder or personality abnormality." [52]

Several reports from India by R. N., G. S., and I. C. Chopra, who sometimes worked in groups of two or three and sometimes worked alone, come to practically the same conclusions with regard to the alleged causal relationship between cannabis and crime. The single most important finding of their series of studies was the existence of an inverse correlation between cannabis use and crime, if any relationship existed at all. Although a 1939 study by R. N. and G. S. Chopra did find that some crimes were committted after the individual had smoked (or ingested) cannabis, the study also showed that "so far as premeditated crime is concerned, especially that of a violent nature, hemp drugs . . . may not only not lead to it, but they actually act as deterrents . . . one of the important actions of these drugs is to quieten and stupify the individual so there is no tendency to violence. . . . The result of continued and excessive use of these drugs in our opinion is to make the individual timid rather than lead him to commit a crime of a violent nature." [53] On the whole, their findings were in direct contradiction to the view that criminals often use marihuana to "boost their nerves" for the commission of a crime.

Most recent reviews of the literature on cannabis state that whereas aggressiveness and antisocial activities are generally agreed to be less common with cannabis than with alcohol,[54] there are three particular types of situation in which the use of cannabis can lead to at least minor violence. The first can occur when a previously marihuana-naive individual develops a sudden panic or phobic state in response to the "hallucinatory" experience(s) which fairly high doses can sometimes spontaneously induce; in this state of extreme fright and bewilderment, the individual is apt to attack anything or anybody.[55] The second possibility occurs during the characteristic stage of increased psychomotor activity and hypersensitivity, when the individual may overreact to unpleasant external stimuli.[56] Finally, sometimes an individual will take cannabis, or any intoxicant, specifically for the enhancement of the ability to act out various repressed or suppressed hostilities. S. Charen and L. Perelman note that the particular form of relief from inferiority feelings that they observed among 55 Negro and 5 white soldiers was actually a continuation and intensification of their delinquent behavior without any drug; they became, under the influence of cannabis, even more psychopathic in their behavior than they normally were. However, it certainly cannot be said that they constituted an unbiased sample, inasmuch as "only 9 were referred for . . . study because of non psychopathic behavior. Twenty were awaiting court martial . . . ; five were referred as part of IRTC policy of study of AWOLs; 16 were referred by company commanders who found them behavior problems or poor soldiers but had not preferred any charges; and 10 had been referred primarily as drug addicts. A total of 85% can be classified as being undesirable army material . . . , and the remaining 15% as potentially unfit because of neurosis or poor morale." [57] However, all three of these types of antisocial or aggressive behavior are atypical of marihuana reactions, and, "Most serious observers agree that cannabis does not, *per se,* induce aggressive or criminal activities, and that the reduction of work drive leads to a negative correlation with criminality rather than a positive one." [58]

It is probably fair to say that emotionally unstable individuals may become more impulsive and irritable when under the influence of cannabis, and that inhibitory defenses which ordinarily hold these people in check, albeit imperfectly, are discarded. But cannabis, like alcohol, does not necessarily generate abnormal behavior. The danger lies in the fact that individuals with certain types of psychopathology, particularly those involving some degree of impulse disorder, make use of this drug in an attempt to temporarily alter their perception of reality; in so doing, the degree to which their behavior is already abnormal may be increased. The basic problem is the abnormal personality, not the drug.

O. M. Andrade studied 120 marihuana-using criminals and found that their criminal actions could not be attributed to use of the drug.[59] In his study in Nigeria, T. Asuni asserts that hashish and crimes are associated, but that this has to do with the fact that there is a higher proportion of both criminals and hashish users in a frustrated and underprivileged community.[60] This simple fact, that there may be a higher prevalence of cannabis users among the noncriminal segment of a given socioeconomic strata from which a sample of criminals derive, was overlooked by E. Stanley in his 1931 study of "marihuana as a developer of criminals" in the United States.[61]

D. D. Shoenfeld, in 1944, could find no positive relationship between violent crime and cannabis use and concluded that the smoking of marihuana was in no way associated with juvenile delinquency. He was the head of the "Sociological Study" branch of the La Guardia Report, which makes the following remarks:

> One of the most important causes of the widespread publicity which marihuana smoking has received is the belief that this practice is directly responsible for the commission of crimes.
>
> During our investigation many law enforcement officers . . . were interviewed and asked for a confidential expression of opinion on the general question of crime and marihuana. In most instances they unhesitatingly stated that there is no proof that major crimes are associated with the practice of smoking marihuana. They did state that many marihuana smokers are guilty of petty crimes, but that the criminal career usually existed prior to the time the individual smoked his first mari-

huana cigarette. These officers further stated that a criminal generally termed as a "real" or "professional" criminal will not associate with marihuana smokers. He considers such a person inferior and unreliable and will not allow him to participate in the commission of a major crime.[62]

The La Guardia investigators also examined the records of the Children's Court of New York City and interviewed "the proper authorities on this subject." They found that "marihuana is not an important factor in the development of delinquency." [63] Of the thirteen conclusions reached by the sociological-study branch of the report, two are of special relevance to the issue of crime:

(10) — Marihuana is not the determining factor in the commission of major crimes.

(12) — Juvenile delinquency is not associated with the practice of smoking marihuana.[64]

The "Clinical Study" of the La Guardia Report, in which both smoked and orally ingested cannabis substances were used, concludes with the statement (in part): "A feeling of apprehension, based on uncertainty regarding the possible effects of the drug and strengthened by any disagreeable sensations present, alternated with the euphoria. If the apprehension developed into a state of real anxiety, a spirit of antagonism was shown. However, any resistance to requests made to the subjects was passive and not physical and there was no aggressive or violent behavior observed." [65]

D. P. Ausubel wrote in 1958 that an accurate summation of all the available evidence on cannabis would indicate that "very rarely do major crimes follow upon the use [of cannabis, and] . . . in instances where they do, the relationship is an indirect one." [66] He does admit that, if a person has already decided to commit a crime, that is, if the crime is premeditated, then the individual may use cannabis to bolster his courage and deaden his awareness of guilt. But he also feels that it is more important that "still another reason for the association of marihuana addiction and crime is the greater use of marihuana in slum-urban areas where delinquency rates tend to be high." He also agrees with the Chopras and others that "marijuana, by virtue of its stupefying effects, may sometimes inhibit the expression of aggressive impulses." [67]

In 1962 L. Kolb noted that the alleged crime-inducing properties of cannabis had been studied at length in at least five well-conducted investigations by competent scientists or doctors in this country, and none of them had found that there was any evidence for a link between cannabis and aggressive crime, and, in particular, none of the investigators had found any evidence for anything that could possibly be labeled a cannabis-induced murder. Kolb believes that the general harmfulness of the drug has been grossly overrated by the antimarihuana laws and their proponents: "Marihuana, like alcohol, releases the user's inhibitions and distorts his judgment . . . , but its potency as an instigator of crime has not been . . . demonstrated in the United States. . . . The tendency to credit a narcotic as the cause of physical, mental, and social disasters is so great in the United States that marihuana-induced crimes are often reported in the press and by police-trained people when there is no causal relation of marihuana to the crime." As an example, he gives a case in which two young men consumed a large amount of whiskey in a hotel room, then smoked one marihuana cigarette, began to quarrel, fought, and one killed the other. The press played up the story as an example of a vicious, marihuana-induced murder.[68]

In 1962 the White House Conference on Narcotic and Drug Abuse stated: "It is the opinion of the Panel that the hazards of marihuana per se have been exaggerated and that long criminal sentences imposed on an occasional user or possessor of the drug are in poor social perspective. Although marihuana has long held the reputation of inciting individuals to commit sexual offenses and other antisocial acts, the evidence is inadequate to substantiate this." [69]

The same year D. W. Maurer and V. H. Vogel wrote: "It would seem that, from the point of view of public health and safety, the effects of marihuana present a very minor problem compared with the abusive use of alcohol, and that the drug has received a disproportionate share of publicity as an inciter of violent crime." [70]

In a recent study, H. Blumer et al. found that, among drug-using juveniles, those who were most delinquent preferred alcohol, whereas the marihuana users tended to be nonaggressive and avoided trouble. Moreover, a shift from the use of alcohol to marihuana tended to be correlated with a change toward less delinquent behavior in other respects.[71]

When S. Abrams was a postgraduate student at Oxford, engaged in writing a book on LSD, he wrote the following:

Another criticism that is frequently made is that cannabis use leads to violence and crime. Professor G. Joachimoglu has stated that "the French word *assassin* for murderer is derived from hashish, because at the crisis, when these people are excited and experiencing the full effect of the hashish, they act criminally." [This preposterous bit of nonsense is an indication of how a myth can be warped and distorted till it is scarcely recognizable.] I find this extremely difficult to believe. During the so-called "crisis," the most violent activity that is likely to occur is uninhibited dancing. I have observed hundreds of persons under the influence of cannabis and have never seen a single act of violence committed. I have known many people who have been arrested for possession of cannabis, but I know of no instance where a person has been arrested, in Oxford at least, for disorderly behaviour under the influence of cannabis. Furthermore, I have had the opportunity of observing the same persons under the influence of both cannabis and alcohol and seen that the latter drug sometimes gives rise to viciousness of many kinds whereas the former leads to a sense of peace. Indeed one of the possible dangers of cannabis is that it may reduce aggressiveness to below the level that is socially acceptable. . . .

I find it hard to think of cannabis as a social menace. Yet a contradictory view is held by the legal authorities, and it must be based on evidence of some kind. There is more than prejudice to it. I think that the answer is that the effects of cannabis have been confused with the people who make use of it. [He might, perhaps more accurately, have written: "the image that the average non-user has of those persons who make use of it."] . . . [Marihuana creates a state of] increased suggestibility. . . . The society of Oxford is probably a highly favourable environment for the use of cannabis, bringing out what is best in the experience. But it is not necessary to accept that in other environments cannabis produces harmful effects. Its use by criminals may be an example. It is true that some criminals smoke cannabis, but that is probably due to the fact that they have special access to illicit channels of supply. I should expect that the use of cannabis would have the effect of reducing the crime rate. This, of course, is an untested hypothesis.[72]

It seems generally true that although there is a diminution of inhibitions during a marihuana high, this is largely verbal, rather than behavioral. The user may say things he ordinarily would not, but he generally will not do things that are foreign to his nature. If he is not a criminal, he will not commit a crime.

When one looks again at the way in which the 1937 law was implemented, and reads some of the remarks of former Commissioner H. J. Anslinger, one can see that another myth concerning marihuana, namely, that it is a catalyst to profligacy and cynically indifferent promiscuity, has quite possibly been largely responsible for the current legislation, and more basically, for the attitudes toward the use of marihuana that lie behind these laws. Anslinger was asked,

What about the alleged connection between drugs and sexual pleasure? . . . What is the real relationship between drugs and sex? ANSLINGER: There isn't any question about marihuana being a sexual stimulant. It has been used throughout the ages for that: in Egypt, for instance. From what we have seen, it is an aphrodisiac, and I believe that the use in colleges today has sexual connotations. A classical example of amatory activities is contained in the article "Hashish Poisoning in England," from the *London Police Journal* of July 1934. In this remarkable case, a young man and his girlfriend planted marijuana seeds in their backyard and when the stalks matured, they crushed the flowering tops and smoked one cigarette and then engaged in such erotic activities that the neighbors called the police and they were taken to jail.[73]

Dr. J. Fort, also included in the same panel discussion on the subject, responded appropriately to Anslinger's confusion:

That's more demonology. Sex isn't degeneracy, Mr. Anslinger; and contrary to your fantasies, no mind-altering drug is in itself a specific aphrodisiac. The most widely used substance to enhance sexuality is alcohol, which is closely associated with a tremendous amount of heterosexual and homosexual behavior, since it loosens inhibitions and reduces guilt and anxiety. In theory, a person could learn to use any one of several drugs to increase sexual pleasure, but the main ingredient would be the user's expectation and knowledge.[74]

Medical opinion as to the capacity of cannabis to act as an aphrodisiac is divided. Robinson wrote in 1912: "In medicinal doses Cannabis has been used as an aphrodisiac."[75] Walton, summarizing the findings of F. Fraenkel and E. Joël, writes simply that "aphrodisiac effects are lacking."[76] Walton himself takes a more judicious stand: "The drug has more of a reputation in this direction than is actually warranted but it is not surprising that this feature should have been particularly attractive to popular fancy. It is true that some individuals experience a marked stimulation of such desires, but in a great proportion of other instances, no such impulses are evident. The effect, again, is very probably due to removal of the usual restraints and correspondingly to the release of the more primitive impulses." However, he goes on to relate that "cases reported by Bromberg experienced marked erotic stimulation. Burton says that the Orientals take it to prolong coition. Posey interviewed some habitual users in New Orleans who described the same effect. Hector France . . . probably developed the most intensely erotic description of the hashish effects. He declares that 'hashish is of course a positive aphrodisiac, the length of the venereal act being at once reinforced and repeated.' Del Favero . . . says the effects are characterized by strong, erotic visions. . . . Stringaris says . . . the drug is a sexual stimulant. . . . Doria, in Brazil, reports instances of women becoming unusually aggressive in sexual affairs while under the influence of the drug."[77] Although Walton writes that there are "numerous" reports of an absence of any such effect, he cites only three: "Bourhill, studying a great many cases in Southern Africa, concluded that the drug did not stimulate sexual activity. Burr observed that sex ideas were entirely absent and said that during the delirium 'Venus herself couldn't have tempted me.' Brunton said: 'cannabis has been regarded as an aphrodisiac, but the trials made of it in this country (England) seem to show that it does not itself at least have any such action and merely induces a condition of partial delirium in which Easterners may possibly have visions of a sexual nature, and indeed, they try to give a sexual direction to the mental disturbance which the cannabis produces by mixing it with musk, ambergris, or cantharides.' "[78]

Allentuck and Bowman state that "marihuana is no more aphro-disiac than is alcohol. Unlike damiana, yohimbin, testosterone propionate, etc. which produce genital engorgement directly, marihuana, like alcohol, acts only indirectly through the cerebral cortex." [79] W. H. McGlothlin claims that any supposed aphro-disiac effects are merely "cerebral" and caused by a reduction of inhibition and an increase in suggestibility.[80] E. R. Bloomquist states that cannabis is not an aphrodisiac, "but it does influence sexual response by releasing restraints and thus permitting greater freedom of participation by the user. By distorting time and space the drug makes the experience of orgasm seem more prolonged and intense.[81] Ausubel states:

> The apparent erotic stimulation induced by marijuana in cer-tain individuals . . . corresponds essentially to the release of inhibited personality trends. These persons prior to drug use tend to be excessively preoccupied with sexual gratification. Many also exhibit infantile and homosexual tendencies. In addition, the drug increases self-confidence and eliminates ap-prehension about the receptivity of the contemplated sex part-ner. Many [users] report that the sensual aspects of sexual enjoyment are prolonged as a consequence of the exaggerated perception of elapsed time. Exhibitions of perverted sexual practices are not an uncommon feature at "tea parties." [82]

Bloomquist also notes that "whatever you were before you took the drug, whatever you had in mind as the goal to reach while on it, is increased and enhanced by the use of the drug." [83] R. D. Johnson asserts that there is no evidence of "increased sexual aggression," although he states that "enjoyment of the sex act is said to be heightened." [84] W. Oursler writes: "The old cry . . . that the drug was aphrodisiac . . . has been discredited. The correct terminology now is that it is an inhibition-releasing drug which often reduces self-inhibition and group-inhibition to levels below socially acceptable behavior." [85] Oursler recounts one of Dr. Moreau's (de Tours) experiments with cannabis, during which he went to the opera and believed that it had taken him an hour to find his box, whereas it had only taken him nine minutes. "Time distortion is said to be one explanation for marijuana's reputation as an aphrodisiac. The sexual act appears to last for a half hour or more when the time is actually only minutes." [86] In an interview, Oursler presents the view of one young male user: "Well, it's what's on your mind. I don't think marijuana is an aphrodisiac or anything, it's just what you might be thinking about. It certainly does multiply, well, what you are thinking about — magnify it, I mean. But I don't think it is an aphrodisiac. If you're thinking about sex it'll make you think about it more and everything, so I suppose it could be called one. But it's not really one taken expressly for that." [87]

The La Guardia Report states: "Although there was an undeniable increase in overt sex interest following the ingestion of marihuana, it seems probable that this interest was not the result of direct sexual stimulation but rather a manifestation of a falling off in inhibiting factors. This sex interest seems to have been due primarily to the fact that these men had been imprisoned for varying periods and had not had access to women. . . . the behavior of these prisoners was more like that which any man deprived of sexual activity for a long time would display under a releasing stimulus and not at all like the behavior shown at marihuana 'tea-pads.' " [88] The report further states: "Some evidence of eroticism was reported in about 10 percent of the 150 instances in which marihuana was administered," but that even though there were females present — nurses, attendants, and others associated with the experiments — there was no "frank expression of sexual stimulation." [89]

McGlothlin recognizes that cannabis is widely believed to have aphrodisiac properties, and he goes on to state: "Whatever aphrodisiac qualities cannabis may possess, virtually all investigators agree that these are cerebral in nature and due to the reduction of inhibition and increased suggestibility." [90] R. J. Bouquet states that in North Africa and Egypt the belief that cannabis will preserve, maintain, or improve sexual powers is an important initiating cause of the habit.[91] In a sample of some 1,200 users, I. C. and G. S. Chopra found that 10 percent listed sexual factors as the exciting cause leading to the cannabis habit.[92] While cannabis intoxication may be sexually stimulating for some, several authors have claimed that the prolonged use of excessive amounts will eventually cause impotence.[93] McGlothlin cites the Chopras again, who claimed that people who wish to renounce all worldly pleasures use cannabis specifically to reduce sexual urges.[94] T. T. Brown, a former policeman turned sociologist, writes: "Tales out of the past to the contrary, marihuana does not act as an aphrodisiac. Smokers, both male and female, have indicated that they experience no change in libido as a result of the drug and do not associate it with sex. . . . The so called sex parties at which marihuana is smoked are often reported in the press as though marihuana was the cause of these orgies. Again, the drug does no more than relax the inhibitions and any promiscuity which may result could just as likely result from over-indulgence in alcohol at a cocktail party." [95] Rosevear notes that the soporific effects of marihuana make it far from the ideal aphrodisiac, and that "inhibition-releasing does not necessarily mean sexual urging." [96] R. Blum believes that sexual aggressiveness operates independently of marihuana's properties.[97] He does not consider the drug in any way an aphrodisiac. According to N. Taylor, "there is no scientific warrant" for charging hemp with being an aphrodisiac. "The plain fact seems to be that pure ganja has the opposite effect, and is taken by Indian priests to quell libido." [98] Bloomquist raises the important, obvious, yet often overlooked point that most of the users of marihuana in this country

are youths between the ages of fourteen and twenty-five. This age span needs no aphrodisiac to stimulate either interest or capacity to perform. If young men have the sex act in mind when they use the drug they will probably move toward a selected partner. The woman, for her part, will find it easier to acquiesce. As for homosexuals, a growing number have found this drug an ideal releaser of restraints and use it to sidetrack the usual inhibitions, suspicions, and guilt associated with socially unapproved sexuality.

The interesting thing is that actual sexual congress by young people while on marijuana is very largely a projection on the part of adults. . . . Contemporary cannabis users have a lot to do while on cannabis, and sex is only one of a long list. As for those who "wouldn't touch a girl while up on pot," well, let's face it; they probably wouldn't have touched her while off pot either.[99]

But there are many, especially among the users of cannabis themselves, who disagree with what is probably the prevailing medical opinion:

Experts agree that marihuana has no aphrodisiac effect, and in this as in a large percentage of their judgments they are entirely wrong. If one is sexually bent, if it occurs to one that it would be pleasant to make love, the judicious use of the drug will stimulate desire and heighten the pleasure immeasurably, for it is perhaps the principal effect of marihuana to take one more intensely into whatever experience. . . . It provokes a more sensual (or aesthetic) kind of concentration, a detailed articulation of minute areas, an ability to adopt play postures. What can be more relevant in the act of love? [100]

Similarly, several of Robinson's friends reported highly erotic sensations.[101] One such subject wrote the following account of part of his experience:

I hear the songs of women. Thousands of maidens pass near me; they bend their bodies in the most charming curves, and scatter beautiful flowers in my fragrant path. Some faces are strange, some I knew on earth, but all are lovely. They smile, and sing and dance. Their bare feet glorify the firmament. It is more than flesh can stand. I grow sensual unto satyriasis. The aphrodisiac effect is astounding in its intensity. I enjoy all the women of the world. I pursue countless maidens through the confines of Heaven. A delicious warmth suffuses my whole body. Hot and blissful I float through the universe, consumed with a resistless passion. And in the midst of this unexampled and unexpected orgy, I think of the case reported by the German doctor Reodel, about a drug-clerk who took a huge dose of hashish to enjoy voluptuous visions, but who heard not even the rustle of Aphrodite's garment, and I laugh at him in scorn and derision.[102]

Two anonymous student reports also mention their own experiences with this "alleged" effect of marihuana: one, a male 22-year-old college student who was enrolled in graduate school at the time, stated that, for him, marihuana was a sexual stimulant only if he was already attracted to the girl he was with; if she had been unattractive or repulsive to him when he was not under the influence of marihuana, he wouldn't think of going near her. He connects this phenomenon with the ability of cannabis to heighten many, if not all, physical sensations, or what he calls "physical impulses": "Sex is more purely physical high, that's the only problem. It's a lust orgy . . . you don't think about the girl at all, you just think about the physical pleasure. But the physical pleasure is just immense. However, it doesn't detract from my straight sex life. I don't say, 'Gee whiz, I wish I were high.' But when you want it to, marihuana acts as a frighteningly powerful aphrodisiac. At least it does for me." [103]

The second anonymous interviewee was an 18-year-old female college student, who smoked marihuana at least once a week. She was smoking during the interview. When questioned concerning sex, she stated that she got "tingly in the sensuous spots, I don't know whether it's psychological, but that's where I feel it usually. It sort of slides down. . . . Pot makes you a sex fiend. You don't necessarily want sex more, but you enjoy it more. You always want it the same. Since it [marihuana] allows your subconscious to express itself subconsciously, you may want sex more, so when you are high, you want more — no not more. You're just more aware of it." [104]

An interesting earlier example of an effect similar to that experienced by Robinson's subject, but differing in at least one important respect, was given by T. Gautier in 1846:

> I was in that blessed state induced by hashish which the Orientals call *al-kief*. I could no longer feel my body; the bonds of matter and spirit were severed; I moved by sheer willpower in an unresisting medium.
>
> Thus I imagined the movement of souls in the world of fragrances to which we shall go after death. A bluish haze, an Elysian light, the reflections of an azure grotto, formed an atmosphere in the room . . . an atmosphere at once cool and warm, moist and perfumed, enveloping me like bath water. . . . When I tried to move away the caressing air made a thousand voluptuous waves about me, a delightful languor gripped my senses and threw me back upon the sofa, where I hung limp. . . .
>
> Nothing material was mingled with this ecstasy; no terrestrial desire marred its purity. Love itself, in fact, could not have increased it. Romeo as a hashisheen would have forgotten his Juliet. The poor child, bending over her jasmines, would have stretched her alabaster arms across the balcony and through the

night in vain. Romeo would have stayed at the foot of the silken ladder, and although I madly love the angel of youth and beauty created by Shakespeare, I must agree that the prettiest girl in Verona, to a hashisheen, is not worth the bother of stirring.

So, with a peaceful though fascinated eye, I watched a garland of ideally beautifully women, who diademed a frieze with their divine nudity; I saw the gleam of their satin shoulders, the sparkle of their silvery breasts, the overhead tripping of small pink feet, the undulation of opulent hips, without feeling the least temptation. The charming spectres that disturbed Saint Anthony would have had no power over me.[105]

In 1969, E. Goode published the results of "an informal survey of about 200 [marihuana] users," in which he asked "some basic questions about the relationship of marijuana to both sexual desire and sexual activity." (When one recalls some of the observations of the La Guardia Report, and the typical lethargy that marihuana frequently produces, one can appreciate the significance of this distinction.) To the question, "Do you think being high on marijuana stimulates your sex interest, or not?", 38 percent answered it did not; 5 percent said it had a decidedly negative effect on their sexual interest; 13 percent replied that the effect depended on either their mood, partner, or both; 44 percent — "a strong plurality" — said that marihuana "definitely increases their sexual desire." Of this group, the breakdown between the men versus the women was as follows: 39 percent of the men claimed increased sexual interest versus 50 percent of the women.

To the question, "Is your enjoyment of sex any different high, or not?", 68 percent indicated that marihuana increased their sexual — particularly orgasmic — enjoyment; 74 percent of the men and 62 percent of the women replied that marihuana increased sexual enjoyment.[106]

In attempting to explain these findings, Goode first notes that they apparently contradict the claims of "most scientists . . . that in physiological terms marijuana lacks an aphrodisiac effect. . . . If, in physiological fact, marijuana is neutral — or even negative — to sexuality, why are so many people sexually turned on by it?" [107]

Goode offers several explanations: first, he considers "the

mythology," noting that the use of marihuana "has traditionally been associated with the dramatic loss of sexual inhibition, and with what were thought to be the inevitable consequences: depravity, degradation, shame." [108] However, the "sex-loaded diatribes" of organizations like the Federal Bureau of Narcotics "may have been a tactical blunder. They seem to have attracted more recruits [to marihuana] than they have discouraged. Sociologists and psychologists stress the power of mood, expectation, social conditioning, setting, and myth in shaping the nature of the drug experience." All these factors have influenced us to associate marihuana use with sexual activity. Goode states: "We have *learned* to associate it [marihuana] with sensuousness, and carnality, with hedonism and physical gratification. And so it stimulates those very reactions. . . . Man's somatic responses are often influenced more by what he thinks than by biological and chemical imperatives; in fact, it can happen that what he thinks actually becomes his biological and chemical imperative. . . . If you believe that sex and marijuana are compatible bedmates, then, for you they probably will be." [109]

Goode readily admits that "in the narrowest sense . . . [marihuana] is not a sexual stimulant; that is, in the sense that it will not excite mindless, laboratory-located animal tissue." But, as Goode points out, given the power of the sex-cannabis myth, "a man and a woman, together, alone, smoking pot — what else could possibly be on their minds? A . . . graduate student . . . said, 'Sex is more taken for granted high.' . . . A . . . sociologist agreed. 'The social situation in which marijuana smoking takes place acts as an aphrodisiac.' " [110]

Goode attempts to explain the seemingly paradoxical finding that a higher percentage of the women said that smoking marihuana increased their sexual desire, whereas a higher percentage of the men said it increased their enjoyment, by postulating a number of hypotheses: First, because of its cultural association with sex, women are more likely to "*think* themselves into becoming excited"; second, "Women need an excuse to justify their desire"; third, men are less concerned with "the ritual of sex, and with what the textbooks refer to as 'foreplay,' " than are women. For them, "these aspects of the sexual act are often more meaningful than the immediate physical gratification it gives her . . . a woman is more preoccupied than a man with the path to sex," whereas for a man, the overture is often only instrumental.[111]

Goode also compared frequent users (smoked marihuana three times a week minimum) and infrequent users along the same two parameters of interest and enjoyment. His findings were that 52 percent of the frequent users stated that marihuana stimulated sexual desire, whereas only 30 percent of the infrequent users agreed with this. With regard to enjoyment, the data indicated the same trend, in more exaggerated form: 77 percent of the frequent users stated that marihuana increased their sexual enjoyment, whereas only 49 percent of the infrequent users agreed.[112]

Goode does not neglect mention of the importance of the strength of the dose, by which he insists one must take into account not only the quality, but also the number of cigarettes smoked. He recognizes that dose-strength is a highly variable factor, "almost impossible to calculate," but, as he notes, there is a limit — imposed by an increasing tendency toward a soporific state hardly compatible with wild amatory adventures — to the amount of marihuana that one normally can smoke. "After two or three good joints, the only erotic experience the pot head will have will be in his dreams." [113]

Goode ties in the enhancement of sex with the general, nonfocal enhancement of all sensory modalities while under the influence of cannabis, although he also states that it is an "impediment to cerebral activity," by which he apparently means higher cognitive tasks, such as reading:

Marijuana seems to allow detours from the customary channels of experience and permit transcendence of some of our peculiar social inhibitions. The middle-class American . . . is warned against belching, flatulating, sweating. Every one of his bodily functions is ringed about by prohibitions and restrictions. Marijuana may unhook some of the rigid associations acquired from a culture ambivalent about bodily things. It loosens the apron strings to the past. "Sex-evil," "sex-dirty," "sex-forbidden" is a class of linkages which, under the influence of the drug, is sometimes replaced by "sex-fun," "sex-nice." This enables a kind of involvement in the act itself which sometimes approaches Total Human Experience. . . .

Many of those I questioned talked about the sudden release of their tactile sensitivity. There was a new awareness of the body as a pleasure-receiving vessel. . . .

The attitude of play, of novel and unusual roles and activities, is also part of the sex-marijuana calculus. A twenty-year-old waitress said, "You do a lot of weird things in bed . . ."

Marijuana cannot create a new mentality, a conscience-less, superego-free psyche. It does endorse some of our more whimsical and carnal tendencies.[114]

Goode goes on to speculate that the condemner of marihuana on sex-related grounds may be one who in "his subterranean self . . . actually regards sex as bestial and violent . . . [and] who . . . probably has a destructive and brutal image of man's inner being. He who, in his inner self condemns sex will, under the influence of marijuana, have basically anti-sexual experiences. Marijuana does not create anew, it only activates what's latent. . . . The factors of 'set' and 'setting' " are of the utmost importance in this, as in most all aspects of the effects of cannabis.[115]

George Bernard Shaw once stated that the vast majority of sexual encounters are due to simple boredom; the individuals can think of nothing else to do. Under the influence of marihuana, users often find that they can become absorbed, with a childlike intensity, in nearly anything, and that it will seem fresh, interesting, and highly pleasurable — even if it is something they have done many times in the past. So it is that if a man and a woman smoke marihuana together with the implicit or explicit expectation of sexual activity, that too is likely to be enhanced.

12 The Campaign against Marihuana

If marihuana is a relatively safe intoxicant that is not addicting, does not in and of itself lead to the use of harder drugs, is not criminogenic, and does not lead to sexual excess, and the evidence that it may lead to personality deterioration and psychosis is quite unconvincing, and indeed there may even be some important clinical utilities for some cannabis derivatives — why then is so much heat generated by its opponents, especially in comparison with the low-key campaign against cigarettes and the practically nonexistent one against alcohol? It is important to attempt to answer this question, because understanding here is a necessary prerequisite to a more rational approach to the problem of the vastly increasing use of cannabis in this country. The present approach is unrealistic, overly punitive, and ineffective.

Any attempt to understand why our reaction to the use of cannabis is overdetermined must be speculative. Nonetheless, I should like to specify some factors which I think may be contributing to the hyperemotionalism that separates cannabis from tobacco and particularly from alcohol. First of all, there is a vast amount of misinformation about the drug. As noted earlier, much of this has its origin in the 1930's with the so-called "educational campaign" of the Federal Bureau of Narcotics (recently reorganized and renamed the Bureau of Narcotics and Dangerous Drugs). Figure 6 shows a poster which typifies the kind of "educational campaign" supported by this bureau in the 1930's. As nearly as I can determine, much of this continuing "educational campaign" is not so much based on what is known about the dangers of cannabis as on a large body of alarming exaggerations, distortions, and mendacities which altogether constitute a kind of latter-day *Malleus Maleficarum*.

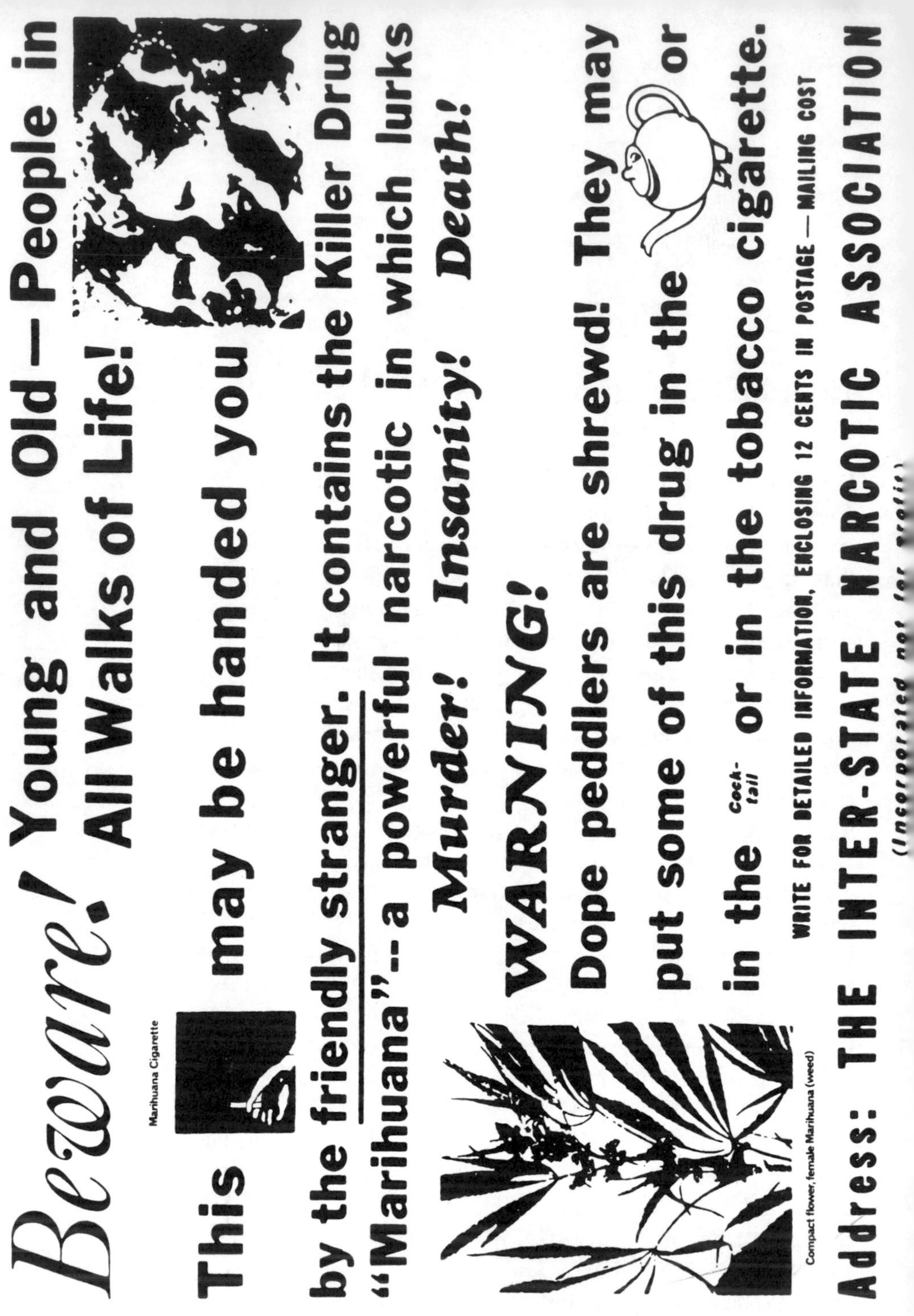

Beware! Young and Old—People in All Walks of Life!

This **[Marihuana Cigarette]** may be handed you by the friendly stranger. It contains the Killer Drug "Marihuana"—a powerful narcotic in which lurks *Murder! Insanity! Death!*

WARNING!

Dope peddlers are shrewd! They may put some of this drug in the cocktail or in the tobacco cigarette.

WRITE FOR DETAILED INFORMATION, ENCLOSING 12 CENTS IN POSTAGE — MAILING COST

Address: **THE INTER-STATE NARCOTIC ASSOCIATION**

(Incorporated not for profit)

Compact flower, female Marihuana (weed)

Fig. 6. This poster illustrates the kind of device supported by the Federal Bureau of Narcotics as part of what it calls "an educational campaign describing the drug, its identification, and evil effects."

Becker has investigated the number of articles condemning cannabis that appeared in United States popular magazines from January 1925 to March 1951. His figures, compiled from the *Reader's Guide to Periodical Literature,* are as follows:

Time Period	Number of Articles
January 1925–December 1928	0
January 1929–June 1932	0
July 1932–June 1935	0
July 1935–June 1937	4
July 1937–June 1939	17
July 1939–June 1941	4
July 1941–June 1943	1
July 1943–April 1945	4
May 1945–April 1947	6
May 1947–April 1949	0
May 1949–March 1951	1

He notes that, of the 17 articles published in the two-year period July 1937 to June 1939, "ten either explicitly acknowledged the help of the [Narcotics] Bureau in furnishing facts and figures or gave implicit evidence of having received help [from it] by using facts and figures that had appeared earlier, either in Bureau publications or in testimony before the Congress on the Marihuana Tax Act." [1] In fact, five of these seventeen articles repeated the identical story, originally told by Commissioner Anslinger:

An entire family was murdered by a youthful [marihuana] addict in Florida. When the officers arrived at the home they found the youth staggering about in a human slaughterhouse. With an ax he had killed his father, mother, two brothers, and a sister. He seemed to be in a daze. . . . He had no recollection of having committed the multiple crime. The officers knew him ordinarily as a sane, rather quiet young man; now he was pitifully crazed. They sought the reason. The boy said he had been in the habit of smoking something which youthful friends called "muggles," a childish name for marihuana.[2]

Various segments of the community are expressing increasing interest in becoming better informed about marihuana. However, most often the only people who can or will lecture on marihuana to, for example, high school or community groups, come from, are recruited by, or have been educated by the Bureau of Narcotics. Illustrative of this kind of "education" was a recent meeting sponsored by the Parent-Teacher Association in a middle-class suburban community. There were two speakers. The first, from the District Attorney's Office, invited the listeners to "take a look at what marihuana's destroying effects are." Among other effects he stated that it "causes fetal damage," that it "causes psychoses in the chronic user," and that it "leads to lethargy and passivity which is incompatible with youth, especially American youth." He compared it to the "relatively harmless drugs, tobacco and alcohol." The second speaker was a policeman, one of six from the town who had attended a two-week seminar on drugs given by the Bureau of Narcotics and Dangerous Drugs for local police. He told the audience that 400 of the 1,300 high school students had tried marihuana and that apparently 150 were on "hard" drugs. When after the meeting he was asked if the 400 figure came from some sort of an anonymous questionnaire, he replied, "Oh no, nothing like that. When I pick up a youngster or one turns himself in, that kid gives me the names of maybe ten others, and in that way I've compiled a list of 400 users." He then emphasized the immunity from prosecution which is granted for confession. He was also asked if any adults in this town smoked marihuana, and he replied that there were absolutely none — if there were, he would know about them. Then the film "Marihuana" (narrated by Sonny Bono of Sonny and Cher), supplied by the District Attorney's Office, was shown. Among its vignettes were scary hallucinations experienced by the marihuana user (someone looked in a mirror and saw himself with a face like a rubber Halloween mask), a girl happily speeding her convertible car off a cliff, and teenagers pulling switchblades in a fight. Although the narrator stated that he was not recommending tobacco, he asked the audience if they would rather fly in a plane with a pilot who had just finished a cigarette or just finished a joint, and if they would rather have a surgeon operating on their brains who had just smoked tobacco or marihuana; these questions were accompanied by shocking action shots which vividly suggested the certain result if one made the wrong choice. The film went on to demonstrate how marihuana is a factor in crime by showing a group breaking into a store after smashing the window. It showed young couples necking while careening down highways and barely missing other cars in loud cinema verité. For the parents who attend such a meeting, the result may be that the concerned uninformed now become the alarmed misinformed. Students who hear about such educational programs scoff and are derisive. Rather than facilitating dialogue between young people and their parents on the subject of marihuana, this kind of "education" merely serves to widen the affective and substantive gaps.

Judging by the published statements of the American Medical Association's Committee on Alcoholism and Drug Dependence approved by the Council on Mental Health,[3] and by the editorials of the *Journal of the American Medical Association*,[4] the medical community has also suffered from the "educational campaign." In their 1967 statement, the Committee on Alcoholism and Drug Dependence of the American Medical Association began with the assertion that "cannabis (marihuana) *has no known use in medical practice in most countries* of the world, including the United States." [5] In my view, this committee either has not done its homework or is making an assertion which is not supported by the facts (see Chap. 8, above). There is an implication of a causal relationship between the use of cannabis and narcotics in the committee's statement that "it is a fact . . . that persons physically dependent on other substances, such as heroin, almost always have had experience with marihuana, although not necessarily prior to experiences with so-called hard drugs." [6] This statement would be no less accurate if the words "Pepsi Cola" were added to or substituted for the word "marihuana." This committee report, which has undoubtedly been important in shaping recent views of physicians toward marihuana, further states that "the use of marihuana among Puerto Ricans and both southern and northern Negroes is reputed to be high. In all likelihood, marihuana use among the poverty-stricken urbanite is concomitant with use of other dependence-inducing substances and a broad range of asocial and antisocial activity." [7] The committee makes no attempt to point out that there is no evidence to indicate that the use of marihuana is causally related to asocial or antisocial behavior. The committee statement is as simplistic and naive in its views on the nature of the treatment as it is in its assumption that everyone who uses marihuana should be treated: "The task of the physician is to learn from the patient *what* really bothers him [i.e., anyone who uses marihuana, even if only once] at both conscious and unconscious levels, and what needs are being spuriously met at both levels by taking marihuana." One should even so treat people who do not use drugs: "If the patient demonstrates a psychopathological condition of such nature which could make him vulnerable to experimentation with drugs or to their abuse, positive confirmation of marihuana or other drug abuse should not be considered prerequisite for treatment of his condition. Such treatment is indicated whether or not he experiments with or has become psychologically dependent on marihuana." [8] Is the committee suggesting that some people should be treated for their curiosity? The naivete of the committee's statement and the degree to which it uses narcotic addiction as a paradigm is indicated in another statement about treatment: "Ordinarily, minimal protection during the period of acute intoxication is all that is required beyond providing appropriate measures for correcting any concurrent physical illnesses, including malnutrition. During the initial phase ambulatory treatment of the person with psychological dependence (as contrasted with the experimenter) is generally not satisfactory because of the tendency to relapse. At least brief hospitalization is usually recommended to separate the patient from his supply, establish relations, and initiate treatment. Complete cessation of the use of the drug is necessary, and circumstances may require the family or others to seek legal means by which the patient can be brought to treatment, in those states where this is possible." [9] It is doubtful that even the confirmed "pot-head" would benefit from such a treatment regime, not to speak of the inappropriateness of these recommendations for the casual user. The statement goes on to caution physicians "to remember that a person who has a psychological dependence on marihuana is sick and deserving of understanding and treatment, even though he may have been involved in unlawful activity." [10] Having satisfied itself that the use of marihuana represents a sickness, that people who use it "are psychiatrically disturbed, and that drug use is but one of a complex of psychological and behavioral symptoms manifested by them," the committee goes on to emphasize the importance of "legal control." [11]

The 1968 position paper of the same committee is equally misleading. For example, the committee states: "Some of the components of the natural resins obtained from the hemp plant are powerful psychoactive agents; hence the resins themselves may be. In dogs and monkeys, they have produced complete anesthesia of several days' duration with quantities of less than ten mg/kg. . . . Although dose-response curves are not so accurately defined in man, the orders of potency on a weight (milligram) basis are greater than those for many other powerful psychoactive agents, such as the barbiturates. They are markedly greater than are those for alcohol." [12] The concept of potency is a relative one which only has meaning in terms of the amount of the substance required to affect an organism in a specific manner. The same effect can be achieved by more of a less potent substance, or less of the same substance in a more potent form. Since the handrolled marihuana cigarette in this country weighs about 500 mg and contains 1–2 percent tetrahydrocannabinol, it has a total dose of about 5–10 mg of tetrahydrocannabinol. One such cigarette is usually sufficiently strong to produce a high; accordingly the animal dose of 10 mg/kg, mentioned above, is of a magnitude of 80 to 160 times that of the usual autotitrated (through smoking) dose as it is used for recreational purposes. The comparison with the animal data is thus meaningless. An 80-kg man would have to smoke over a very short period of time 80 to 160 joints or ingest at least 4 or 5 g of a very potent quality of hashish in a single dose for an equivalent effect.

I have dwelt on the official position of the American Medical Association because this organization is influential with physicians, who in turn are important in shaping the attitudes of people toward various drugs. The tendentiousness of the American Medical Association where marihuana is concerned is revealed not only in its official statements, but equally by the editorial policy of its major organ for the presentation of scientific papers, the *Journal of the American Medical Association*. Bias is evidenced both in the papers it selects and in those it rejects for publication. The only reliable study to date of the relative degrees to which alcohol intoxication and marihuana intoxication affect an individual's ability to operate a motor vehicle demonstrated that cannabis was significantly less dangerous than alcohol in this respect. The study was carefully designed and well controlled and, of course, the results were of great interest. The manuscript was rejected by the *Journal of the American Medical Association* and subsequently accepted for publication in *Science*, one of the country's most prestigious scientific journals, and one with an extremely critical editorial board.[13] During the same year (1969), three papers concerning marihuana were accepted for the *Journal of the American Medical Association*. The first was a case report of two individuals who had boiled marihuana leaves, then drawn off the fluid, injected this substance into their veins, and consequently nearly died.[14] (A third such case was subsequently published in the form of a letter.)[15] These near catastrophes were attributed to cannabis, but it is not certain how much if any of the actual cannabinol derivatives was really contained in the injected solution, inasmuch as they are not water-soluble. Nor is it probable that these solutions were completely free of other plant substances which might be toxic. There is no doubt that the patients experienced severe toxic responses, but to attribute them to cannabinol derivatives is to make an assumption for which the authors have no grounds.* The second paper, that of Talbott and Teague, has been discussed in detail in Chapter 10, above. There it was noted how doubtful it is that the authors are correct in their assertion that all of their cases are toxic psychoses.[16] In the third paper (see Chap. 10) the author attempts to establish that marihuana can cause a psychosis in a person with a "healthy premorbid personality."[17] She is convincing in describing the psychosis this 23-year-old man developed; in fact it appears from the data that he developed a schizophrenic reaction. But she is not at all convincing when she asks us to accept his premorbid personality as healthy. The fact of the matter

---

* A similar case of collapse after the injection of a homemade cannabis brew was reported by A. H. Henderson and D. J. Pugsley. Their patient had symptoms quite similar to the cases reported in the *Journal of the American Medical Association*. However, they did an analysis of the extract (an opalescent brown liquid which the patient had prepared by boiling hashish with water in a saucepan) and found that less than 2 percent of the total cannabinols present in the decoction were in aqueous solution. In addition, the extract contained a number of unidentified phenolic substances. They estimated that the intravenous dose of total cannabinols was only 40 mg, of which less than 0.8 mg was in solution and only a small fraction of this was the relatively insoluble active constituent, tetrahydrocannabinol. "It is likely that the injected particles acted in addition as microemboli, inducing subsequent thromboses. This interpretation is suggested by the delayed onset of symptoms, the evidence of acute pulmonary hypertension and infarction without peripheral venous thrombosis, and the transient thrombocytopenia. The severe circulatory failure produced by a combination of acutely increased pulmonary vascular resistance and fluid loss might then account for many of the clinical features, though the contributory effect of similar vessel occlusion in other organs cannot be excluded" (A. H. Henderson and D. J. Pugsley, "Collapse after Intravenous Injection of Hashish," *Brit. Med. J.*, 3 [1968], 229–230).

is that during the year 1969 the information on the subject of cannabis available in the *Journal of the American Medical Association* was less useful and credible than that published during the same period by the magazine *Playboy*.[18]

Cultural factors play a second role in the campaign against marihuana. Societies and cultures have certain norms for acceptable behavior and performance and tend to sanction for social use those drugs whose psychopharmacological properties are in accord with these norms. In many parts of India the two most prevalent types of intoxication occur side by side in the same community, but the attitude of the users of one toward the other is that of violent antipathy. The two intoxicants are *daru*, a potent distilled alcohol derived from the flowers of the mahwa tree, and *bhang*. Devotees of *daru* are the Rajput, traditionally known for their willingness to fight for the defense of their land and their religion. Members of the other major caste, the Brahmins, unequivocably denounce the use of *daru*, which they say is totally inimical to the pious and contemplative life they feel a special obligation to lead. Among the many forms of self-denial to which they accustom themselves are the avoidance of anger, or any other unseemly expression of personal feelings, and abstinence from alcohol — which is of prime importance. The Brahmins represent the spiritual aristocracy, the Rajput the temporal. The Rajput caste is that of warriors and landlords, and they are accorded certain privileged relaxations from the orthodox Hindu rules, in particular those prohibiting the use of force, the taking of life, the eating of meat, and the use of alcohol. Violence is an integral part of their lives, and they are taught to put great stress on individual bravery and ferocity in the face of danger. They place much emphasis on individual self-assertion. These modes of behavior have been linked with alcohol for ages; manly drinking and fighting occur repeatedly in the armies of ancient Gaul, in Rome, and in the history of the Viking raiders. Westerners, like the Rajputs, are committed to a life of action, and usually regard individual achievement as of primary importance, just as sexual indulgence is considered perfectly acceptable if it is enjoyed within socially prescribed limits.

One Westerner, G. M. Carstairs, an English psychiatrist, lived in a village populated by both Rajputs and Brahmins for a year and was confronted with the importance of cultural differences when he was prevailed upon to share in the Brahmin group's *bhang* potations. "He experienced the time distortion, the tumbling rush of ideas, the intensified significance of sights, sounds and tastes and, more strongly than anything else, the feeling of existing on two planes at once. His body sat or lay in a state of voluptuous indifference to its surroundings, while consciousness alternated between a timeless trancelike state and a painful struggle to keep awake, to keep on observing, and acting (in this case, to keep on writing down notes on his introspective experiences). It became clear to him, in retrospect, that throughout the intoxication his bias of personality, and perhaps his less conscious fears of surrendering to a dream-like state, resisted the somatic pull of the drug; and yet he was able to enter sufficiently into the fringe of the real ecstasy to quicken his future appreciation of what the experience meant to those who welcomed and valued it." [19] He was particularly impressed with feelings of detachment, extreme introspection, and the loss of volition coupled with a dreamlike impression of heightened reality. He recognized his own fear and repudiation of this state and considered that other Western observers might have shared his own reluctance, if not inability, to fully submit to this type of intoxication. "The present writer . . . would have to say that of the two types of intoxication which he witnessed, and in a measure shared, in this Rajasthan village, he had no doubt that that which was indulged in by the Brahmins was the less socially disruptive, less unseemly, and more in harmony with the highest ideas of their race; and yet so alien to his own personal and cultural pattern of ego defenses, that he much preferred the other." [20] It seems clear that to the Hindus, with their vastly different cultural heritage, the experience might represent something entirely different, at once less frightening and more ego syntonic than it is for the casual Westerner. Furthermore, the Rajputs are far from being the only people who dislike cannabis. Indian hemp, which could easily be cultivated in the Far East, is practically unknown to the Japanese. This is understandable when one considers that the Japanese would probably be the last to renounce the active life.

Thus, cannabis has been accepted for centuries among those people in India where cultural background and religious teaching support introspection, meditation, and bodily passivity. The West, with its cultural emphasis on achievement, activity, and aggressiveness, has elected alcohol as its acceptable, semiofficial euphoriant. These cultural differences are consonant with some of the important psychopharmacological differences between the two drugs. Clearly the more introspective, meditative, nonaggressive stereotype associated with marihuana goes against the Western cultural mainstream, particularly in the United States. While this stereotyped view contributes to its attractiveness for some, it makes marihuana repellent for many others who consciously identify with the active, aggressive, manly stereotype; in fact, the implied or actual qualities of introspection, passivity, and the surrendering of volition may be quite threatening to many. Although pharmacological properties do not play a part, much the same can be said of cigarette smoking; the Marlboro man is not easily imagined smoking pot.

In this country alcohol is an agent which lubricates the wheels of commerce and catalyzes social intercourse. Marihuana is considered to be used "just for fun" and, therefore, is in conflict with powerful vestiges of the Protestant ethic which demands self-control (except at specially prescribed times, when the restraints are lowered briefly), hard work, rationality, order, moderation, and future-oriented planning. Drug use is viewed by adherents to this ethic as just one more manifestation of a growing interest in sensual gratification, both esthetic and hedonistic. But in fact increasing numbers of people are genuinely attempting to learn about and do more in art, music, travel, sex, food, and so on. An increasing share of the economy is even devoted to this growing interest in the quality of leisure-time experience. There is a growing "have fun" morality, and, especially among some youth, an increasingly Dionysian orientation. In his recent decision upholding the constitutionality of the marihuana laws of Massachusetts, Judge G. J. Tauro revealed his more traditionally American bias against pleasure. In arguing that the fundamental right to the pursuit of happiness is not violated by the antimarihuana laws, he asserted "that only those rights are to be considered as fundamental whose continuation is essential to ordered liberty . . . and furthermore, those rights which are recognized as fundamental are also, in many instances, closely related to some commonly acknowledged moral or legal duty and not merely to a hedonistic seeking after pleasure." In defending the right of the state to regulate alcohol and at the same time prohibit marihuana, the Judge argued: "The vast majority of alcohol users do not consume it with the intention of becoming intoxicated. It has a social value as a relaxant and, in some instances, as a therapeutic. Marihuana, on the other hand, has no generally recognized medical use and is used solely as a means of intoxication. . . . [Alcohol] is customarily consumed with meals and on social occasions which do not center on the avowed purpose of drinking to the point of intoxication. So ingrained is its use in our culture that all prior statutory and constitutional prohibitions of its use have failed. . . . [Marihuana's] use is not associated with any purpose other than to become intoxicated. Nor has its use become so ingrained in our culture as to make laws strictly prohibiting its use impractical. . . . The ordinary user of marihuana is quite likely to be a marginally adjusted person who turns to the drug to avoid confrontation with and the resolution of his problems. The majority of alcohol users are well adjusted, productively employed individuals who use alcohol for relaxation and as an incident of other social activities." [21] Judge Tauro is incorrect in asserting that alcohol has therapeutic utility and marihuana does not. Alcohol was once considered to have clinical usefulness, but the number of illnesses and symptoms for which it is thought appropriate has dwindled to the point where it is doubtful whether there is now any demonstrable therapeutic value in the drug.[22] Furthermore, in asserting that the major use of alcohol is as a mere "incident of other social activities," Judge Tauro is at odds with those students of alcohol use who agree with D. Horton (in what appears to be another too-general position) that "the release of sexual and aggressive impulses" is the basic role of alcohol in every community which resorts to its use.[23] The point is that it is important to some people to establish that alcohol is not used only as an intoxicant and not used solely for pleasure, and it is these same people who feel threatened by the thought that marihuana may be a short-cut to pleasure, or pleasure for the sake of pleasure, rather than as a reward worked for and earned.

Prejudice is another factor which contributes to the irrational and emotional atmosphere surrounding marihuana. One obvious type exists between the older and younger generations. To the extent that this prejudice exists, each has a bias against the other's use of particular drugs. Alcohol is the traditional, well-established intoxicant of the older generations, whereas marihuana belongs to the younger generation and is viewed by them and their elders as a symbol of youth's social alienation. An illustration of this kind of bias is provided by the accounts of the three-day Woodstock Festival held at White Lake, New York, during the summer of 1969. Reflecting the general tone of the newspaper reporting of this event, an editorial in the *New York Times* was headed "Nightmare in the Catskills." According to the *Times,* "The dreams of marihuana and rock music that drew 300,000 fans and hippies to the Catskills had little more sanity than the impulses that drive the lemmings to march to their deaths in the sea. They ended in a nightmare of mud and stagnation. . . . What kind of culture is it that can produce so colossal a mess?" [24] Almost the only way one could learn the extent to which young people were offended by this kind of editorializing and reporting, and just what the experience meant to the participants, was by talking to them. With rare exception, the newspaper and magazine accounts dwelt on what the rainy, muddy, loud experience would have been as seen and heard through the eyes and ears of an older person. One exception was the *New Yorker* magazine, which briefly carried several interesting accounts of the festival, one of them from a nineteen-year-old university student. "The mud didn't matter, and it was one of the most remarkable experiences I've ever had. The big point was not that pot was passed around openly but that because there was a minimum of force and restriction — the cops were few, and they were friendly — a huge crowd of people handled itself decently. There were no fights, no hassles, no pushing, no stealing. Everybody shared everything he had, and I've never seen such consideration for others. People volunteered for all kinds of jobs — picking up trash, carrying stuff, doing whatever was needed. It was the most extraordinary demonstration of how good people can be — really *want* to be, if they are let alone. It was an ethic shared by a huge mass of people. The *Times* wants to know what kind of culture produces this. In a broad sense, Christian culture produced it." [25]

People who were there were struck by the extraordinary sense of community achieved by these young people, most of them strangers to each other, living for three days in the rain and the mud. A middle-aged man, courageous and curious enough to accept his twelve-year-old son's suggestion that they drive to Woodstock for the festival, was awed by what he observed. Of the enormous traffic jam which began more than ten miles from the festival, he said, "It was comparable to, say, the Long Island Expressway on a Friday night, except that it was devoid of car honkings and anger. Every so often the traffic would come to a total halt, and young people in bare feet and long hair and interesting clothes would wander back along the cavalcade, greeting other people, passing along the news, . . . giving the peace sign, or whatever." [26] He was impressed that there were no ticket takers or sellers. The people simply poured in free of charge. Despite the uncomfortable physical conditions, no one complained, "but that was the spirit of the occasion. Not once did we hear anyone angry or rude or complaining — the universal attitude was one of stoicism, courtesy, and good-will. The benevolence was awesome." [27] A physician who manned the medical aid station, imagining what it would have been like if this had been a three-day football festival with 300,000 to 400,000 spectators using beer and harder liquor, was awestruck by the fact that he saw not one stab wound, punched eye, or bloodied nose.[28]

Groups went about setting up various kinds of creative and ingenious amusements for the free use of others and shared what food and shelter they had. And they were exhilarated by the freedom and camaraderie of this event. When they began to hear news reports over their transistor radios that they were in the midst of a mass disaster, they merely laughed; it seemed such a perfect illustration of the division which exists between them and the "straight" world. The news reports only dramatized the extent of the gap: while the world believed that they were involved in a disaster, these hirsute, colorfully dressed young people knew that they were having one of the most remarkable and marvelous times of their lives. Anyone who is not convinced of the bias of the press need only compare the reporting of the Woodstock Festival to that of the annual Easter vacation gathering at Fort Lauderdale. Here there is much rowdiness and frequent riots, hundreds of arrests, and a great deal of property damage; the major, almost exclusive, intoxicant is beer. The press disapproves but generally conveys a sense that the condemnation is tempered by such attitudes as "boys will be boys" and "young people have to sow their wild oats."

If we look closely, it is possible to get a glimpse at what may be one of the underlying determinants of this prejudice against many of today's young people. If one judges by their physical appearance, they seem to be moving toward a unisex. The popularity and vibrance of such movements as Women's Liberation and others striving for equality of women suggest that more than mere appearance is involved. The "hippie" subculture dress code for women loosely prescribes or, more accurately, endorses with acceptance wearing of the hair in a natural fashion (as opposed to some sort of creation invented in a beauty shop), no makeup (or at least none that is very obvious), a loose-fitting blouse, sweater, or other garment (which only subtly if at all suggests a bosom), beads, and some sort of pants, usually not tight fitting and frequently dungarees. It's as though the wearer were trying to convey the message, "Don't think of me as a sexual object, at least not primarily." The male invariably has long hair, sometimes longer than that of his female companion, and he often has a beard or at least long sideburns. The body garments, including the beads and pants that he wears, are almost completely interchangeable with hers. The girl is seen as a "hippie," and therefore often as dirty, immoral, deviant, slothful, and perhaps disturbed. Because she does not appear to be interested in emphasizing or exploiting her sexual attractiveness, she may also be seen, particularly by "straight" women, as lacking intelligence. But it is the male who is the real problem for the "straight" world — all that hair, those beads and garish colors. If he doesn't wear a beard, he may, at first glance, not be easily distinguishable from his female companion. He is a long way from the shiny, clean-shaven, crew-cut stereotype of American manhood. Although he may, in fact, be generally far less overtly aggressive and destructive than the drinking exemplars of the American manly type, he is paradoxically much more threatening to many people. He is threatening not simply because he appears to have more freedom than they, although that certainly is important, but primarily because with his long hair, his mode of dress, and his pacific stance toward the war in Southeast Asia he is seen as sissified. Men who have gnawing or, more commonly, totally unconscious reservations about their manliness and the totality of their commitment to heterosexuality frequently are, like the adolescent in the process of establishing his masculine identity, threatened by males whose dress, behavior, and concerns appear to them to be passive and effeminate. In its mildest form, the anxiety aroused in this way may be dealt with through derision; in more extreme cases it is dealt with by bullying or an attack on the body of the provocative object. And if long-haired men arouse anxiety in those with serious conflicts around their passive wishes, a drug whose use is commonly associated with them and one which has in fact as one of its properties, whether primarily pharmacological or due to set and setting, that of promoting in the user during the intoxication a more passive state, this drug might be threatening to these same people. It may be more a matter of reaction formation than simple paradox that the common mythology about marihuana is that it does just the opposite, namely that it leads to impulsive and aggressive acts both sexual and criminal.

It is not simply a case of what drug is being used and what its consequences are. Also important in shaping people's feelings about a drug is the question of who uses it. If "hippies" and "yippies" are bad people, they must necessarily use an intoxicant which is bad. In fact, the term "drug abuse" apparently does not necessarily require that the drug have demonstrable ill effects. In the Moslem, Eastern Mediterranean region during the seventeenth century, coffee drinking was strictly forbidden, and those who owned or even visited coffee houses faced the death penalty. The severity of this punishment had nothing to do with the rhetoric about the deleterious effects of coffee, but rather with the coffee house becoming a meeting place for political malcontents assumed to be plotting against established religious and political authorities.[29] The contemporary parallel may be seen when one considers the case of a young "hippie" who organized a communal living arrangement on the lower East Side of New York. Recently, over a period of a few months, his apartment has been raided thirty times by the police who claimed they were searching for drugs. This degree of dedication to duty would appear unusual, and one cannot help but wonder to what extent this zeal was motivated by a desire to destroy the commune which represents such threatening possibilities as premarital sex, mixing of the races, a socialist style of living, and left-wing ideologies.[30]

Opponents of the peyote cult, "The Native American Church," claim dire effects as a result of peyote use: sexual debauchery, slothfulness, mental disease, malformed infants, addiction, and even death. Not one of these claims has ever been substantiated by any of the careful observers of Indian peyote users. Is this simply a misunderstanding of the drug's effects, or is it, as D. F. Aberle argues, a fundamental reflection of a hostile reaction to the cult itself, which is viewed by its opponents as a threat to their values, traditions, and self-interests? [31]

Closely related to this type of reaction is the mechanism of projection, wherein one ascribes to an innocent person, organization, idea, country, or drug impulses which one regards as detrimental, negative, or harmful in oneself. Thus parents are frequently overly concerned about the alleged aphrodisiac properties of marihuana, and some of the questions they most frequently ask suggest an underlying fantasy that if their children use it, they will become sexually promiscuous. Similarly, there is much concern with the possibility that cannabis causes various kinds of aggressive behavior. In fact, one U.S. Senator has attempted to establish that marihuana was responsible for the My Lai massacre. There is a widespread shared fantasy that cannabis use causes loss of self-control and the emergence of primitive impulses. People whose psychic makeup is such that impulse control is precarious may, through the mechanism of projection, display an overconcern about the alleged dangers of marihuana.

Where psychic experience is concerned, what seems desirable or valuable to one person may often seem dangerous to another. Some individuals are fascinated at the prospect of being in touch with primary-process thinking, and perhaps the unconscious in general; to others such a possibility is frightening.

Covert racism is probably another factor that inflames this issue. Until fairly recently marihuana was used in this country primarily by ghetto Negroes and people of Mexican and Puerto Rican descent. Furthermore, users around the world are predominantly non-Caucasian. One cannot avoid questioning to what extent cannabis is viewed, perhaps largely unconsciously, as *the* nonwhite drug which is rapidly invading the white community. It may be no accident that some of the severest penalties for its sale, transfer, and use are found in the southern states, as in Georgia (see Chap. 1). In Louisiana the penalty is death on the first offense, but, if the jury recommends mercy, then there is a mandatory sentencing of 33 years to life imprisonment. Thus, in Louisiana a 21-year-old man who is caught giving some pot to his 20-year-old girlfriend may be legally executed.

It has been said that the truth is a scarce commodity; yet the supply always exceeds the demand. As nearly as can be determined, the truth with regard to the present state of the world is that the very existence of a whole civilization, and perhaps more, is threatened. This view was amplified in 1969 at the American Association for the Advancement of Science meetings in Boston, in a symposium on "Science and the Future of Man." Several prominent scientists, taking into account the staggering and inter-related problems of overpopulation, ecological damage, and the arms race, agreed that this civilization now has a half-life of 20 years; that is, that there is only a 50-50 chance that we shall survive for another two decades. Yet, if one judges by people's behavior, it does not appear as though most of them have grasped or been touched by this fact. If they really believed that their lives and those of their loved ones were so threatened, we would expect them to be seething with concern and activity. C. P. Snow, in his despair before the not too distant consequences of exploding population and the unbridled arms race, alluded to this phenomenon:

> Uneasiness seems to be becoming part of the climate of our time. Uneasiness with an edge of fear? Perhaps. It is a bad state. It can be a paralyzing and self-destructive state. . . . Let us be honest. Most of us are huddling together in our own little groups for comfort's sake. We are turning inward more than is really natural. As I said before, we draw the curtains and take care not to listen to anything which is going on in the streets outside.[32]

This remarkable ability to "draw the curtains" on some of the compelling facts about the world we live in suggests that we are employing some active psychological processes by which we protect ourselves against uncomfortable feelings, against the risk of being overwhelmed by the anxiety which might accompany a full cognitive and affective grasp of the present world situation and its implications for the not-distant future. It serves a man no useful purpose to accept these facts if to do so leads *only* to the development of very disquieting feelings, feelings which interfere with his capacity to be productive, to enjoy life, and to maintain his mental equilibrium. These conscious and unconscious mechanisms involved in the maintenance of men's internal peace are protective and adaptive, and they are employed by that agency of the mind known as the ego. The mechanisms defend and protect the individual against obnoxious or unbearable intrapsychic mental conflicts. Although we sometimes speak of them as though they were directly protecting against external noxious stimuli, they do so only secondarily, insofar as these latter are translated by the individual into internal noxious elements.

Of the psychological mechanisms which protect men from anxiety in the face of threat to their well-being, denial is one of the most primitive and at the same time one of the most important. People use this mechanism when they manage to ignore or dismiss internal or external events the perception of which is painful. Common examples are the avoidance of contemplating one's own inevitable death, or the reluctance to acknowledge the presence of a fatal disease.

Isolation is another mechanism used to defend men against feelings which may be painful. When a man can acknowledge the fact that a continued arms race could lead to a nuclear war, which would probably mean the death of himself, his family, and millions of his countrymen, without experiencing any more affect then he would upon contemplating the effects of DDT upon a population of fruit flies, he is probably making use of the defense mechanism of isolation. In this way people can be quite facile in speaking about the fact that they and their loved ones would undoubtedly lose their lives should a nuclear war break out. They are then speaking of death as something quite apart (isolated) from the feelings associated with the concept of total annihilation. They are speaking rather of an abstraction, of something which has no real connection with themselves.

Rationalization, an ubiquitous defense, accounts for such common attitudes as "I'm sure the authorities know more about it than I do." These rationalizations serve to protect the individual from a genuine engagement with indisputable facts. Another way in which people defend themselves from truths which threaten unmanageable anxiety is through what may be called the defense of dogmatism. Essential to this mechanism is an air-tight system of beliefs which provides an individual with all the answers and does away with uncertainty and anxiety. New facts, however much they have to be distorted, are merely integrated into this system.

There are, of course, many other mechanisms of defense. Among them the one I think most relevant to this discussion is displacement. Through this mechanism people may unconsciously transfer affect from its real object to substitute objects. For example, the hyper-patriot's concern about "the enemy" may, among other things, represent his displaced anxiety about the possibility of nuclear war. Through displacement people can attach affect to substitute objects which allow for its discharge. A case in point may be the fluoridation issue. At least until recently people have been surprisingly complacent about the possible consequences of exposure to various atmospheric and water pollutants, particularly Strontium 90 and other radionucleides, in spite of warnings from medical intelligence of both short- and long-term effects. Contrast this general complacency about pollution of the biosphere with the strong public reaction against fluoridation in some communities in this country. Much public interest and emotion is aroused by both sides in this dispute. The argument against fluoridation is that individuals should not be required to ingest any artifact no matter how beneficial. The objection is to exposing persons en masse to an agent over which they have no control. The equally vociferous arguments in favor of fluoridation hold that the risks are nonexistent or so exceedingly small that they are outweighed by the benefits. It is possible that some concern both for and against fluoridation is actually displaced feeling about pollution and fallout. Notice the similarities between fluoridation of the community's water supply and the contamination of its atmosphere and water supply; in both instances people are faced with imperceptible substances, the ingestion of which they cannot avoid.

Similarly, it is quite possible that some people defend themselves against a full and meaningful, but threatening, affective grasp of these global dangers confronting them — and perhaps particularly their progeny — by unconsciously displacing them onto the issue of drugs. They feel helpless before the issues of overpopulation, ecological damage, racial violence, and the risk of nuclear war; but stamping out marihuana use is a concern one can do something about, and doing something — anything — about it becomes imperative. However, we must acknowledge that the mechanism of displacement works both ways; for example, not only is anxiety about the legal risks of using marihuana for some and the dangers of its use for others displaced, but the risks of the law and the drug themselves may serve as substitute objects for the anxiety of personal internal conflicts. For many people who become actively engaged in fighting for or against the legalization of marihuana, the underlying animus may, to some extent, be the necessity of dealing with their own internal conflicts by substituting for them these seemingly more manageable conflicts. Here involvement in the marihuana issue may be largely determined by displacement.

If it is true that men use drugs to relieve feelings of frustration, anxiety, and helplessness, then we should not be surprised if the increasing use of marihuana is related to the gloomy threats of overcrowding, racial violence, and nuclear war. These same threats may indirectly, through displacement, be contributing affective energy to the repressive campaign against the use of marihuana. To the extent that it is possible for people to defend themselves from distressing facts by unconsciously transferring affect from its real object to substitute objects, it is conceivable that some of the affect which derives from the threat of violence and war is being displaced onto issues such as marihuana. This is especially easy, inasmuch as the drug is typically thought of as essentially evil and leading to all sorts of disaster, and the people who use it are often thought of as "hippies," "yippies," and others who demonstrate, dissent, and in other ways call attention to these gloomy aspects of reality which are too distressing to confront. Thus, the anxiety and helplessness provoked by these frightening facts may be, to a greater or lesser extent, dealt with by some individuals through the *use* of marihuana, and by others, through displacement, by involvement in the crusade *against* the use of this drug. While both may be helpful, and even adaptive as far as individuals are concerned, neither contributes toward the development of a more secure world.

13 The Question of Legalization

The history of punitive-repressive measures to discourage the use of drugs is one which offers little support to those who believe that the best approach to the "problem" of the widespread use of marihuana is Draconian legislation. The spread of tobacco smoking during the sixteenth and seventeenth centuries was the most dramatic "epidemic" of drug use in recorded history. The "foule weed" was adopted by cultures so different — literate and non-literate, for example — that cultural and social determinants must have played a trivial role, if any at all, in its spread. In almost all instances of tobacco use, prohibitions against it failed, whether they were justified on grounds of impairment to health, religion, good taste, or by the threat of inducement to criminal activity. The history of the use of tobacco would seem to indicate that social controls are impotent when a society is confronted by an attractive psychoactive substance, "even if that substance serves no primary physiological need or traditional interpersonal function." [1] In their initial response to the introduction of tobacco into most societies during the sixteenth and seventeenth centuries, the authorities were in fact much more intolerant in their attempts to curb its use than are modern authorities. This is especially surprising when one considers that it is modern evidence which has demonstrated clearly the health dangers arising from tobacco use. Another very similar example is provided by the seventeenth-century spread of coffee drinking in the Arab Near East, in spite of the most extreme penalties, including death. [2]

The impotence of lawmaking in suppressing the use of psychoactive substances is illustrated again by fairly recent North African history. When from 1956–1960 the cultivation of *Cannabis sativa* was prohibited in Tunisia and Algeria, vineyards replaced hemp fields, and alcohol consumption took the place of cannabis with no consequent improvement in public health. B. W. Sigg believes this demonstrates that where large segments of the population are in the habit of using nonaddictive euphoriants, repressive control is futile.[3]

One can go further and consider the possibility that repressive measures may actually be counterproductive, even more harmful to the individual and to his society than the "evil" originally intended to be suppressed. Thus, opium smoking is on the decline around the world, but in the sections of Asia where it has been outlawed, heroin has become the far more dangerous substitute.[4] In India, where the government has been acting slowly by implementing laws to control cultivation and distribution, but not by legally banning cannabis use entirely, a slow reduction in use has been reported. However, this reduction has been accompanied by a rising frequency in the use of alcohol.[5]

At the end of the nineteenth century in Ireland, there was an attempt to suppress the use of hard liquor through temperance campaigns, heavy taxation, and (attempted) strict enforcement of the tax laws. The campaign was a success in that the Irish greatly reduced their intake of hard liquor; instead, they switched to the substitute ethyl ether, which provided a short-lived intoxication involving a "hot all the way down" sensation, followed by thunderous flatus, and, within ten minutes, a high, which could be repeated and which left no hangover. The use of ether became so widespread that in one area of Ulster an eighth of the population were labeled "etheromaniacs." The subsequent alarm over the ether "epidemic" became so great that the various pressure groups which had promoted the campaign reversed their field, and the Irishman happily returned to other psychoactive substances, notably back to his whiskey.[6]

In Japan, after World War II, amphetamines became freely and legally available. Their use began to skyrocket to the point where it was estimated that five million Japanese were habitual users. In response to this medicosocio emergency, a highly punitive law was enacted in 1953 against both users and sellers. But whereas the amphetamine problem was considered solved by 1955, the number of narcotic addicts had begun to rise steadily. The increase in the use of narcotics became so alarming that in 1963 a new law, intended to be as severe as the 1953 antiamphetamine legislation, was passed. It solved the heroin problem, but the number of barbiturate users now began to rise, and in fact is still rising. In addition there is now a sharp increase in the practice of solvent inhalation ("glue-sniffing"). At the present time marihuana is used to a very slight extent in Japan.[7]

Prohibition of alcohol in this country failed because violations were so frequent, blatant, and widespread through all socioeconomic groups. The public increasingly doubted that alcohol was so undesirable, and the cost of and fallout from enforcement became intolerable.

The ostensible reason for the general alarm about the use of marihuana is the belief that it leads to drug abuse, which means that it harms the individual who takes the drug and that he is more likely to inflict injury on society in general. However, regardless of the legal status of its use, if a drug, when taken in its usual doses, is not biologically detrimental, then from a functional (and a common sense) point of view its use cannot constitute "drug abuse." The opiates are in fact truly drugs of abuse in that the addiction they produce is invariably harmful to the individual. However, while the mortality rate for such drug abuse may be from 2 to 10 times that of the non-narcotic-using population, vital statistics in the United States for the year 1965 reveal that deaths resulting from misuse of narcotics and other drugs constitute only 1.5 per 1,000, compared with the figure of 10.7 for alcoholism and its complications.[8] Commonly associated with drug abuse are a variety of disorders, including malnutrition, infection, toxic psychoses, and the precipitation of psychoses. In addition, there are the profound physical and mental changes that may occur upon abrupt withdrawal of drugs of abuse. Drug abuse with opiates is commonly associated with crimes against both people and property, although in fact crimes against people are rare; thievery, forgery, and prostitution are the most common. A common crime among drug users is that of peddling drugs to one another; this is the only one that is common among marihuana users.

Besides crime, other types of social damage commonly associated with drug abuse include automobile accidents, economic losses at all levels, neglect of family and ordinary pursuits and activities, damaged careers, and so forth. Although it is probably impossible to estimate the actual cost of drug abuse, because there are so many factors and variables involved, it seems more than likely that the social cost of abuse of narcotics and other drugs is less than that caused by the widespread addiction to alcohol in this country, where the number of alcoholics is sometimes estimated to be as high as 20 million, although more conservative estimates hover around the 5 to 6 million mark. The possibility that the economic impact of drug abuse of all kinds may be overestimated is supported by the White House Committee on Narcotic and Drug Abuse, which has noted that if the economic aspects alone are considered, there are many other problems deserving of a higher priority.[9]

While there can be no question that the use of psychoactive drugs may be harmful to the social fabric, the harm resulting from the use of marihuana is of a far lower order of magnitude than the harm caused by abuse of narcotics, alcohol, and other drugs. Marihuana itself is not criminogenic; it does not lead to sexual debauchery; it is not addicting; there is no evidence that it leads to the use of narcotics. It does not, under ordinary circumstances, lead to psychoses, and there is no convincing evidence that it causes personality deterioration. Even with respect to automobile driving, although the use of any psychoactive drug must perforce be detrimental to this skill, there exists evidence that marihuana is less so than alcohol. Marihuana use, even over a considerable period of time, does not lead to malnutrition or to any known organic illness. There is no evidence that mortality rates are any higher among users than nonusers; in fact, relative to other psychoactive drugs, it is remarkably safe.

There is, however, a real relationship between crime and cannabis in this country: the criminogenic character of the present laws against the possession, sale, or even the giving away of marihuana; and this constitutes a great irony. The unique nature of this criminogenic effect in the United States is that antimarihuana laws have intensified — and to some extent created — the basic but complex sociological and legal problems they were ostensibly designed to avoid or eliminate. The laws which prohibit the possession, sale, and giving away of cannabis passed by the individual states and the federal government since the mid-1930's have created an entirely new species of "criminal," very often an individual who is truly unable to see himself, in any real sense, as engaged in any criminal activity, and whose typical attitude toward the antimarihuana legislation is a combination of scorn, indifference, and frustration. It is not at all unreasonable to suppose that a government (or, more particularly, a special law-enforcement agency of that government) which strikes marihuana users as downright ludicrous in its extremely punitive approach to prohibition of marihuana will also seem ludicrous in other important respects. We certainly have reason to question how marihuana users will (and do) interpret the pronouncements of various governmental drug-abuse-control agencies concerning other drugs that may well be vastly more dangerous to the individual and to society in terms of both short- and long-term effects.

"When only the poor sought paradise by way of pot, nobody cared about the enhancement and enrichment of perception. They just flung 'em in jail." [10] Increasingly, however, the middle class is experiencing at first hand the unsettling effects (to say perhaps the least) of prohibitions against the use of marihuana. Sometimes it is their own children who are apprehended, sometimes they themselves. It is worth noting that prior to the initial 1937 anti-marihuana legislation, and "despite its increasing popularity in the thirties . . . most middle-class Americans still had no contact with marihuana and knew little, if anything, about it." [11] In fact, in the same year that the Federal Bureau of Narcotics was established (1930), only sixteen states had laws prohibiting or limiting any aspect of marihuana-related activity, and the statutes in these states prescribed what were generally light penalties, and they were laxly — if at all — enforced. But according to one hypothesis:

> The anxiety-producing stresses of the depression had made the country panic-prone. Deprived of the facts and primed on hysteria-provoking, apocryphal horror stories given to the press by the Federal Bureau of Narcotics, Americans were sold a mythological bill of goods. They were told that marihuana was a "killer drug" that triggered crimes of violence and acts of sexual excess; a toxic agent capable of driving normal persons into fits of madness and depraved behavior; a destroyer of the will; a satanically destructive drug which, employing lures of euphoria and heightened sensuality, visited physical degeneration and chronic psychosis upon the habitual user. [12]

As noted in Chapter 12, we live again in uncertain, anxiety-producing times, and it is possible that the increasing alarm about marihuana and its increasingly widespread use are to some extent both a displacement and a symptom of that anxiety.

A. R. Lindesmith, who agrees that "no one, of course, recommends the use of marihuana," also realizes that "the fact that the use of marihuana is outlawed, for example, means that it is often obtained through association with unsavory types, often in an underworld environment, and the user takes the risk of criminal prosecution. . . . The controversy with respect to marihuana is solely concerning the relative potency or frequency of such results [i.e., automobile accidents and "irresponsible and criminal acts"] in comparison to similar consequences following the use of alcoholic beverages. All empirical investigations indicate that alcohol constitutes a far greater social danger than does marihuana." [13]

The critical question with regard to damage to the social fabric is whether the present highly repressive and overly punitive approach is not more damaging and more costly than any dangers or cost inherent in the widespread use of marihuana.

Until recently, the federal laws made distribution, including gifts of marihuana, punishable by from 5 to 20 years imprisonment for a first offense, and 10 to 40 years for a subsequent offense. Furthermore, there were restrictions on probation and suspended sentences. Accordingly, federal penalties for marihuana violations were, with a few minor exceptions, the same as those for violations of the laws relating to opiates and cocaine. The declared intent of Public Law 91-513, which became law on October 27, 1970, is that of reducing penalties for experimenters and increasing them for "pushers." The penalty for simple possession of marihuana is reduced to a prison term of not more than one year and/or a fine of not more than $5,000. The Court can, if it chooses, give a first offender probation instead of a jail sentence. A second conviction of possession is punishable by up to two years of imprisonment and/or a fine of not more than $10,000. The offense of selling marihuana is punishable by a prison sentence of up to 5 years and/or a fine of as much as $15,000. If there is a prior conviction for this offense an offender may be sentenced to 10 years in prison and fined as much as $30,000. In addition, there is a provision, reportedly aimed at professional criminals, which makes it possible to impose a minimum sentence of 10 years and a maximum of life on a person, convicted of a drug offense, who is engaged in a "continuing criminal enterprise." In support of this provision, Representative W. L. Springer noted that individuals dealing in LSD "and especially marihuana" will be subject to its special penalties; he singled out "some of these people . . . who are going around to all of these rock festivals pushing drugs of all types." [14]

Most state legislation makes distribution, including gifts, punishable as a felony — and the felony is often high degree, involving the possibility of a long prison term. Most states define cannabis as a narcotic; the possible punishments for distribution are usually identical with those that apply to the distribution of opiates and cocaine. In fact the degree of permissible punishment for a single small distribution of marihuana is so high in some states that it may approximate those provided for such crimes against person or property as unaggravated robbery, larceny, arson, kidnapping, unaggravated forcible rape, or even, in the state of California, second degree murder.

A conservative estimate is that one-third of the California population between the ages of 16 and 29 have committed the very serious crime (as determined by the legal sanctions, at any rate) of using marihuana and thereby exposed themselves to the possibility of arrest, a felony conviction, and imprisonment. And both the percentage and the age-range are rising each year. As J. Kaplan points out, it is most unhealthy for a society to turn a large percentage of its young people into felons or even define them as such.[15] The young, occasional user of marihuana may have a good deal of trouble adjusting to the official local and federal police view of him as a criminal liable to the most severe punishments, whether fines, imprisonment, or both, of the state or federal government. It is far from unreasonable to suppose that he will feel genuine resentment toward what he feels increasingly forced to view as the "other side" of the law, and that he will see the police less as protectors of rights and property and more as intruders and spies. It is conceivable that this attitude shift might lead to further, more dangerous criminal activity — for if one is already branded a criminal and lives under the threat of a heavy jail sentence and/or fines, what essential difference can it possibly make (or so one might think) if one commits another crime for which the sentence is less (although the actual social cost, and the cost to the new criminal, may well be greater)? Many young marihuana users employ this particular argument.

As noted, there is no way to be sure that those who have once violated laws carrying such severe penalties will not be more likely to violate others (more likely, that is, than they would be — not if they had not smoked — but if they had not in so doing committed such a serious crime). At the very least it must be supposed that current antimarihuana laws have a deleterious effect on the attitude of the young toward the law, and particularly on their respect for it. They are supported in their feeling of alienation by what they can only see as hypocrisy all around them — a judgment that seems to come easily for young people, and which these particular laws in fact help to institutionalize for them. They earnestly believe, and many doctors would agree, that marihuana is, at the very least, less harmful than the alcohol, tobacco, tranquilizers, barbiturates, weight reducing drugs, and so on, which older people, the same who criminalize the young, consume compulsively if not habitually, and for which they are in no way punished or made to feel the weight of social disapproval. To them the prohibition on the use of marihuana represents the imposition by one group in a position of political power of its own standards and norms of morality on another group, one without any effective political power — at least for the present. Furthermore, the ire of the young is increased by the common knowledge that the law prescribes much more serious punishments, in many states, for the use of marihuana than it does for the use of drugs that have been clearly demonstrated to be more harmful, such as the LSD-type drugs, the barbiturates, and the amphetamines — not even to mention alcohol or tobacco. The young see not merely hypocrisy, but outright stupidity. Moreover, they perceive inequities in the distribution of punishments, to which they are extraordinarily sensitive. All these factors combine to induce in the young people a disrespect for these particular laws that usually amounts to outspoken contempt. One cannot help but wonder if and how far they extend their views to consideration of other laws, or even generalize these sentiments in their thinking about allied institutions and society in general.

That the number of people who are experimenting with and using marihuana is increasing at a dramatic rate cannot be denied. Marihuana-arrest statistics cannot be taken at face value because (1) they reflect not just the prevalence of drug use but also such factors as the interest and diligence of enforcement agencies in apprehending users, and (2) they are, for almost all states, either incomplete, not differentiated from narcotics arrests in general, or do not cover a long enough period of time to have any validity. But this statement does not apply to California, where the statistics on marihuana arrests have been distinguished from all others, and the records are accurate back to at least 1962. However, it is also true that any marihuana-arrest statistics, so long as they are not gross misrepresentations, are especially important in at least one other respect: although they are an imperfect barometer of prevalence, they do indicate at least a part of the cost of enforcing laws which make criminals of those who use marihuana. Thus in 1962 there were approximately 3,500 adult arrests in California for violation(s) of the (state) antimarihuana laws; in 1963 there were 4,500; in 1964, 6,500; in 1965, 8,500; in 1966, 14,000; in 1967, 24,000.[16] These figures indicate an increase of almost 700 percent in 6 years.

But the total cost, as Kaplan points out, is not simply in terms of the criminalization of thousands of people; it must also be estimated in terms of the financial costs which usually must be paid from restricted or limited resources that must also maintain law enforcement policies and programs, judicial activities, and correctional and rehabilitative programs. California spent an estimated 75 million dollars in processing marihuana violations in 1968.[17] The California Senate Public Health and Safety Committee met in October 1967 for the purpose of compiling and arranging data, new and old, concerning marihuana use. The usual and expected conflicting testimony was heard, but the comments which are most relevant to the present discussion were made by Los Angeles Deputy District Attorney J. Reichman who first spoke not in his official capacity as the Deputy District Attorney, but as an interested, concerned human being:

> I thought that if I were a legislator, and I had the task of attempting to revise the marijuana laws, I would want to know the answers to some of the questions. I would want to know what the cost of enforcing the marijuana laws is, and how effective that enforcement is. I would want to know whether there is any relationship between the use of marijuana and the commission of subsequent crimes, and I would also want to know what effect the use of marijuana had upon the user.[18]

On the basis of then-current statistics (specifically, that marihuana arrests constituted 17½ percent of all California felonies for
the preceding year), Reichman expressed his view that the cost of
enforcing the marihuana laws was so high that the question of their
continued enforcement was worth genuine and careful consideration:

> Every time an arrest is made [Reichman testified in his official
> capacity], it usually involves two police officers, and several
> hours. . . . There is the initial interrogation, the arrest, the
> transportation of the defendent to the police station, the book-
> ing, the preparation of the police report; two or three hours go
> by without any difficulty at all. A police officer on an eight hour
> shift could normally not handle more than two or three arrests.
> . . . Add . . . the cost of the police officer coming to court.
> They have to appear twice. They have to appear at a preliminary
> hearing. This involves easily a half day. . . .
>
> Then, there is the matter of the trial. That would be another
> day. Add . . . the cost of the deputy district attorneys that had
> to prepare and process these . . . cases. Add the cost of the
> salaries of the Public Defender's Office . . . ; the costs of the
> salaries of the judges and the juries . . . , and the costs that also
> go along with running a court. The cost of the clerk and the
> reporter. There is no doubt in my mind that the cost is stagger-
> ing.
>
> I have spoken with numerous narcotics officers, and they have
> the same opinion that I have: that the effectiveness is almost
> nil. We are barely scratching the surface. For every arrest that
> takes place there are 1,000 or 2,000 other people that are using
> marijuana.
>
> There is no way for me to prove this. The only instance I can
> cite to you is the manner in which most of these arrests take
> place. . . . for the most part, by accident. . . . A person is
> driving an automobile, and he goes through a red light. The
> police give him a ticket, and they notice a marijuana cigarette
> in an ashtray. Then, two hours of time are taken in processing
> the individual. . . . There is no question in my mind that most
> of the arrests occur in this fashion.[19]

However, even though he testified that the enforcement cost was
high and the deterrent effect minimal, Reichman stated that he

thought the guiding principle in determining whether or not the laws against marihuana should be rewritten was in the answer to the question about the nature and extent of any relationship between marihuana and the commission of crime. On the basis of his own experience, he asserted that he sincerely doubted "that the use of marijuana plays a vital factor [sic] in the commission of other crimes." [20] Reichman specifically attacked the current California legislation (and, by implication, the laws of most other states as well):

A man can go out and steal a car and receive a misdemeanor sentence, and a man can . . . commit an assault with a deadly weapon and receive a misdemeanor sentence, but a man that is smoking one marijuana cigarette, he is going to receive a felony. . . . There is a world of difference between someone that possesses three or four kilos of marijuana and somebody that possesses one marijuana cigarette. I feel that the court should be given discretion to impose misdemeanor sentences in marijuana cases if they so desire. . . . I think that such a change will, somewhat, reduce the costs. . . . many of our marijuana cases go to trial because the defendant, who was caught with one or two marijuana cigarettes, doesn't want to have this stigma of a felony facing him for the rest of his life. . . . if there was this misdeameanor alternative, I think many of the cases would terminate in a plea.

[The legislature] . . . should give serious consideration to treating marijuana violations the same way that alcohol violations are concerned. It is my feeling that the marijuana law is just like any other criminal law, whether it is marijuana, whether it is a traffic violation. It is a problem of balancing the interests. On the one hand, the interest of the individual to a freedom of choice and, on the other hand, the interests of society to protect itself.[21]

Roughly three-quarters of those arrested for marihuana violations have had only minor or no difficulty with the law previously. Of those arrested for possession of marihuana in California, about one-third are incarcerated for some period of time.[22] It is an unfortunate fact that most of the jails and prisons in this country are chronically overcrowded and understaffed. To send a person whose behavior presents no essential threat to the fabric of society to such a place is absurd. Worse, it throws someone whose only "crime" may be that he has smoked marihuana into the closest contact with a number of much more serious (from the point of view of the threat of direct social harm) offenders, and increases the likelihood that he will engage in other, perhaps non-drug-related criminal activities, after he is released: the criminogenic nature of the penalties provided by the antimarihuana laws also includes the effects on users of imprisonment. But even those who are not imprisoned have their futures seriously scarred inasmuch as their arrest records follow them through life and jeopardize their chances of getting jobs, gaining entrance to schools, or being accepted as members in many organizations.

Judge J. J. Saunders of California, in an address to a young audience in 1967, stated that he was "heartsick . . . over the number of young people who come into my court charged with narcotics violations. Many of them, I felt, really didn't know the consequences. These consequences . . . can be severe, and the time spent in prison is the least of it. When the convict is released from prison, he becomes a second-class citizen economically. . . . Persons convicted of a felony in narcotics cases will not be licensed by the state in a wide variety of fields, ranging from accounting and medicine to engineering and funeral directing. You can't even be a barber, . . . and most school districts will not hire teachers with a conviction on their records and the government will not give them clearance to work in the defense industry." [23]

Yale University Dean G. May was recently quoted in a national magazine article as saying:

> No amount of discussion . . . can detract from the hard facts that at the present time possession, use or distribution of illegal drugs, including marijuana, makes anyone involved with narcotics, even in a single experiment carried out in the privacy of one's home, liable to arrest, conviction, fine, and imprisonment. Regardless . . . of the disposition, . . . the arrested . . . is immediately faced with . . . bail money and legal fees, which often exceed $1,000. The long range expense to the student may be even greater . . . a conviction for narcotics law violation may preclude consideration for graduate or professional school acceptance, disqualify for graduate fellowships, jeopardize employment opportunities upon graduation, and be

a source of personal disadvantage for the convicted student for the rest of his life.[24]

Even though the Federal Bureau of Narcotics has publicly stated for a number of years that it is not concerned with the prosecution of the student or occasional user, but only the dealer or heavy user, the state laws are usually vigorously implemented, and many young people are convicted under them with a great zeal on the part of the authorities.[25] "There [i.e., in the cases over which the state has jurisdiction], the rigidity of the laws has sometimes resulted in the imposition of penalties that were out of proportion to the seriousness of the crime. This has resulted in senseless prison time being imposed on casual users or juvenile offenders, a punishment that has been both cruel and ineffective. In some instances misguided jurists have sent users to jail to 'cure' a nonexistent 'addiction.' Jails being what they are, these individuals, registered as criminals with all that this label implies, have been forced in some instances into a criminal existence by those very forces sworn to prevent crime." [26]

One can imagine what being arrested for possessing marihuana does to a young person who believes he has been apprehended for doing something which many, if not most, of the other young people he knows do — something which he believes to be quite harmless. If in this most important formative and suggestible period of his life he is already leaning toward social disenchantment, this kind of experience, one would suspect, will very likely push him a long way toward bitter social alienation.

So dramatically is the use of marihuana increasing that one of the most important variables in assessing the results of any poll is the date when it was conducted. The results of a poll conducted in Massachusetts in March 1970 indicated that of those interviewed, about one-half of the college students, one-fourth of the employed persons, and one-fifth of the high school students admitted to having smoked marihuana at least once during the preceding year. When these same young people were asked to express an opinion on the extent of marihuana use, their estimates were even higher than their own personal admissions. Their impression was that among youth in general more than half have experimented with marihuana.[27] It must be expected that at the present rate the use of marihuana will become so widespread and accepted that the present marihuana laws will be labeling a sizable fraction of the population as criminals. This means that some of them will go to jail or prison, or, at the very least, be fined or given a suspended sentence or be placed on probation. In any event, the threat to many people of the possibility of having a criminal record is increasing with the great increase in marihuana use, even if the enforcement of the state laws is (in the future) somewhat relaxed. But even that majority of users who are never arrested are adversely affected by the fact that they are labeled as participating in a criminal activity, and thereby — in many instances — made to feel like criminals. This can only enhance their sense of alienation and bitterness. What is more, one is beginning to perceive among young people today a growing sense of camaraderie concerning their shared status as "criminals." (Along with the public flouting of the antimarihuana laws at smoke-ins and even, recently, by individuals on the main streets of places like Cambridge, Massachusetts, the planting of marihuana has become something of a fad among youth, who in most cases make little or no effort to conceal their gardens even to the point where it has become fashionable to plant cannabis in quite conspicuous places: not only open window boxes and front-yard gardens, but even in "the center strip of Park Avenue in New York City, the lawn in front of a police station in ultra-respectable Westchester county, the United Nations building, and, twice recently, in front of the state capitol in Austin, Texas.")[28]

Many of the young feel that they are all "criminals" together, fighting against the existence of unjust, hypocritical, and irrational laws, and their use of marihuana is carried like a banner. I have talked with some very solid young people who, when told that one risk of marihuana-use concerning which they could be quite certain was the legal one, rejoined with considerable affect that *that* was precisely why they had no intention of stopping. It seems that these laws lend themselves to use by young people as a catalyst both for the enhancement of cohesiveness of a subculture and for alienation from the larger society. Furthermore, the criminalizing of such a large segment of this critical generation promotes in them a sense of distrust which at times may appear to be somewhat paranoid. The hard fact is that the enforcement of these laws involves the use of informers and entrapments. Anyone who is familiar with informing or entrapment or has read of the experiences of Professor Leslie Fiedler will appreciate the basis of this distrust.[29] In fact, it is possible (as noted in Chap. 10) that the paranoid thinking which some people experience while marihuana-intoxicated may have as much to do with the total setting, which in a very real sense cannot be trustworthy, as it has to do with any psychopharmacological property of the drug. In any event, an environment which leads to a paranoidlike stance is decidedly not healthy, and criminalization contributes to this kind of stance.

There are those who are mindful of these and other costs and are particularly sensitive to the short- and long-term effects of the criminalization of a large segment of young people who already have considerable doubt and ambivalence about making a commitment to the values and life-styles that have served their elders; these people wish to change the existing marihuana laws. But they believe that legalizing marihuana use would be too precipitous, and that to whatever extent the present laws act as a deterrent, this would be lost. Instead, they think of reducing the penalties for use or possession, or only for the actual possession, to below the criminal level. M. P. Rosenthal, for example, is willing to accept the risk that some of the deterrent effect of the present laws may be lost in changing the punishment for possession from a felony or a misdemeanor to a civil violation.[30] Under this proposed alternative, people who sell marihuana, however, would still be treated as criminals. One caveat to this proposal is that, among the unorganized distributors particularly, there are and will be many whom one is trying to protect from criminalization; however, the proposal's proponents accept this one price which must be paid if the law is to have any leverage on distribution. But the price might be higher than the proponents of this approach suppose. In a survey of 204 marihuana users, E. Goode found that 44 percent had sold the drug at least once.[31] This type of approach, which makes the real target the dealer rather than the user, is modeled on heroin addiction, where the drug peddler is seen as profiting while he spreads and intensifies human degradation and misery. It assumes that there is a clear-cut distinction between user and seller. But nowadays, at least where marihuana is concerned, the user and seller are largely indistinguishable; almost half of users sell to some extent and almost all sellers use. To think of the marihuana dealer as "preying" on and profiting from a hapless, helpless victim — the pot smoker — is again to use opiate addiction as a paradigm and to entertain a view which is ludicrously inapplicable.

Just what is a civil violation? According to Rosenthal, it is "an official judgment of wrongdoing that is not as severe as the judgment society makes when it convicts of a crime." [32] A civil violation is accordingly not a crime, but rather an official judgment of wrongdoing. But the increasing number of people who use marihuana cannot believe or accept the view that their smoking of marihuana constitutes even wrongdoing. If it were not a felony or misdemeanor, the legal consequences would not be as severe as they are now, but the moral condemnation would remain unchanged. Yet, because the young people using marihuana today seem but little influenced by the risk of punishment and very sensitive to the moral aspects of the legal issues involved, one wonders to what extent they would view such a proposal as constituting a real change over the present approach. Insofar as this proposal would lessen the punishment for use or being under the influence of marihuana, but not for its distribution, it would be based on the premise that while the laws should be designed to limit use, the use, in and of itself, constitutes only a minor dereliction. Distribution would be treated as the real crime, because distribution enables people to use marihuana. But if use is only a minor dereliction, how does it make sense to treat as criminals those who make it possible for others to participate in it? Some are concerned that such a casting-off of most aspects of the punitive approach would be taken as social sanction for the use of marihuana. Again we have to ask, "What are the relative costs?"

If the present trend of increasing popularity of marihuana continues and the demand for it therefore increases, and the government pursues such programs as Operation Intercept, designed to limit the supply — is it not likely that some who would otherwise not have done so will turn, or have already turned, to other and more dangerous drugs? And is it not also likely that the price of marihuana will go up, as it did for a time as a result of Operation Intercept? If this is so, will not organized crime become increasingly involved in its distribution? If this happens, there is more likelihood of the occurrence of such things as paying off of authorities and police, and the lacing of poor grades of marihuana with any number of other substances, a practice against which the consumer is helpless since he can complain neither to the seller nor the authorities. Four factors are most responsible for the fact that so much crime, especially against property, is associated with heroin use: heroin is addicting, its use is illegal, it is expensive, and its distribution is controlled by organized crime. People who are addicted are compelled to get money to buy the addicting drug. Marihuana is not addicting, and therefore could not, even under the worst of circumstances, generate the amount of crime that heroin does. Nonetheless, one can foresee that if its distribution remains a criminal offense, and more Operation Intercept programs are undertaken, the price will continue to go up and organized crime will become more involved in its distribution. Under such circumstances, it would be likely that there would be a considerable increase in crimes against property. What is more, if this were to happen, it might very well provoke more of the young people, the people whom we are trying to protect from criminalization, into applying their vast energy and genius to the problem of developing their own new means of supply and distribution. Fundamentally, the approach which advocates reduction of the penalties for use and possession of marihuana, but retention of those for selling, assumes the existence of two largely distinct and non-overlapping activities and accordingly contradicts empirical reality. There is a great deal of overlap, and it is quite possible that the degree of overlap would be increased rather than decreased by this type of approach.

Before the state interferes with the individual's interest in pursuing his own inclinations, it must have a compelling reason to do so. Those who support prohibitions of liberty must accept the burden of demonstrating the justification for them. I believe that the extent to which marihuana can be demonstrated to be dangerous, both to the individual and to society, does not constitute such a justification. In fact, accepted constitutional doctrine carefully differentiates between self-destructive behavior and behavior which is harmful to society, and claims as the concern of the state only the latter. This doctrine is reflected in the philosophy of John Stuart Mill. He wrote:

[The sole basis society has for] . . . interfering with the liberty of action of any of their number, is self-protection. That the only purpose for which power can be rightfully exercised over any member of a civilised community, against his will, is to prevent harm to others. His own good, either physical or moral, is not a sufficient warrant. He cannot rightfully be compelled to do or forbear because it will be better for him to do so, because it will make him happier, because, in the opinions of others, to do so would be wise or even right. . . . In the part . . . [of his conduct] which merely concerns himself, his independence is, of right, absolute. Over himself, over his own body and mind, the individual is sovereign. . . .

This, then, is the appropriate region of human liberty. It comprises, first, the inward domain of consciousness. . . . Secondly, the principle requires liberty of tastes and pursuits; of framing the plan of our life to suit our own character; of doing as we like, subject to such consequences as may follow: without impediment from our fellow creatures, so long as what we do does not harm them, even though they should think our conduct foolish, perverse, or wrong.[33]

Spinoza, writing long before Mill, stated:

All laws which can be broken without any injury to another, are counted but a laughing-stock, and are so far from bridling the desires and lusts of men, that on the contrary they stimulate them. For "we are ever eager for forbidden fruit, and desire what is denied." Nor do idle men ever lack ability to elude the laws which are instituted about things, which cannot absolutely be forbidden.[34]

In another essay, Spinoza said: "He who seeks to regulate everything by law is more likely to arouse vices than to reform them."[35]

The use of marihuana is a highly personal form of behavior, and as its use does not encourage crime, sexual debauchery, or other antisocial activity, why should its use and distribution be interfered with by the state in more than a regulatory fashion? Perhaps the most unfortunate aspect of the antimarihuana legislation is that it defines a crime which is a crime without any victim. Although marihuana smoking is not usually thought of as a private activity, the small, congenial groups which gather to "turn on" might be considered individuals engaged together in a hobby such as, say, wood-carving, insofar as any detrimental or harmful consequences to society-at-large are concerned. When a bank or grocery store is held up, the police do not have to engage in spy-like activities prior to their knowledge of the crime: the owner or manager will contact them immediately. This is not the situation at all in the case of cannabis use. There is no victim, and in most cases, with the exception of certain hyper-zealous antimarihuana crusaders, no one will call the police to report that marihuana smoking is occurring in the vicinity. The attempt to enforce the antimarihuana legislation entails activities on the part of the police that are very similar to those employed by any police state. As an example, Fort relates how the Chicago police have adopted the practice — a holdover from the days of the "Syndicate" — of using search warrants, obtained in a way that any American court would find intolerable, in order to enter apartments where they believe marihuana is being used and make arrests:

> The police have obtained from the courts the right to use what are called "blank warrants" — warrants in which the witness who alleges he has seen the crime is permitted to sign a false name. This is supposed to be necessary to protect inform-ers. . . .

> As the *Sun-Times* noted: . . . "The police do not have to dis-close the name of the informer or the time when the drugs were bought. There is also a device known as constructive possession: The police can arrest anybody found in the vicinity of pro-hibited drugs, whether he's an innocent visitor or the real cul-prit. The frame-up is easy. Plant the drugs, get the search war-rant, grab everybody in sight. It could happen to you and you'd never have the right to face your accuser." William Braden, a *Sun-Times* reporter, also uncovered one informer, a heroin addict, who admitted signing dozens of such warrants without the names of the accused on them. The narcotics squad could then type in the name of any individual whose apartment they wanted to raid and it would be perfectly "legal" in form — but a terrifying distance in spirit from the actual meaning of the Constitution. Such raids, of course, violate the Sixth Amend-ment — guaranteeing the right "to be confronted with the wit-nesses" against you — as well as the Fourth (no "unreasonable searches"); and they occur everywhere in the nation.[36]

The 1968 "Omnibus" crime bill gave authorization to not only federal but also local police officials to tap the telephones of suspected marihuana users. It is clear that since the use of cannabis has spread throughout the country without any clear relationship or limitation to a particular socioeconomic class, there is scarcely a person outside the Federal Bureau of Narcotics or the White House who is not, in theory, as liable as the known junkie to have his phone tapped for the compiling of evidence that would put him in jail for the rest of his life. This suggests the possibility that police may use the threat of a marihuana "bust," for example, to insure that "undesirable types" — by which is usually meant persons who dress in the "hippie" garb — leave the city limits. And it is not very far-fetched to suppose that the police in some cities would hardly hesitate if they thought they could pin a marihuana rap on members of an organization like the Black Panthers.

Consider a case that is cited by Fort from the point of view, not so much of the chicanery of the law enforcement officials and the absurdity of the lower court, as of fundamental morality — the question of common decency and good faith among men which "peace officers" are supposed to defend:

John Sinclair, a poet, leader of the Ann Arbor hippie community and manager of a rock group called MC-5, became friendly, around October 1966, with Vahan Kapagian and Jane Mumford, who presented themselves to him as members of the hippie-artist-mystic subculture that exists in all of our large cities. Over a period of two months, they worked to secure his confidence and friendship and several times asked him to get them some marijuana. Finally, on December 22, Sinclair, apparently feeling that he could now trust them, gave two marijuana cigarettes to Miss Mumford — one for her and one for Kapagian. He [Sinclair] was immediately arrested; his "friends" were police undercover agents.

Sinclair has been convicted of both "possessing" and "dispensing" marijuana and faces a minimum of 20 years under each statute, and a maximum of life for the sale. If his appeal is not upheld, the very smallest sentence he could receive is 40 years. As his lawyers pointed out in his appeal, "The minimum sentence to which [Sinclair] is subject to imprisonment is 20 times greater than the minimum to which a person may be imprisoned [in Michigan] for such crimes as rape, robbery, arson, kidnapping or second-degree murder. It is more than 20 times greater than the minimum sentence of imprisonment for any other offense in Michigan law, except first-degree murder." [37]

Suppose, for the moment, that the use of marihuana does promote the development of what has been called the "amotivational syndrome," and that the widespread existence of this will change the life style of our society. Even under these circumstances, whether such a change would constitute a "harm" is basically a value judgment about what kind of a society is both possible and ideal. The fact which we must face up to is that it is already clear the younger generation is bringing about a significant change in societal morality. Aside from the question as to whether legislation of morality which appreciably diminishes personal rights is constitutionally proper, there is the serious question as to the effectiveness of such legislation.

Criminal law often prohibits forms of behavior which are pleasurable to some and about which there is considerable doubt as to social harmfulness. Among these forms are the so-called moral offenses, including such behavior as homosexual conduct. This type of legislation comes into existence more out of exaggerated moral concerns and sense of responsibility than from any empirically demonstrated danger to the society. Judging by the paucity of data indicating danger to society and the high pitch of moral concern about its use, the offense represented by the use of this drug appears to be more in the nature of a moral one. And just as it is unlikely that society would disintegrate with the removal of criminal sanctions against homosexuality, so it is unlikely that the striking-out of penalties for the use of marihuana would lead to a similar fate.

Justice Brandeis, as though reaffirming John Stuart Mill, wrote in a dissenting opinion of the Supreme Court:

> The makers of our Constitution undertook to secure conditions favorable to the pursuit of happiness. They recognized the significance of man's spiritual nature, of his feelings, and of his intellect. They knew that only a part of the pain, pleasure, and satisfactions of life are to be found in material things. They sought to protect Americans in their beliefs, their thoughts, their emotions and their sensations. They conferred, as against

the government, the right to be let alone — the most comprehensive of rights and the right most valued by civilized man.
To protect that right, every unjustifiable intrusion by the
government upon the privacy of the individual, whatever the
means employed, must be deemed a violation of the 4th Amendment.[38]

In commenting on the "pursuit of happiness" alluded to by Justice Brandeis, A. D. Brook says:

[It] . . . seems to be the most basic right of the individual
in our society, a right which certainly lies within the penum-
bra of all other rights. It is the right for which all other rights
are designed. It is the right to do with one's entire life what
one wishes, including the right to seek pleasure in whatever
form that pleasure presents itself, provided, of course, that such
a pursuit is not overbalanced by harm done to others. Arguably,
it is also the right to achieve euphoria, the right to get "high,"
the right to experience new sensations, the right to expand
and change one's consciousness, even the right to be silly, and
finally, even the right to withdraw, the right to "cop out." It
is submitted that these are rights that have "redeeming social
value," and that the freedom to engage in behavior leading in
any of these directions outweighs the exaggerated, and in some
cases, fanciful harms that have been attributed to marijuana
use.[39]

New social norms are increasingly and dramatically colliding
with older statutory proscriptions. The legal institution cannot
remain insensitive to these changes without incurring damage to
itself. But, of course, courts lack the flexibility and prerogatives
to provide solutions to social problems; ultimately it is the legislatures which can experiment, improvise, change direction, and
even reverse field when necessary. In fact, just because a court
has so few alternatives, it exercises great caution: a court may
strike down a statute as unconstitutional, but in doing so it may
leave a major social problem without an adequate solution.

As it becomes increasingly accepted that enforcement of the
existing marihuana laws is more costly and dangerous than is use
of the drug itself, at least as it is used at present in the United
States, enforcement will become increasingly difficult. There is
every indication that a great number of people are ignoring these

laws now and that even more will be doing so in the future. It is not simply that more people are using marihuana, but larger numbers of people who are older are also smoking it. The number of people breaking these laws even now is so great that if a substantial fraction of them were arrested, the courts would be overwhelmed with the volume. One can predict that it will not be long before it will be a rare jury that does not have among its members at least one who uses marihuana, is convinced of its relative harmlessness, and will find it difficult to be a party to the conviction of someone else who uses the drug. In the absence of any statutory changes, what may happen is that law enforcement officials faced with increasing numbers of violators and shrinking numbers of convictions will arrive at a point where they decide that any efforts to enforce the laws as written are futile and that the only realistic approach to the widespread use of marihuana will be systematically to ignore it.

Something of this nature recently happened in the Netherlands, where the government has been moving toward the position that at least in the case of marihuana it is more sensible for a society to live with it than to fight its use. Officially marihuana remains outside the law, but even high law enforcement officials acknowledge that this is so because the Netherlands (like the United States) is party to the Single Convention governing traffic in drugs. Compared to the furtiveness and police action associated with drug usage in the United States, the Dutch laissez-faire attitude toward marihuana is striking, and nowhere is it more obvious than in two psychedelically lit, government-subsidized youth clubs, *Paradiso* and *Fantasio,* in downtown Amsterdam. In each of these clubs as many as 1,000 young people 16 years old and over can be found on any night, many of them smoking marihuana while pushers openly ply their trade, offering potential customers free samples. The police are fully aware of the activities and transactions that go on inside but make no effort to interfere. The clubs' managers and staff are alert to the use and sales of harder drugs and eject those so involved. As the man responsible for police affairs says of the present attitude, "It is forbidden to sell drugs but it is difficult to stop. . . . young people had no place to go. Now we have less trouble in the streets." [40] However, the Dutch New Left activists are concerned about the effects that this attitude of the officials and the existence of the clubs may have on their efforts to impress upon young people the need to remake Dutch society. As one of them put it, "One bad effect . . . is that the clubs reduce political pressure. People think that if they've won the fight to have the clubs and drugs, then everything must be all right." [41] As for the extent of marihuana consumption, according to H. Cohen, a researcher at the University of Amsterdam, the dealers in the city handle a supply sufficient for about 10,000 regular users. "The increase in use . . . has not been great since 1960. Numerically, it is not a serious problem." [42]

In view of the present public attitudes toward smoking marihuana in the United States, it seems unlikely that legislatures are going to legalize the use of marihuana in the near future. I think it is likely, then, that this same type of widespread ignoring of the antimarihuana laws will very shortly come to pass. But the laissez-faire approach is no solution. It is mere transitory accommodation with a number of liabilities. First, one must expect that while such an accommodation may become widespread, it will nonetheless remain capricious. Second, since the present laws will presumably still exist, the user, while he may not be pursued, will still be labeled a criminal; and third, such an approach provides no way of imposing any degree of quality control upon distribution.

A more rational approach to the problem of the smoking of marihuana in the United States would include legalization of the use of marihuana, regulation of its distribution, and the development of sound educational programs about it.*

By "legalization" is meant the freedom for people above a certain age, say 18, to use marihuana (*bhang*) of a predetermined potency. The penalties associated with its use, as with alcohol, would deal with those circumstances wherein the user endangers the lives or well-being of others, as, for example, in operating a motor vehicle while intoxicated. Such legalization would immediately put an end to the costs and harmfulness of the present legal approach. It has to be assumed that the legalization of the use

*Although the United States became a party to the Single Convention on the control of narcotic drugs in 1967, it is doubtful that this constitutes a serious obstacle to the legalization of the use of marihuana. In the first place the provisions of the treaty contain the qualification that their application is subject to a signatory's "constitutional limitations," so that a nation reserves for itself the decision of whether or not the Single Convention violates its internal laws; secondly, a signatory may, of course, withdraw from the convention (see Articles 36 and 46, *Multilateral Single Convention on Narcotic Drugs, 1961*, Washington, D.C.: U.S. Government Printing Office, 1967).

of marihuana would result in more widespread use. However, since at the present time the use is increasing explosively, it is at least conceivable that the prevalence of its use will reach roughly the same level sometime in the not too distant future with or without legalization. Furthermore, there is even a possibility that for some groups legalization will mean less use; those young people whose use is largely determined by a need to oppose hypocrisy and the establishment may feel less compelled to smoke pot when it is freely available. And very young people, those for whom its use may be the most harmful, may be more willing to forego its use now with the understanding that they will be able to use it when they reach age 18, just as most of them do not surreptitiously and illegally drive automobiles at a younger age perhaps largely because they know that when they reach 16 they will, with certain restrictions, be able to drive legally. This will by no means bring an end to the use of marihuana among high school and junior high school students, but it is more likely to have a dampening than an accelerating effect on use in this age group.

In this proposed approach the distribution of marihuana is regulated much as that of alcohol is now. The use of cannabis products is generally less dangerous than the use of either tobacco or alcohol, and the use of marihuana, as it is commonly smoked in this country, is the least harmful of all. The regulations controlling the distribution of cannabis would limit it to marihuana (*bhang*), of, say, 1.5-percent tetrahydrocannabinol potency. This would do much to insure the continued use of the milder form through smoking, rather than through the ingestion of more powerful forms such as hashish (*charas*). Just as, with the easy availability of liquors of limited potencies, people do not generally seek out pure ethanol, so it is expected that with the unfettered availability of marihuana, few would seek out hashish. Another important advantage of regulation is that the consumer could be certain not only that he is getting unadulterated marihuana, but also that it is of a potency familiar to him. Thus, there would be no danger of marihuana laced with other drugs. The risk of attaining more of a high through autotitration than the user desires or is prepared for would be minimized if the available product were of a more or less uniform, predictable potency. The risk of the kinds of reactions that have been described earlier, resulting from large amounts of ingested hashish, would be all but impossible under these circumstances.

If this type of approach is to have any effectiveness in stemming the push toward the use of "hallucinogens," amphetamines, and narcotics, it must be accompanied by honest educational programs. To date, such approaches have tended to lump marihuana with the "hallucinogens" or, even more inappropriately, with the true medical narcotics. The law as it presently stands reinforces this when it provides stiffer penalties for the use of marihuana than it does for LSD. Young people who have "learned" for themselves that marihuana is not very harmful then regrettably tend to treat with skepticism information from the same sources about the dangers of other drugs and are more likely to experiment with them. The present laws put the drug educator in a difficult position. He can discuss honestly the dangers of LSD, amphetamines, and heroin. But when he talks about marihuana, and particularly when he is asked about its dangers relative to those of alcohol, he can either be less than candid and risk losing credibility with regard to the other drugs, or he can acknowledge that except for the risk of getting caught, there is little reason on the whole to believe that marihuana as it is used now in the United States is more dangerous than alcohol. If he admits this lack of negative evidence regarding marihuana, he risks being accused by the community (or the school authorities) of encouraging the use of marihuana and thereby criminal behavior. If he tells the students candidly of the relative dangers of marihuana, LSD, amphetamines, and heroin, and he tells them what the penalties are for the use of these, he risks being interpreted as mocking the law. When the use of marihuana is legalized, it will be possible for the drug educator to have more credibility among the young people than he now can have.

However, if he is to be credible for an audience which seems particularly sensitive to breaches of integrity, he must be scrupulously objective about the material he presents. A case in point is an advertisement sponsored by the National Institute of Mental Health which appeared in several campus newspapers in November 1969. It showed the picture of a man and bore the title "Happy Twenty-First Birthday, Johnny." The ad read, "Most people take him for about 35." [43] Then came a few paragraphs of a reasonable description of the dangers of using amphetamines, followed by an invitation to write for free drug booklets to the National Institute of Mental Health. On January 6, 1970, two months later, the *Harvard Crimson,* one of the papers which had published the ad, also published a letter from the man who had posed for the picture, thanking the paper for belatedly recognizing his twenty-first birthday: "I was touched and proud to find your paper commemorating my twenty-first birthday. . . . I guess it just slipped by nine years ago when it happened, and I was a Junior [at Harvard]. But that's all right, I know how busy you are up there, getting out a paper every day, and all." [44] Not only was he in fact thirty years old, he was made up to look even older in the photograph. Needless to say, the student readers treated the incident with derision, and one wonders how seriously they will now consider the reasonably objective information offered in the advertisement. For that matter, one doubts the credibility — as a source of drug information — that they will grant to the National Institute of Mental Health. As mentioned earlier, there is some evidence that students will respond rationally to credible sources of objective evidence concerning the dangers of various drugs. And there is every reason to believe that deceitfulness in drug education will in the long run be counterproductive.

Most people in the United States, at least today, believe that to legalize the use of marihuana would be to invite national tragedy. Among them are those whose attitudes toward the use of this intoxicant are so emotionally overdetermined that they would remain unpersuaded by any amount of evidence of its relative harmlessness or by the most compelling arguments for the sagacity of legalization. Others, who are willing to consider the possibility, believe — as they have heard countless times — that not enough is known about the drug to make such a change which seems to them precipitous and premature. It is quite true that among the hundreds and hundreds of papers dealing with cannabis, there is relatively little methodologically sound research. Yet out of this vast collection of largely unsystematic recordings emerges a very strong impression that no amount of research is likely to prove that cannabis is as dangerous as alcohol and tobacco. The very serious dangers of tobacco, particularly to the pulmonary and cardiovascular systems, are becoming increasingly well known. Alcohol, on the other hand, is generally considered to be a serious danger for "only a minority" of people in this country, namely the alcoholics, who are conservatively estimated to number about 5 to 6 million. Another minority group, the alcohol abstainers, are actually considered by most people to be somewhat deviant. We read in the newspapers of how upper-middle-class parents support and even encourage alcohol use among their teenage children, of how a session of Congress began with cocktails, and, more recently of the exchange between Apollo astronauts and a television comedian, well known for his use of alcohol, during which he gleefully exclaimed that he was higher than they. So-called social drinking is as American as apple pie — this despite the clearly demonstrated dangers of even this kind of drinking.[45] It is a curious fact that the only socially accepted and used drugs known to cause tissue damage (alcohol and tobacco) are the ones whose use Western society sanctions. It is reasonably well established that cannabis causes no tissue damage. There is no evidence that it leads to any cellular damage to any organ. It does not lead to psychoses *de novo,* and the evidence that it promotes personality deterioration is quite unconvincing, particularly in the forms and dosage used in the United States today. Although it is clear that much more must and will be learned about the derivatives of this fascinating psychoactive plant, it is not so clear what specifically needs yet to be learned before we are ready to embark on a more reasoned approach to the social use of marihuana. Given the fact that large segments of any population will use psychoactive drugs and given the psychoactive drugs presently available, marihuana is among the least dangerous. A fortiori, we must consider the enormous harm, both obvious and subtle, short-range and long-term, inflicted on the people, particularly the young, who constitute or will soon constitute the formative and critical members of our society by the present punitive, repressive approach to the use of marihuana. And we must consider the damage inflicted on legal and other institutions when young people react to what they see as a confirmation of their view that those institutions are hypocritical and inequitable. Indeed, the greatest potential for social harm lies in the scarring of so many young people and the reactive, institutional damages that are direct products of present marihuana laws. If we are to avoid having this harm reach the proportions of a real national disaster within the next decade, we must move to make the social use of marihuana legal.

14 Marihuana: Six Years of Reconsideration
by Lester Grinspoon and
James B. Bakalar

When *Marihuana Reconsidered* was published in 1971, attitudes toward cannabis were already changing. Since that time use has continued to increase, and society has become more tolerant toward the users. By 1976, 34 million Americans had smoked marihuana at least once and 12 million could be described as current users: that is, they had smoked at least once in the preceding month and thought they might do so again in the near future. Among young people aged 18 to 25, 53 percent had used marihuana in March 1975, and 25 percent were current users. A nationwide survey of 17,000 members of the high school class of 1976 showed that 8 percent of them used it almost daily.[1] The suggestion in the 1972 report of the National Commission on Marihuana and Drug Abuse that "marihuana use may be a fad, which, if not institutionalized, will recede substantially in time"[2] has proved to be wishful thinking. Now that many middle-class whites use the drug, it no longer inspires the same contempt and fear that it created when it was identified primarily with racial minorities and unkempt hippies. Marihuana has become one of the everyday social drugs, along with alcohol, tobacco, and coffee. A popular slick magazine called *High Times,* devoted to a lighthearted treatment of the pleasures and lore of cannabis and to chronicling the war between romantically heroic smugglers and comically villainous law-enforcement agents, has been on the newsstands since 1974; it already has several imitators. An extensive apparatus of connoisseurship similar to the one applied to wine now surrounds the various grades and geographic varieties of cannabis with their different chemical contents, and attention is also devoted to the subtleties of smoking and ingestion methods. The flourishing small industry that produces accessories like rolling papers, pipes, cleaning devices, and jocular posters continues to grow. The number of social users who take the drug several times a week or less is now probably greater in proportion to the number of people who make it the center of their lives; marihuana has largely lost its former status as a symbol of rebellion and a source of ideological and cultural commitments. The statement at the end of Chapter 6 that most drug use is not ignorant and irrational, does not imply a wish for self-destruction, and will change in response to evidence of danger still seems true to us; the fact that marihuana continues to become more popular is therefore one sign that no convincing evidence of that kind has been produced.

In this area of what might be called the sociology of marihuana use, there have been no surprises; the trends visible in 1971 have simply accelerated, and the predictions made in this book have been more or less confirmed. The law and the official pronouncements of organized medicine and the government are now slowly shifting in response. A major sign of change has been the work of the National Commission on Marihuana and Drug Abuse, established in 1971. At first there was justified skepticism about the objectivity and goals of this commission. Its executive director was quoted as saying before the hearings began that he could "write the report right now," and President Nixon announced, "Even if the commission does recommend that it [marihuana] be legalized, I will not follow the recommendation."[3] Four nationally recognized experts on cannabis were conspicuously absent from the roster of invited witnesses; all four had advocated legalization of social use of marihuana. Many people had come to believe that presidential commissions in any case were created mainly to temporize on important issues and avoid action. So it was an unexpectedly happy outcome when the commission published a report entitled *Marihuana: A Signal of Misunderstanding* (1972), which was fairly accurate in its description and analysis, if politically timid in its recommendations. Since that time many of the misunderstandings have been cleared up. The annual report of the Secretary of Health, Education, and Welfare on "Marihuana and Health" becomes progressively more calm, more rational, and therefore more lenient in its attitudes and recommendations. The director of the National Institute on Drug

Abuse now admits that marihuana is a less serious health hazard than alcohol or tobacco. The *Journal of the American Medical Association* has stopped publishing scientifically dubious papers that purport to show serious dangers in marihuana.

There has also been considerable, though limited, legal progress. By 1974 all states except Nevada were treating possession of small amounts of marihuana as a misdemeanor, a precedent established by the federal government in the Controlled Substances Act of 1970. Many state laws are now facing constitutional challenge in the courts. And eight states, beginning with Oregon in 1973, have adopted a system by which minor marihuana violations are treated like parking violations, with offenders subject only to a citation and fine rather than arrest and a permanent criminal record. Other states are soon to follow suit. This policy of decriminalization has been endorsed by the American Bar Association, the National Council of Churches, the National Education Association, the Governing Board of the American Medical Association, and many other organizations. Although the hunt for smugglers and distributors will continue to give drug-enforcement agents an outlet for their energies and ingenuity, penalties are being applied less often and less harshly to those who are least prepared to cope with them, and there is somewhat less opportunity for the misuse of marihuana charges to make a forceful comment on the accused person's dress, demeanor, or politics.

Nevertheless, the price we pay for continuing the war against cannabis remains high. In 1975 there were over 400,000 arrests on marihuana charges — 70 percent of all drug arrests — and the administrative costs were about $600 million.[4] And still there are occasional outrages, like the case of the "uppity" black man sentenced to 40 years in prison by an all-white jury in Virginia in 1974 for selling a small amount of marihuana to a police informer.[5] This kind of thing is becoming less common, however, and all the signs suggest a rising impatience with the waste of resources involved in enforcing the cannabis laws. According to a federal survey taken in early 1975, for example, 86 percent of the public is against putting minor marihuana offenders in jail;[6] and in fact they are not usually imprisoned now. Legalization is probably still some years off, for several reasons: general public opposition, possible international obligations under the Single Convention on Narcotic Drugs, and controversy about how a legal distribution system should be organized and regulated. The immediate prospect is that drug-enforcement agents will simply start to devote less attention to the marihuana traffic; this has already been suggested in a White Paper issued by a federal committee on drug enforcement in September 1975 and immediately endorsed by President Ford.[7] President Carter is committed to decriminalization of possession at the federal level and may listen sympathetically to advisers who propose that the Drug Enforcement Administration should indulge in a little benign neglect of the commerce in marihuana and find better uses for its talent and money — in bureaucratic terminology, reorder its priorities. The rest of us, it is clear, have already begun to do so.

Several revisions have been proposed in the botanical classification of cannabis described in Chapter 2. The work of Soviet researchers who studied wild hemp plants in the 1920's and 1930's has become widely accepted, and many botanists now believe that the genus *Cannabis* has three species instead of one. The plant described by Linnaeus in 1753 and classified as *Cannabis sativa* was a European specimen; in 1783 Lamarck classified a plant imported from Asia, and quite different in appearance, as *Cannabis indica;* finally, in 1924 the Soviet botanist D. E. Janichewsky suggested the existence of a third species, *Cannabis ruderalis. C. sativa* is tall, gangling, and loosely branched; *C. indica* is shorter, about 3 to 4 feet high, and very densely branched; *C. ruderalis* grows to a height of only 2 feet and has few or no branches. There are also apparent differences in the leaves, stems, and resin. Although all three species are native to western Siberia and central Asia, *C. sativa* has become much more widespread; it is the major species now growing as a weed and cultivated plant in North and South America. Lamarck and the Soviet botanists imply that the resin of *C. indica* has a higher cannabinoid content than that of the other species. An alternative classification, proposed recently by Canadian taxonomists, focuses on differences in the intoxicating properties. This account retains the assumption that the genus *Cannabis* has only one highly variable species (*Cannabis sativa*) and distinguishes two subspecies, *sativa* and *indica*. The first is said to be more northerly and selected for fiber and oil production, the second more southerly and selected for the intoxicating resin; each has domesticated and "wild" (weedy, naturalized, or indigenous) variants.[8]

While use of marihuana continues to increase, and arrests for possession and sale or intent to sell remain at a high level (reaching a maximum of 445,000 in 1974 and declining slightly to 416,000 in 1975, according to the Federal Bureau of Investigation), it has now become more obvious than ever that it presents no danger to society or to the user's mental and physical health that justifies criminal penalties. Therefore the position of advocates of continued prohibition has become defensive rather than offensive. Many old claims about marihuana's deleterious effects have proved unwarranted and are being quietly abandoned; the new ones are often advanced tentatively and based not on clinical observation but on experiments or laboratory analyses that are difficult even for specialists to interpret. In reviewing the contentions about health hazards that are still in circulation, we shall deal briefly with those that are obsolescent and more fully with those that remain popular or have recently become so. The enormously increased amount of research and publicity on cannabis since 1971 has affected public understanding of the issues. As we have indicated, many people have begun to recognize that prohibition is not desirable and does not work anyway; we hope to persuade more of them.

Work since 1971 has substantiated the conclusion (page 347) that cannabis derivatives are "remarkably safe" compared to many other substances, both drugs and nondrugs, that are not subject to criminal penalties. Most impressive are the controlled investigations of heavy cannabis users in Jamaica, Costa Rica, and Greece that have already begun to dispel old prejudices and influence public policy in the United States and elsewhere. During these same years, experiments and tests have been reported that suggest new potentially deleterious effects of cannabis — on the tissues of the brain, on the immune system, on sexuality and testosterone levels, or on chromosomes; these reports are at worst completely unconvincing and at best too inconclusive to serve as a basis for public policy.

The dangers to be considered fall into various categories of acute and chronic psychological, behavioral, and physiological effects.

At one time psychological and behavioral effects were the target on which most accusations were concentrated, and the issues were often confused by law-enforcement zeal and hysterical misrepresentation. Today the results of older work like that of the La Guardia Committee and newer controlled research in Jamaica and elsewhere have become familiar, and it is much harder to persuade people by means of appeals to diffuse fear or social and racial prejudice that either the acute or the chronic psychological and behavioral effects of marihuana are dangerous. When these fears and prejudices are dispelled, there is very little argument for any of the charges; and in fact many of them are being quietly abandoned by advocates of marihuana prohibition.

Effects on cognition and motor coordination. Studies continue to show mild, dose-related impairment of short-term memory, reaction time, attention, time estimation, motor coordination, and number facility. Cannabis reduces driving skill, but possibly not as much as alcohol at intoxicating doses; unlike alcohol, it does not increase aggressiveness.[9] Nevertheless, similar precautions should be taken about driving under the influence. The opinion of experienced marihuana users that they can control the degree and quality of the intoxication by "coming down" when it is necessary to perform some task is confirmed by recent experimental research.[10]

Crime and violence. The contention that marihuana use causes crime, familiar since the days of Harry Anslinger's notorious campaign against the drug and repudiated in Chapter 11, has now been thoroughly discredited, presumably beyond hope of revival. On the matter of aggression, J. R. Tinklenberg concludes: "There is no convincing evidence that the pharmacological properties of marihuana incite or enhance human aggression," defined as intentional acts leading to physical injury.[11]

Acute anxiety reaction and psychosis. As was pointed out in Chapter 10, the most common adverse reaction to marihuana is a state of acute anxiety, sometimes accompanied by paranoid thoughts, which may rarely reach the proportions of panic. The sufferer interprets the perceptual and emotional effects of cannabis as signs that he is ill, dying, or losing his sanity. He may also begin to think that others present are critical, hostile, subtly ridiculing him, or planning to inform on him to the police. These paranoid ideas are usually tenuous and easily dispelled by simple reassurance — the best treatment for the acute anxiety reaction in any case. Someone who is taking the drug for the first time or in an unpleasant or unfamiliar setting is much more likely to react this way than an experienced user who is comfortable with his surroundings and companions; the reaction is very rare where marihuana is a casually accepted part of the social scene. The likelihood varies directly with the dose and inversely with the user's experience; thus the most vulnerable person is the inexperienced user who inadvertently (often precisely because he lacks familiarity with the drug) takes a large dose that produces perceptual and somatic changes for which he is unprepared. Anxiety and paranoia are heightened and to some extent justified in this country by a quite rational fear of arrest; these symptoms are less prominent in areas where penalties for the use of hemp are nonexistent or less severe. The acute anxiety reaction is in no sense a psychosis: there are no "true" hallucinations, and the ability to test reality — necessary if the "treatment" by reassurance is to succeed — remains intact.

The anxiety and paranoid thoughts that characterize the acute panic reaction resemble an attenuated version of the frightening parts of an LSD or other psychedelic experience — the so-called bad trip. Some proponents of the use of LSD in psychotherapy have asserted that the induced altered state of consciousness involves a lifting of repression. Although the occurrence of a global undermining of repression is questionable, many effects of LSD do suggest important alterations in ego defenses. These alterations presumably make new percepts and insights available to the ego; some, particularly those most directly derived from primary process, may be quite threatening, especially if there is no comfortable and supportive setting to facilitate the integration of the new awareness into the ego organization. So psychedelic experiences may be accompanied by a great deal of anxiety, particularly when the drugs are taken under poor conditions of set and setting; to a much lesser extent, the same can be said of cannabis. Frightening LSD experiences are sometimes followed by flashbacks, and these have also been reported (albeit rarely) in connection with cannabis. It is thought that cannabis users who have used LSD or other psychedelics are more likely to experience flashbacks than those who have not used other drugs. It is possible that flashbacks are attempts to deal with primary process derivatives and other unconscious material that have breached the ego defenses during the psychedelic or cannabis experience.

Recent research fails to confirm the existence of the more severe reaction described as a cannabis psychosis that is discussed at length in Chapter 10. Occasional findings to the contrary, when closely examined, can be attributed to pre-existing psychiatric disturbances or the use of other drugs. A survey of 36,000 U. S. soldiers concluded that cannabis alone almost never produces a psychosis; recent studies of chronic heavy users in Jamaica, Greece, and Costa Rica are in agreement. In particular, a study of *ganja*, the powerful cannabis preparation smoked in Jamaica, found no evidence that the drug was a cause of admission to mental hospitals. People who persistently suffer acute anxiety reactions are regarded as "not having the head for *ganja*" and simply avoid it; there is no recognized *ganja* psychosis. A recent review of the literature on cannabis and psychosis concludes that results are "limited and often contradictory." [12] It still seems possible that cannabis can precipitate psychosis in a few people whose egos are so vulnerable that any severe stress or alteration in consciousness would have the same effect. But now that there are 12 million people in the United States who smoke marihuana regularly, as well as many heavy chronic cannabis consumers abroad, if the drug precipitated a psychosis with any regularity there would be unequivocal evidence of the fact.

For some people all this accumulated evidence is less significant than a paper by H. Kolansky and W. T. Moore, published in the *Journal of the American Medical Association* in April 1971.[13] The reception of this study is a part of social history rather than a part of medical and scientific history; for example, a Florida judge declared that the paper established beyond doubt the danger of marihuana and that he would subsequently put in jail all offenders who came before him. Although long since discredited as a scientific work, Kolansky and Moore's study is still occasionally cited by opponents of marihuana use; until very recently, papers attacking marihuana have had a larger circulation and influence than their quality has justified. Kolansky and Moore reported on 38 patients seen in their psychiatric practice; all had used marihuana and later suffered from some form of psychopathology; 8 had become psychotic. The study was not prospective and therefore could not with any certainty establish a causal connection. Still, the inferior retrospective form of experiment can provide controls to eliminate extraneous variables, and Kolansky and Moore failed to do this. There is also a place in clinical research for anecdotal studies as a source of clues for further testing; but the symptoms Kolansky and Moore describe are too varied and ill defined and too insecurely related to cannabis use even to supply hints for further research. For example, when a boy is seduced homosexually by an older man, who also introduces him to marihuana, and the boy later develops a psychosis, most psychiatrists would consider the seduction to be of primary importance; Kolansky and Moore see only marihuana. They further imply that when the boy is hospitalized and recovers, it is withdrawal of marihuana rather than the treatment or the natural course of the illness that restores him to health. The fact that the patients themselves and their parents often attributed their symptoms to marihuana is irrelevant; the parents may have been displacing their own feelings of guilt, and the patients may have been unconsciously providing Kolansky and Moore with the data they needed in order to fulfill the desire to please the therapist that is one consequence of transference. The *Journal of the American Medical Association* would not have accepted this paper for publication if it had had only reasonable medical considerations in mind. It is safe to say — there has actually been some progress since 1971 — that the periodical would not accept a paper of similar quality on this topic today.

An article in the 1976 *Archives of General Psychiatry* by V. R. Thacore and S. R. P. Shukla revives the concept of the cannabis psychosis.[14] The authors compare 25 cases of what they call a paranoid psychosis precipitated by cannabis with an equal number of paranoid schizophrenics. The cannabis psychotics are described as patients in whom there has been a clear temporal relation between prolonged abuse of cannabis and the development of a psychosis on more than two occasions. All had used cannabis heavily for at least 3 years, mainly in the form of *bhang,* the weakest of the three preparations common in India (it is usually drunk as a tea or eaten in doughy pellets). In comparison with the schizophrenics, the cannabis psychotics are described as more panicky, elated, boisterous, and communicative; their behavior is said to be more often violent and bizarre, and their mental processes characterized by rapidity of thought and flight of ideas without schizophrenic thought disorder. The prognosis is said to be good; the symptoms are easily relieved by phenothiazines, and recurrence is prevented by a decision not to use cannabis again. The syndrome is distinguished from an acute toxic reaction by the absence of clouded sensorium, confusion, and disorientation.

Thacore and Shukla do not provide enough information to justify either the identification of their 25 patients' conditions as a single clinical syndrome or the asserted relation to cannabis use. They have little to say about the amount of cannabis used, except that relatives of the patients regarded it as abnormally large; they do not discuss the question of why the psychosis is associated with *bhang* rather than the stronger cannabis preparations *ganja* and *charas*. The meaning of "prolonged abuse on more than two occasions" in the case of men who are constant heavy cannabis users is not clarified, and the temporal relation between this situation and psychosis is not specified. Moreover, the cannabis-taking habits of the control group of schizophrenics are not discussed — a serious omission where use of *bhang* is so common. The patients described as cannabis psychotics are probably a heterogeneous mixture, with acute schizophrenic breaks, acute manic episodes, severe borderline conditions, and a few symptoms actually related to acute cannabis intoxication: mainly anxiety-panic reactions and a few psychoses of the kind that can be precipitated in unstable people by many different experiences of stress or consciousness change. Thacore and Shukla end their paper by writing: "The history of drug abuse among the patients was invariably known to the observers, and this situation could have influenced their observations. Therefore, this study may suffer from limitations that more sophisticated methods could overcome." The tentativeness of this conclusion is justified and welcome.

Addiction and tolerance. Something resembling mild withdrawal symptoms has been reported in laboratory animals given enormous doses of delta-1-tetrahydrocannabinol (Δ^1-THC) for a long time, and occasionally in human beings in a laboratory situation; but as a clinical phenomenon in ordinary recreational use a cannabis abstinence syndrome has not been identified, even among Jamaicans who use up to 420 mg of THC a day.[15] Nor has anyone found evidence of pharmacological tolerance in human beings at recreational doses; instead, it still seems that experienced users are more sensitive to the desired effects at lower doses. "Behavioral tolerance," probably a matter of learning to compensate for or direct the effects of high-dose intoxication when necessary, has been reported in laboratory animals and undoubtedly arises in human beings as well; presumably it enables Jamaicans to do hard physical labor while taking large doses. Some experiments on human beings also reveal dose-related tolerance to various psychological and physiological effects.[16] Whatever may be the nature or degree of the tolerance or reverse tolerance that arises in various circumstances during marihuana use, it does not present a problem to the user or society. There are no reports of a need to increase the dose to recapture the original euphoria or to prevent a relapse into misery.

Although it has long been accepted that cannabis is not physically addictive and does not give rise to significant tolerance, it is often said to create an unhealthy psychological dependency. This term does not tell us much, however; almost any habit that satisfies a need or desire, whether related to drugs or not, can be described as a psychological dependency. Some dependencies are trivial, some benign; the significant question is whether the habit does any harm to the individual or society. One test of this (not, of course, the only one) is whether the person who has the habit wishes he could give it up but feels unable to do so. Marihuana users feel that way much less often than users of more dangerous drugs like alcohol and tobacco. The few who are susceptible to a psychological dependency on cannabis would also be susceptible to other kinds of psychological dependency; they are likely to suffer from anxiety, depression, or feelings of inadequacy. In these cases the original condition is a more serious problem than the attempt to alleviate it by using marihuana. Dependence on cannabis, where it exists, is certainly less dangerous to health than dependence on alcohol or tobacco.

Stepping-stone hypothesis. Since the notion that smoking marihuana somehow leads to the use of opiates and other dangerous drugs is no longer taken very seriously, it might almost seem superfluous to discuss it. Nevertheless, we repeat for the record that no good evidence has been produced either before or since 1971 that any property of marihuana produces a peculiar susceptibility to heroin addiction or that marihuana users tend to "graduate" to heroin. It is true that most heroin users have smoked marihuana first, but an even greater proportion of them have used alcohol, and almost all have drunk milk and Coca-Cola; retrospective associations of this sort provide no evidence of a causal connection. It should hardly be surprising to find, and it usually is found, that anyone who uses any given drug is more likely to use others and that in particular, by a process of cultural selection rather than anything inherent in the drugs, anyone who uses a given *illegal* drug is more likely to use other illegal drugs. When allowances are made for this phenomenon, the relation between marihuana use and heroin use proves to be remarkably slight, more obviously so as marihuana becomes more popular and readily available. The stepping-stone hypothesis, which used to have a life of its own apart from any real evidence — a life largely pumped into it by law-enforcement officials — is now dead or at least playing possum. Nonetheless, it is useful to keep in mind this theory and its fate when considering other charges against marihuana that may be inspired by a need to find justifications for a fixed belief that prohibition is necessary.

Other prolonged adverse reactions. The contention that marihuana use in the long run causes mental, moral, or emotional deterioration of some kind — either cognitive and psychomotor impairment or a personality change like the vaguely defined impairment of mind, emotions, and will known as the "amotivational syndrome" — remains one of the hardest to prove or disprove. The problems of intervening variables and cultural bias are enormous. For example, does smoking marihuana cause personality change or, in our culture, is it the other way around? If there is a personality change, from whose point of view and by what implicit standards is it assumed to be a deterioration? Objective measures of this phenomenon are in short supply, and so are prospective studies that might extricate a causal role for marihuana from the complex web of associations that tie social and psychological conditions to drug use.

Nevertheless, it is safe to say that the favorable conclusions of the Indian Hemp Drugs Commission and other studies reported in Chapter 10 have been confirmed repeatedly. In work done since the publication of *Marihuana Reconsidered,* a survey made in 1972 of a random sample of students at the University of California at Los Angeles (UCLA) showed no difference between users and nonusers in grade-point average. H. B. C. Reed, Jr., found no difference on tests of general intelligence and specific cognitive and motor capacities between casual and heavy users of marihuana. On psychological tests and neurological examination, 47 Greek subjects who had used cannabis heavily for an average of 23 years showed no deficit compared with controls. In a rare controlled prospective study of American college students, C. M. Culver and F. W. King found no deterioration even with frequent cannabis use in scores on a set of psychological tests including the Wechsler Adult Intelligence Scale and tests of spatial perception; this result is subject to the qualification that the period between tests was only a year. A recent controlled study of chronic heavy cannabis users in Costa Rica found no deficit on neuropsychological, intelligence, or personality tests. The results of a prospective study of subjects who smoked large amounts of marihuana daily in a research ward at UCLA for 94 days were similar: no significant effect on learning, performance, or motivation.[17] It is not surprising that the report of the National Commission on Marihuana and Drug Abuse (1973) and the Canadian Government's Le Dain Commission (1974) deny the existence of an amotivational syndrome.

Possibly the most substantial evidence on this subject so far is contained in research recently undertaken in the West Indies and Central America. The landmark study is *Ganja in Jamaica,* by V. Rubin and L. Comitas, published in 1975. Rubin and Comitas compared 30 heavy chronic cannabis users (they had smoked for an average of 17.5 years) with 30 controls matched for age, residence, and socioeconomic status; all were admitted to a hospital for 6 days of medical examinations, psychological questionnaires and tests, and psychiatric interviews; their life histories were taken, and their work habits were observed in the field. There was no evidence that continual heavy use of cannabis (up to 420 mg of THC a day, far more than most heavy users take in the United States) caused violence, psychosis, poverty, intellectual deterioration, or apathy and indolence. *Ganja* does not produce an amotivational condition, but on the contrary is used to provide the will and energy to work. Users showed no significant differences from controls on indices of mental status, social deprivation, extraversion, and neuroticism. There were no signs of brain-function impairment of any kind and no differences between the two groups on 15 intellectual and verbal and 15 neuropsychological tests — including many that are sensitive to the acute effects of cannabis. *Ganja* users expend slightly more energy than nonusers in performing some tasks, because the cannabis makes their movements less efficient; but Rubin and Comitas regard this as much less important than the fact that they often take the drug *in order to* work. (This finding resembles the Indian and African practices reported at the beginning of Chapter 6.) It is worth noting, in view of the conclusion of the Indian Hemp Drugs Commission that "moderate" use of cannabis is harmless, that the daily consumption by these Jamaicans is probably the highest in the world and yet on the evidence does not constitute immoderate use.[18]

A later and more elaborate study of marihuana smokers in Costa Rica by P. Satz, J. M. Fletcher, and L. S. Sutker came to essentially the same conclusions. Satz and his colleagues identified certain methodological deficiencies in the Rubin and Comitas study and tried to develop a set of tests less subject to cultural bias. On 17 neuropsychological tests that measured a variety of functions including immediate and short-term memory, learning, and sensory and motor capacities, 41 marihuana users who had smoked an average of 9 marihuana cigarettes a day for an average of 17 years did just about as well as controls, although on some of the learning and memory tests there was a slight and usually statistically non-significant tendency for the users to score lower. The two groups also scored the same on personality and intelligence tests. Within the marihuana-using group, the tests showed no significant differences between heavy users (7 cigarettes or more a day) and light users (less than 7 cigarettes a day).[19]

The results of these studies should make us skeptical of anecdotal reports from the Old World, especially from Egypt, which suggest what might otherwise be plausible: that cannabis, like alcohol, destroys the mental and physical health of a few who take it to excess. There seems to be no condition among *ganja* users that corresponds to that of the alcoholic or the heroin addict.

As pointed out in Chapter 10, it is very unlikely that the research done a few years ago that showed cannabis users to be more alienated, less well-adjusted academically, more impulsive and rebellious, or more cynical, moody, and bored than other college students indicates an effect of marihuana. Heavy drug users often show more depression, personality disorders, and poor social adjustment; in the case of marihuana, at any rate, excessive use of the drug is symptomatic rather than causative. The personality characteristics associated with marihuana in these studies are partly psychological problems or conditions that existed before the marihuana use began.

As the Jamaican study reveals, it is not even the case that heavy cannabis use must be a product of psychopathology; that depends more on the social role played by the drug and general attitudes toward it than on any characteristic of either the drug or its users. In other words, the personality characteristics associated with marihuana in older American studies are largely a product of its social status and are changing along with that social status. As long as use of marihuana is illegal and heavily stigmatized, those who turn to it are more likely to be different in various ways from more conventional people — either more moody, restless, hostile, bored, and dissatisfied with their lives or simply more self-critical, adventurous, and open to experience and therefore more willing to describe themselves in ways that might seem unflattering from a conventional point of view. Once marihuana use has begun, the reaction of society further shapes user attitudes. Marihuana users who began to take the drug at a time when they were likely to be identified as psychologically aberrant or as criminals, rebels, heroes, or prophets, may have tended to be bitter about the attitudes of the conventional world and hostile toward and fearful of its authority; those who begin to use it in the present era are less rebellious and less distinctive in their attitudes. Now that some of the social views and personal styles of the 1960's drug culture have become more popular, it is obvious that these traits never did imply a decisive change in personality; in particular, now that marihuana use has separated itself from other elements of this cultural pattern and is becoming common among people who otherwise lead conventional lives, it is clear that the drug does not have the capacity to alter personality once attributed to it — hopefully by its friends and fearfully by its enemies. We are already arriving at the situation described in the Rubin and Comitas study of Jamaica, where it is hard to find any significant differences in personality between those who use cannabis and those who do not.

Let us turn now to the physiological effects of cannabis. Marihuana is described in Chapters 3 and 10 as one of the least physiologically toxic of psychoactive drugs. Nothing has happened since 1971 to change that judgment. There is still no well-authenticated case of death from cannabis ingestion in a human being. In one recent incident, a small girl swallowed the enormous dose of 1.5 gm of cannabis resin (about 225 mg of Δ^1-THC, an amount equivalent to 25 or 50 ordinary marihuana cigarettes and rarely obtainable in such concentrated form): her condition was normal after a day.[20] Most of the recent research on health hazards of marihuana concerns long-term physical disease and organic pathology, partly because psychiatric research produced few results and partly because there are new experimental techniques for investigating phenomena like chromosome breaks, immune response, and brain damage. Before reviewing some of this often highly technical work, we should like to point out that clinical observation in marihuana-using populations generally shows no organic disease or deficiency attributable to the drug. The conclusions of the Indian Hemp Drugs Commission reported on page 277 have never been seriously challenged. It should be added that, as in the case of psychiatric illness, no level of use has yet been discovered that qualifies as obviously so immoderate that it causes physical disease. The La Guardia Committee came to the same conclusion as the Indian Hemp Drugs Commission, and the recent studies in Jamaica, Greece, and Costa Rica confirm the observations made in India and New York. An examination of chronic marihuana users in the United States finds no adverse effects on physical health after 2 to 17 years. Laboratory work on animals also indicates no serious pathological changes after chronic use.[21]

Recent investigations have concentrated on brain damage, testosterone levels, immune response, chromosome breakage, birth defects, and pulmonary function.

Brain damage. It is convenient to dispose of the least plausible claim first. We would expect some clinical evidence of serious brain damage if it existed — for example, some effect on neurological and neuropsychological tests in the Jamaican, Greek, and other studies — but none has been found. The recent controversy about brain damage and marihuana had its source in a report by A. M. G. Campbell and his associates in *The Lancet* for November 1971, in which they stated that the brains of 10 heavy marihuana smokers showed evidence of cerebral atrophy as demonstrated by air encephalography. The bias of the authors is indicated by their reference to marihuana users as "addicts" and their approving citation of the dubious work by Kolansky and Moore that associated cannabis use with mental illness. Even aside from this, the deficiencies of the Campbell study are crippling. All 10 subjects were psychiatric patients, and no comparison was made with psychiatric patients who did not use cannabis. At least 1 and maybe 2 were epileptics, several had suffered head injuries, 1 was mentally retarded, and as many as 5 may have been schizophrenic. All had taken LSD, most had used amphetamines, and a few were heavy users of opiates, barbiturates, and tranquilizers. The possible role of alcohol, which is known to be neurotoxic, was not considered. The peculiarity of this sample and the absence of controls make Campbell's results valueless. It would be useful to have controlled prospective studies on cannabis and brain damage, but there is little reason to expect that any connection will be discovered. In a controlled retrospective study of chronic cannabis users in Greece, for example, echoencephalography revealed no evidence of cerebral atrophy.[22]

Testosterone. The question of reduced testosterone levels and possible consequent impotence or sterility in men was raised in an article published by R. C. Kolodny and his associates in the *New England Journal of Medicine* in 1974. Kolodny found that chronic marihuana users had lower plasma testosterone levels than controls and that heavy users had lower levels than light users; he also found that abstention from marihuana after chronic use produced an immediate increase in plasma testosterone. In a later study he found that testosterone began to decline in subjects hospitalized on a research ward in their fifth week of smoking a predetermined amount of marihuana. Other studies failed to replicate these results either in retrospective surveys or on the experimental ward, but this work may have been methodologically inadequate. Cannabis resin in the diet of young male rats at very high doses (10 mg THC per kg per day, the equivalent of 700 mg in a 150-pound man) slows the development of the testes, prostate, and seminal vesicles; but it is apparently not estrogenic, since it does not accelerate uterine development in young female rats.[23]

The significance of these findings is very difficult to determine. Testosterone levels vary considerably from day to day and even from hour to hour without clear cause or obvious effect; it takes a very large decline to affect sexual performance much; even castration has highly variable effects on sexual activity in monkeys. Kolodny himself is cautious about drawing implications from his results. In a public discussion, he mentioned that two of his subjects on the research ward increased their testosterone levels up to 50 percent by lifting weights; he also admits that making a judgment about effects of testosterone depletion from a test taken once a day in like judging a person's behavior from snapshots taken once a day. Even after the reported decline, he found no testosterone levels that could be called subnormal; he concludes that the sexual effects in normal adult males would probably be negligible, but is more apprehensive about effects on children and adolescents and on fetal sex differentiation. In any case, Kolodny did not control for the effects of incarceration, and locking up men apart from women for a month or more might be expected to lower their sex hormone levels whether or not they smoked marihuana. However, he also found decreases in both testosterone and luteinizing hormone as an acute effect of a single marihuana cigarette. He states that the significance of these acute changes is unclear and recommends further investigation of the endocrine effects of marihuana.[24]

In a recent study of chronic heavy marihuana smokers in Costa Rica, W. J. Coggins and his colleagues reached reassuring conclusions about this question. They found no difference in plasma testosterone levels between cannabis-using and control groups, or between heavy and light users of cannabis. The authors suggest that tolerance develops to any possible inhibitory action of marihuana on the hypothalamic-pituitary axis that controls testosterone production. They note that their subjects began using marihuana at an average age of 15.2 years (one began at the age of 9), and they conclude that any transient decrease in testosterone levels that cannabis might have produced apparently had no effect on normal masculine development.[25]

Immune response. The effects of marihuana smoke and cannabinoids on immunological defenses constitute an unusually difficult research issue. Neither the reliability of the available measuring techniques nor the proper way of interpreting the results is agreed upon. Procedural variations in experiments alter the results, or retrospective design makes their significance questionable. Nothing certain can be extracted from the conflicting results of various studies. However, it is not too misleading to summarize as follows: Most evidence that suggests impairment of immune response by cannabis comes from test-tube research; the impairment has not generally been confirmed by studies on live subjects and as far as we know now does not increase susceptibility to infectious diseases or cancer in human marihuana users. For example, the Costa Rica study found no evidence of suppression of cell-mediated immune response. It is not clear whether the damage to lymphocytes observed in some experiments is caused by an ingredient peculiar to marihuana, as opposed to other substances present in the smoked material; the clinical significance is doubtful in any case, since the body has a great deal of reserve lymphocyte capacity. A recent review entitled "Marihuana and Immunity," after discussing in highly technical detail the methods used to examine cells for this purpose, concludes that nothing substantial has been proved.[26] Further information would require prospective studies and possibly full-scale epidemiological surveys, but it is unlikely that any effect will show up. The interest in this subject was created solely by laboratory research; there is no evidence of any kind of unexpected rise in the incidence of infectious disease (say, in the age

group 16 to 25) that might plausibly be traced to increasing marihuana use.

Chromosome damage and fetal defects. Assertions like the contention that marihuana causes violence or is a stepping-stone to
heroin are easy for the user to evaluate and repudiate. The suggestion that it causes chromosome damage in reproductive cells, of a
kind that might lead to birth defects, is very different and much
more frightening, because it represents the insidious unknown.
Studies by M. A. Stenchever and his co-workers reporting chromosome breaks in white blood cells caused by marihuana aroused great
interest and apprehension. But closer examination of this work and
further studies have revealed that marihuana users have very little
reason to worry about genetic damage. A recent review of the literature by S. Matsuyama concludes, "In summary, the available
cytogenetic data provide no definitive evidence for chromosome
damage as a result of marihuana use." In the same symposium A.
Falek states, "At present, genetic findings in drugs of abuse including marihuana are open to question . . . Possibly the equivocal findings are due to the relatively gross methods of analysis now
employed." In the discussion following these papers, Stenchever
himself in effect endorses these conclusions, which are also echoed
by the Fifth Annual Report of the Secretary of Health, Education,
and Welfare on "Marihuana and Health." [27]

Two characteristics of studies associating marihuana with genetic
damage make them questionable: they are based on examination
of body cells (not even reproductive cells in particular) rather than
on observation of actual fetal abnormalities; and they are retrospective, so that it is impossible to separate the effects of marihuana
from other factors. The relation between chromosome breaks in
body cells, or even reproductive cells, and genetic defects is uncertain. Many chemicals other than cannabis constituents, including
aspirin and diazepam (Valium), cause such breaks. Chromosome
breakage in nonreproductive cells or chromosome breakage that
merely creates a nonviable cell and does not lead to a rearrange-
ment of working genetic material is clinically of little importance.
Even on their own terms, cell studies do not support the suggestion
that cannabis causes genetic abnormalities. Although there may be
methodological deficiencies in their work, Rubin and Comitas report no chromosome abnormalities in Jamaican users; and recent
prospective studies on both animals and human beings have shown

no chromosome differences between cannabis users and controls.[28] The outcome here as in other areas of marihuana research seems to be that if we either analyze another culture where heavy marihuana use is not considered deviant or abandon retrospective design in studying our own culture, we find no evidence of health hazards.

Pulmonary function. The only well-documented common adverse effects of prolonged marihuana use are attributable to residual substances in the smoke rather than to the drug itself. Rubin and Comitas found that smokers had a lower postexercise bicarbonate level and reduced lung capacity; they concluded that smoking causes a mild functional hypoxia in body tissues. D. P. Tashkin and his associates found a "mild but statistically significant airway obstruction after 47 to 59 days of heavy smoking." Eleven of his 28 subjects smoked marihuana daily before as well as during the experiment, but none reported coughs, wheezing, or chest illness. Even at the end of the experiment, pulmonary function was still in the normal range.[29] Tobacco smoking has similar effects on the lungs; but they are probably more severe because tobacco does not dilate the bronchi like tetrahydrocannabinols, and also because heavy tobacco users smoke much more than even the heaviest marihuana users.

There is no convincing evidence that chronic use of cannabis does serious damage to the body or the mind. Among the psychoactive drugs available, it seems to be the least dangerous. Even a relatively conservative group of authorities like those who participated in the 1975 symposium headed by Tinklenberg on "Marihuana and Health Hazards" had little ill to speak of it. The question remains whether some pathology has been ignored either because it is too subtle to be detected even with modern laboratory techniques or because it is too rare to be uncovered without full-scale epidemiological analysis. The samples in the Jamaican, Greek, Costa Rican, and other research, it is said, were too small to reveal the kind of association represented by the relation of tobacco smoking to lung cancer; a prospective study on a much larger scale is needed before we can give marihuana a clean bill of health (something that no other drug or medicine has achieved). It has been estimated that this would require at least $2 million and 5 years.[30]

The never-ending call for more research before making policy changes is wearily familiar to advocates of legalization. It can be answered in two ways. First, the chances are poor that we will find out something new and important. Usually a large-scale study is undertaken because some unexpected correlation has been noticed, for example between mothers' use of DES (diethylstilbestrol) during pregnancy and daughters' vaginal cancer. The search for damaging effects of marihuana has been more like a fishing expedition than an attempt to validate a causal connection with an observed clinical abnormality. No one can prove that if we search long enough and hard enough we will not find a relation between marihuana use and some disease or deficiency, but there are more important uses for our medical resources, including those devoted to the study of marihuana.

The second and more important answer is that although continued research on cannabis will undoubtedly be of value — mostly for what it can teach us about the human organism as a biochemical, physiological, and psychological system — the cry that we still do not know enough should no longer be an excuse for delay in the matter of legalization: we *do* know enough about the disastrous effects of present policies. All the consequences cited in Chapter 13 still provide powerful arguments: the failure of deterrence, the financial costs of arrest and punishment, the ruined lives, the promotion of disrespect for the law, the use of police-state tactics by drug-enforcement agents, the economic niches created for organized crime, the dangers of adulteration and the resort to more harmful drugs, the destructive effect on honest drug education. If we balance the concrete, immediate, and substantial harm caused by the present punitive, repressive approach to marihuana against some dubious and nebulous possible cumulative effect of legalized marihuana use, it should be obvious where the weight falls. The prima facie case against such restrictions on liberty is a particularly strong one here. If advocates of prohibition want to continue trying to prove that some effect of legalized marihuana would be worse than the effects of criminal penalities for its use and sale, the burden of proof should be on them. Even this way of posing the question may grant too much to the prohibitionists: decriminalization has not caused use of marihuana to increase in the states where it is law, and full legalization would probably not make any greater difference. So there may be nothing at all to balance against the disadvantages and injustices of prohibition.

The transitory accommodation adumbrated in Chapter 13 as the emerging official policy on marihuana may be about to come into full flower. The formal legal arrangement would be civil penalties for possession of small amounts for personal use and continued prosecution of sale and possession with intent to sell as crimes, possibly misdemeanors when the amounts involved are small. There would also be an implied informal agreement that police should turn their attention elsewhere and especially that the federal government should spend less time and money trying to prevent smuggling. This compromise would undoubtedly be unstable — slightly dishonest, dangerously subject to the caprice of police and judges, and variable from state to state in a way that would create absurd and outrageous anomalies in arrests and sentencing. As long as marihuana use and especially marihuana traffic remain in this peculiar position neither within nor outside the law, demands for a consistent policy would remain strong. We would have to ask ourselves why, if using marihuana is relatively harmless, selling it is a felony; then we would have to decide whether to return to honest prohibition or move on to legalization. It should be clear which choice is preferable.

Since legalization of marihuana would not do any obvious harm and probably would not even affect the rate at which its use is increasing, there now seems to be little reason for opposing it. But reason has had limited influence in this matter. Past crusades against marihuana, as shown in Chapter 12, were often the expression of displaced anxiety, projection, and cultural factors that had nothing to do with the effects of the drug itself. In milder forms, these prejudices remain. For example, Dr. Robert L. DuPont, director of the National Institute on Drug Abuse, who now favors a civil fine for possession and continued criminal prosecution of bulk traffickers, is quoted in an interview in *Science* as warning that marihuana is dangerous because it represents "the leading edge of change in drug-using behavior."[31] This is either a non sequitur stating that marihuana use should remain illegal *because* it is becoming more common; or a revival in modified form of the discredited stepping-stone hypothesis; or, more likely, simply an expression of the kind of vague anxiety that should not be influencing policy. There is also some feeling that legalization would be bad because it would imply official endorsement of marihuana use. As though, after all these years, potential marihuana users are likely to change their attitudes to conform to what they believe is official approval! If anything, it might make them suspicious. Besides, legality would not imply endorsement in the case of marihuana any more than it does in the case of tobacco or alcohol. Again, it is the emotional symbolism involved rather than any anticipated actual effects of legalization that gives this kind of argument what weight it has.

Rigorously impartial scientific investigation is important to counteract the prejudice and irrationality that have characterized much of the debate about marihuana, but this impartiality should not be allowed to degenerate into a false objectivity that declares it unscientific to make policy recommendations. We should take the scientific conclusions where they lead us as citizens, and stop the increasingly unjustifiable persecution of marihuana users and sellers.

The increase in recreational use of marihuana has helped to revive interest in its medical uses. Although the possible dangers of marihuana when taken for pleasure and its possible usefulness as a medicine are two separate issues, they are historically and practically interrelated: historically, because the arguments used to justify public and official disapproval of recreational use have had unwarranted influence on opinions of its medical potential; and practically, because the more evidence accumulates that marihuana is relatively benign even when used chronically in large quantities, the more clear it becomes that the first requirement for a medicine — that it be safe — is satisfied. The medical history of cannabis derivatives outlined in Chapter 8 has become much more familiar to physicians and the public in the last few years, new research has been undertaken, and marihuana now looks more promising than ever as a therapeutic agent. We must qualify the following optimistic remarks by admitting that most recent research is tentative and that initial enthusiasm for drugs is often disappointed after further investigation. Nevertheless, it is not as though cannabis were an entirely new agent with unknown properties; its safety is well attested and there is plenty of informal evidence of its effectiveness in treating a variety of conditions over a period of thousands of years. In fact, it can be argued that its medical uses, including the seemingly new ones, are merely being rediscovered. It is still too soon to make a careful methodological analysis and evaluation of recent research, so our comments will be brief and in most cases only suggestive; but undoubtedly the weight of past and contemporary evidence combined will prove cannabis to be valuable as a medicine in several ways. Right now, removing bureaucratic and legal obstacles to its therapeutic use is particularly important.

As the discussion on pages 219–222 indicates, cannabis was used in the nineteenth century mainly as a sedative and analgesic. In Jamaica and elsewhere today, it serves as a skin liniment and a medicine for muscle pains and rheumatism. Research in Czechoslovakia in the 1950's (see page 223) suggested that the combined analgesic and antibiotic properties of cannabis made it useful in treating periodontal pain, middle ear infections, and burns. Cannabis was replaced in medical practice toward the end of the nineteenth century by the apparently more reliable hypodermic administration of opiates and then by synthetic drugs like aspirin and barbiturates; now that the dangers and disadvantages of these drugs are clearer, and cannabis derivatives that are easier to administer and more consistent in quality have become available, we should be reconsidering the use of cannabinoids for these purposes. A recent controlled double-blind experiment showed that smoking marihuana heightens pain tolerance, and paraplegics at a Veterans Administration hospital have reported some relief of phantom pain, spastic movements, and headache. Delta-1-tetrahydrocannabinol at the level of 15 mg relieves the pain of cancer patients, by an action that seems to be distinct from its sedative and euphoriant effects.[32]

Prospects for the use of cannabis derivatives as antidepressants are not so good. Recent controlled studies suggest doubt about their effectiveness in cases of moderate to severe depression; for example, in one experiment Δ^1-THC at 0.3 mg per kg (a fairly high dose) administered twice a day to depressed patients for a week in a double-blind experiment produced no mood change. Cannabinoids may be more useful when depression is a reaction to illness rather than the primary diagnosis; for example, THC improves the mood of cancer patients receiving chemotherapy.[33] Because these drugs are so safe, we should not give up hope too quickly for their use as antidepressants. Nevertheless, optimism is not justifiable at the moment.

Another potential use of cannabis discussed in Chapter 8 and still incompletely explored is its use for the relief of opiate and alcohol withdrawal symptoms and as a benign alternative for alcoholics and addicts. The legal and emotional obstacles to pursuing this application are now less formidable, but there is still very little recent research to report. Rubin and Comitas suggest that *ganja* in Jamaica provides protection from alcoholism and its consequences. It appears that there are almost no admissions to mental hospitals for alcoholism in Jamaica, even though many people there drink rum. A recent study in Boston concludes that alcoholics neither want to substitute marihuana for alcohol nor find it particularly useful by itself. However, there is some hope for the use of marihuana in combination with disulfiram (Antabuse), which protects the alcoholic by producing uncomfortable symptoms whenever he drinks.[34] For people who cannot avoid dependence on a drug but are able to substitute one drug for another, a cannabis habit would unquestionably be preferable to an alcohol or opiate (or tobacco) habit.

The medical literature on cannabis as an anticonvulsant remains sparse, and recent research has produced oddly conflicting results. One report describes a patient who needed marihuana as well as phenobarbitol and diphenylhydantoin (Dilantin) to control his epileptic seizures. Both delta-1-tetrahydrocannabinol and cannabidiol have been shown to raise the threshold of convulsive reaction to electric shock in mice. However, other experiments indicate that Δ^1-THC can activate seizures in naturally epileptic dogs, and one clinical case history suggests the same effect in a human marihuana smoker.[35] This capacity of Δ^1-THC to be either convulsant or anticonvulsant, another sign of the complexity of its pharmacological activity, reduces its prospects as an antiepileptic drug. Cannabidiol does not seem to have convulsant activity and may be useful for this purpose.

Although it is still almost universally reported that cannabis stimulates appetite and would therefore be useful in any illness where appetite loss is a problem — especially in the symptomatic treatment of anorexia nervosa — psychiatrists have not yet begun to experiment with marihuana or cannabinoids in treating this syndrome; they should certainly consider it.

Another possible use of cannabis is suggested by its dilation of the bronchi, which makes breathing easier. K. Vachon and his associates found that smoked marihuana reversed the bronchial constriction of asthmatic patients for hours. D. P. Tashkin and his associates, in a controlled study, determined that in asthmatics "inhaled delta-9-THC [delta-1-THC, in the notation we prefer] (in the form of marihuana) caused a prompt, complete, and sustained reversal of methacholine-induced bronchospasm and correction of the associated hyperinflation." Cannabinoids seem to relax bronchial smooth muscle by a mechanism different from that of the bronchodilators in current medical use. Smoking marihuana is a dubious way of treating asthma because of the chronic pulmonary effects, so some recent research has been aimed at finding a better method of administration. Delta-1-THC in the form of an aerosol spray works just as well as marihuana as a bronchodilator and produces less change in heart rate and less intoxicating central nervous system effect.[36]

One of the most promising medical uses for marihuana was unknown at the time *Marihuana Reconsidered* was published: reduction of intraocular pressure in cases of glaucoma. Glaucoma is a disease in which fluid pressure within the eyeball increases until it damages the optic nerve; it is the second leading cause of blindness in the United States. Experiments show that smoking marihuana causes a dose-related, clinically significant drop in intraocular pressure that lasts several hours in both normal subjects and those with the abnormally high ocular tension produced by glaucoma. Oral or intravenous Δ^1-THC has the same effect, which is apparently specific to cannabis constituents rather than a consequence of general euphoria and sedation, since diazepam (Valium), for example, does not produce it. About a million Americans suffer from wide-angle glaucoma, the most common form (90 percent of all cases) and the one treatable with cannabis. Cannabis does not cure the disease but can retard the progressive loss of sight when conventional medication fails and surgery is too dangerous. Topical application to the eyeball of Δ^1-THC or a synthetic cannabinoid may eventually prove preferable to smoking marihuana for this purpose.[37]

Some minor notoriety was achieved by a recent case which showed that unnecessary obstacles are still being put in the way of therapeutic use of cannabis, but also that the situation is improving. A young glaucoma sufferer named Bob Randall discovered while at college that smoking marihuana relieved some of his symptoms, especially visual distortions. He later took part in a research project in which marihuana was used to treat glaucoma; when that project ended, he had to go back to smoking it on his own — illegally. In the summer of 1976 he was arrested and charged with growing a few cannabis plants on his back porch. In November he was acquitted in the District of Columbia Superior Court on the rare defense of "necessity" to commit a criminal act. In effect, the court admitted that Randall needed marihuana to save his sight. Meanwhile he was petitioning the federal government to supply him with legal marihuana. After months of red tape and negotiations, during which officials of the three federal agencies involved suggested, among other "compromises," that he come to his doctor's office five times a day to smoke it, he was finally provided with government-grown marihuana under the auspices of a special research project directed by an ophthalmologist at Howard University, who will also be permitted to succor other glaucoma sufferers.[38] It is time we enabled ourselves to reach happy endings like this one by less complicated and devious means.

If the results of L. S. Harris and his associates in experiments on mice are confirmed, cannabinoids may even have some use in the treatment of cancer. They found that oral Δ^1-THC, Δ^6-THC and cannabinol reduced the size of lung tumors and lengthened survival time by a quarter to a third. Delta-1-THC also inhibited the growth of one kind of leukemia virus. The authors conclude that cannabinoids may be antineoplastic because they preferentially inhibit RNA and DNA synthesis in tumor cells.[39]

Probably the most promising use of cannabis in cancer treatment is to prevent vomiting in patients undergoing chemotherapy. In a study using placebo controls, oral Δ^1-THC prevented nausea and vomiting in 14 of 20 cancer victims who were not helped by conventional antiemetics; the dose was 15 mg every 4 hours.[40] Since cannabis also reduces pain, tranquilizes, sedates, and stimulates appetite, it might be helpful in many ways to these patients. So far it has proved impossible to get an Investigational New Drug application approved for a project that would allow similar research on children who have cancer. While this bureaucratic delay continues, an ironic contrast is provided by the widespread use of potentially more dangerous drugs like dextroamphetamine (Dexedrine) and methylphenidate (Ritalin) on children said to suffer from hyperkinesis or minimal brain dysfunction.

The greatest general advantage of cannabis as a medicine remains its unusual safety for a drug with such powerful effects: no addiction, no tolerance, extraordinarily high ratio of lethal to effective dose, practically no disturbance of physiological functions or organ toxicity. The main disadvantages are deterioration in potency (about 6 percent a year), insolubility in water and consequent difficulty in penetrating the bloodstream from the digestive tract, and the fact that marihuana contains so many ingredients with possible therapeutically disadvantageous effects (including too high a degree of intoxication). This last fact constitutes a problem but also an opportunity, since it suggests the manufacture of different cannabinoids, synthetic or natural, with properties useful for particular purposes. The other problems too should be easy to overcome by suitable technical advances.

Recreational use of cannabis has affected physicians' opinions of its medical potential in some irrational ways. When marihuana was regarded as the drug of blacks, Mexican Americans, and bohemians, doctors were ready to go along with the Federal Bureau of Narcotics, ignore its medical uses, and urge prohibition. The results of this alliance are incorporated in the Controlled Substances Act of 1970, which governs federal policy on psychoactive drugs; it places cannabis and its derivatives in Schedule I as drugs with a high potential for abuse and no current medical use. For years the National Organization for the Reform of Marihuana Laws (NORML) has been petitioning the federal government to change this classification, and it may soon succeed. Now that marihuana has become so popular among middle-class youth, we are more willing to investigate its therapeutic value seriously; recreational use is spurring medical interest instead of medical hostility. Whatever the cultural conditions that have made it possible, there is no doubt that the discussion about marihuana has become much more sensible. We are gradually becoming conscious of the irrationality of classifying this drug as one with a high abuse potential and no medical value. If the trend continues, it is likely that within a decade marihuana will be sold in the United States as a legal intoxicant. Even before that cannabis-derived compounds, possibly in the form of synthetic homologues of the natural cannabis constituents, will be available to physicians as prescription drugs.

Abbreviations

Selected Bibliography

Notes

Index

Abbreviations

Advance. Sci.	*Advancement of Science*
Amer. J. Med. Sci.	*American Journal of the Medical Sciences*
Amer. J. Nurs.	*American Journal of Nursing*
Amer. J. Obstet. Gynecol.	*American Journal of Obstetrics and Gynecology*
Amer. J. Orthopsychiat.	*American Journal of Orthopsychiatry*
Amer. J. Pharm.	*American Journal of Pharmacy*
Amer. J. Pharmacol.	*American Journal of Pharmacology*
Amer. J. Psychiat.	*American Journal of Psychiatry*
Amer. Rev. Resper. Dis.	*American Review of Respiratory Disease*
Ann. Intern. Med.	*Annals of Internal Medicine*
Ann. Medicopsychol.	*Annales Medico-Psychologiques* (Paris)
Arch. Gen. Psychiat.	*Archives of General Psychiatry*
Arch. Ges. Physiol.	*Archiv für Gesamte Physiologie*
Arch. Inst. Pasteur de Tunis	*Archives de l'institut Pasteur de Tunis*
Arch. Int. Pharmacodyn.	*Archives Internationales de Pharmacodynamie et de Therapie*
Arch. Neurol. Psychiat.	*Archives of Neurology and Psychiatry*
Arch. Pharm. Berl.	*Archiv der Pharmazie und Berichte der Deutschen Pharmazeutischen Gesellschaft* (Berlin)
Arch. Psychiat. Nervkrankh.	*Archive für Psychiatric und Nervenkrankheiten*
Behav. Neuropsychiat.	*Behavioral Neuropsychiatry*
Brit. Med. J.	*British Medical Journal*
Bull. Narcotics	*Bulletin on Narcotics*
Bull. Probl. Drug Dependence	*Bulletin, Problems of Drug Dependence*
Bull. WHO	*Bulletin of the World Health Organization*
Calif. Med.	*California Medicine*
Canad. Psychiat. Ass. J.	*Canadian Psychiatric Association Journal*
Chem. Commun.	*Chemical Communications*
Clin. Pharmacol. Ther.	*Clinical Pharmacology and Therapeutics*
Clin. Toxicol.	*Clinical Toxicology*
Compr. Psychiat.	*Comprehensive Psychiatry*

Dis. Nerv. Syst.	*Diseases of the Nervous System*
E. Afr. Med. J.	*East African Medical Journal*
Fed. Proc.	*Federation Proceedings*
Gaz. Nat. Moniteur Univ.	*Gazette Nationale, ou Le Moniteur Universel*
Guy. Hosp. Rep.	*Guy's Hospital Reports*
Harvey Lect.	*Harvey Lectures*
Indian J. Med. Res.	*Indian Journal of Medical Research*
Indian Med. Gaz.	*Indian Medical Gazette*
Indian Med. Res. Mem.	*Indian Medical Research Memoirs*
J. Abnorm. Soc. Psychol.	*Journal of Abnormal and Social Psychology*
J.A.M.A.	*Journal of the American Medical Association*
J. Amer. Chem. Soc.	*Journal of the American Chemical Society*
J. Amer. Coll. Health Ass.	*Journal of the American College Health Association*
J. Chem. Soc.	*Journal of the Chemical Society*
J. Clin. Pharmacol.	*Journal of Clinical Pharmacology*
J. Clin. Pharmacol. J. New Drugs	*Journal of Clinical Pharmacology and Journal of New Drugs*
J. Clin. Psychopathology	*Journal of Clinical Psychopathology*
J. Health Soc. Behav.	*Journal of Health and Social Behavior*
J. Kansas Med. Soc.	*Journal of the Kansas Medical Society*
J. Ment. Sci.	*Journal of Mental Science*
J. Mich. State Med. Soc.	*Journal of the Michigan State Medical Society*
J. Nerv. Ment. Dis.	*Journal of Nervous and Mental Disease*
J. Neurol. Neurosurg. Psychiat.	*Journal of Neurology, Neurosurgery and Psychiatry*
J. Pharm. Belg.	*Journal de Pharmacie de Belgique*
J. Pharmacol. Exp. Ther.	*Journal of Pharmacology and Experimental Therapeutics*
J. Psychedelic Drugs	*Journal of Psychedelic Drugs*
J. Travis County Med. Soc.	*Journal of the Travis County Medical Society*
J. Washington Acad. Sci.	*Journal of the Washington Academy of Science*
Life Sci.	*Life Sciences*
Medicoleg. J.	*Medico-Legal Journal*
Med. J. Rec.	*Medical Journal and Record*
Med. Sci.	*Medical Science*
Ment. Hyg.	*Mental Hygiene*
Milit. Surg.	*The Military Surgeon*
Mutat. Res.	*Mutation Research*
N. Carolina Med. J.	*North Carolina Medical Journal*
New Eng. J. Med.	*New England Journal of Medicine*
New Orleans Med. Surg. J.	*New Orleans Medical and Surgical Journal*
Pensiero med.	*Pensiero medico*
Pharm. J.	*Pharmaceutical Journal*
Pharmacol. Rev.	*Pharmacological Reviews*
Proc. Chem. Soc.	*Proceedings of the Chemical Society* (London)

Psychiat. Quart.	Psychiatric Quarterly
Public Health Rep.	Public Health Reports
Quart. J. Stud. Alcohol	Quarterly Journal of Studies on Alcohol
Quart. Rev.	Quarterly Review
Rev. Americana	Revista Americana (Rio de Janeiro)
Rhode Island Med. J.	Rhode Island Medical Journal
S. Afr. Med. J.	South African Medical Journal
St. Louis Med. Surg. J.	St. Louis Medical and Surgical Journal
Ther. Gaz.	Therapeutic Gazette
Toxicol. Appl. Pharmacol.	Toxicology and Applied Pharmacology
Vietnam Med. Bull.	Vietnam Medical Bulletin
W. Virginia Med. J.	West Virginia Medical Journal
War Med.	War Medicine
Z. Naturforsch.	Zeitschrift für Naturforschung; Teil B

Selected Bibliography

Abrams, S. "The Case Against Paton." *Student Magazine,* 2 (1969), 49–50.

Adams, R. "Marihuana." *Harvey Lect.,* 37 (1942), 168–197.

Adams, R., and B. R. Baker. "The Structure of Cannabinol VII. A Method of Synthesis of a Tetrahydrocannabinol Which Possesses Marihuana Activity." *J. Amer. Chem. Soc.,* 62 (1940), 2405–2408.

Adams, R., M. Harfenist, and S. Loewe. "New Analogs of Tetrahydrocannabinol." *J. Amer. Chem. Soc.,* 71 (1949), 1624–1628.

Aldrich, C. K. "The Effect of a Synthetic Marihuana-like Compound on Musical Talent as Measured by the Seashore Test." *Public Health Rep.,* 59 (1944), 431–433.

Allen, J. R., and L. J. West. "Flight from Violence: Hippies and the Green Rebellion." *Amer. J. Psychiat.,* 125 (1968), 364–370.

Allentuck, S., and K. M. Bowman. "The Psychiatric Aspects of Marihuana Intoxication." *Amer. J. Psychiat.,* 99 (1942), 248–251.

Ames, F. "A Clinical and Metabolic Study of Acute Intoxication with *Cannabis Sativa.*" *J. Ment. Sci.,* 104 (1958), 972–999.

Andrade, O. M. "The Criminogenic Action of Cannabis (Marihuana) and Narcotics." *Bull. Narcotics,* 16 (1964), 23–28.

Andrews, G., and S. Vinkenoog, eds. *The Book of Grass: An Anthology of Indian Hemp.* New York: Grove Press, 1967.

Anslinger, H. J., and C. R. Cooper. "Marihuana: Assassin of Youth." *American Magazine,* 124 (1937), 19–20, 150–153.

Anslinger, H. J., and W. F. Tompkins. *The Traffic in Narcotics.* New York: Funk and Wagnalls, 1953.

Asuni, T. "Socio-Psychiatric Problems of Cannabis in Nigeria." *Bull. Narcotics,* 16 (1964), 17–28.

Ausubel, D. P. "Controversial Issues in the Management of Drug Addiction: Legalization, Ambulatory Treatment, and the British System." *Ment. Hyg.,* 44 (1960), 535–544.

————— *Drug Addiction: Physiological, Psychological, and Sociological Aspects.* New York: Random House, 1958.

Baudelaire, C. "De l'ideal artificiel." *La Révue contemporaine,* Paris, 1858.

Becker, H. S. "History, Culture and Subjective Experience: An Exploration of the Social Bases of Drug-Induced Experiences." *J. Health Soc. Behav.,* 8 (1967), 163–176.

————— *Outsiders: Studies in the Sociology of Deviance.* New York: Macmillan, 1963.

Benabud, A. "Psycho-pathological Aspects of the Cannabis Situation in Morocco. Statistical Data for 1956." *Bull. Narcotics,* 9 (1957), 1–16.

Birch, E. A. "The Use of Indian Hemp in the Treatment of Chronic Chloral and Chronic Opium Poisoning." *Lancet,* 1 (1889), 625.

Blatt, A. H. "A Critical Survey of the Literature Dealing with the Chemical Constituents of *Cannabis Sativa.*" *J. Washington Acad. Sci.,* 28 (1938), 465–477.

Bloomquist, E. R. *Marijuana.* Beverly Hills, Calif.: Glencoe Press, 1968.

—— "Marijuana: Social Benefit or Social Detriment?" *Calif. Med.,* 106 (1967), 346–353.

Blum, R. H., and associates. "Drugs, Behavior, and Crime." *Society and Drugs: Social and Cultural Observations,* I (San Francisco: Jossey-Bass, 1969), 66.

Blumer, H., A. Sutter, S. Ahmed, and R. Smith. *The World of Youthful Drug Use.* ADD Center Project — Final Report. Berkeley: University of California, Jan. 1967.

Bose, B. C., A. Q. Saifi, and A. W. Bhagwat. "Observations on the Pharmacological Actions of Cannabis Indica. Part II." *Arch. Int. Pharmacodyn.,* 147 (1964), 285–290.

—— "Studies on Pharmacological Actions of *Cannabis Indica* (Linn.). Part III." *Arch. Int. Pharmacodyn.,* 147 (1964), 291–297.

Bouquet, R. J. "Cannabis." *Bull. Narcotics,* 2 (1950), 14–30.

—— "Cannabis, Part III–V." *Bull. Narcotics,* 3 (1951), 22–45.

Boyd, E. S., and D. A. Merritt. "Effects of a Tetrahydrocannabinol Derivative on Some Motor Systems in the Cat." *Arch. Int. Pharmacodyn.,* 153 (1965), 1–12.

—— "Effects of Barbiturates and a Tetrahydrocannabinol Derivative on Recovery Cycles of Medial Lemniscus, Thalamus, and Reticular Formation in the Cat." *J. Pharmacol. Exp. Ther.,* 151 (1966), 376–384.

Braude, M. C., and S. Szara, eds., *Pharmacology of Marihuana.* 2 vols. New York: Raven Press, 1976.

Brill, H. "Misapprehensions about Drug Addiction: Some Opinions and Repercussions." *Compr. Psychiat.,* 4 (1963), 157.

Bromberg, W. "Marihuana, a Psychiatric Study." *J.A.M.A.,* 113 (1939), 4–12.

—— "Marihuana Intoxication: A Clinical Study of Cannabis Sativa Intoxication." *Amer. J. Psychiat.,* 91 (1934), 303–330.

Bromberg, W., and T. C. Rogers. "Marihuana and Aggressive Crime." *Amer. J. Psychiat.,* 102 (1946), 825–827.

Burr, C. W. "Two Cases of Cannabis Indica Intoxication." *Ther. Gaz.,* 40 (1916), 554–556.

Burroughs, W. "Points of Distinction between Sedative and Consciousness-Expanding Drugs." *Evergreen Review,* Dec. 1964.

Cahn, R. S. "*Cannabis Indica* Resin, Part III: The Constitution of Cannabinol." *J. Chem. Soc.* (1932), pp. 1342–1353.

Caldwell, D. F., S. A. Myers, E. F. Domino, et al. "Auditory and Visual Threshold Effects of Marihuana in Man." *Perceptive Motor Skills,* 29 (1969), 755–759.

"Cannabis: Report by the Advisory Committee on Drug Dependence." London: Her Majesty's Stationery Office, 1968.

Carey, J. T. *The College Drug Scene.* Englewood Cliffs, N.J.: Prentice-Hall, 1968.

Carlini, E. A., and C. Kramer. "Effects of Cannabis Sativa (Marihuana) on Maze Performance of the Rat." *Psychopharmacologia,* 7 (1965), 175–181.

Carstairs, G. M. "Daru and Bhang: Cultural Factors in the Choice of Intoxicants." *Quart. J. Stud. Alcohol,* 15 (1954), 220–237.

Cary, E. H. "Report of the Committee on Legislative Activities." *J.A.M.A.,* 108 (1937), 2214–2215.

Charen, S., and L. Perelman. "Personality Studies of Marihuana Addicts." *Amer. J. Psychiat.,* 102 (1946), 674–682.

Chein, I., D. L. Gerard, R. S. Lee, and E. Rosenfeld, with the collaboration of D. M. Wilner. *The Road to H: Narcotics, Delinquency, and Social Policy.* New York: Basic Books, 1964.

Chopra, I. C., and R. N. Chopra. "The Use of Cannabis Drugs in India." *Bull. Narcotics,* 9 (1957), 4–29.

Chopra, R. N., and G. S. Chopra. "The Present Position of Hemp Drug Addiction in India." *Indian Med. Res. Mem.,* 31 (1939), 1–119.

Christison, A. "On the Natural History, Action, and Uses of Indian Hemp." *Monthly Journal of Medical Science,* 13 (1851), 26–45, 117–121.

Clarke, L. D., and E. N. Nakashima. "Experimental Studies of *Marihuana.*" *Amer. J. Psychiat.,* 125 (1968), 379–384.

Cohen, M., and D. F. Klein. "Drug Abuse in a Young Psychiatric Population." *Amer. J. Orthopsychiat.,* 40 (1970), 448–455.

Cohen, S. "Pot, Acid, Speed." *Med. Sci.,* 19 (1968), 30–35.

———— *The Beyond Within: The LSD Story.* New York: Atheneum, 1965.

———— and R. C. Stillman, eds. *The Therapeutic Potential of Marihuana.* New York: Plenum Publishing, 1976.

Connell, K. H. "Ether Drinking in Ulster." *Quart. J. Stud. Alcohol,* 26 (1965), 629–653.

Connery, G. "Control of Narcotic Addiction." *J.A.M.A.,* 147 (1951), 1162–1165.

Corey, M. J., J. C. Andrews, M. J. McLeod, J. R. MacLean, and W. E. Wilby. "Chromosome Studies on Patients (in Vivo) and Cells (in Vitro) Treated with Lysergic Acid Diethylamide." *New Eng. J. Med.,* 282 (1970), 939–941.

Council on Mental Health and Committee on Alcoholism and Drug Dependence, American Medical Association. "Dependence on Cannabis (Marihuana)." *J.A.M.A.,* 201 (1967), 368–371.

———— "Marihuana and Society." *J.A.M.A.,* 204 (1968), 1181–1182.

Crancer, A., J. M. Dille, J. C. Delay, J. E. Wallace, and M. D. Haykin. "Comparison of the Effects of Marihuana and Alcohol on Simulated Driving Performance." *Science,* 164 (1969), 851–854.

Creighton, C. "On Indications of the Hasheesh Vice in the Old Testament." *Janus* (Amsterdam) 8 (1903), 241–246, 297–303.

Crépet, M. J., ed. *Oeuvres complètes de Charles Baudelaire.* Paris: Louis Conard, 1928.

Culliton, B. J. "Pot Facing Stringent Scientific Examination." *Science News,* 97 (1970), 102–105.

Dally, P. "Undesirable Effects of Marijuana." *Brit. Med. J.,* 3 (1967), 367.

Davidson, C., ed. *Union Worthies, Number Eight Fitz Hugh Ludlow (Class of 1856).* New York: Union College, 1953.

Davis, J. P., and H. H. Ramsey. "Antiepileptic Action of Marijuana-Active Substances." *Fed. Proc.,* 8 (1949), 284–285.

Deakin, S. "Death from Taking Indian Hemp." *Indian Med. Gaz.,* 15 (1880), 71.

deRopp, R. S. *Drugs and the Mind.* New York: Saint Martin's Press, 1957.

Dhunjibhoy, J. E. "A Brief Resume of the Types of Insanity Commonly Met with in India, with a Full Description of Indian Hemp Insanity Peculiar to the Country." *J. Ment. Sci.,* 76 (1930), 254–264.

Dornbush, R. L., A. M. Freedman, and M. Fink, eds. *Chronic Cannabis Use.* New York: Annals of the New York Academy of Sciences, 1977.

Dorrance, D., O. Janiger, and R. L. Teplitz. "In Vivo Effects of Illicit Hallucinogens on Human Lymphocyte Chromosomes." *J.A.M.A.,* 212 (1970), 1488–1527.

Downing, D. F. "The Chemistry of the Psychotomimetic Substances." *Quart. Rev.,* 16 (1962), 132–162.

Drewry, P. H. "Some Psychiatric Aspects of Marihuana Intoxication." *Psychiat. Quart.,* 10 (1936), 232–242.

Dwarkanath, C. "The Use of Opium and Cannabis in the Traditional Systems of Medicine in India." *Bull. Narcotics,* 17 (1965), 15–19.

Ebin, D., ed. *The Drug Experience.* New York: Grove Press, 1961.

Eddy, N. B., H. Halbach, H. Isbell, and M. H. Seevers. "Drug Dependence: Its Significance and Characteristics." *Bull. WHO,* 32 (1965), 721–733.

"Effects of Alcohol and Cannabis during Labor." Editorial. *J.A.M.A.,* 94 (1930), 1165.

Epstein, S. S., and J. Lederburg. "Chronic Non-Psychiatric Hazards of Drugs of Abuse." *Science,* 168 (1970), 507–509.

Ewens, G. F. W. "Insanity following the Use of Indian Hemp." *Indian Med. Gaz.,* 39 (1904), 401–413.

———— *Insanity in India, Its Symptoms and Diagnosis with Reference to the Relation of Crime and Insanity.* Calcutta: Thacker, Spink, and Co., 1908.

Farnsworth, D. L. "The Drug Problem among Young People." *W. Virginia Med. J.,* 63 (1967), 433–437.

Farnsworth, N. R. "Hallucinogenic Plants." *Science,* 162 (1968), 1086–1092.

Fiedler, L. *On Being Busted.* New York: Stein and Day, 1970.

Fort, J. "Pot: A Rational Approach." *Playboy,* Oct. 1969, pp. 131, 154, 216–228.

Fossier, A. E. "The Marihuana Menace." *New Orleans Med. Surg. J.,* 84 (1931), 247–252.

Freedman, H. L., and M. J. Rockmore. "Marihuana: A Factor in Personality Evaluation and Army Maladjustment." *J. Clin. Psychopathology,* 7 (1946), 765–782 (Part I), and 8 (1946), 221–236 (Part II).

Gaoni, Y., and R. Mechoulam. "Cannabichromene, a New Active Principle in Hashish." *Chem. Commun.,* 1 (1966), 20–22.

———— "The Structure and Synthesis of Cannabigerol, a New Hashish Constituent." *Proc. Chem. Soc.* (1964), p. 82.

Garriott, J. C., L. J. King, R. B. Forney, and F. W. Hughes. "Effects of Some Tetrahydrocannabinols on Hexobarbital Sleeping Time and Amphetamine Induced Hyperactivity in Mice." *Life Sci.,* 6 (1967), 2119–2128.

Gaskill, H. S. "Marihuana, an Intoxicant." *Amer. J. Psychiat.,* 102 (1945), 202–204.

Geller, A., and M. Boas. *The Drug Beat.* New York: Cowles Book Co., 1969.

Gershon, S. "On the Pharmacology of Marihuana." *Behav. Neuropsychiat.,* 1 (1970), 9–18.

"Allen Ginsberg." Interview by T. Clark in *Writers at Work: The Paris Review Interviews, Third Series,* ed. G. Plimpton, introd. Alfred Kazin (New York, 1967), pp. 291–294.

Ginsberg, A. "The Great Marihuana Hoax: First Manifesto to End the Bringdown." *Atlantic Monthly,* Nov. 1966, pp. 104, 107–112.

Goode, E., ed. *Marijuana.* New York: Atherton Press, 1969.

———— "Marijuana and Sex." *Evergreen,* 66 (1969), 19–21, 72–74.

———— "The Marijuana Market." *Columbia Forum,* 7 (1969), 4–8.

———— "Multiple Drug Use among Marijuana Smokers." *Social Problems,* 17 (1969), 48–64.

Goodman, L. S., and A. Gilman, eds. *The Pharmacological Basis of Therapeutics.* New York: Macmillan, 1965.

Greenberg, D. S. "Hash in Holland: The Dutch Find It Easier to Let Traffic Flourish." *Science,* 165 (1969), 476–478.

Grinspoon, L. "Marihuana." *Scientific American,* 221 (1969), 17–25.

———— "The Psychiatric Aspects of the Use of Marihuana." Paper presented at the 123rd Annual Meeting of the American Psychiatric Association, San Francisco, Calif., May 1970.

———— "Marihuana." In *International Journal of Psychiatry: Current Issues in Psychiatry,* ed. J. Aronson. Vol. 9. New York: Science House, 1970.

Grlic, L. "Recent Advances in Chemical Research of Cannabis." *Bull. Narcotics,* 16 (1964), 29–38.

Grlic, L., and A. Andrec. "The Content of Acid Fraction in Cannabis Resin of Various Age and Provenance." *Experientia,* 17 (1961), 325–326.

Grossman, W. "Adverse Reactions Associated with Cannabis Products in India." *Ann. Intern. Med.,* 70 (1969), 529–533.

Hare, H. A. "Clinical and Physiological Notes on the Action of Cannabis Indica." *Ther. Gaz.,* 11 (1887), 225–228.

"Hasheesh Eater, The." *Putnam's Magazine,* Sept. 1856, pp. 233–239.

Hayman, M. "The Myth of Social Drinking." *Amer. J. Psychiat.,* 124 (1967), 585–594.

Hekimian, L. J., and S. Gershon. "Characteristics of Drug Abusers Admitted to a Psychiatric Hospital." *J.A.M.A.,* 205 (1968), 125–130.

Hensela, J. D., L. J. Epstein, and K. H. Blacker. "LSD and Psychiatric Inpatients." *Arch. Gen. Psychiat.,* 16 (1967), 554–559.

Hermon, H. C. "Psychedelicoanalysis." *J. Travis County Med. Soc.,* 13 (1968), 5, 21–25.

Heyndrickx, A., C. Scheiris, and P. Schepens. "Toxicological Study of a Fatal Intoxication by Man Due to Cannabis Smoking." *J. Pharm. Belg.,* 24 (1969), 371–377.

Hinkley, R. G. "Nonmedical Drug Use and the College Student." *J. Amer. Coll. Health Ass.,* 17 (1968), 35–42.

Hively, R. L., W. A. Mosher, and F. W. Hoffman. "Isolation of *trans*-Δ^6-Tetrahydrocannabinol from Marihuana." *J. Amer. Chem. Soc.,* 88 (1966), 1832–1833.

Hoch, P. H. "Comments on Narcotic Addiction." *Compr. Psychiat.,* 4 (1963), 143.

Hogan, R., D. Mankin, J. Conway, and S. Fox. "Personality Correlates of Undergraduate Marijuana Use." Paper presented at the Spring Meetings of the Eastern Psychological Association, Philadelphia, Pa., 1969.

Hollister, L. E. "Criminal Laws and the Control of Drugs of Abuse: An Historical View of the Law (Or, It's the Lawyer's Fault)." *J. Clin. Pharmacol. J. New Drugs,* 9 (1969), 345–348.

Hopkins, J. F. *A History of the Hemp Industry in Kentucky.* Lexington: University of Kentucky Press, 1951.

Horman, R. E., and A. M. Fox. *Drug Awareness.* New York: Avon Books, 1970.

Horton, D. "The Functions of Alcohol in Primitive Societies: A Cross-Cultural

Study." *Quart. J. Stud. Alcohol,* 4 (1943), 199–320.

Houghton, E. M., and H. C. Hamilton. "A Pharmacological Study of Cannabis Americana." *Amer. J. Pharm.,* 80 (1908), 16–20.

Isbell, H., C. W. Gorodetzsky, D. Jasinski, U. Claussen, F. von Spulak, and F. Korte. "Effects of (-) Δ^9-*trans*-tetrahydrocannabinol in Man." *Psychopharmacologia,* 11 (1967), 184–188.

Isbell, H., D. J. Jasinsky, C. W. Gorodetzky, F. Korte, U. Claussen, M. Haage, H. Sieper, and F. von Spulak. "Committee on Problems of Drug Dependence: Minutes of the 29th Meeting, 13, 14, 15, and 16 February, 1967. Lexington, Kentucky." *Bull. Probl. Drug Dependence* (1967), pp. 4836–4837.

James, G., and T. Rosenthal, eds. *Tobacco and Health.* Springfield, Ill.: Charles C Thomas, 1962.

Johnson, R. D. "Medico-Social Aspects of Marijuana." *Rhode Island Med. J.,* 51 (1968), 171–178.

Kabelík, J., Z. Krejčí, and F. Santavý. "Cannabis as a Medicament." *Bull. Narcotics,* 12 (1960), 5–23.

Kalant, O. J. *An Interim Guide to the Cannabis (Marihuana) Literature.* Addiction Research Foundation Bibliographic Series No. 2. Toronto, 1968.

Kaufman, J., J. R. Allen, and L. J. West. "Runaways, Hippies, and Marihuana." *Amer. J. Psychiat.,* 126 (1969), 717–720.

Keeler, M. H. "Adverse Reaction to Marijuana." *Amer. J. Psychiat.,* 124 (1967), 674–677.

——— "Motivation for Marihuana Use: A Correlate of Adverse Reaction." *Amer. J. Psychiat.,* 125 (1968), 386–390.

Keniston, K. "Alienation in American Youth." Paper presented at the Annual Convention of the American Psychological Association. New York, Sept. 1966.

——— "Heads and Seekers: Drugs on Campus, Counter-Cultures and American Society." *The American Scholar,* 38 (1968–69), 97–112.

Keup, W. "Psychotic Symptoms Due to Cannabis Abuse." *Dis. Nerv. Syst.,* 30 (1970), 119–126.

King, A. B., and D. R. Corven. "Effect of Intravenous Injection of Marihuana." *J.A.M.A.,* 215 (1969), 724–725.

King, F. W. "Marijuana and LSD Usage among Male College Students: Prevalence Rate, Frequency, and Self-Estimates of Future Use." *Psychiatry,* 32 (1969), 265–276.

Kingman, R. "The Green Goddess: A Study in Dreams, Drugs, and Dementia." *Med. J. Rec.,* 126 (1927), 470–475.

Klee, G. D. "Marihuana Psychosis: A Case Study." *Psychiat. Quart.,* 43 (1969), 719–733.

Kolb, L. "Marihuana." *Federal Prohibition,* 2 (1938), 22–25.

Krejčí, Z., M. Horak, and F. Santavý. "Hemp (Cannabis Sativa) — An Antibiotic. 3 Isolation and Constitution of Two Acids from Cannabis sativa." *Pharmazie,* 14 (1959), 349–355.

Laurie, P. *Drugs: Medical, Psychological, and Social Facts.* Middlesex, England: Penguin, 1967.

Loewe, S. "Studies on the Pharmacology and Acute Toxicity of Compounds with Marihuana Activity." *J. Pharmacol. Exp. Ther.,* 88 (1946), 154–161.

Louria, D. B. *Nightmare Drugs.* New York: Pocket Books, 1966.

Ludlow, F. H. *The Hasheesh Eater: Being Passages from the Life of a Pythagorean.* New York: Harper and Bros., 1857.

Mandel, J. "Hashish, Assassins, and the Love of God." *Issues in Criminology,* 2 (1966), 149–156.

—— "Who Says Marijuana Use Leads to Heroin Addiction?" *Journal of Secondary Education,* 43 (1968), 211–217.

Marcovitz, E., and H. J. Myers. "The Marihuana Addict in the Army." *War Med.,* 6 (1944), 382–391.

Margolis, J. S., and R. Clorfene. *A Child's Garden of Grass.* North Hollywood, Calif.: Contact Books, 1969.

"Marihuana Problem in the City of New York, The" (book review). *Science,* 101 (1945), 538.

"Marihuana Problems." Editorial. *J.A.M.A.,* 127 (1945), 1129.

"Marihuana Thing." Editorial. *J.A.M.A.,* 204 (1968), 1187.

Marshall, C. R. "A Review of Recent Work on *Cannabis Indica.*" *Pharm. J.,* 69 (1902), 131–132.

Mattison, J. B. "Cannabis Indica as an Anodyne and Hypnotic." *St. Louis Med. Surg. J.,* 61 (1891), 265–271.

Mayor's Committee on Marihuana. *The Marihuana Problem in the City of New York.* Lancaster, Pa.: Jaques Cattell Press, 1944.

McArthur, C., E. Waldron, and J. Dickinson. "The Psychology of Smoking." *J. Abnorm. Psychol.,* 56 (1958), 267–275.

McGlothlin, W. H. "Toward a Rational View of Hallucinogenic Drugs." MR-83 Institute of Government and Public Affairs, University of California, Los Angeles.

McGlothlin, W. H., and L. J. West. "The Marihuana Problem: An Overview." *Amer. J. Psychiat.,* 125 (1968), 370–378.

McMorris, S. C. "What Price Euphoria?: The Case against Marihuana." *Medicoleg. J.,* 34 (1966), 74–79.

Mechoulam, R. "Marihuana Chemistry." *Science,* 168 (1970), 1159–1166.

Mechoulam, R., and Y. Gaoni. "A Total Synthesis of *dl*-Δ^1-tetrahydrocannabinol, the Active Constituent of Hashish." *J. Amer. Chem. Soc.,* 87 (1965), 3273–3275.

Melges, F. T., J. R. Tinklenberg, L. E. Hollister, and H. K. Gillespie. "Marihuana and Temporal Disintegration." *Science,* 168 (1970), 1118–1120.

Mendelson, J. H., A. M. Rossi, and R. E. Meyer, eds. *The Use of Marihuana: A Physiological and Psychological Inquiry.* New York: Plenum Publishing, 1974.

Merrill, F. T. *Marihuana, the New Dangerous Drug.* Opium Research Committee, Foreign Policy Association, Inc., Washington Office, 1200 National Press Building, Washington, D.C. (March 1938).

Michaux, Henri. *Light through Darkness.* Trans. Haakon Chevalier. New York: Orion Press, 1961. (Originally published in France by Librairie Gallimard under the title *Connaissance par les gouffres.*)

—— *Miserable Miracle.* Trans. L. Varese. San Francisco: City Lights Books, 1953.

Mikuriya, T. H. "Historical Aspects of Cannabis Sativa in Western Medicine." *The New Physician* (Nov. 1969), pp. 902–908.

Miller, L. L., ed. *Marijuana: Effects on Human Behavior.* New York: Academic Press, 1974.

Mirin, S. M., L. M. Shapiro, R. E. Meyer, and R. C. Pillard. "Casual Versus Heavy Use of Marihuana: A Redefinition of the Marihuana Problem." Paper presented at the 123rd Annual Meeting of the American Psychiatric Association, San Francisco, Calif., May 1970.

Mizner, G. L., J. T. Barter, and P. H. Werme. "Patterns of Drug Use among College Students: A Preliminary Report." *Amer. J. Psychiat.*, 127 (1970), 15–24.

M'Meens, R. R. "Report of the Committee on Cannabis Indica." *Transactions of the Fifteenth Annual Meeting of the Ohio State Medical Society*, 15 (1860), 75–100.

Moreau, J. J. (de Tours). "Du Haschisch et de l'alienation mentale." Paris, 1845. Later published as a chapter in *La Psychologie morbide dans ses rapports avec la philosophie de l'histoire; ou de l'influence des neuropathies sur le dynamisme intellectuel*, Paris, 1859.

———— "Lypemanie avec stupeur; tendance à la démence — Traitement par l'extrait (principe résineux) de cannabis indica — Guérison." *Lancette Gaz. Hop.*, 30 (1857), 391.

Murphy, H. B. M. "The Cannabis Habit: A Review of the Recent Psychiatric Literature." *Addiction*, 13 (1966), 3–25.

Nowlis, H. H. *Drugs on the College Campus*. New York: Doubleday, 1969.

O'Donnell, J. A., and J. C. Ball, eds. *Narcotic Addiction*. New York: Harper and Row, 1966.

O'Shaughnessy, W. B. "On the Preparation of the Indian Hemp or Gunjah (*Cannabis Indica*): The Effects on the Animal System in Health, and Their Utility in the Treatment of Tetanus and Other Convulsive Diseases." *Transactions of the Medical and Physical Society of Bombay*, 8 (1842), 421–461.

Oursler, W. *Marijuana: The Facts, The Truth*. New York: Paul S. Eriksson, 1968.

Parker, C. S., and F. W. Wrigley. "Synthetic Cannabis Preparations in Psychiatry: I Synhexyl." *J. Ment. Sci.*, 99 (1950), 276–279.

Paton, W. D. M. "Drug Dependence — A Socio-Pharmacological Assessment." *Advance. Sci.* (Dec. 1968), pp. 200–212.

Perna, D. "Psychotogenic Effect of Marihuana." *J.A.M.A.*, 209 (1969), 1085–1086.

Phalen, J. M. "The Marihuana Bugaboo." *Milit. Surg.*, 93 (1943), 94–95. "Playboy Panel: The Drug Revolution." *Playboy*, Feb. 1970, pp. 53–74, 200–201.

Pond, D. A. "Psychological Effects in Depressive Patients of the Marihuana Homologue Synhexyl." *J. Neurol. Neurosurg. Psychiat.*, 11 (1948), 271–279.

Porche, F. *Charles Baudelaire*. Trans. J. Mavin. New York: Horace Liveright, 1928.

Postell, Wilfred. "Marihuana Use in Vietnam: A Preliminary Report." *Vietnam Med. Bull.* (1969).

Proceedings of the White House Conference on Narcotic and Drug Abuse. Washington: G.P.O., 1962.

Rand, M. E., J. D. Hammond, and P. J. Moscou. "A Survey of Drug Use at Ithaca College." *J. Amer. Coll. Health Ass.*, 17 (1968), 43–51.

"Recent Investigation of Marihuana." Editorial. *J.A.M.A.*, 120 (1942), 1128–1129.

Reichman, J. Testimony given before the Senate Public Health and Safety Committee. Los Angeles, Calif., Oct. 18, 1967.

Reynolds, J. R. "Therapeutic Uses and Toxic Effects of Cannabis Indica." *Lancet*, 1 (1890), 637–638.

Robbins, E. S., L. Robbins, W. A. Frosch, and M. Stern. "College Student Drug Use." *Amer. J. Psychiat.*, 126 (1970), 1743–1751.

Robinson, Victor. *An Essay on Hasheesh*. New York: Dingwall-Rock, 1925.

——— "Experiments with Hashish." *Ciba Symposia,* 8 (1946), 387–396, 404.

Rolls, E. J., and D. S. Clark. "Depersonalization Treated by Cannabis Indica and Psychotherapy." *Guy Hosp. Rep.,* 103 (1954), 330–336.

Rosevear, J. *Pot: A Handbook of Marihuana.* New York: University Books, 1967.

Rubin, V., and L. Comitas. *Ganja in Jamaica.* The Hague: Mouton, 1975.

Russell, P. B., A. R. Todd, S. Wilkinson, A. D. MacDonald, and G. Woolfe. *"Cannabis Indica.* Part VIII. Further Analogues of Tetrahydrocannabinol." *J. Chem. Soc.* (1941), pp. 826–829.

Schultes, R. E. "Hallucinogens of Plant Origin." *Science,* 163 (1969), 245–254.

Schwarz, C. J. "Toward a Medical Understanding of Marihuana." *Canad. Psychiat. Ass. J.,* 14 (1969), 591–600.

Siler, J. F., W. L. Sheep, L. B. Bates, G. F. Clark, G. W. Cook, and W. A. Smith. "Marihuana Smoking in Panama." *Milit. Surg.,* 73 (1933), 269–280.

Simon, W., and J. H. Gagnon. "Children of the Drug Age." *Saturday Review,* Sept. 21, 1968, pp. 60–63, 75.

Smith, A. E. W. *The Drug Users: The Psychopharmacology of Turning on.* Wheaton, Ill.: Harold Shaw Publishers, 1969.

Smith, D. E. "Acute and Chronic Toxicity of Marijuana." *J. Psychedelic Drugs,* 2 (1968), 37–47.

Solomon, D., ed. *The Marihuana Papers.* Indianapolis: Bobbs-Merrill, 1966.

Souief, M. I. "Hashish Consumption in Egypt, with Special Reference to Psychological Aspects." *Bull. Narcotics,* 19 (1967), 1–12.

Stanley, E. "Marihuana as a Developer of Criminals." *American Journal of Police Science,* 2 (1931), 252–261.

Starkie, E. *Baudelaire.* Norfolk, Conn.: New Directions, 1958.

Stockings, G. T. "A New Euphoriant for Depressive Mental States." *Brit. Med. J.,* 1 (1947), 918–922.

Symons, A., trans. *Baudelaire: Prose and Poetry.* New York: Albert and Charles Boni, 1926.

Talbott, J. A., and J. W. Teague. "Marihuana Psychosis: Acute Psychosis Associated with the Use of Cannabis Derivatives." *J.A.M.A.,* 210 (1969), 299–302.

Tauro, G. Joseph. "A Judicial Opinion: Commonwealth v. Joseph D. Leis and Ivan Weiss." *Suffolk University Law Review,* 3 (1968), 23–41.

Taylor, B. *The Land of the Saracens; or, Pictures of Palestine, Asia Minor, Sicily, and Spain.* New York: G. P. Putnam and Sons, 1855.

Taylor, E. C., K. Leonard, and Y. Sbvo. "Active Constituents of Hashish Synthesis of *dl-Δ⁶-3,* 4-trans-tetrahydrocannabinol." *J. Amer. Chem. Soc.,* 88 (1966), 367–369.

Taylor, E. C., and E. J. Strojny. "The Synthesis of Some Model Compounds Related to Tetrahydrocannabinol." *J. Amer. Chem. Soc.,* 82 (1960), 5198–5202.

Taylor, Norman. *Narcotics: Nature's Dangerous Gifts,* rev. ed. New York: Dell, 1963. (Earlier version published under the title *Flight from Reality* [New York: Duell, Sloan, and Pearce, 1949]).

Thompson, L. J., and R. C. Proctor. "Pyrahexyl in the Treatment of Alcoholic and Drug Withdrawal Conditions." *N. Carolina Med. J.,* 14 (1953), 520–523.

Tiffany, W. J., Jr. "The Mental Health of Army Troops in Viet Nam." *Amer. J. Psychiat.,* 123 (1967), 1585–1586.

Tinklenberg, J. R., ed. *Marijuana and Health Hazards: Methodological Issues in Current Research.* New York: Academic Press, 1975.

——— F. T. Melges, L. E. Hollister, and H. K. Gillespie. "Marihuana and Immediate Memory." *Nature,* 226 (1970), 1171–1172.

Todd, A. R. "The Hemp Drugs." *Endeavor,* 2 (1943), 69–72.

Tull-Walsh, J. H. "Hemp Drugs and Insanity." *J. Ment. Sci.,* 40 (1894), 21–36.

United Nations Single Convention on Narcotic Drugs, U. N. Doc. Sales No. 62, XI (1962).

U.S., Congress, House, Ways and Means Committee, *Taxation of Marihuana, Hearings on H.R. 6385,* 75th Cong., 1st sess., April 27, 1937.

Walton, R. P. *Marihuana, America's New Drug Problem.* Philadelphia: Lippincott, 1938.

Warnoch, J. "Insanity from Hasheesh." *J. Ment. Sci.,* 49 (1903), 96–110.

Waskow, I., J. E. Olson, C. Salzman, and M. M. Katz. "Psychological Effects of Tetrahydrocannabinol." *Arch. Gen. Psychiat.,* 22 (1970), 97–107.

Watts, A. W. *The Joyous Cosmology: Adventures in the Chemistry of Consciousness.* New York: Random House, 1965.

Weil, A. T. "Adverse Reactions to Marihuana." *New Eng. J. Med.,* 282 (1970), 997–1000.

Weil, A. T., and N. E. Zinberg. "A Scientific Report — The Effects of Marihuana on Human Beings." *New York Times Magazine,* May 11, 1969, pp. 28–29, 79–94.

Weil, A. T., N. E. Zinberg, and J. M. Nelsen. "Clinical and Psychological Effects of Marihuana in Man." *Science,* 162 (1968), 1234–1242.

West, L. J., and J. R. Allen. "Three Rebellions: Red, Black, and Green." In *The Dynamics of Dissent: Scientific Proceedings of the American Academy of Psychoanalysis,* ed. Jules H. Masserman. New York: Grune and Stratton, 1968.

Williams, E. G., C. K. Himmelsbach, A. Wikler, D. C. Ruble, and B. J. Lloyd. "Studies on Marihuana and Pyrahexyl Compound." *Public Health Rep.,* 61 (1946), 1059–1083.

Winick, C. "The Use of Drugs by Jazz Musicians." *Social Problems,* 7 (1960), 240–253.

Wittenborn, J. R., H. Brill, Y. P. Smith, and S. A. Wittenborn, eds. *Drugs and Youth: Proceedings of the Rutgers Symposium on Drug Abuse.* Springfield, Ill., Charles C Thomas, 1969.

Wolk, D. J. "Marijuana on the Campus: A Study at One University." *J. Amer. Coll. Health Ass.,* 17 (1968), 144–149.

Wolstenholme, G. E. W., and Julie Knight, eds. *Hashish: Its Chemistry and Pharmacology.* Ciba Foundation Study Group, No. 21. London: J. and A. Churchill, 1965.

Wood, T. B., W. T. N. Spivey, and T. H. Easterfield. "Charas: The Resin of Indian Hemp." *J. Chem. Soc.,* 69 (1896), 539–546.

Yawger, N. S. "Marihuana, Our New Addiction." *Amer. J. Med. Sci.,* 195 (1938), 351–357.

Zimmering, P., J. Toolan, R. Safrin, and S. B. Wortis. "Heroin Addiction in Adolescent Boys." *J. Nerv. Ment. Dis.,* 144 (1951), 19–34.

Zinberg, N. E., and A. T. Weil. "A Comparison of Marijuana Users and Non-Users." *Nature,* 226 (1970), 119–123.

Notes

INTRODUCTION

1. O. J. Kalant, *An Interim Guide to the Cannabis (Marihuana) Literature,* Addiction Research Foundation Bibliographic Series No. 2 (Toronto, 1968).
2. R. Adams, "Marihuana," *Harvey Lect.,* 37 (1942), 168–197.
3. E. R. Bloomquist, "Marijuana: Social Benefit or Social Detriment?", *Calif. Med.,* 106 (1967), 346–353.

1. THE HISTORY OF MARIHUANA IN THE UNITED STATES

1. R. H. Blum and associates, "Drugs, Behavior, and Crime," *Society and Drugs: Social and Cultural Observations* (San Francisco, 1969), I, 66.
2. B. Moore, *The Hemp Industry in Kentucky* (Lexington, Ky., 1905), p. 11.
3. J. Rosevear, *Pot: A Handbook of Marihuana* (New Hyde Park, N.Y., 1967), pp. 20–21.
4. G. Washington, "Diary Notes," in *The Book of Grass: An Anthology of Indian Hemp,* ed. G. Andrews and S. Vinkenoog (New York, 1967), p. 34.
5. E. M. Houghton and H. C. Hamilton, "A Pharmacological Study of Cannabis Americana," *Amer. J. Pharmacol.,* 80 (1908), 17.
6. J. F. Hopkins, *A History of the Hemp Industry in Kentucky* (Lexington, Ky., 1951), pp. 67, 95, 156–158.
7. V. Robinson, *An Essay on Hasheesh* (New York, 1925), p. 21.
8. Houghton and Hamilton, "Pharmacological Study of Cannabis Americana," pp. 16–20.
9. E. H. Cary, "Report of the Committee on Legislative Activities," *J.A.M.A.,* 108 (1937), 2214.
10. R. P. Walton, *Marihuana, America's New Drug Problem* (Philadelphia, 1938), p. 31
11. M. Mezzrow and B. Wolfe, *Really the Blues* (New York, 1946), p. 72.
12. Ibid., pp. 262–263.
13. Walton, *Marihuana,* p. 30.
14. A. E. Fossier, "The Marihuana Menace," *New Orleans Med. Surg. J.,* 84 (1931), 249.
15. "Editor's Foreword: The Marihuana Myths," in *The Marihuana Papers,* ed. D. Solomon (Indianapolis, 1966), p. xv.
16. V. Vaughn, "Prey on Children with New 'Killer Drug,'" *Boston Herald,* Feb. 28, 1937.

17. Walton, *Marihuana,* p. 31.
18. *FBI Law Enforcement Bulletin,* 6 (1937), 14–15; F. T. Merrill, *Marihuana, The New Dangerous Drug,* Opium Research Committee, Foreign Policy Association, Inc., Washington Office, 1200 National Press Building, Washington, D.C. (March, 1938), pp. 3, 15, 28; W. Bromberg, "Marihuana: A Psychiatric Study," *J.A.M.A.,* 113 (1939), 9.
19. Bromberg, "Marihuana: A Psychiatric Study," p. 9.
20. W. Bromberg, "Marihuana Intoxication," *Amer. J. Psychiat.,* 91 (1934), 307.
21. H. S. Becker, *Outsiders: Studies in the Sociology of Deviance* (New York, 1963), p. 141.
22. H. J. Anslinger and W. F. Tompkins, *The Traffic in Narcotics* (New York, 1953), pp. 23–24.
23. J. F. Siler et al., "Marihuana Smoking in Panama," *Milit. Surg.,* 73 (1933), 269–280.
24. "Marihuana, Amazing Drug," *World Digest,* Jan. 1937, p. 7.
25. Becker, *Outsiders,* pp. 140–141.
26. U.S. Congress, House, Ways and Means Committee, *Taxation of Marihuana, Hearings on H.R. 6385,* 75th Cong., 1st sess., April 27, 1937, statement of C. Hester, Ass't. General Counsel for the Treasury Dept., pp. 12–13; "The Marihuana Tax Act of 1937," in *Marihuana Papers,* ed. Solomon, pp. 424–438.
27. *Taxation of Marihuana, Hearings on H.R. 6385,* p. 18.
28. R. Fitzgerald, trans., *The Odyssey* (Garden City, N.Y., 1961), pp. 160, 184.
29. J. Mandel, "Hashish, Assassins, and the Love of God," *Issues in Criminology,* 2 (1966), 149–156.
30. *Taxation of Marihuana, Hearings on H.R. 6385,* p. 24.
31. Bromberg, "Marihuana Intoxication," pp. 327–328.
32. *Taxation of Marihuana, Hearings on H.R. 6385,* p. 50.
33. Ibid., pp. 91, 94.
34. Ibid., p. 117.
35. Ibid., p. 116.
36. Mayor's Committee on Marihuana, *The Marihuana Problem in the City of New York* (Lancaster, Pa., 1944), pp. 214–220.
37. J. M. Phalen, "The Marihuana Bugaboo," *Milit. Surg.,* 93 (1943), 94–95.
38. Anslinger and Tompkins, *Traffic in Narcotics,* p. 168.
39. S. Allentuck and K. M. Bowman, "The Psychiatric Aspects of Marihuana Intoxication," *Amer. J. Psychiat.,* 99 (1942), 248–251; editorial, "Recent Investigation of Marihuana," *J.A.M.A.,* 120 (1942), 1128–1129; letter, Anslinger, "The Psychiatric Aspects of Marihuana Intoxication," *J.A.M.A.,* 121 (1943), 212–213; letter, Bouquet, "Marihuana Intoxication," *J.A.M.A.,* 124 (1944), 1010–1011; editorial, "Marihuana Problems," *J.A.M.A.,* 127 (1945), 1129; R. S. deRopp, *Drugs and the Mind* (New York, 1957), pp. 108–109.
40. "The Marihuana Problem," *Science,* 101 (1945), 538.
41. Council on Mental Health and Committee on Alcoholism and Drug Dependence, American Medical Association, "Dependence on Cannabis (Marihuana)," *J.A.M.A.,* 201 (1967), 368–371; Council on Mental Health and Committee on Alcoholism and Drug Dependence, American Medical Association, "Marihuana and Society," *J.A.M.A.,* 204 (1968), 1181–1182.

2. FROM PLANT TO INTOXICANT

1. D. B. Louria, *Nightmare Drugs* (New York, 1966), p. 32.
2. Ibid., p. 32 (citing R. G. Wasson, *Soma: The Divine Mushroom of Immortality* [New York, 1968]).
3. R. E. Schultes, "Hallucinogens of Plant Origin," *Science,* 163 (1969), 245.
4. Ibid., p. 246; N. R. Farnsworth, "Hallucinogenic Plants," *Science,* 162 (1968), p. 1089.
5. Schultes, "Hallucinogens of Plant Origin," p. 247; Farnsworth, "Hallucinogenic Plants," p. 1089.
6. W. H. McGlothlin, "Toward a Rational View of Hallucinogenic Drugs," MR-83 Institute of Government and Public Affairs, University of California, Los Angeles, p. 9; also in J. L. Simmons, ed., *Marihuana Myths and Realities* (Hollywood, Calif., 1967), pp. 163–214; W. H. McGlothlin, *Hallucinogenic Drugs: A Perspective with Special Reference to Peyote and Cannabis* (July 1964; chap. 2 covers the history of peyote use); Farnsworth, "Hallucinogenic Plants," p. 1089.
7. Farnsworth, "Hallucinogenic Plants," pp. 1090–1091.
8. Schultes, "Hallucinogens of Plant Origin," p. 246; Farnsworth, "Hallucinogenic Plants," p. 1092.
9. E. R. Bloomquist, *Marijuana* (Beverly Hills, Calif., 1968), p. 4; N. S. Yawger, "Marihuana, Our New Addiction," *Amer. J. Med. Sci.,* 195 (1938), 351; J. Rosevear, *Pot: A Handbook of Marihuana* (New Hyde Park, N.Y., 1967), pp. 38, 42.
10. J. W. Folstad, "Spectrum," *Environment,* 12 (1970), S-1, S-2.
11. F. Rabelais, "The Herb Pantagruelion," trans. Samuel Putnam, in *The Marihuana Papers,* ed. D. Solomon (Indianapolis, 1966), p. 114.
12. Ibid., p. 107.
13. Ibid.
14. H. Carter, trans., *The Histories of Herodotus* (New York, 1958), 1. 4. 75 (p. 256).
15. R. J. Bouquet, "Cannabis," *Bull. Narcotics,* 2 (1950), p. 17.
16. Rabelais, "The Herb Pantagruelion," p. 107.
17. Yawger, "Marihuana, Our New Addiction," p. 352.
18. Ibid., p. 352. "When ripe, the small, whitish flowers at the top of the female plant are found to yield a sticky greenish, resinous substance which contains the active principle of marihuana; however, recent research by Munch showed definitely that the substance may also be obtained from the male plant."
19. Bouquet, "Cannabis," p. 19.
20. J. H. Schaffner, "The Influence of Relative Length of Daylight on the Reversal of Sex in Hemp," *Ecology,* 4 (1923), 323.
21. Bouquet, "Cannabis," p. 15.
22. Ibid., p. 19.
23. *Les Remedes galeniques* (Paris, 1925), p. 926, as cited by Bouquet, "Cannabis," p. 20.
24. Bloomquist, *Marijuana,* p. 3.
25. Ibid., pp. 3–4.
26. Bouquet, "Cannabis," p. 22 (citing League of Nations document O. C. 15420).

27. Ibid., p. 23; see Farnsworth, "Hallucinogenic Plants," p. 1087, for general description of *bhang, ganja,* and *charas.*
28. W. B. O'Shaughnessy, "On the Preparation of the Indian Hemp, or Gunjah (*Cannabis Indica*): The Effects on the Animal System in Health, and Their Utility in the Treatment of Tetanus and Other Convulsive Diseases," *Transactions of the Medical and Physical Society of Bombay* (Calcutta, 1842), p. 425.
29. R. Adams, "Marihuana," *Science,* 92 (1940), 116.
30. Quoted in A. Christison, "On the Natural History, Action and Uses of Indian Hemp," *Monthly Journal of Medical Science,* 13 (1851), 32.
31. Many articles comment upon these processes, including the following: Bouquet, "Cannabis," p. 24; N. Taylor, "The Pleasant Assassin," in *Marihuana Papers,* ed. Solomon, pp. 3–17, see esp. p. 8.

3. CHEMISTRY AND PHARMACOLOGY

1. Chemical investigation of cannabis products has evolved with the science of chemistry. A series of reviews has appeared over the years; some of the more notable include the following: C. R. Marshall, "A Review of Recent Work on *Cannabis Indica,*" *Pharm. J.,* 69 (1902), 131; A. H. Blatt, "A Critical Survey of the Literature Dealing with the Chemical Constituents of *Cannabis Sativa,*" *J. Washington Acad. Sci.,* 28 (1938), 465–477; R. Adams, "Marihuana," *Harvey Lect.,* 37 (1942), 168–197; A. R. Todd, "The Hemp Drugs," *Endeavor,* 2 (1943), 69–72; D. F. Downing, "The Chemistry of the Psychotomimetic Substances," *Quart. Rev.,* 16 (1962), 132–162; N. R. Farnsworth, "Hallucinogenic Plants," *Science,* 162 (1968), 1086–1092; S. Gershon, "On the Pharmacology of Marihuana," *Behav. Neuropsychiat.,* 1 (1970), 9–18; R. Mechoulam, "Marihuana Chemistry," *Science,* 168 (1970), 1159–1166.
2. T. B. Wood, W. T. N. Spivey, and T. H. Easterfield, "Charas: The Resin of Indian Hemp," *J. Chem. Soc.,* 69 (1896), 539–546; T. B. Wood, W. T. N. Spivey, and T. H. Easterfield, "Cannabinol, Part I," *J. Chem. Soc.,* 75 (1899), 20–36.
3. R. P. Walton, *Marihuana, America's New Drug Problem* (Philadelphia, 1938), p. 187.
4. R. S. Cahn, "*Cannabis Indica* Resin, Part III; The Constitution of Cannabinol," *J. Chem. Soc.* (1932), pp. 1342–1353.
5. R. Adams and B. R. Baker, "The Structure of Cannabinol. VII. A Method of Synthesis of a Tetrahydrocannabinol Which Possesses Marihuana Activity," *J. Amer. Chem. Soc.,* 62 (1940), 2405; Adams, "Marihuana," pp. 168–197; R. Adams, M. Harfenist, and S. Loewe, "New Analogs of Tetrahydrocannabinol," *J. Amer. Chem. Soc.,* 71 (1949), 1624–1628.
6. D. F. Downing, "The Chemistry of Psychotomimetic Substances," *Quart. Rev.,* 16 (1962), 132–162.
7. A. R. Todd, "Hashish," *Experientia,* 2 (1946), 55–60.
8. Adams, Harfenist, and Loewe, "New Analogs of Tetrahydrocannabinol."
9. E. C. Taylor and E. J. Strojny, "The Synthesis of Some Model Compounds Related to Tetrahydrocannabinol," *J. Amer. Chem. Soc.,* 82 (1960), 5198–5202.
10. P. B. Russell et al., "*Cannabis indica.* Part VIII. Further Analogues of Tetrahydrocannabinol," *J. Chem. Soc.* (1941), pp. 826–829; Adams,

Harfenist, and Loewe, "New Analogs of Tetrahydrocannabinol," pp. 1624–1628.

11. D. F. Downing, "The Chemistry of the Psychotomimetic Substances," *Quart. Rev.*, 16 (1962), 156. Downing cites S. Loewe, "Studies on the Pharmacology and Acute Toxicity of Compounds with Marihuana Activity," *J. Pharmacol. Exp. Ther.*, 88 (1946), 154–161, but this citation appears to be inadequate substantiation for his claim.

12. Adams, "Marihuana," p. 170.

13. R. Mechoulam and Y. Gaoni, "A Total Synthesis of *dl*-Δ^1-tetrahydrocannabinol, the Active Constituent of Hashish," *J. Amer. Chem. Soc.*, 87 (1965), 3273–3275.

14. Y. Gaoni and R. Mechoulam, "Cannabichromene, a New Active Principle in Hashish," *Chem. Commun.*, 1 (1966), 20–22.

15. Y. Gaoni and R. Mechoulam, "The Structure and Synthesis of Cannabigerol, a New Hashish Constituent," *Proc. Chem. Soc.* (March 1964), p. 82.

16. R. L. Hively et al., "Isolation of *trans*-Δ^6-tetrahydrocannabinol from Marihuana," *J. Amer. Chem. Soc.*, 88 (1966), 1832–1833.

17. E. C. Taylor, K. Leonard, and Y. Sbvo, "Active Constituents of Hashish Synthesis of *dl*-Δ^6-*3,4,-trans*-tetrahydrocannabinol," *J. Amer. Chem. Soc.*, 88 (1966), 367.

18. R. Mechoulam, "Marihuana Chemistry," *Science*, 168 (1970), 1160–1161.

19. Ibid., p. 1161.

20. F. Korte and H. Sieper, "Recent Results of Hashish Analysis," in *Hashish: Its Chemistry and Pharmacology*, ed. G. E. W. Wolstenholme and J. Knight (Boston, 1965), pp. 15–30; O.-E. Schultz and G. Haffner, "Zur Kenntnis eines sedativen und antibakteriellen Wirkstoffes aus dem deutschen Faserhanf (*Cannabis sativa*)," *Z. Naturforsch.*, 14b (1959), 99.

21. L. Grlic and A. Andrec, "The Content of Acid Fraction in Cannabis Resin of Various Age and Provenance," *Experientia*, 17 (1961), 325–326; L. Grlic, "Recent Advances in Chemical Research of Cannabis," *Bull. Narcotics*, 16 (1964), 29–38.

22. O.-E. Schultz and G. Haffner, "Zur Kenntnis eines sedativen Wirkstoffes aus dem deutschen Faserhanf (*Cannabis sativa*)," *Arch. Pharm. Berl.*, 291 (1958), 391–403; Korte and Sieper, "Recent Results of Hashish Analysis," pp. 15–30.

23. Z. Krejčí, M. Horak, and F. Santavý, "Hemp (Cannabis Sativa) — An Antibiotic. 3 Isolation and Constitution of Two Acids from Cannabis Sativa," *Pharmazie*, 14 (1959), 349.

24. Gershon, "Pharmacology of Marihuana," pp. 9–18.

25. S. Loewe, "Pharmacological Study," in Mayor's Committee on Marihuana, *The Marihuana Problem in the City of New York* (Lancaster, Pa., 1944), p. 207.

26. J. C. Garriott et al., "Effects of Some Tetrahydrocannabinols on Hexobarbital Sleeping Time and Amphetamine Induced Hyperactivity in Mice," *Life Sci.*, 6 (1967), 2119–2128.

27. S. P. Epstein and J. Lederberg, "Chronic Non-Psychiatric Hazards of Drugs of Abuse," *Science*, 168 (1970), 507–509.

28. E. Joël, "Beitrage sur Pharmakologie der Korperstellung und der Labyrinthreflexe. XIII. Haschisch," *Arch. Ges. Physiol.*, 209 (1925), 526.

29. B. C. Bose, A. Q. Saifi, and A. W. Bhagwat, "Studies on Pharmacological

Actions of *Cannabis indica* (Linn.) Part III," *Arch. Int. Pharmacodyn.*, 147 (1964), 291.

30. B. C. Bose, A. Q. Saifi, and A. W. Bhagwat, "Observations on the Pharmacological Actions of Cannabis Indica. Part II," *Arch. Int. Pharmacodyn.*, 147 (1964), 285–290.

31. Gershon, "Pharmacology of Marihuana," p. 13.

32. C. J. Miras, "Some Aspects of Cannabis Action," in *Hashish,* ed. Wolstenholme and Knight, p. 43.

33. E. S. Boyd and D. A. Merritt, "Effects of a Tetrahydrocannabinol Derivative on Some Motor Systems in the Cat," *Arch. Int. Pharmacodyn.*, 153 (1965), 1; E. S. Boyd and D. A. Merritt, "Effects of Barbiturates and a Tetrahydrocannabinol Derivative on Recovery Cycles of Medical Lemniscus, Thalamus, and Reticular Formation in the Cat," *J. Pharmacol. Exp. Ther.*, 151 (1966), 376.

34. E. A. Carlini and C. Kramer, "Effects of *Cannabis Sativa* (Marihuana) on Maze Performance of the Rat," *Psychopharmacologica,* 7 (1965), 175.

35. L. J. Thompson and R. C. Proctor, "Pyrahexyl in the Treatment of Alcoholic and Drug Withdrawal Conditions," *N. Carolina Med. J.,* 14 (1953), 521.

36. E. G. Williams et al., "Studies on Marihuana and Pyrahexyl Compound," *Public Health Rep.,* 61 (1946), 1064–1067.

37. Ibid., p. 1074.

38. Ibid., pp. 1073–1074.

39. Adams, "Marihuana," pp. 168–197.

40. A. T. Weil et al., "A Scientific Report — The Effects of Marijuana on Human Beings," *New York Times Magazine,* May 11, 1969, p. 79.

41. A. T. Weil et al., "Clinical and Psychological Effects of Marihuana in Man," *Science,* 162 (1968), 1240.

42. H. Isbell et al., "Committee on Problems of Drug Dependence: Minutes of the 29th Meeting, 13, 14, 15 and 16 February, 1967. Lexington, Kentucky," *Bull. Prob. Drug Dependence* (1967), pp. 4836–4837.

43. Ibid., p. 4834.

44. Weil et al., "Clinical and Psychological Effects," p. 1240.

45. S. Allentuck and K. M. Bowman, "The Psychiatric Aspects of Marihuana Intoxication," *Amer. J. Psychiat.*, 99 (1942), 248.

46. Weil et al., "Scientific Report," p. 89.

47. On an increase in blood pressure, see Walton, *Marihuana,* p. 105; J. H. Jaffe, "Cannabis (Marijuana)," in *The Pharmacological Basis of Therapeutics,* ed. L. S. Goodman and A. Gilman, 3rd ed. (New York, 1965), p. 300 (also in *Marijuana,* ed. E. Goode [New York, 1969], p. 49); Allentuck and Bowman, "Psychiatric Aspects of Marihuana Intoxication," p. 248; J. Rosevear, *Pot: A Handbook of Marihuana* (New York, 1967), p. 84; Thompson and Proctor, "Pyrahexyl in Treatment of Withdrawal," pp. 522–523. On a decrease in blood pressure: Walton, *Marihuana,* p. 125; H. S. Gaskill, "Marihuana, an Intoxicant." *Amer. J. Psychiat.*, 102 (1945), 202–203; I. Waskow et al., "Psychological Effects of Tetrahydrocannabinol," *Arch. Gen. Psychiat.*, 22 (1970), 100. On no change in blood pressure: J. F. Siler et al., "Marihuana Smoking in Panama," *Milit. Surg.*, 73 (1933), 278; Adams, "Marihuana," p. 169; Isabell et al., "Committee on Drug Dependence," p. 4836.

48. Walton, *Marihuana,* p. 125; Jaffe, "Cannabis (Marijuana)," p. 300; Allentuck and Bowman, "Psychiatric Aspects of Marihuana Intoxication," p.

248; Siler et al., "Marihuana Smoking in Panama," p. 278; S. F. Yolles, "Recent Research on LSD, Marijuana, and Other Dangerous Drugs," in *Drug Awareness,* ed. R. E. Horman and A. M. Fox (New York, 1970), p. 77; M. H. Keeler, "Adverse Reaction to Marijuana," *Amer. J. Psychiat.,* 124 (1967), 675; Thompson and Proctor, "Pyrahexyl in Treatment of Withdrawal," pp. 432–433; Waskow et al., "Psychological Effects of Tetrahydrocannabinol," p. 9.

49. Weil et al., "Clinical and Psychological Effects," pp. 1239, 1242.
50. Isbell et al., "Committee on Drug Dependence," p. 4836.
51. On hypoglycemia: Walton, *Marihuana,* p. 123; N. B. Eddy et al., "Drug Dependence: Its Significance and Characteristics," *Bull. WHO,* 32 (1965), 729; S. Cohen, "Pot, Acid, and Speed," *Med Sci.,* 19 (1968), 32; E. R. Bloomquist, "Marijuana, Social Benefit or Social Detriment?" *Calif Med.,* 106 (1967), 347. On hyperglycemia: Jaffe, "Cannabis (Marijuana)," p. 300; S. Allentuck, "Medical Aspects: Symptoms and Behavior," in Mayor's Committee, *The Marihuana Problem,* p. 50.
52. Weil et al., "Clinical and Psychological Effects," p. 1242.
53. H. Isbell et al., "Effects of (-)Δ⁹-*trans*-tetrahydrocannabinol in man," *Psychopharmacologica,* 11 (1967), 181; H. Isbell et al., "Studies on Tetrahydrocannabinol. 1. Method of Assay in Human Subjects and Results with Crude Extracts, Purified Tetrahydrocannabinols and Synthetic Compounds," in "The Committee on Problems of Drug Dependence, Minutes of the 29th Meeting, 13, 14, 15, and 16 February, 1967, Lexington, Kentucky," National Academy of Sciences, National Research Council, Washington, D.C., *Bull. Probl. Drug Dependence* (1967), pp. 4832–4846.
54. Isbell et al., "Studies on Tetrahydrocannabinol," pp. 4832–4846.

4. THE ACUTE INTOXICATION: LITERARY AND OTHER REPORTS

1. W. B. O'Shaughnessy, "On the Preparation of the Indian Hemp, or Gunjah (*Cannabis Indica*): The Effects on the Animal System in Health, and Their Utility in the Treatment of Tetanus and Other Convulsive Diseases," *Transactions of the Medical and Physical Society of Bombay* (Calcutta, 1842), pp. 421–469.
2. Introduction to Théophile Gautier, *Captain Fracasse,* trans. and ed. F. C. de Sumichrast (New York, 1902), p. xi.
3. Théophile Gautier, *Memoirs of Mademoiselle de Maupin* (London, 1835), p. 38.
4. J. J. Moreau (de Tours), *Du Haschisch et de l'aliénation mentale* (Paris, 1845). Later published as a chapter in *La Psychologie morbide dans ses rapports avec la philosophie de l'histoire; ou de l'influence des neuropathies sur le dynamisme intellectuel* (Paris, 1859).
5. D. Ebin, ed., *The Drug Experience* (New York, 1961), p. 5.
6. Théophile Gautier, "Le Club des hachichins," trans. R. J. Gladstone, in *The Marihuana Papers,* ed. D. Solomon (Indianapolis, 1966), p. 122.
7. F. Rabelais, *The Histories of Gargantua and Pantagruel,* trans. and introd. J. M. Cohen (Baltimore, 1957), pp. 421–432. Rabelais, among his various other accomplishments, was a physician, and his slightly disguised account of hashish (or more correctly, cannabis) is interesting in that it anticipates by over 400 years the report of Yugoslav investigators (see Chap. 8) that cannabis possesses surprising antibiotic qualities: "The juice of this herb

. . . kills every kind of vermin . . . [it is] a prompt remedy for horses with colic and broken wind. Its root, boiled in water, softens hardened sinews, contracted joints, sclerotic gout, and gouty swellings. If you want quickly to heal a scald or burn, apply some Pantagruelion raw," that is, just as it is cut. Rabelais introduces his account by stating that "Pantagruelion" is "the exemplar and paragon of perfect jollity." He finds in Pantagruelion "so many virtues, so much vigour, so many perfections, so many admirable effects, that if its full worth had been known when, as the Prophet tells us, the trees elected a wooden king . . . it would have no doubt gained the majority of their votes." He does not deal directly with the acute intoxication, or with "hallucinations," preferring to express himself by metaphor: "By means of this herb, invisible substances are visibly stopped, caught, detained, and, as it were, imprisoned; . . . By its help nations which Nature seemed to keep hidden, inaccessible, and unknown, have come to us, and we to them: something beyond the power of birds, however light of wing, and whatever freedom to swim down the air Nature may have given them." The only typical symptom of the cannabis intoxication that Rabelais refers to (and this is slight and indirect) is its thirst-provoking qualities.

8. B. Taylor, *The Land of the Saracens, or Pictures of Palestine, Asia Minor, Sicily and Spain* (New York, 1855); C. Baudelaire, *Les Paradis artificiels,* in *Oeuvres complètes de Charles Baudelaire,* ed. M. J. Crépet (Paris, 1928), pp. v–196 (trans. for the author by P. Hedblom); C. Baudelaire, "Du Vin et du haschisch: comparés comme moyens de multiplication de l'individualité," in *Oeuvres complètes,* ed. Crépet, pp. 199–233.

9. B. Taylor, "The Visions of Hasheesh," in *The Drug Experience,* ed. Ebin, p. 43.

10. F. Porché, *Charles Baudelaire,* trans. J. Mavin (New York, 1928), pp. 24–25. Also L. P. Shanks, *Baudelaire: Flesh and Spirit* (Boston, 1930), p. 13; J.-P. Sartre, *Baudelaire,* trans. M. Turnell (New York, 1950), p. 17.

11. E. Starkie, *Baudelaire* (Norfolk, Conn., 1958), p. 40.

12. Ibid., pp. 57, 77.

13. Ibid., p. 57.

14. Ibid., pp. 57–58.

15. Ibid., p. 69.

16. A. Symons, trans., *Baudelaire: Prose and Poetry* (New York, 1926), pp. 244–246.

17. Ibid., p. 247.

18. Ibid., pp. 247–248.

19. C. Baudelaire, "Du Vin et du haschisch," in *Oeuvres complètes,* ed. Crépet, p. 219.

20. Symons, trans., *Baudelaire: Prose and Poetry,* pp. 250–252.

21. Ibid., p. 252.

22. Ibid., pp. 253–255.

23. Ibid., pp. 256–258.

24. Ibid., p. 256.

25. Ibid., p. 256.

26. F. H. Ludlow, *The Hasheesh Eater: Being Passages from the Life of a Pythagorean* (New York, 1857), p. 179.

27. Symons, trans., *Baudelaire: Prose and Poetry,* p. 256.

28. Ibid., p. 262.

29. Ibid., p. 262.
30. A. W. Watts, *The Joyous Cosmology: Adventures in the Chemistry of Consciousness* (New York, 1965), pp. xviii, 22–24.
31. A. Huxley, *The Doors of Perception* (New York, 1954), p. 18.
32. Symons, trans., *Baudelaire: Prose and Poetry*, pp. 272–273.
33. Ibid., p. 275.
34. Ibid., pp. 267–268.
35. Ibid., pp. 275–278.
36. Ibid., pp. 278–279.
37. d'Argonne, Levavasseur, and Prarond, *Vers retrouvés* (printed privately in Paris, 1842); also ed. J. Mouquet (Paris, 1929), p. 15.
38. Starkie, *Baudelaire*, p. 327 (citing T. Varlet, *Au Paradis du haschisch* [Paris, 1930]).
39. Ibid., p. 372 (citing A. Marx, *Indiscrétions parisiennes*).
40. Starkie, *Baudelaire*, pp. 164–167, 372.
41. Ibid., pp. 372–373.
42. Ibid.
43. Baudelaire's *Lettres inédites à sa mère* (Paris, 1918), p. 383.
44. C. Baudelaire, "De L'Idéal artificiel," *La Revue contemporaine* (Paris, 1858). Also in Porché, *Charles Baudelaire*, p. 176, and Starkie, *Baudelaire*, p. 368.
45. C. Baudelaire, *Les Paradis artificiels*, in *Oeuvres complètes*, ed. Crépet, pp. 231–232.
46. Shanks, *Baudelaire: Flesh and Spirit*, p. 71; Porché, *Charles Baudelaire*, pp. 80–81.
47. Starkie, *Baudelaire*, p. 372 (citing T. Varlet, *Au Paradis du haschisch*).
48. Baudelaire, *Les Paradis artificiels*, in *Oeuvres complètes*, ed. Crépet, p. 217.
49. Ibid., pp. 284–291.
50. Starkie, *Baudelaire*, p. 368.
51. Ibid., p. 368, n. 4.
52. Ibid., p. 374. Starkie also notes that "while he admits, however, that he no longer knows to what extent he has identified himself with his author's [De Quincey's] personality, his intention was certainly not to give a picture of his own dreams." Her source is an article by Henri in *Le Temps*, Feb. 27, 1923 (ibid., p. 374). Baudelaire admitted this in a letter to Vigny, written in 1861. He also wrote Poulet Malassis "that it was a matter of blending his own sensations with those of his author [De Quincey] . . ." Feb. 16, 1860 (ibid., p. 374, n. 32).
53. Ibid., pp. 79–83.
54. Ibid., pp. 372–373.
55. Ibid., p. 373 (citing G. T. Clapton, *Baudelaire et De Quincey* [Paris, 1931] and T. Varlet, *Au Paradis du haschisch*).
56. Sartre, *Baudelaire*, p. 192.
57. Starkie, *Baudelaire*, p. 411. On page 56, she writes: "It was probably at this time that Baudelaire contracted the venereal disease from which he was to die 25 years later." He died Aug. 31, 1867; 25 years earlier would have been sometime around 1842, although Baudelaire must have contracted the disease before June 9, 1841, when he set sail, but after the fall of 1839, when he left home. Porché writes: "In a letter from Baudelaire to his mother (1861), we find this statement: 'It seems then, that

426 Notes to Pages 84–108

this misfortune, which had such disastrous effects on the poet's life and in the end perhaps hastened his death, should be placed in the period of his first excesses (1839–41)' " (*Charles Baudelaire*, pp. 37–38). Both Porché and Starkie quote the epitaph that Baudelaire wrote during this period: "Ci -gît qui pour avoir par trop aime les gaupes; Descendit jeune encore au royaume des taupes" (Here lies one who because he loved the whores too well; Descended too young to the realm of the moles). Shanks (*Baudelaire*, pp. 28–39) agrees with the others with regard to the date, and goes so far as to pin the blame on "a Jewess called Louchette because of a squint," who was likely the frequently mentioned "first mistress" of Baudelaire. Starkie and Porché mention the mistress, but not by name, and do not seem to think that there is any real evidence that she was the infecting agent.

58. Symons, trans., *Baudelaire: Prose and Poetry*, p. 239.
59. Sartre, *Baudelaire*, p. 192.
60. M. Bishop, "Fitz Hugh Ludlow," in *Union Worthies, Number Eight Fitz Hugh Ludlow (Class of 1856)*, ed. C. Davidson (Schenectady, New York, 1953), p. 14.
61. Ludlow, *The Hasheesh Eater*, pp. v–viii.
62. R. S. deRopp, *Drugs and the Mind* (New York, 1957), pp. 78–79.
63. "The Hasheesh Eater," *Putnam's Magazine*, Sept. 1856.
64. Ibid., p. 233.
65. Bishop, "Fitz Hugh Ludlow," p. 16. (Bishop writes: "From San Francisco Ludlow pushed north to the Columbia River. In his account of the journey he mentions suffering from 'pulmonary spasms,' an indication of the tuberculosis that was to cause his death.")
66. A. Ginsberg, "The Great Marijuana Hoax: First Manifesto to End the Bringdown," *Atlantic Monthly*, Nov. 1966, pp. 104, 107–112 (long version, "The First Manifesto to End the Bringdown," in *Marihuana Papers*, ed. Solomon, pp. 183–200).
67. Ginsberg, "First Manifesto," p. 184–185.
68. Ibid., p. 196.
69. "Playboy Interview: Allen Ginsberg," *Playboy*, April 1969, p. 82.
70. Ginsberg, "Great Marihuana Hoax," p. 109.
71. "Allen Ginsberg," interview by T. Clark in *Writers at Work: The Paris Review Interviews, Third Series*, ed. G. Plimpton, introd. Alfred Kazin (New York, 1967), pp. 291–294.
72. Ibid., pp. 296–297.
73. Ibid., p. 292.
74. Ibid., pp. 311–313.
75. Ibid., pp. 314–316. The poem reads as follows: "Yes I am that worm soul under/the heel of the daemon horses/I am that man trembling to die/in vomit & trance in bamboo/eternities belly ripped by/red hands of courteous/chinamen kids — Come sweetly/now back to my Self as I was — /Allen Ginsberg says this: I am/a mass of sores and worms/& baldness & belly & smell/I am false Name the prey/of Yamantaka Devourer of/Strange dreams, the prey of/radiation & Police Hells of Law/ . . . In my train seat I renounce/my power, so I am/to be so — /My own Identity now nameless/neither man nor dragon or/God/but the dreaming Me . . ." ("The Change: Kyoto–Tokyo Express," *Planet News*, pp. 59–63).
76. Ginsberg, "Great Marihuana Hoax," pp. 109–110.

77. J. Kramer, *Allen Ginsberg in America* (New York, 1968), p. 21.
78. Ginsberg, "Great Marihuana Hoax," p. 107.
79. Ginsberg, "First Manifesto," p. 189.
80. Ginsberg, "Great Marihuana Hoax," pp. 108–109.
81. Ginsberg, "First Manifesto," p. 195.
82. Ibid., p. 185.

5. THE ACUTE INTOXICATION: ITS PROPERTIES

1. On the "properties" of acute intoxication, see E. R. Bloomquist, *Marijuana* (Beverly Hills, Calif., 1968), pp. 12, 71; J. Rosevear, *Pot: A Handbook of Marihuana* (New York, 1967), pp. 85, 89; J. H. Jaffe, "Cannabis (Marijuana)," in *The Pharmacological Basis of Therapeutics,* ed. L. S. Goodman and A. Gilman, 3rd ed. (New York, 1965), p. 300 (also in *Marijuana,* ed. E. Goode [New York, 1969], p. 49); C. J. Schwarz, "Toward a Medical Understanding of Marihuana," *Canad. Psychiat. Ass. J.,* 14 (1969), 593; F. Ames, "A Clinical and Metabolic Study of Acute Intoxication with *Cannabis Sativa,*" *J. Ment. Sci.,* 104 (1958), 993; L. D. Clarke and E. N. Nakashima, "Experimental Studies of *Marihuana,*" *Amer. J. Psychiat.,* 125 (1968), 384; R. P. Walton, *Marihuana, America's New Drug Problem* (Philadelphia, 1938), pp. 96–103, 115; A. Geller and M. Boas, *The Drug Beat* (New York, 1969), pp. 187–189; S. Cholst, "Notes on the Use of Hashish," chap. 9 in *The Marihuana Papers,* ed. D. Solomon (Indianapolis, 1966), pp. 219–220.
2. S. Allentuck and K. M. Bowman, "The Psychiatric Aspects of Marihuana Intoxication," *Amer. J. Psychiat.,* 99 (1942), 248.
3. R. Adams, "Marihuana," *Harvey Lect.,* 37 (1942), 169.
4. W. Bromberg, "Marihuana Intoxication: A Clinical Study of Cannabis Sativa Intoxication," *Amer. J. Psychiat.,* 91 (1934), 309.
5. Bloomquist, *Marijuana,* pp. 167–216.
6. C. K. Aldrich, "The Effect of a Synthetic Marihuana-like Compound on Musical Talent as Measured by the Seashore Test," *Public Health Rep.,* 59 (1944), 431.
7. G. Piel, "Narcotics: War Has Brought Illicit Traffic to All-Time Low, but U.S. Treasury Fears Rising Postwar Addiction," *Life* magazine, July 19, 1943, pp. 82, 84; Walton, *Marihuana,* pp. 121–122.
8. C. Winick, "The Use of Drugs by Jazz Musicians," *Social Problems,* 7 (1960), 243.
9. Geller and Boas, *Drug Beat,* p. 41.
10. Walton, *Marihuana,* p. 103.
11. R. S. deRopp, *Drugs and the Mind* (New York, 1957), p. 101.
12. W. Oursler, *Marijuana: The Facts, the Truth* (New York, 1968), p. 51 (pub. simultaneously in Canada); Bloomquist, *Marijuana,* p. 63; Rosevear, *Pot: A Handbook,* p. 144; H. H. Nowlis, *Drugs on the College Campus* (Garden City, N.Y., 1969), p. 94.
13. W. Surface, *The Poisoned Ivy* (New York, 1968; paper reissue, 1969), p. 184.
14. S. Allentuck, "Medical Aspects: Symptoms and Behavior," in Mayor's Committee on Marihuana, *The Marihuana Problem in the City of New York* (Lancaster, Pa., 1944), p. 64; F. Halpern, "Intellectual Functioning," ibid., p. 106; Geller and Boas, *Drug Beat,* pp. 48, 49.

15. Geller and Boas, *Drug Beat,* pp. 51, 46.

16. H. Isbell et al., "Studies on Tetrahydrocannabinol," *Bull., Probl. Drug Dependence* (1967), p. 4839.

17. E. C. Taylor et al., "Active Constituents of Hashish, Synthesis of *dl-∆⁶-³-4-trans*-tetrahydrocannabinol," *J. Amer. Chem. Soc.,* 88 (1966), 367.

18. Nowlis, *Drugs on the College Campus,* p. 95, citing Isbell et al., "Studies on Tetrahydrocannabinol," p. 4843.

19. *Hashish: Its Chemistry and Pharmacology,* ed. G. E. W. Wolstenholme and J. Knight (London, 1965), p. 81.

20. H. S. Becker, *Outsiders: Studies in the Sociology of Deviance* (New York, 1963), pp. 46–58; see also A. T. Weil et al., "Clinical and Psychological Effects of Marihuana in Man," *Science,* 162 (1968), 1241.

21. Weil et al., "Clinical and Psychological Effects," p. 1241.

22. Geller and Boas, *Drug Beat,* p. 54.

23. N. R. Farnsworth, "Hallucinogenic Plants," *Science,* 162 (1968), 1088; see also L. Grlic, "Recent Advances in the Chemical Research of *Cannabis,*" *Bull. Narcotics,* 16 (1964), 29–38; R. Mechoulam, "Marihuana Chemistry," *Science,* 168 (1970), 1160.

24. Becker, *Outsiders,* pp. 49–50; Oursler, *Marijuana: The Facts,* pp. 76–77; R. D. Johnson, "Medico-Social Aspects of Marijuana," *Rhode Island Med. J.,* 51 (1968), 173; R. J. Bouquet, "Cannabis," *Bull. Narcotics,* 3 (1951), 27.

25. Walton, *Marihuana,* p. 110.

26. Winick, "Use of Drugs by Jazz Musicians," p. 248.

27. Johnson, "Medico-Social Aspects," p. 173; also E. Goode, "Multiple Drug Use among Marijuana Smokers," *Social Problems,* 17 (1969), 55.

28. P. Laurie, *Drugs: Medical, Psychological and Social Facts* (Harmondsworth, England, 1967), p. 83.

29. Allentuck and Bowman, "Psychiatric Aspects of Marihuana Intoxication," p. 248; Ames, "Clinical and Metabolic Study," p. 984; Bouquet, "Cannabis," pp. 22, 26; Bromberg, "Marihuana Intoxication," p. 309; I. C. Chopra and R. N. Chopra, "The Use of Cannabis Drugs in India," *Bull. Narcotics,* 9 (1957), 9–29; H. L. Freedman and M. J. Rockmore, "Marihuana: A Factor in Personality Evaluation and Army Maladjustment," *J. Clin. Psychopathology,* 7 (1946), 776, and 8 (1946), 229–230; W. H. McGlothlin and L. J. West, "The Marihuana Problem: An Overview," *Amer. J. Psychiat.,* 125 (1968), 374; Allentuck, "Medical Aspects," p. 41.

30. Bloomquist, *Marijuana,* p. 71; Rosevear, *Pot: A Handbook,* p. 85; Allentuck and Bowman, "Psychiatric Aspects of Marihuana Intoxication," p. 249.

31. Bromberg, "Marihuana Intoxication," p. 309; Ames, "Clinical and Metabolic Study," pp. 981, 984; Bromberg, "Marihuana: A Psychiatric Study," p. 5; S. Charen and L. Perelman, "Personality Studies of Marihuana Addicts," *Amer. J. Psychiat.,* 102 (1946), 679; Allentuck, "Medical Aspects," pp. 38–39.

32. Walton, *Marihuana,* p. 104 (summary of findings of F. Fraenkel and E. Joël).

33. Ibid., p. 104.

34. Ibid., p. 117; Bromberg, "Marihuana Intoxication," p. 309; H. S. Gaskill, "Marihuana, an Intoxicant," *Amer. J. Psychiat.* 102 (1945), 203; Allentuck, "Medical Aspects," pp. 50–51.

35. Walton, *Marihuana,* p. 117.

36. Allentuck, "Medical Aspects," pp. 37, 39; Ames, "Clinical and Metabolic Study," p. 984.
37. Allentuck, "Medical Aspects," p. 37.
38. W. H. McGlothlin, "Cannabis Intoxication and its Similarity to That of Peyote and LSD," in *Hallucinogenic Drugs: A Perspective with Special Reference to Peyote and Cannabis* (July 1964), pp. 40–41.
39. Walton, *Marihuana*, p. 117; Schwarz, "Toward a Medical Understanding," p. 593; Ames, "Clinical and Metabolic Study," p. 979.
40. Jaffe, "Cannabis (Marijuana)," p. 300 (also in *Marijuana*, ed. Goode, p. 49).
41. Walton, *Marihuana*, p. 104–105.
42. Ibid., p. 117.
43. Ibid., p. 115.
44. Jaffe, "Cannabis (Marijuana)," p. 300 (also in *Marijuana*, ed. Goode, p. 49); S. Cohen, "Pot, Acid, and Speed," *Med. Sci.*, 19 (1968), 32; S. Yolles, "Recent Research on LSD, Marijuana, and Other Dangerous Drugs," in *Drug Awareness*, ed. R. E. Horman and A. M. Fox (New York, 1970), p. 77; Walton, *Marihuana*, p. 104 (summary of F. Fraenkel and E Joël); see also Ames, "Clinical and Metabolic Study," p. 980.
45. Walton, *Marihuana*, p. 115.
46. Bromberg, "Marihuana Intoxication," p. 309; Walton, *Marihuana*, p. 107.
47. Bromberg, "Marihuana Intoxication," pp. 310, 326.
48. Allentuck and Bowman, "Psychiatric Aspects of Marihuana Intoxication," p. 248.
49. E. R. Bloomquist, "Marijuana: Social Benefit or Social Detriment?" *Calif. Med.*, 106 (1967), 348.
50. Jaffe, "Cannabis (Marijuana)," p. 300 (also in *Marijuana*, ed. Goode, p. 50); Johnson, "Medico-Social Aspects," p. 173; V. Robinson, "Experiments with Hashish," *Ciba Symposia*, 8 (1946), 392; ibid., p. 394; ibid., p. 391.
51. Oursler, *Marijuana: The Facts*, pp. 32–33, quoting Goodman and Gilman's *Pharmacological Basis of Therapeutics*.
52. *Marihuana Papers*, ed. Solomon, p. 228.
53. Allentuck, "Medical Aspects," p. 39; Geller and Boas, *Drug Beat*, p. 51.
54. F. Halpern, "Emotional Reactions and General Personality Structure," in *The Marihuana Problem*, p. 120.
55. H. Michaux, *Miserable Miracle*, trans. L. Varese (San Francisco, 1963), pp. 48–49.
56. Walton, *Marihuana*, pp. 119, 105–106.
57. Bromberg, "Marihuana Intoxication," pp. 324, 309.
58. N. B. Eddy et al., "Drug Dependence: Its Significance and Characteristics," *Bull. WHO*, 32 (1965), 729; also quoted in "Dependence on Cannabis," *J.A.M.A.*, 201 (1967), 370; also quoted in *Marijuana*, ed. Goode, p. 21.
59. Allentuck and Bowman, "Psychiatric Aspects of Marihuana Intoxication," pp. 248–249; Jaffe, "Cannabis (Marijuana)," p. 301 (also in *Marijuana*, ed. Goode, p. 50).
60. Adams, "Marihuana," p. 194; Laurie, *Drugs*, p. 83; Allentuck, "Medical Aspects," p. 37; Allentuck and Bowman, "Psychiatric Aspects of Marihuana Intoxication," p. 249; Bromberg, "Marihuana Intoxication," p. 309.

61. Oursler, *Marihuana: The Facts,* p. 59.
62. *Hashish: Its Chemistry and Pharmacology,* ed. Wolstenholme and Knight, pp. 75–77.
63. Halpern, "Emotional Reactions and General Personality Structure," p. 132; Geller and Boas, *Drug Beat,* p. 47.
64. Geller and Boas, *Drug Beat,* p. 47; A. R. Lindesmith, "The Marihuana Problem: Myth or Reality?" in *Marihuana Papers,* ed. Solomon, pp. 19, 22–23; G. M. Carstairs, "Daru and Bhang: Cultural Factors in the Choice of Intoxicants," *Quart. J. Stud. Alcohol,* 15 (1954), 220–237; A. T. Weil et al., "A Scientific Report — The Effects of Marijuana on Human Beings," *New York Times Magazine,* May 11, 1969, p. 92, especially regarding brief reference to the findings of a soon-to-be published study conducted by the Department of Motor Vehicles of the State of Washington and the University of Washington; A. Storr, "Marijuana and Alcohol," in *The Book of Grass: An Anthology of Indian Hemp,* ed. G. Andrews and S. Vinkenoog (New York, 1967), pp. 234–235.
65. Walton, *Marihuana,* pp. 105, 123; Allentuck and Bowman, "Psychiatric Aspects of Marihuana Intoxication," p. 249; J. F. Siler et al., "Marihuana Smoking in Panama," *Milit. Surg.,* 73 (1933), 269–280, referred to in Weil et al., "Clinical and Psychological Effects," pp. 1235; Jaffe, "Cannabis (Marijuana)," p. 300 (in *Marijuana,* ed. Goode, p. 49); Eddy, "Drug Dependence," pp. 728–729 (also quoted in *Marijuana,* ed. Goode, p. 22); V. Robinson, "Concerning Cannabis Indica," in *Book of Grass,* ed. Andrews and Vinkenoog, p. 138; Adams, "Marihuana," p. 193; Cohen, "Pot, Acid, and Speed," p. 32; Bloomquist, "Marijuana: Social Benefit or Social Detriment?", p. 347; Johnson, "Medico-Social Aspects," p. 173; Geller and Boas, *Drug Beat,* p. 47; Laurie, *Drugs,* p. 83; L. S. Thompson and R. C. Proctor, "Pyrahexyl in the Treatment of Alcoholic and Drug Withdrawal Conditions," *N. Carolina Med. J.,* 14 (1953), 520; Rosevear, *Pot: A Handbook* pp. 62, 88; Allentuck, "Medical Aspects," pp. 40, 50.
66. Weil et al., "A Scientific Report," p. 89; Council on Mental Health and Committee on Alcoholism and Drug Dependence, American Medical Association, "Dependence on Cannabis (Marihuana)," *J.A.M.A.,* 201 (1967), 370 (quoting Eddy et al.).
67. Weil et al., "Clinical and Psychological Effects," pp. 1240, 1241.
68. See Keeler, "Adverse Reaction to Marijuana," p. 675; Ames, "Clinical and Metabolic Study," p. 984.
69. D. E. Miller, "Narcotic Drug and Marijuana Controls," in *Drug Awareness,* ed. Horman and Fox, pp. 412–413.
70. Allentuck, "Medical Aspects," p. 64; Geller and Boas, *Drug Beat,* p. 48.
71. deRopp, *Drugs and the Mind,* p. 105; D. D. Shoenfeld, "The Sociological Study," in Mayor's Committee, *The Marihuana Problem,* p. 13; N. Taylor, *Narcotics: Nature's Dangerous Gift* (New York, 1963), p. 29; Geller and Boas, *Drug Beat,* p. 47.
72. Walton, *Marihuana,* p. 123.
73. Mayor's Committee, *The Marihuana Problem,* pp. 217.
74. Halpern, "Emotional Reactions and General Personality Structure," p. 131; Allentuck and Bowman, "Psychiatric Aspects of Marihuana Intoxication," p. 249; Gaskill, "Marihuana, an Intoxicant," p. 202.
75. Robinson, "Experiments with Hashish," p. 393; Ames, "Clinical and Metabolic Study," pp. 990–991.

76. Halpern, "Emotional Reactions and General Personality Structure," p. 128.
77. Allentuck, "Medical Aspects," p. 37.
78. Walton, *Marihuana*, p. 115.
79. H. Isbell et al., "Studies on Tetrahydrocannabinol," p. 4839.
80. J. S. Margolis and R. Clorfene, *A Child's Garden of Grass* (North Hollywood, Calif., 1969), pp. 26–27; Bouquet, "Cannabis," p. 26.
81. Oursler, *Marijuana: The Facts*, p. 11; Bouquet, "Cannabis," p. 22; McGlothlin, "Cannabis Intoxication and Its Similarity," pp. 42–43; Lindesmith, "Marihuana Problem: Myth or Reality?" p. 19; Cohen, "Pot, Acid, and Speed," p. 47.
82. Winick, "Use of Drugs by Jazz Musicians," p. 247.
83. Halpern, "Emotional Reactions and General Personality Structure," p. 130.
84. Ibid., pp. 130–131.
85. Bromberg, "Marihuana Intoxication," p. 309.
86. Bloomquist, *Marijuana*, p. 72; Jaffe, "Cannabis (Marijuana)," p. 300 (also in *Marijuana*, ed. Goode, p. 49); Thompson and Proctor, "Pyrahexyl in Treatment of Withdrawal," p. 520; Bouquet, "Cannabis," p. 23.
87. Bloomquist, "Marijuana: Social Benefit or Social Detriment?" p. 347; Geller and Boas, *Drug Beat*, pp. 46–47.
88. H. Michaux, *Light through Darkness*, trans. H. Chevalier (New York, 1961), pp. 100–101.
89. Michaux, *Miserable Miracle*, pp. 46–47.
90. Robinson, "Experiments with Hashish," p. 389.
91. Ibid., p. 393.
92. Oursler, *Marijuana: The Facts*, p. 11.
93. H. France, *Musk, Hashish and Blood* (privately printed), quoted in Rosevear, *Pot: A Handbook*, pp. 82–83; Walton, *Marihuana*, p. 84.
94. Cholst, "Notes on the Use of Hashish," pp. 217–219.
95. Walton, *Marihuana*, p. 117; also, Jaffe, "Cannabis (Marijuana)," p. 300 (also in *Marijuana*, ed. Goode, p. 50); McGlothlin, "Cannabis Intoxication and Its Similarity," pp. 40–41; Oursler, *Marijuana: The Facts*, p. 33; Robinson, "Experiments with Hashish," pp. 202, 209, 213–214; Isbell et al., "Studies on Tetrahydrocannabinol," pp. 4838–4839.
96. Oursler, *Marijuana: The Facts*, p. 59; see also: Ames, "Clinical and Metabolic Study," pp. 983–984; Bouquet, "Cannabis," p. 24.
97. McGlothlin, "Cannabis Intoxication and Its Similarity," p. 40–41.
98. Oursler, *Marijuana: The Facts*, p. 78.
99. Ibid., p. 84.
100. Jaffe, "Cannabis (Marijuana)," p. 300 (also in *Marijuana*, ed. Goode, p. 50); Oursler, *Marijuana: The Facts*, p. 33.
101. Robinson, "Experiments with Hashish," p. 393.
102. France, *Musk, Hashish and Blood*, as quoted in Rosevear, *Pot: A Handbook*, p. 83.
103. Robinson, "Experiments with Hashish," pp. 393–394.
104. Isbell et al., "Studies on Tetrahydrocannabinol," p. 4838.
105. Walton, *Marihuana*, p. 105 (summary of findings of F. Fraenkel and E. Joël); see also Bouquet, "Cannabis," pp. 22–23; Bromberg, "Marihuana Intoxication," pp. 309–310, 324.
106. Allentuck and Bowman, "Psychiatric Aspects of Marihuana Intoxication," p. 249.

107. Bromberg, "Marihuana Intoxication," pp. 309, 324, citing K. Beringer, *Der Mescalinrausch* (Berlin, 1927), and K. Beringer, V. Bryer, and H. Marx: "Zur Klinik des Haschish Rausches," *Nervenarzt,* 5 (1932), 337.
108. Weil et al., "A Scientific Report," p. 94.
109. Jaffe, "Cannabis (Marijuana)," p. 301; also in *Marijuana,* ed. Goode, p. 50.
110. Bloomquist, "Marijuana: Social Benefit or Social Detriment?" p. 347; see also Souief, "Hashish Consumption in Egypt," pp. 8–9; Bromberg, "Marihuana Intoxication," p. 310.
111. Geller and Boas, *Drug Beat,* p. 59; Rosevear, *Pot: A Handbook,* pp. 85–86.
112. Robinson, "Experiments in Hashish," pp. 395–396.
113. Michaux, *Light through Darkness,* pp. 124–127.
114. Halpern, "Emotional Reactions and General Personality Structure," p. 131.
115. Walton, *Marihuana,* p. 105 (summary of findings of F. Fraenkel and E. Joël).
116. F. T. Melges et al., "Marihuana and Temporal Disintegration," *Science,* 168 (1970), 1118–1120; also, J. R. Tinklenberg et al., "Marihuana and Immediate Memory," accepted for publication in *Nature.*
117. Walton, *Marihuana,* p. 116; Bromberg, "Marihuana Intoxication," pp. 310–311.
118. H. S. Gaskill, "Marihuana: An Intoxicant," p. 203; Council on Mental Health and Committee on Alcoholism and Drug Dependence, "Dependence on Cannabis *(Marihuana),*" *J.A.M.A.,* 201 (1967), 370; Yolles, "Recent Research on LSD," p. 77.
119. Allentuck and Bowman, "Psychiatric Aspects of Marihuana Intoxication," p. 249.
120. McGlothlin, "Cannabis Intoxication and Its Similarity," pp. 40–41.
121. Jaffe, "Cannabis (Marijuana)," p. 300; also in *Marijuana,* ed. Goode, p. 49.
122. Cohen, "Pot, Acid, and Speed," p. 47.
123. Bloomquist, "Marijuana: Social Benefit or Social Detriment?" p. 347; Bloomquist, *Marijuana,* p. 72.
124. Keeler, "Adverse Reaction," p. 675 (quoting Bouquet).
125. Lindesmith, "Marihuana Problem: Myth or Reality?" p. 19.
126. Laurie, *Drugs,* p. 83 (quoting Murphy, *U.N. Bulletin on Narcotics,* Jan.–March, 1963).
127. deRopp, *Drugs and the Mind,* quoting E. J. Rolls and D. Stafford-Clark, pp. 111–112.
128. Isbell et al., "Studies on Tetrahydrocannabinol," p. 4838.
129. Winick, "Use of Drugs by Jazz Musicians," p. 244.
130. Weil et al., "Clinical and Psychological Effects," p. 1240.
131. Michaux, *Light through Darkness,* pp. 64, 87–88.
132. Michaux, *Miserable Miracle,* p. 52.
133. Melges et al., "Marihuana and Temporal Disintegration," pp. 1118–1119.
134. Ibid., p. 1119.
135. Ibid., pp. 1119–1120.
136. Ibid., p. 1120.
137. Melges et al., "Marihuana and Immediate Memory," pp. 2–3 (of preprint).

138. Bromberg, "Marihuana Intoxication," pp. 310–311, 324.
139. Walton, *Marihuana*, p. 104.
140. Ibid., p. 116.
141. Jaffe, "Cannabis (Marijuana)," p. 300 (also in *Marijuana*, ed. Goode, p. 49); Bloomquist, "Marijuana: Social Benefit or Social Detriment?" pp. 347–348; Rosevear, *Pot: A Handbook*, p. 86; N. S. Yawger, "Marihuana: Our New Addiction," *Amer. J. Med. Sci.*, 195 (1938), 353.
142. Halpern, "Intellectual Functioning," pp. 100–105.
143. Ibid.
144. Ibid., p. 105.
145. Ibid., pp. 101, 105.
146. Ibid., pp. 101, 105.
147. Walton, *Marihuana*, p. 116.
148. Allentuck and Bowman, "Psychiatric Aspects of Marihuana Intoxication," p. 249.
149. Jaffe, "Cannabis (Marijuana)," p. 300; also in *Marijuana*, ed. Goode, p. 49.
150. deRopp, *Drugs and the Mind*, p. 111; P. H. Drewry, "Some Psychiatric Aspects of Marijuana Intoxication," *Psychiat. Quart.*, 10 (1936), 234.
151. Keeler, "Adverse Reaction," p. 675 (citing Bouquet); Bloomquist, "Marijuana: Social Benefit or Social Detriment?" p. 347.
152. McGlothlin, "Cannabis Intoxication and Its Similarity," pp. 40–41; Yolles, "Recent Research on LSD," p. 77.
153. Michaux, *Light through Darkness*, p. 104.
154. Ibid., pp. 118–119; see also Bouquet, "Cannabis," 23–24.
155. Bromberg, "Marihuana Intoxication," p. 310.
156. Ibid., pp. 310–311.
157. Bromberg, "Marihuana Intoxication," p. 325; he cites L. Kanner and P. Schilder, "Optic Movements and Movements in Optic Images," *J. Nerv. Ment. Dis.*, cited ibid., ref. 28, p. 330. Apparently the article Bromberg is referring to is "Movements in Optic Images and the Optic Imagination of Movements," 72 (1930), 489–517.
158. Walton, *Marihuana*, p. 104 (summary of findings of F. Fraenkel and E. Joël).
159. Ibid., pp. 105, 105–107.
160. Allentuck and Bowman, "Psychiatric Aspects of Marihuana Intoxication," p. 249; Walton, *Marihuana*, p. 109; Bromberg, "Marihuana: A Psychiatric Study," p. 6; Drewry, "Some Psychiatric Aspects of Marijuana Intoxication," p. 234.
161. Bloomquist, "Marijuana: Social Benefit or Social Detriment?" pp. 347–348.
162. Isbell et al., "Studies on Tetrahydrocannabinol," p. 4838.
163. Walton, *Marihuana*, p. 104; Allentuck and Bowman, "Psychiatric Aspects of Marihuana Intoxication," p. 249; Jaffe, "Cannabis (Marijuana)," p. 300 (also in *Marijuana*, ed. Goode, p. 49); Eddy et al., "Drug Dependence," pp. 728–729; McGlothlin, "Cannabis Intoxication and Its Similarity," pp. 40–41; Yolles, "Recent Research on LSD," p. 77; Bloomquist, *Marijuana*, p. 73; Keeler, "Adverse Reaction," p. 675 (citing Bouquet); Robinson, "Experiments with Hashish," pp. 387–296, 404.
164. Oursler, *Marijuana: The Facts*, pp. 65 (quoting A. Ginsberg, "The Great Marihuana Hoax: First Manifesto to End the Bringdown," in *Marihuana Papers*, ed. Solomon, p. 197), 89–90, 180, 206, 228.

165. Walton, *Marihuana,* pp. 105–106.
166. Ibid., p. 120 (see F. H. Ludlow, *The Hasheesh Eater* [New York, 1857], p. 162).
167. Walton, *Marihuana,* pp. 121–122 (citing Ludlow, *The Hasheesh Eater,* p. 117).
168. Walton, *Marihuana,* p. 122 (citing *Confessions of an English Hachish-Eater* [London, 1884]).
169. Eddy et al., "Drug Dependence," pp. 728–729; McGlothlin, "Cannabis Intoxication and Its Similarity," pp. 40–41; Halpern, "Intellectual Functioning," p. 81; Allentuck, "Medical Aspects," p. 39; France, *Musk, Hashish and Blood,* as cited in Rosevear, *Pot: A Handbook,* pp. 82–83; Michaux, *Miserable Miracle,* p. 49.
170. Walton, *Marihuana,* p. 104.
171. Ibid., p. 107.
172. Ibid., p. 120.
173. Bromberg, "Marihuana Intoxication," pp. 326–327.
174. "Effects of Alcohol and Cannabis During Labor," editor, *J.A.M.A.,* 94 (1930), 1165; Allentuck and Bowman, "Psychiatric Aspects of Marihuana Intoxication," p. 248; Jaffe, "Cannabis (Marijuana)," p. 300–301 (also in *Marijuana,* ed. Goode, pp. 49–50); McGlothlin, "Cannabis: A Reference," p. 403; Isbell et al., "Studies on Tetrahydrocannabinol," p. 4838; Robinson, "Experiments with Hashish," p. 393; Keeler, "Adverse Reaction," p. 675; Carstairs, "Daru and Bhang," p. 223.
175. Weil et al., "A Scientific Report," p. 92–94.
176. Allentuck and Bowman, "Psychiatric Aspects of Marihuana Intoxication," p. 249.
177. Robinson, "Experiments with Hashish," p. 395.
178. Anonymous, "Some Thoughts on Marijuana and the Artist," in *Marijuana,* ed. Goode, pp. 177–182.
179. Mental Health and Committee on Alcoholism and Drug Dependence, American Medical Association, "Dependence on Cannabis (Marihuana)," *J.A.M.A.,* 201 (1967), 370; Cohen, "Pot, Acid, and Speed," p. 47; Yolles, "Recent Research on LSD," p. 71.
180. Gaskill, "Marihuana: An Intoxicant," p. 203; Jaffe, "Cannabis (Marijuana)," p. 300 (also in *Marijuana,* ed. Goode, p. 49); Bloomquist, "Marijuana: Social Benefit or Social Detriment?" p. 347; Bromberg, "Marihuana Intoxication," pp. 309–310, 324 (citing R. Meunier [*sic*], "Le Haschich Essai sur la psychologie des paradis ephèmieres," [Paris, 1909]).
181. Laurie, *Drugs,* p. 83, citing H. B. M. Murphy, "The Cannabis Habit," *Bull. Narcotics,* 15 (1963), 15–23; Laurie, *Drugs,* p. 86; E. G. Williams et al., "Studies on Marihuana and Pyrahexyl Compounds," *Pub. Health Rep.,* 61 (1946), 1059.
182. Halpern, "Emotional Reactions and General Personality Structure," p. 128; Halpern, "Intellectual Functioning," p. 106; Keeler, "Adverse Reaction," p. 675; Johnson, "Medico-Social Aspects," pp. 173–174.
183. McGlothlin, "Cannabis Intoxication and Its Similarity," pp. 40–41.
184. Weil et al., "Clinical and Psychological Effects," p. 1235, referring to Siler et al., "Marihuana Smoking in Panama," pp. 269–280.
185. W. Burroughs, "Points of Distinction between Sedative and Consciousness-Expanding Drugs," *Evergreen Review,* Dec. 1964, reprinted in part in *Book of Grass,* ed. Andrews and Vinkenoog, pp. 207–208.

186. Eddy et al., "Drug Dependence," pp. 728–729; Council on Mental Health and Committee on Alcoholism and Drug Dependence, American Medical Association, "Dependence on Cannabis (Marihuana)," *J.A.M.A.*, 201 (1967), p. 370; Bloomquist, *Marijuana*, pp. 187–189 (C. K. Aldrich, "The Effect of a Synthetic Marihuana-like Compound on Musical Talent as Measured by the Seashore Test," *Public Health Rep.*, 59 [1944], 431–433); Winick, "Use of Drugs by Jazz Musicians," pp. 251–252, 249.
187. Walton, *Marihuana*, p. 114.
188. Allen Ginsberg, "First Manifesto to End the Bringdown" in *Marihuana Papers*, ed. Solomon, pp. 184–185.
189. Halpern, "Emotional Reactions and General Personality Structure," pp. 116–117.
190. Bob Dylan, "Ballad of a Thin Man," in *Bob Dylan: Highway 61 Revisited* (New York, 1965), pp. 18–19.
191. Rosevear, *Pot: A Handbook*, pp. 88–89, 98–99.
192. Bloomquist, "Marijuana: Social Benefit or Social Detriment?" p. 350.
193. A. Crancer, Jr., *Predicting Driving Performance with a Driver Simulator Test* (Washington State Department of Motor Vehicles, Olympia, Wash., 1968).
194. A Crancer et al., "Comparison of the Effects of Marihuana and Alcohol on Simulated Driving Performance," *Science*, 164 (1969), "Abstract," p. 851.
195. Ibid., p. 852.
196. Ibid., p. 854.
197. Ibid., p. 854.
198. Ibid., p. 853.
199. Ibid., "Abstract," p. 851.
200. Ibid., p. 854.
201. D. F. Caldwell et al., "Auditory and Visual Threshold Effects of Marihuana in Man," *Perceptive and Motor Skills*, 29 (1969), 758–759. He cites Weil et al., "Clinical and Psychological Effects," and Crancer et al., "Effects of Marihuana and Alcohol."
202. Laurie, *Drugs*, p. 86.
203. Halpern, "Emotional Reactions and General Personality Structure," p. 129.
204. Bromberg, "Marihuana Intoxication," p. 324; Walton, *Marihuana*, p. 116; McGlothlin, "Cannabis: A Reference," p. 403; Robinson, "Experiments with Hashish," p. 394.
205. Walton, *Marihuana*, p. 115.
206. Johnson, "Medico-Social Aspects," p. 173.
207. Bloomquist, "Marijuana: Social Benefit or Social Detriment?" p. 347; Bloomquist, *Marijuana*, p. 71.
208. Rosevear, *Pot: A Handbook*, p. 85; "Effects of Alcohol and Cannabis During Labor," editor, *J.A.M.A.*, 94 (1930), 1165; Robinson, "Experiments with Hashish," p. 387; Robinson, "Concerning Cannabis Indica," p. 138; Lindesmith, "Marihuana Problem: Myth or Reality?" p. 19; E. J. Waring, "Pharmacopoeia of India, 1868," in *Book of Grass*, ed. Andrews and Vinkenoog, p. 139.
209. Walton, *Marihuana*, p. 116; Geller and Boas, *Drug Beat*, p. 81; "Effects of Alcohol and Cannabis During Labor," p. 1165; Waring, "Pharmacopoeia of India, 1868," p. 139; E. Bertherand, "Pharmacopee Arabe,

1900," in *Book of Grass,* ed. Andrews and Vinkenoog, p. 145; Oursler, *Marijuana: The Facts,* p. 206.

210. Jaffe, "Cannabis (Marijuana)," p. 300 (also in *Marijuana,* ed. Goode, p. 49); Weil et al., "Clinical and Psychological Effects," p. 1242; Bloomquist, *Marijuana,* p. 74; Allentuck, "Medical Aspects," pp. 36–37, 40, 44; Morrow, "Psychological and Other Functions," in Mayor's Committee, *The Marihuana Problem,* pp. 80–81; Wallace, "Summary," in Mayor's Committee, *The Marihuana Problem,* pp. 217–219; Geller and Boas, *Drug Beat,* p. 46; Oursler, *Marijuana: The Facts,* pp. 80–81; Johnson, "Medico-Social Aspects," p. 173.

211. Allentuck and Bowman, "Psychiatric Aspects of Marihuana Intoxication," p. 248; see also Bloomquist, *Marijuana,* p. 74.

212. Rosevear, *Pot: A Handbook,* p. 84; Jaffe, "Cannabis (Marijuana)," p. 300 (also in *Marijuana,* ed. Goode, p. 49); Weil et al., "Clinical and Psychological Effects," p. 1235; Allentuck, "Medical Aspects," pp. 36–37, 40, 44; Morrow, "Psychological and Other Functions," pp. 80–81; Halpern, "Intellectual Functioning," pp. 96, 97.

213. Walton, *Marihuana,* p. 125; Bromberg, "Marihuana Intoxication," p. 310; Allentuck and Bowman, "Psychiatric Aspects of Marihuana Intoxication," p. 249; Gaskill, "Marihuana: An Intoxicant," p. 202; Siler et al., "Marihuana Smoking in Panama," mentioned in Weil et al., "Clinical and Psychological Effects," p. 1235; Jaffe, "Cannabis (Marijuana)," p. 301 (also in *Marijuana,* ed. Goode, p. 50); Adams, "Marihuana," p. 194; McGlothlin, "Cannabis Intoxication and Its Similarity," pp. 42–43; Cohen, "Pot, Acid, and Speed," p. 47; Yolles, "Recent Research on LSD," p. 77; Bloomquist, "Marijuana: Social Benefit or Social Detriment?", p. 347; Johnson, "Medico-Social Aspects," p. 173; Robinson, "Experiments with Hashish," p. 394; Laurie, *Drugs,* p. 83.

214. Walton, *Marihuana,* pp. 105, 125.

215. Allentuck and Bowman, "Psychiatric Aspects of Marihuana Intoxication," p. 249.

216. Johnson, "Medico-Social Aspects," p. 173; Laurie, *Drugs,* p. 85; Robinson, "Experiments with Hashish," pp. 385, 389, 396.

217. Oursler, *Marijuana: The Facts,* pp. 57, 85.

218. Gaskill, "Marihuana: An Intoxicant," p. 202.

219. Halpern, "Intellectual Functioning," p. 94.

220. Emmitt G. Warner, "Sources of Hallucinogenic Drugs, including Marihuana: The Nature and Economic Significance of the Trade," in *Drugs and Youth: Proceedings of the Rutgers Symposium on Drug Abuse,* ed. J. R. Wittenborn et al. (Springfield, Ill., 1969), pp. 163–167.

221. deRopp, *Drugs and the Mind,* p. 72.

222. S. Cohen, *The Beyond Within* (New York, 1965), pp. 11–12.

223. N. R. Farnsworth, "Hallucinogenic Plants," *Science,* 162 (1968), 1092, n. 2.

224. Cohen, *The Beyond Within,* pp. 12–13.

225. Michaux, *Light through Darkness,* p. 209.

226. Allentuck, "Medical Aspects," p. 41.

6. MOTIVATION OF THE USER

1. C. Dwarkanath, "The Use of Opium and Cannabis in the Traditional Systems of Medicine in India," *Bull. Narcotics,* 17 (1965), 15–19.

2. I. C. Chopra and R. N. Chopra, "The use of Cannabis Drugs in India," *Bull. Narcotics,* 9 (1957), 13.
3. C. J. G. Bourhill, thesis submitted for the degree of Doctor of Medicine, Edinburgh University, 1913.
4. R. P. Walton, *Marihuana, America's New Drug Problem* (Philadelphia, 1938), p. 117.
5. The ritualistic use of peyote for the care of the sick was introduced into the U.S. from Mexico around 1870 and spread rapidly among the Plains Indians. Soon the ritual procedures, which were of a tribal nature in Mexico, were standardized into a religious cult. As the cult spread northward, a number of Christian elements were added, and the religion was incorporated in 1914 under the name of "The First-Born Church of Christ," later to become "The Native American Church." The attitude one should possess before receiving the peyote in the religious ceremony is similar to that emphasized in other Christian churches before communion, i.e., consciousness of personal inadequacy, humility, and sincerity. The denouement of the experience is the surrender of the individual to the powers of peyote, at which point individuals often rise to confess their sins. Peyote, by its power of direct revelation, is considered a teacher that will lead the individual to an ethical stance strikingly similar to that of Christian belief, that is, emphasizing brotherly love, care of family, and self-reliance.
6. Walton, *Marihuana,* p. 30.
7. E. Marcovitz and H. J. Myers, "The Marihuana Addict in the Army," *War Med.,* 6 (1944), 391; S. Charen and L. Perelman, "Personality Studies of Marihuana Addicts," *Amer. J. Psychiat.,* 102 (1946), 682; H. L. Freedman and M. J. Rockmore, "Marihuana: A Factor in Personality Evaluation and Army Maladjustment," *J. Clin. Psychopathology,* 7 (1946), 772, and 8 (1946), 222; H. F. Gaskill, "Marihuana, an Intoxicant," *Amer. J. Psychiat.,* 102 (1945), 202.
8. Freedman and Rockmore, "Marihuana: A Factor in Personality Evaluation," 7 (1946), 765–781.
9. Ibid.
10. M. H. Keeler, "Motivation for Marihuana Use: A Correlate of Adverse Reaction," *Amer. J. Psychiat.,* 125 (1968), 386–390.
11. "Fifty Percent of College Students Have Smoked Marihuana," *Boston Globe,* poll conducted by Becker Research Corporation, March 16, 1970.
12. K. Keniston, "Heads and Seekers: Drugs on Campus, Counter-Cultures and American Society," *American Scholar,* 38 (1968–69), 98.
13. M. E. Rand, J. D. Hammond, and P. J. Moscou, "A Survey of Drug Use at Ithaca College," *J. Amer. Coll. Health Ass.,* 17 (1968), 47; D. J. Wolk, "Marijuana on the Campus: A Study at Ore University," *J. Amer. Coll. Health Ass.,* 17 (1968), 145; R. G. Hinckley, "Nonmedical Drug Use and the College Student," *J. Amer. Coll. Health Ass.,* 17 (1968), 41; G. L. Mizner, J. T. Barter, and P. H. Werme, "Patterns of Drug Use Among College Students: A Preliminary Report," *Amer. J. Psychiat.,* 127 (1970), 15–24.
14. Keniston, "Heads and Seekers," p. 99.
15. Ibid., p. 101.
16. Ibid., p. 102.
17. D. L. Farnsworth and T. W. Scott, "Marihuana: The Conditions and Consequences of Use and the Treatment of Users," in *Drugs and Youth:*

Proceedings of the Rutgers Symposium on Drug Abuse, ed. J. R. Wittenborn et al. (Springfield, Ill., 1969), pp. 168–177.

18. M. J. Corey et al., "Chromosome Studies on Patients (in Vivo) and Cells
(in Vitro) Treated with Lysergic Acid Diethylamide," *New Eng. J. Med.,*
282 (1970), 939–941; D. Dorrance, O. Janiger, and R. L. Teplitz, "In
Vivo Effects of Illicit Hallucinogens on Human Lymphocyte Chromosomes," *J.A.M.A.,* 212 (1970), 1488–1527.

7. TURNING ON

1. A. T. Weil et al., "Clinical and Psychological Effects of Marihuana in
Man," *Science,* 162 (1968), 1241; H. S. Becker, *Outsiders: Studies in the
Sociology of Deviance* (New York, 1963), p. 46; J. Rosevear, *Pot:A Hand-
book of Marihuana* (New York, 1967), p. 86; P. Laurie, *Drugs: Medical,
Psychological and Social Facts* (Harmondsworth, Eng., 1967), p. 94; E.
Goode, "Introduction" to *Marijuana* (New York, 1969), p. 9.
2. Weil et al., "Clinical and Psychological Effects," p. 1241.
3. Becker, *Outsiders,* pp. 41–42.
4. E. Marcovitz and H. J. Myers, "The Marihuana Addict in the Army,"
War Med., 6 (1944), 382–391; H. S. Gaskill, "Marihuana, an Intoxicant,"
Amer. J. Psychiat., 102 (1945), 202–203; S. Charen and L. Perelman, "Personality Studies of Marihuana Addicts," *Amer. J. Psychiat.,* 102 (1946),
674–682.
5. E. R. Bloomquist, *Marijuana* (Beverly Hills, Calif., 1968), pp. 48–49.
6. Becker, *Outsiders,* p. 58.
7. For these traits, see W. Bromberg, "Marihuana: A Psychiatric Study,"
J.A.M.A., 113 (1939), 11; L. Kolb, "Marihuana," *Federal Prohibition,* 2
(1938), pp. 22–25.
8. Becker, *Outsiders,* pp. 44–45.
9. Ibid., p. 46.
10. Ibid., pp. 46–48.
11. Ibid., pp. 48–49.
12. Ibid., p. 50.
13. Ibid., pp. 50–52.
14. Ibid., pp. 52–53.
15. Ibid., pp. 53–55. Becker sites Charen and Perelman, "Personality Studies
of Marihuana Addicts," p. 679.
16. Ibid., p. 55.
17. Ibid., pp. 55–56.
18. Ibid., pp. 56–58.
19. E. Goode, "Multiple Drug Use Among Marihuana Smokers," *Social
Problems,* 17 (1969), 54.
20. Ibid., p. 50.
21. Ibid., p. 55.
22. Ibid., p. 55.
23. Ibid., p. 56.
24. Weil et al., "Clinical and Psychological Effects," p. 1241.
25. Ibid., p. 1241.
26. *The Hippies,* ed. J. D. Brown (New York, 1967), p. 182.
27. J. S. Margolis and R. Clorfene, *A Child's Garden of Grass* (N. Hollywood, Calif., 1969), p. 155.
28. Goode, "Multiple Drug Use," p. 61.

29. Weil et al., "Clinical and Psychological Effects," p. 1241.
30. D. D. Shoenfeld, "The Sociological Study," in Mayor's Committee on Marihuana, *The Marihuana Problem in the City of New York* (Lancaster, Pa., 1944), p. 9.
31. Ibid., p. 10.
32. Ibid., p. 11.
33. Ibid.
34. G. B. Wallace, "The Clinical Study," in Mayor's Committee, *The Marihuana Problem*, p. 30.
35. Ibid.
36. Rosevear, *Pot: A Handbook*, pp. 23–24.
37. Bloomquist, *Marijuana*, p. 33.
38. A. Ginsberg, "The First Manifesto to End the Bringdown," in *The Marihuana Papers*, ed. D. Solomon (Indianapolis, 1966), p. 196.
39. Bloomquist, *Marijuana*, p. 33.
40. Brown, ed., *The Hippies*, p. 9. See N. Mailer, "The White Negro," *Advertisements for Myself* (New York, 1959), pp. 337–358.
41. A. Geller and M. Boas, *The Drug Beat* (New York, 1969), p. 147.
42. Ibid., p. 146.
43. J. F. Siler et al., "Marihuana Smoking in Panama," *Milit. Surg.*, 73 (1933), 278.
44. Geller and Boas, *Drug Beat*, p. 147.
45. J. M. Phalen, "The Marihuana Bugaboo," *Milit. Surg.*, 93 (1943), 94–95.
46. Geller and Boas, *Drug Beat*, p. 147.
47. Ibid., pp. 28–29.
48. Ibid., pp. 147–148.
49. Ibid., p. 148; J. Steinbeck IV, *In Touch* (New York, 1969), p. 97.
50. Geller and Boas, *Drug Beat*, p. 148.
51. Steinbeck, *In Touch*, p. 98.
52. Geller and Boas, *Drug Beat*, p. 148.
53. Ibid.
54. Geller and Boas, *Drug Beat*, p. 148, citing Wilfred Postell, "Marihuana Use in Vietnam: A Preliminary Report," *Vietnam Med. Bull.*, (1969).
55. Geller and Boas, *Drug Beat*, p. 151.
56. Ibid., p. 152.
57. Ibid.
58. Ibid.
59. J. Rubin, *Do It!, Scenarios of the Revolution* (New York, 1970), p. 99.
60. Rosevear, *Pot: A Handbook*, p. 58.
61. Ibid., p. 63.
62. Geller and Boas, *Drug Beat*, p. 69.
63. Ibid., pp. 69–70.
64. Rosevear, *Pot: A Handbook*, pp. 63–64.
65. Geller and Boas, *Drug Beat*, p. 70.
66. Margolis and Clorfene, *Child's Garden of Grass*, p. 120.
67. Geller and Boas, *Drug Beat*, p. 70.
68. Rosevear, *Pot: A Handbook*, p. 66.
69. Ibid.
70. Ibid.
71. Ibid., pp. 66–67.
72. Ibid., p. 67.
73. Weil et al., "Clinical and Psychological Effects," p. 1237.

74. Rosevear, *Pot: A Handbook,* pp. 67–68.
75. M. Mezzrow, *Really the Blues* (New York, 1946), as quoted in *The Drug Experience,* ed. D. Ebin (New York, 1967), p. 87.
76. Geller and Boas, *Drug Beat,* p. 71.
77. Rosevear, *Pot: A Handbook,* pp. 70–72.
78. Geller and Boas, *Drug Beat,* p. 73.
79. Rosevear, *Pot: A Handbook,* pp. 76–78.
80. Ibid., p. 77.
81. Geller and Boas, *Drug Beat,* p. 73.
82. Ibid., p. 63.
83. Ibid., p. 64.
84. Ibid., p. 30.
85. Ibid., pp. 143–144.
86. Ibid., p. 62.
87. Ibid., p. 108.
88. Ibid., p. 108.
89. Ibid.
90. Bloomquist, *Marijuana,* p. 49.
91. Shoenfeld, "Sociological Study," p. 10.
92. S. Cholst, "Notes on the Use of Hashish," in *Marihuana Papers,* ed. Solomon, pp. 217–219.
93. Becker, *Outsiders,* p. 61.
94. Ibid.
95. Ibid., p. 68.
96. Ibid., p. 76.
97. Ibid., p. 77.
98. Geller and Boas, *Drug Beat,* p. 66.
99. Ibid.
100. Ibid., pp. 66–67.
101. Ibid., pp. 67–68.
102. W. Simon and J. H. Gagnon, "Children of the Drug Age," *Saturday Review,* Sept. 21, 1968, p. 61.
103. Becker, *Outsiders,* p. 100.
104. Geller and Boas, *Drug Beat,* p. 129.
105. Ibid.
106. Ibid., p. 130.
107. Ibid., p. 130; *United Nations Single Convention on Narcotic Drugs* (1961), U.N. Doc. Sales No. 62, XI.I (1962).
108. Geller and Boas, *Drug Beat,* p. 130.
109. W. Oursler, *Marijuana: The Facts, The Truth* (New York, 1968), p. 110.
110. Ibid., p. 122.
111. Ibid., pp. 122–123.
112. Geller and Boas, *Drug Beat,* p. 130.
113. Ibid., pp. 132–133.
114. Ibid., p. 64.
115. Shoenfeld, "Sociological Study," p. 9.
116. Geller and Boas, *Drug Beat,* p. 128.
117. Ibid., p. 129.
118. Ibid., p. 138.
119. "Ric," "I Turned on 200 Fellow Students at the University of Michigan," *Esquire,* Sept. 1967, p. 101.

8. THE PLACE OF CANNABIS IN MEDICINE

1. W. B. O'Shaughnessy, "On the Preparations of the Indian Hemp, or Gunjah (*Cannabis Indica*): The Effects on the Animal System in Health, and Their Utility in the Treatment of Tetanus and Other Convulsive Diseases," *Transactions of the Medical and Physical Society of Bombay* (Calcutta, 1842), p. 460.

2. R. R. M'Meens, "Report of the Committee on Cannabis Indica," from *Transactions of the Fifteenth Annual Meeting of the Ohio State Medical Society* (Columbus, Ohio, 1860), pp. 94, 95.

3. Ibid., p. 76.

4. J. B. Mattison, "Cannabis Indica as an Anodyne and Hypnotic," *St. Louis Med. Surg. J.*, 61 (1891), 266.

5. Ibid., p. 268.

6. E. A. Birch, "The Use of Indian Hemp in the Treatment of Chronic Chloral and Chronic Opium Poisoning," *Lancet*, 1 (1889), 625.

7. Mattison, "Cannabis Indica as Anodyne," pp. 266–267.

8. W. Osler, *The Principles and Practice of Medicine*, 8th ed. (New York, 1913), p. 1089.

9. Mattison, "Cannabis Indica as Anodyne," p. 271.

10. J. R. Reynolds, "Therapeutic Uses and Toxic Effects of Cannabis Indica," *Lancet*, 1 (1890), 637.

11. Ibid.

12. Ibid., p. 638.

13. H. A. Hare, "Clinical and Physiological Notes on the Action of Cannabis Indica," *Ther. Gaz.*, 11 (1887), 225.

14. Ibid., pp. 225–226.

15. Ibid., p. 226.

16. Ibid., p. 228.

17. J. P. Davis and H. H. Ramsey, "Antiepileptic Action of Marijuana-Active Substances," *Fed. Proc.*, 8 (1949), 284–285.

18. J. Kabelík, Z. Krejčí, and F. Santavý, "Cannabis as a Medicament," *Bull. Narcotics*, 12 (1960), 20–22.

19. H. H. Kane, *Drugs That Enslave* (Philadelphia, 1881), p. 208–210.

20. S. Allentuck and K. M. Bowman, "The Psychiatric Aspects of Marihuana Intoxication," *Amer. J. Psychiat.*, 99 (1942), 250.

21. L. J. Thompson and R. C. Proctor, "Pyrahexyl in the Treatment of Alcoholic and Drug Withdrawal Conditions," *N. Carolina Med. J.*, 14 (1953), 520–523.

22. J. Moreau (de Tours), "Lypémanie avec stupeur; tendance à la démence. — Traitement par l'extrait (principle résineux) de cannabis indica — Guérison," *Lancette Gaz. Hop.*, 30 (1857), 391.

23. G. T. Stockings, "A New Euphoriant for Depressive Mental States," *Brit. Med. J.*, 1 (1947), 918–922.

24. D. A. Pond, "Psychological Effects in Depressive Patients of the Marihuana Homologue Synhexyl," *J. Neurol. Neurosurg. Psychiat.*, 11 (1948), 279.

25. C. S. Parker and F. W. Wrigley, "Synthetic Cannabis Preparations in Psychiatry: I Synhexyl," *J. Ment. Sci.*, 99 (1950), 276–279.

26. D. F. Downing, "The Chemistry of the Psychotomimetic Substances," *Quart. Rev.*, 16 (1962), 156. Downing cites S. Loewe, "Studies on the Pharmacology and Acute Toxicity of Compounds with Marihuana Activ-

ity," *J. Pharmacol. Exp. Ther.*, 88 (1946), 154–161. Downing's citation of Loewe, however, appears to be inadequate substantiation for his claims.

27. H. C. Hermon, "Psychedelicoanalysis," *J. Travis County Med. Soc.*, 13 (1968), 5, 21–25; E. J. Rolls and D. Stafford-Clark, "Depersonalization Treated by Cannabis Indica and Psychotherapy," *Guy. Hosp. Rep.*, 103 (1954), 330–336.

28. T. H. Mikuriya, "Historical Aspects of Cannabis Sativa in Western Medicine," *New Physician* (1969), p. 904.

29. E. H. Cary, "Report of the Committee on Legislative Activities," *J.A.M.A.*, 108 (1937), 2214–2215.

30. Council on Mental Health and Committee on Alcoholism and Drug Dependence, American Medical Association, "Dependence on Cannabis (Marihuana)," *J.A.M.A.*, 201 (1967), 368.

31. Council on Mental Health and Committee on Alcoholism and Drug Dependence, American Medical Association, "Marihuana and Society," *J.A.M.A.*, 204 (1968), 1181.

32. Mikuriya, "Historical Aspects," p. 905.

33. G. F. Ewens, *Insanity in India, Its Symptoms and Diagnosis with Reference to the Relation of Crime and Insanity* (Calcutta, 1908), p. 405.

34. S. Deakin, "Death from Taking Indian Hemp," *Indian Med. Gaz.*, 15 (1880), 71.

35. A. Heyndrickx, C. Scheiris, and P. Schepens, "Toxicological Study of a Fatal Intoxication by Man Due to Cannabis Smoking," *J. Pharm. Belg.*, 24 (1969), 375.

36. J. F. Howes, "A Study of Two Water Soluble Derivatives of Δ^9- Tetrahydrocannabinol," Arthur D. Little, Inc., Life Sciences Division, Cambridge, Mass. Paper presented at the Fall Meeting of the American Society for Pharmacology and Experimental Therapeutics, 1970.

37. B. J. Culliton, "Pot Facing Stringent Scientific Examination," *Science News*, 97 (1970), 105.

9. ADDICTION, DEPENDENCE, AND THE STEPPING-STONE HYPOTHESIS

1. H. Isbell and H. F. Fraser, "Addiction to Analgesics and Barbiturates," *Pharmacol. Rev.*, 2 (1950), p. 356; M. H. Seevers, "Possible Mechanisms of Physical Dependence to Narcotics," in *Origins of Resistance to Toxic Agents*, ed. M. G. Sevag, R. D. Reid, and O. E. Reynolds (New York, 1955), pp. 244–263; M. H. Seevers and G. A. Deneau, "A Critique of the 'Dual Action' Hypothesis of Morphine Physical Dependence," *Arch. Int. Pharmacodyn.*, 140 (1962), 514–520; M. H. Seevers and G. A. Deneau, "Physiological Aspects of Tolerance and Physical Dependence," in *Physiological Pharmacology*, ed. W. S. Root and F. G. Hoffman (New York, 1963), 1, 565–640; H. Isbell, "Medical Aspects of Opiate Addiction," in *Narcotic Addiction*, ed. J. A. O'Donnell and J. C. Ball (New York, 1966), p. 68.

2. W. R. Martin, "Drug Addiction," in *Drill's Pharmacology in Medicine*, ed. J. R. DiPalma, 3rd ed. (New York, 1958), pp. 281–282.

3. A. R. Lindesmith, "Basic Problems in the Social Psychology of Addiction and a Theory," in *Narcotic Addiction*, ed. O'Donnell and Ball, pp. 93, 97.

4. World Health Organization, Expert Committee on Drugs Liable to Pro-

duce Addiction: Report on the Second Session, *Tech. Rep. Ser.*, no. 21 (1950), pp. 6–7.

5. A. E. W. Smith, *The Drug Users: The Psychopharmacology of Turning On* (Wheaton, Ill., 1969), p. 109; also in R. W. Rosor, "Narcotic Addiction in Young People in the U.S.A.," and P. H. Connell, "Clinical Aspects of Amphetamine Dependence," in *Adolescent Drug Dependence*, ed. C. W. M. Wilson (London, 1968), pp. 21, 43.

6. G. F. W. Ewens, "Insanity Following the Use of Indian Hemp," *Indian Med. Gaz.*, 39 (1904), 402.

7. Panama Canal Zone Governor's Committee, April–December 1925; J. F. Siler et al., "Marihuana Smoking in Panama," *Milit. Surg.*, 73 (1933), 274.

8. *Cannabis: Report by the Advisory Committee on Drug Dependence*, Sir Edward Wayne, chairman (London, 1968), p. 76.

9. A. T. Weil, N. E. Zinberg, and J. M. Nelson, "Clinical and Psychological Effects of Marihuana in Man," *Science*, 162 (1968), 1241.

10. W. Bromberg, "Marihuana Intoxication: A Clinical Study of Cannabis Sativa Intoxication," *Amer. J. Psychiat.*, 91 (1934), 308–309.

11. W. D. M. Paton, "Drug Dependence — A Socio-Pharmacological Assessment," *Advance. Sci.*, (December 1968), 201.

12. M. I. Soueiff, "Hashish Consumption in Egypt, with Special Reference to Psychological Aspects," *Bull. Narcotics*, 19 (1967), 8; S. Allentuck and K. M. Bowman, "The Psychiatric Aspects of Marihuana Intoxication," *Amer. J. Psychiat.*, 99 (1942), 249.

13. Siler et al., "Marihuana Smoking in Panama," p. 277.

14. *The Pharmacological Basis of Therapeutics*, ed. L. S. Goodman and A. Gilman, 3rd ed. (New York, 1965), p. 301.

15. M. Hayman, "The Myth of Social Drinking," *Amer. J. Psychiat.*, 124 (1967), 585–594.

16. F. R. Gomila, "Present Status of the Marihuana Vice in the United States," in *Marihuana, America's New Drug Problem*, by R. P. Walton (Philadelphia, 1938), pp. 27–39; Paton, "Drug Dependence," p. 207.

17. U.S. Congress, House, Ways and Means Committee, *Taxation of Marihuana, Hearings on H.R. 6385*, 75th Cong., 1st sess., April 27, 28, 29, 30, and May 4, 1937, statement of H. J. Anslinger, Commissioner of Narcotics, Bureau of Narcotics, Department of the Treasury, p. 24.

18. A. R. Lindesmith, "The Marihuana Problem: Myth or Reality?" in *The Marihuana Papers*, ed. D. Solomon (Indianapolis, 1966), p. 25; also, A. Lindesmith, "Introduction," ibid., p. xxiii.

19. H. J. Anslinger and C. R. Cooper, "Marihuana: Assassin of Youth," *American Magazine*, July 1937, pp. 19–20, 150–153.

20. J. Mandel, "Who Says Marijuana Use Leads to Heroin Addiction?" *Journal of Secondary Education*, 43 (1968), 217; citing Dep. Com. G. W. Cunningham, testifying before the Congressional Committee on Appropriations, Jan. 9, 1950, fn. 10.

21. Ibid., pp. 211–212; citations p. 216. Professional literature: *Merck's Index* (1930); Torwald's *Manual of Pharmacology* (1932 or 1936); *Milit. Surg.* (1933); *Amer. J. Nurs.* (1936); *U.S. Dispensatory* (pre-1937 edition); *J. Mich. State Med. Soc.* (1937); *J. Ment. Sci.* (1938); *J. Kansas Med. Soc.* (1939); Cushny's *Pharmacology and Therapeutics* (1940); Wilson and Bruce's *Neurology* (1940); Yunken's *Textbook of Pharmacognosy* (1943); *War Med.* (1944); *Amer. J. Psychiat.* (3 articles in 1945, 1 in 1946); *Amer. J. Pharm.* (1945); and *J. Clin. Psychopathology* (1946). Lay articles and

books: *New York Police Journal* (1929 and 1937); *American Journal of Police Science* (1931); *Journal of Criminal Law and Criminology* (1933); *San Francisco Police and Peace Officers Journal* (1934); FBI's *Law Enforcement Bulletin* (1937 and 1938); and *Federal Probation* (1946). Eighteen other publications: Payne's *The Menace of Narcotic Drugs* (1931); *Good Housekeeping* (1935); *American Mercury* (1935); Donnelly's *Alcohol and the Habit-forming Drugs* (1936); *Popular Science Monthly* (1936); *Literary Digest* (1936); *Newsweek* (1937 and 1946); *Hygeia* (1937 and 1940); Hearst's *International Cosmopolitan* (1938); *Christian Century* (1938); *New York Herald Tribune Forum* (1938); *Scientific American* (1938); *Hansen's Conspiracy of Silence* (1938); *Forum and Century* (1939); *Almack's Facts First on Narcotics* (1939); and *Life* (1943).

22. A. E. Fossier, "The Marihuana Menace," *New Orleans Med. Surg. J.*, 84 (1931), 249.
23. Mandel, "Who Says Marijuana Leads to Heroin," p. 212.
24. F. R. Gomila, "Present Status of Marihuana Vice," in Walton, *Marihuana*, pp. 27–39.
25. Mandel, "Who Says Marijuana Leads to Heroin," p. 212 (citing P. O. Wolff, *Journal of Criminal Law and Criminology*, 34 [1943]).
26. *Social Work Technique*, 1937, as mentioned by Mandel, "Who Says Marijuana Leads to Heroin," p. 212.
27. Mandel, "Who Says Marijuana Leads to Heroin," p. 212.
28. Lindesmith, "Marihuana Problem: Myth or Reality?" p. 23.
29. Ibid.
30. A. Geller and M. Boas, *The Drug Beat* (New York, 1969), p. 89.
31. Mandel, "Who Says Marihuana Leads to Heroin," pp. 212–213, citing 3 articles: Bromberg, "Marihuana Intoxication," pp. 303–330; S. Charen and L. Perelman, "Personality Studies of Marihuana Addicts," *Amer. J. Psychiat.*, 102 (1946), 674–682; P. H. Drewry, "Some Psychiatric Aspects of Marijuana Intoxication," *Psychiat. Quart.*, 10 (1936), 232–242.
32. D. D. Shoenfeld, "The Sociological Study," in Mayor's Committee on Marihuana, *The Marihuana Problem in the City of New York* (Lancaster, Pa., 1944), p. 13.
33. Mandel, "Who Says Marijuana Leads to Heroin," p. 213.
34. Ibid.
35. Ibid., p. 217, reference 11, citing *Newsweek*, Nov. 20, 1950, June 11, 1951, and July 9, 1951; *Woman's Home Companion* (June 1951); *Life* (June 16, 1961); *U.S. News and World Report* (June 29, 1951); *New Yorker* (Aug. 11, 1951); *Science Digest* (April 1952); *Saturday Review* (Sept. 19, 1953); and reference 12, citing *Fortnight* (Aug. 1951); *Reader's Digest* (Oct. 1951); Vogel's *Facts about Narcotics* (1951); *California Peace Officer* (May–June 1952); and Deutsch's *Public Affairs Pamphlet* on drugs (1952).
36. Mandel, "Who Says Marijuana Leads to Heroin," p. 213.
37. Ibid.
38. G. Piel, "Narcotics: War Has Brought Illicit Traffic to All-Time Low, but U.S. Treasury Fears Rising Postwar Addiction," *Life* magazine, July 19, 1943, p. 83.
39. Mandel, "Who Says Marijuana Leads to Heroin," p. 213.
40. G. Connery, "Control of Narcotic Addiction," *J.A.M.A.*, 147 (1951), 1162.
41. Mandel, "Who Says Marijuana Leads to Heroin," p. 214.
42. Ibid.

43. Lindesmith, "Marihuana Problem: Myth or Reality?" p. 24.
44. Ibid., p. 25.
45. H. J. Anslinger, "Teenage Addicts: New Problem?" in *U.S. News and World Report*, June 1951, p. 18.
46. U.S. Congress, House, Committee on Appropriations, *Department of Treasury and Post Office and Executive Office of the President Appropriations for 1968*, Hearings before a Subcommittee of the Committee on Appropriations, 90th Cong., 1st sess., Feb. 8, 1967, p. 477.
47. "Interview with John E. Ingersoll, Director, Federal Bureau of Narcotics: Dangers in Dope, Teen-Age Addicts: Drug Menace: How Serious?", *U.S. News and World Report*, May 25, 1970, p. 41.
48. R. W. Emerson, *Selections from Ralph Waldo Emerson*, in *An Organic Anthology*, ed. S. E. Whicher (Boston, 1957), p. 153.
49. E. Goode, "Multiple Drug Use among Marihuana Smokers," *Social Problems*, 17 (1969), 52.
50. "Interview with John E. Ingersoll," p. 42.
51. Mandel, "Who Says Marijuana Leads to Heroin," p. 214.
52. Ibid., p. 215.
53. Ibid.
54. MacFarland and Hall, *Journal of Criminal Law, Criminology, and Police Science* (1953), as cited in Mandel, "Who Says Marijuana Leads to Heroin," p. 214.
55. P. Zimmering et al., "Heroin Addiction in Adolescent Boys," *J. Nerv. Ment. Dis.*, 114 (1951), 20.
56. New York City Youth Board, *Reaching the Teen-Age Addict* (1960 or later), cited in Mandel, "Who Says Marijuana Leads to Heroin," p. 215.
57. L. Bender, "Drug Addiction in Adolescence," *Compr. Psychiat.*, 4 (June 1963), 181–193; I. Chein et al., *The Road to H.: Narcotics, Delinquency, and Social Policy* (New York, 1964), pp. 149–150.
58. Mandel, "Who Says Marijuana Leads to Heroin," p. 216.
59. U.S. Congress, House, Ways and Means Committee, *Control of Narcotics, Marihuana, and Barbiturates, Hearings on H.R. 3490 and H.R. 348*, 82nd Cong., 1st sess., April 7, 14, and 17, 1951, statement of George W. Cunningham, Deputy Commissioner, Bureau of Narcotics, Treasury Department, p. 64.
60. Task Force on Narcotics and Drug Abuse, The President's Commission on Law Enforcement and Administration of Justice, *Task Force Report, Narcotics and Drug Abuse (Annotation and Consultants' Papers)* (Washington, 1967), p. 13.
61. N. E. Zinberg and A. T. Weil, "A Comparison of Marijuana Users and Non-Users," *Nature*, 226, (1970), 122.
62. Paton, "Drug Dependence," pp. 207–208.
63. Ibid., p. 207.
64. Ibid.
65. Ibid., pp. 207–208.
66. Ibid., p. 201, table #3.
67. D. P. Ausubel, "Controversial Issues in the Management of Drug Addiction: Legalization, Ambulatory Treatment, and the British System," *Ment. Hyg.*, 44 (1960), 542 (quoting A. R. Lindesmith, "The British System of Narcotics Control," *Law and Contemporary Problems*, 22 [1957], 140).

68. Ibid.
69. P. Laurie, *Drugs: Medical, Psychological and Social Facts* (Baltimore, 1967), pp. 19–20, 52–53.
70. Paton, "Drug Dependence," p. 208.
71. S. Abrams, "The Case Against Paton," *Student Magazine*, summer issue, 2, (1969), 50.
72. Ibid.
73. Ibid.
74. J. T. Carey, *The College Drug Scene* (Englewood Cliffs, N.J., 1968), p. 43.
75. Goode, "Multiple Drug Use," p. 52.
76. Ibid., p. 59.
77. Ibid., p. 60.
78. H. H. Nowlis, *Drugs on the College Campus* (Garden City, N.Y., 1969), p. 36.
79. J. H. Jaffe, "Drug Addiction and Drug Abuse," in *Pharmacological Basis of Therapeutics,* ed. Goodman and Gilman, 3rd ed., p. 286.
80. P. H. Hoch, "Comments on Narcotic Addiction," *Compr. Psychiat.,* 4 (1963), 143.
81. H. Brill, "Misapprehensions About Drug Addiction: Some Opinions and Repurcussions," *Compr. Psychiat.,* 4 (1963), 157.
82. Nowlis, *Drugs on the College Campus,* p. 36; quoting D. P. Ausubel, "Some Future Directions for Research in Adolescent Drug Addiction," *Adolescence,* 1 (1966), 70–78.
83. E. Goode, "Multiple Drug Use," p. 50.
84. "The Crutch that Cripples," Committee on Alcoholism and Drug Dependence, Council on Mental Health, American Medical Association (1968), reprinted in *Drug Awareness,* ed. R. E. Horman and A. M. Fox (New York, 1970), p. 204.
85. Ibid., p. 215.
86. Ibid., p. 216.
87. Mandel, "Who Says Marijuana Leads to Heroin," p. 216.

10. PSYCHOSES, ADVERSE REACTIONS, AND PERSONALITY DETERIORATION

1. J. H. Tull-Walsh, "Hemp Drugs and Insanity," *J. Ment. Sci.,* 40 (1894), 21–36. He cites A. Simpson, "Annual Report Dacca Lunatic Asylum for 1862"; A Fleming, "Annual Report Moorshedabad Lunatic Asylum, 1862"; J. McClelland, Officiating Principal Inspector General Medical Department, "Annual Report on Lunatic Asylums, Bengal, 1863"; A. Simpson, "Annual Report Dacca Lunatic Asylum for 1863"; W. B. Beatson, "Annual Report Dacca Lunatic Asylum for 1864"; R. F. Hutchinson, "Annual Report Patna Lunatic Asylum for 1865"; A. Eden, "Government Resolution, 1866"; N. Jackson, "Annual Report Cuttack Lunatic Asylum for 1866"; J. Wise, "Annual Report Dacca Lunatic Asylum for 1867"; H. C. Cutcliffe, "Annual Report Dacca Lunatic Asylum for 1869"; W. D. Stewart, "Annual Report Cuttack Lunatic Asylum for 1867"; J. D. Wise, "Annual Report Dacca Lunatic Asylum for 1868"; R. F. Hutchinson, "Annual Report Patna Lunatic Asylum for 1868"; A. J. Payne, "Annual Report Dallanda Lunatic Asylum for 1871"; A. Mackenzie, "Government Resolution on Asylum Report, 1871"; J. Campbell Brown, Inspector General of

Hospitals, Bengal, "Annual Report on Asylums, 1872"; J. Wise, "Annual Report Dacan Lunatic Asylum for 1872."

2. R. P. Walton, *Marihuana, America's New Drug Problem* (Philadelphia, 1938), p. 142.

3. A. Eden, "Government Resolution, 1866," in Tull-Walsh, "Hemp Drugs and Insanity," p. 25.

4. A. Simpson, "Annual Report Dacca Lunatic Asylum for 1863," in Tull-Walsh, "Hemp Drugs and Insanity," p. 24; H. C. Cutcliffe, "Annual Report Dacca Lunatic Asylum for 1869," in Tull-Walsh, "Hemp Drugs and Insanity," p. 30.

5. G. F. W. Ewens, "Insanity Following the Use of Indian Hemp," *Indian Med. Gaz.,* 39 (1904), 404.

6. R. F. Hutchinson, "Annual Report Patna Lunatic Asylum for 1865," in Tull-Walsh, "Hemp Drugs and Insanity," p. 25.

7. Ibid., citing A. Simpson, "Annual Report Dacca Lunatic Asylum for 1862"; A. Fleming, "Annual Report Moorshedabad Lunatic Asylum, 1862"; A. Eden, "Government Resolution, 1866"; R. F. Hutchinson, "Annual Report Patna Lunatic Asylum for 1868"; J. Coates, "Annual Report Moydapore Lunatic Asylum for 1871"; A. MacKenzie, "Government Resolution on Asylum Reports, 1871"; J. Wise, "Annual Report Dacan Lunatic Asylum for 1872."

8. A. J. Payne, "Annual Report Dallanda Lunatic Asylum for 1871," in Tull-Walsh, "Hemp Drugs and Insanity," p. 30.

9. Ibid.

10. J. Wise, "Annual Report Dacan Lunatic Asylum for 1872," in Tull-Walsh, "Hemp Drugs and Insanity," p. 32.

11. Tull-Walsh, "Hemp Drugs and Insanity," p. 34.

12. A. MacKenzie, "Government Resolution on Asylum Reports, 1871, Bengal," in Tull-Walsh, "Hemp Drugs and Insanity," p. 31.

13. J. Warnoch, "Insanity from Hasheesh," *J. Ment. Sci.,* 49 (1903), 101–102.

14. J. E. Dhunjibhoy, "A Brief Resume of the Types of Insanity Commonly Met with in India, with a Full Description of Indian Hemp Insanity Peculiar to the Country," *J. Ment. Sci.,* 76 (1930), 263.

15. Walton, *Marihuana,* p. 147.

16. Warnoch, "Insanity from Hasheesh," pp. 99–100.

17. A. Benabud, "Psycho-pathological Aspects of the Cannabis Situation in Morocco: Statistical Data for 1956," *Bull. Narcotics,* 9 (1957), 2–16.

18. The existence of this particular type of psychosis has been seriously questioned. See J. F. Siler et al., "Marihuana Smoking in Panama," *Milit. Surg.,* 73 (1933), 269–280; J. R. Bouquet, "Cannabis," *Bull. Narcotics,* 3 (1951), 22–45; and A. Porot, "Le cannabisme," *Ann. Medicopsychol.,* 1 (1942), 1–24.

19. H. B. M. Murphy, "The Cannabis Habit: A Review of the Recent Psychiatric Literature," *Addictions,* 13 (1966), 13 (citing R. N. Chopra and G. S. Chopra, "The Present Position of Hemp Drug Addiction in India," *Indian Med. Res. Mem.,* 31 (1939).

20. Lin Tsung-yi and C. C. Standley, "The Scope of Epidemiology in Psychiatry," *Public Health Papers,* 16 (1962), 9–76.

21. Ewens, "Insanity Following Use of Hemp," p. 404.

22. Warnoch, "Insanity from Hasheesh," p. 109.

23. Tull-Walsh, "Hemp Drugs and Insanity," p. 35.

24. W. Grossman, "Adverse Reactions Associated with Cannabis Products in India," *Ann. Intern. Med.,* 70 (1969), 532.
25. Ibid.
26. Tull-Walsh, "Hemp Drugs and Insanity," p. 23.
27. Warnoch, "Insanity from Hasheesh," p. 109; A. Boroffka, "Mental Illness and Indian Hemp in Lagos," *E. Afr. Med. J.,* 43 (1966), 377–384.
28. Tull-Walsh, "Hemp Drugs and Insanity," pp. 34–35.
29. Ibid., p. 36.
30. J. Wise, "Annual Report Dacan Lunatic Asylum for 1872," in Tull-Walsh, "Hemp Drugs and Insanity," p. 32.
31. W. Keup, "Psychotic Symptoms Due to Cannabis Abuse," *Dis. Nerv. Syst.,* 30 (1970), 119.
32. H. S. Becker, "History, Culture and Subjective Experience: An Elaboration of the Social Bases of Drug-Induced Experiences," *J. Health Soc. Behav.,* 8 (1967), 172.
33. H. L. Freedman and M. J. Rockmore, "Marihuana: A Factor in Personality Evaluation and Army Maladjustment," *J. Clin. Psychopathology,* 7 (1946), 765–782, and 8 (1946), 233.
34. S. Charen and L. Perelman, "Personality Studies of Marihuana Addicts," *Amer. J. Psychiat.,* 102 (1946), 674–682.
35. H. S. Gaskill, "Marihuana, an Intoxicant," *Amer. J. Psychiat.,* 102 (1945), 204.
36. Siler et al., "Marihuana Smoking in Panama," p. 278.
37. S. Allentuck, "Medical Aspects: Symptoms and Behavior," in Mayor's Committee on Marihuana, *The Marihuana Problem in the City of New York* (Lancaster, Pa., 1944), pp. 45–51.
38. S. Allentuck and K. M. Bowman, "The Psychiatric Aspects of Marihuana Intoxication," *Amer. J. Psychiat.,* 99 (1942), 249.
39. W. Bromberg, "Marihuana, A Psychiatric Study," *J.A.M.A.,* 113 (1939), 4–12.
40. H. B. M. Murphy, "The Cannabis Habit: A Review of Recent Psychiatric Literature," *Bull. Narcotics,* 15 (1963), 12.
41. D. Perna, "Psychotogenic Effect of Marihuana," *J.A.M.A.,* 209 (1969), 1086.
42. G. D. Klee, "Marihuana Psychosis: A Case Study," *Psychiat. Quart.,* 43 (1969), 719.
43. Ibid., p. 720.
44. Ibid., pp. 720–725.
45. Ibid., p. 727.
46. Ibid., pp. 727–728.
47. Ibid., p. 730.
48. P. Dally, "Undesirable Effects of Marijuana," *Brit. Med. J.,* 3 (1967), 367.
49. Ibid.
50. Ibid.
51. Ibid.
52. Ibid.
53. J. A. Talbott and J. W. Teague, "Marihuana Psychosis: Acute Psychosis Associated with the Use of *Cannabis* Derivatives," *J.A.M.A.,* 210 (1969), 301.

54. Ibid., p. 302.
55. W. J. Tiffany, Jr., "The Mental Health of Army Troops in Viet Nam," *Amer. J. Psychiat.*, 123 (1967), 1585–1586.
56. Personal correspondence.
57. Murphy, "Cannabis Habit," p. 14.
58. L. J. Hekimian and S. Gershon, "Characteristics of Drug Abusers Admitted to a Psychiatric Hospital," *J.A.M.A.*, 205 (1968), 125–130.
59. Keup, "Psychotic Symptoms," p. 120.
60. Ibid., p. 125.
61. D. E. Smith, "Acute and Chronic Toxicity of Marijuana," *J. Psychedelic Drugs*, 2 (1968), 41.
62. H. Isbell et al., "Studies on Tetrahydrocannabinol," *Bull. Probl. Drug Dependence* (1967), p. 4838.
63. Ibid.
64. Ibid.
65. Ibid., p. 4833.
66. Becker, "History, Culture and Subjective Experience," pp. 168–169.
67. S. C. McMorris, "What Price Euphoria?: The Case Against Marihuana," *Medicoleg. J.*, 34 (1966), 78.
68. A. T. Weil, "Adverse Reactions to Marihuana," *New Eng. J. Med.*, 282 (1970), 998.
69. A. Ginsberg, "The Great Marijuana Hoax: First Manifesto to End the Bringdown," *Atlantic Monthly*, Nov. 1966, p. 109.
70. D. L. Farnsworth and T. W. Scott, "Marijuana: The Conditions and Consequences of Use and the Treatment of Users," in *Drugs and Youth: Proceedings of the Rutgers Symposium on Drug Abuse*, ed. J. R. Wittenborn et al. (Springfield, Ill., 1969), p. 172.
71. M. H. Keeler, "Adverse Reaction to Marihuana," *Amer. J. Psychiat.*, 124 (1967), 674–677.
72. Weil, "Adverse Reactions to Marihuana," pp. 999–1000.
73. N. Taylor, *Narcotics: Nature's Dangerous Gifts* (New York, 1963), p. 26.
74. N. Taylor, "The Pleasant Assassin: The Story of Marihuana," in *The Marihuana Papers*, ed. D. Solomon (Indianapolis, 1966), p. 11.
75. Mayor's Committee, *The Marihuana Problem*, pp. 142–143.
76. Freedman and Rockmore, "Marihuana: Factor in Personality Evaluation," pp. 7, 765–782; 8, 221–236.
77. Bromberg, "Marihuana: A Psychiatric Study," pp. 4–12.
78. Siler et al., "Marihuana Smoking in Panama," pp. 269–280.
79. D. L. Farnsworth, "The Drug Problem among Young People," presented at the Centennial Meeting of West Virginia State Medical Association in White Sulphur Springs, W. Va., Aug. 25, 1967.
80. M. Cohen and D. F. Klein, "Drug Abuse in a Young Psychiatric Population," *Amer. J. Orthopsychiat.*, 40 (1970), 449.
81. Ibid., p. 450.
82. Ibid., pp. 452–453.
83. Ibid., p. 452 (Table 3).
84. R. Hogan et al., "Personality Correlates of Undergraduate Marijuana Use," paper presented at the Spring Meetings of the Eastern Psychological Association, Philadelphia, 1969. Quotation from preprint, p. 8.
85. S. M. Mirin et al., "Casual versus Heavy Use of Marihuana: A Redefi-

nition of the Marihuana Problem," Psychopharmacology Laboratory, Division of Psychiatry, Boston University School of Medicine, Boston, Mass., 1970, p. 9 (preprint).

86. Ibid., p. 13.

87. See, e.g., E. Goode, "Multiple Drug Use Among Marijuana Smokers," *Social Problems*, 17 (1969), 60–61; F. W. King, "Marijuana and LSD Usage Among Male College Students: Prevalence Rate, Frequency, and Self-Estimates of Future Use," *Psychiatry*, 32 (1969), 265–276; J. D. Hensela, L. J. Epstein, and K. H. Blacker, "LSD and Psychiatric Inpatients," *Arch. Gen. Psychiat.*, 16 (1967), 554–559.

88. Mirin et al., "Casual versus Heavy Use of Marihuana," p. 10.

89. Ibid., p. 11.

90. Ibid., p. 14.

91. N. E. Zinberg and A. T. Weil, "A Comparison of Marijuana Users and Non-Users," *Nature*, 226 (1970), 119.

92. Ibid., p. 120.

93. Ibid.

94. Ibid., pp. 120–121.

95. Ibid., p. 121.

96. Ibid., p. 122.

97. Ibid.

98. A. Friendly, "Daily Pot-Smokers Erode in Intellect, Researchers Claim," *Washington Post*, April 14, 1970.

99. Zinberg and Weil, "Comparison of Marijuana Users and Non-Users," p. 122.

100. Ibid.

101. Ibid.

102. Ibid.

103. Ibid.

104. Ibid., p. 123.

105. E. S. Robbins et al., "College Student Drug Use," *Amer. J. Psychiat.*, 126 (1970), 88.

106. Ibid., p. 90.

107. Ibid., p. 91.

108. K. Keniston, "Alienation in American Youth," paper presented at the Annual Convention of the American Psychological Association, New York, Sept. 4, 1966. Braiman's discussion followed the paper.

109. Ibid.

110. C. McArthur, E. Waldron, and J. Dickinson, "The Psychology of Smoking," *J. Abnorm. Soc. Psychol.*, 56 (1958), 267.

111. Ibid., p. 272.

112. Ibid.

113. C. C. McArthur, "The Personal and Social Psychology of Smoking," in *Tobacco and Health*, ed. G. James and T. Rosenthal (Springfield, Ill., 1962), p. 294.

114. McArthur et al., "Psychology of Smoking," p. 274.

115. Ibid.

116. J. Kaufman, J. R. Allen, and L. J. West, "Runaways, Hippies, and Marihuana," *Amer. J. Psychiat.*, 126 (1969), 717–720; L. J. West and J. R. Allen, "Three Rebellions: Red, Black, and Green," in *The Dynamics of Dissent: Scientific Proceedings of the American Academy of*

Psychoanalysis, ed. Jules H. Masserman, (New York, 1968), pp. 99–119; J. R. Allen and L. J. West, "Flight From Violence: Hippies and the Green Rebellion," *Amer. J. Psychiat.,* 125 (1968), 364–370; W. H. Mc-Glothlin and L. J. West, "The Marihuana Problem: An Overview," *Amer. J. Psychiat.,* 125 (1968), 126–134; Benabud, "Psycho-pathological Aspects," pp. 10–16.

117. Allen and West, "Flight from Violence," p. 369; West and Allen, "Three Rebellions," p. 110.

118. McGlothlin and West, "Marihuana Problem," p. 128.

119. Allen and West, "Flight from Violence," p. 366.

11. CRIME AND SEXUAL EXCESS

1. H. Anslinger and C. R. Cooper, "Marihuana: Assassin of Youth," *American Magazine,* July 1937, p. 150.

2. *The Book of Ser Marco Polo The Venetian Concerning the Kingdoms and Marvels of the East,* ed. and trans. H. Yule, 3rd ed. (New York, 1903), Vol. I, book 1, chap. 23, n. 1, p. 141.

3. P. K. Hitti, *The History of the Arabs* (London, 1937), p. 446.

4. Ibid.

5. Ibid.

6. Ibid., pp. 447–448. See Yule, *Book of Marco Polo,* I, 140–142, for a discussion of just who was called the "Old Man of the Mountain."

7. Yule, *Book of Marco Polo,* I, 139–143.

8. J. Mandel, "Hashish, Assassins, and the Love of God," *Issues in Criminology,* 2 (1966), 153.

9. Ibid., p. 153. The footnote reads as follows: "Although the Ricci translation of Marco Polo quoted in this article does not describe the 'potion' in any detail, several other editions of Polo refer to the potion as 'opium' or 'an opiate.'"

10. *The Travels of Marco Polo,* ed. M. Komroff (New York, 1926), pp. xxi, xxii.

11. Ibid., p. 53.

12. *The Travels of Marco Polo,* ed. J. Masefield (London, 1926), p. 75.

13. Mandel, "Hashish, Assassins," p. 153.

14. Chronica Slavor. Arnoldi Abbatis Lubecensis, Lib. III, Cap. XXVII, p. 379, Lib. VII, Cap. X, p. 523 (1659), cited in R. Walton, *Marihuana, America's New Drug Problem* (Philadelphia, 1938), p. 15.

15. Ibid., p. 15.

16. E. R. Bloomquist, *Marijuana* (Beverly Hills, Calif., 1968), p. 27.

17. *The Rubaiyat of Omar Khayyam,* trans. E. Fitzgerald (Garden City, N.Y., 1952), pp. 29–30.

18. B. Lewis, "The Sources for the History of the Syrian Assassins," *Speculum,* 27 (1952), 475–489.

19. C. Creighton, "On Indications of the Hasheesh Vice in the Old Testament," *Janus* (Amsterdam), 8 (1903), 301.

20. Ibid., pp. 243–246; 297–301.

21. Walton, *Marihuana,* p. 15, citing S. DeSacy, "Memoires sur le dynastie des Assassins et sur l'origine de leur nom," *Gaz. Nat. Moniteur Univ.,* 210 (1809), 828–830.

22. A. Dumas, *Le Comte de Monte Cristo* (1845), chap. 31.

23. B. Lewis, "The Isma'ilites and the Assassins," in *A History of the Crusades: The First 100 Years,* ed. M. Baldwin, vol. I, cited in Mandel, "Hashish, Assassins," pp. 153–154.

24. Yule, *Book of Marco Polo,* I, 143, n. 1.

25. Ibid., p. 144.

26. Mandel, "Hashish, Assassins," p. 154.

27. Lewis, "Isma'ilites and Assassins," cited ibid., pp. 154–155.

28. Mandel, "Hashish, Assassins," p. 155.

29. *Webster's Seventh New Collegiate Dictionary,* s.v. "myth."

30. A. E. Fossier, "The Marihuana Menace," *New Orleans Med. Surg. J.,* 84 (1931), 247.

31. R. Kingman, "The Green Goddess: A Study in Dreams, Drugs and Dementia," *Med. J. Rec.,* 126 (1927), 472.

32. V. Robinson, "An Essay on Hasheesh," *Medical Review of Reviews* (1912), cited in Mandel, "Hashish, Assassins," pp. 151–152.

33. A. Parry, "Menace of Marihuana," *American Mercury,* Dec. 1935, pp. 487–490.

34. W. Gard, "Youth Gone Loco; Villain is Marihuana," *Christian Century,* June 29, 1938, cited in Mandel, "Hashish, Assassins," p. 150.

35. G. R. McCormack, "Marihuana," *Hygeia* (Oct. 1937), pp. 898–900.

36. H. G. Leach, "One More Peril for Youth," *Forum and Century,* Jan. 1939, pp. 1–2.

37. W. Wolf, "Uncle Sam Fights a New Drug Menace: Marihuana," *Popular Science Magazine,* May 1936, cited in Mandel, "Hashish, Assassins," p. 151.

38. D. Maurer and V. Vogel, *Narcotics and Narcotic Addiction,* XIV (Springfield, Ill., 1954), 219 (cited ibid., p. 150).

39. T. Brown, *The Enigma of Drug Addiction* (Springfield, Ill., 1964), cited in Mandel, "Hashish, Assassins," p. 150.

40. F. T. Merrill, *Marihuana, The New Dangerous Drug,* Opium Research Committee, Foreign Policy Association, Inc., Washington Office, 1200 National Press Building, Washington, D.C. (March 1928), p. 28.

41. W. Bromberg, "Marihuana, A Psychiatric Study," *J.A.M.A.,* 113 (1939), 9.

42. Ibid., p. 10.

43. Ibid.

44. J. F. Siler et al., "Marijuana Smoking in Panama," *Milit. Surg.,* 73 (1933), 274.

45. Ibid., pp. 279–280.

46. W. Bromberg and T. C. Rodgers, "Marihuana and Aggressive Crime," *Amer. J. Psychiat.,* 102 (1946), 825.

47. Ibid., citing R. Bouquet, "L'Etude de la cannabis," *Arch. Inst. Pasteur de Tunis,* 26 (1937), 288, n. 6; E. Stanley, "Marihuana as a Developer of Criminals"; E. Marcovitz and H. J. Myers, "The Marihuana Addict in the Army," *War Med.,* 6 (1944), 382–394; Mayor's Committee on Marihuana, *The Marihuana Problem in the City of New York* (Lancaster, Pa., 1944); K. M. Bowman, "Letter to the Editor," *J.A.M.A.,* 128 (1945), 899–900; R. N. Chopra et al., "Cannabis Sativa in Relation to Mental Diseases and Crime in India," *Indian J. Med. Res.,* 30 (1942), 155–171; Bromberg, "Marihuana: A Psychiatric Study," pp. 4–12.

48. Bromberg and Rodgers, "Marihuana and Aggressive Crime," p. 825.

49. Ibid.

50. Ibid., p. 826.
51. Ibid.
52. Ibid.
53. R. N. Chopra and G. S. Chopra, "The Present Position of Hemp Drug Addiction in India," *Indian Med. Res. Mem.*, 31 (1939), 92.
54. Chopra and Chopra, "Present Position of Hemp Drug Addiction," p. 92; H. L. Freedman and M. J. Rockmore, "Marihuana: A Factor in Personality Evaluation and Army Maladjustment," *J. Clin. Psychopathology*, 8 (1946), 231, 233; H. L. Freedman and M. J. Rockmore, "Marihuana: A Factor in Personality Evaluation and Army Maladjustment," *J. Clin. Psychopathology*, 7 (1946), 782; Siler et al., "Marihuana Smoking in Panama," p. 278.
55. Bromberg, "Marihuana: A Psychiatric Study," pp. 4–12.
56. Allentuck and Bowman, "Psychiatric Aspects of Marihuana Intoxication," *Amer. J. Psychiat.*, 99 (1942), 249–250.
57. S. Charen and L. Perelman, "Personality Studies of Marihuana Addicts," *Amer. J. Psychiat.*, 102 (1946), 674.
58. H. B. M. Murphy, "The Cannabis Habit: A Review of Recent Psychiatric Literature," *Addictions*, 13 (1966), 6; also mentioned in Allentuck and Bowman, "Psychiatric Aspects of Marihuana Intoxication," p. 250.
59. O. M. Andrade, "The Criminogenic Action of Cannabis (Marihuana) and Narcotics," *Bull. Narcotics*, 16 (1964), 23–28.
60. T. Asuni, "Socio-Psychiatric Problems of Cannabis in Nigeria," *Bull. Narcotics*, 16 (1964), 28.
61. E. Stanley, "Marihuana as a Developer of Criminals," *American Journal of Police Science*, 2 (1931), 256.
62. D. D. Schoenfeld, "The Sociological Study," in Mayor's Committee, *The Marihuana Problem*, pp. 14–15.
63. Ibid., p. 24.
64. Ibid., p. 25.
65. S. Allentuck, "Medical Aspects: Symptoms and Behavior," in Mayor's Committee, *The Marihuana Problem*, p. 50.
66. D. P. Ausubel, *Drug Addiction: Physiological, Psychological, and Sociological Aspects* (New York, 1958), p. 103.
67. Ibid., p. 104.
68. L. Kolb, *Drug Addiction: A Medical Problem* (Springfield, Ill., 1962), pp. 23–24.
69. "Proceedings: White House Conference on Narcotic and Drug Abuse, September 27–28, 1962," State Department Auditorium, Washington, D.C. (Washington, G.P.O., 1963), p. 286.
70. D. W. Maurer and V. H. Vogel, *Narcotics and Narcotics Addiction* (Springfield, Ill., 1962), p. 245.
71. H. Blumer et al., *The World of Youthful Drug Use*, ADD Center Project, Final Report (Berkeley, University of California, Jan. 1967).
72. S. Abrams, "The Oxford Scene and the Law: The Oxford Scene," in *The Book of Grass: An Anthology of Indian Hemp*, ed. G. Andrews and S. Vinkenoog (New York, 1967), pp. 240–242. The quotation by G. Joachimoglu is taken from *Hashish: Its Chemistry and Pharmacology*, ed. G. E. W. Wolstenholme and J. Knight, p. 14.
73. "Playboy Panel: The Drug Revolution," *Playboy*, Feb. 1970, p. 72.
74. Ibid.

75. V. Robinson, "Concerning Cannabis Indica," in *Book of Grass*, ed. Andrews and Vinkenoog, p. 138.

76. Walton, *Marihuana*, p. 105.

77. Ibid., p. 122, citing W. Bromberg, "Marihuana Intoxication: A Clinical Study of Cannabis Sativa Intoxication," *Amer. J. Psychiat.*, 91 (1934), 303–330; R. F. Burton, trans., *The Book of the Thousand Nights and a Night*, vol. X (Kamashasta Society, Benares, 1885); H. T. Posey, "Marihuana," Ph.D. dissertation Tulane University, 1937; H. France, *Musk, Hashish, and Blood* (Falstaff, New York); E. del Favero, "Alteratzioni mentali da haschich e loro gravi conseguenze tra i negri dell' Africa Centrale," *Pensiezo Med.*, 17 (1928), 270–277; M. G. Stringaris, "Zur Klinik der Haschischpsychosen (Nach Studien in Griechenland)," *Arch. Psychiat. Nervkrankh.*, 100 (1933), 522–532, abstract in *Arch. Neurol. Psychiat.*, 34 (1935), 1085; R. Doria, "Os Fumadores de Machona, effeites e Males do vicio," *Rev. Americana* (Rio de Janeiro, 1916), pp. 64–85.

78. Walton, *Marihuana*, p. 122, citing J. M. Watt and M. G. Breyer-Brandwijk, "Forensic and Sociological Aspects of the Dagga Problem in South Africa," *S. Afr. Med. J.*, 10 (1936), 573–579 (quoting Bourhill); C. W. Burr, "Two Cases of Cannabis Indica Intoxication," *Ther. Gaz.*, 40 (1916), 554; L. Brunton, *Pharmacology, Therapeutics and Materia Medica*, 3rd ed. (1888), p. 450.

79. Allentuck and Bowman, "Psychiatric Aspects of Marihuana Intoxication," p. 249.

80. W. H. McGlothlin, "Cannabis Intoxication and Its Similarity to that of Peyote and LSD," in *Hallucinogenic Drugs: A Perspective with Special Reference to Peyote and Cannabis* (July 1964), pp. 42–47.

81. E. R. Bloomquist, "Marijuana: Social Benefit or Social Detriment?" *Calif. Med.*, 106 (1967), 348.

82. D. P. Ausubel, *Drug Addiction: Physiological, Psychological and Sociological Aspects* (New York, 1964), pp. 102–103. (Also in Bloomquist, *Marijuana*, p. 182.)

83. Bloomquist, *Marijuana*, p. 183.

84. R. D. Johnson, "Medico-Social Aspects of Marijuana," *Rhode Island Med. J.*, 51 (1968), 173.

85. W. Oursler, *Marijuana: The Facts, The Truth* (New York, 1968), p. 10.

86. Ibid., p. 37.

87. Ibid., pp. 77–78.

88. F. Halpern, "Emotional Reactions and General Personality Structure," in Mayor's Committee, *The Marihuana Problem*, p. 130.

89. Allentuck, "Medical Aspects," p. 38.

90. W. H. McGlothlin, "Cannabis: A Reference," in *The Marihuana Papers*, ed. D. Solomon (Indianapolis, 1966), pp. 405–406.

91. R. J. Bouquet, "Cannabis, Parts III–V," *Bull. Narcotics*, 3 (1951), 32.

92. I. C. Chopra and R. N. Chopra, "The Use of Cannabis Drugs in India," *Bull. Narcotics*, 9 (1957), 9–29, in *Marihuana Papers*, ed. Solomon, p. 405.

93. McGlothlin, "Cannabis: A Reference," p. 405; A. Benabud, "Psychopathological Aspects of the Cannabis Situation in Morocco. Statistical Data for 1956," *Bull. Narcotics*, 9 (1957), 1–16; Bouquet, "Cannabis, Parts III–V," pp. 22–43; Chopra and Chopra, "Cannabis Drugs in India," pp. 4–29.

94. McGlothlin, "Cannabis: A Reference," p. 405.

95. T. T. Brown, *The Enigma of Drug Addiction* (Springfield, Ill., 1961), pp. 68–69.

96. J. Rosevear, *Pot: A Handbook of Marihuana* (New York, 1967), p. 91.

97. Blum quoted in A. Geller and M. Boas, *The Drug Beat* (New York, 1969), p. 104.

98. N. Taylor, *Narcotics: Nature's Dangerous Gifts* (New York, 1963), p. 32.

99. Bloomquist, *Marijuana*, p. 183.

100. A. Trocchi, "Marihuana and Sex," in *Book of Grass*, ed. Andrews and Vinkenoog, p. 108.

101. V. Robinson, "Experiments with Hashish," *Ciba Symposia*, 8 (1946), 388.

102. Ibid., p. 395.

103. Anonymous, "The Smoker's View," in *Marijuana*, ed. E. Goode (New York, 1969), p. 55.

104. Ibid., p. 57.

105. T. Gautier, "Le Club des Haschischins," *Review des Deux Mondes*, Feb. 1, 1846, quoted in *Marihuana Papers*, ed. Solomon, pp. 130–131.

106. E. Goode, "Marijuana and Sex," *Evergreen*, 66 (May 1969), 19–20.

107. Ibid., p. 20.

108. Ibid.

109. Ibid.

110. Ibid.

111. Ibid., pp. 20–21.

112. Ibid., p. 21.

113. Ibid.

114. Ibid., p. 72.

115. Ibid., pp. 72–73.

12. THE CAMPAIGN AGAINST MARIHUANA

1. H. S. Becker, *Outsiders: Studies in the Sociology of Deviance* (New York, 1963), p. 141.

2. H. J. Anslinger and C. R. Cooper, "Marihuana: Assassin of Youth," *American Magazine*, July 1937, pp. 19, 50.

3. Council on Mental Health and Committee on Alcoholism and Drug Dependence, American Medical Association, "Dependence on Cannabis (Marihuana)," *J.A.M.A.*, 201 (1967), 368–371; Council on Mental Health and Committee on Alcoholism and Drug Dependence, American Medical Association, "Marihuana and Society," *J.A.M.A.*, 204 (1968), 1181–1182.

4. E.g., "Marihuana Thing," *J.A.M.A.*, 204 (1968), 1187.

5. "Dependence on Cannabis (Marihuana), p. 368.

6. Ibid., p. 369.

7. Ibid., p. 370.

8. Ibid., p. 370.

9. Ibid., p. 370.

10. Ibid., p. 371.

11. Ibid., p. 369.

12. "Marihuana and Society," pp. 1181–1182.

13. A. Crancer et al., "Comparison of the Effects of Marihuana and Alcohol on Simulated Driving Performance," *Science*, 164 (1969), 851–854.

14. A. B. King and D. R. Corven, "Effect of Intravenous Injection of Marihuana," *J.A.M.A.*, 210 (1969), 724–725.

15. N. E. Gary and V. Keylon, "Intravenous Administration of Marihuana," *J.A.M.A.*, 211 (1970), 501.

16. J. A. Talbott and J. W. Teague, "Marihuana Psychosis: Acute Toxic Psychosis Associated with the Use of Cannabis Derivatives," *J.A.M.A.*, 210 (1969), 299–302.

17. D. Perna, "Psychotogenic Effect of Marihuana," *J.A.M.A.*, 209 (1969), 1085–1086.

18. J. Fort, "Pot: A Rational Approach," *Playboy*, Oct. 1969, pp. 131, 154, 216–228.

19. G. M. Carstairs, "Daru and Bhang: Cultural Factors in the Choice of Intoxicants," *Quart. J. Stud. Alcohol*, 15 (1954), 224–226.

20. Ibid., pp. 235–236.

21. G. J. Tauro, "A Judicial Opinion: Commonwealth v. Joseph D. Leis and Ivan Weiss," *Suffolk University Law Review* 3 (1968), 23–41.

22. M. Hayman, "The Myth of Social Drinking," *Amer. J. Psychiat.*, 124 (1967), 585–594.

23. D. Horton, "The Functions of Alcohol in Primitive Societies: A Cross-Cultural Study," *Quart. J. Stud. Alcohol*, 4 (1943), 199–320.

24. "Nightmare in the Catskills," editorial, *New York Times*, Aug. 18, 1969.

25. "Notes and Comments," *New Yorker*, Aug. 30, 1969, p. 19.

26. Ibid., p. 17.

27. Ibid., p. 19.

28. J. L. Titchener, "A Remarkable Assemblage," paper presented at the Fall Meetings of the American Psychoanalytic Association, Dec. 11–14, 1969, New York.

29. T. Eli Mahi, "A Preliminary Study on Khat Together with the Institutional History of Coffee as a Beverage in Relation to Khat," World Health Organization Regional Office for the Eastern Mediterranean, March 1962.

30. "At a Commune for Diggers Rules are Ten and Simple," *New York Times*, June 1, 1967.

31. D. F. Aberle, *The Peyote Religion among the Navaho* (Chicago, 1966), pp. 210–214. Unlike the use of alcohol in religious ritual, the practice of using peyote has undergone frequent attack by lawmakers. The federal opposition to peyotism was spearheaded by the Indian Bureau, which made several unsuccessful attempts, beginning in 1908, to have peyote included in the Liquor Suppression Act. This was accomplished in 1923 and repealed in 1935. Nine Congressional bills to prohibit peyote were defeated between the years 1916 and 1937. Under strong pressure from Christian missionaries, the Indian Bureau disseminated antipeyote propaganda. In 1933, John Collier became Commissioner of Indian Affairs and was instrumental in bringing about a more tolerant attitude toward peyotism. Since 1937, opposition at the federal level has largely disappeared, although a bill to make peyote illegal was introduced in the House as late as 1963. Recent action by the state supreme courts of Arizona and California has virtually eliminated resistance at the state level. The case against the religious use of peyote is a weak one. There has never been a study conducted of the long-term effects on humans. Immediate physiological effects are minor (nausea and vomiting), and claims of peyote-induced psychoses, though not totally without foun-

dation, are typically of a vague and general nature. Most observers regard the introduction of alcohol to the Indians to be much more devastating than peyote.

32. Excerpts from a lecture on world problems by C. P. Snow at Westminster College, Fulton, Mo., Nov., 12, 1968, J. Findley Green Lecture, *New York Times*, Nov. 13, 1968.

13. THE QUESTION OF LEGALIZATION

1. R. H. Blum and associates, "Drugs, Behavior, and Crime," *Society and Drugs: Social and Cultural Observations* (San Francisco, 1969), I, 277–291.
2. Ibid., pp. 100–101.
3. Ibid., p. 74, citing B. W. Sigg, *Le Cannabisme chronique: Fruit du sous developpement et du capitalisme* (Marrakesch, 1960; Algiers, 1963).
4. Ibid., p. 55, citing *Narcotic Addiction*, ed. J. A. O'Donnell and J. C. Ball (New York, 1966).
5. R. N. Chopra and G. S. Chopra, "The Present Position of Hemp Drug Addiction in India," *Indian Med. Res. Mem.*, 31 (1939), 1–119.
6. Blum et al., *Society and Drugs*, pp. 35–36, citing K. H. Connell, "Ether Drinking in Ulster," *Quart. J. Stud. Alcohol*, 26 (1965), 629–653.
7. L. E. Hollister, "Criminal Laws and the Control of Drugs of Abuse: An Historical View of the Law (Or, It's the Lawyer's Fault)," *J. Clin. Pharmacol. J. New Drugs* (1969), pp. 345–348.
8. F. M. Berger and J. Potterfield, "Drug Abuse and Society," in *Drugs and Youth: Proceedings of the Rutgers Symposium on Drug Abuse*, ed. J. R. Wittenborn et al., (Springfield, Ill., 1969), p. 41, citing *Vital Statistics in the United States* (Washington: G.P.O., 1965).
9. *Proceedings of the White House Conference on Narcotic and Drug Abuse* (Washington, G.P.O., 1962).
10. F. Mount, "The Wild Grass Chase," *National Review*, Jan. 30, 1968, p. 83.
11. "Editor's Foreword: The Marihuana Myths," in *The Marihuana Papers*, ed. D. Solomon (Indianapolis, 1966), p. xv.
12. Ibid.
13. A. R. Lindesmith, "The Marihuana Problem: Myth or Reality?" in *Marihuana Papers*, ed. Solomon, p. 27.
14. "House OKs Drug Bill Favoring Treatment Prevention: Attempts to Limit Amphetamine Production Torpedoed," *Drugs and Drug Abuse Education Newsletter*, 1 (1970), 14–15. Public Law 91-513, 91st Cong., H.R. 18583, Oct. 27, 1970.
15. J. Kaplan, "What Legislators Should Consider," in *Drugs and Youth*, ed. Wittenborn et al., p. 254.
16. Kaplan, "What Legislators Should Consider," p. 256.
17. Ibid.
18. J. Reichman, testimony given before the Senate Public Health and Safety Committee, Los Angeles, Calif., Oct. 18, 1967, pp. 5–6.
19. Ibid.
20. Ibid.
21. Ibid.
22. N. L. Chayet, "Legal Aspects of Drug Abuse," in *Drugs and Youth*, ed. Wittenborn et al., p. 241.
23. J. Glenn, "Narcotics Conviction Can Hurt Job Chances Students Warned,"

Los Angeles Times, Nov. 29, 1967; also in E. R. Bloomquist, *Marijuana,* p. 133.

24. L. Shearer, "Why Students Take Pot," *Parade,* June 4, 1967, p. 10, quoting Dean George May.

25. J. E. Ingersoll, interview, *U.S. News and World Report,* May 25, 1970, p. 42.

26. Bloomquist, *Marijuana,* p. 134.

27. "Fifty Percent of College Students Have Smoked Marihuana," *Boston Globe,* poll conducted by Becker Research Corporation, March 13, 1970.

28. J. Fort, "Pot: A Rational Approach," *Playboy,* Oct. 1969, p. 222.

29. L. Fiedler, *On Being Busted* (New York, 1970).

30. Rosenthal, "Marihuana: Some Alternatives," in *Drugs and Youth,* ed. Wittenborn et. al., pp. 260–279.

31. E. Goode, "The Marijuana Market," *Columbia Forum,* 7 (1969), 6.

32. Rosenthal, "Marihuana: Some Alternatives," p. 272.

33. J. S. Mill, "On Liberty," in *Great Books of the Western World,* ed. R. Maynard Hutchins, 43 (New York, 1952), 271–273.

34. B. de Spinoza, "Of Aristocracy," in *The Chief Works of Benedict de Spinoza,* trans. R. H. M. Elwes (New York, 1951), p. 381. (Quotes Ovid, *Amores,* 3. 4. 17.)

35. B. de Spinoza, "Freedom of Thought and Speech," in *Chief Works of Benedict de Spinoza,* trans. Elwes, p. 261.

36. Fort, "Pot: A Rational Approach," pp. 22, 225.

37. Ibid., p. 225.

38. Mr. Justice Brandeis, Dissenting Opinion, Olmstead et al. v. United States, 277 U.S. 438, 471 (1927).

39. A. D. Brooks, "Marihuana and the Constitution: Individual Liberties and Puritan Virtues," in *Drugs and Youth,* ed. Wittenborn et al., p. 297.

40. D. S. Greenberg, "Hash in Holland: The Dutch Find It Easier to Let Traffic Flourish," *Science,* 165 (1969), 476.

41. Ibid.

42. Ibid., p. 478.

43. Harvard *Crimson,* Jan. 6, 1970, pp. 1, 4.

44. Ibid.

45. M. Hayman, "The Myth of Social Drinking," *Amer. J. Psychiat.,* 124 (1967), 585–594.

14. MARIHUANA: SIX YEARS OF RECONSIDERATION

1. National Institute on Drug Abuse, "Public Experience with Psychoactive Substances: A Nationwide Study Among Adults and Youth" (Washington, D.C.: Government Printing Office, 1975), cited in "NORML Memo," May 1976, pp. 2, 3.

2. *Marihuana: A Signal of Misunderstanding,* Official Report of the National Commission on Marihuana and Drug Abuse (New York: New American Library, 1972), p. 165.

3. Statement by L. Grinspoon, M.D., before the National Commission on Marihuana and Drug Abuse, 1972.

4. California Legislature Select Committee on Control of Marijuana, *Marijuana: Beyond Misunderstanding* (May 1974), p. 118.

5. *The Leaflet* (publication of the National Organization for the Reform of Marijuana Laws) 5(3), 1976, p. 10.

6. "Public Experience with Psychoactive Substances," cited in "NORML Memo," p. 4.

7. Strategy Council on Drug Abuse, *Federal Strategy for Drug Abuse and Drug Traffic Prevention* (Washington, D.C.: Government Printing Office, 1976) pp. v, 1.

8. R. E. Schultes, W. M. Klein, T. Plowman, and T. E. Lockwood, "Cannabis: An Example of Taxonomic Neglect," *Botanical Museum Leaflets,* Harvard University, vol. 3, no. 9 (1974), pp. 337–367; E. Small and A. Cronquist, "A Practical and Natural Taxonomy for Cannabis," *Taxonomy,* 25 (1976), pp. 405–435.

9. H. Klonoff and M. D. Low, "Psychological and Neurophysiological Effects of Marijuana in Man: An Interaction Model," and H. Klonoff, "Effects of Marijuana on Driving in a Restricted Area and on City Streets," in *Marijuana: Effects on Human Behavior,* ed. L. L. Miller; A. B. Dott, "Effects on Marijuana on Aggression and Risk Acceptance in an Automotive Simulator," *Clin. Toxicol.* 7 (1974), 289.

10. T. F. Babor, A. M. Rossi, G. Sagotsky, and R. E. Meyer, "Group Behavior: Problem Solving Efficiency," in *The Use of Marihuana: A Physiological and Psychological Inquiry,* ed. J. H. Mendelson, A. M. Rossi, and R. E. Meyer; M. J. Cohen and W. H. Rickles, Jr., "Performance on a Verbal Learning Task by Subjects of Heavy Past Marihuana Usage," *Psychopharmacologia,* 37 (1974), 323–330.

11. "Marijuana and Human Aggression," in *Marijuana: Effects on Human Behavior,* p. 354.

12. F. S. Tennant, Jr., and C. S. Groesbeck, "Psychiatric Effects of Hashish," *Arch. Gen. Psychiat.,* 27 (1972), 133–136; V. Rubin and L. Comitas, *Ganja in Jamaica,* p. 155; J. A. Halikas, "Marijuana Use and Psychiatric Illness," in *Marijuana: Effects on Human Behavior.*

13. "Effects of Marihuana on Adolescents and Young Adults," *J.A.M.A.,* 216 (1971), 486–492.

14. "Cannabis Psychosis and Paranoid Schizophrenia," *Arch. Gen. Psychiat.,* 33 (1976), 383–386.

15. N. L. Benowitz and R. T. Jones, "Cardiovascular Effects of Prolonged Delta-9-tetrahydrocannabinol Ingestion," *Clin. Pharmacol. Ther.,* 18 (1975), 287–297; Rubin and Comitas, *Ganja in Jamaica,* p. 130.

16. Benowitz and Jones, "Cardiovascular Effects."

17. H. B. C. Reed, Jr., "Cognitive Effects of Marijuana," in *The Use of Marihuana: A Physiological and Psychological Inquiry;* C. Stefanis, J. Boulougouris, and A. Liakos, "Clinical and Psychophysiological Effects of Cannabis in Longterm Users," in *Pharmacology of Marihuana,* ed. M. C. Braude and S. Szara; C. M. Culver and F. W. King, "Neurophysiological Assessment of Undergraduate Marihuana and LSD Users," *Arch. Gen. Psychiat.,* 31 (1974), 707–711; P. Satz, J. M. Fletcher, and L. S. Sutker, "Neurophysiologic, Intellectual, and Personality Correlates of Chronic Marihuana Use in Native Costa Ricans," in *Chronic Cannabis Use,* ed. R. L. Dornbush, A. M. Freedman, and M. Fink; P. J. Lessin and S. Thomas, "Assessment of the Chronic Effects of Marihuana on Motivation and Achievement: A Preliminary Report," in *Pharmacology of Marihuana.*

18. Rubin and Comitas, *Ganja in Jamaica, passim,* esp. pp. 68, 104–106, 118, 192.

19. Satz et al., "Neurophysiological, Intellectual, and Personality Correlates."

20. P. Bro, J. Schon, and G. Topp, "Cannabis Poisoning with Analytical Veri-

fication," *New Eng. J. Med.,* 293 (1975), 1049–1050.

21. Rubin and Comitas, *Ganja in Jamaica;* Stefanis et al., "Clinical and Psychophysiological Effects"; W. S. Coggins, E. W. Swenson, W. W. Dawson, A. Fernandez-Salaz, J. Hernandez-Bolanos, E. F. Jimenez-Antellon, J. R. Solano, R. Vinocur, and F. Faerron-Valdez, "Health Status of Heavy Cannabis Users," in *Chronic Cannabis Use;* J. G. Bernstein, R. E. Meyer, and J. H. Mendelson, "Physiological Assessments: General Medical Survey," in *The Use of Marihuana: A Physiological and Psychological Inquiry;* H. Rosenkrantz, R. A. Sprague, R. W. Fleischman, and M. C. Braude, "Oral Delta-9-tetrahydrocannabinol Toxicity in Rats Treated for Periods of up to 6 Months," *Toxicol. Appl. Pharmacol.,* 32 (1975), 399–417.

22. A. M. G. Campbell, M. Evans, J. L. G. Thomson, and M. J. Williams, "Cerebral Atrophy in Young Cannabis Smokers," *Lancet,* 2 (1971), 1219–1224; Stefanis et al., "Clinical and Psychophysiological Effects."

23. R. Kolodny, W. Masters, R. M. Kolodner, and G. Toro, "Decreased Testosterone after Chronic Marihuana Use," *New Eng. J. Med.,* 290 (1974), 872–874; R. Kolodny, "Research Issues in the Study of Marihuana and Male Reproductive Physiology in Humans," in *Marijuana and Health Hazards: Methodological Issues in Current Research,* ed. J. R. Tinklenberg; J. H. Mendelson, J. Kuehle, J. Ellingboe, and T. F. Babor, "Effects of Marijuana on Plasma Testosterone," in *Marijuana and Health Hazards;* C. F. Schaefer, C. S. Gunn, and K. M. Dubrowski, "Normal Plasma Testosterone Concentrations after Marihuana Smoking," *New Eng. J. Med.,* 292 (1975), 867–868; R. C. Kolodny, P. Lessin, G. Toro, W. H. Masters, and S. Cohen, "Depression of Plasma Testosterone with Acute Marihuana Administration," in *Pharmacology of Marihuana;* A. B. Okey and G. S. Truant, "Cannabis Demasculinizes Rats But Is Not Estrogenic," *Life Sci.,* 17 (1975), 1113–1118.

24. Kolodny, "Research Issues"; Kolodny et al., "Depression of Plasma Testosterone."

25. Coggins et al., "Health Status of Heavy Cannabis Users."

26. Ibid.; A. E. Munsen, "Marijuana and Immunity," in *Marijuana and Health Hazards.*

27. M. A. Stenchever and M. Allen, "The Effect of Delta-9-tetrahydrocannabinol in the Chromosomes of Human Lymphocytes *in vitro,*" *Amer. J. Obstet. Gynecol.,* 114 (1972), 821; M. A. Stenchever, T. J. Kunysz, and M. Allen, "Chromosome Breakage in Users of Marijuana," *Amer. J. Obstet. Gynecol.,* 118 (1974), 106–113; S. Matsuyama, "Cytogenetic Studies of Marijuana," A. Falek, "Genetic Studies of Marijuana: Current Findings and New Directions," and M. A. Stenchever, "Observations on the Cytogenetic Effects of Marijuana," all in *Marijuana and Health Hazards.*

28. Rubin and Comitas, *Ganja in Jamaica,* p. 85; W. W. Nichols, R. C. Miller, W. Heneen, C. Bradt, L. Hollister, and S. Kanter, "Cytogenetic Studies on Human Subjects Receiving Marihuana and Delta-9-tetrahydrocannabinol," *Mutat. Res.,* 26 (1974), 413–417; S. Matsuyama, "Cytogenetic Studies."

29. Rubin and Comitas, *Ganja in Jamaica,* pp. 85–101; D. P. Tashkin, B. J. Shapiro, Y. E. Lee, and C. E. Harper, "Subacute Effects of Heavy Marihuana Smoking on Pulmonary Function in Healthy Men," *New Eng. J. Med.,* 294 (1976), 125–128.

30. T. H. Maugh II, "A Conversation with NIDA's Robert L. DuPont," *Science,* 192 (1976), 647–649.

31. Ibid., p. 648.

32. V. Rubin, "Cross-Cultural Perspectives on Therapeutic Uses of Cannabis,"

in *The Therapeutic Potential of Marihuana,* ed. S. Cohen and R. C. Still-man; S. Milstein, "Pain Tolerance and Cannabis," reported at the Collegium Internationale Neuropsychopharmacologicum Convention, Paris, 1975; M. Dunn and R. Davis, "The Perceived Effects of Marijuana on Spinal Cord Injured Males," *Paraplegia,* 12 (1974), 175; R. Noyes, F. Brunk, D. A. Baram, and A. Canter, "Analgesic Effect of Delta-9-tetrahydrocannabinol," *J. Clin. Pharmacol.,* 15 (1975), 139–143.

33. J. Kotin, R. M. Post, and F. K. Goodwin, "Delta-9-tetrahydrocannabinol in Depressed Patients," *Arch. Gen. Psychiat.,* 28 (1973), 345–348; W. Regelson, J. R. Butler, J. Schulz, T. Kirk, L. Peek, M. L. Green, and M. D. Zalis, "Δ^9-Tetrahydrocannabinol as an Effective Antidepressant and Appetite Stimulation Agent in Advanced Cancer Patients," in *Pharmacology of Marihuana.*

34. Rubin and Comitas, *Ganja in Jamaica,* pp. 155–156, 163; C. M. Rosenberg, "The Use of Marihuana in the Treatment of Alcoholism," in *Therapeutic Potential of Marihuana.*

35. P. F. Consroe, G. P. Wood, and H. Buchsbaum, "Anticonvulsant Nature of Marihuana Smoking," *J.A.M.A.,* 234 (1975), 306–307; R. Karler, W. Cely, S. A. Turkanis, "The Anticonvulsant Activity of Cannabinol and Cannabidiol," *Life Sci.,* 13 (1973), 1527–1531; D. M. Feeney, M. Spiker, and G. Weiss, "Marihuana and Epilepsy: Activation of Symptoms by Delta-9-THC," in *Therapeutic Potential of Marihuana;* P. F. Consroe, B. Jones, H. Laird III, and J. Reinking, "Anticonvulsant-Convulsant Effects of Delta-9-Tetrahydrocannabinol," in *Therapeutic Potential,* p. 375; R. Karler and S. Turkanis, "The Antiepileptic Potential of the Cannabinoids," in *Therapeutic Potential.*

36. K. Vachon, M. X. Fitzgerald, N. H. Solliday, I. A. Gould, and E. A. Gaensler, "Single Dose Effect of Marihuana Smoke," *New Eng. J. Med.,* 288 (1973), 985–989; D. P. Tashkin, B. J. Shapiro, Y. E. Lee, and C. E. Harger, "Effects of Smoked Marijuana in Experimentally Induced Asthma," *Amer. Rev. Respir. Dis.,* 112 (1975), 377–386; D. P. Tashkin, B. Shapiro, S. Reiss, J. Olsen, and J. Lodge, "Bronchial Effects of Aerosolized Delta-9-Tetrahydrocannabinol," in *Therapeutic Potential of Marihuana.*

37. R. S. Hepler and I. M. Frank, "Marihuana Smoking and Intraocular Pressure," *J.A.M.A.,* 217 (1971), 1392; R. S. Hepler, I. M. Frank, and R. Petrus, "Ocular Effects of Marihuana Smoking" in *Pharmacology of Marihuana.*

38. Randall's story is told in *The Leaflet,* 5 (3), 1976, p. 9.

39. L. S. Harris, A. E. Munsen, and R. A. Carchman, "Anti-tumor Properties of Cannabinoids," in *Pharmacology of Marihuana.*

40. S. E. Sallan, N. E. Zinberg, and E. Frei III, "Antiemetic Effect of Delta-9-tetrahydrocannabinol in Patients Receiving Cancer Chemotherapy," *New Eng. J. Med.,* 293 (1975), 795–797.

Index

Aberle, D. F., 339
Abrams, S., 311–312
Adams, R., 5, 42–44, 46, 51, 126
Addiction, 231–233, 381–382. *See also* Marihuana, effects of (addiction); Hashish, effects of (addiction)
Adverse reactions, *see* Mental illness and marihuana (acute panic states, depressive reaction, psychoses, toxic psychoses)
Africa, 202, 218, 308, 313, 344–345
Alarmist propaganda, 16–19, 23, 28, 236–238, 299–302, 310, 312, 325–327, 348. *See also* American Medical Association; Bias and prejudice against marihuana; Federal Bureau of Narcotics; Newspapers and popular literature as antimarihuana forces; White Cross
Alcohol, 254, 264–265, 312, 323, 331, 372; Baudelaire's use of, 71, 79, 80; compared to marihuana, 117, 127, 159–161, 164–165, 176, 204, 227, 228, 277, 307–329 *passim*, 349, 351, 369, 370, 374, 377, 382, 385, 396; habituation to, 27, 233, 234, 250–251, 347; legislation concerning, 184, 236, 345, 346, 354, 367, 368; lobby, 16; related to marihuana, 187, 282, 285, 334; and "stepping-stone hypothesis," 243, 244; in U.S., 174, 235, 333, 334, 371; used with marihuana, 128, 282. *See also* Classified Abstract Archive of the Alcohol Literature
Alcoholism, treatment, 223–224, 395–396
Aldrich, C. K., 157
Al-kief, 62, 318
Allen, J. R., 288
Allentuck, S., 27, 51–52, 126, 147–165 *passim*, 224, 234, 262
American Association for the Advancement of Science, 340
American Bar Association, 374
American Medical Association, 27, 228, 240, 301; on LaGuardia Report, 28, 304; on Marihuana Tax Act of *1937*, 14, 24–25, 226–227; published statements on marihuana, 29, 138, 151, 154, 157, 164, 227–228, 252, 327–331. *See also Journal of the American Medical Association*
Amphetamines, 233, 245, 278, 285, 369, 370; in Japan, 345–346; literature, 4; related to marihuana, 243, 248, 282, 351
Andrade, O. M., 308
Andrews, G., 12
Animals, effects of cannabis on, 13–14, 48–50, 127, 219, 329, 381, 398
Anslinger, Harry, 19, 238, 240–241, 377; on Assassins, 21–22, 291, 295, 296, 299; on LaGuardia Report, 27; on Marihuana Tax Act of *1937*, 11, 21–23, 236, 312, 325
Aphrodisiac, marihuana as, 58, 62, 129, 157, 312–322, 339
Arabian Nights, 85–87
Archives of General Psychiatry, 380
Armed Forces of U.S., marihuana and, 19, 156, 174–175, 195–196, 262, 304–306. *See also* Vietnam, use of marihuana in
Arrests involving marihuana, 240, 242–243, 246, 302–303, 350–356, 362–363, 366, 374, 375–376, 397–398
Aspirin, 2, 223
Assassin, 59, 311. *See also* Assassins
Assassini, *see* Assassins
Assassins, 22, 291–302
Assissini, *see* Assassins
Asuni, T., 308
Ausubel, D. P., 309–310, 314
Autotitration, 116, 128, 165, 171, 368

Balzac, 58. *See also* "Club des Haschischins"
Barbiturates, 233, 278, 285; in Japan,
346; related to marihuana, 187, 222,
227, 243, 248, 329, 351
Baudelaire, Charles, 55, 56, 64, 69–72,
79–85, 102, 108, 119; description of
acute intoxication, 72–79; on hallucination, 57–58, 168–170
Becker, H. S., 207, 211–212, 262; on
enjoyment of marihuana as learning
process, 120, 185–190, 192, 206, 271;
on Federal Bureau of Narcotics, 19,
20, 325
Becker Research Corporation, 177
Benabud, A., 258
Bhang, 37, 41, 173, 234, 254, 259, 260,
277, 331, 332, 367, 380–381
Bias and prejudice against marihuana,
15–16, 118, 119, 123, 138, 159, 269,
329, 332–339, 372–375
Biblical references, 297
Birch, E., 220, 224
"Blank warrants," 362
Bloomquist, E. R.; on acute intoxica-
tion, 130, 136, 143, 146, 147, 155,
157, 159, 164, 314, 316; on classifi-
cation of users, 186, 189, 204, 205
Blum, R., 10, 316
Blumen, H., et al., 310
Boas, M., 121, 212, 216
Boissard, Fernand, 58, 72
Boroffka, A., 260–261
Bose, B. C., et al., 49
Botanical description of cannabis, 31–
37, 375. *See also* Preparation of can-
nabis
Bouquet, R. J., 27–28, 35, 129, 147,
304, 315
Bourhill, C. J. G., 173, 313
Bowman, K. M., 27, 51–52, 126, 147–
165 *passim*, 224, 234, 262, 304
Boyd, E. S., et al., 49
Braden, William, 362
Brahmins, 331, 332
Braiman, A., 286
Brain damage, and marihuana use, 387
Brain Report, *1968*, 247–248
Brandeis, Justice Louis D., 364, 365
Brill, H., 251
"Bring down," 134, 162, 191–192, 208
Bromberg, W., 277; on acute intoxica-
tion, 123–145 *passim*, 151, 155, 163,
313; on crime and marihuana, 18,
22–23, 302–305; on dependence on
marihuana, 233–234; on psychoto-
genic effects of marihuana, 263

Brook, A. D., 365
Brown, T. T., 301–302, 315, 316
Brunton, L., 313
"Bummer," 192
Bureau of Narcotics and Dangerous
Drugs (U.S.), 19, 213, 235, 302, 323,
326. *See also* Federal Bureau of Nar-
cotics
Burroughs, William, 156, 166
Burton, R. F., 313
"Busted," 199, 363

Cahn, R. S., 42
Campbell, A. M. G., 387
Cannabichromene, 46, 53
Cannabidiol, 43, 48, 121, 396
Cannabidiolcarboxylic acid, 48
Cannabidiolic acid, 48, 121, 223
Cannabigerol, 46
Cannabinol, 42–44, 48, 121
Cannabinol derivatives, 5, 218, 230, 330.
See also Cannabichromene; Canna-
bidiol; Cannabidiolcarboxylic acid;
Cannabidiolic acid; Cannabigerol;
Cannabinol; Tetrahydrocannabinol
Cannabis, tincture of, 10
Cannabis indica, 13, 35, 220, 222, 226,
375
Cannabis ruderalis, 375
Cannabis sativa, 1, 27–48 *passim*, 121,
168, 196, 344, 375. *See also* Ter-
minology for cannabis
Cantharides, 58, 313. *See also* Aphro-
disiac
Carey, J. T., 249
Carlini, E. A., 49–50
Carstairs, G. M., 151, 331–332
Carter, President James E., 375
Cazotte, 81
Cézanne, 104–106
Charas, 37–41, 119, 137, 228, 259–261,
368, 381. *See also* Hashish
Charen, S., 262, 307
Charras, *see* Charas
Chemistry of marihuana, 42–50, 121
Chira, *see* Charas
Chloral-hydrate, 220, 222, 224
Cholst, S., 132–133
Chopra, G. S., 306, 309, 315
Chopra, I. C., 173, 259, 306, 309, 315
Chopra, R. N., 173, 259, 306, 309
Chromosome damage, marihuana use
and, 390–391
Churrus, *see* Charas
Clapton, G. T., 83
Class attitudes to marihuana, *see* Mari-
huana users (ethnic minorities)

Classified Abstract Archive of the Alcohol Literature, 4
"Club des Haschischins, Le," 58–64, 72, 108
Cocaine, 25, 30, 114, 233, 236, 238, 272, 349, 350
Coffee, 338, 344, 372
Coggins, W. J., 389
Cohen, M., 278–280
Cohen, S., 129, 154, 169, 170
Collins, Judy, 204
Comitas, L., 384, 386, 390, 391, 396
Committee on Alcoholism and Drug Dependence, see American Medical Association
Committee on Legislative Activities, 14
Confessions of an English Opium Eater, see De Quincey
Controlled Substances Act of 1970, 374, 399
Cooper, C. R., 236, 238
Costa Rica, cannabis users in, 376, 379, 383, 384–385, 387, 389, 391
Council on Mental Health, see American Medical Association
Crancer, A., et al., 161, 162
Creativity and marihuana, see Marihuana, effects of (specific: creativity). See also Music, musicians, and marihuana
Creighton, C., 297
Crépet, M. J., 80
Crime and marihuana use, 15, 17–19, 24, 29, 252, 326, 347, 361, 377; and the Assassins, 22, 291, 299–302; and Federal Bureau of Narcotics, 15, 17–19, 22–23, 236, 239, 241, 291, 299; and juvenile delinquency, 308–311; and LaGuardia Report, 26, 308–309; marihuana as deterrent to crime, 306–307; possession, sale, or giving away of cannabis as a crime, 212–213, 245, 251, 274, 347–371, 374–375, 375–376. See also Social risks in using marihuana
Criminalization of youth, 350–351, 355–358, 363–364. See also Crime and marihuana use (possession, sale, or giving away of cannabis as a crime)
Culver, C. M., 383
Cunningham, G. W., 236
Cur-ganja, see Ganja
Curiosités esthétiques, 81
Cutcliffe, H. C., 254

Dagga, 32, 173. See also Terminology for cannabis

Dally, P., 265
Dangerous Drugs Act of 1920 (Great Britain), 247
Daniel, Price (Senator), 240–241
Daru, 331
Datura, 259, 260
Davis, J. P., 223
Dawamesk, 58. See also Hashish, effects of (admixed)
Deakin, S., 228
Deaths due to cannabis, 228, 330, 347
De Boisdenier, F. B., 58
De Boismont, Brierre, 81
Del Favero, E., 313
De Nerval, Gerard, 57, 58
De Quincey, Thomas, 56, 69, 81–83, 86
DeRopp, A. S., 28
DeSacy, Sylvester, 80, 297
DET (N,N-diethyltryptamine), 168, 176
Devil's weed, 13. See also Uses for cultivated hemp
Dhunjibhoy, J. E., 256–258
Dingell, John (Representative), 25, 236
Dioxins, see 2,4–D
DMT (N,N-dimethyltryptamine), 168, 171, 176, 179
DOM, see STP
Doria, R., 313
Dose, 108, 346, 371; effective dose, 6, 227–228; and effects of marihuana, 52, 119–130 passim, 139–165 passim, 171, 221, 225, 228, 307, 321, 377; and experience of user, 116, 122; lethal, 6, 54, 227–228, 386; toxic, 6; and toxic psychosis, 259, 271, 273. See also Potency
Doughton (Representative), 20
Dow Chemical Company, 168
Downing, D. F., 46, 225
DPT (dipropyltryptamine), 168
Drug Enforcement Administration, 375
Dumas, Alexander, 58, 297
DuPont, Robert L., 393
Dylan, Bob, 159

Easterfield, T. H., 42
Eddy, N. B., et. al., 126, 127, 147, 150, 157
Eden, A., 254
Effects of hashish, see Hashish, effects of
Effects of marihuana, see Marihuana, effects of
Egypt, 218, 253, 255–258, 261
"Etheromaniacs," 345
Ethyl ether, 345
Ewens, G. F. W., 228, 233, 254, 256, 259

Falek, A., 390
Faqir, 259
Farnsworth, D. L., 181, 274, 278
Farnsworth, N. R., 121
Federal Bureau of Investigation (U.S.),
    17, 376
Federal Bureau of Narcotics (U.S.), 11,
    16–20, 27–29, 236–244 passim, 291,
    301, 320, 323, 325, 348, 356, 363.
    See also Bureau of Narcotics and
    Dangerous Drugs
"Fidawi," see Assassins
Fiedler, Leslie, 358
Fitzgerald, B., 214
Fitzgerald, E., 296
Flashbacks, 266, 275
Fletcher, J. M., 384–385
Ford, President Gerald R., 375
Foreign Policy Association, 17, 18, 302
Fort, J., 312–313, 363
Fossier, A. E., 236, 237, 299
Fraenkel, F., on acute intoxication, 123,
    135–158 passim, 165, 313
France, H., 150, 313
Freedman, H. L., 175, 262, 277
Freud, Sigmund, 114
Friedenberg, E. Z., 204

Ganja, 37, 38, 173, 254, 255, 260, 261,
    277, 304, 379, 384, 385, 396
"Ganja doctor," 36
Ganja in Jamaica, 384
Gaoni, Y., 46, 162
Gaskill, H. S., 165, 262
Gautier, Théophile, 55–58, 108, 119,
    169, 260, 318; description of acute
    intoxication, 58–64
Geller, A., 121, 212, 216
Gershon, S., 48, 49, 269
Gilman, A., 125, 234
Ginsberg, Allen, 103–109, 147, 156–
    158, 274
Giordano, H. L., 241
"Glue-sniffing," 346
Gomila, F. R., 237
Goode, E., 189, 190, 192, 249, 319–322,
    358
Goodman, L. S., 125, 234
Greece, cannabis users in, 376, 379,
    383, 387, 391
Grlic, L., et al., 48
Grossman, W., 260
Gunjah, see Ganja

Habituation, see Hashish, effects of (ad-
    diction); Marihuana, effects of (addic-
    tion); "Psychic dependence"

Haffner, G., 48
Haight-Ashbury Medical Clinic, 270
Hallucinations, see Baudelaire (on hallu-
    cination); Hashish, effects of (specific:
    hallucinations); Marihuana, effects of
    (specific: hallucinations)
"Hallucinogens," 30, 31, 62, 108, 167–
    183 passim, 252, 369; compared to
    marihuana, 164, 168, 170–171, 252;
    and flashbacks and psychotic reac-
    tions, 275; and "stepping-stone hy-
    pothesis," 180, 249, 281–282. See also
    DET, DMT, DPT, Hawaiian Wood-
    rose, LSD, MDA, mescaline, nutmeg,
    PCP, peyote, psilocybin, STP
Hamilton, H. C., 12–14
Hammer, see Von Hammer-Purgstall, J.
Hare, H. A., 221–222
Harris, L. S., 398
Harvard Crimson, 370
Hasan, 292, 293, 296–301
Hashish, 40, 55–103 passim, 119, 132–
    133, 146–148, 157–158, 169, 234,
    241–260 passim, 304, 368–369; and
    the Assassins, 296, 298, 300, 301;
    Michaux's use, 125–126, 137–138,
    140, 171; in treatment of alcoholism,
    223–224. See also Charas
Hashish, effects of: addiction, 86–87;
    admixed, 55, 58, 71, 80, 82–84; dosage,
    62–72 passim, 86, 94, 100, 101, 137;
    tolerance, 94. Specific: aftereffects,
    69, 77–78, 93, 95; age regression, 132–
    133; agitation, 60; appreciation, 137;
    attention to detail, 158; benevolence,
    73, 98; burning (stomach), 65, 66;
    coldness, 73; delirium, 63, 94; delu-
    sions, 147; depersonalization, 62, 75;
    dilation of pupils, 73; dizziness, 63,
    125; double-consciousness, 67, 68, 89;
    dreamlike, 89; dry throat, 68; euphoria,
    66; expanded consciousness, 74, 76,
    98; expansiveness, 65, 66; face (pallid),
    73; fear, 73, 90, 91; hallucinations,
    57, 58, 60–63, 66–68, 72, 74, 89–99,
    147–148, 169; heightening of senses,
    74; hilarity, 72, 73; hunger, 75; in-
    sanity (feeling of), 63, 68; insight, 75,
    94, 98, 137; interruption of digestion,
    79; joy, 133; laughter, 66, 130–131;
    lightness (feeling of), 64, 126; objec-
    tivity loss, 94; panic, 260; paranoia,
    89, 98; perception of ludicrous, 64;
    power and triumph (sense of), 66–67,
    76–77, 95; psychosis, 253, 255–258;
    pulse increase, 68, 91; rapid mental
    associations, 73, 90; relaxation, 133;

sexuality, 62; sleep, 64, 65; space distortion, 63, 89, 90, 140; strangeness (sense of), 88; stupor, 60, 73; suicide, 68, 96; synesthesia, 62, 74–75, 98; taste augmentation, 60; tension, 67; terror, 73, 88; thirst, 68, 73, 75; thrill, 60, 65, 66, 88; throbbing heart, 68, 90; time distortion, 63, 65, 67, 89, 90; toxic psychosis, 259–260, 262; visions, 94; visual changes, 60, 146; wavelike aspect, 60, 73, 89, 91, 94; weakness, 73, 79–80. *See also* Marihuana, effects of
"Hashish insanity," *see* Mental illness and marihuana ("cannabis insanity")
Hashshashin, *see* Assassins
Hassan, *see* Hasan
Hawaiian Woodrose, 168
Heissessin, 296. *See also* Assassins
Hekimian, L. J., 269
Hemp, cultivated, *see* Uses for cultivated hemp
"Hemp insanity," *see* Mental illness and marihuana ("cannabis insanity")
Henderson, A. H., 330
Herbal, 1, 143
Herodotus, 33–34
Heroin, 122, 369, 385; addiction, 233, 272, 360; on campus, 250; and crimes against property, 360; legislation, 245–248, 251–252, 345, 346, 358; and "stepping-stone hypothesis," 236–239, 241–246, 249, 251, 301, 327, 382–383
Hester, C., 21
Hiding cannabis intoxication, 133, 159, 167, 207
High Times, 372
History of marihuana: Chinese Turkestan and Hindustan, 38–39; England, 11; Russia, 12; United States, 10–29. *See also* Assassins
Hively, R. L., 47
Hoch, P. H., 251
Hogan, R., et al., 280
Homer, 21, 22
Horak, M., 48
Horton, D., 334
Houghton, E. M., 12–14
H. R. *6906*, 20–26. *See also* Legislation against marihuana
Hugo, 57, 58
Hutchinson, R. F., 254

Idée fixe, 225
Immune response, marihuana use and, 389–390

India, 173, 218, 253–261 *passim*, 306, 331–332
Indian hemp, *see* Terminology for cannabis
Indian Hemp Drugs Commission Study of *1894*, 19, 125, 276, 383, 384, 386, 387
Ingersoll, J. E., 241, 242
Insanity and marihuana use, *see* Mental illness and marihuana
Isbell, H., et al., 51, 52, 120, 128, 135–151 *passim*, 270–271

Jaffe, J. H., 123–143 *passim*, 147, 155, 250
Jamaica, cannabis users in, 376, 379, 381, 384, 385, 386, 387, 390, 391, 395, 396
Janichewsky, D. E., 375
Joachimoglu, G., 311
Joël, E., 49, 123, 135–150 *passim*, 165, 313
Johnson, R. D., 124, 156, 314
Joint, 41. *See also* Bhang
Journal of the American Medical Association, 27–29, 227, 304, 327, 329–331, 374, 379, 380. *See also* American Medical Association
Justice Department (U.S.), 32

Kabelík, J., 223
Kalant, O. J., 3
Kane, H. H., 223
Kanner, L., 145–146
Kant, F., 126, 148–149
Kaplan, J., 350, 352
Keeler, M. H., 147, 151, 156
Keniston, K., 177–180, 286
Kerim, F., 257
Keup, W., 269
Kief, *see* Al-kief
Kif, 258, 259
"Kilo," 206
King, F. W., 383
Kingman, R., 300
Klee, G. D., 263–265
Klein, D. F., 278–280
Kolansky, H., 379–380, 387
Kolb, L., 310
Kolodny, R. C., 388–389
Korte, F., 47–48
Kramer, C., 49–50
Krapf, E., 126, 148–149
Krejčí, Z., 48, 223

La Guardia, Fiorello H., 26. *See also* La Guardia Report

La Guardia Report, 26–28, 121, 277, 376, 387; on acquisition of marihuana, 212, 215, 216; on acute intoxication, 125–130, 138, 143–165 *passim;* on crime and marihuana, 308–309; on psychoses and marihuana, 262; on rolling a joint, 199–200; on sex and marihuana, 315; on self-titration, 128, 171; on "stepping-stone hypothesis," 238; on users of marihuana, 192–194, 198

Lamarck, 375

Lancet, 387

Laudanum, 56, 71, 82, 84

Laurie, P., 122, 155

Leary, Timothy, 72

Le Dain Commission (*1974*), 384

Legalization of marihuana, 367–371, 374, 391–394

Legislation against marihuana, 1–2, 8, 16, 27, 246, 247, 310, 339, 347–363 *passim;* Tunisia and Algeria, 344–345. *See also* Arrests involving marihuana; H. R. *6906; Marihuana Tax Act of 1937; Public Law 91–513;* United Nations Single Convention Narcotic and Drug Act of *1961*

LEMAR, 199

Lewis, B., 296–298

Lindesmith, A. R., 129, 164, 349

Linnaeus, 1, 375

Loewe, S., 48

LSD (lysergic acid diethylamide), 167, 182–184, 210, 212, 269, 278, 311; and consciousness expansion, 76; marihuana in relation to, 62, 116, 170–172, 176, 189, 191, 265–266, 275, 378; and morning glory seeds, 31, 168; penalties for use, 349–351, 369; psychotherapy and, 378; and set and setting, 72, 378; and "stepping-stone hypothesis," 179, 192, 241–242, 249, 250, 252; and tolerance, 232

Lubecensis, A. A., 296

Ludlow, Fitz Hugh, 55, 56, 60, 69–88 *passim,* 102–103, 108, 119, 133, 149–150, 260, 273; description of acute intoxication, 85–101

McArthur, C., et al., 286

McCormack, John (Representative), 23

McGlothlin, W. H., 129, 150, 151, 163, 288, 314, 315

MacKenzie, A., 255

M'Meens, R. R., 219, 220

Mailer, Norman, 195

Mandel, J.: on Assassins, 22, 295, 296; on "stepping-stone hypothesis," 236, 238–240, 243, 252

Marco Polo, 291, 293–297, 299–301

Marcovitz, F., 304

Marihuana: A Signal of Misunderstanding, 373

Marihuana, as found in U.S., 1, 32, 119, 148, 171, 375

Marihuana, botanical description, *see* Botanical description of cannabis

Marihuana, effects of: addiction, 1, 14, 24, 29, 110, 117, 196, 224–236 *passim,* 347, 360, 381–382 (*see also* "Stepping-stone hypothesis"); admixed, 119, 313, 368; alternation of pleasant and unpleasant effects, 122, 123, 126; dosage, *see* Dose; duration of effect, 164, 166; influential factors, 117, 120, 121, 147, 151 (*see also* Set and setting); neurological action, 50–51, 128, 156, 163, 164, 383; potency, *see* Potency; safety, 1, 2, 117, 219; tolerance, 27, 29, 119, 172, 229, 232–234, 237, 381–382; variability of effects, 117, 118, 120, 121, 186; withdrawal symptoms, 224, 233. *Specific:* after-effects, 116, 164–165, 176; agitation, 122, 166; aggression, 26, 130, 305–307, 309–311, 377, 384; amnesia, 165; amotivational syndrome, 125, 129, 287–289, 364, 383–386; antagonism, 171; antisocial tendencies, 26, 147, 182, 307, 310, 327, 361; anxiety, 109, 120, 122, 124, 151–176 *passim,* 273, 309, 377–378; appetite, 121, 127, 128, 173, 219, 220, 396; appreciation, 112, 115, 149–167 *passim,* 179; apprehension, 122; ataxia, 167; attention span, 152–153, 155, 166, 377; autistic thinking, 135, 147; awareness of surroundings and meaning, 113, 156–157, 170, 206; benevolence, 132; bliss, 129, 132; blood pressure, 52, 171; blood sugar, 52, 127; bodily integrity, 124, 150, 151, 170, 270; brain damage, 387; calmness, 122; cellular damage, 54; chemical age regression, 135; chromosome damage, 390–391; concentration, difficulty in, 136, 152, 155, 156; confusion, 142, 154, 155; conjunctivae, 51, 167; consciousness expansion, 103, 104, 106, 159; craving for sweets, 128; creativity, 111, 114, 118, 149, 150, 154–157, 166; delirium, 123, 169, 313; delusions, 53, 135, 146, 147, 169,

270; depersonalization, 53, 133, 151, 170; depression, 123, 164, 176, 179; detachment, 332; details, emphasis on, 157–159, 166; diarrhea, 167; disinhibition, 118, 127–149 passim, 154, 157, 176, 310–316, 321; dizziness, 124, 125, 166, 187; double-consciousness, 111, 116, 133–135, 167; dreaming, 122, 123, 138; dream-like, 136, 138, 166, 332; drive, loss of, 130; drowsiness, 122, 171; dryness of mouth and throat, 128, 167; effort required, 126, 136; effortlessness (sense of), 126, 166; elation, 155, 166; euphoria, 110, 121, 122, 123, 126, 129, 135, 165, 166, 171, 282, 309, 348; excitation, et cetera, 123, 124, 129, 164; eyes, effect on, 51–52, 167; false reality, 123; fantasies, 123, 146; fatigue, 173, 174, 384; fear, 147, 188, 307; fear of death, 122, 166; fear of discovery, 206, 207; floating sensation, 124–126, 150, 166; free and rapid association thinking, 136, 156, 166, 176, 205; goodwill, 132; grandiosity, 129, 135; hallucinations, 124, 135, 145–148, 168–170, 270, 274; headache, 165; hearing, 148–150, 170, 203; heat, 150; heaviness, 123–125, 166; heightened reality, 332; heightening of senses, 106, 112–113, 153; "high," 187, 191; hilarity, 122, 130, 132, 166, 222; hunger, 127, 128, 167, 187; hyperactivity, 122, 126, 307, 311; hypermotility, 126; hypoxia, 391; illusions, 122, 145–147, 270; imagination, 155; immune response impaired, 389–390; impulsiveness, 126; incoordination, 127, 159–160, 377; indolence, 136, 384; insanity (feeling of), 113, 115, 187, 188, 273; insecurity, 120; insight, 103–109, 113, 114, 135, 153–176 passim, 205, 270, 282; intellectual impairment, 152–153, 155, 156, 385; introspection, 130, 134, 332; irritability, 23, 154, 171; joy, 123; judgement impaired, 154; lassitude, 129; laughter, 121, 122, 130–132, 134, 135, 166; lethargy, 319; lightness (feeling of), 123–126, 150, 151, 166; macropsia, 146, 166; memory, 113, 114, 123, 135, 136, 138, 140–144, 154, 155, 377, 385; micropsia, 146, 166; mood shifts, 53, 122, 123, 129, 166; nausea, 120, 128, 167; negativism, 120; numbness, 150; objectvity loss, 124, 130; overestimate

of capabilities, 129, 154, 155; panic, 111, 122, 124, 151, 273; paranoid reaction, 109, 167, 170, 274–275, 358, 377–378; parathesia, 123, 124, 126, 187; passivity, 126, 136, 309, 311; perceptions heightened, 147, 176, 179; personality changes, 23, 26–27, 124, 130, 151, 289–290, 347, 383; phobias, 135, 147, 307; pressure (head), 125, 166; pulse increase, 167, 171; pupil dilation, 51, 167; rapidity of ideas and speech, 135, 136, 138, 155; relaxation, 129, 130, 171, 282; respiratory rate, 52; restlessness, 127; ringing (ears), 150; self-awareness, 179; self-confidence, 120, 129, 130, 142, 155, 157, 158, 314; sensory acuity, 151, 307, 385; sensory anesthesia, 123; sexuality, 112–113, 313, 315, 316–322; sexuality, overt, 182, 310, 315; sexual stimulant, 312, 313, 315, 317–321; sleep, 164, 165, 219, 220; smell, 112; sociability, 116, 171; space distortion, 138–145 passim, 160, 163, 170, 187, 314; speech difficulty, 135–136, 140–142; stimulation, 163–164, 173–174; strength, 126, 307; stupor, 306, 309–310; suggestibility, 155, 156, 170, 311, 314, 315; swollen head (feeling of), 124, 125; synesthesia, 17, 142, 163, 170; task performance, 157–162; taste, 112, 127; testosterone reduction, 388–389; thirst, 121, 127, 128, 167, 187; time distortion, 109, 113, 135–144 passim, 160–170 passim, 187, 314, 377; touch, 139, 150–151; tremors, 124, 167; universality of attitudes, 132; vision, 124, 145, 146, 166; visions, 110–111, 135, 264, 313; volition, 332; volubility, 122, 135, 166; vomiting, 128, 167; wavelike aspects, 123–125, 166, 170; well-being (sense of), 123, 129, 155, 162, 166, 171, 173, 176. See also Hashish, effects of; Smoking versus ingestion of cannabis

Marihuana, reasons for using: awareness (increase), 103, 104; to belong, 175, 178, 181; creativity, see Marihuana, effects of (specific: creativity); cultural, 173; defy authority, 181; escapism, 175–197 passim, 204, 205; experiment, 181, 194; fatigue (alleviation), 173, 174, 384; hallucinogenic experience, 176, 186, 204; internal world, 183, 186, 204, 205, 282; medical, 173–175; mystical, 106, 176,

Marihuana, reasons for using (cont'd)
180; perception heightening, 103,
104, 176, 179; pleasure, 174–194
passim, 205, 235, 282, 333; prestige,
178; psychic pain (relief), 175, 176,
179, 185, 198, 204, 235; religious,
173, 174; sexual depressant, 315, 316;
stimulation, 173–175; tension or boredom (release), 176, 181, 197. See also
Aphrodisiac; Uses for cultivated hemp
"Marihuana Bugaboo, The," 27, 196
"Marihuana Problem in the City of
New York," see La Guardia Report
Marihuana Tax Act of 1937, 4–26 passim, 218, 226, 251, 312, 325, 348
Marihuana terminology, see Terminology for cannabis
Marihuana users: attitudes, 189, 209,
280–281, 285–286, 385–386; children,
16, 24, 309; college educated, 175–
184, 186, 196, 212–213, 250, 356,
383; creative people, 194, 196, 204,
212; ethnic minorities, 15, 16, 20,
174, 193–195, 212, 327, 339; frequent
or "social" users, 174, 178–179, 190,
206–208, 281–282, 283, 373; group
characteristics, 178, 186–187, 189–
192, 208, 271, 361; introduction to
marihuana, 178, 186–189, 190; laborers, 173, 174; middle class, 2, 194–
198, 203, 204, 212–213, 348, 366,
372; occasional users, 178, 190, 206,
281–282, 356; the poor, 174, 193–
195, 249, 308, 309, 327, 348; "pot-
heads," 178–181, 191, 201, 206, 208–
210, 278–284 passim, 328, 356; techniques and manners, 186, 200–202
(see also Autotitration); youth, 175–
184, 202–204, 212, 356, 372. See also
Armed Forces of U.S.; Becker, H. S.
(on enjoyment of marihuana as learning process); Novice user of marihuana; Pharmacological sensitization
Marx, A., 79
Mattison, J. B., 220, 221, 224
Matsuyama, S., 390
Maurer, D. W., 310
May, G. (Dean), 355–356
Mayor's Committee on Marihuana, see
La Guardia Report
MDA (3,4-methylenedioxyamphetamine),
168
Mechoulam, R., 46, 47, 162
Medical uses of marihuana, 4, 12–14,
24, 173–175, 219–230, 327, 334, 394–
399; analgesic, 164, 219–229 passim,
395; antibiotic, 223, 226, 395; anticonvulsant, 164, 219, 223, 226, 396;
antidepressant, 27, 395; antitussive,
219, 226; appetite stimulant, 27, 219,
396; hypnotic, 219, 223, 226; muscle
relaxant, 219; oxytoxic, 226; psychotherapeutic aid, 175, 219, 224–226;
sedative, 164, 171, 175, 220, 222, 225,
226; soporific, 163, 220, 321; topical
anesthetic, 222, 226; withdrawal in
addictions to opiates and alcohol, 27,
126, 220, 223, 224, 226, 395–396;
Specific: anorexia nervosa, 27, 219,
396; asthma, 219–221, 226, 396–397;
bronchitis, 219, 226; cancer, 396;
convulsions, 219; delirium tremens,
220; depression, 27, 221, 225, 226,
229; dysmenorrhoea, 219–221; epileptoid states, 219, 221, 223; gastric
ulcer, 220; glaucoma, 397–398;
gonorrhea, 219; hemorrhage (uterine),
219; hyperkinesis, 398; hypertension,
229; labor pains, 219; migrane headache, 175, 220–222, 226; neuralgias,
219, 221, 226, post partem psychosis,
219; psychiatric illnesses, 224–226;
rabies, 219; rheumatism, 219, 220;
senile insomnia, 221; tetanus, 219
Melges, F. T., et al., 140–142
Mennier, R., 155
Mental illness and marihuana: acute
panic states, 267, 270, 273–274, 307;
"cannabis insanity," 254–258, 262;
"cannabis psychosis," 258–261, 272;
degeneracy, 276–278; depressive reaction, 275; Eastern reports, 253–262,
270, 272, 277; "five day schizophrenia," 263; manic-depressive psychoses,
257, 263; "marihuana psychosis,"
263–265, 269, 270, 378–379, 380–
381, 384; psychoses, 253, 262, 263,
267–269, 272, 276, 347, 348, 371;
psychoses, predisposing factors in,
260–266, 269, 271; psychosis, protection against, 268–269; schizophrenia,
257, 260, 261, 263, 266, 269, 276;
toxic psychoses, 259, 260, 262, 263,
267, 270–273, 330; U.S. reports, 253,
262–271. See also Personality deterioration and marihuana use
Merrill, F. T., 17, 238
Mescaline, 30, 140, 167–179 passim,
212, 275, 285
Methedrine, 248
"Mexican grass," 119, 213–216
Mezzrow, Milton, 15, 201. See also
Music, musicians, and marihuana
Michaux, Henri, 125–126, 130, 137–

140, 144–145, 150, 171

Mikuriya, T. H., 226, 227

Mill, John Stuart, 143, 360–361, 364

Mirin, S. M., et al., 281–282

Misinformation on marihuana, see Alarmist propaganda; American Medical Association; Assassins; Bias and prejudice against marihuana; Newspapers and popular literature as antimarihuana influences

Moore, W. T., 379–380, 387

Moreau, M. le Dr. Henri, 81

Moreau (de Tours), Jacques Joseph, 58, 59, 80, 225, 314

Morning glory seeds, see LSD (and morning glory seeds)

Morphine, 117, 164, 220, 233, 236, 238, 272

Munch, J. C., 23

Murphy, H. B. M., 155, 263, 268

Mushroom worshippers, see Psilocybin

Music, musicians, and marihuana, 15, 98, 104, 112, 118, 129, 139, 149, 150, 157, 167, 194. See also Marihuana, effects of (specific: creativity; hearing)

Myers, H. J., 304

National Commission on Marihuana and Drug Abuse, 372, 373

National Council of Churches, 374

National Education Association, 374

National Formulary, 10, 14, 218

National Institutes of Health, 3, 369, 370

National Organization for the Reform of Marihuana Laws (NORML), 399

Native American Church, see Peyote

Nevada, 374

New England Journal of Medicine, 388

New Orleans, 14–15, 17, 174, 194, 237, 299, 304, 313

Newspapers and popular literature as antimarihuana influences, 15–20, 24, 25, 238–240, 271–272, 300–325 passim, 335–336, 348

"Nightmare in the Catskills," see Woodstock Festival

Nixon, President Richard M., 373

Novice user of marihuana, 122, 136, 162, 185–189, 200–201, 307; compared to chronic user, 121–122, 135–136, 144, 152, 156, 158–159, 233; initial experiences, 72, 110, 121, 178, 185

Nowlis, H. H., 250, 251

Nung, Chinese Emperor, 143

Nutmeg, 31, 168

Odoric, 297

Operation Intercept, 359, 360

Opiates, 14, 187, 278, 396; addiction to, 250, 251, 346, 359; and the Assassins, 295; legislation against, 349, 350; and "stepping-stone hypothesis," 238–240, 243, 244, 382–383. See also Heroin; Morphine; Opium

Opium: addiction to, 30, 196, 220, 224, 231, 233, 236; and the Assassins, 296; and Baudelaire, 71, 79–84; cause of death and insanity, 228, 254; and De Quincey, 56, 81, 86; legislation against, 25, 214, 345; and Ludlow, 88; as medicine, 219, 222

Oregon, 374

O'Shaughnessy, W. B., 37, 56, 219

Osler, William, 220

Oursler, W., 133, 147, 148, 165, 314, 315

Parahexyl, see Pyrahexyl

Parke-Davis and Company, 168

Parker, C. S., 225

Paton, W. D. M., 234, 244–246, 248, 249

Payne, A. J., 254

PCP (phencyclidine hydrochloride), 168

Perelman, L., 262, 307

Perma, D., 263

Personality deterioration and marihuana use, 278–290. See also Marihuana, effects of (specific: personality changes)

Peyote, 30, 31, 167–176 passim, 212, 338–339

Phalen, J. M., 27

Pharmacological sensitization, 120, 121, 190–192

Playboy, 331

Pond, D. A., 225

Posey, H. T., 313

Potency, 128, 227, 329; of bhang, ganja, and charas compared, 37–38, 41, 380, 381; and fertilization of hemp plant, 12; and legalization of marihuana, 368; and location and climate, 13–14, 35, 36, 121, 215; of marihuana in food, 202; of "Mexican grass," 119; of the "roach," 201; and toxic psychoses, 259–260. See also Dose

"Pot-heads," see Marihuana users ("pot-heads")

Preparation of cannabis, 37–41

President's Commission on Law Enforcement and Administration of Justice, 244

Proctor, R. C., 50, 224

Protestant ethic, as antimarihuana influence, 333
Psilocybin, 30, 31, 167, 171, 172, 176
"Psychedelics," 30, 116, 176. *See also* "Hallucinogens"
"Psychic dependence," 78, 83, 231–235, 282, 328; and Ludlow, 87, 102
Psychotomimetics, 30, 111, 135, 170, 176. *See also* "Hallucinogens"
Psychotropic drugs, 30
Public Law *91–513*, 349–350
Pugsley, D. J., 330
Pulmonary function, 391
Pyrahexyl, 45, 50, 118, 119, 224, 225, 235. *See also* Tetrahydrocannabinol (homologues)

Rabelais, Francois, 32–33, 61, 131
Rajput, 331, 332
Ramawats, 261
Ramsey, H. H., 223
Randall, Bob, 397–398
"Red oil" of hemp, 46
Reed, H. B. C., Jr., 383
Reichman, J., 352–354
Remèdes galéniques, Les, 35
Reynolds, J. R., 221
Rig Veda, 31
"Roach," 201
Robbins, E. S., 285
Robinson, V.: and acute intoxication, 124–135 *passim,* 147, 151, 153, 163, 164; on the Assassins, 300–301; on hemp seed uses, 13; on marihuana as aphrodisiac, 313, 317, 318
Rockmore, M. J., 175, 262, 277
Rodgers, T. C., 304–305
Romantic movement in France, influence, 55–57, 64, 103
Rora, *see* Ganja
Rosenthal, M. P., 358, 359
Rosevear, J., 143, 159, 164, 316
Rowell, Earle Albert, 237
Rubin, Jerry, 198
Rubin, V., 384, 386, 390, 391, 396

Santavý, F. 48, 223
Sartre, Jean-Paul, 84–85
Satz, P., 384–385
Saunders, J. J. (Judge), 355
Schilder, P., 145–146
Schultz, O. E., 48
Secobarbital, 227–228
"Self-retent," 94. *See also* Hiding cannabis intoxication
Sernyl, *see* PCP

Set and setting, 5, 117, 122, 136, 162, 166, 186–192; influence on Baudelaire, 72; influence on Gautier, 58; influence on paranoia and acute anxiety states, 273–275, 358, 377–378; influence on sexuality, 320, 322
Sexuality and marihuana, 17–29 *passim,* 112–113, 157, 241, 312–322, 338, 339, 347, 361
Shoenfeld, D. D., 308–309
Shukla, S. R. P., 380–381
Sieper, H., 47–48
Sigg, B. W., 345
Siler, J. F., et al., 234, 262, 277
Sinensis, 35. *See also* Terminology for cannabis
Smith, D. E., 270
Smoking versus ingestion of cannabis, 5, 47, 52, 120, 128–129, 143–144, 147, 164–166, 171, 202, 273
Snow, C. P., 340
Social risks in using marihuana, 2, 21, 109, 176, 181, 184, 204, 235, 251, 355, 359
"Sociogenic" drug, marihuana as, 189
Soma, 31. *See also* Terminology for cannabis
Souquère, M., 80
Speed, 212. *See also* Methedrine
Spinoza, 361
Spivey, W. T. N., 42
Springer, W. L. (Representative), 350
Stanley, E., 17, 304, 308
Starkie, E., 79
"Stash," 199
Steinbeck, John IV, 196, 197
Stenchever, M. A., 390
"Stepping-stone hypothesis," 235–252, 281–282, 284, 327, 347, 382–383. *See also* Marihuana, effects of (addiction)
Stockings, G. T., 225
STP   (2,5-dimethoxy-4-methamphetamine), 168, 176, 179
Straub, W., 126
Stringaris, M. G., 313
Strojny, E. J., 44
Subculture, marihuana and development of, 178, 180–181, 209–212, 271, 337–338, 357. *See also* Marihuana users ("pot-heads")
Sutker, L. S., 384–385
Synhexyl, *see* Pyrahexyl
Synthetic hypnotics, *see* Barbiturates; Chloral-hydrate

Talbott, J. A., 267, 330
Tashkin, D. P., 391, 396

Tauro, G. J. (Judge), 333, 334
Taylor, Bayard, 55, 60, 85, 88, 101–119
  passim, 260, 272; description of acute
  intoxication, 64–70
Taylor, E. C., 44, 46, 47
Taylor, N., 276, 316
Tax Act of 1937, see Marihuana Tax
  Act of 1937
Teague, J. W., 267, 330
"Tea-pad," 193, 216, 315
Terminology for cannabis, 1, 14, 15,
  30–32, 35, 40. See also Bhang; Can-
  nabis indica; Cannabis sativa; Charas;
  Ganja
Testosterone, marihuana and, 388–389
Tests used in cannabis study: Beam
  Test, 42; Buss-Durkee Scale, 281;
  California Psychological Inventory,
  280; Continuous Performance Test,
  152; Dog Ataxia, 45; Digit Symbol
  Substitution, 152; Digits Span For-
  ward and Backward (DSFB), 141;
  Downey Will-and-Temperament, 130;
  Gayer "Corneal anaesthesia test," 45;
  Goal Directed Serial Alternation
  (GDSA), 141, 142; Psychiatric Outpatient Mood Scale, 281; Pursuit
  Rotor Test, 152; Regular Serial Subtraction of Sevens (RSSS), 141; Rorschach, 157–158; Seashore, 118, 157;
  Wechsler Adult Intelligence Scale,
  383
Tetrahydrocannabinol, 121, 260, 330,
  381–382, 391, 395, 396–397, 398;
  homologues, 45–46; isolation and
  identification, 4, 5, 43, 44, 222;
  isomers, 46–47; in marihuana cigarette, 329, 368; recent research, 228,
  229; use in studies, 48–53 passim, 120,
  126, 139–142, 146, 162, 223, 270–
  271. See also Cannabinol derivatives;
  Pyrahexyl
Thacore, V. R., 380–381
Thompson, L. S., 50, 224
Tilden's Extract, 87, 94, 95. See also
  Ludlow, Fitz Hugh
Tinklenberg, J. R., 377
Tobacco, 323, 371, 372; compared with
  cannabis, 27, 196, 326, 351, 368, 370,
  374, 382, 391, 396; and DMT and
  DET, 168; habituation, 27, 233, 234;
  history, 344; lobby, 184; and "stepping-stone hypothesis," 237, 244;
  users compared with cannabis users,
  286–287, 333
Todd, A. R., 43
Toklas, Alice B., 41, 202

Tolerance, see Marihuana, effects of
  (tolerance)
Traffic, marihuana, 14, 198, 213–216
Tranquilizers, 351
Tull-Walsh, J. H., 254, 255, 259–261
Turbahs, 40
Turn-off phenomenon, 116, 161, 162
2,4-D, 32

United Nations bibliography on cannabis, 3
United Nations Single Convention Narcotic and Drug Act of 1961, 213, 214,
  366, 374
University of California at Los Angeles
  (UCLA), 383
Uses for cultivated hemp, 10, 11, 13, 33,
  34, 40–41; in folk medicine, 173–174;
  in religion, 173–174. See also Medical
  uses of marihuana
U.S. Pharmacopoeia, 1, 10, 14, 218

Vachon, K., 396
Varlet, T., 79, 80, 83
Vietnam, use of marihuana in, 195–198,
  267–268, 339. See also Armed Forces
  of U.S.
Vinkenoog, S., 12
Vogel, V. H., 310
Volstead Act, 3, 16
Von Hammer-Purgstall, J., 297

Walton, R. P., 19, 173; on acute in-
  toxication, 118–138 passim, 143, 144,
  146–150, 157–158, 163–164, 165; on
  Assassins, 296; on New Orleans and
  marihuana, 14, 16, 17; on "stepping-
  stone hypothesis," 237
Waring, E. J., 164
Warnoch, J., 255–260
Washington, George, 12
Wasson, R., 30
Watts, Alan, 76
Wechsler Adult Intelligence Scale, 383
Weight reducing drugs, 351
Weil, A. T.: on acute intoxication, 127,
  135–136, 139, 152–161 passim; on
  chronic users, 282–285; on effect of
  marihuana on eyes, 51–52; on novice
  users, 185, 200–201, 282–285; on
  panic reactions, 273; on pharmacological sensitization, 190–192; on psychotic reactions and flashbacks, 275–
  276; on "stepping-stone hypothesis,"
  244
Welker (Senator), 241
West, L. J., 288

White Cross, 237–238
White House Committee on Narcotic and Drug Abuse, 347
Williams, E. G., et al., 50
Wilson, Earl, 238–239
Winick, C., 118, 129, 139, 157
Wise, J., 254, 255
Wolff, P. O., 237
Women's Liberation, 337
Wood, T. B., 42
Woodstock Festival, 199, 335–336
Woodward, W. C., 24–26

Wootton Committee, 248
World Health Organization, 232, 233, 250
Wriggly, F. W., 225

X, Mr., 109–116, 260

Yawger, N. S., 143
Yolles, S. F., 147, 154–155

Zinberg, N. E., 244, 283